The Apostolic Fathers

The Apostolic Fathers

Clement, Ignatius, and Polycarp

Revised Texts with Introductions, Notes,
Dissertations, and Translations

Edited and Translated by Joseph B. Lightfoot

Second Edition

2 Parts in 5 Volumes

Part One

Clement

Volume 1

WIPF & STOCK · Eugene, Oregon

Wipf and Stock Publishers
199 W 8th Ave, Suite 3
Eugene, OR 97401

The Apostolic Fathers, Second Edition, Part 1, Volume 1
Clement
By Lightfoot, Joseph B.
Softcover ISBN-13: 979-8-3852-0950-7
Hardcover ISBN-13: 979-8-3852-0951-4
eBook ISBN-13: 979-8-3852-0952-1
Publication date 12/6/2023
Previously published by Baker Book House, 1889

This edition is a scanned facsimile of the original edition published in 1889.

PREFATORY NOTE.

THE present volumes complete a work of which the first part was issued in 1869. In that year Bishop Lightfoot, being then Hulsean Professor of Divinity at Cambridge, published 'a revised text' of 'Clement of Rome—the two Epistles 'to the Corinthians—with introduction and notes.' Six years afterwards the first complete text of 'the Epistles' was published by Bryennios (1875)[1], and in the following year a complete Syrian translation was found by Prof. Bensly in a MS. purchased for the University Library at Cambridge, and prepared by him for publication. In 1877 Dr Lightfoot embodied the chief results of these important discoveries in "An Appendix "containing the newly recovered portions [of the Epistles of "Clement], with introductions, notes and translations." In 1879 he was called away from Cambridge to undertake the Bishopric of Durham. At that time a large portion of the edition of the Epistles of Ignatius and Polycarp was already printed[2]. He steadily pressed forward the completion of this second part of the whole work as he had originally planned it in the scanty leisure left by his official duties, and it was issued in 1885 (second edition, revised and somewhat enlarged, 1889). He then resumed his labours on Clement, and continued them with unflagging interest and zeal up to the time of his illness in the Autumn of

[1] An autotype of the part of the 'Constantinopolitan' MS. which contains the two Epistles is given I. pp. 425—474.

[2] He had also made preparations for an edition of Barnabas and Hermas; but I always understood him to draw a line between these writings and the Epistles of Clement, Ignatius, and Polycarp, perhaps from school associations with the edition of Jacobson in which he first studied them.

1888 and after his partial recovery. Even when he was suffering from the relapse in the following year which proved speedily fatal, he retained his passion for work and was busy with Clement till he fell into a half-unconscious state three days before his death. The last words which he wrote formed part of an imperfect sentence of the fragmentary Essay on St Peter's Visit to Rome. But, in spite of some gaps, the book was substantially finished before the end came. He was happily allowed to treat of 'Clement the Doctor,' 'Ignatius the Martyr,' 'Polycarp the Elder,' in a manner answering to his own noble ideal; and the "complete edition of the Apostolic Fathers," such as he had designed more than thirty years before, was ready at his death to be a monument of learning, sagacity and judgment unsurpassed in the present age[1].

It is worth while to recal these dates in order that the student may realise how the purpose which the work embodies extended through the Bishop's whole literary life. Before he was appointed to the Hulsean Chair in 1861 he was keenly interested in the Ignatian controversy; and after his appointment he devoted even more time to the study of sub-apostolic Christian literature than to his Commentaries on St Paul. Whatever his friends might think or plead, he held that his discussion of the Ignatian Epistles was the task of his life. This, as he said, was "the motive and core" of the work which is now finished; and in breadth and thoroughness of treatment, in vigour and independence, in suggestiveness and fertility of resource, this new edition of Clement will justly rank beside the "monumental edition" of Ignatius.

A comparison of the edition of Clement in its three stages is an instructive lesson in the development of a scholar's work. The commentary remains essentially unchanged from first to last. Fresh illustrations, and a few new notes, were added in the Appendix and in this edition, but a judgment on interpre-

[1] It was the Bishop's intention to superintend an edition of 'The Clementines', and he made a collection of critical materials for this purpose, which it is hoped may still be used.

tation once formed has very rarely been changed. On the other hand the broad historic relations of the First Epistle have been examined again and again with increasing fulness. The Essays on 'Clement the Doctor,' on the 'Early Roman Succession,' and on 'Hippolytus,' which appear now for the first time and form nearly half of the present book, supply an exhaustive study of the chief records of the history of the Roman Church to the third century. They deal with many questions which have been keenly debated; and, to single out one only, perhaps it is not too much to say that the problem of the order of the first five Bishops of Rome is now finally settled.

The section on the 'Philosophumena' of Hippolytus is wholly wanting, and the Essay on 'St Peter in Rome' is unfinished; but though it would have been a great gain to have had in detail Bishop Lightfoot's views on these subjects, he has expressed his general opinion on the main questions which are involved in them (see Index). With these we must be content, for he has left no other indication of the lines which his fuller investigation would have taken. His method of work was characteristic. When a subject was chosen, he mastered, stored, arranged in his mind, all the materials which were available for its complete treatment, but he drew up no systematic notes, and sketched no plan. As soon as the scope of the Essay was distinctly conceived, he wrote continuously and rapidly, trusting to his memory for the authorities which he used, and adding them as he went forward, but so that every reference was again carefully verified in proof. One subject in which he was deeply interested he has touched lightly, the relation of the Early Liturgies to the Synagogue Service (I. 384 ff). There is, I venture to think, no subject which would better reward thorough discussion, and it may be that Bishop Lightfoot's last work will encourage some young student to make it his own[1].

[1] The indices have been prepared by the Rev. J. R. Harmer, Fellow of Corpus Christi College, and late Fellow of King's College, Cambridge, who also prepared the indices to the second part of the work; and to him the best thanks of every reader are due.

To write these few lines is a task of singular pathos. Here indeed the parts are inverted. But at least no one can have the knowledge which I have of the self-forgetful generosity of Dr Lightfoot's work at Cambridge, and of the abiding effect of his episcopal work in Durham. He called me to Cambridge to occupy a place which was his own by right; and having done this he spared no pains to secure for his colleague favourable opportunities for action while he himself withdrew in some sense from the position which he had long virtually occupied. And now when I have been charged to fulfil according to the measure of my strength the office which he held here, I find in every parish an inheritance of reverence and affection which he has bequeathed to his successor.

So it is that from the historic house which he delighted to fill with the memorials of his predecessors, under the shadow of the Chapel, which he made a true symbol of our Church in its foundation and its catholicity, surrounded by personal relics which speak of common labours through twenty years, it is my duty to commend to the welcome of all serious students the last mature fruit of labours pursued with unwearied devotion at Cambridge, at St Paul's, and at Durham, by one whose "sole desire" it was, in his own words written a few months before his death, in "great things and in small, to be found *συνεργὸς τῇ ἀληθείᾳ*."

B. F. DUNELM.

AUCKLAND CASTLE,
BISHOP AUCKLAND,
Sept. 12th, 1890.

TABLE OF CONTENTS.

FIRST VOLUME.

PAGE

1. *THE APOSTOLIC FATHERS.* 1—13

Fragmentary character of early Christian literature; the writings of the sub-apostolic age neglected [1]. The epithet 'apostolic' [2]. The title 'Apostolic Fathers', writings so designated [3—6]. Their external form [6]. Their internal character and spirit [7, 8]. Their relation to the apostolic teaching and the Canon [8—11]. Their currency and importance [11—13].

2. *CLEMENT THE DOCTOR.* 14—103

Story of Clement the bishop in the Clementine romance [14—16]. It leads us to the imperial palace [16]. The stemma Flaviorum, and Flavius Clemens [16—21]. The identification of Clement the bishop, theories disposed of [22—25]. His social status [25]. Christianity in the imperial household [25—29]. Its upward social tendency [29, 30]. Pomponia Græcina, a Christian [30—33]. Flavia Domitilla and Flavius Clemens, Christians [33—35]. The evidence of the catacombs to other Christian Flavii [35—39]. Domitian's assassination due to his treatment of Flavia Domitilla [39—42]. Domitilla the Virgin [42—44]. Her existence traceable to Eusebius, and improbable; Eusebius's authorities Bruttius and Africanus [45—51]. Clement the consul and Clement the bishop distinct [52—58]. The writer of the Epistle a Hellenist Jew [58—60]. Probably a freedman of the household of Flavius Clemens [61]. Social status of early bishops [61, 62]. Date of Clement's episcopate and order in the episcopal succession [63—67]. Nature of his episcopal office [67—69]. The Roman Church at this time [69—72]. Events in his life; S. Peter and S. Paul at Rome, the Neronian persecution, the episcopates of Linus and Anencletus [72—81]. His episcopate and the persecution of Domitian [81]. His Epistle to the Corinthians [82—84]. His death [84]. Legend of his martyrdom and reliques [85—91]. His basilica at Rome [91—95]. Characteristics of his Epistle [95—98]. His memory neglected in the West [98]. Writings assigned to him [99—102]. The designation 'the Doctor' [103].

I.

THE APOSTOLIC FATHERS.

'LITERATURE', says Goethe, 'is the fragment of fragments. Only a very small portion of what was uttered was written down, and of what was written down only a very small portion survives[1].' This is preeminently true of early Christian literature. The Christian teachers in primitive ages were evangelists, not authors, preachers, not historians. The written literature was only the casual efflorescence of the spoken. Literary distinction and posthumous fame were the last thoughts which could have had any place in their minds. They were too intensely occupied with the present and the immediate to spare a glance for the more remote future. When the heavens might part asunder at any moment, and reveal the final doom, it was a matter of infinitely little consequence how after-ages—if after-ages there should be—would estimate their written words.

Moreover time has pressed with a heavy hand upon such literature as the early Church produced. The unique position of the Apostles and Evangelists might shield their writings from its ravages; but the literature of the succeeding generation had no such immunity. It was too desultory in form and too vague in doctrine to satisfy the requirements of more literary circles and a more dogmatic age. Hence, while Athanasius and Basil and Chrysostom, Jerome and Augustine and Ambrose, were widely read and frequently transcribed, comparatively little attention was paid to those writings of the first and second centuries which were not included in the sacred Canon. The literary remains of the primitive ages of Christianity, which to ourselves are of priceless value, were suffered to perish from neglect—a few fragments here and there alone escaping the general fate, like the scattered Sibylline leaves in the old story.

[1] *Sprüche in Prosa*, Goethe's *Werke* III. p. 196.

The epithet 'apostolic' (ἀποστολικός) does not occur in the canonical writings, but is found first, as might have been expected, in the vocabulary of the succeeding generation, when the Apostles could be regarded in the light of history. Its first occurrence is in Ignatius, who tells his correspondents that he writes to them 'after the apostolic manner' (*Trall.* inscr. ἐν ἀποστολικῷ χαρακτῆρι), where he seems to refer to the epistolary form of his communication. At the close of the second century and beginning of the third its use is very frequent. It is often found in conjunction with and in contrast to other similarly formed adjectives, such as κυριακός, προφητικός, εὐαγγελικός, and the like. More especially it is used in three different connexions. (i) *Writings* are called 'apostolic.' Thus one passage from an epistle of S. Paul is quoted as ἡ ἀποστολικὴ γραφή by one father (Clem. Alex. *Coh. ad Gent.*, *Op.* I. p. 2), and another is designated τὸ ἀποστολικόν by another (Orig. *de Princ.* iii. 8, *Op.* I. p. 115; comp. *In Jerem. Hom.* v. § 4, *Op.* III. p. 150, τοῦ ἀποστολικοῦ ῥητοῦ, *c. Cels.* ii. 65 τοῖς ἀποστολικοῖς λόγοις). The books of the New Testament accordingly are divided into 'the evangelic' and 'the apostolic' (Iren. *Haer.* i. 3. 6 ἐκ τῶν εὐαγγελικῶν καὶ τῶν ἀποστολικῶν; comp. Orig. *de Orat.* 29, *Op.* I. p. 259, ἀποστ. καὶ εὐαγγ. ἀναγνώσματα, ib. *Comm. in Matth.* x. § 12, *Op.* III. p. 455); and in this division the Acts falls among the 'apostolica' (Tertull. *adv. Marc.* v. 2). (ii) *Churches* are likewise designated 'apostolic,' where they could trace their origin to an Apostle as their founder. This is more especially the case with the Smyrnæan Church, which derived its lineage through Polycarp from S. John, and with the Roman, which in like manner claimed descent from S. Peter through Clement (*de Praescr.* 32). Such churches were called in the language of Tertullian 'ecclesiae apostolicae' or 'ecclesiae matrices' (*de Praescr.* 21, 22; comp. *adv. Marc.* i. 21, iv. 5), and sometimes 'apostolicae' alone (*de Praescr.* 32). (iii) Lastly, *individual men* are likewise so designated. Thus Tertullian divides the writers of the four gospels into two classes, Matthew and John being 'apostoli' but Luke and Mark 'apostolici' or 'apostolici viri' (*adv. Marc.* iv. 2, 3, *de Praescr.* 32). Thus again in the Smyrnæan Letter giving an account of Polycarp's death, this father is called (§ 16) διδάσκαλος ἀποστολικός, and similarly Irenæus styles him ἀποστολικός πρεσβύτερος (*Ep. ad Florin.* in Euseb. *H. E.* v. 20); while Clement of Alexandria (see below, p. 5) designates Barnabas ὁ ἀποστολικὸς Βαρνάβας. In such cases it generally signifies direct personal connexion with Apostles, but it need not necessarily imply so much. It may be a question for instance whether Tertullian (*de Carn. Christ.* 2), when he addresses Marcion, 'si propheta es, praenuntia aliquid; si apostolus, praedica publice; si apostolicus, cum apostolis senti; si tantum Christianus es, crede quod traditum est,' refers to any claims put forward by this heretic to direct communication with Apostles[1].

Though the familiar sense of the term 'Apostolic Fathers' is based on this ancient use of the word 'apostolicus,' yet the expression itself does not occur, so far as I have observed, until comparatively recent times. Its origin, or at least its general currency, should probably be traced to the idea of gathering together the literary remains of those who flourished in the age immediately succeeding the Apostles, and who presumably therefore were their direct personal disciples. This idea first took shape in the edition of Cotelier during the last half of the seventeenth century (A.D. 1672). Indeed such a collection would have been an impossibility a few years earlier. The first half of that century saw in print for the first time the Epistles of Clement (A.D. 1633), and of Barnabas (A.D. 1645), to say nothing of the original Greek of Polycarp's Epistle (A.D. 1633) and the Ignatian Letters in their genuine form (A.D. 1644, 1646). The materials therefore would have been too scanty for such a project at any previous epoch. In his title-page however Cotelier does not use the actual expression, though he approximates to it, '*SS. Patrum qui temporibus Apostolicis floruerunt opera*'; but the next editor, Ittig (1699), adopts as his title *Patres Apostolici*, and thenceforward it becomes common.

After the history of the term itself, which I have thus briefly sketched, a few words may fitly be allowed a place here by way of introduction to the present work under the following heads: (i) The writings comprised under the designation; (ii) The external form of these writings; (iii) Their internal character and spirit; (iv) Their relation to the Apostolic teaching and to the Canonical Scriptures; and lastly; (v) Their currency and importance at different epochs.

(i) *Writings so designated.*

The term itself, as we have seen, is sufficiently elastic. It might denote more generally those fathers whose doctrinal teaching was in accord with the Apostles, or with a more restricted meaning those who were historically connected with the Apostles. Common consent however has agreed to accept it in this latter sense and to confine

[1] Free use is made in this paragraph, and throughout the chapter, of an article on the *Apostolic Fathers* which I wrote some time ago for Smith and Wace's *Dict. of Christ. Biogr.* I. p. 147 sq.

it to those who are known, or may reasonably be presumed, to have associated with and derived their teaching directly from some Apostle, or at least to those who were coeval with the Apostles. Accordingly it will embrace more or fewer names according to the historical views of the writer who employs it.

Three names preeminently challenge acceptance among the ranks of the Apostolic Fathers, CLEMENT, IGNATIUS, and POLYCARP. In none of these cases does there seem to be reasonable ground for hesitation. Though the identification of Clement, the writer of the letter to the Corinthians, with the person mentioned by S. Paul (*Phil.* iv. 3) is less than probable, though the authority of the Clementine romance is worthless to establish his connexion with S. Peter, yet the tradition that he was the disciple of one or both of these Apostles is early, constant, and definite; and it is borne out by the character and contents of the epistle itself. Again, in the case of Ignatius, though the tradition which represents him as a disciple of S. John rests only on the authority of late writings, like the spurious *Antiochene Acts*[1], yet his early date and his connexion with Antioch, a chief centre of apostolic activity, render his personal intercourse with Apostles at least probable. Lastly, Polycarp's claim to the title seems indisputable, since his own pupil Irenæus states that he was a scholar of the beloved disciple, and that the writer himself had heard from his master many anecdotes of the Apostle, which he had carefully stored up in his memory[2].

Other aspirants to a place in this inner circle will not so easily establish their claim. Thus, at an earlier stage the works of DIONYSIUS THE AREOPAGITE would have asserted their right to rank among the writings of the Apostolic Fathers; but these are now universally condemned as spurious. The same is the case with certain apocryphal works, which for this reason may be neglected from our consideration. The SHEPHERD OF HERMAS again owes its place among the writings of the Apostolic Fathers to another cause. The case here is not one of fraud, but of misapprehension, not of false impersonation, but of mistaken identity. It was supposed to have been written by the person of this name mentioned by S. Paul (Rom. xvi. 14)[3]; whereas a seemingly authentic tradition ascribes it to the brother of Pius, who was bishop of Rome about the middle of the second century[4]. Again, the claim of

[1] See *Ign. and Polyc.* I. pp. 29, 390, II. pp. 448, 473 sq.

[2] See *Ign. and Polyc.* I. p. 424 sq.

[3] So Origen *ad loc.*, *Op.* IV. p. 683.

[4] *Canon Murat.* p. 58, ed. Tregelles; *Catal. Liberian.* p. 635, ed. Mommsen; Anon. *adv. Marc.* iii. 294 in Tertull. *Op.* II. p. 792, ed. Oehler.

PAPIAS to be considered an Apostolic Father rests on the supposition that he was a disciple of S. John the Evangelist, as Irenæus apparently believes (*Haer.* v. 33. 4); but Eusebius has pointed out that the inference of Irenæus from the language of Papias is more than questionable, and that the teacher of Papias was not the Apostle S. John, but the Presbyter of the same name (*H. E.* iii. 39). Again, the anonymous EPISTLE TO DIOGNETUS derives its claim from an error of another kind. It is founded on an expression occurring towards the close, which has been interpreted literally as implying that the writer was a personal disciple of one or other of the Apostles[1]. But, in the first place, the context shows that this literal interpretation is unwarranted, and the passage must be explained as follows; 'I do not make any strange discourses nor indulge in unreasonable questionings, but having learnt my lessons from Apostles, I stand forward as a teacher of the nations.' And secondly, this is no part of the Epistle to Diognetus proper (§§ 1—10), but belongs to a later writing, which has only been accidentally attached to this epistle owing to the loss of some leaves in the manuscript. This latter fact is conclusive. If therefore this epistle has any title to a place among the Apostolic Fathers, it must be established by internal evidence. But, though the internal character suggests an early date, yet there is no hint of any historical connexion between the writer and the Apostles. Again, the EPISTLE OF BARNABAS occupies a unique position. If the writer had been the companion of S. Paul bearing the same name, then he would be more properly called not an 'apostolic man,' as he is once designated by Clement of Alexandria, but an 'Apostle,' as this same father elsewhere styles him[2] in accordance with the language of S. Luke (Acts xiv. 14). But if the writer be not the 'Apostle' Barnabas, then we have no evidence of his personal relations with the Apostles, though the early date of the epistle, which seems to have been written during the epoch of the Flavian dynasty, would render such connexion far from improbable. Lastly; the recently discovered work, the TEACHING OF THE APOSTLES, is second in importance to none of the writings enumerated in this paragraph, and perhaps may be dated as early as any. Yet it is difficult to say what the writer's position was with reference to those properly called Apostles, though he claims to reproduce their teaching, and though in his ordinances he mentions as his contemporaries certain persons bearing the apostolic title[3].

[1] § 11 οὐ ξένα ὁμιλῶ οὐδὲ παραλόγως ζητῶ, ἀλλὰ ἀποστόλων γενόμενος μαθητὴς γίνομαι διδάσκαλος ἐθνῶν.

[2] *Strom.* ii. 20 (p. 489) ὁ ἀποστολικὸς Βαρνάβας, *Strom.* ii. 6 (p. 445) ὁ ἀπόστολος Βαρνάβας, comp. *ib.* ii. 7 (p. 447).

[3] *Doctr. Duod. Apost.* xi. 3 πᾶς δὲ ἀπόστολος ἐρχόμενος κ.τ.λ.

Thus besides the epistles of the three Apostolic Fathers properly so called, which are comprised in the first and second parts of the present work, it has been the practice of editors to include in their collections several other early Christian writings. For this practice there is good reason. Though the designation 'Apostolic Fathers' may be seriously strained to admit these writings, yet it is highly convenient to have, gathered together in one whole, the Church literature which belongs to the sub-apostolic times and thus bridges over the chasm which separates the age of the Apostles from the age of the Apologists.

(ii) *Their external form.*

All the genuine writings of the three Apostolic Fathers are epistolary in form. When Ignatius, in an expression already quoted (p. 2), describes his own letters as 'written after the apostolic manner,' he gives a description which applies equally well to Clement and Polycarp. They are all modelled upon the Canonical Epistles, more especially upon those of S. Paul. Like the Canonical letters they are called forth by pressing temporary needs, and in no case is any literary motive apparent. A famous teacher writes, in the name of the community over which he presides, to quell the dissensions in a distant but friendly church. An aged disciple on his way to martyrdom pours forth a few parting words to the Christian congregations with whom he has been brought in contact on his journey. A bishop of a leading church, having occasion to send a parcel to another brotherhood at a distance, takes the opportunity of writing, in answer to their solicitations, a few plain words of advice and instruction. Such is the simple account of the letters of Clement, Ignatius, and Polycarp, respectively.

Even when we extend the term 'Apostolic Fathers,' so as to include the two other writings which have the next claim to the title, this same form is preserved. The Epistle of Barnabas and the Letter to Diognetus are no departure from the rule. But though the form is preserved, the spirit is different. They no longer represent the natural outpouring of personal feeling arising out of personal relations, but are rather treatises clothed in an epistolary dress, the aim of the one being polemical, of the other apologetic. In this respect they resemble rather the Epistle to the Hebrews, than the letters of S. Paul.

The other writings, which find a place in collections of the Apostolic Fathers, diverge from this normal type. The *Teaching of the Apostles* is a primitive book of Church discipline and ordinances; the *Shepherd* of

Hermas is the first Christian allegory; while the *Expositions* of Papias were among the earliest forerunners of commentaries, partly explanatory, partly illustrative, on portions of the New Testament.

(iii) *Their internal character and spirit.*

'The Apostolic Fathers,' it has been justly said, 'are not great writers, but great characters[1].' Their style is loose; there is a want of arrangement in their topics and an absence of system in their teaching. On the one hand they present a marked contrast to the depth and clearness of conception with which the several Apostolic writers place before us different aspects of the Gospel, and by which their title to a special inspiration is vindicated. On the other they lack the scientific spirit which distinguished the fathers of the fourth and fifth centuries, and enabled them to formulate the doctrines of the faith as a bulwark against lawless speculation. But though they are deficient in distinctness of conception and power of exposition, 'this inferiority' to the later fathers 'is amply compensated by a certain naïveté and simplicity which forms the charm of their letters. If they have not the precision of the scientific spirit, they are free from its narrowness[2].' There is a breadth of moral sympathy, an earnest sense of personal responsibility, a fervour of Christian devotion, which are the noblest testimony to the influence of the Gospel on characters obviously very diverse, and will always command for their writings a respect wholly disproportionate to their literary merits. The gentleness and serenity of Clement, whose whole spirit is absorbed in contemplating the harmonies of nature and of grace; the fiery zeal of Ignatius, in whom the one over-mastering desire of martyrdom has crushed all human passion; the unbroken constancy of Polycarp, whose protracted life is spent in maintaining the faith once delivered to the saints—these are lessons which can never become antiquated or lose their value.

This freshness and reality is especially striking in the three cases just named, where we are brought face to face with the personality of the writers; but the remark applies likewise, though in different degrees, to those other writings of the group, which are practically anonymous. The moral earnestness and the simple fervour of the *Shepherd* of Hermas and of the *Teaching of the Apostles* will arrest the attention at once. The intensity of conviction, which breathes in the Epistle to

[1] De Pressensé *Trois Premiers Siècles* II. p. 384.

[2] *Ib.* p. 411.

Diognetus, is nowhere more conspicuous than in the lofty utterance—recalling the very tones of the great Apostle himself—in which the writer contrasts the helpless isolation and the universal sovereignty of the Christian[1]. Only in the Epistle of Barnabas is the moral and spiritual element overlaid by a rigid and extravagant allegorism; yet even here we cannot fail to recognise a very genuine underlying faith. Of the *Expositions* of Papias we have not sufficient data to express an opinion. It would be unfair to the writer to judge him from the few extant fragments, consisting chiefly of anecdotes, which do not leave a favourable impression of his theological depth.

(iv) *Their relation to the Apostolic teaching and the Canon.*

If we had to describe briefly the respective provinces of the three great Apostolic Fathers, we might say that it was the work of Clement to co-ordinate the different elements of Christian teaching as left by the Apostles; and of Ignatius to consolidate the structure of ecclesiastical polity as sketched out by them; while for Polycarp, whose active career was just beginning as theirs ended, and who lived on for some half century after their deaths, was reserved the task of handing down unimpaired to a later generation the Apostolic doctrine and order thus co-ordinated and consolidated by his elder contemporaries—a task for which he was eminently fitted by his passive and receptive character[2].

The writings of all these three fathers lie well within the main stream of Catholic teaching. They are the proper link between the Canonical Scriptures and the Church Fathers who succeeded them. They recognise all the different elements of the Apostolic teaching, though they combine them in different proportions. 'They prove that Christianity was Catholic from the very first, uniting a variety of forms in one faith. They show that the great facts of the Gospel narrative, and the substance of the Apostolic letters, formed the basis and moulded the expression of the common creed[3].'

But when we turn to the other writings for which a place has been claimed among the Apostolic Fathers the case is different. Though the writers are all apparently within the pale of the Church, yet there is a tendency to a one-sided exaggeration, either in the direction of Judaism or of the opposite, which stands on the verge of heresy. In the

[1] § 5 πατρίδας οἰκοῦσιν ἰδίας, ἀλλ' ὡς πάροικοι, κ.τ.λ.

[2] See *Ign. and Polyc.* I. p. 458 sq.

[3] Westcott *History of the Canon* p. 55.

Epistle of Barnabas and in the Letter to Diognetus the repulsion to Judaism is so violent that one step further would have carried the writers into Gnostic or Marcionite dualism. On the other hand, in the *Teaching of the Apostles*, in the *Shepherd* of Hermas, and possibly in the *Expositions* of Papias (for in this last instance the inferences drawn from a few scanty fragments must be precarious), the sympathy with the Old Dispensation is unduly strong, and the distinctive features of the Gospel are somewhat obscured by the shadow of the Law thus projected upon them. In Clement, Ignatius, and Polycarp, both extremes alike are avoided.

The crucial test of this central position occupied by them is their relation to the Apostles S. Peter and S. Paul. These two great names were adopted as the watchwords of antagonistic heresies in the latter half of the second century, and even earlier. Some passages in the Apostolic history itself gave a colour to this abuse of their authority (Gal. ii. 11 sq., 1 Cor. i. 12 sq.). Hence an extreme school of modern critics has explained the origin of the Catholic Church as the result of a late amalgamation between these two opposing elements, after several generations of conflict, in which each lost its more exaggerated features. This theory can be upheld only by trampling under foot all the best authenticated testimony. The three Apostolic Fathers more especially are a strong phalanx barring the way. The two Apostles are directly named by Clement (1 *Cor.* 5) and by Ignatius (*Rom.* 4), as of equal authority; while the remaining father, Polycarp, though as writing to a Church founded by this Apostle (*Phil.* 3) he mentions S. Paul alone by name, yet adopts the language and the thoughts of S. Peter again and again. Thus we have the concurrent testimony of Rome, of Syria, of Asia Minor, to the co-ordinate rank of the two great Apostles in the estimate of the Christian Church at the close of the first and beginning of the second century.

The relation of these writers to the Canonical Scriptures of the New Testament may be briefly summed up as follows: (1) They assign a special and preeminent authority to the Apostles, while distinctly disclaiming any such exceptional position for themselves. This is the case with Clement (1 *Cor.* 5, 47), and Ignatius (*Rom.* 4), speaking of S. Peter and S. Paul, and with Polycarp (*Phil.* 3), speaking of S. Paul, these being the only Apostles mentioned by name in their writings. (2) On the other hand, there is no evidence that these fathers recognised a Canon of the New Testament, as a well-defined body of writings. The misinterpretation of a passage in Ignatius (*Philad.* 8), which has been supposed to imply such a recognition, is dealt with in its proper place and shown to be an error[1]. (3) As a rule the Apostolic Fathers do not quote the New Testament Scriptures by name. The exceptions are just what we should expect to find. Clement, writing to the Corinthians, mentions S. Paul's injunctions to this same church on a kindred occasion (§ 47); Ignatius, addressing the Ephesians, speaks of their having been initiated in the mysteries of the faith with S. Paul, and remarks on the large space which they occupy in his letters (§ 12); lastly Polycarp, writing to the Philippians, calls attention to the instructions which S. Paul had given them by letter, and mentions his praising them to other churches (§ 3, 11). Besides these passages there is only one other exception (Polyc. *Phil.* 11, 'sicut Paulus docet'), and this is possibly due to a transcriber. But while (with these exceptions) there is no direct reference to the books of the New Testament, yet fragments of most of the Canonical Epistles are embedded in the writings of these fathers, whose language moreover is thoroughly leavened with the Apostolic diction. The usual formula of Scriptural quotation, 'as it is written' (ὡς γέγραπται), is still confined to the Old Testament. The only real exception to this rule is *Barnab.* 4, where our Lord's words, as recorded in Matt. xxii. 14, are introduced in this way. The passage in Polyc. *Phil.* 12, not extant in the Greek, where a combined quotation of Ps. iv. 4 and Ephes. iv. 26 is prefaced by the words 'ut his scripturis dictum est,' can hardly be regarded in this light, even if we could feel quite certain that the original was correctly represented in the Latin. (4) Lastly: there is not a single Evangelical quotation which can be safely referred to any apocryphal source. The two exceptions to this rule, which were at one time adduced from Barnabas, have both vanished in the fuller light of criticism. In § 4 the Latin text reads 'sicut dicit filius Dei,' but the recovery of the Greek original, ὡς πρέπει υἱοῖς Θεοῦ, shows that we have here a corruption of 'sicut decet filios Dei,' and thus the quotation altogether disappears. The second supposed example in this same writer (§ 7) is due to a misinterpretation of the formula φησίν, 'he saith,' which here introduces not a quotation but an interpretation, 'he meaneth,' according to the usage elsewhere in this same epistle (§ 10, 11). The passages in Ignatius, which seem to be taken from apocryphal writings, may perhaps more probably be ascribed to oral tradition. They are discussed in their proper places[2]. At all events, though Ignatius incidentally refers to a large number of facts in the Evangelical history, they all are

[1] *Ign. and Polyc.* I. p. 388, II. p. 271 sq.

[2] See *Ign. and Polyc.* I. p. 388 sq., II. pp. 294 sq., 299 sq.

found in the Canonical Gospels[1]. Even the supposed apocryphal quotation in *Smyrn.* 4 has its counterpart in Luke xxiv. 39, being an independent report of the same saying. So far as we are able to judge, his range of knowledge in the province of evangelical history was practically coextensive with our own. This absence of any unmistakeable traces of a New Testament Apocrypha in the Apostolic Fathers is the more remarkable, because the references to pre-Christian apocryphal writings are not unfrequent, as for example several prophetical passages quoted by Clement, and the book of Eldad and Modad mentioned by name in Hermas.

In this investigation I have said nothing about Papias, for he requires a separate treatment. But the main result would be the same. Though he illustrated the Gospel narratives with very many oral traditions, there is no evidence that he had any other written sources of information before him besides those which we possess in the New Testament.

(v) *Their currency and importance.*

For reasons which have been suggested already, the writings of the Apostolic Fathers were consigned to comparative neglect for many centuries. To Eusebius, the historian of the early Church, these Christian remains of the primitive ages had yielded the most valuable results; but no later writer inherited his mantle. Ages of dogmatic definition and conflict succeeded. The interest in the early struggles of the Church with heathendom had given way to the interest in the doctrinal combats then raging within the Church herself; and owing to their lack of dogmatic precision these early writings contained little or nothing of value for the combatants. Here and there a passage—more especially in Ignatius—might be made to serve the purpose of a disputant; but these were the rare exceptions. In the West this neglect reached its climax. Those Latin fathers, who were well acquainted with Greek, directed their knowledge of the language to other channels. Jerome seems never to have read any of the three Apostolic Fathers. Rufinus translated the spurious Clementine writings, the Recognitions and the Letter to James, but entirely neglected the genuine Epistle to the Corinthians. The medieval Latin translations did something for Ignatius and Polycarp, but Clement's Epistle was altogether forgotten.

[1] The embellishments (*Ephes.* 19) of the star seen by the shepherds ought perhaps to be excepted.

Yet his personal fame was great, not in the West only, but throughout Christendom.

The Reformation brought a great change. The exigencies of the crisis turned the attention of both the contending parties to questions of Church order and polity; and the first appeal was naturally to those writers who lived on the confines of the Apostolic age. Happily the supply followed quickly upon the demand. The discovery and publication of large portions of the Apostolic Fathers in the first half of the seventeenth century was opportune, and the literature thus recovered was discussed with eager interest. In the present century the controversy has taken another turn, but the writings of the earliest Christian ages are still the battle-field. The attack has been directed against the authenticity and early date of the Canonical writings; and again assailants and defenders alike have sought weapons from the armoury of these primitive writings. Never has the interest in the Apostolic Fathers been so keen as during the last half century; and in this period again large accessions have been made to the available materials by a succession of fresh discoveries. The publication of the Syriac Ignatius by Cureton in 1845, and more fully in 1849, led the way. Almost simultaneously with his later work, in 1849, appeared Petermann's edition of the Armenian Ignatius, which, though not a new discovery, was then for the first time rendered available to scholars and supplied a factor of the highest moment in the solution of the Ignatian question. These were followed by the lost ending of the Clementine Homilies, recovered and given to the world by Dressel in 1853. Then came the publication of the Codex Lipsiensis and the accompanying transcript by Anger in 1856, and of the Codex Sinaiticus by Tischendorf in 1862, thus giving for the first time nearly the whole of Hermas and the beginning of Barnabas in the original Greek. About the same time, large additional materials for the Greek and Latin texts of the Apostolic Fathers—notably a second Latin Version of Hermas hitherto unnoticed—and for the literature connected therewith, were contributed to the common stock by Dressel in his edition in 1857. Within two or three years also followed the Æthiopic Hermas edited by A. d'Abbadie in 1860. Then, after a longer interval, Bryennios published for the first time a text of the two Epistles of Clement entire in 1875, and this was followed immediately by the discovery of a Syriac Version, likewise complete, of these same two Epistles, of which I was able by the aid of Bensly to give the first full account in 1877. Mention should also be made of the Coptic additions to the Ignatian matter published for the first time partly by Ciasca in 1883 and partly by myself in 1885;

nor does this list exhaust the accessions to the apparatus criticus of these fathers which have been made during the period under review. To crown all came the *Teaching of the Apostles*, a hitherto unknown work of the sub-apostolic age, of which the editio princeps was given to the world by Bryennios in 1883. In this summary I have not included other highly important publications, like the *Philosophumena*, published in 1851, which, though not directly connected with the Apostolic Fathers, throw great light on these primitive ages of the Church.

This rapid accumulation of fresh materials has furnished abundant fuel to feed and sustain the interest in the Apostolic Fathers, which the chief theological controversy of the age had aroused. During the last half-century they have received an amount of attention which goes far to compensate for many ages of neglect in the past. Within these fifty years some twenty editions have appeared—a larger number than during the two preceding centuries—besides monographs, versions, and treatises of various kinds; and no signs can be discerned of the interest flagging.

2.

CLEMENT THE DOCTOR.

CLEMENT, a noble Roman citizen, was connected by birth with the family of the Cæsars. His father Faustus was a near relation and a foster brother of the reigning emperor, and had married one Mattidia, likewise Cæsar's kinswoman. From this union had sprung two elder sons, Faustinus and Faustinianus[1], who were twins, and our hero Clement, who was born many years after his brothers. At the time when Clement first comes before our notice, he is alone in the world. Many years ago, when he was still an infant, his mother had left home to escape dishonourable overtures from her husband's brother, and had taken her two elder sons with her. Not wishing to reveal his brother's turpitude to Faustus, she feigned a dream which warned her to leave home for a time with her twin children. Accordingly she set sail for Athens. After her departure her brother-in-law accused her to her husband of infidelity to her marriage vows. A storm arose at sea, the vessel was wrecked on the shores of Palestine, and she was separated from her children, whom she supposed to have been drowned. Thus she was left a lone woman dependent on the charity of others. The two sons were captured by pirates and sold to Justa the Syrophœnician woman mentioned in the Gospels, who educated them as her own children, giving them the names Aquila and Nicetes. As they grew up they became fellow-disciples of Simon Magus, whose doctrines they imbibed. Eventually however they were brought to a better mind by the teaching of Zacchæus, then a visitor to those parts; and through his influence they attached themselves to S. Peter, whom they accompanied from that time forward on his missionary circuits. They were so engaged at the moment when the narrative, to which we owe this account of their career, presents them to our notice.

[1] These are the names in the *Homilies*. On the other hand in the *Recognitions* the father is Faustinianus, while the brothers are Faustinus and Faustus.

Their father Faustus, as the years rolled on and he obtained no tidings of his wife and two elder children, determined after many fruitless enquiries to go in search of them himself. Accordingly he set sail for the East, leaving at home under the charge of guardians his youngest son Clement, then a boy of twelve years. From that time forward Clement heard nothing more of his father and suspected that he had died of grief or been drowned in the sea.

Thus Clement grew up to man's estate a lonely orphan. From his childhood he had pondered the deep questions of philosophy, till they took such hold on his mind that he could not shake them off. On the immortality of the soul more especially he had spent much anxious thought to no purpose. The prevailing philosophical systems had all failed to give him the satisfaction which his heart craved. At length—it was during the reign of Tiberius Cæsar—a rumour reached the imperial city, that an inspired teacher had appeared in Judæa, working miracles and enlisting recruits for the kingdom of God. This report determined him to sail to Judæa. Driven by stress of wind to Alexandria and landing there, he fell in with one Barnabas, a Hebrew and a disciple of the Divine teacher, and from him received his first lessons in the Gospel. From Alexandria he sailed to Cæsarea, where he found Peter, to whom he had been commended by Barnabas. By S. Peter he was further instructed in the faith, and from him he received baptism. He attached himself to his company, and attended him on his subsequent journeys.

At the moment when Clement makes the acquaintance of S. Peter, the Apostle has arranged to hold a public discussion with Simon Magus. Clement desires to know something about this false teacher, and is referred to Aquila and Nicetes, who give him an account of Simon's antecedents and of their own previous connexion with him. The public discussion commences, but is broken off abruptly by Simon who escapes from Cæsarea by stealth. S. Peter follows him from city to city, providing the antidote to his baneful teaching. On the shores of the island of Aradus, Peter falls in with a beggar woman, who had lost the use of her hands. In answer to his enquiries she tells him that she was the wife of a powerful nobleman, that she left home with her two elder sons for reasons which she explains, and that she was shipwrecked and had lost her children at sea. Peter is put off the right scent for the time by her giving feigned names from shame. But the recognition is only delayed. Clement finds in this beggar woman his long-lost mother, and the Apostle heals her ailment.

Aquila and Nicetes had preceded the Apostle to Laodicea. When he arrives there, they are surprised to find a strange woman in his company. He relates her story. They are astounded and overjoyed. They declare themselves to be the lost Faustinus and Faustinianus, and she is their mother. It is needless to add that she is converted and baptised. After her baptism they betake themselves to prayer. While they are returning, Peter enters into conversation with an old man whom he had observed watching the proceedings by stealth. The old man denies the power of prayer. Everything, he says, depends on a man's nativity. A friend of his, a noble Roman, had had the horoscope of his wife cast. It foretold that she would prove unfaithful to him and be drowned at sea. Everything had come to pass in accordance with the prediction. Peter's suspicions are roused by the story; he asks this friend's name, and finds that he was none other than Faustus the husband of Mattidia. The reader's penetration will probably by this time have gone a step farther and divined the truth, which appears shortly afterwards. The narrator is himself Faustus, and he had represented the circumstances as happening to a friend, in order to conceal his identity. Thus Clement has recovered the last of his lost relatives, and the 'recognitions' are complete. One other incident however is necessary to crown the story. Faustus is still a heathen. But the failure of Mattidia's horoscope has made a breach in the citadel of his fatalism, and it is stormed by S. Peter. He yields to the assault and is baptised.

This romance of Clement's life was published within two or three generations of his death—at all events some years before the close of the second century. It is embodied in two extant works, the Clementine *Homilies*, and the Clementine *Recognitions*, with insignificant differences of detail. Yet it has no claim to be regarded as authentic; and we may even question whether its author ever intended it to be accepted as a narrative of facts.

But though we may without misgiving reject this story as a pure fiction, discredited by its crude anachronisms, yet in one respect it has guided us in the right direction. It has led us to the doors of the imperial palace, where we shall have occasion to stay for a while. Our investigations will bring us from time to time across prominent members of the Flavian dynasty; and a knowledge of the family genealogy is needed as a preliminary.

The founder of the Flavian family was T. Flavius Petro[1], a native of the second-rate provincial town Reate, who had fought in the civil

[1] See Sueton. *Vespas.* 1, who is the authority for the main facts in this paragraph.

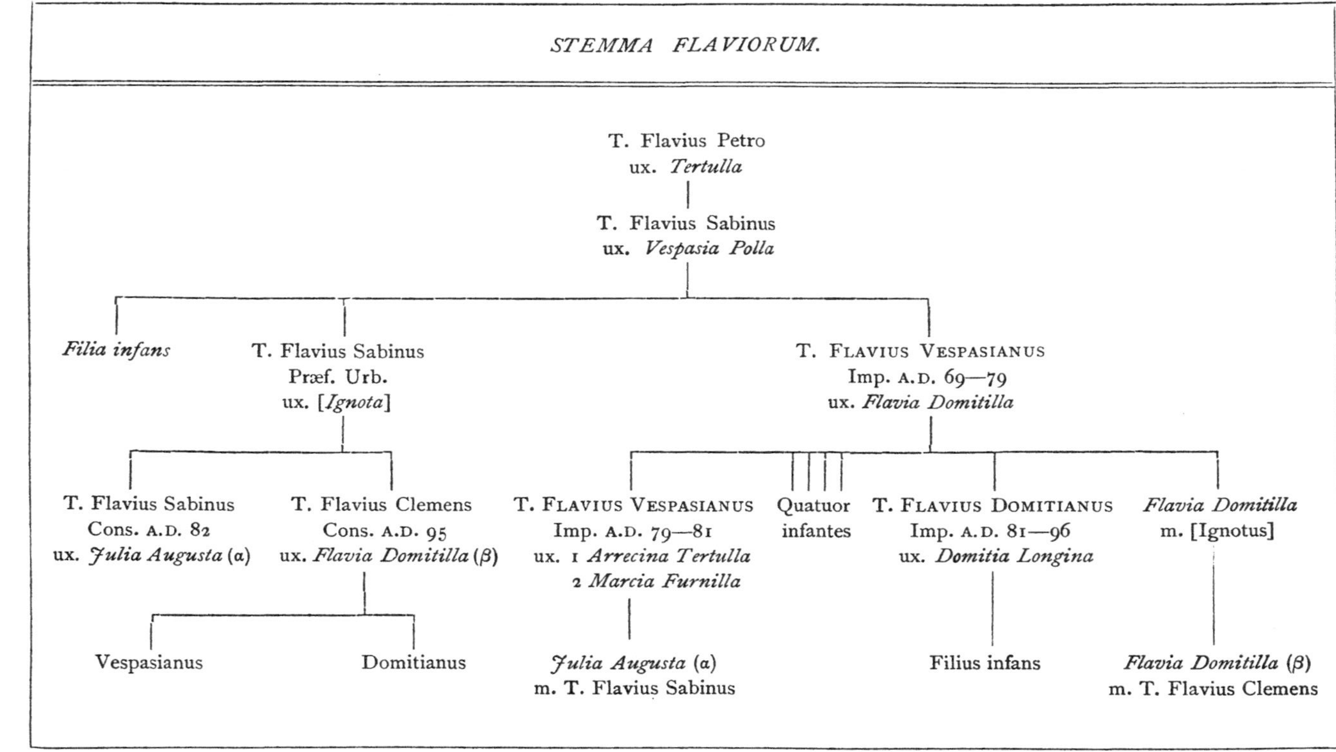
STEMMA FLAVIORUM.
T. Flavius Petro
ux. *Tertulla*
T. Flavius Sabinus
ux. *Vespasia Polla*
Filia infans
T. Flavius Sabinus
Præf. Urb.
ux. [*Ignota*]
T. Flavius Vespasianus
Imp. A.D. 69—79
ux. *Flavia Domitilla*
T. Flavius Sabinus
Cons. A.D. 82
ux. *Julia Augusta* (α)
T. Flavius Clemens
Cons. A.D. 95
ux. *Flavia Domitilla* (β)
T. Flavius Vespasianus
Imp. A.D. 79—81
ux. 1 *Arrecina Tertulla*
2 *Marcia Furnilla*
Quatuor
infantes
T. Flavius Domitianus
Imp. A.D. 81—96
ux. *Domitia Longina*
Flavia Domitilla
m. [Ignotus]
Vespasianus
Domitianus
Julia Augusta (α)
m. T. Flavius Sabinus
Filius infans
Flavia Domitilla (β)
m. T. Flavius Clemens

wars on the side of Pompeius, but after the battle of Pharsalia laid down his arms and went into business. His son Sabinus was a pure civilian. Apparently a thrifty man like his father before him, he amassed some money and married a lady of superior rank to himself, Vespasia Polla, by whom he had three children, a daughter who died an infant in her first year[1] and two sons who both became famous in history—the elder, T. Flavius Sabinus, who held the City prefecture for several years, and the younger, T. Flavius Vespasianus, who attained to the imperial throne.

T. Flavius Sabinus, the elder brother, was prefect of the City at the time of the Neronian persecution and retained this office with one short interruption until his death[2]. The name of his wife is not known. Having been deprived of the City prefecture by Galba and restored by his successor, he was put to death by Vitellius on account of his near relationship to the rival aspirant to the imperial throne[3]. He left two sons, T. Flavius Sabinus and T. Flavius Clemens. The elder, Sabinus, married Julia the daughter of the emperor Titus[4]. He held the consulate in A.D. 82, and was put to death by Domitian, because on his election to this office the herald had inadvertently saluted him as emperor instead of consul[5]. The

[1] Sueton. *Vespas.* 5 'puella nata non perannavit.'

[2] On his tenure of the prefecture see Borghesi *Œuvres* III. p. 327 sq, IX. p. 264 sq. He was appointed to this office by Nero, deprived by Galba, and restored again under Otho (Plutarch. *Otho* 5). Tacitus *Hist.* iii. 75 writes, 'septem annis quibus Moesiam, duodecim quibus praefecturam urbis obtinuit,' but this is inconsistent with his statement elsewhere (*Ann.* xiv. 42), that Pedanius Secundus the prefect of the City was assassinated in A.D. 61. Sabinus seems to have been his immediate successor, and Borghesi therefore proposes to read either 'totidem' for 'duodecim' or vii for xii.

[3] Tacit. *Hist.* iii. 74, Sueton. *Vitell.* 15.

[4] Philostr. *Vit. Apoll.* vii. 7 (p. 284) *Σαβῖνον ἀπεκτονὼς ἕνα τῶν ἑαυτοῦ ξυγγενῶν, Ἰουλίαν ἤγετο, ἡ δὲ Ἰουλία γυνὴ μὲν ἦν τοῦ πεφονευμένου Δομετιανοῦ δὲ ἀδελφιδῆ, μία τῶν Τίτου θυγατέρων.* The last clause is loosely worded, as Titus does not appear to have had any other children.

[5] Sueton. *Domit.* 10 'Flavium Sabinum alterum e patruelibus [occidit], quod eum comitiorum consularium die destinatum perperam praeco non consulem ad populum sed imperatorem pronunciasset.' The herald might have stumbled the more easily, because the emperor was his colleague in the consulship.

Philostratus (l. c.) implies that the emperor's object was to get possession of the murdered man's wife Julia, his own niece. She had been offered to him in marriage earlier, but declined. Afterwards he is said to have had guilty relations with her (Sueton. *Domit.* 22, Dion Cass. lxvii. 3), though he did not actually marry her, as Philostratus' language (*ἤγετο*) might suggest. After her death she was deified by him. Perhaps he acted from mixed motives. The murder does not appear to have taken place immediately after the herald's blunder.

younger brother Clemens married Domitilla, the daughter of Domitian's sister. Of her I shall have to speak presently. With this married couple we are more especially concerned, as they appear—both husband and wife—to have been converts to Christianity, and are intimately connected with our subject.

T. Flavius Vespasianus, the younger son of the first mentioned Sabinus, became emperor in due time and reigned from A.D. 69 to A.D. 79. He married Flavia Domitilla, a daughter of one Flavius Liberalis, a quæstor's clerk and a native of Ferentum[1]. From her name she would seem to have been some relation of her husband, but this is not stated. She is the first of three persons in three successive generations bearing the same name, Flavia Domitilla, mother, daughter, and grand-daughter. By her Vespasian appears to have had seven children[2], but four must have died in infancy or childhood. Only three have any place in history—two sons, T. Flavius Vespasianus and T. Flavius Domitianus, the future emperors, known respectively as Titus and Domitian, and a daughter Domitilla. Both the wife Domitilla and the daughter Domitilla died before A.D. 69, when Vespasian ascended the imperial throne[3]. Either the mother or the daughter—more probably the latter—attained to the honours of apotheosis, and appears on the coins as DIVA DOMITILLA. This distinction had never before been conferred on one who died in a private station, but it served as a precedent which was followed occasionally[4].

The emperor Titus was twice married[5]. By his second wife he

[1] Sueton. *Vespas.* 3.

[2] See the inscription given below, p. 114, with the note upon it.

[3] Sueton. *Vespas.* 3.

[4] In *C. I. L.* v. 2829 mention is made of a SACERDOS . DIVAE . DOMITILLAE, and coins bear the inscription DIVA . DOMITILLA . AVG . (Eckhel VI. p. 345 sq, Cohen I. 337). This deified Domitilla is generally supposed to be the wife of Vespasian. So for instance Eckhel (l. c.). But Statius *Silv.* i. 1. 97, imagining the apotheosis of Domitian, writes 'Ibit in amplexus natus, fraterque, paterque, et soror,' where his sister Domitilla is mentioned among the inhabitants of heaven and his mother is not. For this reason Mommsen (*Staatsrecht* II. p. 794 sq, note) maintains confidently that this deified Domitilla was not the wife, but the daughter of Vespasian. In this case the name Augusta here given to her would have a parallel in Julia Augusta the daughter of Titus. If however the DIVA . DOMITILLA . AVG. is the wife of Vespasian, then probably the other form of inscription found on coins MEMORIAE . DOMITILLAE refers to the daughter, as Eckhel takes it. So far as I can see, it is just possible to refer all the inscriptions on the genuine coins to the daughter, as the passage in Statius suggests, though the connexion sometimes points rather to the mother. Those coins bearing such inscriptions as DOMITILLAE . AVG . MATRI . etc. are spurious.

[5] Sueton. *Tit.* 4. His first wife was Arrecina Tertulla, daughter of the Ar-

left a daughter Julia, who, as we have seen, became the wife of her father's first cousin, the third Sabinus[1]. The emperor Domitian took to wife Domitia Longina. A son, the offspring of this marriage, died in infancy, was received into the ranks of the gods, and appears on the coins as DIVVS CAESAR[2]. There are reasons also for believing that another child was born of this union; but if so, it did not survive long[3]. The sister of the two emperors, Flavia Domitilla, likewise was married. Her husband's name is not recorded, but she left a daughter called after her. This third Flavia Domitilla, the grand-daughter of Vespasian, was wedded, as I have already mentioned, to her mother's first cousin Flavius Clemens, and became famous in Christian circles.

Of this union between Flavius Clemens and Flavia Domitilla two sons were born. They were committed by the emperor Domitian to the tuition of the distinguished rhetorician Quintilian[4]; and we learn

recinus Clemens who was prefect of the prætorium under Gaius, and sister of the Arrecinus Clemens who held the same office under Domitian (Tac. *Hist.* iv. 68) and was put to death by this tyrant (Sueton. *Domit.* 11). Tacitus (*l. c.*) describes the brother as 'domui Vespasiani per affinitatem innexum.' Not only does her father's and brother's name Clemens occur elsewhere in the Flavian pedigree, but her own name Tertulla likewise. Her first name is diversely written Arricidia, Arretina, etc., in different texts. The correct form is decided in an inscription in which she is mentioned (Orelli-Henzen 5429); see De-Vit's Forcellini *Onomast.* s. v. Arrecina. The mother of Julia was Titus' second wife Marcia Furnilla.

[1] See above, p. 18, note 4.

[2] Sueton. *Domit.* 3 'Uxorem suam Domitiam, ex qua in secundo suo consulatu filium tulerat, alteroque anno consalutaverat ut Augustam etc.' The second consulship of Domitian was as early as A.D. 73, some 8 or 9 years before he became emperor. But 'altero anno' ought to mean 'in the second' or 'following year,' and yet the incident implies that he was already Augustus. Either therefore there is some mistake in the figure, or Eckhel (*Doctr. Num.* VI. p. 400) may be right in supposing that Suetonius means the second consulate after he came to the throne, i.e. A.D. 82, when he was consul for the 8th time. Friedländer however without misgiving places it A.D. 73 (*Sittengesch.* III. p. 392). The birth and apotheosis of this son are alluded to in Mart. *Epigr.* iv. 3 (written A.D. 88), in Stat. *Silv.* i. 1. 97 (written A.D. 89 or 90), and in Sil. Ital. *Pun.* iii. 629. Domitia appears on the coins as DIVI . CAESARIS . MATER (Eckhel VI. p. 401, Cohen I. p. 459 sq.). There must be some mistake about the coins described by Cohen I. p. 461, for COS. VI is not chronologically reconcilable with DOMITIANVS AVG.

[3] At all events there was an expectation of another child at a later date, A.D. 89 or 90, soon after the death of Julia, Mart. *Epigr.* vi. 3 (see Friedländer *Sittengesch.* III. pp. 381, 392, and his note on the passage). Eckhel (VI. p. 400) refers this passage to the son who was deified, but this is chronologically impossible.

[4] Quintil. *Instit. Orat.* iv. Prooem. given below, p. 112.

incidentally that the influence of their father Flavius Clemens procured for their tutor the honour of the consular fasces[1]. When they were little children, the emperor had designated them as his successors in the imperial purple, and had commanded them to assume the names Vespasianus and Domitianus[2]. They appear to have been still very young at the time of Domitian's death; and as we hear nothing more of them, they must either have died early or retired into private life. More than a hundred and seventy years later than this epoch, one Domitianus, the general of the usurper Aureolus (A.D. 267), is said to have boasted that he was descended 'from Domitian and from Domitilla'[3]. If this boast was well founded, the person intended was probably the son of Clemens and Domitilla, the younger Domitian, whom the historian confused with his more famous namesake the emperor. A glance at the genealogical tree will show that no one could have traced his direct descent both from the emperor Domitian and from Domitilla; for the Domitilla here mentioned cannot have been the wife of Vespasian[4]. Moreover, there is no record of the emperor Domitian having any children except one, or perhaps more than one, who died in earliest infancy.

Who then was this Clement of Rome, the assumed writer of the Epistle to the Corinthians and the leading man in the Church of Rome in the ages immediately succeeding the Apostolic times? Recent discoveries in two different directions—the one literary, the other archæological—have not only stimulated this enquiry but have furnished more adequate data for an answer to it.

In the first place, the publication of the lost ending to the genuine epistle (A.D. 1875) has enabled us to realize more fully the position

[1] Auson. *Orat. Act. ad Gratian.* 31 'Quintilianus consularia per Clementem ornamenta sortitus, honestamenta nominis potius videtur quam insignia potestatis habuisse.' To this Juvenal probably alludes, *Sat.* vii. 197 'Si fortuna volet, fies de rhetore consul,' as Quintilian is mentioned in his context.

[2] Sueton. *Domit.* 15, quoted below, p. 111 sq. This Vespasianus is probably the ΟΥΕCΠΑCΙΑΝΟC . ΝΕωΤΕΡΟC commemorated on a Smyrnæan coin (Cohen I. p. 462), unless the future emperor Titus before his accession be meant.

[3] Trebell. Poll. *Tyr. Trig.* 12, quoted below, p. 113.

[4] This seems impossible on two accounts; (1) There could be no reason for mentioning the eldest Domitilla, the wife of Vespasian, as she was not famous in any way, whereas the youngest Domitilla, her grand-daughter, had a wide reputation as shown by ancient inscriptions and Christian records alike; (2) If the historian had intended this eldest Domitilla, he would have mentioned not her son Domitian but her husband Vespasian, as the forefather of Domitianus the general.

of the writer. The liturgical prayer in the concluding part, the notices respecting the bearers of the letter, and the attitude assumed towards the persons addressed, all have a bearing upon this question. Then secondly, the recent excavations in the Cemetery of Domitilla at Rome have thrown some light on the surroundings of the writer and on the society among which he lived. The archæological discovery is hardly less important than the literary; and the two combined are a valuable aid in solving the problem.

Before attempting to give the probable answer to this question, it may be well to dispose of other solutions which have been offered from time to time.

1. Origen, without any misgiving, identifies him with the Clement mentioned by S. Paul writing to the Philippians (iv. 3) as among those 'fellow labourers whose names are in the book of life'[1]. This was a very obvious solution. As Hermas the writer of the *Shepherd* was identified with his namesake who appears in the salutations of the Epistle to the Romans[2], so in like manner Clement the writer of the Epistle was assumed to be the same with the Apostle's companion to whom he sends greeting in the Epistle to the Philippians. It is not improbable that others may have made this same identification before Origen. At all events many writers from Eusebius onward adopted it after him[3]. But we have no reason to suppose that it was based on any historical evidence, and we may therefore consider it on its own merits. So considered, it has no claim to acceptance. The chronological difficulty indeed is not insurmountable. A young disciple who had rendered the Apostle efficient aid as early as A.D. 61 or 62, when St Paul wrote to the Philippians, might well have been the chief ruler of the Roman Church as late as A.D. 95 or 96, about which time Clement seems to have written the Epistle to the Corinthians, and might even have survived the close of the first century, as he is reported to have done. But the locality is a more formidable objection. The Clement of S. Paul's epistle is evidently a member of the Philippian Church; the Clement who writes to the Corinthians was head of the Roman community, and would seem to have lived the whole or the main part of his life in Rome. If indeed the name had been very rare, the identification would still have deserved respect notwithstanding the difference of locality; but this is far from being the case. Common even before this epoch, especially among slaves and

[1] *In Joann.* vi. § 36, *Op.* IV. p. 153 (ed. Delarue).

[2] See above, p. 4.

[3] See *Philippians*, p. 168, note 4.

freedmen, it became doubly common during the age of the Flavian dynasty, when it was borne by members of the reigning family[1].

2. A wholly different answer is given in the romance of which I have already sketched the plot. Though earlier than the other authorities which give information about Clement, it is more manifestly false than any. Its anachronisms alone would condemn it. The Clement who wrote the epistle in the latest years of Domitian could not have been a young man at the time of Christ's ministry, nearly seventy years before. Moreover it is inconsistent with itself in its chronology. While Clement's youth and early manhood are placed under Tiberius, the names of his relations, Mattidia and Faustinus, are borrowed from the imperial family of Hadrian and the Antonines. The one date is too early, as the other is too late, for the genuine Clement.

3. A third solution identifies the writer of the epistle with Flavius Clemens, the cousin of Domitian, who held the consulship in the year 95, and was put to death by the emperor immediately after the expiration of his term of office. This identification never occurred to any ancient writer, but it has found much favour among recent critics and therefore demands a full discussion. To this question it will be necessary to return at a later point, when it can be considered with greater advantage. At present I must content myself with saying that, in addition to the other difficulties with which this theory is burdened, it is hardly conceivable that, if a person of the rank and position of Flavius Clemens had been head of the Roman Church, the fact would have escaped the notice of all contemporary and later writers, whether heathen or Christian.

4. Ewald has propounded a theory of his own[2]. He believes that Clement the bishop was not Flavius Clemens himself, but his son. No ancient authority supports this view, and no subsequent critic, so far as I am aware, has accepted it. This identification is based solely on a parallelism with the story in the *Homilies* and *Recognitions*. As Clement's father Faustus (Faustinianus) is there described as a near kinsman of Tiberius[3], so was Flavius Clemens a near kinsman of Domitian. As Mattidia, the wife of Faustus, is

[1] The number of persons bearing this name in one volume alone (V) of the *Corpus Inscriptionum Latinarum* is over fifty, in another (X) it is between forty and fifty. These refer to different parts of Italy. The portion comprising Rome itself is still incomplete and without an index.

[2] *Gesch. d. Volkes Israel* VII. p. 297 sq.

[3] *Hom.* xii. 8, xiv. 6, 10, comp. iv. 7; *Recogn.* vii. 8, ix. 35.

stated herself to have been a blood relation of Tiberius[1], so was Flavia Domitilla, the wife of Flavius Clemens, a blood relation of Domitian. The parallelism might have been pressed somewhat farther, though Ewald himself stops here. Lipsius, though using the parallel for another purpose, points out that Faustus in this romance is represented as having two sons besides Clement, just as Flavius Clemens is known to have had two sons, and that in this fiction these two are said to have changed their names to Aquila and Nicetes, just as in actual history the two sons of Flavius Clemens are recorded to have taken new names, Vespasianus and Domitianus[2]. This parallel however, notwithstanding its ingenuity, need not occupy our time; for the identification which it is intended to support is chronologically impossible. The two sons of Flavius Clemens were boys under the tuition of Quintilian when this rhetorician wrote his great work (about A.D. 90). They are described by Suetonius as young children when their father was put to death (A.D. 95 or 96), or at all events when they were adopted by Domitian as his successors[3]. Indeed this will appear from another consideration, independently of the historian's testimony. Their grandmother was the sister of Titus and Domitian, born A.D. 41 and A.D. 51 respectively. It has been assumed that she was younger than either, because her name is mentioned after her brothers'[4]; but this assumption is precarious. At all events she died before A.D. 69, leaving a daughter behind her. Having regard to these facts, we cannot with any probability place the birth of this daughter, the third Flavia Domitilla, before A.D. 60 or thereabouts; so that her sons must have been mere striplings, even if they were not still children, at the time when their father died and when the Epistle of the Roman Church to the Corinthians was written. But the writer of this epistle was evidently a man of great influence and position, and it is a fair inference that he had passed middle life, even if he was not already advanced in years. Ewald's theory therefore may safely be discarded.

5. A fifth answer is supplied by the spurious Acts of Nereus and Achilleus[5], which are followed by De Rossi[6]. These persons are there

[1] *Hom.* xii. 8, *Recogn.* vii. 8.

[2] *Chronol. d. Röm. Bisch.* p. 153.

[3] Sueton. *Domit.* 15 (see below, p. 111 sq). His expression 'etiam tum parvulos' is commonly referred to the time of their father's death. This is perhaps the more probable reference, but it might refer to the time of their adoption by Domitian.

[4] Hasenclever in *Jahrb. f. Prot. Theol.* VIII. p. 72; see Sueton. *Vespas.* 3 'ex hac liberos tulit Titum et Domitianum et Domitillam.'

[5] See below, p. 42.

[6] *Bull. di Archeol. Crist.* 1865, p. 20 sq.

related to have reminded Clement the bishop that 'Clement the consul was his father's brother.' He is thus represented to be the grandson of Sabinus the City prefect, and son of Sabinus the consul; for no other brother of Flavius Clemens is mentioned elsewhere except Flavius Sabinus the consul. Indeed the language of Suetonius seems to imply two sons, and two only[1], of the elder Sabinus. Moreover this answer is open to the same chronological objection as the last, though not to the same degree. As these Acts are manifestly spurious and cannot date before the fifth or sixth century, and as the statement is unconfirmed by any other authority, we may without misgiving dismiss it from our consideration.

Hitherto the object of our search has eluded us. Our guides have led us to seek our hero among the scions of the imperial family itself. But the palace of the Cæsars comprised men of all grades; and considering the station of life from which the ranks of the Christians were mainly recruited, we should do well to descend to a lower social level in our quest.

The imperial household occupied a large and conspicuous place in the life of ancient Rome. The extant inscriptions show that its members formed a very appreciable fraction of the whole population of the city and neighbourhood. Not only do we find separate columbaria, devoted solely to the interment of slaves and freedmen of a single prince or princess, as Livia or Claudius for instance; but epitaphs of servants and dependants of the imperial family are strewn broadcast among the sepulchral monuments of the suburbs. Obviously this connexion is recorded as a subject of pride on these monumental inscriptions. The 'verna' or the 'servus' or the 'libertus' of Cæsar or of Cæsar's near relations did not wish the fact to be forgotten. Hence the extant inscriptions furnish a vast amount of information, where extant literature is comparatively silent. The most elaborately organized of modern royal establishments would give only a faint idea of the multiplicity and variety of the offices in the palace of the Cæsars[2]. The departments in the household are divided and subdivided; the offices are numberless. The 'tasters' are a separate class of servants under their own chief. Even the pet dog has a functionary assigned to him. The aggregate of imperial residences on or near

[1] Sueton. *Domit.* 10 'Flavium Sabinum *alterum* e patruelibus.'

[2] See the discussion on 'Cæsar's Household' in *Philippians* p. 171 sq.; comp. also Orelli-Henzen *Inscr.* I. 488, III. 245, *C. I. L.* VI. p. 1113 sq, where the Roman inscriptions relating to the subject are given.

the Palatine formed a small city in itself; but these were not the only palaces even in Rome. Moreover the country houses and estates of the imperial family all contributed to swell the numbers of the 'domus Augusta.' But, besides the household in its more restricted sense, the emperor had in his employ a countless number of officials, clerks, and servants of every degree, required for the work of the several departments, civil and military, which were concentrated in him, as the head of the state.

Only a small proportion of these numerous offices were held by Romans. The clever, handy, versatile Greek abounded everywhere. If the Quirites looked with dismay on an invasion which threatened to turn their own Rome into a Greek city, assuredly the danger was not least on the Palatine and in its dependencies. But the Greeks formed only a small portion of these foreign 'dregs'[1], which were so loathsome to the taste of the patriotic Roman. We have ample evidence that Orientals of diverse nations, Egyptians, Syrians, Samaritans, and Jews, held positions of influence in the court and household at the time with which we are concerned. They had all the gifts, for which the multifarious exigencies of Roman civilization would find scope.

It is just here, among this miscellaneous gathering of nationalities, that we should expect Christianity to effect an early lodgment. Nor are we disappointed in our expectation. When S. Paul writes from his Roman captivity to Philippi about midway in Nero's reign, the only special greeting which he is commissioned to send comes from the members 'of Cæsar's household' (iv. 22). We may safely infer from the language thus used that their existence was well known to his distant correspondents. Obviously they were no very recent converts to Christianity. But we may go further than this. I have given reasons elsewhere, not absolutely conclusive indeed but suggesting a high degree of probability, that in the long list of greetings which four years earlier (A.D. 58) the Apostle had sent to the Roman Church, we have some names at least of servants and dependants of the imperial family[2].

More than thirty years had rolled by since the Epistle to the Romans was sent from Corinth, when Clement wrote his letter to the Corinthians in the name of the Roman Christians and from Rome. For a quarter of a century or more the Roman Church had enjoyed comparative peace, if not absolute immunity from persecution[3]. During

[1] Juvenal *Sat.* iii. 61 'Quamvis quota portio faecis Achaei'; comp. Lucr. vii. 405.

[2] *Philippians* p. 171 sq.

[3] See *Ign. and Polyc.* I. p. 15.

the reigns of Vespasian and Titus, and in the early years of Domitian, there is every reason to believe that Christianity had made rapid advances in the metropolis of the world. In its great stronghold—the household of the Cæsars—more especially its progress would be felt. Have we not indications of this in Clement's letter itself?

At the close of the epistle mention is made of the bearers of the letter, two members of the Roman Church, Claudius Ephebus and Valerius Bito, who are despatched to Corinth with one Fortunatus (§ 65). In an earlier passage of the epistle (§ 63) these delegates are described as 'faithful and prudent men, who have walked among us (the Roman Christians) from youth unto old age unblameably (*ἄνδρας πιστοὺς καὶ σώφρονας ἀπὸ νεότητος ἀναστραφέντας ἕως γήρους ἀμέμπτως ἐν ἡμῖν*).' Now the date of this epistle, as determined by internal and external evidence alike, is about A.D. 95 or 96; and, as old age could hardly be predicated of persons under sixty, they must have been born as early as the year 35, and probably some few years earlier. They would therefore have been young men of thirty or thereabouts, when S. Paul sent his salutation to the Philippians. It is clear likewise from Clement's language that they had been converted to Christianity before that time. But their names, Claudius and Valerius, suggest some important considerations. The fourth Cæsar reigned from A.D. 41 to A.D. 54, and till A.D. 48 Messalina was his consort. Like his two predecessors, Tiberius and Gaius, he was a member of the Claudian gens, while Messalina belonged to the Valerian. Consequently we find among the freedmen of the Cæsars and their descendants both names, Claudius (Claudia) and Valerius (Valeria), in great frequency. Moreover they occur together, as the names of parent and child (*C. I. L.* VI. 4923),

D . M .	D . M .
CLAVDIAE . AVG . LIB . NEREIDI	M . VALERIO . SYNTROPHO
M . VALERIVS . FVTIANVS	FVTIANVS
MATRI . CARISSIMAE	LIB . OPTIMO,

or of husband and wife (*C. I. L.* VI. 8943),

VALERIA . HILARIA
NVTRIX
OCTAVIAE . CAESARIS . AVGVSTI
HIC . REQVIESCIT . CVM
TI . CLAVDIO . FRVCTO . VIRO . SVO . CARISSIMO,

where the Octavia, whom this Valeria nursed, is the ill-fated daughter of Claudius and wife of Nero. To these should be added another inscription (*C. I. L.* x. 2271),

D . M .
CLAVDI . GEMELLI
ANNIS . XIX
VALERIVS . VITALIS
HERES . B . M .

not only for the connexion of the names Claudius and Valerius, but because Vitalis (elsewhere written Bitalis *C. I. L.* vi. 4532, where likewise it is mentioned in the same inscription with a Valeria) may possibly be connected with Vito (Bito)[1].

The same combination likewise occurs in *C. I. L.* vi. 4548,

CLAVDIAE . PIERIDI . ET
FILIAE . EIVS
M . VALERIVS
SECVNDIO . FEC.

as also in *C. I. L.* vi. 15174,

DIIS . MAN . SACR.
TI . CLAVDI . ONESIMI . FEC.
VALERIA . ATHENAIS
CONIVGI . SVO . KARISSIMO,

and again in *C. I. L.* vi. 15304,

DIIS . MANIBVS
TI . CLAVDII . TI . F . QVI
VALERIANI
VIXIT . ANN . VIIII . MENS . VI
D . VALERIVS . EVTYCHES,

and likewise in *C. I. L.* vi. 15351,

CLAVDIAE . AMMIAE
L . VALERIVS . GLYCON . FEC.
COIVGI . CARISSIMAE.

[1] We have this combination 'Claudius Vitalis' again in vi. 9151, 9152, in connexion with a freedman of the emperor (comp. x. 8397). So also 'Claudia Vitalis,' vi. 15654, 15655. In like manner x. 2261 TI . CLAVDIO . BITONI, though BITO is not a common name (*C. I. L.* v. 6913, 8110(56), ix. 85). Similarly we meet with 'Valerius Vitalis' in viii. 2562 (15) and 'Valeria Vitalis' in vi. 4674, while 'Bitalis' and 'Valeria' appear in the same inscription vi. 4532. The names 'Vitus' (Βίτος) and 'Vitalis' (Βιτάλιος) are used of the same person in the spurious Ignatian Epistles, *Philipp.* 14, *Hero* 8.

Probably many other examples also might be found, exhibiting this same combination of names. The connexion of persons bearing the name Valerius, Valeria, with the household of Messalina is patent in several cases, either from the context of the inscription or from the locality in which it is found (see *C. I. L.* VI. p. 909). Of the Jewish origin of many slaves and freedmen of the imperial palace I have already spoken. This appears in the case of one CLAVDIA SABBATHIS (*C. I. L.* VI. 8494), who erects a monument to her son described as a 'slave of our Cæsars'. The name here clearly betrays its Jewish origin, and indeed we find it in other places borne by Jews[1]. Elsewhere likewise we meet with evidence of the presence of Jews among slaves and dependants of the Valerian gens[2]. All these facts combined seem to invest the opinion which I have ventured to offer, that these messengers who carried the Roman letter to Corinth were brought up in the imperial household, with a high degree of probability[3]. When S. Paul wrote from Rome to the Philippians about A.D. 62, they would be, as we have seen, in the prime of life; their consistent course would mark them out as the future hope of the Roman Church; they could hardly be unknown to the Apostle; and their names along with others would be present to his mind when he dictated the words, 'They that are of Cæsar's household salute you.' The Claudia of 2 Tim. iv. 21 likewise was not improbably connected with the imperial palace.

Hitherto we have not risen above the lower grades in the social scale. But it is the tendency of religious movements to work their way upwards from beneath, and Christianity was no exception to the general

[1] Boeckh *C. I. G.* 9910 ΕΝΘΑΔΕ . ΚΕΙΘΕΙ . CΑΒΒΑΤΙC . ΔΙCΑΡΧΩΝ (comp. Garrucci *Dissert. Archäol.* II. p. 189), where Σαββάτις is a man's name, as belonging to a ruler of a synagogue (see also *ib.* p. 182 Σαβάτιος). In *C. I. G.* 9723 it is a Christian name; and elsewhere we meet with Σαββάτιος, Σαββατία, De Rossi *Rom. Sotterr.* I. p. 326, III. pp. 173, 288, and Tav. xviii. 57.

[2] We find the Jewish names, L VALERIVS BARICHA, L. VALERIVS ZABDA, L. VALERIVS ACHIBA, as freedmen of one L. Valerius, in an inscription on the Appian way (Canina *Via Appia* I. p. 224).

[3] Along with Claudius Ephebus and Valerius Bito a third person, Fortunatus, is mentioned. The form of expression (*σὺν καὶ Φορτουνάτῳ*), which dissociates him from the other two, suggests that he was a Corinthian, as I have pointed out in my note on the passage (§ 65). If not, the name might be illustrated by *C. I. L.* V. 4103 TI . CLAVDIVS . TI . L[IB]. FORTVNATVS, or by *C. I. L.* VI. 15082 TI . CLAVDIO . AVG . L . FORTVNATO, where this cognomen is not only connected with the name of one of his fellow-messengers but likewise with the imperial household. For the combination of 'Fortunatus' with 'Claudius' see also *C. I. L.* V. 7281, VI. 15067, 15070—15081, IX. 338, 4255, 4995. For its connexion with the other name Valerius, see below, p. 62, note 1.

rule. Starting from slaves and dependants, it advanced silently step by step, till at length it laid hands on the princes of the imperial house[1]. Even before S. Paul's visit to Rome the Gospel seems to have numbered at least one lady of high rank among its converts[2]. Pomponia Græcina, the wife of Plautius the conqueror of Britain, was arraigned of 'foreign superstition' before the Senate and handed over to a domestic tribunal, by which however she was acquitted[3]. Many years earlier her friend Julia, the daughter of Drusus, had been put to death by the wiles of Messalina[4]. From that time forward she cherished a life-long grief, and never appeared in public except in deep mourning. These

[1] This is a convenient place to refer to two articles by Hasenclever, entitled *Christliche Proselyten der höheren Stände im ersten Jahrhundert* in *Jahrb. f. Protest. Theol.* VIII. p. 34—78, p. 230—271. They go over the whole ground and are well worth reading, though not free from inaccuracies.

[2] Tac. *Ann.* xiii. 32 'Pomponia Graecina, insignis femina, Plautio qui ovans se de Brittaniis rettulit nupta ac superstitionis externae rea, mariti judicio permissa; isque prisco instituto, propinquis coram, de capite famaque conjugis cognovit et insontem nuntiavit. Longa huic Pomponiae aetas et continua tristitia fuit; nam post Juliam Drusi filiam dolo Messalinae interfectam per quadraginta annos non cultu nisi lugubri, non animo nisi maesto egit; idque illi imperitante Claudio impune, mox ad gloriam vertit.'

[3] Wandinger (p. 30 sq.) appears to me to give the most probable account of the trial before the domestic tribunal. As Judaism was a religion recognised by Roman law, and as Christianity was not yet distinguished from Judaism, Pomponia was entitled to an acquittal on the purely religious ground. But rumours were already abroad, which accused the Christians of flagitious and impure orgies in secret, and the participation in these was the matter referred to the domestic tribunal. The domestic court was charged with the cognizance of this very class of crimes, more especially of the violation of the marriage vow. On this ancient institution see Dionys. Hal. *Ant.* ii. 25 *ἁμαρτάνουσα δέ τι δικαστὴν τὸν ἀδικούμενον ἐλάμβανε καὶ τοῦ μεγέθους τῆς τιμωρίας κύριον· ταῦτα δὲ οἱ συγγενεῖς μετὰ τοῦ ἀνδρὸς ἐδίκαζον· ἐν οἷς ἦν φθορα σώματος κ.τ.λ.*, M. Cato in Aul. Gell. *Noct.* x. 23 'Vir cum divortium facit, mulieri judex pro censore est...si quid perverse taetreque factum est a muliere, multitatur; si vinum bibit, si cum alieno viro probri quid fecit, condempnatur,' Tac. *Ann.* ii. 50 'adulterii graviorem poenam deprecatus, ut exemplo majorum propinquis suis ultra ducentesimum lapidem removeretur suasit,' Sueton. *Tib.* 35 'Matronas prostratae pudicitiae...ut propinqui more majorum de communi sententia coercerent, auctor fuit.'

[4] Sueton. *Claud.* 29 'Julias, alteram Drusi, alteram Germanici filiam, crimine incerto nec defensione ulla data occidit'; comp. Senec. *Apocol.* 10, where Augustus is made to say, 'ut duas Julias proneptes meas occideret, alteram ferro, alteram fame.' Of these two Julias, who were put to death by Claudius, the former was the friend of Pomponia Græcina. She appears also to have been a relation; for Drusus was descended from Pomponius Atticus, the friend of Cicero (Tac. *Ann.* ii. 43). On her death see (besides the passage of Tacitus quoted in note 2) Dion Cass. lx. 18, Tac. *Ann.* xiii. 43, Incert. *Octav.* 970 sq.

two traits combined—the seriousness of demeanour and the imputation of a strange religion—had led many modern critics of repute to suppose that she was a convert to Christianity[1]. This surmise, which seemed probable in itself, has been converted almost into a certainty by an archæological discovery of recent years[2].

The earliest portion of the catacombs of Callistus, the so-called crypt of Lucina, shows by its character and construction that it must have been built in the first century of the Christian Church. Its early date appears alike in the better taste of its architecture and decorations and in its exposure above ground. But in this crypt a sepulchral inscription has been found belonging to the close of the second or beginning of the third century, unquestionably bearing the name Pomponius Græcinus[3], though somewhat mutilated; while other neighbouring monuments record the names of members of the Pomponian gens or of families allied to it. It is clear therefore that this burial place was constructed by some Christian lady of rank, probably before the close of the first century, for her fellow-religionists; and that among these fellow-religionists within a generation or two a descendant or near kinsman of Pomponia Græcina was buried. De Rossi, to whom we owe this discovery and the inferences drawn from it, himself goes a step farther. The name Lucina does not occur elsewhere in Roman history, and yet the foundress of this cemetery must have been a person of rank and means, to erect so costly a place of sepulture and to secure its immunity when erected. He suggests therefore that Lucina was none other than Pomponia Græcina herself, and that this name was assumed by her to commemorate her baptismal privileges, in accordance with the early Christian language which habitually spoke of baptism as an 'enlightening' (φωτισμός). Without following him in this precarious identification, which indeed he puts forward with some diffidence, we shall still find in his archæological discoveries a strong confirmation of the conjecture, to

[1] So Merivale *Hist. of Rom.* VI. p. 272 sq.; see *Philippians* p. 21. Monographs on this subject are Friedländer *De Pomp. Graecin. superstitionis externae rea* 1868, and Wandinger *Pomponia Graecina* 1873. It is also fully discussed in Hasenclever p. 47 sq. Friedländer's tract was written without any knowledge of De Rossi's discoveries, and he disputed the Christianity of Pomponia. After making acquaintance with these discoveries he speaks differently (*Sittengesch. Roms* III. p. 534). Wandinger writes to refute Friedländer's tract. Among recent writers, Hausrath *Neutest. Zeitgesch.* III. p. 300, and Schiller *Röm. Kaiserz.* I. p. 446, still speak doubtfully.

[2] De Rossi *Rom. Sotterr.* I. p. 306 sq., II. p. 280 sq, 360 sq; comp. *ib.* II. Anal. Geol. Archit. p. 20 sq.

[3] See the plate *Rom. Sotterr.* II. Tav. xlix, Π[Ο]ΜΠΩΝΙΟϹ ΓΡΗ[Κ]Ε[ΙΝΟ]Ϲ, where however some of the letters not included in brackets are much mutilated.

which the notice in Tacitus had given rise, that Pomponia was a Christian[1].

The death of her friend Julia took place in A.D. 43[2]; the charge of 'foreign superstition' was brought against her in A.D. 57; and she herself must have died about A.D. 83[3], for she is stated to have worn her mourning for her friend forty years. We are thus brought into the reign of Domitian. But some reasons exist for supposing that she was related to the Flavian family. In the *Acts of SS. Nereus and Achilleus* (May 12) we are told that Plautilla was sister of Flavius Clemens the consul, and mother of Domitilla the virgin[4]. This statement is accepted by De Rossi and others. Plautilla would thus be the daughter of Vespasian's brother, Sabinus the City prefect; and, as his wife's name is not otherwise known, De Rossi weds him to a supposed daughter of Aulus Plautius and Pomponia Græcina, whom he designates Plautia, and who thus becomes the mother of Plautilla[5]. This theory however is somewhat frail and shadowy. The Acts of Nereus and

[1] By a process which I am unable to follow, Hasenclever (p. 47 sq) arrives at the conclusion that at the time of her trial Pomponia was only a proselytess to Judaism, but that she afterwards became a Christian. He sees an allusion to this change in the final sentence of the notice in Tacitus, 'idque illi imperitante Claudio impune, mox ad gloriam vertit,' referring the last clause to her deeds of charity as a Christian which gave her a great reputation even among the heathen (p. 63). Surely the sentence means nothing more than that her constancy to Julia's memory somehow escaped punishment during the lifetime of the tyrant by whom her friend was murdered, and obtained its proper meed of praise, when men's tongues were untied by his death.

[2] Dion Cass. lx. 18. The sequence of events requires A.D. 43, not A.D. 44, as Hasenclever (p. 49) gives it.

[3] Hasenclever (pp. 61, 63) places her death in A.D. 97 or 98, on the authority of Tacitus, apparently reckoning the forty years from the date of her trial; but this is evidently not the historian's meaning.

[4] Bolland. *Act. Sanct.* Maii III. p. 8 'Hujus [Clementis consulis] soror Plautilla nos [Nereum et Achilleum] in famulos comparavit... et nos simul secum et cum filia Domitilla sancto baptismate consecravit.' The passage is given in full below, p. 111.

One Plautilla, described as 'nobilissima matrona...apostolorum ferventissima dilectrix et religionis divinae cultrix,' appears in the *Passio Pauli* (De la Bigne *Magn. Bibl. Vet. Patr.* I. p. 75 sq) of the pseudo-Linus, where she lends S. Paul the veil wherewith he binds his eyes. She plays the same part for S. Paul, which Veronica does for our Lord. Nothing is said of her family connexions. As the author of the *Acts of Nereus and Achilleus* was acquainted with the work of this spurious Linus (see Lipsius *Apokryph. Apostelgesch.* II. i. p. 106, 200 sq), he probably derived the name thence. On the Plautilla legend see Lipsius *ib.* pp. 95 sq, 158, 170 sq. He does not seem to me to have given adequate reasons for his view that this legend, though absent from some recensions, formed part of the original *Passio Pauli*.

[5] *Bull. di Archeol. Crist.* 1865, p. 20 sq.

Achilleus are, as I have already stated, late and devoid of authority[1]; the existence of Domitilla the virgin, as distinguished from Domitilla the wife of Flavius Clemens, is highly questionable; and Plautia herself, who does not appear outside this theory, is a mere critical postulate to account for the name of Plautilla. Still it remains possible that the Plautilla of these Acts was not a pure fiction; and in this case De Rossi's handling of the pedigree, which thus links together the Pomponian and Flavian families, is at least plausible. A connexion of another kind between these families is a matter of history. The two brothers, Sabinus and Vespasian, both served under Aulus Plautius in Britain as his lieutenants[2].

But, whether from the upward moral pressure of slaves and freedmen in the household itself or through the intercourse with friends of a higher social rank like Pomponia Græcina, the new religion before long fastened upon certain members of the imperial family itself with tragic results. The innate cruelty of Domitian had a merciless and unscrupulous ally in his ever growing jealousy. Any one who towered above his fellows in moral or intellectual stature, or whose social or official influence excited his suspicions, was at once marked out for destruction. Philosophers and men of letters, nobles and statesmen, alike were struck down. Ladies of rank were driven into banishment[3]. In such cases the most trivial charge was sufficient to procure condemnation. The adoption of an unrecognized religion or the practice of foreign rites was a convenient handle. I have spoken elsewhere of the persecution against the Jews in this reign and of its indirect consequences to the Christians[4]. But the Jewish religion at all events was tolerated by the law. The profession of Christianity enjoyed no such immunity. A charge was brought by the emperor against Flavius Clemens and Flavia Domitilla his wife[5]—the former his first cousin, the latter his niece. A childless monarch, he seems to have scanned his own relations with especial jealousy. The brother of Flavius Clemens, a man of consular rank, had been put to death by Domitian some years before. Clemens himself was the emperor's colleague

[1] See above, p. 24, and below, p. 42 sq. Lipsius places them as far back as the 5th century, and they cannot well be dated earlier; *Quellen d. Röm. Petrussage* p. 152 sq, *Apokr. Apostelgesch.* II. i. p. 107.

[2] Dion Cass. lx. 20.

[3] Tacit. *Agric.* 45 'tot *consularium* caedes, tot *nobilissimarum feminarum* exsilia et fugas,' where the connexion suggests that Tacitus had prominently in his mind Domitian's treatment of Clemens and Domitilla.

[4] See *Ignat. and Polyc.* I. p. 11 sq.

[5] The authorities for this incident are given in full below, p. 104 sq.

in the consulship, and had only just resigned his office[1], when he found himself the victim of his cousin's malignity. His two children had been designated by the emperor as his successors in the purple, and bidden to assume the names Vespasianus and Domitianus accordingly[2]. The charge against him, so Suetonius reports, was the flimsiest possible. Dion Cassius tells us more explicitly that the husband and wife alike were accused of atheism[3], and connects this charge with the adoption of Jewish rites and customs. This combination can hardly point to anything else but the profession of Christianity[4]. Judaism, as distinguished from Christianity, will not meet the case[5], both because Judaism was a religion recognized by law and because 'atheism' would be out of place in this case. Indeed the authorities used by Eusebius—notably Bruttius—seem to have

[1] Dion Cassius says ὑπατεύοντα, 'while he was consul,' but Suetonius 'tantum non in ipso ejus consulatu'. He was 'consul ordinarius' with Domitian in A.D. 95; and the two statements may be reconciled by supposing that he died in the year which was named after his consulate, though he had retired to make way for a 'suffectus.' Domitian died on Sept. 18, A.D. 96, and Suetonius apparently speaks of the interval after the execution of Clemens as eight months (*Domit.* 15 'continuis octo mensibus'); see Imhof *Domitianus* p. 116. If therefore he was executed in A.D. 95, it must have been quite at the close of the year. It does not seem to me necessary to interpret the eight months rigidly with Lipsius (*Chron.* pp. 153, 161), so as to place his death in January 96.

[2] See above, pp. 21, 24, and below pp. 42, 112.

[3] *Domit.* 14 *ἐπηνέχθη δὲ ἀμφοῖν ἔγκλημα ἀθεότητος ὑφ' ἧς καὶ ἄλλοι ἐς τὰ τῶν Ἰουδαίων ἔθη ἐξοκέλλοντες πολλοὶ κατεδικάσθησαν.*

For the charge of 'atheism' brought against the Christians see the note on Ignat. *Trall.* 3.

[4] The combination of the two charges is accepted by Gibbon *Decline and Fall* c. xvi, as showing that they were Christians. So too Baur *Paulus* p. 472, and most writers. Renan, *Les Évangiles* p. 226 sq, treats them as only Christians in a very vague way.

[5] Grätz (*Geschichte der Juden* IV. p. 120, 435 sq; comp. *Monatsschr. f. Gesch. u. Wiss. d. Judenth.* April 1869, p. 169) would make him a convert to Judaism. He connects the account of Clemens with a story in the Talmud (*Gittin* 56b, *Abodah Sarah* 11a) of one Onkelos son of Calonicus or Cleonicus קלוניקוס, or of Calonymus or Cleonymus קלונימוס (for it is differently written in the two passages), and nephew of the emperor Titus, who was converted to Judaism; and he supposes this to represent the name Clemens. The story however has nothing else in common with the account of Fl. Clemens, and the hero is not this Calonicus (Calonymus) himself, but his son Onkelos. The two Talmudic passages will be found in F. C. Ewald's *Abodah Sarah* p. 77 sq. There is indeed the bare possibility that this Talmudic legend has grown out of the account of Clemens as given for example by Dion Cassius, but it cannot have any value in determining the actual facts. Other Talmudic stories, in which Grätz finds a reference to Clemens and Domitilla, are even more foreign to the subject.

stated this distinctly, at least of the wife. Clemens himself was put to death; Domitilla was banished to one of the islands, Pontia or Pandateria[1]. Of the husband Suetonius speaks as a man of 'utterly contemptible indolence.' This inactive temperament may have been partially hereditary; for his father Sabinus, the City prefect, is said to have been deficient in energy[2]. But it is much more likely to have been the result of his equivocal position. He would be debarred by his principles from sharing the vicious amusements which were popular among his fellow countrymen, and he must have found himself checked again and again in his political functions by his religious scruples. To be at once a Roman consul and a Christian convert in this age was a position which might well tax the consistency of a sincere and upright man. The Christian apologists in these early times are obliged constantly to defend themselves against the charge of indifference to their political and civil duties[3].

But any shadow of doubt, which might have rested on the Christianity of Clemens and Domitilla after the perusal of the historical notices, has been altogether removed (at least as regards the wife) by the antiquarian discoveries of recent years.

Among the early burial places of the Roman Christians was one called the *Coemeterium Domitillae*. This has been identified beyond question by the investigations of De Rossi with the catacombs of the Tor Marancia near the Ardeatine Way[4]. With characteristic patience and acuteness the eminent archæologist has traced the early history of this cemetery; and it throws a flood of light on the matter in question[5].

[1] Dion banishes her to Pandateria; Eusebius, following Bruttius, to Pontia. This discrepancy is discussed below, p. 49 sq.

[2] Tacit. *Hist.* ii. 63 'Sabinus suopte ingenio mitis, ubi formido incessisset, facilis mutatu' etc, iii. 59 'Sabinus inhabilem labori et audaciae valetudinem causabatur,' iii. 65 'melior interpretatio mitem virum abhorrere a sanguine et caedibus,' iii. 75 'in fine vitae alii segnem, multi moderatum et civium sanguinis parcum credidere.' The expression which Suetonius applies to his son is 'contemptissimae inertiae.'

[3] Tertull. *Apol.* 42 'infructuosi in negotiis dicimur,' against which charge he defends the Christians at length; see also Minuc. Fel. *Octav.* 8 'latebrosa et lucifuga natio, in publicum muta, in angulis garrula.' Some difficult problem confronted the Christian at every turn in connexion with his duties to the state; see Neander *Hist.* I. p. 274 sq.

[4] On what grounds Hasenclever (p. 261) can call this identification 'more than questionable,' I cannot understand in the face of the evidence. Yet Lipsius (*Apokr. Apostelgesch.* II. i. p. 205, note 2) says the same. By the way Hasenclever calls it 'Tor Mancia,' and has misled Lipsius.

[5] De Rossi's investigations will be found in the *Bullettino di Archeologia Cristiana* 1865, pp. 17 sq, 33 sq, 41 sq, 89 sq; 1874, pp. 5 sq, 68 sq,

Inscriptions have been discovered which show that these catacombs are situated on an estate once belonging to the Flavia Domitilla who was banished on account of her faith. Thus one inscription records that the plot of ground on which the cippus stood had been granted to P. Calvisius Philotas as the burial place of himself and others, EX. INDVLGENTIA. FLAVIAE. DOMITILL[AE]. Another monumental tablet is put up by one Tatia in the name of herself and her freedmen and freedwomen. This Tatia is described as [NV]TRIX. SEPTEM. LIB[ERORVM]. DIVI. VESPASIAN[I. ATQUE]. FLAVIAE. DOMITIL[LAE]. VESPASIANI. NEPTIS, and the sepulchre is stated to be erected EIVS. BENEFICIO, i.e. by the concession of the said Flavia Domitilla, to whom the land belonged. A third inscription runs as follows...FILIA. FLAVIAE. DOMITILLAE...... [VESPASI]ANI. NEPTIS. FECIT. GLYCERAE. L. This last indeed was not found on the same site with the others, having been embedded in the pavement of the Basilica of San Clemente in Rome: but there is some reason for thinking that it was transferred thither at an early date with other remains from the Cemetery of Domitilla. Even without the confirmation of this last monument however, the connexion of this Christian cemetery with the wife of Flavius Clemens is established beyond any reasonable doubt. And recent excavations have supplied further links of evidence. This cemetery was approached by an above ground vestibule, which leads to a hypogæum, and to which are attached chambers, supposed to have been used by the custodian of the place and by the mourners assembled at funerals. From the architecture and the paintings De Rossi infers that the vestibule itself belongs to the first century. Moreover the publicity of the building, so unlike the obscure doorways and dark underground passages which lead to other catacombs, seems to justify the belief that it was erected under the protection of some important personage and during a period of quiet such as intervened between the death of Nero and the persecution of Domitian. The underground vaults and passages contain remains which in De Rossi's opinion point to the first half of the second century. Here also are sepulchral memorials, which seem to belong to the time of the Antonines, and imply a connexion with the Flavian household. Thus one exhibits the monogram of a FLAVILLA; another bears the inscription ΦΛ. CΑΒΕΙΝΟC. ΚΑΙ. ΤΙΤΙΑΝΗ. ΑΔΕΛΦΟΙ; a third, ΦΛ. ΠΤΟΛΕΜΑΙΟC.

122 sq; 1875, pp. 5 sq, 46 sq; 1877, p. 128 sq; 1878, p. 126 sq; 1879, pp. 5 sq, 139 sq; 1880, pp. 69, 169 sq; 1881, p. 57 sq: comp. *Roma Sotterranea* I. p. 186 sq, 266 sq. The Cemetery of Domitilla and its surroundings will form the main subject of the 4th volume of *Roma Sotterranea*, which has not yet appeared.

ΠΡ. ΚΑΙ ΟΥΛΠΙ. ΚΟΝΚΟΡΔΙΑ. As regards the second, it will be remembered that the father of Flavius Clemens and brother of Vespasian bore this name T. Flavius Sabinus; and De Rossi therefore supposes that we have here the graves of actual descendants, grandchildren or great grandchildren, of this Flavius Sabinus, through his son Flavius Clemens the Christian martyr. In illustration of the name Titiane again, he remarks that three prefects of Egypt during the second century bore the name Flavius Titianus, and that the wife of the emperor Pertinax was a Flavia Titiana. We may hesitate to accept these facts as evidence that the persons in question were actual descendants of the imperial house; but if not, the names will at all events point to connexions or retainers of the family. The restoration of another inscription, [SEPVLC]RVM [FLAVI]ORVM, which is followed by a cruciform anchor and therefore points to a Christian place of sepulture, may indeed be correct, but it is far too uncertain to be accepted as evidence.

Connected also with this same cemetery from very early times was the cultus of one Petronilla[1]. Here, between the years 390 and 395[2], Pope Siricius erected over her tomb a spacious basilica with three aisles, of which very considerable remains have been laid bare by recent explorations. The tomb itself was a very ancient sarcophagus bearing the inscription[3]

AVR . PETRONILLAE . FILIAE . DVLCISSIMAE .

This Petronilla for some reason or other was the patron saint of the Carlovingian kings of France. To commemorate the alliance between king Pepin and the Papacy, the reigning pope Stephen II undertook to translate the remains of S. Petronilla to the Vatican; and this pledge was fulfilled by his brother and immediate successor Paul I (A.D. 758). Her new resting-place however at the Vatican was not a recent erection, but an imperial mausoleum, already some centuries old, as De Rossi has shown[4]. This Church of S. Petronilla, and with it the ancient

1 For the discovery of the basilica of S. Petronilla and for her cultus within the Cemetery of Domitilla, as also for the memorials of SS. Nereus and Achilleus within the same cemetery, see *Bull. di Archeol. Crist.* 1874, pp. 5 sq, 68 sq, 122 sq, 1875, p. 5 sq.

2 These limits of time are established by the position of the dated monuments; see De Rossi *Bull. di Archeol. Crist.* 1874, p. 27 sq, 1875, p. 46.

3 For the sarcophagus and its inscription, for the translation of the remains, and for the church at the Vatican, see *Bull. di Archeol. Crist.* 1878, p. 125 sq, 1879, p. 5 sq, p. 139 sq.

4 *Bull. di Archeol. Crist.* 1878, p. 139 sq. A ground plan of the ancient basilica of S. Peter, with the buildings connected with it, including this Church of S. Petronilla, is given in Duchesne's *Liber Pontificalis* I. p. 192.

sarcophagus which had been transferred from the Cemetery of Domitilla, perished in the ruthless and wholesale vandalism, which swept away the original basilica of Constantine with other priceless memorials of early Christendom, to make room for the modern Church of S. Peter in the sixteenth century. This Petronilla in legendary story was called the daughter of S. Peter. Some modern critics have sought to explain this designation by a spiritual fatherhood, just as the same Apostle speaks of his 'son Marcus' (1 Pet. v. 13). But the legend has obviously arisen from the similarity of the names Petros, Petronilla[1], and thus it implies a natural relationship. The removal of her sarcophagus to the Vatican, and the extraordinary honours there paid to her, are only explicable on this supposition. Of this personage De Rossi has given a probable account. It had been remarked by Baronius, that the name Petronilla is connected etymologically not with *Petros* but with *Petronius;* and De Rossi calls attention to the fact, which has been mentioned already[2], that the founder of the Flavian family was T. Flavius Petro. This Petronilla therefore, whom the later legend connects with S. Peter, may have been some scion of the Flavian house, who, like her relations Fl. Clemens and Fl. Domitilla, became a convert to Christianity. The name Aurelia suggests a later date than the Apostolic times, and points rather to the age of the Antonines than to the age of S. Peter. If, as seems to have been the case, it was given in its contracted form AVR., this indicates an epoch, when the name had already become common, being borne by the imperial family, just as under similar circumstances we have CL. for CLAVDIVS and FL. for FLAVIVS[3]. Even the simple fact of a conspicuous tomb bearing the name Petronilla, and the dedication to a 'darling daughter', would have been a sufficient starting-point for the legend of her relationship to S. Peter, when the glorification of that apostle had become a dominant idea[4].

[1] *Bull. di Archeol. Crist.* 1865, p. 22, 1879, p. 141. De Rossi seems still to attach weight to the opinion that Petronilla was a spiritual daughter of S. Peter; but he himself has deprived this hypothesis of its *raison d'être* by pointing out the true derivation of the name. The spiritual relationship is a mere invention of modern critics, following Baronius (ann. 69, § xxxiii). To this writer it was an offence that a daughter should have been born to S. Peter after his call to the apostleship, and he argues against the natural relationship accordingly. The old legend had no such scruple.

[2] See above, p. 16.

[3] *Bull. di Archeol. Crist.* 1879, pp. 147, 155. These considerations, as favouring a later date, suggest a misgiving to De Rossi whether S. Petronilla can have been a personal disciple of S. Peter, as his theory requires.

[4] The Acts of S. Petronilla are incorporated in those of SS. Nereus and Achil-

Of the connexion of Nereus and Achilleus, the legendary chamberlains of Domitilla, with this basilica of Petronilla, I shall have occasion to speak presently. Still more interesting is the slab bearing the name AMPLIATVS, as raising the question whether this may not be the very person named in S. Paul's salutations to the Romans[1]; but, except that the form of the letters and the character of the surroundings betoken a very early date, and thus furnish additional evidence that this locality was a primitive burial-place of the Christians[2], it has no direct bearing on the question before us. The name itself is common.

The account which I have given will suffice as an outline of the principal facts which De Rossi has either discovered or emphasized, and of the inferences which he has drawn from them, so far as they bear on my subject. He has also endeavoured to strengthen his position by other critical combinations; but I have preferred to pass them over as shadowy and precarious. Even of those which I have given, some perhaps will not command general assent. But the main facts seem to be established on grounds which can hardly be questioned; that we have here a burial place of Christian Flavii of the second century; that it stands on ground which once belonged to Flavia Domitilla; and that it was probably granted by her to her dependents and co-religionists for a cemetery. There is reason for believing that in the earliest ages the Christians secured their places of sepulture from disturbance under the shelter of great personages, whose property was protected by the law during their life time, and whose testamentary dispositions were respected after their death[3].

With the blood of Clemens the cup of Domitian's iniquities overflowed. The day of retribution came full soon. His hand had long been reeking with the noblest blood of Rome; but his doom was sealed, when he became a terror to men in humbler walks of life[4]. His own domestics no longer felt themselves safe from his jealous suspicions. Among these the conspiracy was hatched, which put an

leus, for which see below, p. 42. See also *Act. SS. Bolland.* Maii xxxi, VII. p. 413 sq, this being her own day. Comp. Lipsius *Apokr. Apostelgesch.* II. i. p. 203 sq.

[1] xvi. 8, where the weight of authority is in favour of 'Ampliatus' rather than the contracted form 'Amplias.'

[2] See *Bull. di Archeol. Crist.* 1881, p. 57 sq. De Rossi has promised (p. 74) to discuss this question in the 4th volume of *Roma Sotterranea*.

[3] De Rossi *Bull. di Archeol. Crist.* 1864, p. 25 sq, *Rom. Sotterr.* I. p. 102 sq.

[4] Juv. *Sat.* iv. 153 'Periit postquam Cerdonibus esse timendus Coeperat; hoc nocuit Lamiarum caede madenti,' where Cerdo seems to be used as a slave's name (see Mayor's note).

end to his life[1]. It is worth observing that both Suetonius and Philostratus connect his fate directly with his treatment of Clemens and Domitilla. The chief assassin at all events was one Stephanus, a steward and freedman of Domitilla[2]. This is stated by all our authorities. Carrying his left arm bandaged as if it were broken, he went in to the emperor's presence with a dagger concealed in the wrappings, engaged his attention with a pretended revelation of a conspiracy, and while Domitian was reading the document, plunged the dagger into his body. The wound was not fatal. Domitian grappled with the assassin in mortal conflict, tried to wrench the dagger from his hand, and with gashed fingers strove to tear out his eyes. Meanwhile the other accomplices, gladiators and servants of the household, entered. The tyrant was despatched by seven wounds, but not before Stephanus had been slain in the fray. The motives which led Stephanus to play the assassin's part are differently stated. Suetonius says that he had been accused of peculation. The account of Philostratus puts another complexion on his act. He compares the feat to the glorious achievements of Harmodius and Aristogeiton. The emperor had desired Domitilla to wed another man only three days after he had murdered her husband[3]; the assassination was an act of vengeance for this indecent refinement of cruelty. Bandaged as I have described, he went up to Domitian and said 'I wish to speak to you, Sire, on an important matter.' The emperor took him aside. 'Your great enemy Clement,' continued Stephanus, 'is not dead, as you suppose, but is I know where, and he is arraying himself against you.' Saying this, he smote him. Then ensued the death struggle, which he describes in language closely resembling the narrative of Suetonius, though obviously not taken from this author. The two representations of Stephanus' motive are not irreconcilable, and may perhaps be accepted as supplementary the one to the other. Philostratus' account of the words uttered by Stephanus, when he dealt the blow, cannot, I think, be a pure fiction. The reference to Clement,

[1] For Domitian's death see Sueton. *Domit.* 17, Dion Cass. lxvii. 15—18, Philostr. *Vit. Apoll.* viii. 25.

[2] Sueton. *l.c.* 'Stephanus Domitillae procurator...consilium operamque obtulit,' Dion *l.c.* Στέφανον ἐρρωμενέστερον τῶν ἄλλων ὄντα εἰσέπεμψεν [ὁ Παρθένιος] κ.τ.λ. (where however his relation to Domitilla is not stated), Philostr. *l.c.* Στέφανος...ἀπελεύθερος τῆς γυναικὸς [Δομιτίλλας] κ.τ.λ. So too Georg. Syncell. p. 650 (ed. Bonn.) τούτου [τοῦ Κλήμεντος] Στέφανός τις τῶν ἀπελευθέρων εἶς τῇ πρὸς τὸν δεσπότην εὐνοίᾳ Κλήμεντα κ.τ.λ. In Tertull. *Apol.* 35 the reading 'Stephanis' for 'Sigeriis' is purely conjectural and quite unnecessary.

[3] See the passage as quoted below, p. 112 sq; where the meaning of the expression ἐς ἀνδρὸς φοιτᾶν is considered.

as still living, has a Christian ring. If it does not report the language actually used by Stephanus over his victim, it doubtless represents the thoughts aroused by the incident in the minds of Christians at the time. Philostratus might well have derived his account from some Christian source. But was Stephanus himself a Christian? If so, the still untamed nature of the man, goaded by the menace of personal danger or stung to a chivalrous resentment of his mistress' wrongs, asserted itself against the higher dictates of his faith. There is no ground for charging Domitilla herself with complicity in the plot[1].

The tyrant's death brought immediate relief to the Christians. As the victims of his cruelty, and indirectly as the avengers of his wrong-doings, they might for the moment be regarded even with favour. A late writer, who however seems to have drawn from some earlier source, tells us that the senate conferred honours on Stephanus, as 'having delivered the Romans from shame[2].' If so, the honours must have been posthumous, for he himself had passed beyond the reach of human praise or blame. The dead could not be revived, but the exiles were restored to their homes[3]. Domitilla would find herself once more in the midst of her dependants, free to exercise towards them a kindly generosity, which was nowhere more appreciated by ancient sentiment than in the due provision made for the repose of the dead. In this respect she seems not to have confined her benefactions to her co-religionists, but to have provided impartially likewise for her domestics who still remained pagans[4]. But her banishment was not forgotten. The sufferings of herself, if not of her husband, were recorded by one Bruttius—whether a heathen or a Christian historian, I shall consider presently—who would seem to have been in some way allied with her family[5]. Even after the lapse of three centuries Paula, the friend of

[1] As Renan does, *Les Évangiles* p. 297, where quite a fancy picture is drawn; 'Venger son mari, sauver ses enfants, compromis par les caprices d'un monstre fantasque, lui parut un devoir,' with more to the same effect.

[2] Georg. Syncell. l.c.; see below, p. 110 sq.

[3] Tertullian (*Apol.* 5) speaks as if Domitian himself had recalled the exiles (see below, p. 105). This father must, I imagine, have had in his mind the story which Hegesippus tells (Euseb. *H.E.* iii. 19; see below, p. 107), how Domitian was so impressed with the poverty and simplicity of the grandsons of Jude that he not only set them free but also 'by an injunction stopped the persecution of the Church.' But this is inconsistent with the representations of all other writers, both heathen and Christian, who ascribe the restitution of Domitian's victims to his successor Nerva; e.g. Dion lxviii. 1, Plin. *Paneg.* 46, *Ep.* iv. 9, Melito in Euseb. *H. E.* iv. 26, Lactant. *de Mort. Pers.* 3, Euseb. *H. E.* iii. 20.

[4] See for instance the inscription on one Hector, quoted below, p. 113.

[5] See below, p. 47.

Jerome, was shown in the island of Pontia the cells in which she 'suffered a protracted martyrdom[1].' This language however is a flourish of rhetoric, since she cannot have remained an exile more than a few months, except by her own choice. What became of her two young sons, Vespasianus and Domitianus, who had been destined to the imperial purple, we know not. Their Christian profession, by discountenancing political ambition, would disarm suspicion, and they would be suffered to live unmolested as private citizens. Mention has been made already of a Domitian who appears in history some generations later, and may have been a descendant of one of them[2].

But before we pass away from this subject a question of some interest bars our path and presses for a solution. Besides the Domitilla of history, the wife of Flavius Clemens, of whom I have already spoken, ecclesiastical legend mentions another Domitilla, a virgin niece of this matron, as an exile to one of the islands and a confessor for the faith. Were there then really two Domitillas—aunt and niece—who suffered in the same way[3]? Or have we here a confusion, of which a reasonable explanation can be given?

The story of Domitilla the virgin, as related in the Acts of Nereus and Achilleus, runs as follows[4]:

Domitilla, the daughter of Plautilla and niece of Clemens the consul, was betrothed to one Aurelian. The preparations had already been made for the wedding, when her chamberlains Nereus and Achilleus, converts of S. Peter, succeeded in persuading her to renounce Aurelian and to prefer a heavenly bridegroom to an earthly. So Domitilla re-

[1] Hieron. *Epist.* cviii. 7; see the passage quoted below, p. 108.

[2] See above, p. 21.

[3] It is not surprising that the ecclesiastical tradition which recognizes two Domitillas, the matron and the virgin, should have decided the opinion of most Roman Catholic writers. So Tillemont *Mémoires* II. p. 124 sq, De Rossi *Bull. di Archeol. Crist.* 1865, p. 17 sq, 1875, p. 69 sq, and Doulcet *Rapports de l'Église Chrétienne avec l'État Romain* p. 40 sq. Funk is an exception (*Theolog. Quartalschr.* LXI. p. 562 sq, 1879). Two Domitillas are also maintained by Imhof *Domitianus* p. 116, and by Wieseler *Jahrb. f. Deutsche Theol.* XXII. p. 404, comp. *Christenverfolgung.* p. 5. Most writers however, following Scaliger, receive only one Domitilla; e.g. Lardner *Testimonies* c. XXVII (*Works* VII. p. 344 sq), Zahn *Hermas* p. 49 sq, Renan *Évangiles* p. 227, Aubé *Persécutions de l'Église* p. 178 sq, p. 427 sq, Lipsius *Chronologie* p. 154 sq, Hasenclever *l. c.* p. 231 sq, and so commonly. For the most part they accept Dion's statement that this Domitilla was the wife of Clemens, but Lipsius (p. 155) prefers the authority of Bruttius(?) and regards her as his niece.

[4] See the Bollandist *Act. Sanct.* Maii III. p. 4 sq; comp. Aubé *Persécutions* p. 429 sq, Lipsius *Apokr. Apostelgesch.* II. i. p. 106 sq, p. 200 sq.

ceives the veil at the hands of her cousin Clement the bishop. Aurelian, enraged at being thus rejected, instigates Domitian to banish her to the island of Pontia for refusing to sacrifice. She is accompanied thither by Nereus and Achilleus. They there have an altercation with two disciples of Simon Magus, Furius and Priscus, who denounce the ill-treatment of their master by S. Peter. The question is referred to Marcellus, a former disciple of Simon Magus and a son of Marcus the City prefect. He writes a long letter in reply, relating how he had been converted by S. Peter's miracles; and he adds an account of the death of Petronilla, S. Peter's daughter, with her companions[1]. Here again it was a question between marriage and virginity, and Petronilla had chosen the latter, though at the cost of martyrdom. But before Marcellus' letter arrived at its destination, Nereus and Achilleus had been put to death by the machinations of Aurelian. Their bodies were brought back to Rome and buried in the plot of Domitilla by one Auspicius their disciple. Information of these facts is sent to Rome to Marcellus by Eutyches, Victorinus, and Maro, likewise their disciples.

[1] The story of S. Petronilla, as told by Marcellus in these Acts, is as follows:

Petronilla was bed-ridden with paralysis. Titus remonstrated with S. Peter for not healing his daughter. He replied that her sickness was for her good, but that, as an evidence of his power, she should be cured temporarily and should wait upon them. This was done; she rose and ministered to them, and then retired again to her bed. After her discipline was completed, she was finally healed. Her beauty attracted Flaccus the Count, who came with armed men to carry her away and marry her by force. She asked a respite of three days. It was granted. On the third day she died. Then Flaccus sought her foster-sister Felicula in marriage. Felicula declined, declaring herself to be a 'virgin of Christ.' For this she was tortured and put to death.

With this story should be compared the notice in Augustine (*c. Adim.* 17, *Op.* VIII. p. 139), who tells us that the Manicheans, while rejecting the account of the death of Ananias and Sapphira in the Acts, yet read with satisfaction in their own apocryphal books a story 'ipsius Petri filiam paralyticam sanam factam precibus patris, et hortulani filiam ad precem ipsius Petri esse mortuam,' and alleged 'quod hoc eis expediebat ut et illa solveretur paralysi et illa moreretur.' There is likewise an allusion to S. Peter smiting his daughter with paralysis, because her beauty had become a stumbling-block, in *Acta Philippi* pp. 149, 155 (Tischendorf's *Apocalypses Apocryphae* 1866).

The legend of S. Petronilla then, as told in the Acts, appears to be due to a combination of two elements; (1) The story in the Manichean writings that S. Peter miraculously healed his daughter (whose name is not given) of the palsy. This story seems to be suggested by the incident in Mark i. 29 sq, Luke iv. 38 sq. (2) The discovery of a sarcophagus in the Cemetery of Domitilla with the inscription AVR . PETRONILLAE . FILIAE . DVLCISSIMAE. The identification with S. Peter's daughter would naturally arise out of this inscription, which was supposed to have been engraved by the Apostle's own hand.

These three again are denounced by Aurelian, and put to death by the emperor Nerva for refusing to offer sacrifice. Hereupon Aurelian fetches Domitilla from Pontia to Terracina, where she falls in with two other maidens Euphrosyne and Theodora, who were betrothed to two young men Sulpitius and Servilianus. She persuades them to follow her example, and to repudiate the marriages which awaited them. In this case the intended bridegrooms likewise acquiesce, and are converted to Christianity. Aurelian now attempts to overpower her by violence, but is seized with a fit and dies before two days are over. His brother Luxurius avenges his death. Sulpitius and Severianus are beheaded; while Domitilla, Euphrosyne, and Theodora, are burnt to death in their cells.

These Acts are evidently late and inauthentic. The details of the story betray their fictitious character, and are almost universally rejected. But the question still remains whether the main fact—the virginity and persecution of a niece of Flavius Clemens—may not be historical. This opinion is maintained by many who reject the story as a whole; and it receives some countenance from statements in earlier and more authentic writers.

Domitilla, the wife of Flavius Clemens, whom Domitian banished, when he put her husband to death, is stated by Dion to have been a relation of Domitian, but he does not define her relationship[1]. We infer however from Quintilian that she was his sister's daughter[2]; and this is confirmed by inscriptions, which more than once name one Domitilla as VESPASIANI NEPTIS[3]. This point therefore we may consider as settled. Philostratus, a much inferior authority, as read in his present text, says that she was Domitian's sister, but either he has blundered or (as seems more probable) his transcribers have carelessly substituted ἀδελφήν for ἀδελφιδῆν[4]. His sister she cannot have been; for the only

[1] lxvii. 14 *καὶ αὐτὴν συγγενῆ ἑαυτοῦ*, see below, p. 104.

[2] He calls her children 'sororis suae nepotes,' 'the grandchildren of his sister,' speaking of Domitian. Though at a much later date 'nepos,' 'neptis,' came to be used in the sense 'nephew,' 'niece' (e.g. Beda *H. E.* iii. 6 'nepos ex sorore Acha'), no decisive example of this sense is produced till a later age. Such passages as Sueton. *Caes.* 83, Spartian. *Hadr.* 2, *C. I. L.* III. 6480, are wrongly alleged for this meaning. When we find these words in connexion with 'avunculus' (*C. I. L.* III. 3684, 4321), we must remember that 'avunculus' sometimes denotes 'a great uncle.'

[3] See below, p. 114.

[4] *Vit. Apoll.* viii. 25 Κλήμεντα...ᾧ τὴν ἀδελφὴν τὴν ἑαυτοῦ ἐδεδώκει. The whole passage is given below, p. 112 sq. We have the choice of substituting either ἀδελφιδῆν or ἐξαδέλφην, for both would mean the same relationship in the language of this age. The former is the more probable, since the missing letters might

daughter of Vespasian who grew up to womanhood had died before her father[1].

On the other hand Eusebius, speaking of the defeat of Flavius Clemens, says nothing at all about a wife of Clemens, but mentions a niece (a sister's daughter) of Clemens, as being exiled at the same time. In other words the banished Domitilla of Eusebius bears the same relationship to Clemens, which the banished Domitilla of contemporary authorities and of the Roman historian bears to Domitian. Have we not here the key to the confusion?

easily slip out, when the word was still written in uncials.

It may be well here once for all to distinguish those terms implying relationship, which are liable to confusion. (1) ἀνεψιός. The word is carefully defined by Pollux *Onom.* iii. 2. 8. It denotes *first cousins*, the children whether of two brothers or of two sisters or of brother and sister. Though αὐτανέψιοι is more precise, it signifies nothing more (οὐδὲν πλέον τῶν ἀνεψιῶν). The children of ἀνεψιοί are ἀνεψιαδοῖ (or ἀνεψιάδαι), *second cousins*. The children of ἀνεψιαδοῖ are ἐξανέψιοι. For more on ἀνεψιός see the note to Col. iv. 10. (2) ἀδελφιδοῦς, ἀδελφιδῆ. This signifies a son or daughter of a sister or brother, a *nephew* or a *niece*. Thus Octavianus (Augustus) is called ὁ της ἀδελφιδῆς υἱὸς of Julius; Plutarch. *Marc. Anton.* 11. He was his grand-nephew. Thus also Julia the daughter of Titus is ἀδελφιδῆ of Domitian; Dion Cass. lxvii. 3, Philostr. *Vit. Apoll.* vii. 7. Thus again in Josephus the two childless wives of Herod are called in *Antiq.* i. 1. 3 ἀδελφοῦ παῖς καὶ ἀνεψιά, but in *Bell. Jud.* i. 28. 4 ἀνεψιά τε καὶ ἀδελφιδῆ. (3) ἐξάδελφος, ἐξαδέλφη. These are treated by Phrynichus (p. 306, Lobeck) as synonymes of ἀνεψιός, ἀνεψιά, and are denounced by him as solœcisms; ἐξάδελφος ἀποδιοπομπητέον, ἀνεψιὸς δὲ ῥητέον. This account of their meaning however is not borne out by usage. The words indeed are of Hellenistic origin, but in the earliest examples and for some centuries they signify *nephew*, *niece*, not *cousins*, and are therefore synonymes of ἀδελφιδοῦς, ἀδελφιδῆ. Thus in Tobit i. 22 (comp. xi. 17) ἐξάδελφος is a brother's son. Again in Justin *Dial.* 49 (p. 268) the relationship of Herodias' daughter to Herod is described by τῆς ἐξαδέλφης αὐτοῦ, where the reading τῆς ἐξ ἀδελφῆς αὐτοῦ cannot stand on any showing. Again in Jos. *Ant.* xx. 10 the relationship of Onias who founded the temple near Heliopolis to the high priest his namesake recently deceased is described in the words, ὁ Ὀνίας ὁ τοῦ τετελευτηκότος Ὀνίου ἐξάδελφος, while we learn elsewhere that he was his brother's son (*Antiq.* xii. 5. 1, xiii. 3. 1). This is also the sense in which Eusebius uses the term, as appears from the parallel passages. In the *History* Domitilla's relationship to Flavius Clemens is described by ἐξ ἀδελφῆς γεγονυῖα Φλαουΐου Κλήμεντος, but in the *Chronicle* by ἐξαδέλφη Φλαουΐου Κλήμεντος. For the accent of ἐξάδελφος see Chandler *Greek Accentuation* p. 127.

In later writers there is much confusion, and all the three words ἀνεψιοί, ἀδελφιδοῖ, ἐξάδελφοι, are found in both senses. Hence the error in the A. V. of Col. iv. 10, where ὁ ἀνεψιὸς Βαρνάβα is translated 'sister's son to Barnabas.'

[1] Sueton. *Vespas.* 3 'Ex hac [uxore] liberos tulit [Vespasianus] Titum et Domitianum et Domitillam. Uxori ac filiae superstes fuit, atque utramque adhuc privatus amisit.' Vespasian came to the throne A.D. 69.

Eusebius gives his authority. He refers in the *Chronicle* to one Bruttius or Brettius. In the *History* on the other hand he does not mention any name, but states in general terms that even historians unconnected with the Christian faith (καὶ τοὺς ἄποθεν τοῦ καθ' ἡμᾶς λόγου συγγραφεῖς) had not shrunk from recording the persecution under Domitian and the martyrdoms resulting from it. We may infer however from the context, as well as from the parallel passage in the *Chronicle*, that he had in his mind chiefly, though perhaps not solely, this same chronicler Bruttius [1].

Who then was this Bruttius? When did he live? Was he a heathen or a Christian writer? He is cited as an authority three times by Malalas [2]. The first passage relates to the legend of Danae, which Bruttius explains in a rationalistic sense, and where he identifies Picus with Zeus. In the second passage, referring to the conquests of Alexander, he describes him as subduing 'all the kingdoms of the earth,' while in the context there is an obvious allusion to the prophecy of Daniel. The third contains the notice of the banishment of the Christians under Domitian with which we are more directly concerned. Thus Bruttius in his chronography covered the whole period from the beginnings of history to the close of the first Christian century at least. The Bruttian family attained their greatest prominence in the second century [3]. One C. Bruttius Praesens was consul for the second time in A.D. 139; and among the friends and correspondents of the younger Pliny [4] we meet with a Praesens, who doubtless belonged to this same

[1] It may be a question whether Eusebius was not acquainted with Dion (Hasenclever p. 258); but there is no indication that he was thinking of him here.

[2] Joann. Malalas pp. 34, 193, 262 (ed. Bonn.). The last passage is given in full below, p. 109. The writer is called ὁ σοφώτατος Βούττιος ἱστορικὸς χρονογράφος, Βόττιος ὁ σοφώτατος, and Βώττιος ὁ σοφὸς χρονογράφος, in the three passages respectively. The comparison of the last passage with Eusebius shows that Bruttius is meant, and that the forms therefore are corrupt in the existing text of Malalas. This appears also from the fact that the first reference is found likewise in the *Chron. Pasch.* p. 69 (ed. Bonn), where the authority is given as ὁ σοφώτατος Βρούττιος ὁ ἱστορικὸς καὶ χρονογράφος.

[3] For the Bruttian gens see De-Vit *Onomast. Lex. Forcell.* I. p. 764 sq. The relationships given in my text are not in all respects absolutely ascertained, as there may be some doubt about the identification of the different persons bearing the name C. Bruttius Praesens; but the only point of importance is quite certain, namely, that the second C. Bruttius Praesens who was twice consul was the father of L. Bruttius Crispinus the consul (*C. I. L.* VI. 7582) and of Bruttia Crispina the empress (*C. I. L.* X. 408, Capitol. *M. Anton.* 27). His wife's name Crispina is given in another inscription (*C. I. L.* VIII. 110). In this way the Praesentes and Crispini of the Bruttian gens are closely related.

[4] *Epist.* vii. 3.

family and may have been this same person. Critics not uncommonly, following Scaliger, identify Pliny's friend with the chronographer mentioned by Eusebius and Malalas, but for this identification there is no sufficient ground. A second C. Bruttius Praesens, apparently a son of the former, was also twice consul A.D. 153 and 180. He was the father of L. Bruttius Crispinus, whose name appears in the consular fasti for A.D. 187, and of Bruttia Crispina, who became consort of the emperor Commodus. A third C. Bruttius Praesens, who held the consulate in A.D. 217, seems also to have been his son[1]. The family continued to hold a distinguished position after this date, for we find the name more than once in the consular lists[2]. The chronographer might have been any one of the persons already named, or he might have been an entirely different person, perhaps some freedman or descendant of a freedman attached to the house. The extant inscriptions suggest that there was a numerous clientele belonging to this family[3]. It is a curious coincidence, if it be nothing more, that De Rossi has discovered, in immediate proximity to and even within the limits of the Cemetery of Domitilla, the graves of certain members of the Bruttian clan, especially one BRVTTIVS CRISPINVS[4]. There is indeed no direct indication that these were Christian graves, but the locality suggests some connexion, or at least explains how Bruttius the chronographer should have taken a special interest in the career of Domitilla. But was not this Bruttius himself a Christian[5]? Eusebius

[1] *C. I. L.* IX. 4512.

[2] One C. Bruttius Crispinus is consul A.D. 224, and one C. Bruttius Praesens A.D. 246. For this last see *Ephem. Epigr.* IV. p. 185, V. p. 610.

[3] See for Rome the *Monumentum Bruttiorum* in *C. I. L.* VI. 7582 sq, also VI. 13640 sq; and compare the indices to volumes IX, X, relating to Italy.

[4] *C. I. L.* VI. 7589 BRVTTIE . MERCA[TIL]LE . Q . V . A . V . M . X . D . X[...] ET . BRVTTIO . CRISPI[NO . Q] . V . A . V . M . IIII . D . XXII . FILI[IS . CARISSI]MIS . ROMANV[S . ET .] GENICE . PA[REN]TES . FECER[VNT], where Bruttius Crispinus is evidently a child of servile descent, though he bears the cognomen Crispinus of his family's patron (see below, p. 61, note). In another of these inscriptions (no. 5786) we meet with C . BRVTTIVS C . L . in connexion with the name CLEMEN[S]. One Q . BRITTIVS . CLEMENS also appears in an inscription found at Puteoli (X. 2177). In another (VI. 7583) one C. Bruttius bears the same surname Telesphorus as an early pope, who was martyred in the last years of Hadrian. With this last compare *C. I. L.* VI. 13649, C . BRVTIVS . BAROCHAS . ET . CLAVDIA . TELESPHORIS, where the name Barochas points to an Eastern origin.

[5] Lardner *Testimonies* c. xii (*Works* VII. p. 103) writes, 'I suppose no one will hesitate to allow that Bruttius was an heathen historian.' So Tillemont *Mém.* II. p. 117, De Rossi *Bull.* 1875, p. 74, Zahn *Hermas* p. 53, Lipsius *Chronol.* pp. 154, 159, Hasenclever p. 257, and this is the almost universal view. On the other hand Volkmar (*Theolog. Jahrb.* 1856, p. 301 sq) makes him a Christian

indeed, as we have seen, in his *History* speaks generally of his authorities for the persecution under Domitian as unconnected with Christianity, while we learn from his *Chronicle* that the most important of these authorities was Bruttius. It would appear then that he regarded Bruttius as a heathen, though this inference is not absolutely certain. But was he well acquainted with the facts? Had he the work of Bruttius before him, or did he only quote it at second hand? I believe that the latter alternative is correct. We have seen that Malalas three times refers to Bruttius as his authority. It is highly improbable that he at all events should have been directly acquainted with the work of Bruttius; and the conjecture of Gutschmidt that he derived his information from Julius Africanus seems very probable[1]. But, if Malalas owed this notice of the persecution of Domitian to Africanus, why may not Eusebius also have drawn it from the same source? He was certainly well acquainted with the chronography of Africanus, whom he uses largely in his *Chronicle* and of whose writings he gives an account in his *History*[2]. On the other hand he never mentions Bruttius except in the *Chronicle*, and there only in this single passage relating to Domitilla.

This consideration must affect our answer to the question whether Bruttius was a heathen or a Christian writer. Eusebius, as we have seen, seems to have set him down as a heathen; but, if he was unacquainted with the work itself, his opinion ceases to have any value. The references in Malalas appear to me to point very decidedly to a Christian writer[3]. The first is an attempt to explain heathen mythology by Euhemeristic methods, a common and characteristic expedient in the Christian apologists and chronographers[4]. The second evidently treats the empire of Alexander as fulfilling the prophecy of the third beast, the leopard, in Daniel[5]. We cannot indeed feel sure that the

writer, as do C. Müller (*Fragm. Hist. Graec.* IV. p. 352), and Erbes (*Jahrb. f. Prot. Theol.* 1878, p. 715). Gelzer (*Sextus Julius Africanus* I. p. 282), if I understand him rightly, takes up an intermediate position. He supposes that the passage relating to the persecution under Domitian was a later Christian fiction appended to a genuine chronography written by a heathen writer. For this conjecture there seems to be no ground.

[1] Gutschmidt's opinion is given in Lipsius *Chronol.* p. 155, note. If this be correct, it gives, as a *terminus ad quem* for the date of Bruttius, A.D. 221, when the work of Africanus was published.

[2] *H. E.* vi. 31, comp. i. 6, 7; also *Ecl. Proph.* iii. 26 (pp. 151 sq, 158). See Gelzer I. p. 23 sq.

[3] See above p. 46, note 2.

[4] See the notes on *Act. Mart. Ignat. Rom.* 3 sq, passim.

[5] p. 193 ὡς πάρδαλις ἐκεῖθεν ὁρμήσας ὁ Ἀλέξανδρος: comp. Dan. vii. 6 (LXX) ἐθεώρουν θηρίον ἄλλο ὡσεὶ πάρδαλιν. The expression 'all the kingdoms of the earth'

more obvious references to Daniel were not due to Africanus or to Malalas himself, but the part of Bruttius is inseparable from the rest. The direct reference to the Christians in the third passage needs no comment. Thus Bruttius would appear to have been a precursor of Africanus and Eusebius, as a Christian chronographer.

But, if the notice had already passed through two hands before it reached Eusebius, the chances of error are greatly increased. Now it is a suspicious fact (which I have already noticed), that in Eusebius the niece Domitilla, the virgin of ecclesiastical legend, bears exactly the same relationship to Clement which the aunt Domitilla, the widow of authentic history, bears to Domitian in classical authorities. Must we not suspect then, that by some carelessness the relationship has been transferred from the one to the other? Our suspicions are deepened, when we examine the form of the notice. The Armenian of the *Chronicle*, as given by Petermann, is much confused; but the sense is doubtless correctly rendered by Jerome 'et Flaviam Domitillam Flavii Clementis consulis ex sorore neptem in insulam Pontianam relegatam,' while the form is probably preserved, at least in its main character by Syncellus, καὶ Φλαουία Δομετίλλα ἐξαδέλφη Κλήμεντος Φλαουίου ὑπατικοῦ...εἰς νῆσον Ποντίαν φυγαδεύεται. The error might be rectified by the repetition of a single letter, ἐξαδέλφη ἡ Κλήμεντος, 'a niece, the *wife* of Clement', the person to whom she stood in the relation of ἐξαδέλφη being explained by the context[1], or the name of Domitian having been omitted by a clerical blunder owing to the similar letters, so that the sentence would run Φλαουία Δομετίλλα [Δομετιανοῦ] ἐξαδέλφη ἡ Κλήμεντος κ. τ. λ. Or again, the mistake might be explained by an ambiguity of expression, as thus; καὶ τὴν γυναῖκα Φλαουίαν Δομετίλλαν, ἐξαδέλφην οὖσαν αὐτοῦ, φυγαδεύει, after a notice of the death of the husband Clemens[2].

But, besides the difficulty of the relationship, there remains the difference of locality. Dion makes Pandateria her place of exile, while Eusebius and Christian writers banish her to Pontia. These were two neighbouring islands in the Tyrrhene sea[3]. They were both used as places of exile for members of the imperial family during the first

is followed immediately by 'as the exceedingly wise Bottius (Bruttius) hath recorded'.

[1] See *Philippians* p. 22 sq, where the solution of the two Domitillas given in the text is suggested.

[2] For this last suggestion see Zahn *Hermas* p. 50, note 3.

[3] Strabo v. p. 233 Πανδατερία τε καὶ Ποντία οὐ πολὺ ἀπ' ἀλλήλων διέχουσαι. Hence they are constantly mentioned together; e.g. Strabo ii. p. 123, Varro *R. R.* ii. 5, Suet. *Calig.* 15, Mela ii. 7, Plin. *N. H.* iii. 6, Ptolem. iii. 1. 79.

century. To the former were banished Julia the daughter of Augustus, Agrippina the wife of Germanicus, and Octavia the wife of Nero; to the latter, Nero the son of Germanicus was exiled by Tiberius, and the sisters of Caligula by their brother[1]. The two are constantly mentioned together, and a confusion would be easy. Though Dion's account of this transaction is generally the more authentic, yet I am disposed to think that on this point he has gone wrong. Bruttius, who is the primary authority for Pontia, seems to have lived before Dion, and may perhaps be credited with a special knowledge of Domitilla's career. This locality likewise is confirmed by the fact that three centuries later Jerome's friend Paula, visiting the island of Pontia, was shown the cells which Domitilla occupied in her exile[2]. Not much stress however can be laid on such a confirmation as this. The cicerone of the fourth century was at least as complaisant and inventive as his counterpart in medieval or modern times.

It should be observed that neither Eusebius nor Jerome says anything about the virginity of this Domitilla, which occupies so prominent a place in the later legend. It is a stale incident, which occurs in dozens of stories of female martyrdoms[3]. Yet in this instance it is not altogether without a foundation in fact. Philostratus relates of the historical Domitilla, that Domitian attempted in vain to force her to a second marriage immediately after the death of Clemens. As the true Domitilla thus cherishes the virginity of widowhood, so the legendary Domitilla retains the virginity of maidenhood, despite the commands of the same tyrant[4].

The existence of this younger Domitilla depends on Eusebius alone. All later writers—both Greek and Latin—have derived their information from him. If he breaks down, the last thread of her frail life is snapped. But strong reasons have been given for suspecting a blunder. The blunder however is evidently as old as Eusebius himself (as the comparison of his two works shows) and cannot have been due to later copyists of his text. He may have inherited it from Africanus or Africanus' transcribers, or he may have originated it himself. The true history of the relations of Nereus and

[1] For the imperial exiles in Pandateria see Tac. *Ann.* i. 53, xiv. 63, Sueton. *Tib.* 53, *Calig.* 15, Dion Cass. lv. 10; for those in Pontia or Pontiæ (for there was a group of three islands, of which Pontia was the chief), Sueton. *Tib.* 54, *Calig.* 15, Dion Cass. lix. 22.

[2] See below, p. 108.

[3] See for instance the case of S. Cæcilia; *Ign. and Polyc.* I. p. 500.

[4] See Hasenclever p. 235. On a chaste widowhood, regarded as a second virginity, see the note on Ignat. *Smyrn.* 13.

Achilleus to Domitilla is beyond the reach of recovery without fresh evidence. The later legend, as we have seen, makes them her chamberlains. This however seems to have been unknown to Damasus (A.D. 366—384), whose inscription[1], placed in the Cemetery of Domitilla, implies that they were soldiers of the tyrant who refused to be the instruments of his cruelty, and resigned their military honours in consequence. Of their connexion with Domitilla it says nothing. Perhaps this connexion was originally one of locality alone. There were, we may conjecture, two prominent tombs bearing the names NEREVS and ACHILLEVS[2] in this Cemetery of Domitilla; and a romance writer, giving the rein to his fancy, invented the relation which appears in their Acts. Whether this Nereus was the same with or related to the Nereus of S. Paul's epistle (Rom. xvi. 15), it were vain to speculate. Exactly the same problem has presented itself already with regard to Ampliatus, who was likewise buried in this cemetery.

[1] The inscription (see *Bull. di Archeol. Crist.* 1874, p. 20 sq) runs thus;

Militiae nomen dederant saevumque gerebant
Officium, pariter spectantes jussa tyranni,
Praeceptis pulsante metu servire parati.
Mira fides rerum, subito posuere furorem;
Conversi fugiunt, ducis impia castra relinquunt,
Projiciunt clypeos faleras telaque cruenta;
Confessi gaudent Christi portare triumfos.
Credite per Damasum, possit quid gloria Christi.

It will be seen at once that the heroes of this inscription have nothing in common with the heroes of the Bollandist Acts except their names. The inscription is preserved in full in old manuscripts, and a fragment of it was found by De Rossi in the Cemetery of Domitilla.

[2] A marble column has been discovered, which apparently was one of four supporting the ciborium, and on which is a sculpture of a martyr with the name ACILLEVS over his head. The lower part of a corresponding column has likewise been found with the feet of a figure, but the main part of the sculpture and the superscription are wanting. It was doubtless NEREVS. The style of the sculpture points to the 4th or the beginning of the 5th century. See *Bull. di Archeol. Crist.* 1875 p. 8 sq, with plate iv for the same year.

The names, Nereus and Achilleus, like other designations of Greek heroes and deities, suggest that the bearers were in the humbler walks of life, slaves or freedmen, or common soldiers, or the like. In *C. I. L.* VI. 4344 I find one NEREVS . NAT . GERMAN . PEVCENNVS . GERMANICIANVS . NERONIS . CAESARIS, a slave of the imperial family. A native of Germany, he had been first a slave of Germanicus and was afterwards transferred to his son Nero. In *C. I. L.* VI. 12992, 12993, are persons bearing the name M. Aur. Achilleus and T. Aur. Achilleus; and in *C. I. L.* VI. 1058 (pp. 206, 207) there are two city watches, M. Valerius Achillaeus and C. Valerius Achilleus, these last of the time of Caracalla. The Latin proper name is sometimes Achilles (='Αχιλλεύς), but rather more frequently Achilleus (='Αχιλλεῖος, and sometimes written Achillaeus), the two vowels making separate syllables. The martyr's name, so far as I have observed, is always the quadrisyllable Achilleus.

Having solved the question of the two Domitillas, we find ourselves confronted with a similar problem affecting the persons bearing the name Clemens. Clement the consul and Clement the bishop—should these be identified or not? Until recent years the question was never asked. Their separate existence was assumed without misgiving. But latterly the identification has found considerable favour. A recent German writer can even say that 'later Protestant theology almost without exception has declared itself for the identification[1]'. I suppose the remark must be confined to German theological critics; for I cannot find that it has met with any favour in England or France[2]. Even as restricted to Germans, it seems to be much overstated. But a view which reckons among its supporters Volkmar and Hilgenfeld and has been favourably entertained by Lipsius and Harnack, not to mention other writers, has achieved considerable distinction, if not popularity[3]. On this account it claims a consideration, to which it would not be entitled by its own intrinsic merits.

[1] Hasenclever p. 255. When Hasenclever asserts that 'the identity of the bishop and the consul was originally maintained in the Roman Church and adopted into the *Liber Pontificalis* and Roman Breviary,' and contrasts with this supposed earlier opinion the later view of the Roman Church, separating the two Clements, of which he speaks as gaining ground since Baronius and Tillemont, till it has almost become an article of faith, he seems to me to use language which is altogether misleading. Clement the bishop, as represented in the *Liber Pontificalis* and the Roman Breviary, is certainly not Clement the consul. He has not a single characteristic feature in common with him. Not even his connexion with the imperial family is recognized. He is the son of Faustinus, whereas the consul was the son of Sabinus. He is the fellow-labourer of S. Paul greeted in the Philippian letter, whereas the consul must have resided at Rome and can only have been a mere child, even if he were born, when the apostle wrote. He is banished by Trajan, whereas the consul died some years before Trajan came to the throne. He is put to death in the Chersonese, whereas the consul suffered in Rome. In fact there is not the smallest approach to an identification in these Roman books. They merely assign to Clement the bishop some traits borrowed from the Clementine romance and from the later legend, while they ignore Clement the consul altogether.

[2] Thus Renan (*Les Évangiles* p. 311 sq) says strongly, but not too strongly, 'il faut écarter absolument...l'imagination de certains critiques modernes qui ne veulent voir dans l'évêque Clément qu'un personnage fictif, un dédoublement de Flavius Clemens.' See also Aubé *Persécutions* p. 164 sq.

[3] If we set aside Baur, whose position is quite different, and of whose speculations I shall have to speak presently (p. 55, note 2), the first writer I believe, who suggested this theory of the identity, was R. A. Lipsius *De Clem. Rom. Epist.* p. 184 sq (1855), but he was careful to put it forward as a conjecture and nothing more. In his *Chronol.* p. 156 sq (1869) he again discusses this identification more fully, and still leaves it an open question. Soon after the

The two personalities, which this theory seeks to combine, are definite and well authenticated. On the one hand there is the consul, a near relative of the emperor, who was put to death towards the close of Domitian's reign on some vague charge. These facts we have on strictly contemporary authority. The nature of the charge is more particularly defined by a later historian Dion in a way which is strictly consistent with the account of the contemporary Suetonius, and which points, though not with absolute certainty, to Christianity. Moreover it is distinctly stated that his wife suffered banishment for the same crime. But recent archæological discovery has made it clear that she at all events was a Christian. This Clement then died by a violent death; and, if a Christian, may be regarded as a martyr. On the other hand there is a person of the same name holding high official position, not in the Roman State, but in the Roman Church, at this same time. His existence likewise is well authenticated, and the authentication is almost, though not quite, contemporary. In the tradition which prevailed in the Roman Church a little more than half a century later, when Irenæus resided in Rome, he is represented as the third in the succession of the Roman episcopate after the Apostles S. Peter and S. Paul. Consistently with this notice, an epistle, which bears traces of having been written during or immediately after the persecution of Domitian, has been assigned to him by an unbroken tradition. He is mentioned as the writer of it by Dionysius of Corinth, who flourished about A.D. 170, and who represents the city to which the letter was addressed[1]. His hand in it is also recognized by two other writers of the same age, Hegesippus and Irenæus[2]. Probably not

earlier work of Lipsius, Volkmar (*Theolog. Jahrb.* 1856, p. 304) with characteristic courage accepted it as an established fact. It was adopted likewise by Hilgenfeld *Nov. Test. extr. Can. Rec.* i. p. xxvii sq, ed. 1, 1866 (p. xxxii sq, ed. 2, 1876), comp. *Zeitschr. f. Wiss. Theol.* XII. p. 233 sq (1869), and has also been eagerly maintained by Erbes *Jahrb. f. Protest. Theol.* IV. p. 690 sq, (1878) and by Hasenclever *ib.* VIII. p. 250 sq (1882). On the other hand it has been not less strenuously opposed by Zahn *Hermas* p. 49 sq. (1868), by Wieseler *Jahrb. f. Deutsch. Theol.* 1878, p. 375, and by Funk *Theolog. Quartalschr.* XLI. p. 531 sq, 1879, who makes it the subject of a special article. Harnack, *Patr. Apost.* I. i. p. lxi sq., ed. 2 (1876), holds his judgment in suspense. On the whole I cannot find that the facts justify Hasenclever's expression. In criticism, as in politics, the voice of the innovators, even though they may not be numerous, cries aloud, and thus gives an impression of numbers; while the conservative opinion of the majority is unheard and unnoticed.

[1] Dionys. Cor. in Euseb. *H. E.* iv. 23. The passage is given below, p. 155.

[2] For Hegesippus, see below, p. 154, and for Irenæus, p. 156. The bearing of their testimony on the authorship of the letter will be discussed at a later point.

without reference to this letter, he is described by one who professes to have been his contemporary, Hermas the author of the Shepherd, as the foreign secretary of the Roman Church[1]. Partly no doubt owing to this same cause, he had become so famous by the middle of the second century, that a romance was written in Syria or Palestine giving a fictitious account of his doings and sayings[2]. But he was not a martyr. Some centuries later indeed a story of his martyrdom was invented; but the early Church betrays no knowledge of any such incident. The silence of Irenæus who devotes more space to Clement than to any other Roman bishop and yet says nothing on this point, though he goes out of his way to emphasize the martyrdom of Telesphorus, would almost alone be conclusive.

Hitherto we have seen nothing which would suggest an identification, except the fact that they both bore the same name Clemens, and both lived in Rome at the same time. In every other respect they are as wide apart, as it was possible for any two persons to be under the circumstances.

Yet the mere identity of names counts for little or nothing. Was not Pius the Christian bishop contemporary with Pius the heathen emperor, though no other namesake occupied the papal chair for more than thirteen centuries and none known by this name ever again mounted the imperial throne? Did not Leo the First, pope of Rome, flourish at the same time with Leo the First, emperor of Rome, both busying themselves in the great doctrinal questions of the day? Was not one Azariah high priest, while another Azariah was king, in Jerusalem, though the name does not ever occur again in the long roll either of the sacerdotal or of the regal office? Was not one Honorius pope 'alterius orbis,' while another Honorius was pope of Rome, though the see of Canterbury was never again occupied by a namesake and the see of Rome only after half a millennium had past? But indeed history teems with illustrations[3]. Yet the examples of duplication, which I have given, were a thousand times more improbable on any

[1] Hermas *Vis.* ii. 4. 3 *πέμψει οὖν Κλήμης εἰς τὰς ἔξω πόλεις, ἐκείνῳ γὰρ ἐπιτέτραπται.* The bearing of this notice on the personality and date of S. Clement will be considered hereafter.

[2] See the outline of the story in the Clementine *Homilies* and *Recognitions* given above, p. 14 sq.

[3] To a bishop of Durham it occurs to quote *Hist. Dunelm. Script. Tres* Appendix p. xiv 'Ego Willielmus Dei gratia Dunelmensis episcopus...in praesentia domini mei regis Willielmi,' William I of Durham being contemporary with William I of England. We may further note that the last William bishop of Durham (1826—1836) was contemporary with the last William king of England (1830—1837).

mathematical doctrine of chances than the coincidence of the two Clements in the respective positions assigned to them—this being an extremely common name.

Only one authority, if it deserves the name, seems to confuse the two. The Clementine romance, which we find incorporated in the existing *Homilies* and *Recognitions*, and to which I have already alluded, must have been written soon after the middle of the second century. The hero Clement, the future bishop of Rome, is here represented as sprung from parents who were both scions of the imperial house[1]. Does not this look like a counterpart of Flavius Clemens and Domitilla[2]? But what is the value of this coincidence? This romance probably emanates from a distant part of the world. The local knowledge which it possesses is confined to the easternmost shores of the Mediterranean. Of Rome and of Roman history it

[1] See above, p. 23 sq.

[2] Baur, *Paulus* p. 471 sq, maintained, as Cotelier (on *Recogn.* vii. 8) had pointed out long before him, that the 'fundus fabulae,' as regards the imperial relationships ascribed to Clement the bishop in the romance, was to be sought in the accounts of Flavius Clemens. So far he was probably right. But his own solution has long been abandoned, and only deserves a passing notice. The steps of his argument may be given as follows.

(1) The germ of the Christian legend of Clement the Roman bishop is the account of Flavius Clemens, as he appears in the secular historians—a member of the imperial family converted to Christianity in the primitive ages. (2) The Clement of Phil. iv. 3 points to Flavius Clemens; for the reference must be connected with the mention of the prætorium and of Cæsar's household in other parts of this same Epistle (i. 1, iv. 22). Thus the writer intends to represent him as a member of the imperial family and as a disciple of S. Paul. (3) The story in the Clementine romance is another representation of this same personage. Here the imperial relationship is distinctly stated. But in accordance with the general tendency of this writing he is here described as a disciple of S. Peter. In order so to represent him, without violating chronology, the author makes him a relative not of Domitian but of Tiberius. As this romance was the product of Roman Christianity, its origin gives it a special value. (4) The writer of the Philippian letter has not been careful in like manner to mend or explain the chronology. In representing one who was converted to Christianity under Domitian as a συνεργὸς of S. Paul in the reign of Nero, he has fallen into an anachronism. *Therefore* the Epistle to the Philippians is a forgery.

Of Baur's theory respecting Clement, I have spoken more at length elsewhere (*Philippians* p. 169 sq.). It is sufficient to say here that his two main positions have broken down. (i) His condemnation of the Philippian Epistle as spurious has been rejected with a consent which is practically unanimous; (ii) His theory of the Roman origin of the Clementine romance is finding less favour daily. Its ignorance of everything Roman is its fatal condemnation. This however will be a subject for consideration in its proper place.

betrays gross ignorance. It is full of anachronisms. It makes his father and mother relatives not of Domitian, but of Tiberius. Its hero cannot be identified with Flavius Clemens, who was the son of Flavius Sabinus, for it gives to his father the name Faustus or Faustinianus.

What account then shall we give of this ascription of imperial relationships to Clement the bishop? It is the confusion of ignorance. The writer, presumably an Ebionite Christian in the distant East, invents a romance as the vehicle of certain ideas which he desires to disseminate. For his hero he chooses Clement, as the best known name among the leading Christians of the generation succeeding the Apostles. His Epistle to the Corinthians had a wide circulation, and appears to have been in the hands of the writer himself. But of this Clement he knows nothing except that he was bishop of the Roman Church. A vague rumour also may have reached him of one Clement, a member of the imperial family, who had professed the faith of Christ. If so, he would have no scruple, where all else was fiction, in ascribing this imperial relationship to his hero. Where everything else which he tells us is palpably false, it is unreasonable to set any value on this one statement, if it is improbable in itself or conflicts with other evidence.

The confusion however did not end with this Clementine writer. Certain features were adopted from this romance into the later accounts of Clement the bishop. Thus the name of his father Faustinus[1] and the discipleship to S. Peter are borrowed in the *Liber Pontificalis*; but no sign of an identification appears even here, and some of the facts are inconsistent with it. Not a single authenticated writer for many centuries favours this identity. The silence of Irenæus is against it. The express language of Eusebius, as also of his two translators Jerome and Rufinus, contradicts it. Rufinus indeed speaks of Clement as a 'martyr,' and possibly (though this is not certain) this martyrdom may have been imported indirectly by transference from his namesake Flavius Clemens. But this very example ought to be a warning against the identification theory. Confusion is not fusion. The confusion of ancient writers does not justify the fusion of modern critics.

But it is urged in favour of this fusion that Christian writers betray no knowledge of the consul as a Christian, unless he were the same person as the bishop. This ignorance however, supposing it to have

[1] The father's name is Faustus in the *Homilies* and Faustinianus in the *Recognitions*, while the *Liber Pontificalis* calls him Faustinus, which is the name of one or other of the twin-brothers in both these works.

existed, would not in any degree justify the identification, if the identification presents any difficulty in itself. But is it not burdened with this great improbability, that a bishop of Rome in the first century should not only have held the consular office, but have been so intimately connected with the reigning emperor, as to have sons designated for the imperial purple, and that nevertheless all authentic writers who mention Clement the bishop should have overlooked the fact? Is it easy to conceive for instance that Irenæus, who visited Rome a little more than half a century after the consul's death, who gives the Roman succession to his own time, and who goes out of his way to mention some facts about Clement, should have omitted all reference to his high position in the state? In short, the argument to be drawn from ignorance in Christian writers is far more fatal to the identification than to its opposite. Moreover, we may well believe that the husband's Christianity was less definite than the wife's—indeed the notices seem to imply this[1]—and thus, while Domitilla (though not without some confusion as to her relationship) has a place in Christian records as a confessor, Flavius Clemens has none as a martyr.

Again it is urged that, just as Christian writers betray entire ignorance of the consul, so heathen writers show themselves equally ignorant of the bishop. This reciprocity of ignorance is supposed in some way or other to favour the identity. Yet it is difficult to see why this conclusion should be drawn. Heathen writers equally ignore all the Roman bishops without exception for the first two or three centuries, though several of these were condemned and executed by the civil government. Not one even of the Apostles, so far as I remember, is mentioned by any classical writer before the age of Constantine.

But, besides the difficulty of explaining the ignorance of Christian writers, supposing the bishop to have stood so near the throne, a still greater objection remains. This is the incompatibility of the two

[1] Those who adopt the identification theory strongly uphold the Christianity of Flavius Clemens. Their theory obliges them to take up this position. There obviously was a Christian Clement, and on their hypothesis no other person remains. So for instance Baur, Volkmar, Hilgenfeld, Erbes, Hasenclever, and others, and (though less strenuously) Lipsius. On the other hand those who oppose this theory are tempted to question or to deny that Flavius Clemens was a Christian, and thus to cut the ground from under their opponents. This is the position of Zahn and of Wieseler. Funk resists this temptation. The logical order of investigation, as it seems to me, is *first* to enquire whether there are two distinct Clements, and *then* (in the event of this question being answered in the affirmative) to enquire whether Flavius Clemens was or was not a Christian.

functions, which would thus be united in one person. It would have strained the conscience and taxed the resources of any man in that age to reconcile even the profession of a Christian with the duties of the consular magistracy; but to unite with it the highest office of the Christian ministry in the most prominent Church of Christendom would have been to attempt a sheer impossibility, and only the clearest evidence would justify us in postulating such an anomaly[1].

Then again what we know of Clement the consul is not easily reconcilable with what we know of Clement the bishop. I have already referred to the martyrdom of the former as inconsistent with the traditions of the career of the latter. But this is not the only difficulty. According to ancient testimony, which it would be sceptical to question, Clement the bishop is the author of the letter to the Corinthians. This letter however declares at the outset that the persecution had been going on for some time; that the attacks on the Church had been sudden and repeated; that this communication with the Corinthians had been long delayed in consequence; and that now there was a cessation or at least a respite[2]. The language of the letter indeed—both in the opening reference to the persecution and in the closing prayers for their secular rulers—leaves the impression that it was written immediately after the end of the persecution and probably after the death of Domitian, when the Christians were yet uncertain what would be the attitude of the new ruler towards the Church. At all events it is difficult to imagine as the product of one who himself was martyred eight months before the tyrant's death.

But a still graver and to my mind insuperable objection to the theory, which identifies the writer of the epistle with the cousin of Domitian, is the style and character of the document itself.

Is it possible to conceive this letter as written by one, who had received the education and who occupied the position of Flavius Clemens; who had grown up to manhood, perhaps to middle life, as a heathen; who was imbued with the thoughts and feelings of the Roman noble;

[1] This objection appears to me to hold, whatever view we take of Clement's office, consistently with the facts; for on any showing it was exceptionally prominent. Its validity does not depend, as Hasenclever seems to think (p. 255), on his being invested with the supremacy of the later papal office, though undoubtedly it would be greatly increased thereby.

[2] See especially § 1 Διὰ τὰς αἰφνιδίους καὶ ἐπαλλήλους γενομένας ἡμῖν συμφορὰς κ.τ.λ., as read in C. A is mutilated here. In my former edition (*Appendix* p. 269) I assigned too much weight to the Syriac rendering, which gives a present, 'which are befalling,' as this may be a mere carelessness, and not denote a different reading γινομένας. But the force of the argument is qualified by the doubt respecting the reading.

who about this very time held the most ancient and honourable office in the state in conjunction with the emperor; who lived in an age of literary dilettantism and of Greek culture; who must have mixed in the same circles with Martial and Statius and Juvenal, with Tacitus and the younger Pliny; and in whose house Quintilian lived as the tutor of his sons, then designated by the emperor as the future rulers of the world[1]? Would not the style, the diction, the thoughts, the whole complexion of the letter, have been very different? It might not perhaps have been less Christian, but it would certainly have been more classical—at once more Roman and more Greek—and less Jewish, than it is.

The question, whether the writer of this epistle was of Jewish or Gentile origin, has been frequently discussed and answered in opposite ways. The special points, which have been singled out on either side, will not bear the stress which has been laid upon them. On the one hand, critics have pleaded that the writer betrays his Jewish parentage, when he speaks of 'our father Jacob,' 'our father Abraham' (§§ 4, 31); but this language is found to be common to early Christian writers, whether Jewish or Gentile[2]. On the other hand, it has been inferred from the order 'day and night' (§§ 2, 20, 24), that he must have been a Gentile; but examples from the Apostolic writings show that this argument also is quite invalid[3]. Or again, this latter conclusion has been drawn from the mention of 'our generals' (§ 37), by which expression the writer is supposed to indicate his position as 'before all things a Roman born'[4]. But this language would be equally appropriate on the lips of any Hellenist Jew who was a native of Rome. Setting aside these special expressions however, and looking to the general character of the letter, we can hardly be mistaken, I think, in regarding it as the natural outpouring of one whose mind was saturated with the knowledge of the Old Testament. The writer indeed, like the author of the Book of Wisdom, is not without a certain amount of Classical culture (§§ 20, 25, 33, 37, 38, 55); but this is more or less superficial. The thoughts and diction alike are moulded on 'the Law and the Prophets and the Psalms.' He is a Hellenist indeed, for he betrays no acquaintance with the Scriptures in their original tongue: but of the Septuagint Version his knowledge is very thorough and

[1] Observe what language Quintilian uses of the Jews, iii. 7. 21 'Est conditoribus urbium infame contraxisse aliquam perniciosam ceteris gentem, qualis est primus Judaicae superstitionis auctor.'

[2] See the note on § 4 ὁ πατὴρ ἡμῶν.

[3] See the note on § 2 ἡμέρας τε καὶ νυκτός.

[4] Ewald *Gesch. d. V. Israel*, VII. p. 206.

intimate. It is not confined to any one part, but ranges freely over the whole. He quotes profusely, and sometimes his quotations are obviously made from memory. He is acquainted with traditional interpretations of the sacred text (§§ 7, 9, 11, 31). He teems with words and phrases borrowed from the Greek Bible, even where he is not directly quoting it. His style has caught a strong Hebraistic tinge from its constant study. All this points to an author of Jewish or proselyte parentage, who from a child had been reared in the knowledge of this one book[1].

It has been remarked above, that Jews were found in large numbers at this time among the slaves and freedmen of the great houses, even of the imperial palace. I observe this very name Clemens borne by one such person, a slave of the Cæsars, on a monument, to which I have already referred (p. 29) for another purpose (*C. I. L.* VI. 8494),

D. M.
CLEMETI . CAESAR
VM . N̄. SERVO . CASTE
LLARIO . AQVAE . CL
AVDIAE . FECIT . CLAV
DIA . SABBATHIS . ET . SI
BI . ET . SVIS,

for his nationality may be inferred from the name of his relative Sabbathis, who sets up the monument. And elsewhere there is abundant evidence that the name at all events was not uncommon among the dependants of the Cæsars about this time. Thus we read in a missive of Vespasian (*C. I. L.* X. 8038), DE . CONTROVERSIA ... VT . FINIRET . CLAVDIVS . CLEMENS . PROCVRATOR . MEVS . SCRIPSI . EI. In another inscription (*C. I. L.* VI. 1962) we have, EVTACTO . AVG . LIB . PROC .. ACCENSO . DELAT . A. DIVO . VESPASIANO . PATRI . OPTIMO . CLEMENS .

[1] This conviction of a Jewish training in the author is strengthened in my mind every time I read the epistle. Since I expressed myself in this sense in my *Appendix* p. 264 (1877), I have been glad to find that this view is strongly maintained by Renan *Les Évangiles* p. 311 sq (see also *Journal des Savants*, Janvier 1877). Funk considers the argument so far valid, that the letter could only have been written after a long Christian training, which is inconsistent with what we know of Flavius Clemens (*Theolog. Quartalschr.* LXI. p. 544, 1879); see also Aubé *Persécutions* p. 170. On the other hand Harnack says (p. lxiii, ed. 2), 'rectius ex elegante sermonis genere et e cc. 37, 55, judices eum nobili loco natum fuisse, patria Romanum'; and Ewald (l. c.) argues (I think, somewhat perversely) that the length of the writer's quotations from the Old Testament shows that the book was novel to him. But in fact the direct quotations are only a very small part, and the least convincing part of the evidence.

FILIVS; in another (*C. I. L.* VI. 9049), CLEMENS . AVG . AD . SVPELECT; in another (*C. I. L.* VI. 9079), D. M . SEDATI . TI . CL . SECVNDINI . PROC . AVG . TABVL . CLEMENS . ADFINIS; in another (*C. I. L.* VI. 940), PRO . SALVTE . T . CAESARIS . AVG . F . IMP . VESPASIANI . TI . CLAVDIVS . CLEMENS . FECIT; in another (*C. I. L.* III. 5215), T . VARIO . CLEMENTI . AB . EPISTVLIS . AVGVSTOR., this last however dating in the reign of M. Aurelius and L. Verus A. D. 161—169; while in another, found in the columbarium of the Freedmen of Livia, and therefore perhaps belonging to an earlier date than our Clement, we read (*C. I. L.* VI. 4145), IVLIA . CALLITYCHE . STORGE . CLAVDI . EROTIS . DAT . CLEMENTI . CONIVGI . CALLITYCHES. I venture therefore to conjecture that Clement the bishop was a man of Jewish descent, a freedman or the son of a freedman belonging to the household of Flavius Clemens the emperor's cousin[1]. It is easy to imagine how under these circumstances the leaven of Christianity would work upwards from beneath, as it has done in so many other cases; and from their domestics and dependants the master and mistress would learn their perilous lessons in the Gospel. Even a much greater degree of culture than is exhibited in this epistle would be quite consistent with such an origin; for amongst these freedmen were frequently found the most intelligent and cultivated men of their day. Nor is this social status inconsistent with the position of the chief ruler of the most important church in Christendom. A generation later Hermas, the brother of bishop Pius, unless indeed he is investing himself with

[1] The coincidence in the *cognomen* may have been accidental, owing to the fact that he or his father or grandfather had borne it as a slave; for it was a common slave name (e.g. *C. I. L.* V. 6021, IX. 3051). As a rule the manumitted slave took the *nomen* of his master, but retained his own name as the *cognomen*. This is a difficulty raised by Lipsius *Chronol.* p. 161, and others. Thus Renan (*Les Évangiles* p. 311) objects that our Clement in this case 'se serait appelé Flavius et non pas Clemens,' forgetting that he himself in an earlier passage (p. 255) has explained the name of S. Luke (Lucas, Lucanus) by saying that it 'peut se rattacher, par un lien de clientèle ou d'affranchissement, à quelque M. Annæus Lucanus, parent du célèbre poëte.' We meet occasionally with examples where the freedmen or their descendants bear the same *cognomen* with the master (see above, p. 47, note 4), though these are the exceptions. It is impossible for instance that all, and not very likely that any, of the Flavii Clementes mentioned in the inscriptions were descendants of Domitian's nephew.

Still the conjecture that Clement the bishop was a dependant of Clement the consul must remain a conjecture. His connexion with the imperial household in some way or other has a much higher degree of probability. But being so connected, he may nevertheless not have been a Flavius, but a Claudius or a Valerius, as the examples given in the next note will show.

a fictitious personality, speaks of himself as having been a slave (*Vis.* i. 1); and this involves the servile origin of Pius also. At a still later date, more than a century after Clement's time, the papal chair was occupied by Callistus, who had been a slave of one Carpophorus an officer in the imperial palace (Hippol. *Haer.* ix. 12). The Christianity which had thus taken root in the household of Domitian's cousin left a memorial behind in another distinguished person also. The famous Alexandrian father, who flourished a century later than the bishop of Rome, bore all the three names of this martyr prince, Titus Flavius Clemens[1]. He too was doubtless a descendant of some servant in the family, who according to custom would be named after his patron when he obtained his freedom.

The imperial household was henceforward a chief centre of Christianity in the metropolis. Irenæus writing during the episcopate of Eleutherus (circ. A.D. 175—189), and therefore under M. Aurelius or Commodus, speaks of 'the faithful in the royal court' in language which seems to imply that they were a considerable body there (iv. 30. 1). Marcia, the concubine of this last-mentioned emperor, was herself a Christian, and exerted her influence over Commodus in alleviating the sufferings of the confessors (Hippol. *Haer.* l. c.). At this same time also another Christian, Carpophorus, already mentioned, whose name seems to betray a servile origin, but who was evidently a man of con-

[1] This conjunction of names occurs also in an inscription found at Augsburg, T. FL. PRIMANO. PATRI. ET. TRAIAN. CLEMENTINAE. MATRI. ET. T. FL. CLEMENTI. FRATRI (*C. I. L.* III. 5812), where the name *Traiana* is another link of connexion with the imperial household. Compare also T. FL. LONGINVS...ET. FLAVI. LONGINVS. CLEMENTINA. MARCELLINA. FIL[I] (*C. I. L.* III. 1100); MATRI. PIENTISSIMAE. LVCRETIVS. CLEMENS. ET. FL. FORTVNATVS. FILI (*C. I. L.* III. 5844). The name FLAVIVS. CLEMENS occurs also in another inscription (Murat. CDXCIV. 4), along with many other names which point to the household of the Cæsars, though at a later date. So too *C. I. L.* III. 5783, VIII. 2869, 9470, 10470. Comp. also D. M. C. VALERIO. CLEMENTI. C. IVLIVS. FELIX. ET. FLAVIA. FORTVNATA. HEREDES (Murat. MDV. 12).

This last inscription illustrates the connexion of names *Valerius* and *Clemens* which appears in our epistle. Of this phenomenon also we have other examples: e.g. a memorial erected C. VALERIO. C. F. STEL. CLEMENTI by the DECVRIONES. ALAE. GETVLORVM. QVIBVS. PRAEFVIT. BELLO. IVDAICO. SVB. DIVO. VESPASIANO. AVG. PATRE (*C. I. L.* 7007), found at Turin. This Valerius Clemens therefore was a contemporary of our Clement. For other instances of the combination Valerius Clemens see *C. I. L.* III. 633, 2572, 6162, 6179, V. 3977, 7007, 7681, VIII. 5121, X. 3401, 3646, Muratori MCDXV. 1, MDLXIV. 12. So too Valerius Clementinus *C. I. L.* III. 3524, and Valeria Clementina, *ib.* 2580. For examples of Claudius Clemens, besides X. 8038 quoted in the text, see VIII. 5404, X. 6331, 8397.

siderable wealth and influence, held some office in the imperial household. A little later the emperor Severus is stated to have been cured by a physician Proculus, a Christian slave, whom he kept in the palace ever afterwards to the day of his death: while the son and successor of this emperor, Caracalla, had a Christian woman for his foster-mother (Tertull. *ad Scap.* 4). Again, the Christian sympathies of Alexander Severus and Philip, and the still more decided leanings of the ladies of their families, are well known. And so it continued to the last. When in an evil hour for himself Diocletian was induced to raise his hand against the Church, the first to suffer were his confidential servants, the first to abjure on compulsion were his own wife and daughter[1].

I have spoken throughout of this Clement, the writer of the letter, as bishop of the Roman Church. But two questions here arise; *First*, What do we know from other sources of his date and order in the episcopal succession? and *Secondly*, What was the nature of this episcopal office which he exercised.

1. The first of these questions will be more fully answered in a later chapter, on the Roman Succession, where the various problems offered by the discrepancies in the early lists are discussed. It will be sufficient here to sum up the results, so far as they affect our answer.

Confining ourselves then to the earliest names, we are confronted with three different representations which assign three several positions to Clement. Not counting the Apostles, he is placed third, first, and second, in the series respectively.

(1) The first of these appears among extant writers as early as Irenæus, who wrote during the episcopate of Eleutherus (about A.D. 175—190). The order here is Linus, Anencletus, Clemens, Euarestus[2], the first mentioned having received his commission from the Apostles S. Peter and S. Paul (iii. 1. 1, iii. 3. 3). But some years earlier than Irenæus, the Jewish Christian Hegesippus had drawn up a list of the Roman succession[3]. He was well acquainted with Clement's letter and visited both Corinth and Rome—the place from which and the place to which it was addressed. He arrived there soon after the middle of the second century, during the episcopate of Anicetus (c. A.D. 160) and remained till the accession of Eleutherus. We should expect there-

[1] Mason *Persecution of Diocletian* p. 121 sq.

[2] The word PLACEAS will serve as a convenient memoria technica, giving the initial letters of the first seven (including the Apostles) according to the order preserved in the earliest tradition; Petrus et Paulus, Linus, Anencletus, Clemens, Euarestus, Alexander, Sixtus (Xystus).

[3] See the passage given below, p. 154.

fore that his list would not differ essentially from that of Irenæus, since his information was obtained about the same time and in the same place. Elsewhere I have given reasons, which seem to me to be strong, for believing that his list is preserved in Epiphanius. If this supposition be correct, after the Apostles S. Peter and S. Paul came Linus, then Cletus, then Clemens, then Euarestus. Thus these two earliest lists are identical, except that the same person is called in the one Cletus and in the other Anencletus. This is the order likewise which appears in Eusebius and in Jerome after him. It is adopted during the fourth century by Epiphanius in the East, and by Rufinus in the West. Altogether we may call it the *traditional* order. Indeed none other was ever current in the East.

(ii) The Clementine romance emanated, as I have already said, from Syria or some neighbouring country, and betrays no knowledge of Rome or the Roman Church. A leading idea in this fiction is the exaltation of its hero Clement, whom it makes the depositary of the apostolic tradition. The author's ignorance left him free to indulge his invention. He therefore represented Clement as the immediate successor of S. Peter, consecrated by the Apostle in his own life time. Though the date of this work cannot have been earlier than the middle of the second century, yet the glorification of Rome and the Roman bishop obtained for it an early and wide circulation in the West. Accordingly even Tertullian speaks of Clement as the immediate successor of S. Peter. This position however is not assigned to him in any list of the Roman bishops, but only appears in this father as an isolated statement.

(iii) The Liberian list dates from the year 354, during the episcopate of the pope by whose name it is commonly designated. It gives the order, Linus, Clemens, Cletus, Anacletus, Aristus; where Clemens is placed neither first nor third but second, where the single bishop next in order is duplicated, thus making Cletus and Anacletus, and where the following name (a matter of no moment for our purpose) is abridged from Euarestus into Aristus. This list appears with a certain show of authority. It was illustrated by Furius Filocalus, the calligrapher whom we find employed in the catacombs by Pope Damasus the successor of Liberius. Moreover it had a great influence on later opinion in Rome and the West. It coincides in some respects with the list of the African fathers Optatus and Augustine. It was followed in many of its peculiarities by the catalogues of the succeeding centuries. It influenced the order of the popes in the famous series of mosaics in the basilica of S. Paul at Rome. It formed the ground-work of the

Liber Pontificalis, which was first compiled in the end of the fifth or beginning of the sixth century, but revised from time to time, and which, though not strictly official, had a sort of recognition as a summary of the Papal history. But quite independently of its subsequent influence, this Liberian Catalogue claims consideration on its own account. It is circumstantial, it is early, and it is local. On these three grounds it challenges special investigation.

It is *circumstantial.* It gives not only the names of the several bishops in succession, but also their term of office in each case. The duration is precisely defined, not only the years but the months and days being given. Moreover it adds data of relative chronology. It mentions the imperial reigns during which each bishop held office, and also the consulships which mark the first and last years of his episcopate.

It is *early.* The date already mentioned (A.D. 354) gives the time when the collection was made and the several tracts contained in it assumed their present form; but it comprises much more ancient elements. The papal list falls into two or three parts, of which the first, comprising the period from the accession of Peter to the accession of Pontianus (A.D. 230), must have been drawn up in its original form shortly after this latter date.

It is *local.* Bound up in this collection is another treatise, a 'chronicle,' which on good grounds is ascribed to Hippolytus. Moreover there is somewhat strong, though not absolutely conclusive evidence, that Hippolytus drew up a catalogue of the Roman bishops, and that this catalogue was attached to the chronicle. Moreover the date at which (as already mentioned) the first part of the papal list ends, the episcopate of Pontianus (A.D. 230—235), coincides with the termination of this chronicle, which was brought down to the 13th year of Alexander (A.D. 234). Thus incorporated in this Liberian document, we apparently have the episcopal list of Hippolytus, who was bishop of Portus the harbour of Rome, and was closely mixed up with the politics of the Roman Church in his day. At all events, if not the work of Hippolytus himself, it must have been compiled by some contemporary, who like him had a direct acquaintance with the affairs of the Roman Church.

If this were all, the Liberian list would claim the highest consideration on the threefold ground of particularity, of antiquity, and of proximity. But further examination diminishes our estimate of its value. Its details are confused; its statements are often at variance with known history; its notices of time are irreconcilable one with another.

It has obviously passed through many vicissitudes of transcription and of editing, till its original character is quite changed. This is especially the case with the more ancient portion. This very sequence of the earliest bishops, so far as we can judge, is simply the result of blundering. Whether and how far Hippolytus himself was responsible for these errors, we cannot say with absolute confidence ; but examination seems to show that the document, which was the original groundwork of this list, gave the same sequence of names as we find in Irenæus and Eusebius and Epiphanius, and that any departures from it are due to the blunders and misconceptions of successive scribes and editors.

These results, which I have thus briefly gathered up, will be set forth more fully in their proper place. If they are substantially correct, the immediate problem which lies before us is simple enough. We have to reckon with three conflicting statements, so far as regards the position of Clement in the Roman succession—a *tradition*, the Irenæan—a *fiction*, the Clementine—and a *blunder*, the Liberian, or perhaps the Hippolytean. Under these circumstances we cannot hesitate for a moment in our verdict. Whether the value of the tradition be great or small, it alone deserves to be considered. The sequence therefore which commends itself for acceptance is, Linus, Anencletus or Cletus, Clemens, Euarestus. It has moreover this negative argument in its favour. The temptation with hagiologers would be great to place Clement as early as possible in the list. Least of all would there be any inducement to insert before him the name of a person otherwise unknown, Cletus or Anencletus.

Nor can the tradition be treated otherwise than with the highest respect. We can trace it back to a few years later than the middle of the second century. It comes from Rome itself. It was diligently gathered there and deliberately recorded by two several writers from different parts of Christendom. At the time when Hegesippus and Irenæus visited the metropolis, members of the Roman Church must still have been living, who in childhood or youth, or even in early manhood, had seen Clement himself.

But, besides the sequence of the names, we have likewise the durations of the several episcopates. It will be shown, when the time comes, that the numbers of years assigned to the early bishops in lists as wide apart as the Eusebian and the Liberian can be traced to one common tradition, dating before the close of the second century at all events. If the reasons which I shall give be accepted as valid, the tradition of the term-numbers was probably coeval with the earliest evidence for the tradition of the succession, and was recorded by the pen of Hegesippus himself. This tradition assigns twelve years to Linus, twelve to Cletus or Anencletus, and nine to Clement. As the accession of Linus was coeval, or nearly so, with the martyrdom of the two Apostles, which is placed about A.D. 65 (strictly speaking A.D. 64 or A.D. 67), the accession of Clement would be about A.D. 90. Thus, roughly speaking, his episcopate would span the last decade of the first century. This agrees with the evidence of Clement's epistle itself, which appears to have been written immediately after, if not during, the persecution, i.e. A.D. 95 or 96.

2. The discussion of the first question has paved the way for the consideration of the second, What was the position which Clement held? Was he bishop of Rome in the later sense of the term 'bishop'? and, if bishop, was he pope, as the papal office was understood in after ages?

We have seen that tradition—very early tradition—gives by name the holders of the episcopal office in Rome from the time of the Apostles' death. The tradition itself is not confused. Linus, Cletus or Anencletus, and Clemens, are bishops in succession one to the other. The discrepancies of order in the later papal lists do not require to be explained by any hypothesis which supposes more than one person to have exercised the same episcopal office simultaneously; as for instance the theory which represents them as at the same time leading members of the Roman presbytery, the term 'bishop' being understood in the earlier sense, when it was a synonyme for 'presbyter[1]'; or the theory which supposes Linus and Cletus to have been suffragans under S. Peter during his life-time[2]; or the theory which suggests that Clement, though ordained bishop before Linus and Cletus, yet voluntarily waived his episcopal rights in their favour for the sake of peace[3]; or lastly the theory which postulates two distinct Christian communities in Rome—a Jewish and a Gentile Church—in the ages immediately succeeding the Apostles, placing one bishop as the successor of S. Peter at the head of the Jewish congregation, and another as the successor of S. Paul at the

[1] This is a not uncommon theory of modern critics. It was also maintained by the French and English Protestants of the 17th century arguing against episcopacy.

[2] This theory was first propounded by Rufinus *Praef. in Recogn.*, quoted below, p. 174 sq. It is adopted in the later recension of the *Liber Pontificalis*; see below, p. 191.

[3] This view is propounded by Epiphanius, who however only offers it as a suggestion, *Haeres.* xxvii. 6, quoted below, p. 169. It has found favour with Baronius (ann. 69, § xliii), Tillemont (*Mémoires* II. p. 548), and others.

head of the Gentile, and supposing the two communities to have been afterwards fused under the headship of Clement[1]. However attractive and plausible such theories may be in themselves, their foundation is withdrawn, and they can no longer justify their existence, when it is once ascertained that the tradition of the Roman succession was one and single, and that all variations in the order of the names are the product of invention or of blundering.

The value of the tradition will necessarily be less for the earlier names than for the later. Though, so far as I can see, no adequate reason can be advanced why Linus and Anencletus should not have been bishops in the later sense, as single rulers of the Church, yet here the tradition, if unsupported by any other considerations, cannot inspire any great confidence. But with Clement the case is different. The testimony of the succeeding ages is strong and united. Even the exaggerations of the Clementine story point to a basis of fact.

By this Clementine writer indeed he is placed on a very high eminence. Not only is the episcopal office, which he holds, monarchical; but he is represented as a bishop not of his own Church alone, but in some degree also of Christendom. S. Peter is the missionary preacher of the whole world, the vanquisher of all the heresies; and S. Clement, as his direct successor, inherits his position and responsibilities. But over the head of the pope of Rome (if he may be so styled) is a still higher authority—the pope of Jerusalem. Even Peter himself—and *a fortiori* Peter's successor—is required to give an account of all his missionary labours to James the Lord's brother, the occupant of the mother-see of Christendom.

The language and the silence alike of Clement himself and of writers in his own and immediately succeeding ages are wholly irreconcilable with this extravagant estimate of his position[2]. Even the opinion, which has found favour with certain modern critics, more especially of the Tübingen school, that the episcopate, as a monarchical

[1] This theory receives some support from the statement in *Apost. Const.* vii. 46 τῆς δὲ Ῥωμαίων ἐκκλησίας Λίνος μὲν ὁ Κλαυδίας πρῶτος ὑπὸ Παύλου, Κλήμης δὲ μετὰ τὸν Λίνου θάνατον ὑπ' ἐμοῦ Πέτρου δεύτερος κεχειροτόνηται, though it is not this writer's own view. It was propounded, I believe, first by Hammond *de Episcopatus Juribus* p. 257 (London 1651); see Cotelier on *Apost. Const.* l. c., and Tillemont *Mémoires* II. p. 547. Hammond's theory with some modifications has found favour with several recent writers, e. g. Bunsen *Hippolytus* I. pp. xxiv, 44 (ed. 2), Baring-Gould *Lives of Saints* Nov. II. p. 507. I had myself put it forward tentatively as a possible solution of the discrepancies in the early lists of Roman bishops; *Galatians* p. 337 sq, *Philippians* p. 221.

[2] See on this point *Philippians* p. 217 sq, *Ignat. and Polyc.* I. p. 383 sq.

office, was developed more rapidly at Rome than elsewhere, finds no support from authentic testimony. Whatever plausibility there may be in the contention that the monarchical spirit, which dominated the State, would by contact and sympathy infuse itself into the Church, known facts all suggest the opposite conclusion. In Clement's letter itself—the earliest document issuing from the Roman Church after the apostolic times—no mention is made of episcopacy properly so called. Only two orders are enumerated, and these are styled bishops and deacons respectively, where the term 'bishop' is still a synonyme for 'presbyter'[1]. Yet the adoption of different names and the consequent separation in meaning between 'bishop' and 'presbyter' must, it would seem, have followed closely upon the institution or development of the episcopate, as a monarchical office. Nevertheless the language of this letter, though itself inconsistent with the possession of papal authority in the person of the writer, enables us to understand the secret of the growth of papal domination. It does not proceed from the bishop of Rome, but from the Church of Rome. There is every reason to believe the early tradition which points to S. Clement as its author, and yet he is not once named. The first person plural is maintained throughout, 'We consider,' 'We have sent.' Accordingly writers of the second century speak of it as a letter from the community, not from the individual. Thus Dionysius, bishop of Corinth, writing to the Romans about A.D. 170, refers to it as the epistle 'which you wrote to us by Clement (Euseb. *H. E.* iv. 23)'; and Irenæus soon afterwards similarly describes it, 'In the time of this Clement, no small dissension having arisen among the brethren in Corinth, the Church in Rome sent a very adequate letter to the Corinthians urging them to peace (iii. 3. 3).' Even later than this, Clement of Alexandria calls it in one passage 'the Epistle of the Romans to the Corinthians' (*Strom.* v. 12, p. 693), though elsewhere he ascribes it to Clement. Still it might have been expected that somewhere towards the close mention would have been made (though in the third person) of the famous man who was at once the actual writer of the letter and the chief ruler of the church in whose name it was written. Now however that we possess the work complete, we see that his existence is not once hinted at from beginning to end. The name and personality of Clement are absorbed in the church of which he is the spokesman.

This being so, it is the more instructive to observe the urgent and almost imperious tone which the Romans adopt in addressing their Corinthian brethren during the closing years of the first century. They

[1] See *Philippians* p. 95 sq, 196.

exhort the offenders to submit 'not to them, but to the will of God' (§ 56). 'Receive our counsel,' they write again, 'and ye shall have no occasion of regret' (§ 58). Then shortly afterwards; 'But if certain persons should be disobedient unto the words spoken by Him (i.e. by God) through us, let them understand that they will entangle themselves in no slight transgression and danger, but we shall be guiltless of this sin' (§ 59). At a later point again they return to the subject and use still stronger language; 'Ye will give us great joy and gladness, if ye render obedience unto the things written by us through the Holy Spirit, and root out the unrighteous anger of your jealousy, according to the entreaty which we have made for peace and concord in this letter; and we have also sent unto you faithful and prudent men, that have walked among us from youth unto old age unblameably, who shall be witnesses between you and us. And this we have done, that ye might know, that we have had and still have every solicitude, that ye may speedily be at peace (§ 63).' It may perhaps seem strange to describe this noble remonstrance as the first step towards papal domination. And yet undoubtedly this is the case. There is all the difference in the world between the attitude of Rome towards other churches at the close of the first century, when the Romans as a community remonstrate on terms of equality with the Corinthians on their irregularities, strong only in the righteousness of their cause, and feeling, as they had a right to feel, that these counsels of peace were the dictation of the Holy Spirit, and its attitude at the close of the second century, when Victor the bishop excommunicates the Churches of Asia Minor for clinging to a usage in regard to the celebration of Easter which had been handed down to them from the Apostles, and thus foments instead of healing dissensions (Euseb. *H. E.* v. 23, 24). Even this second stage has carried the power of Rome only a very small step in advance towards the assumptions of a Hildebrand or an Innocent or a Boniface, or even of a Leo: but it is nevertheless a decided step. The substitution of the bishop of Rome for the Church of Rome is an all important point. The later Roman theory supposes that the Church of Rome derives all its authority from the bishop of Rome, as the successor of S. Peter. History inverts this relation and shows that, as a matter of fact, the power of the bishop of Rome was built upon the power of the Church of Rome. It was originally a primacy, not of the episcopate, but of the church. The position of the Roman Church, which this newly recovered ending of Clement's epistle throws out in such strong relief, accords entirely with the notices in other early documents. A very few years later—from ten to twenty—Ignatius writes to Rome. He is a staunch advocate of episcopacy. Of his six remaining letters, one is addressed to a bishop as bishop; and the other five all enforce the duty of the churches whom he addresses to their respective bishops. Yet in the letter to the Church of Rome there is not the faintest allusion to the episcopal office from first to last. He entreats the Roman Christians not to intercede and thus by obtaining a pardon or commutation of sentence to rob him of the crown of martyrdom. In the course of his entreaty he uses words which doubtless refer in part to Clement's epistle, and which the newly recovered ending enables us to appreciate more fully; 'Ye never yet,' he writes, 'envied any one,' i.e. grudged him the glory of a consistent course of endurance and self-sacrifice, 'ye were the teachers of others (οὐδέποτε ἐβασκάνατε οὐδενί· ἄλλους ἐδιδάξατε, § 3).' They would therefore be inconsistent with their former selves, he implies, if in his own case they departed from those counsels of self-renunciation and patience which they had urged so strongly on the Corinthians and others. But, though Clement's letter is apparently in his mind, there is no mention of Clement or Clement's successor throughout. Yet at the same time he assigns a primacy to Rome. The church is addressed in the opening salutation as 'she who hath the presidency (προκάθηται) in the place of the region of the Romans.' But immediately afterwards the nature of this supremacy is defined. The presidency of this church is declared to be a presidency of love (προκαθημένη τῆς ἀγάπης). This then was the original primacy of Rome—a primacy not of the bishop but of the whole church, a primacy not of official authority but of practical goodness, backed however by the prestige and the advantages which were necessarily enjoyed by the church of the metropolis. The reserve of Clement in his epistle harmonizes also with the very modest estimate of his dignity implied in the language of one who appears to have been a younger contemporary, but who wrote (if tradition can be trusted) at a somewhat later date[1]. Thou shalt therefore, says the personified Church to Hermas, 'write two little books,' i.e. copies of this work containing the revelation, 'and thou shalt send one to Clement and one to Grapte. So Clement shall send it to the cities abroad, for this charge is committed unto him, and Grapte shall instruct the widows and the orphans; while thou shalt read it to this city together with the presbyters who preside over the church.' And so it remains till the close of the second century. When, some seventy years later than the date of our epistle, a second letter is written from Rome to Corinth during the episcopate of Soter (about A.D. 165—175), it is still written

[1] Herm. *Vis.* ii. 4.

in the name of the Church, not the bishop, of Rome; and as such is acknowledged by Dionysius of Corinth. 'We have read your letter' (ὑμῶν τὴν ἐπιστολήν), he writes in reply to the Romans. At the same time he bears a noble testimony to that moral ascendancy of the early Roman Church which was the historical foundation of its primacy; 'This hath been your practice from the beginning; to do good to all the brethren in the various ways, and to send supplies (ἐφόδια) to many churches in divers cities, in one place recruiting the poverty of those that are in want, in another assisting brethren that are in the mines by the supplies that ye have been in the habit of sending to them from the first, thus keeping up, as becometh Romans, a hereditary practice of Romans, which your blessed bishop Soter hath not only maintained, but also advanced,' with more to the same effect[1].

The results of the previous investigations will enable us in some degree to realize the probable career of Clement, the writer of the epistle; but the lines of our portrait will differ widely from the imaginary picture which the author of the Clementine romance has drawn. The date of his birth, we may suppose, would synchronize roughly with the death of the Saviour. A few years on the one side or on the other would probably span the difference. He would be educated, not like this imaginary Clement on the subtleties of the schools, but like Timothy on the Scriptures of the Old Testament. He would indeed be more or less closely attached to the palace of the Cæsars, not however as a scion of the imperial family itself, but as a humbler dependent of the household. When he arrived at manhood, his inward doubts and anxieties would be moral rather than metaphysical. His questioning would not take the form 'Is the soul immortal?' but rather 'What shall I do to be saved?' He would enquire not 'To what philosophy shall I betake myself—to the Academy or to the Lyceum or to the Porch?', but 'Where shall I find the Christ?' How soon he discovered the object of his search, we cannot tell; but he was probably

[1] Euseb. *H. E.* iv. 23 quoted below, p. 155. Harnack (p. xxix, ed. 2) says that this letter of Dionysius 'non Soteris tempore sed paullo post Soteris mortem (175—180) Romam missa esse videtur.' I see nothing in the passage which suggests this inference. On the contrary the perfect tenses (διατετήρηκεν, ἐπηύξηκεν), used in preference to aorists, seem to imply that he was living. The epithet μακάριος, applied to Soter, confessedly proves nothing; for it was used at this time and later not less of the living than of the dead (e.g. Alexander in Euseb. *H. E.* vi. 11). Eusebius himself, who had the whole letter before him, seems certainly to have supposed that Soter was living, for he speaks of it as ἐπιστολὴ...ἐπισκόπῳ τῷ τότε Σωτῆρι προσφωνοῦσα. See below, p. 154 sq.

grown or growing up to manhood when the Messianic disturbances among the Jews at Rome led to the edict of expulsion under Claudius (about A.D. 52)[1]. If he had not known the name of Jesus of Nazareth hitherto, he could no longer have remained ignorant that one claiming to be the Christ had been born and lived and died in Palestine, of whom His disciples asserted that, though dead, He was alive—alive for evermore. The edict was only very partial in its effects[2]. It was not seriously carried out; and, though some Jews, especially those of migratory habits like Aquila and Priscilla, were driven away by it, yet it did not permanently disturb or diminish the Jewish colony in Rome. Meanwhile the temporary displacements and migrations, which it caused, would materially assist in the diffusion of the Gospel.

A few years later (A.D. 58) the arrival of a letter from the Apostle Paul, announcing his intended visit to Rome, marked an epoch in the career of the Roman Church. When at length his pledge was redeemed, he came as a prisoner; but his prison-house for two long years was the home and rallying point of missionary zeal in Rome. More especially did he find himself surrounded by members of Cæsar's household. The visit of Paul was followed after an interval (we know not how long) by the visit of Peter. Now at all events Clement must have been a Christian, so that he would have associated directly with both these great preachers of Christianity. Indeed his own language seems to imply as much. He speaks of them as 'the *good* Apostles[3]'—an epithet which suggests a personal acquaintance with them. The later traditions, which represent him as having been consecrated bishop by one or other of these Apostles, cannot be literally true; but they are explained by the underlying fact of his immediate discipleship[4]. Around

[1] Sueton. *Claud.* 25; comp. Acts xviii. 2, and see *Philippians* p. 19.

[2] See Lewin *Fasti Sacri* p. 295, for the date of this decree and for its effects. This most useful book is not as well known as it deserves to be.

[3] § 5 τοὺς ἀγαθοὺς ἀποστόλους. The epithet has caused much uneasiness to critics, and emendations have been freely offered. It is confirmed however by the recently discovered authorities (the Constantinople MS and the Syriac version), and must be explained by the writer's personal relations to the Apostles.

[4] Lipsius again and again insists that the tradition which makes Clement the third in the succession of Roman bishops is inconsistent with the tradition which makes him an immediate disciple of one or other Apostle, treating this assumed inconsistency as if it were a postulate beyond the reach of controversy; *Chronologie* pp. 147, 149, 150. But what havock would be made by the application of this principle to contemporary history. The death of the Apostles Peter and Paul is placed A.D. 64 at the earliest; and the date of Clement's epistle is somewhere about A.D. 95. There is thus an interval of a little more than thirty

these great leaders were grouped many distinguished followers from the distant East, with whom Clement would thus become acquainted. Peter was attended more especially by Mark, who acted as his interpreter. Sylvanus was also in his company at least for a time[1]. Paul was visited by a succession of disciples from Greece and Asia Minor and Syria, of whom Timothy and Titus, Luke and Apollos, besides Mark who has been already mentioned, are among the most prominent names in the history of the Church[2].

Then came the great trial of Christian constancy, the persecution of Nero. Of the untold horrors of this crisis we can hardly doubt, from his own description, that he was an eye-witness. The suspenses and anxieties of that terrible season when the informer was abroad and every Christian carried his life in his hand must have stamped themselves vividly on his memory. The refined cruelty of the tortures—the impalements and the pitchy tunics, the living torches making night hideous with the lurid flames and piercing cries, the human victims clad in the skins of wild beasts and hunted in the arena, while the populace gloated over these revels and the emperor indulged his mad orgies—these were scenes which no lapse of time could efface. Above all—the climax of horrors—were the outrages, far worse than death itself, inflicted on weak women and innocent girls[3].

As the central figures in this noble army of martyrs, towering head and shoulders above the rest, Clement mentions the Apostles

years. Must we reject as erroneous the common belief, which assumes that a famous statesman still living as I write (A.D. 1887) was a political disciple of Sir R. Peel, who died in 1850, and even held office under him sixteen years before his death? Is it credible, that certain Englishmen occupying prominent positions in Church or State, apparently with a prospect of many years of life still before them, were (as they are reported to have been) pupils of Arnold, the great schoolmaster, who died not less than forty-five years ago? Above all who will venture to maintain that the Emperor William entered Paris with the victorious Prussian troops after the surrender seventy-three years ago (A.D. 1814), seeing that the story may be explained by a confusion with another entry of a triumphant German army into Paris more than half a century later (A.D. 1871), on which occasion there are good reasons for believing that he was actually present?

[1] 1 Pet. v. 12, 15, on the supposition, which seems to me highly probable, that this epistle was written from Rome. See also Papias in Euseb. *H. E.* iii. 39, Iren. *Haer.* iii. 1. 1, iii. 10. 6.

[2] For Timothy see Phil. i. 1, Col. i. 1, Philem. 1, comp. 2 Tim. iii. 9 sq, Heb. xiii. 23; for Mark, Col. iv. 10, Philem. 24, 2 Tim. iv. 11; for Luke, Col. iv. 14, Philem. 24, 2 Tim. iv. 11; for Titus, 2 Tim. iii. 10, comp. Tit. iii. 12; for Apollos, Tit. iii. 13, in conjunction with his not improbable authorship of the Epistle to the Hebrews.

[3] See the note on § 6 Δαναΐδες καὶ Δίρκαι.

Peter and Paul; for I cannot doubt that he speaks of both these as sealing their testimony with their blood[1]. Whether they died in the general persecution at the time of the great fire, or whether their martyrdoms were due to some later isolated outbreak of violence, it is unnecessary for my present purpose to enquire. There are solid reasons however—at least in the case of S. Paul—for supposing that a considerable interval elapsed[2].

The Christian Church emerged from this fiery trial refined and strengthened. Even the common people at length were moved with pity for the crowds of sufferers, whom all regarded as innocent of the particular offence for which they were punished, and against whom no definite crime was alleged, though in a vague way they were charged with a universal hatred of their species[3]. But on more thoughtful and calm-judging spirits their constancy must have made a deep impression. One there was, whose position would not suffer him to witness this spectacle unmoved. Flavius Sabinus, the City prefect, must by virtue of his position have been the instrument—we cannot doubt, the unwilling instrument—of Nero's cruelty at this crisis[4]. He was naturally

[1] See the notes on the passage (§ 5) relating to the two Apostles.

[2] The main reasons for this view are; (1) The confident expectations of release which the Apostle entertains (Phil. i. 25, Philem. 22): (2) The visit to the far West, more especially to Spain; see the note on § 5 τὸ τέρμα τῆς δύσεως: (3) The phenomena of the Pastoral Epistles, which require a place after the close of the period contained in the Acts.

[3] Tac. *Ann.* xv. 44 'indicio eorum multitudo ingens, haud perinde in crimine incendii quam *odio humani generis*, convicti sunt......unde quamquam adversus sontes et novissima exempla meritos miseratio oriebatur, tamquam non utilitate publica sed in saevitiam unius absumérentur.' It is clear that 'humani generis' is the objective not the subjective genitive, and that the phrase is correctly rendered in the text, for several reasons; (1) The parallelism of the context requires that this phrase should express a charge against the Christians; (2) The parallel passages elsewhere point to this interpretation, e.g. *Hist.* v. 5 'apud ipsos fides obstinata, misericordia in promptu, sed *adversus omnes alios hostile odium*' of the Jews, with which compare 1 Thess. ii. 15 πᾶσιν ἀνθρώποις ἐναντίων, Juv. *Sat.* xiv. 103 sq, with the passages quoted in Mayor's note. Tillemont (*Mémoires* II. p. 74) wrongly interprets it 'victimes de la haine du genre humain,' and this is likewise the meaning attached to it by some commentators on Tacitus.

I need not stop to consider the vagary of Hochart (*Persécution des Chrétiens sous Néron*, Paris 1885), who maintains that the passage in Tacitus relating to the Christians is a medieval interpolation. It will go the way of Father Hardouin's theories that Terence's Plays and Virgil's Aeneid and Horace's Odes, and I know not what besides, were monkish forgeries; though it may possibly have a momentary notoriety before its departure.

[4] See above, p. 18, note 2, for his tenure of office, and p. 35, note 2, for his humane disposition.

of a humane and gentle nature. Indifferent spectators considered him deficient in promptitude and energy in the exercise of his office. Doubtless it imposed upon him many duties which he could not perform without reluctance; and we may well suppose that the attitude and bearing of these Christians inspired him at all events with a passive admiration. This may have been the first impulse which produced momentous consequences in his family. Thirty years later his son Flavius Clemens was put to death by another tyrant and persecutor—a near relation of his own—on this very charge of complicity with the Christians.

On the death of the two Apostles the government of the Roman Church came into the hands of LINUS, the same who sends greeting to Timothy on the eve of S. Paul's martyrdom. The name Linus itself, like the names of other mythical heroes, would be a fit designation of a slave or freedman[1]; and thus it suggests the social rank of himself or his parents. An early venture, or perhaps an early tradition, makes him the son of Claudia whose name is mentioned in the same salutations[2]. If so, he, like so many others, may have been connected with the imperial household, as his mother's name suggests. But the relationship was perhaps a mere guess of the writer, who had no better ground for it than the proximity of the two names in S. Paul's epistle. Modern critics are not satisfied with this[3]. They have seen in Pudens who is mentioned in the same context the husband of Claudia; and they have identified him with a certain Aulus Pudens, the friend of Martial, who

[1] See *C. I. L.* x. 6637, where it is apparently a slave's name. This same inscription gives five Claudias, contemporaries of S. Paul.

[2] 2 Tim. iv. 21 ἀσπάζεταί σε Εὔβουλος καὶ Πούδης καὶ Λίνος καὶ Κλαυδία καὶ οἱ ἀδελφοὶ [πάντες]: comp. *Apost. Const.* vii. 46 Λίνος ὁ Κλαυδίας, where presumably the relationship intended is that of son and mother, though this is not certain.

[3] The theory that Pudens and Claudia were connected with Britain, and thus were the evangelists of the British Church, had a controversial value with the older generation of English critics and historians. The origin of the British Church was thus traced back to an apostolic foundation, and in this way they met the contention of Romanist writers who maintained that it was founded by missionaries sent by pope Eleutherus on the invitation of the British prince Lucius. See e.g. Ussher *Britann. Eccles. Antiq.* cc. 1, 3 (*Works* v. p. 22 sq, p. 49 sq), Fuller *Church History* i. § 9 (I. p. 13 sq, ed. Brewer, 1845), Collier *Eccles. Hist. of Great Britain* I. p. 7 sq (ed. Barham, 1840). 'Father Parsons,' writes Fuller, 'will not admit hereof, because willingly he would not allow any sprinkling of Christianity but what was raised from Rome'; but he himself adds sensibly, 'He that is more than lukewarm is too hot in a case of so little consequence.' In urging the chronological objection to the identification of Pudens and Claudia Parsons was right; but the mission under Lucius seems to be equally untenable

married the British maiden Claudia Rufina[1]. Before following these speculations farther, it should be observed that the interposition of Linus between Pudens and Claudia removes any presumption in favour of their being regarded as man and wife[2]. The only ground, on which such a relationship could still be maintained, is the statement of the *Apostolic Constitutions*, which would make Linus their son; and even then the order would be strange. Their son however he cannot have been; for, as the immediate successor of the apostles in the government of the Roman Church, he must have been thirty years old at least at the time of the Neronian persecution (A.D. 64), and probably was much older. Yet the epigram of Martial, celebrating the marriage of Pudens and Claudia, was not written at this time, and probably dates many years later[3]. But not only is the oldest tradition respecting Claudia ignored by this hypothesis. It equally disregards the oldest tradition respecting Pudens, which attributes to him wholly different family relations, a wife Sabinella, two sons Timotheus and Novatus, and two daughters Pudentiana and Praxedis[4]. I do not say that these traditions are trustworthy; but they have at least a negative value as showing that antiquity had no knowledge whatever of this marriage of Pudens and Claudia. Several English writers however have gone beyond this. Not content with identifying the Pudens and Claudia of S. Paul with the Pudens and Claudia of Martial, they have discovered a history for the couple whom they have thus married together. It had been the

with the mission under Pudens and Claudia; see Hallam *Archaeologia* XXXIII. p. 308 sq.

[1] *Epigr.* iv. 13 'Claudia, Rufe, meo nubit peregrina Pudenti.' In order to maintain this theory it is necessary to identify this Claudia with the person mentioned in *Epigr.* xi. 53, 'Claudia caeruleis cum sit Rufina Britannis Edita quam Latiae pectora gentis habet!' Friedlaender however (Martial *Epigr.* I. p. 342, II. p. 375) regards them as different persons, printing 'Peregrina' as a proper name. The identification of the two Claudias of Martial seems to me probable in itself.

[2] Conybeare and Howson (II. p. 592) consider this 'not a conclusive objection, for the names of Linus and Pudens may easily have been transposed in rapid dictation.' Alford accounts for the interposed Linus by saying, 'They apparently were not married at this time,' III. p. 105. But what reason is there for supposing that they were married afterwards?

[3] For the chronology of Martial's epigrams see Friedlaender *Sittengesch.* III. p. 376 sq, and also his edition of this poet, I. p. 50 sq (1886). The date of publication of the several books in order is there traced. There is no ground for the contention of some English writers that epigrams in the later books were written long before, though not published at the time. The instances alleged do not prove the point.

[4] See Ussher l.c. p. 51 sq, Tillemont *Mémoires* II. p. 615 sq. It should be added that in the *Liber Pontificalis* the father of Linus is called 'Herculanus.'

fashion with the older generation of English critics to regard this Claudia as the daughter of the British king Caractacus; and some more adventurous spirits considered Linus to be none other than Llin, a person appearing in British hagiography as the son of Caractacus. The discovery however, in the year 1722, of an inscription at Chichester gave another direction to these speculations. This inscription records (*C. I. L.* VII. 11, p. 18) how a certain temple was erected to Neptune and Minerva [EX .] AVCTORITATE . [TI.] CLAVD[I . CO]GIDVBNI . R . LEGA[TI]. AVG . IN . BRIT., by a guild of smiths, DONANTE . AREAM . [PVD]ENTE . PVDENTINI . FIL. The British king Cogidubnus, who is here designated a 'legate of Augustus', is doubtless the same whom Tacitus mentions[1] as a faithful ally of the Romans during the campaigns of Aulus Plautius and Ostorius Scapula (A.D. 43—51); and he appears to have taken the name of his suzerain, the emperor Claudius. Assuming that this Cogidubnus had a daughter, she would probably be called Claudia; and assuming also that the name of the donor is correctly supplied [PVD]ENTE[2], we have here a Pudens who might very well have married this Claudia. This doubtful Pudens and imaginary Claudia are not only identified with the Pudens and Claudia of Martial, for which identification there is something to be said, but also with the Pudens and Claudia of S. Paul, which seems altogether impossible[3].

[1] Tacit. *Agric.* 14 'Consularium primus A. Plautius praepositus, ac subinde Ostorius Scapula, uterque bello egregius; redactaque paullatim in formam provinciae proxima pars Britanniae...quaedam civitates Cogidumno regi donatae (is ad nostram usque memoriam fidissimus mansit), vetere ac jam pridem recepta populi Romani consuetudine ut haberet instrumenta servitutis et reges.' This person is described accordingly in our inscription; 'r(egis), lega(ti) Aug(usti) in Brit(annia).'

[2] This restoration seems likely enough, though Huebner says 'majore fortasse cum probabilitate credideris Pudentinum fuisse filium Pudentis secundum consuetudinem nomenclaturae in hominibus peregrinis observandam,' and himself suggests [CLEM]ENTE (*C. I. L.* VII. p. 19).

[3] This theory, which had found favour with previous writers, is strenuously maintained in a pamphlet by Archdeacon J. Williams *Claudia and Pudens* etc. (Llandovery, 1848), where it is seen in its best and final form. It has been taken up with avidity by more recent English writers on S. Paul; e.g. by Alford (Excursus on 2 Tim. iv. 21), by Conybeare and Howson (*Life and Epistles of S. Paul* II. p. 594 sq, ed. 2), by Lewin (*Life and Epistles of S. Paul* II. p. 392 sq), and by Plumptre (Bp Ellicott *New Testament Commentary* II. p. 185 sq, Excursus on Acts). Lewin sums up, 'Upon the whole we should say that Claudia may have been the daughter of Cogidunus, or may have been the daughter of Caractacus, and that in all probability she was either the one or the other' (p. 397). At all hazards the Claudia of S. Paul must be made out to be a British princess. Yet the arguments which go to show that she was a daughter of Caractacus, must to the same extent go to show that she was not a daughter of Cogidubnus, and conversely.

The chronology alone is a fatal objection. Martial only came to Rome about the year 65; the epigram which records the marriage of Pudens and Claudia did not appear till A.D. 88; and the epigram addressed to her as a young mother, if indeed this be the same Claudia, was published as late as A.D. 96[1]. To these chronological difficulties it should be added that Martial unblushingly imputes to his friend Pudens the foulest vices of heathendom, and addresses to him some of his grossest epigrams, obviously without fear of incurring his displeasure. Under these circumstances it is not easy to see how this identification can be upheld, especially when we remember that there is not only no ground for supposing the Pudens and Claudia of S. Paul to have been man and wife, but the contrary, and that both names are very frequent, Claudia especially being the commonest of all female names at this period. Here is an inscription where a married pair, connected with the imperial household, bear these same two names (*C. I. L.* VI. 15066);

TI.CL.TI.LIB.PVDENS
ET . CL . QVINTILLA
FILIO . DVLCISSIMO.

In this inscription we have the basis of a more plausible identification; and probably a careful search would reveal others bearing the same combination of names. But we are barred at the outset by the improbability that the Pudens and Claudia of S. Paul were man and wife.

Of the episcopate of this Linus absolutely nothing is recorded on trustworthy authority. Even the *Liber Pontificalis* can only tell us—beyond the usual notice of ordinations—that he issued an order to women to appear in church with their heads veiled[2]; and he alone of the early Roman bishops is wholly unrepresented in the forged letters of the *False Decretals*. On the other hand he acquires a certain prominence, as the reputed author of the spurious Acts of S. Peter and S. Paul, though we learn from them nothing about Linus himself[3].

Of Linus' successor in the direction of the Roman Church we know absolutely nothing except the name, or rather the names, which he bore.

This theory has been controverted by Hallam (*Archaeologia* XXXIII. p. 323 sq, 1849), by myself (*Journ. of Class. and Sacr. Philol.* IV. p. 73 sq, 1857), and by Huebner (*Rheinisches Museum* XIV. p. 358, 1859; comp. *C. I. L.* VII. p. 19).

[1] See the references in p. 77, note 3. I had formerly (l. c. p. 73) spoken lightly of the chronological difficulty, but it now appears to me insuperable.

[2] *Lib. Pont.* I. pp. 53, 121, ed. Duchesne.

[3] *Magn. Bibl. Vat. Patr.* I. p. 69 sq. (De la Bigne).

He is called ANENCLETUS or CLETUS in the several authorities. Anencletus is found in Irenaeus; Cletus, though among extant writings it appears first in Epiphanius, would seem to have been as old as Hegesippus[1]. His original designation probably was Anencletus, 'the blameless,' which, though it occurs but rarely, represents a type of names familiar among slaves and freedmen[2]. As a slave's name it appears on a Roman inscription, found in London and now preserved in the Guildhall (*C. I. L.* VII. 28). It occurs likewise, not indeed as a slave's name, but perhaps a freedman's, in a more interesting inscription of the year A.D. 101 found in Central Italy, among the Ligures Baebiani, in connexion with a 'Flavian estate' (*C. I. L.* IX. 1455); L. VIBBIO. ANENCLETO. FVND. FLAVIANI. And a few other examples of the name appear elsewhere, but it is not common[3]. If this were his original name, Cletus would be no inappropriate substitution. Over and above the general tendency to abbreviation, a designation which reminded him of his Christian 'calling' would commend itself; whereas his own name might jar with Christian sentiment, which bids the true disciple, after doing all, to call himself an 'unprofitable servant'. Had not S. Paul, writing to this very Roman Church, called himself κλητὸς as an apostle of Christ, and his readers κλητοὶ as a people of Christ? On the other hand the word κλητὸς is not such as we should expect to find adopted as a proper name, except in its Christian bearing[4]. But, whatever may have been the origin of the second name, there can be no reasonable doubt that the two are alternative designations of the same person. The documents which make two persons out of the two

[1] See above, p. 64.

[2] Such as Amemptus, Amomus, Amerimnus, Abascantus, Anicetus, etc.

[3] *C. I. L.* III. 6220, V. 8110, 40 (p. 960). This last is a tile, across which likewise is written Q. IVN. PASTOR. It has given rise to an amusing mistake. The words have been read continuously QVIN. PASTOR. ANACLETVS (Muratori CDXCVIII. 6); and, as Anencletus is the fifth in the succession as given in the *Liber Pontificalis*, they have been referred to him. This name occurs twice in a Spartan inscription of the imperial times, Boeckh *Corp. Inscr. Graec.* 1240.

The Latin *Anacletus* is a mere corruption of Ἀνέγκλητος. The Greek ἀνάκλητος 'called back' is never, so far as I can discover, used as a proper name, nor would it be appropriate. In Dion Cass. xlv. 12 it is given as a translation of the military term 'evocatus.'

[4] Κλῆτος is given in *Corp. Inscr. Graec.* 6847, but the inscription is mutilated and of the date nothing is said. One of the two Laconian Graces was called Κλήτα, if indeed the reading be correct (Pausan. iii. 18. 6, ix. 35. 1). In Mionnet *Suppl.* VI. p. 324 (a Smyrnæan coin) ΕΠΙ. ΚΛΗΤΟΥ there is perhaps a mistake, as the next coin has ΕΠΙΚΤΗΤΟΥ. In the Latin inscriptions we meet with Claetus, Cleta (II. 2268, 2903). Clitus also occurs. The possible confusion with the more common names Κλεῖτος, Κλύτος, when transliterated into Latin, was great.

names are comparatively late, and they carry on their face the explanation of the error—the fusion of two separate lists.

The tradition, as I have already mentioned, assigns a duration of twenty-four years to the episcopates of Linus and Anencletus, twelve to each. Probably these should be regarded as round numbers. It was a period of steady and peaceful progress for the Church. In a later writer indeed we stumble upon a notice of a persecution under Vespasian; but, if this be not altogether an error, the trouble can only have been momentary, as we do not find any record of it elsewhere[1]. On the whole the two earlier Flavian emperors—father and son—the conquerors of Judæa, would not be hostilely disposed to the Christians, who had dissociated themselves from their Jewish fellow-countrymen in their fatal conflict with the Romans[2]. When Clement succeeded to the government of the Church, the reign of Domitian would be more than half over. The term of years assigned to him in all forms of the tradition is nine; and here probably we may accept the number as at least approximately correct, if not strictly accurate. If so, his episcopate would extend into the reign of Trajan. The most trustworthy form of the tradition places his death in the third year of this emperor, which was the last year of the century[3].

Domitian proved another Nero[4]. The second persecution of the Church is by general consent of Christian writers ascribed to him. It was however very different in character from the Neronian. The Neronian persecution had been a wholesale onslaught of reckless fury. Domitian directed against the Christians a succession of sharp, sudden, partial assaults[5], striking down one here and one there from malice or jealousy or caprice, and harassing the Church with an agony of suspense. In the execution of his cousin, the consul, Flavius Clemens, the persecution culminated; but he was only one, though the most conspicuous, of a large number who suffered for their faith[6].

[1] See *Ignat. and Polyc.* I. p. 15 sq.

[2] Euseb. *H. E.* iii. 5.

[3] Euseb. *H. E.* iii. 34.

[4] See Juv. *Sat.* iv. 38, with Mayor's note, for heathen writers; comp. Euseb. *H. E.* iii. 17. When Tertullian calls him 'Subnero' (*de Pall.* 4) and 'portio Neronis de crudelitate' (*Apol.* 5), he is influenced by the story which gave Domitian the credit of having stopped the persecution; see above, p. 41, note 3.

[5] See the note on § 1 *Διὰ τὰς αἰφνιδίους καὶ ἐπαλλήλους κ.τ.λ.*

[6] See especially Dion Cass. lxvii. 14 *ἄλλοι...πολλοὶ κατεδικάσθησαν κ.τ.λ.*, given in full below, p. 104. Whether Acilius Glabrio, whom Dion mentions by name immediately afterwards, was put to death for his Christianity or for some other cause, is a matter of dispute. Dion speaks of him as *κατηγορηθέντα τά τε ἄλλα καὶ οἷα οἱ πολλοὶ καὶ ὅτι θηρίοις ἐμάχετο.* In the former part of the sentence (*τά τε ἄλλα κ.τ.λ.*) it might be possible to see

In the midst of these troubles disastrous news arrived from Corinth. The old spirit of faction in the Corinthian Christians, as it appears in S. Paul's epistle, had reasserted itself. They had risen up against the duly commissioned rulers of their Church—presbyters who had been appointed by the Apostles themselves or by those immediately so appointed—and had ejected them from their office. It does not appear that any doctrinal question was directly involved, unless indeed their old scepticism with respect to the Resurrection had revived[1]. The quarrel, so far as we can judge, was personal or political. However this may have been, the ejection was wholly unjustifiable, for the persons deposed had executed their office blamelessly. Corinth was an important Roman colony. The communication between Rome and Corinth was easy and frequent. If the journey were rapidly accomplished, it need not take more than a week; though the average length was doubtless greater[2]. The alliances within the Christian Church were

a charge of Christianity, for previously he has mentioned 'Jewish practices' and 'atheism' in connexion with Flavius Clemens and others; but there is no ground for confining οἷα οἱ πολλοὶ to these cases, and it is more naturally interpreted 'the same sort of charges as the majority of his victims.' The account of Domitian's victims has extended over several chapters, and the pretexts for their destruction are various. The last point (ὅτι καὶ θηρίοις ἐμάχετο) has nothing to do with Christianity, though some have connected it with the cry 'Christianos ad leones.' Dion explains himself in the next sentence. Domitian had compelled Glabrio, when consul (he was colleague of the future emperor Trajan, A.D. 91), to kill a huge lion at the Juvenalia (νεανισκεύματα), and he had despatched the beast with consummate skill and without receiving any wound himself. The emperor's real motive therefore was partly jealousy at his success, and partly (we may suppose) dread of his future ascendancy; his ostensible reason was the degradation of the consul's office by fighting in the arena, though he himself had compelled him to do this. This is the way of tyrants. Suetonius (*Domit.* 10) says of this Acilius Glabrio, that he and another were put to death in exile by Domitian 'quasi molitores novarum rerum.' He is the 'juvenis indignus quem mors tam saeva maneret' of Juv. *Sat.* iv. 95. The Christianity of Acilius Glabrio is favoured by De Rossi, *Rom. Sotterr.* I. 319, and more strenuously maintained by Hasenclever, p. 267 sq. Zahn takes the opposite view (*Hermas* p. 57). The case seems to me to break down altogether.

[1] Some prominence is given to the subject, and analogies in nature are brought forward, § 24 sq.

[2] Helius, having important news to convey to Nero who was then in Corinth, left Rome and arrived in Greece ἑβδόμῃ ἡμέρᾳ, Dion Cass. lxiii. 19. This however was extraordinary speed. Commonly it occupied a longer time. With very favourable winds it took five days from Corinth to Puteoli (Philostr. *Vit. Ap.* vii. 10); and setting sail at evening from Puteoli a vessel would arrive at Ostia on the third day (*ib.* vii. 15, 16). The land route from Puteoli to Rome was 138 miles and would occupy about the same time as the journey by water (*ib.* vii. 41). The route by way of Brundusium would take a longer time than if the traveller

determined to a great degree by political and ethnical affinities. Thus the Churches of Asia Minor were closely connected with the Churches of Gaul, notwithstanding the wide intervening space, because Gaul had been studded at an early date with Greek settlements from Asia Minor[1]. In the same way the strong Roman element at Corinth attached the Corinthian Church closely to the Roman. It was therefore natural that at this critical juncture the Roman Christians should take a lively interest in the troubles which harassed the Corinthian brotherhood. For a time however they were deterred from writing by their anxieties at home. At length a respite or a cessation of the persecution enabled them to take the matter up. Clement writes a long letter to them, not however in his own name, but on behalf of the Church which he represents, rebuking the offenders and counselling the restoration of the ejected officers.

Clement's letter is only one of several communications which passed between these two Churches in the earliest ages of Christianity, and of which a record is preserved. Of four links in this epistolary chain we have direct knowledge. (1) The Epistle of S. Paul to the Romans was written from Corinth. It contains the earliest intimation of the Apostle's intention to visit Rome. It comprises a far larger number of salutations to and from individual Christians, than any other of his epistles. (2) An interval of less than forty years separates the Epistle of Clement from the Epistle of S. Paul. It is addressed from the Romans to the Corinthians. For some generations it continued to be read from time to time in the Corinthian Church on Sundays[2]. (3) We pass over another interval of seventy or eighty years; and we find Soter, the Roman bishop, addressing a letter to the Corinthians. What was the immediate occasion which called it forth we do not know. From the language of the reply it would appear, like the earlier letter of Clement, to have been written not in the name of the bishop, but of the Church of Rome[3]. (4) This letter of Soter called forth a reply from Dionysius, bishop of Corinth, written (as we may infer from the language) not long after the letter was received. In this reply he associates the Corinthian Church with himself, using the first person

sailed from one of the ports on the Western coast under favourable conditions of weather. See for some facts bearing on this question, *Philippians* p. 38, note.

[1] See *Contemporary Review*, August 1876, p. 406, *Ignat. and Polyc.* I. p. 430 sq.

[2] Dionys. Cor. in Euseb. *H. E.* iv. 23; see below, p. 155.

[3] Dionys. Cor. in Euseb. *H. E.* ii. 25, iv. 23, *ὑμεῖς...συνεκεράσατε, ὑμῖν ἔθος ἐστί, ὁ μακάριος ὑμῶν ἐπίσκοπος Σωτήρ, ἀνέγνωμεν ὑμῶν τὴν ἐπιστολήν*. See above p. 72.

plural 'we,' 'us'; but whether the address was in his own name or in theirs or (as is most probable) in both conjointly, we cannot say. He reminds the Romans of their common inheritance with the Corinthians in the instruction of S. Peter and S. Paul, saying that, as both Apostles had visited Corinth and preached there, so both had taught at Rome and had sealed their teaching there by martyrdom[1]. He extols the 'hereditary' liberality of the Roman Christians, and commends the fatherly care of the bishop Soter for strangers who visit the metropolis. He informs them that on that very day—being Sunday—their recent epistle had been publicly read in the congregation, just as it was the custom of his Church to read their earlier letter written by Clement; and he promises them that it shall be so read again and again for the edification of the Corinthian brotherhood[2].

We have no explicit information as to the result of Clement's affectionate remonstrances with the Corinthians. But an indirect notice would lead to the hope that it had not been ineffectual. More than half a century later Hegesippus visited Corinth on his way to Rome. Thus he made himself acquainted with the condition of the Church at both places. He mentioned the feuds at Corinth in the age of Domitian and the letter written by Clement in consequence. To this he added, 'And the Church of Corinth remained steadfast in the true doctrine (ἐπέμενεν...ἐν τῷ ὀρθῷ λόγῳ) till the episcopate of Primus in Corinth[3]'. The inference is that the Corinthian Church was restored to its integrity by Clement's remonstrance, and continued true to its higher self up to the time of his own visit. This inference is further confirmed by the fact already mentioned, that Clement's letter was read regularly on Sundays in the Church of Corinth.

This letter to the Corinthians is the only authentic incident in Clement's administration of the Roman Church[4]. The persecution ceased at the death of the tyrant. The victims of his displeasure were recalled from banishment. Domitilla would return from her exile in Pontia or Pandateria; and the Church would once more resume its career of progress.

Clement survived only a few years, and died (it would appear) a

[1] Dionys. Cor. in Euseb. *H. E.* ii. 25, quoted below, p. 155. See also above, p. 72.

[2] Dionys. Cor. in Euseb. *H. E.* iv. 23.

[3] Hegesipp. in Euseb. *H. E.* iv. 22; see below, p. 154.

[4] For the acts ascribed to him in the *Liber Pontificalis*, see below, pp. 186, 191. He is there represented as dividing the city into seven regions, and as collecting the acts of the martyrs.

natural death. We do not hear anything of his martyrdom till about three centuries after his death. Probably in the first instance the story arose from a confusion with his namesake, Flavius Clemens. In its complete form it runs as follows ;

The preaching of Clement was attended with brilliant successes among Jews and Gentiles alike. Among other converts, whom he 'charmed with the siren of his tongue,' was one Theodora, the wife of Sisinnius, an intimate friend of the emperor Nerva. On one occasion her husband, moved by jealousy, stealthily followed her into the church where Clement was celebrating the holy mysteries. He was suddenly struck blind and dumb for his impertinent curiosity. His servants attempted to lead him out of the building, but all the doors were miraculously closed against them. Only in answer to his wife's prayers was an exit found ; and on her petition also Clement afterwards restored to him both sight and speech. For this act of healing he was so far from showing gratitude, that he ordered his servants to seize and bind Clement, as a magician. In a phrensied state, they began binding and hauling about stocks and stones, leaving 'the patriarch' himself unscathed. Meanwhile Theodora prayed earnestly for her husband, and in the midst of her prayers S. Peter appeared to her, promising his conversion. Accordingly Sisinnius is converted. His devotion to the patriarch from this time forward is not less marked than his hatred had been heretofore. With Sisinnius were baptised not less than 423 persons of high rank, courtiers of Nerva, with their wives and children.

Upon this 'the Count of the Offices,' Publius Tarquitianus, alarmed at the progress of the new faith, stirs up the people against Clement. Owing to the popular excitement Mamertinus, the Prefect, refers the matter to Trajan, who is now emperor, and Clement is banished for life 'beyond the Pontus' to a desolate region of Cherson, where more than two thousand Christians are working in the marble quarries. Many devout believers follow him voluntarily into exile. There, in this parched region, a fountain of sweet water is opened by Clement, and pours forth in copious streams to slake the thirst of the toilers. A great impulse is given to the Gospel by this miracle. Not less than seventy-five churches are built ; the idol-temples are razed to the ground ; the groves are burnt with fire. Trajan, hearing of these facts, sends Aufidianus, the governor, to put a stop to Clement's doings. The saint is thrown into the deep sea with an iron anchor about his neck, so that 'not so much as a relique of him may be left for the Christians.'

These precautions are all in vain. His disciples Cornelius and

Phœbus pray earnestly that it may be revealed to them where the body lies. Their prayer is answered. Year by year, as the anniversary of the martyrdom comes round, the sea recedes more than two miles, so that the resting place of the saint is visited by crowds of people dry-shod. He lies beneath a stone shrine, not reared by mortal hands. At one of these annual commemorations a child was left behind by his God-fearing parents through inadvertence, and overwhelmed with the returning tide. They went home disconsolate. The next anniversary, as the sea retired, they hastened to the spot, not without the hope that they might find some traces of the corpse of their child. They found him—not a corpse, but skipping about, full of life. In answer to their enquiries, he told them that the saint who lay within the shrine had been his nurse and guardian. How could they do otherwise than echo the cry of the Psalmist, 'God is wonderful in His saints'[1]?

These Acts are evidently fictitious from beginning to end. The mention of the 'Comes Officiorum' alone would show that they cannot have been written before the second half of the fourth century at the earliest[2]. It is therefore a matter of no moment, whether or not the portion relating to the Chersonese was originally written for a supposed namesake Clement of Cherson, and afterwards applied to our hero Clement of Rome[3]. The story must have been translated into Latin before many generations were past; for it is well known to Gregory of Tours (c. A.D. 590) and it has a place in early Gallican service books[4]. By the close of the fourth century indeed S. Clement is regarded as a

[1] These Acts of Clement are sometimes found separately, and sometimes attached to an Epitome of Clement's doings taken from the spurious *Epistle to James* and the *Homilies* or *Recognitions*. They may be conveniently read in Cotelier's *Patr. Apost.* I. p. 808 sq (ed. Clericus, A.D. 1724), reprinted by Migne *Patrol. Graec.* II. p. 617 sq; or in Dressel's *Clementinorum Epitomae Duae* pp. 100 sq, p. 222 sq (1859); or again in Funk's *Patr. Apost.* II. p. 28 sq, comp. p. vii sq (1881).

[2] § 164 ὁ πονηρότατος...τῶν ὀφφικίων κόμης (p. 108, ed. Dressel). The 'comes officiorum' is the same with the 'magister officiorum'; Gothofred *Cod. Theodos.* VI. ii. p. 16. For his functions see Gibbon *Decline and Fall* c. xvii, II. p. 326 (ed. W. Smith), Hodgkin *Italy and her Invaders* I. p. 215. He does not appear till the age of Constantine. For other anachronisms in these Acts see Tillemont *Mémoires* II. p. 564 sq.

[3] See Tillemont *Mémoires* II. p. 566, Duchesne *Lib. Pontif.* I. p. xci. I cannot find that this theory of a confusion of two Clements is based on any foundation of fact, nor is it required to explain the locality. The passages of De Rossi *Bull. di Archeol. Crist.* 1864, 5 sq, 1868, p. 18, to which Duchesne refers, do not bear it out.

[4] See the passage of Gregory given below, p. 186; and for the Gallican service books, Duchesne *Lib. Pontif.* I. pp. xci, 124.

martyr, being so designated both by Rufinus (c. A.D. 400) and by Zosimus (A.D. 417)[1]; and a little earlier, during the episcopate of Siricius (A.D. 384–394), an inscription in his own basilica, of which only fragments remain, seems to have recorded a dedication [SANCTO .] MARTYR[I . CLEMENTI], though the name has disappeared[2]. But the attribution of martyrdom would probably be due, as I have already said[3], to a confusion with Flavius Clemens the consul. The fact of the martyrdom being first accepted, the details would be filled in afterwards; and a considerable interval may well have elapsed before the story about the Chersonese was written. We seem to see an explanation of the exile of Clement to this distant region in a very obvious blunder. An ancient writer, Bruttius, mentioned the banishment of Domitilla, the wife of Flavius Clemens, who together with her husband was condemned for her religion, to 'Pontia'[4]. A later extant Greek chronographer, Malalas, unacquainted with the islands of the Tyrrhene sea, represents this Bruttius as stating that many Christians were banished under Domitian to Pontus or to 'the Pontus' (*ἐπὶ τὸν Πόντον*)[5]; and accordingly we find Clement's place of exile and death elsewhere called 'Pontus'[6]. In these very Acts he is related to have been banished 'beyond the Pontus,' i.e. the Euxine (*πέραν τοῦ Πόντου*). The ambiguity of *νῆσος Ποντία*, 'the island Pontia,' and 'an island of Pontus,' would easily lend itself to confusion. It does not therefore follow that, where later writers speak of Pontus or some equivalent as the scene of his banishment and martyrdom, they were already in possession of the full-blown story in the Acts of Clement. Thus it is impossible to say how much or how little was known to the author of the *Liber Pontificalis*, who records that Clement was martyred in the 3rd year of Trajan and 'buried in Greece' (sepultus est in Grecias)[7]. The panegyric, which bears the name of Ephraim bishop of Cherson[8],

[1] For the passages of Rufinus and Zosimus, see below, pp. 174, 176.

[2] See De Rossi *Bull. di Archeol. Crist.* 1870, p. 147 sq, where the reasons are given for filling in the name CLEMENTI. Duchesne *Lib. Pontif.* I. p. 124 calls this restoration 'à peu près certaine.'

[3] See above, pp. 53, 56.

[4] See Euseb. *H. E.* iii. 18 *εἰς νῆσον Ποντίαν*, and so too *Chron.* II. p. 160, the authority being Bruttius. For the passages see below, p. 105 sq.

[5] Joann. Malalas, quoted below, p. 109.

[6] The resting place of Clement is given 'In pontu (sic), in mari,' corrupted sometimes into 'In portu, in mari.' See Duchesne *Lib. Pontif.* I. pp. xlvii, clvii.

[7] The passages in both recensions of the *Liber Pontificalis* are given below, pp. 186, 192.

[8] This is printed by Cotelier *Patr. Apost.* I. p. 815 sq (comp. Migne *Patrol. Graec.* II. p. 634). It has the heading *τοῦ ἐν ἁγίοις ἡμῶν Ἐφραὶμ ἀρχιεπισκόπου Χερσῶνος περὶ τοῦ θαύματος κ.τ.λ.*, and begins Θαυμαστὸς (v. l. Εὐλογητὸς) ὁ Θεὸς

is certainly based on the Acts of Clement, as we possess them; but except in connexion with the praises of Clement we never hear of this person[1]. If the author of this panegyric really bore the name Ephraim, he cannot have belonged to Cherson; for he speaks of the annual recession of the tide on the anniversary of Clement's death as a miracle repeated on the spot in his own time[2]. Obviously he is a romancer, living at a distance, whether measured by time or by space. The Chersonese was doubtless a favourite place of banishment in the age when the Acts were composed. A later pope, Martin I, died in exile there (A.D. 655).

This story has a curious sequel[3]. Between seven and eight centuries had elapsed since Clement's death. Cyril and Methodius, the evangelists of the Slavonian people and the inventors of the Slavonian alphabet[4], appear on the scene. The more famous of the two brothers, Constantine surnamed the Philosopher, but better known by his other name Cyril, which he assumed shortly before his death, was sent to evangelize the Chazars. He halted in the Crimea, in order to learn the language of the people among whom he was to preach. Being acquainted with the account of Clement's martyrdom, he made diligent enquiry about the incidents and the locality, but could learn nothing.

κ.τ.λ. Another panegyric of Clement bearing the name of this same Ephraim, and commencing Ἐξελθόντος Φιλίππου τοῦ ἀποστόλου τῆς Γαλιλαίας, is mentioned by Allatius, but has never been published. Cotelier could not find it. See Fabric. *Bibl. Graec.* VII. p. 21 sq, VIII. p. 254 (ed. Harles).

1 Lequien, *Oriens Christianus* I. p. 1330, says of this person, 'quo tempore Ephraem ille vixerit, *si tamdem aliquando vixerit*, incertum est.' The words which I have italicized express a misgiving which I had felt independently. See also Tillemont II. p. 565.

2 § 5 ἔκτοτε γὰρ...μέχρι τῆς σήμερον ἡμέρας ἑκάστῳ χρόνῳ τὸ θαυμαστὸν τοῦτο τελεῖται θεουργικῶς μεγαλούργημα.

3 The account of the translation of the reliques is given in a document printed in the Bollandist *Act. Sanct.* Martii II. p. *19 sq. It is a Life of S. Cyril, though largely occupied with these reliques, and is one of the most important authorities for his history. It was taken from a MS belonging to F. Duchesne. Another account printed likewise in the *Act. Sanct.* ib. p. *22 from a MS belonging to the monastery of Blaubeuern (?) near Ulm, is obviously later and has no value.

4 For the authorities for the history of Cyril and Methodius see Potthast *Bibl. Histor. Med. Ævi* p. 664, with Suppl. p. 138, Ginzel *Geschichte der Slavenaposteln* (Vienna, 1861), and Leger *Cyrille et Méthode* (Paris, 1868). This last mentioned work contains a useful account of the sources of information ancient and modern, as well as of the history of the two brothers. It is sufficient to refer those readers who desire to pursue the point further to its references. The matter with which we are concerned, the translation of S. Clement's reliques, is treated only cursorily by this writer.

Successive invasions of barbarians had swept over the country, and wiped out the memory of the event. After praying, however, he was directed in a dream to go to a certain island lying off the coast. He obeyed, and his obedience was rewarded. Arrived there, he and his companions began digging in a mound in which they suspected that the treasure lay, and soon they saw something sparkling like a star in the sand. It was one of the saint's ribs. Then the skull was exhumed; then the other bones, not however all lying together. Lastly, the anchor was found. At the same time they were gladdened by a fragrance of surpassing sweetness. From this time forward the precious reliques were Cyril's constant companions of travel in his missionary journeys. After his labours were ended in these parts, he and his brother were sent to convert the Moravians and Bohemians. Here magnificent spiritual victories were achieved. As time went on they were summoned to Rome by the reigning pontiff Nicholas I (A.D. 858—867) to give an account of their stewardship. Nicholas himself died before their arrival, but his successor Adrian II (A.D. 867—872) gave them an honorable welcome. Hearing that they brought with them the remains of his ancient predecessor, he went forth with the clergy and people in solemn procession, met them outside the walls, and escorted them into the city. The bones of Clement were deposited in his own basilica, his long-lost home, after an absence of nearly eight centuries.

Cyril died in Rome, and his body was placed in a sarcophagus in the Vatican. Methodius set forth to resume his missionary labours in Moravia. But before departing, he requested that he might carry his brother Cyril's bones back with him—this having been their mother's special request, if either brother should die in a foreign land. The pope consented; but an earnest remonstrance from the Roman clergy, who could not patiently suffer the loss of so great a treasure, barred the way. Methodius yielded to this pressure, asking however that his brother's bones might be laid in the church of the blessed Clement, whose reliques he had recovered. A tomb was accordingly prepared for Cyril in the basilica of S. Clement, by the right of the high altar, and there he was laid[1].

The story of the martyrdom and its miraculous consequences is a wild fiction; but this pendant, relating to the translation of the reliques, seems to be in the main points true history. The narrative, which

[1] A tomb has been discovered in the subterranean basilica (see below, p. 92 sq.), which may have been that of S. Cyril. The claim of this basilica to the possession of the tomb of Methodius rests on no historical foundation.

contains the account, has every appearance of being a contemporary document. Indeed there is ground for surmising that it was compiled by Gaudericus bishop of Velitræ, whose cathedral is dedicated to S. Clement and who was himself an eye-witness of the deposition of the bones in Rome[1]. There is also an allusion to the event in a letter written a few years later by Anastasius the Librarian (A.D. 875)[2]. An account of the discovery and transportation of the reliques, coinciding with, if not taken from, this narrative, was given by Leo bishop of Ostia, who has been represented as a contemporary, but seems to have lived at least a century later[3]. Again the internal character of the narrative is altogether favourable to its authenticity. The confession that the people of the place knew nothing of the martyrdom or of the portentous miracle recurring annually is a token of sincerity[4]. Moreover there is no attempt to bridge over the discrepancy as regards the locality. The legend of the martyrdom spoke of a submerged tomb; the account of the discovery relates that the bones were found scattered about in a mound on an island[5]. Moreover it is frankly stated that the spot was chosen for digging for no better reason than that it was a *likely* place. It was, we may suppose, a sepulchral mound on the sea-shore, where bones had been accidentally turned up before. Thus, while

[1] See *Act. Sanct.* l. c. p. * 15, where the reasons for assigning this narrative to Gaudericus are given. His date is fixed by the fact that his name appears attached to acts of the 8th General Council, A.D. 869. See also Leger, pp. xxxii, 106.

[2] *Anastas. Biblioth.* Op. III. p. 741 (Migne *Patrol. Lat.* CXXIX).

[3] Baron. *Annal.* ann. 867 § cxxxii, *Act. Sanct.* l. c. p. 41. For his date see Ughelli *Ital. Sacr.* I. p. 55 note, ed. Coleti 1717.

[4] *Act. Sanct.* l.c. p. *20 'Ad quem praefati omnes, utpote non indigenae sed diversis ex gentibus advenae, se quod requireret omnino nescire professi sunt. Siquidem ex longo jam tempore ob culpam et negligentiam incolarum miraculum illud marini recessus, quod in historia passionis praefati pontificis celebre satis habetur, fieri destiterat, et mare fluctus suos in pristinas stationes refuderat. Praeterea et ob multitudinem incursantium barbarorum locus ille desertus est, et templum neglectum atque destructum, et magna pars regionis illius fere desolata et inhabitabilis reddita; ac propterea ipsa sancti martyris arca cum corpore ipsius fluctibus obruta fuerat'.

[5] *ib.* 'Navigantes igitur...pervenerunt ad insulam in qua videlicet *aestimabant* sancti corpus martyris esse. Eam igitur undique circumdantes...coeperunt...in acervo illo, quo tantum thesaurum quiescere *suspicari* dabatur, curiose satis et instantissime fodere'.

'Tandem ex improviso velut clarissimum quoddam sidus, donante Deo, una de costis martyris pretiosi resplenduit ...magisque ac amplius...terram certatim eruderantibus sanctum quoque caput ipsius consequenter apparuit...ecce post paullulum rursus quasi ex quibusdam abditis sanctarum reliquiarum particulis paullatim et per modica intervalla omnes repertae sunt. Ad ultimum quoque ipsa etiam anchora' etc.

there are the best possible grounds for holding that Clement's body never lay in the Crimea, there is no adequate reason for doubting that the Apostle of Slavonia brought some bones from the Crimea, and deposited them in Rome, believing them to be Clement's[1].

The foregoing account has brought us in contact with a historical monument of the highest interest, connected with S. Clement—the basilica bearing his name at Rome. Jerome, writing A.D. 392, after referring to the death of Clement, adds, 'A church erected at Rome preserves to this day the memory of his name,' or perhaps we should translate it, 'protects to this day the memorial chapel built in his name[2],' since 'memoria' is frequently used to denote the small oratory or chapel built over the tomb or otherwise commemorative of martyrs and other saints[3]. To the existence of this basilica in Jerome's time more than one extant inscription bears witness[4]; and indeed his expression 'usque hodie' shows that it was no recent erection when he wrote. A quarter of a century after this date it is mentioned by

[1] This incident seems to have left only a confused tradition in the country itself. When in the year 1058 Henry I of France sent Roger bishop of Châlons as ambassador to Jaroslav, one of the dukes of Kiov, the predecessors of the Czars of Russia, to claim the duke's daughter as his bride, enquiry was expressly made by the bishop (who by the way must have been ignorant of Cyril's doings) whether Clement's body still lay in Cherson, and whether the sea still parted asunder annually on his 'birthday.' The reply was that pope Julius [A.D. 337—352] had visited those regions to put down heresy; that, as he was departing, he was admonished by an angel to return and remove the body of Clement; that he hesitated because the parting of the sea only took place on the day of the martyrdom; that the angel assured him the miracle would be wrought specially for his benefit; that accordingly he went to the place dryshod, brought the body to the shore, and built a church there; and that he carried a portion of the reliques (de corpore ejus reliquias) to Rome. It is added that on the very day when the Roman people received the reliques, the ground on which the tomb stood rose above the surface of the sea and became an island, and that the people of the place erected a basilica there. The duke moreover told the bishop that he himself had once visited this place and had carried away the heads of S. Clement and S. Phœbus his disciple and had deposited them in the city of Kiov, where he showed them to the bishop.

This story is given in a marginal note of a S. Omer MS, quoted *Act. Boll.* l.c. p. *14 sq. The visit of Pope Julius to these parts is mythical.

[2] Hieron. *Vir. Illustr.* 15 'nominis ejus memoriam usque hodie Romae exstructa ecclesia custodit'.

[3] See the numerous examples in Ducange *Gloss. Med. et Infim. Latin.* s. v. 'memoria'; comp. also De Rossi *Rom. Sotterr.* III. p. 455. This sense is given to 'memoria' in the passage of Jerome by De Rossi *Bull. di Archeol. Crist.* 1870, p. 149 sq.

[4] De Rossi *Bull. di Archeol. Crist.* 1863, p. 25, 1870, p. 147 sq; see Duchesne l. c. p. 21.

Pope Zosimus, who held a court here (A.D. 417) to consider the case of Cælestius the Pelagian[1]. Some generations later we find Gregory the Great delivering more than one of his homilies in this building[2]. And in the succeeding centuries it occupies a position of prominence among the ecclesiastical buildings of Rome.

There can be no doubt that the existing basilica of San Clemente, situated in the dip between the Esquiline and Cælian hills, marks the locality to which S. Jerome refers. Until quite recently indeed it was supposed to be essentially the same church, subject to such changes of repair and rebuilding as the vicissitudes of time and circumstance had required. It preserves the features of the ancient basilica more completely than any other church in Rome; and the archaic character naturally favoured the idea of its great antiquity. The discoveries of recent years have corrected this error[3].

The excavations have revealed three distinct levels, one below the other. The floor of the existing basilica is nearly even with the surrounding soil, the church itself being above ground. Beneath this is an earlier basilica, of which the columns are still standing and help to support the upper building. It is altogether below the surface, but was at one time above ground, as the existing basilica now is. Thus it was not a crypt or subterranean storey to the present church, nor was it used simultaneously; but was an integral building in itself, disused at some distant epoch and filled up so as to support the present church when erected. Under this earlier basilica is a third and still lower storey. This is occupied partly by solid masonry of tufa, belonging to

[1] See the passage quoted below, p. 176.

[2] Greg. Magn. *Hom. in Evang.* ii. 33, 38.

[3] These excavations were carried on by the zeal and energy of J. Mullooly, the Irish prior of the monastery of San Clemente, who published an account of the discoveries in a work entitled *Saint Clement Pope and Martyr and his Basilica in Rome* (Rome, 1869). The book is provokingly uncritical. The subject however has been discussed in a series of notices and articles by the great master of Christian archæology in Rome, De Rossi, who has brought his great knowledge and penetration to bear on the subject; *Bull. di Archeol. Crist.* 1863, pp. 8 sq, 25 sq; 1864, pp. 1 sq, 39 sq; 1865, pp. 23, 32; 1867, p. 35; 1870, pp. 125, 130 sq. The last article more especially gives a complete survey of these discoveries. See also a description with plates by Th. Roller, *Saint Clément de Rome, Description de la Basilique Souterraine récemment découverte* (Paris, 1873), and for the decorations Parker's *Archæology of Rome*, XI. p. 58 sq. English readers will find a useful and succinct account with plans in the later editions of Murray's *Handbook for Rome*. When I was last in Rome (1885), the lowest storey was flooded and inaccessible. For the early notices of this basilica see Duchesne *Notes sur la Topographie de Rome au Moyen-Age* p. 21 (Rome, 1887), extracted from *Mélanges d'Archéologie et d'Histoire* VII.

the regal or republican period, and partly by certain chambers of the imperial age, of which I shall have to speak presently.

The history of the two upper storeys—the disused and the existing basilicas—can be satisfactorily explained. The lower of these, the now subterranean church, belongs to the Constantinian age. It is the same church of which Jerome speaks, though renovated from time to time. On its walls are frescoes representing (among other subjects) the martyrdom and miracles of S. Clement, as related in his Acts. These however are much later than the building itself. They are stated in the accompanying inscriptions to have been given by BENO DE RAPIZA and his wife. But surnames were not used till the tenth century, and even then only sparingly; and this particular surname first makes its appearance in Rome in the eleventh century. Moreover there is in this lower church a sepulchral inscription bearing the date A.D. 1059[1]. The lower basilica therefore must have been still used at this comparatively late date. On the other hand the upper church contains an inscription, misread and misinterpreted until recently, which ascribes the erection of the new basilica to Anastasius the Cardinal presbyter of the church, whom we know to have been alive as late as A.D. 1125[2]. Between these two dates therefore the change must have taken place. What had happened meanwhile to cause the substitution of the new building for the old?

In A.D. 1084 Rome was stormed and set on fire by Robert Guiscard. 'Neither Goth nor Vandal, neither Greek nor German, brought such desolation on the city as this capture by the Normans'[3]. From the Lateran to the Capitol the city was one mass of smoking ruins. This was the beginning of that general migration which transferred the bulk of the people from the older and now desolate parts of Rome to the Campus Martius. The level of the ground in the dips of the hills was heaped up with the debris; and thus the old basilica was half buried beneath the soil.

Hence, phœnix like, this new basilica rose out of the bosom of the old. But not only was the general character of the old building retained in the new—the narthex, the semicircular apse, the arrangement of the choir and presbytery[4]. A large portion of the furniture also was

[1] *Bull. di Archeol. Crist.* 1870, p. 138; comp. Mullooly, p. 220.

[2] *Bull. di Archeol. Crist.* 1870, pp. 138, 141 sq.

[3] Milman's *Latin Christianity* III. p. 100.

[4] The lines of the upper church are not traced exactly on the lines of the lower, the dimensions of the lower being somewhat greater. This may be seen from the plans given in the works mentioned above, p. 92, note 3.

transferred thither—the candelabrum, the ambones, the pierced stone fences or transennae. Carved slabs have had their sculptures or their mouldings hewn away to shape them for their new surroundings. Inscriptions from the previous edifice are found in strange incongruous places. One such describes the dedication of an altar during the papacy of Hormisdas (A.D. 514—523) by MERCVRIVS PRESBYTER, who himself afterwards succeeded Hormisdas as Pope John II[1].

The history of the third and lowest storey, beneath the old Constantinian basilica, is not so easy to decipher. Of the very ancient masonry belonging to regal or republican periods I say nothing, for without further excavations all conjecture is futile. A flight of steps near the high altar led down to some chambers of the imperial times. One of these is immediately below the altar, and this De Rossi supposes to have been the original 'memoria' of Clement. Extending to the west of it and therefore beyond the apse of the superposed basilica is a long vaulted chamber, which has evidently been used for the celebration of the rites of Mithras. It is De Rossi's hypothesis that this chapel originally belonged to the house of Clement and was therefore Christian property; that it was confiscated and devoted to these Mithraic rites in the second or third century, when they became fashionable; that so it remained till the close of the last persecution; and that at length it was restored to the Christians with the general restoration of Church property under Constantine, at which time also the first basilica was built over the 'memoria' of the saint.

On these points it is well to suspend judgment. The relation of the Mithraic chapel to the house of Clement more especially needs confirmation. It remains still only a guess; but it is entitled to the consideration due even to the guesses of one who has shown a singular power of divination in questions of archæology. For the rest I would venture on a suggestion. The basilica would most probably be built over some place which in early times was consecrated to Christian worship, whether an oratory or a tomb bearing the name of Clement. But was it not the house, or part of the house, not of Clement the bishop, but of Flavius Clemens and Domitilla? Whether the two Clements, the consul and the bishop, stood to each other in the relation of patron and client, as I have supposed, or not, it is not unnatural that the Christian congregation in this quarter of the city should have met under Clement the bishop in the house of Clement the consul, either during the lifetime or after the death of the latter,

[1] *Bull. di Archeol. Crist.* 1870, p. 143 sq.

seeing that his wife or widow Domitilla bore a distinguished part in the early Roman Church. If so, we have an account of the confusion which transferred the martyrdom of Clement the consul to Clement the bishop. We have likewise an explanation of the tradition that Flavius Clemens lies buried in this same basilica, which is called after his namesake and is said to cover his namesake's bones. A dedication of a portion of a private house to purposes of Christian worship was at least not uncommon in early Christian times. In the Flavian family it might claim a precedent even in heathen devotion. The emperor Domitian, the head of the clan, converted the house in which he was born into a temple of the Flavian race; and after his tragical death his own ashes were laid there by a faithful nurse[1].

A truer and nobler monument of the man, even than these architectural remains, is his extant letter to the Corinthians. This document will be considered from other aspects at a later stage. We are only concerned with it here, in so far as it throws light on his character and position in the history of the Church. From this point of view, we may single out three characteristics, its comprehensiveness, its sense of order, and its moderation.

(i) The *comprehensiveness* is tested by the range of the Apostolic writings, with which the author is conversant and of which he makes use. Mention has already been made (p. 9) of his co-ordinating the two Apostles S. Peter and S. Paul (§ 5) in distinction to the Ebionism of a later age, which placed them in direct antagonism, and to the factiousness of certain persons even in the apostolic times, which perverted their names into party watchwords notwithstanding their own protests. This mention is the fit prelude to the use made of their writings in the body of the letter. The influence of S. Peter's First Epistle may be traced in more than one passage; while expressions scattered up and down Clement's letter recall the language of several of S. Paul's epistles belonging to different epochs and representing different types in his literary career[2]. Nor is the comprehensiveness of Clement's letter restricted to a recognition of these two leading Apostles. It is so largely interspersed with thoughts and expressions from the Epistle to the Hebrews, that many ancient writers attributed this Canonical epistle to Clement. Again, the writer shows himself

[1] Sueton. *Domit.* 1 'Domitianus natus est...domo quam postea in templum gentis Flaviae convertit' (comp. *ib.* 5, 15); *ib.* 17 'Phyllis nutrix...reliquias templo Flaviae gentis clam intulit.'

[2] For the justification of the statements in this paragraph see the passages in Lardner *Works* II. p. 40 sq, or the index of Biblical passages at the end of this volume.

conversant with the type of doctrine and modes of expression characteristic of the Epistle of S. James. Just as he coordinates the authority of S. Peter and S. Paul, as leaders of the Church, so in like manner he combines the teaching of S. Paul and S. James on the great doctrines of salvation[1]. The same examples of Abraham and of Rahab, which suggested to the one Apostle the necessity of faith, as the principle, suggested to the other the presence of works, as the indispensable condition, of acceptance. The teaching of the two Apostles, which is thus verbally, though not essentially, antagonistic, is 'coincidently affirmed'[2] by Clement. It was 'by reason of faith *and* hospitality' (διὰ πίστιν καὶ φιλοξενίαν) that both the one and the other found favour with God. 'Wherefore,' he asks elsewhere (§ 31), 'was our father Abraham blessed? was it not because he wrought righteousness (δικαιοσύνην) and truth by faith (διὰ πίστεως)?' With the same comprehensiveness of view (§§ 32, 33) he directly states in one paragraph the doctrine of S. Paul, 'Being called by His will (διὰ θελήματος αὐτοῦ) in Christ Jesus, we are not justified by ourselves (οὐ δι' ἑαυτῶν δικαιούμεθα) nor by...works which we wrought in holiness of heart but by our faith (διὰ τῆς πίστεως)'; while in the next he affirms the main contention of S. James, 'We have seen that all the righteous (πάντες οἱ δίκαιοι) have been adorned with good works,' following up this statement with the injunction 'Let us work the work of righteousness (justification) with all our strength' (ἐξ ὅλης ἰσχύος ἡμῶν ἐργασώμεθα ἔργον δικαιοσύνης). We have thus a full recognition of four out of the five types of Apostolic teaching, which confront us in the Canonical writings. If the fifth, of which S. John is the exponent, is not clearly affirmed in Clement's letter, the reason is that the Gospel and Epistles of this Apostle had not yet been written, or if written had not been circulated beyond his own immediate band of personal disciples.

(ii) The *sense of order* is not less prominent as a characteristic of this epistle. Its motive and purpose was the maintenance of harmony. A great breach of discipline had been committed in the Corinthian Church, and the letter was written to restore this disorganized and factious community to peace. It was not unnatural that under these circumstances the writer should refer to the Mosaic dispensation as enforcing this principle of order by its careful regulations respecting persons, places, and seasons. It creates no surprise when we see him

[1] See especially Westcott *History of the Canon* p. 25.

[2] Westcott, l. c. He also calls attention to the distinctions between the *final cause* and the *instrument*, as expressed by διὰ with the accusative and genitive respectively in these passages of Clement.

going beyond this and seeking illustrations likewise in the civil government and military organization of his age and country. But we should hardly expect to find him insisting with such emphasis on this principle as dominating the course of nature. Nowhere is 'the reign of law' more strenuously asserted. The succession of day and night, the sequence of the seasons, the growth of plants, the ebb and flow of the tides, all tell the same tale. The kingdom of nature preaches harmony, as well as the kingdom of grace. 'Hitherto shalt thou come, and no further' is only a physical type of a moral obligation. We may smile, as we read the unquestioning simplicity which accepts the story of the phœnix and uses it as an illustration; but we are apt to forget that among his most cultivated heathen contemporaries many accepted it as true and others left it an open question[1]. With this aspect of the matter however we are not at present concerned. The point to be observed here is that it is adduced as an illustration of natural law. It was not a miracle in our sense of the term, as an interruption of the course of nature. It was a regularly recurrent phenomenon. The time, the place, the manner, all were prescribed.

(iii) The third characteristic of the writer is *moderation*, the sobriety of temper and reasonableness of conduct, which is expressed by the word ἐπιείκεια. This was the practical outcome of the other two. One who takes a comprehensive view of all the elements in the problem before him, and is moreover pervaded by a sense of the principle of harmony and order, cannot well be extravagant or impulsive or fanatical. He may be zealous, but his zeal will burn with a steady glow. This is not a quality which we should predicate of Ignatius or even of Polycarp, but it is eminently characteristic of Clement[2]. The words ἐπιεικής, ἐπιείκεια, occur many times in his epistle[3]. In two several passages the substantive is qualified by a striking epithet, which seems to be its contradiction, ἐκτενὴς ἐπιείκεια, 'intense moderation'[4]. The verbal paradox describes his own character. This gentleness and equability, this 'sweet reasonableness,' was a passion with him.

The importance of the position which he occupied in the Church in his own age will have been sufficiently evident from this investigation. The theory of some modern writers that the Roman Christians had hitherto formed two separate organizations, a Petrine and a Pauline, and that they were united for the first time under his direction, cannot be maintained[5]; but it probably represents in an exaggerated form the

[1] See the notes on the passage, § 25.

[2] See *Ignat. and Polyc.* I. p. 1 sq.

[3] See the notes on §§ 1, 56, 58.

[4] §§ 58, 62 μετὰ ἐκτενοῦς ἐπιεικείας.

[5] See above, p. 67 sq.

actual condition of this church. Not separate organizations, but divergent tendencies and parties within the same organization—this would be the truer description. Under such circumstances Clement was the man to deal with the emergency. At home and abroad, by letter and in action, in his doctrinal teaching and in his official relations, his work was to combine, to harmonize, and to reconcile.

The posthumous fame of Clement presents many interesting features for study. Notwithstanding his position as a ruler and his prominence as a writer, his personality was shrouded in the West by a veil of unmerited neglect. His genuine epistle was never translated into the Latin language; and hence it became a dead letter to the church over which he presided, when that church ceased to speak Greek and adopted the vernacular tongue. His personal history was forgotten—so entirely forgotten, that his own church was content to supply its place with a fictitious story imported from the far East. Even his order in the episcopate was obscured and confused, though that episcopate was the most renowned and powerful in the world. Meanwhile however his basilica kept his fame alive in Rome itself, giving its name to one of the seven ecclesiastical divisions of the city and furnishing his title to one of the chief members of the College of Cardinals. His personal name too was adopted by not a few of his successors in the papacy, but nearly a whole millennium passed before another Clement mounted the papal throne—the first pope (it is said) who was consecrated outside of Rome; and he only occupied it for a few brief months[1]. This second Clement was the 147th pope, and reigned on the eve of the Norman invasion. Yet in this interval there had been many Johns, many Stephens, many Benedicts and Gregories and Leos. Elsewhere than in Rome his name appears not unfrequently in the dedications of churches; and in Bohemia more especially the connexion of his supposed reliques with Cyril the evangelist of those regions invested him with exceptional popularity at an early date[2].

Meanwhile a place was given to him in the commemorations of the Roman Sacramentaries, where after the Apostles are mentioned 'Linus, Cletus, Clemens, Xystus, Cornelius, Cyprianus,' etc.[3], the correct traditional order of the early Roman bishops being thus preserved notwithstanding the confusions of the Liberian Catalogue. At what date this commemoration was introduced we cannot say; but it is found

[1] Clement II was pope from 25 Dec. A.D. 1046 to 9 Oct. A.D. 1047.

[2] See Leger *Cyrille et Méthode* p. 132; comp. p. 101.

[3] See Muratori *Lit. Rom.* I. p. 696, II. pp. 3, 693, 777.

in the earliest of these Sacramentaries. His day is recorded in Western Calendars also with exceptional unanimity on ix Kal. Dec. (Nov. 23). It does not indeed appear in the Liberian list, for the Clement commemorated there on v Id. Nov. (Nov. 9) must be a different person, unless it be altogether an error. But the martyrdom of Clement was probably not yet known; and martyrs alone have a place in this list. This however is the one exception among the earlier Western martyrologies. In the early Carthaginian Calendar[1] and in the Old Roman and Hieronymian Martyrologies, Nov. 23 is duly assigned to him. In the last-mentioned document we have a double entry

xi Kal. Dec. [Nov. 21] Romae, natalis S. Clementis Confessoris,
ix Kal. Dec. [Nov. 23] Romae...natalis S. Clementis Episcopi et Martyris,

but such duplications abound in this document. The later Western calendars and martyrologies follow the earlier. In the early Syriac Martyrology his name is not found at all. In the Greek books his festival undergoes a slight displacement, as frequently happens, and appears as Nov. 24 or Nov. 25, the former being the day assigned to him in the Menæa. In the Coptic Calendar it is Hathor 29, corresponding to Nov. 25[2], and in the Armenian the day seems to be Nov. 26. All these are evidently derived mediately or immediately from the Roman day. At what date and for what reason this day, Nov. 23, was adopted, we have no means of ascertaining.

But while the neglect of the West robbed him of the honour which was his due, the East by way of compensation invested him with a renown—a questionable renown—to which he had no claim. His genuine letter was written in Greek and addressed to a Greek city, though a Roman colony. Its chief circulation therefore was among Greek-speaking peoples, not in Greece only, or in Asia Minor, but in Syria and the farther East. It dated from the confines of the apostolic age. It was issued from the metropolis of the world. It was the most elaborate composition of its kind which appeared in these primitive times. Hence we may account for the attribution to Clement of not a few fictitious or anonymous writings which stood in need of a sponsor.

[1] The date given in this Calendar is... Kal. Dec., the number having disappeared; but, as the next entry is S. Chrysogonus, whose day was Nov. 24 (viii Kal. Dec.), there can be no doubt that the missing number is ix.

[2] See Malan's *Calendar of the Coptic Church* p. 13; comp. Wüstenfeld's *Synaxarium d. Coptischen Christen* p. 144 sq (translated from the Arabic), where the story of the martyrdom and miracles is given from the Acts.

(i) The earliest of these literary ventures was singularly bold. A writer living about the middle of the second century wanted a hero for a religious romance, and no more imposing name than Clement's could suggest itself for his purpose. So arose the Clementine fiction, having for its plot the hero's journeys in search of his parents, which brought him in contact with S. Peter. The story was only the peg on which the doctrinal and practical lessons were hung. The writer had certain Ebionite views which he wished to enforce; and he rightly judged that they would attract more attention if presented in the seductive form of a novel[1]. The work is not extant in its original form; but we possess two separate early recensions—the *Homilies* and the *Recognitions*—both Ebionite, though representing different types of Ebionism. As he and his immediate readers were far removed from the scene of Clement's actual life, he could invent persons and incidents with all the greater freedom. Hence this Clementine story is the last place where we should look for any trustworthy information as regards either the life or the doctrine of Clement.

(ii) Not improbably this early forgery suggested a similar use of Clement's name to later writers. The device which served one extreme might be employed with equal success to promote the other. The true Clement was equally removed from both. The author of the Clementine romance had laid stress on the importance of early marriage in all cases. It occurred to another writer, who was bent on exalting virginity at the expense of marriage, to recommend his views by an appeal to the same great authority. The *Epistles to Virgins*, written in Clement's name, are extant only in Syriac, and contain no certain indications which enable us to assign a date to them with confidence. Perhaps we shall not be far wrong if we ascribe them to the first half of the third century. They must certainly be younger than the Clementine romance, of which I have spoken already; and they are probably older than the Apostolic Constitutions, of which I am now about to speak.

(iii) In the *Apostolical Constitutions* the Apostles are represented as communicating to Clement their ordinances and directions for the future administration of the Church. The Apostles describe him as their 'fellow minister,' their 'most faithful and like-minded child in the Lord' (vi. 18. 5). Rules are given relating to manners and discipline, to the various Church officers, their qualifications and duties, to the conduct to be observed towards the heathen and towards heretics, to the times of fasting and of festival, to the eucharist, and other matters affecting the worship of the Church. Clement is the mouthpiece of

[1] The story is given above, p. 14 sq; see also pp. 55 sq, 64, 68.

the Apostles to succeeding generations of Christians. As a rule, he is mentioned in the third person (vi. 8. 3, vi. 18. 5, vii. 46. 1, viii. 10. 2); while the Apostles themselves, notably S. Peter, speak in the first. But in one place (vii. 46. 7) he comes forward in his own person, 'I Clement.' The *Apostolical Canons* may be regarded as a corollary to the Constitutions. At least they proceed on the same lines, though they were compiled many generations later. Here towards the close of the list of Canonical Scriptures, the professed author thus describes the work to which these Canons are appended; 'The ordinances addressed to you the bishops in eight books by the hand of me Clement (δι' ἐμοῦ Κλήμεντος), which ye ought not to publish before all men by reason of the mysteries contained therein (διὰ τὰ ἐν αὐτοῖς μυστικά).'

(iv) Three distinct groups of spurious writings attributed to Clement have been described. But these do not nearly exhaust the literary productions with which he has been credited. There is the so-called *Second Epistle to the Corinthians*, not certainly an epistle nor written by Clement, but a homily dating perhaps half a century after his time. Unlike the works already enumerated, this is not a fictitious writing. It does not pretend to be anything but what it is, and its early attribution to Clement seems to be due to an accidental error. It will be considered more fully in its proper place.

(v) This enumeration would be incomplete, if we failed to mention the *Canonical writings* attributed to Clement. The anonymous *Epistle to the Hebrews*, its parentage being unknown, was not unnaturally fathered upon Clement. This attribution was earlier than the time of Origen, who mentions it[1], and may therefore have been maintained by Clement of Alexandria or even by Pantænus. It is due to the fact that the Roman Clement shows familiarity with this Canonical epistle and borrows from it. But it does not deserve serious consideration. The differences between the two writings are far greater than the resemblances. More especially do we miss in the Roman Clement, except where he is quoting from it, the Alexandrian type of thought and expression which is eminently characteristic of this Canonical epistle. The part of Clement however is otherwise stated by Eusebius. He mentions the fact that certain persons regard him as the *translator* of this epistle, the author being S. Paul himself[2]. This view again

[1] Quoted in Euseb. *H. E.* vi. 25; see below, p. 161 sq. Origen describes this opinion as ἡ εἰς ἡμᾶς φθάσασα ἱστορία ὑπό τινων λεγόντων κ.τ.λ. See the statement of Stephanus Gobarus (quoted below, p. 188), who seems to ascribe this opinion to Clement of Alexandria, though the passage is confused.

[2] *H. E.* iii. 37, quoted below, p. 166. Eusebius himself speaks favorably of this

need not detain us. There is every reason to believe that the Epistle to the Hebrews was written originally in Greek and not written by S. Paul. But whether Clement be regarded as author or as translator, we must take this attribution, however early, not as a historical tradition, but as a critical inference. When a later writer, Photius, says that Clement was supposed by some to have been the author of the *Acts of the Apostles*, the form of his statement leads me to suspect that he is guilty of some confusion with the Epistle to the Hebrews[1].

(vi) All the writings hitherto mentioned as falsely ascribed to Clement were written in the Greek language and apparently in the East. But besides these there were other Western fabrications of which I shall have to speak again at a later point. It is sufficient to say here that the 'Letter to James' which is prefixed to the Clementine Homilies was translated into Latin by Rufinus; that somewhat later a second letter was forged as a companion to it; that they were subsequently amplified and three others added to them; and that these five Latin letters thus ascribed to Clement formed the basis of the collection of spurious papal documents known as the *False Decretals*, the most portentous of medieval forgeries—portentous alike in their character and their results. Thus the Clementine romance of the second century was the direct progenitor of the forged Papal Letters of the ninth—a monstrous parent of a monstrous brood[2].

If then we seek to describe in few words the place which tradition, as interpreted by the various forgeries written in his name, assigns to

opinion. Jerome (*de Vir. Ill.* 15) appropriates the judgment of Eusebius ('mihi videtur') without acknowledgment.

[1] *Amphiloch.* 122; see below, p. 128. The three persons, whom he mentions as the authors of the Acts according to different authorities, Clement, Barnabas, and Luke, are the same to whom the Epistle to the Hebrews was actually assigned by various ancient writers.

[2] Besides these well-known Clementine writings, he is credited with others by isolated writers. Thus Theodorus the Studite (see below, p. 195) ascribes to him a narrative of the Apostles watching at the tomb of the Virgin, similar to that which is found in the Pseudo-Melito. Again Georgius Hamartolus (see below, p. 196) makes him the author of a story relating to Abraham. These ascriptions may have been mere blunders. It is certainly a blunder, when S. Thomas Aquinas in the thirteenth century speaks of some Antenicene writers as having attributed the Epistle to the Hebrews to Clement the Pope, because 'ipse scripsit *Atheniensibus* quasi per omnia secundum stilum istum' (*Prol. ad Hebr.*), though the statement is repeated by Nicolas of Lyra († 1340) *de Libr. Bibl. Can.* (see the passages in Credner's *Einl. in das N. T.* pp. 511, 512). This mistake shows how little was known of Clement's genuine Epistle even by the ablest and most learned medieval writers in the West.

Clement, we may say that he was regarded as *the interpreter of the Apostolic teaching and the codifier of the Apostolic ordinances.*

In dealing with Ignatius and Polycarp I sought for some one term, which might express the leading conception of either, entertained by his own and immediately succeeding ages. I was thus led to describe Ignatius as 'the Martyr' and Polycarp as 'the Elder.' It is not so easy to find a corresponding designation for Clement. The previous examination will have shown that the traditional Clement is in this respect an exaggeration of the historical Clement, but the picture is drawn on the same lines. The one digests and codifies the spurious apostolic doctrine and ordinances, as the other combines and co-ordinates their true teaching. Again, the practical side of his character and work, as we have seen, corresponds to the doctrinal. From this point of view he may be regarded as the moderator between diverse parties and tendencies in the Church. In both respects he is a *harmonizer.* Yet the term is hardly suitable for my purpose, as it unduly restricts the scope of his position. But he stands out as the earliest of a long line of worthies who, having no authority in themselves to originate, have been recognized as interpreters of the Apostolic precepts 'once delivered,' and whom it is customary to call the 'doctors' of the Church. By right of priority therefore Clement is essentially 'the Doctor.'

Notices of the Persecution under Domitian and of the Family of Flavius Clemens.

1.

Dion Cassius *Hist.* lxvii. 14.

Κἀν τῷ αὐτῷ ἔτει ἄλλους τε πολλοὺς καὶ τὸν Φλαούϊον Κλήμεντα ὑπατεύοντα, καίπερ ἀνεψιὸν ὄντα καὶ γυναῖκα καὶ αὐτὴν συγγενῆ ἑαυτοῦ Φλαουΐαν Δομιτίλλαν ἔχοντα, κατέσφαξεν ὁ Δομιτιανός. ἐπηνέχθη δὲ ἀμφοῖν ἔγκλημα ἀθεότητος, ὑφ' ἧς καὶ ἄλλοι ἐς τὰ τῶν Ἰουδαίων ἔθη ἐξοκέλλοντες πολλοὶ κατεδικάσθησαν, καὶ οἱ μὲν ἀπέθανον, οἱ δὲ τῶν γοῦν οὐσιῶν ἐστερήθησαν· ἡ δὲ Δομιτίλλα ὑπερωρίσθη μόνον ἐς Πανδατερίαν. τὸν δὲ δὴ Γλαβρίωνα τὸν μετὰ τοῦ Τραϊανοῦ ἄρξαντα, κατηγορηθέντα τά τε ἄλλα καὶ οἷα οἱ πολλοὶ καὶ ὅτι καὶ θηρίοις ἐμάχετο, ἀπέκτεινεν. ἐφ' ᾧ που καὶ τὰ μάλιστα ὀργὴν αὐτῷ ὑπὸ φθόνου ἔσχεν, ὅτι ὑπατεύοντα αὐτὸν ἐς τὸ Ἀλβανὸν ἐπὶ τὰ νεανισκεύματα ὠνομασμένα καλέσας λέοντα ἀποκτεῖναι μέγαν ἠνάγκασε, καὶ ὃς οὐ μόνον οὐδὲν ἐλυμάνθη ἀλλὰ καὶ εὐστοχώτατα αὐτὸν κατειργάσατο.

For the bearing of this passage see the investigations, pp. 33 sq, 81 sq, above.

2.

Melito *Apol. ad M. Antonin.* (Euseb. *H. E.* iv. 26).

Μόνοι πάντων ἀναπεισθέντες ὑπό τινων βασκάνων ἀνθρώπων τὸν καθ' ἡμᾶς ἐν διαβολῇ καταστῆσαι λόγον ἠθέλησαν Νέρων καὶ Δομετιανός· ἀφ' ὧν καὶ τὸ τῆς συκοφαντίας ἀλόγῳ συνηθείᾳ περὶ τοὺς τοιούτους ῥυῆναι συμβέβηκε ψεῦδος. ἀλλὰ τὴν ἐκείνων ἄγνοιαν οἱ σοὶ εὐσεβεῖς πατέρες ἐπηνωρθώσαντο, πολλάκις πολλοῖς ἐπιπλήξαντες ἐγγράφως, ὅσοι περὶ τούτων νεωτερίσαι ἐτόλμησαν.

3.

TERTULLIANUS *Apol.* 5.

Temptaverat et Domitianus, portio Neronis de crudelitate; sed qua et homo, facile coeptum repressit, restitutis etiam quos relegaverat.

Again elsewhere, *de Pall.* 4, he uses the expression 'Subneronem,' apparently referring to Domitian. See above, p. 81, note 4.

4.

LACTANTIUS *de Mort. Persec.* 3.

Post hunc [Neronem], interjectis aliquot annis, alter non minor tyrannus ortus est; qui cum exerceret injustam dominationem, subjectorum tamen cervicibus incubavit quam diutissime, tutusque regnavit, donec impias manus adversus Dominum tenderet. Postquam vero ad persequendum justum populum instinctu daemonum incitatus est, tunc traditus in manus inimicorum luit poenas.

5.

EUSEBIUS *Chronicon* II. p. 160, ed. Schöne.

Dometianus stirpem Davidis interfici praecepit, ne quis successor regni Judaeorum maneret. Refert autem Brettius, multos Christianorum sub Dometiano subiisse martyrium; Flavia vero Dometila et Flavus Clementis consulis sororis filius in insulam Pontiam fugit (fugerunt?) quia se Christianum (Christianos?) esse professus est (professi sunt?).

This notice is placed after Ann. Abr. 2110, Domit. 14.

The text is confused in the Armenian Version, of which this Latin is a translation. It must be corrected by the texts of Syncellus (see below, p. 110 sq) and of Jerome (see below, p. 108).

6.

EUSEBIUS *Hist. Eccl.* iii. 17, 18, 19, 20.

17. Πολλήν γε μὴν εἰς πολλοὺς ἐπιδειξάμενος ὁ Δομετιανὸς ὠμότητα, οὐκ ὀλίγον τε τῶν ἐπὶ Ῥώμης εὐπατριδῶν τε καὶ ἐπισήμων ἀνδρῶν πλῆθος οὐ μετ' εὐλόγου κρίσεως κτείνας, μυρίους τε ἄλλους ἐπιφανεῖς ἄνδρας ταῖς ὑπὲρ τὴν

ἐνορίαν ζημιώσας φυγαῖς καὶ ταῖς τῶν οὐσιῶν ἀποβολαῖς ἀναιτίως, τελευτῶν τῆς Νέρωνος θεοεχθρίας τε καὶ θεομαχίας διάδοχον ἑαυτὸν κατεστήσατο. δεύτερος δῆτα τὸν καθ' ἡμῶν ἀνεκίνει διωγμόν, καίπερ τοῦ πατρὸς αὐτοῦ Οὐεσπασιανοῦ μηδὲν καθ' ἡμῶν ἄτοπον ἐπινοήσαντος.

18. Ἐν τούτῳ κατέχει λόγος τὸν ἀπόστολον ἅμα καὶ εὐαγγελιστὴν Ἰωάννην ἔτι τῷ βίῳ ἐνδιατρίβοντα τῆς εἰς τὸν θεῖον λόγον ἕνεκεν μαρτυρίας Πάτμον οἰκεῖν καταδικασθῆναι τὴν νῆσον. γράφων γέ τοι ὁ Εἰρηναῖος περὶ τῆς ψήφου τῆς κατὰ τὸν ἀντίχριστον προσηγορίας φερομένης ἐν τῇ Ἰωάννου λεγομένῃ Ἀποκαλύψει, αὐταῖς συλλαβαῖς ἐν πέμπτῳ τῶν πρὸς τὰς αἱρέσεις ταῦτα περὶ τοῦ Ἰωάννου φησίν·

> εἰ δὲ ἔδει ἀναφανδὸν ἐν τῷ νῦν καιρῷ κηρύττεσθαι τοὔνομα αὐτοῦ, δι' ἐκείνου ἂν ἐρρέθη τοῦ καὶ τὴν ἀποκάλυψιν ἑωρακότος. οὐδὲ γὰρ πρὸ πολλοῦ χρόνου ἑωράθη, ἀλλὰ σχεδὸν ἐπὶ τῆς ἡμετέρας γενεᾶς πρὸς τῷ τέλει τῆς Δομετιανοῦ ἀρχῆς.

εἰς τοσοῦτον δὲ ἄρα κατὰ τοὺς δηλουμένους ἡ τῆς ἡμετέρας πίστεως διέλαμπε διδασκαλία, ὡς καὶ τοὺς ἄποθεν τοῦ καθ' ἡμᾶς λόγου συγγραφεῖς μὴ ἀποκνῆσαι ταῖς αὐτῶν ἱστορίαις τόν τε διωγμὸν καὶ τὰ ἐν αὐτῷ μαρτύρια παραδοῦναι. οἵγε καὶ τὸν καιρὸν ἐπ' ἀκριβὲς ἐπεσημήναντο, ἐν ἔτει πεντεκαιδεκάτῳ Δομετιανοῦ μετὰ πλείστων ἑτέρων καὶ Φλαυΐαν Δομετίλλαν ἱστορήσαντες, ἐξ ἀδελφῆς γεγονυῖαν Φλαυΐου Κλήμεντος, ἑνὸς τῶν τηνικάδε ἐπὶ Ῥώμης ὑπάτων, τῆς εἰς Χριστὸν μαρτυρίας ἕνεκεν εἰς νῆσον Ποντίαν κατὰ τιμωρίαν δεδόσθαι.

19. Τοῦ δ' αὐτοῦ Δομετιανοῦ τοὺς ἀπὸ γένους Δαυὶδ ἀναιρεῖσθαι προστάξαντος, παλαιὸς κατέχει λόγος τῶν αἱρετικῶν τινὰς κατηγορῆσαι τῶν ἀπογόνων Ἰούδα (τοῦτον δὲ εἶναι ἀδελφὸν κατὰ σάρκα τοῦ σωτῆρος), ὡς ἀπὸ γένους τυγχανόντων Δαυίδ, καὶ ὡς αὐτοῦ συγγένειαν τοῦ Χριστοῦ φερόντων. ταῦτα δὲ δηλοῖ κατὰ λέξιν ὧδέ πως λέγων ὁ Ἡγήσιππος·

20. ἔτι δὲ περιῆσαν οἱ ἀπὸ γένους τοῦ Κυρίου υἱωνοὶ Ἰούδα τοῦ κατὰ σάρκα λεγομένου αὐτοῦ ἀδελφοῦ, οὓς ἐδηλατόρευσαν ὡς ἐκ γένους ὄντας Δαυίδ. τούτους δ' ὁ ἰουόκατος ἤγαγε πρὸς Δομετιανὸν Καίσαρα· ἐφοβεῖτο γὰρ τὴν παρουσίαν τοῦ Χριστοῦ, ὡς καὶ Ἡρώδης· καὶ ἐπηρώτησεν αὐτοὺς εἰ ἐκ Δαυίδ εἰσι, καὶ ὡμολόγησαν· τότε ἐπηρώτησεν αὐτοὺς πόσας κτήσεις ἔχουσιν, ἢ πόσων χρημάτων κυριεύουσιν· οἱ δὲ εἶπον ἀμφότεροι ἐννακισχίλια δηνάρια ὑπάρχειν αὐτοῖς μόνα, ἑκάστῳ αὐτῶν ἀνήκοντος τοῦ ἡμίσεως. καὶ ταῦτα οὐκ ἐν ἀργυρίοις ἔφασκον ἔχειν, ἀλλ' ἐν διατιμήσει γῆς πλέθρων τριάκοντα ἐννέα μόνων, ἐξ ὧν καὶ τοὺς φόρους ἀναφέρειν, καὶ αὐτοὺς αὐτουργοῦντας διατρέφεσθαι. εἶτα δὲ καὶ τὰς χεῖρας τὰς ἑαυτῶν ἐπιδεικνύναι, μαρτύριον τῆς αὐτουργίας τὴν τοῦ σώματος σκληρίαν καὶ τοὺς ἀπὸ τῆς συνεχοῦς ἐργασίας ἐναποτυπωθέντας ἐπὶ τῶν ἰδίων χειρῶν τύλους παριστάντας. ἐρωτηθέντας δὲ περὶ τοῦ Χριστοῦ καὶ τῆς βασιλείας αὐτοῦ, ὁποία τις εἴη καὶ ποῖ καὶ πότε φανησομένη, λόγον δοῦναι ὡς οὐ κοσμικὴ μὲν οὐδ' ἐπίγειος, ἐπουράνιος δὲ καὶ ἀγγελικὴ τυγχάνει, ἐπὶ συντελείᾳ τοῦ αἰῶνος γενησομένη, ὁπηνίκα ἐλθὼν ἐν δόξῃ κρινεῖ ζῶντας καὶ νεκρούς, καὶ ἀποδώσει ἑκάστῳ κατὰ τὰ ἐπιτηδεύματα αὐτοῦ. ἐφ' οἷς μηδὲν αὐτῶν κατεγνωκότα τὸν Δομετιανόν, ἀλλὰ καὶ ὡς εὐτελῶν καταφρονήσαντα, ἐλευθέρους μὲν αὐτοὺς ἀνεῖναι, καταπαῦσαι δὲ διὰ προστάγματος τὸν κατὰ τῆς ἐκκλησίας διωγμόν. τοὺς δὲ ἀπολυθέντας ἡγήσασθαι τῶν ἐκκλησιῶν, ὡς ἂν δὴ μάρτυρας ὁμοῦ καὶ ἀπὸ γένους ὄντας τοῦ Κυρίου, γενομένης δὲ εἰρήνης μέχρι Τραϊανοῦ παραμεῖναι αὐτοὺς τῷ βίῳ.

ταῦτα μὲν ὁ Ἡγήσιππος. οὐ μὴν ἀλλὰ καὶ ὁ Τερτυλλιανὸς τοῦ Δομετιανοῦ τοιαύτην πεποίηται μνήμην·

πεπειράκει ποτὲ καὶ Δομετιανὸς ταὐτὸ ποιεῖν ἐκείνῳ, μέρος ὢν τῆς Νέρωνος ὠμότητος. ἀλλ' οἶμαι, ἅτε ἔχων τι συνέσεως, τάχιστα ἐπαύσατο, ἀνακαλεσάμενος καὶ οὓς ἐξ[ελ]ηλάκει.

μετὰ δὲ τὸν Δομετιανὸν πεντεκαίδεκα ἔτεσιν ἐπικρατήσαντα, Νερούα τὴν ἀρχὴν διαδεξαμένου, καθαιρεθῆναι μὲν τὰς Δομετιανοῦ τιμάς, ἐπανελθεῖν δὲ ἐπὶ τὰ οἰκεῖα μετὰ τοῦ καὶ τὰς οὐσίας ἀπολαβεῖν τοὺς ἀδίκως ἐξεληλαμένους, ἡ Ῥωμαίων σύγκλητος βουλὴ ψηφίζεται· ἱστοροῦσιν οἱ γραφῇ τὰ κατὰ τοὺς χρόνους παραδόντες. τότε δὴ οὖν καὶ τὸν ἀπόστολον Ἰωάννην ἀπὸ τῆς κατὰ τὴν νῆσον φυγῆς τὴν ἐπὶ τῆς Ἐφέσου διατριβὴν ἀπειληφέναι ὁ τῶν παρ' ἡμῖν ἀρχαίων παραδίδωσι λόγος.

The passage at the close of the 18th chapter is translated by Rufinus; 'quintodecimo anno Domitiani principis cum aliis plurimis ab eo etiam Flaviam Domitillam sororis filiam Flavii Clementis unius hinc ex consulibus viri ob testimonium, quod Christo perhibebat, in insulam Pontiam nomine deportatam.'

For the passage in Tertullian see above, p. 105.

7.

Hieronymus *Epist.* cviii. 7 (*Op.* I. p. 695).

Delata ad insulam Pontiam quam clarissimae quondam feminarum sub Domitiano principe pro confessione nominis Christiani Flaviae Domitillae nobilitavit exilium, vidensque cellulas, in quibus illa longum martyrium duxerat, sumtis fidei alis Ierosolymam et sancta loca videre cupiebat.

Jerome is here giving an account of the travels of Paula (A.D. 385). The date of the letter itself is A.D. 404.

There is a v. l. 'insulas Pontias'; see above, p. 50, note 1.

8.

Hieronymus *Chronicon* (II. p. 163, Schöne).
Ann. Abr. 2112, Domit. 16.

Domicianus eos qui de genere David erant interfici praecipit, ut nullus Iudaeorum regni reliquus foret. Scribit Bruttius plurimos Christianorum sub Domiciano fecisse martyrium, inter quos et Flaviam Domitillam Flavii Clementis consulis ex sorore neptem in insulam Pontianam relegatam, quia se Christianam esse testata sit.

9.

THEODORET *Graec. Affect. Cur.* ix (Op. IV. p. 931, ed. Schulze).

τὸν Πέτρον ἐκεῖνος [ὁ Νέρων] καὶ τὸν Παῦλον ἀνεῖλεν· ἀλλ' οὐ ξυνανεῖλε τοῖς νομοθέταις τοὺς νόμους· οὐκ Οὐεσπασιανός, οὐ Τίτος, οὐ Δομετιανός, καὶ ταῦτα πολλοῖς κατ' αὐτῶν καὶ παντοδαποῖς χρησάμενος μηχανήμασι. πολλοὺς γὰρ δὴ τούτους ἀσπαζομένους τῷ θανάτῳ παρέπεμψε, παντοδαπαῖς κολαστηρίων ἰδέαις χρησάμενος.

10.

MART. IGN. ANTIOCH. 1 (*Ignat. and Polyc.* II. p. 474).

ὃς [Ἰγνάτιος] τοὺς πάλαι χειμῶνας μόλις παραγαγὼν τῶν πολλῶν ἐπὶ Δομετιανοῦ διωγμῶν, καθάπερ κυβερνήτης ἀγαθός, τῷ οἴακι τῆς προσευχῆς καὶ τῆς νηστείας, τῇ συνεχείᾳ τῆς διδασκαλίας, τῷ τόνῳ τῷ πνευματικῷ, πρὸς τὴν ζάλην τῆς ἀντικειμένης ἀντεῖχεν δυνάμεως, δεδοικὼς μή τινα τῶν ὀλιγοψύχων ἢ ἀκεραιοτέρων ἀποβάλῃ.

11.

JOANNES MALALAS *Chronographia* x. p. 262 (ed. Bonn.).

Ἐπὶ δὲ τῆς αὐτοῦ βασιλείας διωγμὸς Χριστιανῶν ἐγένετο· ὅστις καὶ τὸν ἅγιον Ἰωάννην τὸν θεόλογον ἀνήνεγκεν ἐν τῇ Ῥώμῃ καὶ ἐξήτασεν αὐτόν. καὶ θαυμάσας τοῦ αὐτοῦ ἀποστόλου τὴν σοφίαν ἀπέλυσεν αὐτὸν λάθρᾳ ἀπελθεῖν εἰς Ἔφεσον, εἰπὼν αὐτῷ, Ἄπελθε καὶ ἡσύχασον, ὅθεν ἦλθες. καὶ ἐλοιδορήθη· καὶ ἐξώρισεν αὐτὸν εἰς Πάτμον. πολλοὺς δὲ ἄλλους Χριστιανοὺς ἐτιμωρήσατο, ὥστε φυγεῖν ἐξ αὐτῶν πλῆθος ἐπὶ τὸν Πόντον, καλῶς Βώττιος ὁ σοφὸς χρονογράφος συνεγράψατο κατ' αὐτῶν.

See above, pp. 48 sq, 87.

12.

CHRONICON PASCHALE I. p. 467 sq (ed. Bonn.).

Ἰνδ. ε΄. ιγ΄. ὑπ. Δομετιανοῦ Αὐγούστου τὸ ιγ΄ καὶ Φλαβίου Κλήμεντος.

Δεύτερος μετὰ Νέρωνα Δομετιανὸς Χριστιανοὺς ἐδίωξεν.

Ἐπ' αὐτοῦ δὲ καὶ ὁ ἀπόστολος Ἰωάννης εἰς Πάτμον ἐξορίζεται τὴν νῆσον, ἔνθα τὴν ἀποκάλυψιν ἑωρακέναι λέγεται, ὡς δηλοῖ Εἰρηναῖος.

Δομετιανὸς τοὺς ἀπὸ γένους Δαυὶδ ἀναιρεῖσθαι προσέταξεν, ἵνα μή τις διαμείνῃ διάδοχος τῆς τῶν Ἰουδαίων βασιλικῆς φυλῆς.

Ἰνδ. ϛ΄. ιδ΄. ὑπ. Ἀσπρενάτου καὶ Λατεράνου.

Ἱστορεῖ ὁ Βρούττιος πολλοὺς Χριστιανοὺς κατὰ τὸ ιδ΄ ἔτος Δομετιανοῦ μεμαρτυρηκέναι.

Ἰνδ. ζ΄. ιε΄. ὑπ. Δομετιανοῦ Αὐγούστου τὸ ιδ΄ καὶ Κλήμεντος τὸ β΄.

The three years intended are A.D. 93–95. The 14th year of Domitian began Id. Sept. A.D. 94. The names of the consuls for A.D. 93 are wrongly given. They were Collega and Priscus (or Priscinus); see Tac. *Agric.* 44. The consuls for A.D. 94 were Asprenas and Lateranus, as here named. In the following year, A.D. 95, Domitian and Flavius Clemens were consuls together for the first and only time. It was the 17th consulate of Domitian, and the 1st of Clemens.

13.

GEORGIUS SYNCELLUS *Chronogr.* p. 650 (ed. Bonn.).

Δομετιανὸς τοὺς ἀπὸ γένους Δαυὶδ ἀναιρεῖσθαι προσέταξεν, ἵνα μή τις Ἰουδαίων βασιλικοῦ γένους ἀπολειφθῇ.

Οὗτος μετὰ Νέρωνα δεύτερος Χριστιανοὺς ἐδίωξε, καὶ Ἰωάννην τὸν θεολόγον ἄπολιν ἐν Πάτμῳ τῇ νήσῳ περιώρισεν, ἔνθα τὴν ἀποκάλυψιν ἑώρακεν, ὡς ὁ ἅγιος Εἰρηναῖός φησι· πολλοὶ δὲ Χριστιανῶν ἐμαρτύρησαν κατὰ Δομετιανόν, ὡς ὁ Βρέττιος ἱστορεῖ· ἐν οἷς καὶ Φλαουΐα Δομετίλλα ἐξαδελφὴ Κλήμεντος Φλαουΐου ὑπατικοῦ ὡς Χριστιανὴ εἰς νῆσον Ποντίαν φυγαδεύεται, αὐτός τε Κλήμης ὑπὲρ Χριστοῦ ἀναιρεῖται. τούτου δὲ Στέφανός τις τῶν ἀπελευθέρων εἷς τῇ πρὸς τὸν δεσπότην εὐνοίᾳ Κλήμεντα ἐνεδρεύσας τὸν Δομετιανὸν ἀνεῖλε, τιμῆς τε παρὰ τῆς συγκλήτου ἠξιώθη ὡς αἴσχους Ῥωμαίους ἀπαλλάξας.

14.

GEORGIUS HAMARTOLUS *Chronicon* iii. 131 (*Patrol. Graec.* cx. p. 517, ed. Migne).

Ἐφ' οὗ [Δομετιανοῦ] Τιμόθεος ὁ ἀπόστολος καὶ Ὀνήσιμος ἐμαρτύρησαν, καὶ Ἰωάννης ὁ θεόλογος καὶ εὐαγγελιστὴς ἐν Πάτμῳ τῇ νήσῳ ἐξορίζεται.

15.

DE SS. NEREO, ACHILLEO, DOMITILLA, ETC. (*Act. Sanct. Bolland.* Maius III. p. 4 sq.).

§ 9. Tunc Nereus et Achilleus perrexerunt ad S. Clementem episcopum et dixerunt ei; Licet gloria tua tota in Domino nostro Iesu Christo sit posita et non de humana sed de divina dignitate glorieris, scimus tamen Clementem consulem patris tui fuisse germanum; hujus soror Plautilla nos in famulos comparavit, et tunc quando a domino Petro apostolo verbum vitae audiens credidit et baptizata est, et nos simul secum et cum filia Domitilla sancto baptismate consecravit. Eodem anno dominus Petrus apostolus ad coronam martyrii properavit ad Christum et Plautilla corpus terrenum deseruit. Domitilla vero filia ejus, cum Aurelianum illustrem haberet sponsum, a nostra parvitate didicit sermonem quem nos ex ore apostoli didicimus, quia virgo, quae propter amorem Domini in virginitate perseveraverit, Christum mereatur habere sponsum, etc.

16.

SUETONIUS *Domitianus* 15, 17.

15. Denique Flavium Clementem patruelem suum, contemptissimae inertiae, cujus filios, etiam tum parvulos, successores palam destinaverat,

et, abolito priore nomine, alterum Vespasianum appellari jusserat, alterum Domitianum, repente ex tenuissima suspicione tantum non in ipso ejus consulatu interemit. Quo maxime facto maturavit sibi exitum...

17. De insidiarum caedisque genere haec fere divulgata sunt. Cunctantibus conspiratis, quando et quomodo, id est, lavantem an coenantem, aggrederentur, Stephanus Domitillae procurator et tunc interceptarum rerum reus, consilium operamque obtulit.

17.

QUINTILIANUS *Inst. Orat.* iv. prooem.

Cum vero mihi Domitianus Augustus sororis suae nepotum delegaverit curam, non satis honorem judiciorum caelestium intelligam, nisi ex hoc oneris quoque magnitudinem metiar. Quis enim mihi aut mores excolendi sit modus, ut eos non immerito probaverit sanctissimus censor? aut studia, ne fefellisse in his videar principem ut in omnibus ita in eloquentia quoque eminentissimum?

18.

PHILOSTRATUS *Vit. Apollon.* viii. 25 (p. 170).

Ἐώθουν δὲ οἱ θεοὶ Δομετιανὸν ἤδη τῆς τῶν ἀνθρώπων προεδρίας. ἔτυχε μὲν γὰρ Κλήμεντα ἀπεκτονὼς ἄνδρα ὕπατον, ᾧ τὴν ἀδελφὴν τὴν ἑαυτοῦ ἐδεδώκει, πρόσταγμα δὲ ἐπεποίητο περὶ τὴν τρίτην ἢ τετάρτην ἡμέραν τοῦ φόνου κἀκείνην ἐς ἀνδρὸς φοιτᾶν· Στέφανος τοίνυν ἀπελεύθερος τῆς γυναικός, ὃν ἐδήλου τὸ τῆς διοσημίας σχῆμα, εἴτε τὸν τεθνεῶτα ἐνθυμηθεὶς εἴτε πάντας, ὥρμησε μὲν ἴσα τοῖς ἐλευθερωτάτοις Ἀθηναίοις ἐπὶ τὸν τύραννον, ξίφος δ' ὑφείρας τῷ τῆς ἀριστερᾶς πήχει καὶ τὴν χεῖρα ἐπιδέσμοις ἀναλαβὼν οἷον κατεαγυῖαν ἀπιόντι τοῦ δικαστηρίου προσελθών, Δέομαί σου, ἔφη, βασιλεῦ, μόνου, μεγαλὰ γὰρ ὑπὲρ ὧν ἀκούσῃ. οὐκ ἀπαξιώσαντος δὲ τοῦ τυράννου τὴν ἀκρόασιν ἀπολαβὼν αὐτὸν ἐς τὸν ἀνδρῶνα, οὗ τὰ βασίλεια, Οὐ τέθνηκεν, εἶπεν, ὁ πολεμιώτατός σοι Κλήμης, ὡς σὺ οἴει, ἀλλ' ἔστιν οὗ ἐγὼ οἶδα, καὶ ξυντάττει ἑαυτὸν ἐπί σε. μέγα δ' αὐτοῦ βοήσαντος περὶ ὧν ἤκουσε, τεταραγμένῳ προσπεσὼν ὁ Στέφανος καὶ τὸ ξίφος τῆς ἐσκευασμένης χειρὸς ἀνασπάσας διῆκε τοῦ μηροῦ κ.τ.λ.

For ἀδελφὴν we should probably read ἀδελφιδὴν 'niece', as Domitilla, the wife of Flavius Clemens, appears from other authorities to have been the daughter of Domitian's sister; see above, p. 44. Zahn (*Der Hirt des Hermas* p. 45, note 4) supposes Philostratus to have confused her with her mother.

The expression ἐς ἀνδρὸς φοιτᾶν is sometimes translated 'to go and join her husband', i.e. 'to put herself to death'; e.g. by Hausrath *Neutest. Zeitsgesch.* III. p. 301, Renan *Les Évangiles* p. 296, note 5, and others. Erbes (*Jahrb. f. Prot. Theol.* IV. p. 700 sq., 1878) rightly objects to this interpretation. It is untenable for two reasons. (1) It would require πρὸς τὸν ἄνδρα instead of ἐς ἀνδρός. The definite article at all events is wanted. (2) The verb φοιτᾶν signifies 'to go to and fro,' and could not signify 'to depart.' On the other hand it is used especially in the sense 'to have intercourse with'; see Steph. Thes. s.v. φοιτᾶν (ed. Hase and Dind.). It must therefore mean 'to marry another husband,' as it is correctly taken by Zahn (*l. c.*), Lipsius (*Chronol.* p. 156), and Hasenclever (p. 235).

19.

TREBELLIUS POLLIO *Tyr. Trig.* 12.

Domitianus...dux Aureoli fortissimus et vehementissimus, qui se originem diceret a Domitiano trahere atque a Domitilla.

20.

ANTHOLOGIA LATINA 1435 (II. p. 160, ed. Meyer).

Qui colitis Cybelen et qui Phryga plangitis Attin,
  Dum vacat et tacita Dindyma nocte silent,
Flete meos cineres. Non est alienus in illis
  Hector, et hoc tumulo Mygdonis umbra tegor.
Ille ego, qui magni parvus cognominis heres
  Corpore in exiguo res numerosa fui;
Flectere doctus equos, nitida certare palaestra,
  Ferre jocos, astu fallere, nosse fidem.
At tibi dent superi quantum, Domitilla, mereris,
  Quae facis, exigua ne jaceamus humo.

This epigram is headed 'Domitilla Hectori'. It was, I suppose, the inscription placed on the grave of a Phrygian slave or freedman, to whom Domitilla had given a plot of ground for burial; see above, p. 41.

21.

CORP. INSCR. LAT. VI. 948 (v. p. 172 sq.).

FL. DOMITILLA | FILIA . FLAVIAE . DOMITILLAE |
DIVI . VESPASI | ANI . NEPTIS . FECIT . GLYCERAE . L . ET |

See also Orelli 776. This inscription was formerly in the Church of S. Clemente in Rome on the steps of the episcopal chair, but is now in the Vatican. Another fragment of an inscription, attached to this by Cittadini (see Mommsen *ad loc.*), seems not to have any connexion with it. It contains, or did contain, the words CVRANTE . T . FLAVIO . ONESIMO . CONIVGI . BENEMER, whence Zahn (p. 48) and Lipsius (*Chronol.* p. 155) make this Onesimus the husband of 'Domitilla filia'. But surely his wife would be Glycera, not Domitilla, if this were part of the same inscription.

Mommsen (*l. c.*) takes 'neptis' as the genitive on account of the order. He thus gives to the wife of Fl. Clemens a daughter besides her two sons Vespasianus and Domitianus (see above, p. 21). Zahn takes it in the same way, and weds this fourth Fl. Domitilla to T. Flavius Onesimus. It seems to me simpler to suppose with De Rossi that the 'filia' is herself the wife of Clemens and granddaughter of Vespasian, her mother being Vespasian's daughter Fl. Domitilla.

Commenting on this inscription, Mommsen drew up a *stemma* of the Flavii, which contradicted all the authorities, Philostratus, Dion, Eusebius, and Quintilian alike, It seemed to myself 'to have nothing to recommend it except the name of that truly great scholar' (*Philippians* p. 23). It was criticized by De Rossi (*Bull. di Arch. Crist.* 1875, p. 70 sq), and has since been withdrawn by Mommsen himself (*Corp. Inscr. Lat.* VI. 8942, p. 1187).

The Flavia Domitilla of *C. I. L.* X. 1419 seems to be the wife of Vespasian.

22.

CORP. INSCR. LAT. VI. 8942 (p. 1187).

T A T I A . B A V C Y L
T R I X . S E P T E M . L I B
D I V I . V E S P A S I A N
F L A V I A E . D O M I T I L
V E S P A S I A N I . N E P T I S . A
IVS . BENEFICIO . HOC . SEPHVLCRU | M FECI
MEIS . LIBERTIS . LIBERTABVS . PO | STERISQ.

See also Orelli-Henzen 5423. This inscription is now restored by Mommsen as follows: TATIA BAUCYL . . [NU]TRIX SEPTEM LIB[ERORUM PRONEPOTUM] DIVI VESPASIAN[I, FILIORUM FL. CLEMENTIS ET] FLAVIAE DOMITIL[LAE UXORIS EJUS, DIVI] VESPASIANI NEPTIS A[CCEPTO LOCO E]JUS BENEFICIO HOC SEPHULCRU[M] ETC.

This restoration seems to me to be open to two objections. (1) The expression 'liberorum nepotum' is awkward and unusual. (2) The words supplied are greatly in excess of the available space. I should restore it [NV]TRIX . SEPTEM . LIB[ERO-RVM] . DIVI . VESPASIAN[I . ATQVE] FLAVIAE . DOMITILLAE . etc. This person had nursed two generations, the seven children of Vespasian and his grandchild Domitilla, just as we read of one Phyllis, who nursed not only his son Domitian but his grand-daughter Julia (Sueton. *Domit.* 17). It is no objection to this interpretation that only three children of Vespasian are mentioned in history (see above, p. 19). The other four may have died in infancy. Indeed the long interval (ten years) between the births of Titus and Domitian suggests that there were other children born between them. Nor again is it any objection that in Suetonius (l. c.) Phyllis is mentioned as the nurse of Domitian. He would have more than one nurse. De Rossi (*Bull. di Archeol. Crist.* 1875, p. 67, note) so far agrees with Mommsen as to suppose that the inscription speaks of seven children of Fl. Clemens and Fl. Domitilla.

23.

CORP. INSCR. LAT. VI. 16246 (p. 1836).

SER . CORNELIO . IVLIANO . FRAT.
PIISSIMO . ET . CAL[VISI]AE . EIVS
P. CALVISIVS . PHILO[T]AS . ET . SIBI
EX . INDVLGENTIA . FLAVIAE . DOMITILL .
IN . FR . P . XXXV . IN AGR . P . XXXX.

See also Orelli-Henzen III. p. 72. Found at Tor Marancia, and published in the *Bull. Inst. Arch.* 1835, p. 155.

24.

CORP. INSCR. LAT. VI. 5. 3468.

GRATTE . C . F. DOMITILLAE
[F]ILIAE . LENTINI . SABINI
V . FORT . LEGT . ASCALON .
CONIVG . SATRI . SILON
IS . V . RELIG . PROMAGIST .
NEPTI . VESPASIANI . IM

This inscription is here printed as a warning. It was published by Vignoli *De Columna Imperatoris Antonini Pii* p. 318 (Romae 1705) among *Inscriptiones Variae.* From this work it was extracted in a mutilated form by Reimar on Dion Cass. lxvii. 14 'Est et DOMITILLA . CONJVX . SATRI . SILONIS . NEPTIS . VESPASIANI . IM . apud Jo. Vignolium in Inscriptt. p. 318, quae an haec nostra esse potest, eruditiores judicent.' From Reimar it passed into the hands of Lipsius *Chron.* pp. 155, 156, and of Zahn *Hermas* p. 48, who both entertain the question whether Domitian's niece may not be here intended, and Satrius Silo have been her second husband after the death of Flavius Clemens, the former suggesting that he was perhaps the person whom Domitian (according to Philostratus, see above, pp. 40, 112) compelled her to marry. The inscription is spurious; see *C. I. L.* VI. 5, p. 240*. It is included however in the collections of Muratori DCCV. 4 and Orelli 2430 without misgiving.

3.

MANUSCRIPTS AND VERSIONS.

A PERIOD of nearly two centuries and a half elapsed since the Epistles of S. Clement of Rome were first published (A.D. 1633) from the Alexandrian MS, or as the editor describes it, 'ex laceris reliquiis vetustissimi exemplaris Bibliothecae Regiae.' In this mutilated condition the two epistles remained till a few years ago. The First Epistle had lost one leaf near the end, while the surviving portion occupied nine leaves, so that about a tenth of the whole had perished. The Second Epistle ended abruptly in the middle, the last leaves of the MS having disappeared. It is now ascertained that the lost ending amounted to a little more than two-fifths of the whole. Moreover the MS in different parts was very much torn, and the writing was blurred or obliterated by time and ill usage, so that the ingenuity of successive editors had been sorely exercised in supplying the lacunæ.

After so long a lapse of time it seemed almost beyond hope, that the epistles would ever be restored to their entirety. Yet within a few months they were discovered whole in two distinct documents. The students of early patristic literature had scarcely realized the surprise which the publication of the complete text from a Greek MS at Constantinople had caused (A.D. 1875), when it was announced that the University of Cambridge had procured by purchase a MS containing the two epistles whole in a Syriac Version. Of these three authorities for the text I proceed to give an account.

1. *The Alexandrian Manuscript.*

The Alexandrian MS (A) of the Greek Bible was presented to King Charles I by Cyril Lucar, Patriarch first of Alexandria and then of Constantinople, and brought to England in the year 1628. It was transferred from the King's Library and placed in the British Museum, where it now is, in 1753. More detailed accounts of this MS will be found in the Introductions and Prolegomena to the Greek Testament (e.g. Tregelles *Horne's Introduction to the N.T.* p. 152 sq; Scrivener *Introduction to the N.T.* p. 93 sq, ed. 3; C. R. Gregory *Proleg. Tischend. Nov. Test. Graec.* III. p. 354 sq). It contained originally the whole of the Old and New Testaments, but both have suffered from mutilation. This MS is assigned by the most competent authorities to the 5th century ('the beginning or middle of the 5th century...though it may be referred even to the fourth century and is certainly not much later,' Scrivener p. 97; 'the middle of the fifth century or a little later,' Tregelles p. 155; 'saeculi v ejusque fere exeuntis,' Tischendorf p. ix, ed. 8; 'saeculo quinto medio vel exeunte,' Gregory p. 356). Hilgenfeld is alone in placing it, together with the *Sinaiticus*, in the 6th century; *Zeitschr. f. Wiss. Theol.* VII. p. 214 sq (1864), *Einleitung in das N.T.* p. 793, *Clem. Rom. Epist.* Prol. p. xi, ed. 2.

The two Epistles of Clement stand (fol. 159 a) at the close of the New Testament and immediately after the Apocalypse. The title of the First is mutilated, so that it begins ... C ΚΟΡΙΝΘΙΟΥC Α̅. It ends towards the bottom of fol. 168 a. col. 1; and below is written

ΚΛΗΜΕΝΤΟCΠΡΟCΚΟ

ΡΙΝΘΙΟΥCΕΠΙCΤΟΛΗ

Α.

The Second commences fol. 168 a. col. 2, without any heading. As the end leaves of the MS are wanting, this Second Epistle is only a fragment and terminates abruptly in the middle of a sentence, § 12 οὔτε θῆλυ τοῦτο (fol. 169 b). Both epistles are included in the table of contents prefixed by the scribe to the MS, where the list of books under the heading Η ΚΑΙΝΗ ΔΙΑΘΗΚΗ ends thus:

ΑΠΟΚΑΛΥΨΙC[ΙΩΑ]ΝΝΟΥ
ΚΛΗΜΕΝΤΟCΕ[ΠΙCΤ]ΟΛΗ Α̅
ΚΛΗΜΕΝΤΟCΕ[ΠΙCΤΟΛ]Η Β̅

[ΟΜ]ΟΥΒΙΒΛΙΑ[......]

ΨΑΛΜΟΙCΟΛΟΜΩΝΤΟC

ΙΗ

As the edges of the leaves are worn in many places and the vellum is in other parts very fragile, words or parts of words have occasionally disappeared. Moreover the use of galls by the first editor, Patrick Young, has rendered some passages wholly or in part illegible. In addition to this, a leaf is wanting towards the close of the First Epistle, between fol. 167 and fol. 168, § 57 ἀνθ' ὧν γὰρ ἠδίκουν...§ 63 ὑμᾶς εἰρηνεῦσαι. The hiatus is detected by the numerals in ancient Arabic characters at the foot of the verso of each leaf, where 834 (fol. 167) is followed immediately by 836 (fol. 168)[1]. My attention was first called to this fact respecting the Arabic numerals by the late H. Bradshaw, the distinguished librarian of the Cambridge University Library; and it has since been noticed by Tischendorf (p. xv). The first editor, Patrick Young, had said 'Desideratur hic in exemplari antiquo folium integrum.' Jacobson accounts for this statement by remarking, 'Forte codicem conferre contigit priusquam a bibliopego Anglico praescissus fuerat et in corio compactus,' which was perhaps the case. It is strange however that the Arabic numerals, which set the question at rest, should have been so long overlooked.

The Epistles of Clement were transcribed with tolerable but not strict accuracy, and the lacunæ supplied for the most part with felicity, by the first editor, Patricius Junius (Patrick Young), A.D. 1633. But an *editio princeps* necessarily left much to be done. Collations were accordingly made by Mill and Grabe; and Wotton, in preparing his edition (A.D. 1718), not only employed these collations, but also examined the MS itself. Lastly, Jacobson (1st ed., 1838) recollated it throughout and corrected many inaccuracies which had run through previous editions. Hitherto however, while facsimiles had been made of the text of the New Testament in this MS by Woide (1786) and subsequently of the Old by Baber (1816—1821), nothing of the kind had been done for the Epistles of Clement, though here the MS was unique. But in the year 1856 Sir F. Madden, the keeper of the MSS at the British Museum, in answer to a memorial from the Divinity Professors and others of Oxford and Cambridge and by permission of the Trustees of the Museum, published a photograph of this portion of the MS. Hilgenfeld, when he first edited these epistles (1866), seems to have been unaware of the existence of this photograph, though it had appeared ten years before; but in a foreigner this ignorance was very excusable. Where the MS has not been injured by time or by the application of galls, the photograph was all that could be desired; but passages which have suffered in this way may often be read accu-

[1] The numbering is carried through continuously from the Old Testament. Hence the high numbers. Tischendorf (p. x) misreads the first figure (1 for 8) and gives 134, 136.

rately in the MS itself, though wholly illegible in the photograph. For this reason Tischendorf's reproduction of these epistles, published in his *Appendix Codicum Celeberrimorum Sinaitici, Vaticani, Alexandrini* (Lips. 1867), was not superfluous, but supplied fresh materials for a more accurate text. Before I was aware that Tischendorf was engaged upon this facsimile, I had with a view to my first edition procured a new and thorough collation of the text of these epistles through the kindness of the late Mr A. A. Vansittart, who at my request undertook the work; and we found that notwithstanding the labours of previous editors the gleanings were still a sufficient reward for the trouble. On the appearance of Tischendorf's facsimile, I compared it with Vansittart's collation, and found that they agreed in the great majority of instances where there was a divergence from previous editors (e.g. in the reading τίς ἀρκετὸς ἐξειπεῖν § 49, where the printed texts had previously read τίς ἀρκεῖ ὡς δεῖ εἰπεῖν). In some readings however they differed: and in such cases I myself inspected the MS (repeating the inspection at three different times, where the writing was much defaced), in order to get the result as accurate as possible. Tischendorf's text contained several errors, which however were for the most part corrected in the preface. A few still remained, of which the most important is διακονιαν (§ 35), where the MS has διανοιαν, as even the photograph shows.

My first edition appeared in 1869. A few years later Tischendorf again edited these epistles under the title, *Clementis Romani Epistulae; Ad ipsius Codicis Alexandrini fidem ac modum repetitis curis* (Lipsiae 1873). In his 'prolegomena' and 'commentarius' he discusses the points of difference between us as to the readings of the Alexandrian MS. At his request our common friend, Dr W. Wright, had consulted the MS in the more important and doubtful passages; and in some points he decided in favour of Tischendorf, while in others he confirmed my reading. While preparing for my Appendix, which appeared in 1876, I again consulted the MS, where doubtful points still remained, and the results were given in that work. Lastly; in 1879 an autotype *Facsimile of the Codex Alexandrinus* (*New Testament and Clementine Epistles*) was published 'by order of the Trustees of the British Museum,' and was followed later by the Old Testament. This is admirably executed, and all is now done for the deciphering of the MS which photography can do. I congratulate myself on having had the criticisms on my work from a writer so competent in this department as Tischendorf; and probably the Alexandrian MS has now by successive labours been deciphered almost as fully and correctly as it ever will be. It is a happy incident that this result was mainly achieved before the discovery of a second

Greek MS and of the Syriac Version furnished new data for the construction of the text.

On the whole this MS appears to give a good text. The shortcomings of the scribe are generally such that they can be easily corrected; for they arise from petty carelessness and ignorance, and not from perverse ingenuity. Thus there are errors of the ordinary type arising from repetition or omission, where the same letters recur, e.g. § 2 αμαμνησικακοι, § 11 ετερογνωμοσ, § 12 υποτοτοεγοσ, § 17 δομενου, § 19 ταπεινοφρονον, § 25 τελευτηκοτοσ, § 32 ημερασ, § 35 μον, αδελφουσσου, § 48 διακριακρισει, § 50 μακακαριοι, ii § 1 ποιουν (for ποιουνουν), ii § 9 αιωνιον (for αινυναιωνιον), ii § 11 ασουκ (for ασουσουκ): there is the usual substitution of wrong case endings, arising mostly from confusion with the context, e.g. § 3 τησ, § 16 ελθοντοσ, § 19 αλλασ, § 32 του, § 43 κεκοσμημενω, § 44 μεμαρτυρημενοισ, ii § 1 εχοντεσ, ii § 6 αιχμαλωσιᾱ; there is now and then a transposition, e.g. § 4 ζηλοσ and διαζηλοσ, § 39 σητον τροποσ for σητοσ τροπον; there are several paltry blunders of omission or miswriting or substitution, which cannot be classed under any of these heads, e.g. § 1 ξενοισ, § 2 εστερνισμενοι, εδεδετο, πεποιηθησεωσ, § 3 δοθη, απεγαλακτισεν, § 8 λαω αγιω, διελεχθωμεν, § 10 πιστισ, § 15 αναστησομεν, § 16 εψεται, § 20 κρυματα, § 21 λυχνον, εγκαυχωμενοι εν, § 23 εξαιχνησ, § 25 μονογενησ, διανευει, § 29 αριθον, § 30 αγνουσ, εδεηθη, § 33 εγγοισ, § 34 λιτουργουν, § 35 καταλιλιασ, φιλοξενιαν, εξαβαλλεσ, § 38 τμμελειτω, § 41 συνειδησιν, καταξιωθημεν, § 44 μετοξυ, μεταγαγετε, § 45 επιτασθαι, στυητοι, § 51 οικιαισ, οι, § 56 ουκοψεται, § 57 οταρ, § 59 ανεπεμψατε, ii § 7 αιων, θι, θωμεν, ii § 9 πουντες; there is the occasional dropping of words owing to homœoteleuton or other causes, e.g. § 3 τησ καρδιασ, § 5 δια, § 15 τα λαλουντα κ.τ.λ., § 35 δια, and probably § 40 επιμελωσ; there is lastly the common phenomenon of debased and ungrammatical forms, e.g. § 1 ασφαλην, § 14 ασεβην, § 18 πλυνιεισ, § 26 (comp. ii § 8) σαρκαν, §§ 1, 29 επιεικην, § 32 αυτων, § 40 υπερτατω, § 42 καθεστανον, § 59 επιποθητην, ii § 1 ελπιδαν, ii § 12 δηλοσ, with several others, though in some cases they may be attributed to the author rather than the scribe. In these instances the correct text is generally obvious. But one or two deeper corruptions remain, e.g. § 2 μετελεουσ, § 12 φωνησ, § 45 επαφροι, and perhaps § 6 δαναιδεσκαιδιρκαι.

This MS also exhibits the usual interchanges of like-sounding vowels and diphthongs; of ο and ω, as § 48 εξομολογησωμαι, § 54 τοπωσ, ii § 4 αυτων, and on the other hand, § 25 βασταζον, § 45 ειπομεν, ii § 6 οιομεθα; of η and ι, as § 1 αιφνηδιουσ, καθικουσαν, § 4 ηυλησθησαν, § 8 προστηθεισ, § 39 μυκτιρηζουσιν, § 47 προσκλησεισ, ii § 10 ηληκην; of ε and αι, as § 14 αιπερομενον (for επαιρομενον), § 6 οσταιων, § 10 οραιων, §§ 21, 52 ναιουσ, ναιον, §§ 25, 26 ορναιον, ορναιου, § 39 επεσεν (for ἔπαισεν), § 4 παιδιον, παιδιω (for πεδίον, πεδίῳ), §§ 2, 9, 18, 22, ii § 3 ελαιοσ, ελαιουσ, etc. (for ἔλεος, ἐλέους, etc.); and lastly, of ι and ει, e.g. § 26 το μεγαλιον τησ επαγγελειασ, § 27 ποιησειν for ποιησιν, § 40 λειτουργειασ, but § 41 λιτουργιασ and § 44 λιτουργειασ, § 2 ειλεικρινεισ, but § 32 ιλικριν[ωσ] and ii. § 9 ιλικρινουσ, § 14 στασισ for στασεισ, but §§ 6, 44 ερεισ for ερισ. In all such cases I have substituted the ordinary classical spelling: but when we call to mind that half a century later the heretic Marcus (Iren. *Haer.* i. 15. 1, Hippol. *Ref.* vi. 49) founds a theory on the fact that σιγὴ contains five letters (ϲειγη) and Χριστὸς eight (χρειϲτοϲ), and that about this very time the Roman biographer confuses Χριστὸς and Χρηστὸς (Suet. *Claud.* 25), we cannot feel at all sure that Clement might not in this respect have allowed himself the same latitude in spelling which we find in our scribe.

The contractions which I have noted in these epistles (besides the line over the previous letter as a substitute for the final ν) are the following; ανοϲ, ανογ, etc., for ανθρωπος, ανθρωπου, etc.; ογνοϲ, ογνογ, etc., for ουρανος, ουρανου, etc.; πηρ, προϲ, etc., for πατηρ, πατρος, etc.; μηρ for μητηρ; θϲ, θγ, etc., κϲ, κγ, etc., χϲ, χγ, etc., ιϲ, ιγ, etc., for θεος, θεου, etc., κυριος, κυριου, etc., χριστος, χριστου, etc., ιησους, ιησου, etc. (but, where Joshua is meant § 12, it is written in full); πνα, πνϲ, πνι, etc., for πνευμα, πνευματος, πνευματι, etc.; δαδ for δαυειδ; ιλημ for ιερουσαλημ; ιϲλ (§§ 4, 29, 43, 55) and ιηλ (§ 8) for ισραηλ.

2. *Constantinopolitan Manuscript.*

At the close of the year 1875 a volume was published at Constantinople, bearing the title:

Τοῦ ἐν ἁγίοις πατρὸς ἡμῶν Κλήμεντος ἐπισκόπου Ῥώμης αἱ δύο πρὸς Κορινθίους ἐπιστολαί. Ἐκ χειρογράφου τῆς ἐν Φαναρίῳ Κωνσταντινουπόλεως βιβλιοθήκης τοῦ Παναγίου Τάφου νῦν πρῶτον ἐκδιδόμεναι πλήρεις μετὰ προλεγομένων καὶ σημειώσεων ὑπὸ Φιλοθέου Βρυεννίου μητροπολίτου Σερρῶν κ.τ.λ. Ἐν Κωνσταντινουπόλει, 1875.

['The Two Epistles of our holy father Clement Bishop of Rome to the Corinthians; from a manuscript in the Library of the Most Holy Sepulchre in Fanar of Constantinople; now for the first time published complete, with prolegomena and notes, by Philotheos Bryennios, Metropolitan of Serrae. Constantinople, 1875'.]

This important MS is numbered 456 in the library to which it belongs. It is an 8vo volume, written on parchment in cursive characters, and consists of 120 leaves. Its contents, as given by Bryennios, are as follows:

fol. 1 a—32 b Τοῦ ἐν ἁγίοις Ἰωάννου τοῦ Χρυσοστόμου σύνοψις τῆς παλαιᾶς καὶ καινῆς διαθήκης ἐν τάξει ὑπομνηστικοῦ[1].

fol. 33 a—51 b Βαρνάβα ἐπιστολή.

fol. 51 b—70 a Κλήμεντος πρὸς Κορινθίους Α′.

fol. 70 a—76 a Κλήμεντος πρὸς Κορινθίους Β′.

fol. 76 a—80 b Διδαχὴ τῶν δώδεκα Ἀποστόλων.

fol. 81 a—82 a Ἐπιστολὴ Μαρίας Κασσοβόλων πρὸς τὸν ἅγιον καὶ ἱερομάρτυρα Ἰγνάτιον ἀρχιεπίσκοπον Θεουπόλεως Ἀντιοχείας.

fol. 82 a—120 a Τοῦ ἁγίου Ἰγνατίου Θεουπόλεως Ἀντιοχείας
πρὸς Μαρίαν
πρὸς Τραλλιανούς
πρὸς Μαγνησίους
πρὸς τοὺς ἐν Ταρσῷ
πρὸς Φιλιππησίους περὶ βαπτίσματος
πρὸς Φιλαδελφεῖς
πρὸς Σμυρναίους
πρὸς Πολύκαρπον ἐπίσκοπον Σμύρνης
πρὸς Ἀντιοχεῖς
πρὸς Ἥρωνα διάκονον Ἀντιοχέα
πρὸς Ἐφεσίους
πρὸς Ῥωμαίους.

The genuine Epistle of Clement is headed Κλήμεντος πρὸς Κορινθίους Α′; the so-called Second Epistle likewise has a corresponding title, Κλήμεντος πρὸς Κορινθίους Β′. At the close of the Second Epistle is written, Στίχοι χ. ῥητὰ κ′ε. At the end of the volume is the colophon; Ἐτελειώθη μηνὶ Ἰουνίῳ εἰς τὰς ια′. ἡμέραν γ′. Ἰνδ. θ′. ἔτους ͵στφξδ′. χειρὶ Λέοντος νοταρίου καὶ ἀλείτου. The date A.M. 6564 is here given according to the Byzantine reckoning, and corresponds to A.D. 1056, which is therefore the date of the completion of the MS.

A facsimile of a page of this manuscript is given in the plates of the *Palæographical Society* 2nd Series, no. 48 (1880). A full account of it, likewise containing a facsimile, will be found in Schaff's *Teaching of the Twelve Apostles* p. 1—7.

It is strange that this discovery should not have been made before.

[1] This is the same work which is printed in Montfaucon's edition of S. Chrysostom, VI. p. 314 sq. The treatise in this MS contains only the Old Testament and ends with Malachi. Montfaucon stops short at Nahum. For a full account see Bryennios *Didache* p. 109 sq.

The Library of the Most Holy Sepulchre at Constantinople is attached to the Patriarchate of Jerusalem in that city, and therefore has something of a public character. It has moreover been examined more than once by learned men from Western Europe. A catalogue of its MSS, compiled in 1845 by Bethmann, appeared in Pertz *Archiv der Gesellsch. f. ältere deutsche Geschichtskunde* IX. p. 645 sq.; but it does not mention this volume (see *Patr. Apost. Op.* I. i. p. xi sq., Gebhardt u. Harnack, ed. 2). Some years later, in 1856, M. Guigniant read a report of the contents of this library before the French Academy of Inscriptions, which is published in the *Journal Général de l'Instruction Publique* 1856, XXV. p. 419; and again this MS is unnoticed. M. Guigniant seems to have attended chiefly to classical literature, and to have made only the most superficial examination of the Christian writings in this collection; for he says, somewhat contemptuously, that these MSS 'unfortunately comprise little besides Homilies, Prayers, Theological and Controversial Treatises, written at times not very remote from our own,' with more to the same effect (as quoted in the *Academy*, May 6, 1876). Again, two years later, the Rev. H. O. Coxe, the Librarian of the Bodleian, visited this library and wrote a report of his visit (*Report to H. M. Government on the Greek MSS in the Libraries of the Levant* pp. 32, 75, 1858); but he too passes over this volume in silence. A serious illness during his stay at Constantinople prevented him from thoroughly examining the libraries there.

This MS is designated I (Ἱεροσολυμιτικός) by Bryennios, and by Hilgenfeld after him. But this designation is misleading, and I shall therefore call it C (Constantinopolitanus) with Gebhardt and Harnack.

Facsimiles of C are given by Bryennios at the end of his volume. He has added a fuller account of the minor features of the MS in a later publication, *Didache* p. 93 sq. (1883), where also he gives (p. 103) *Addenda and Corrigenda* to the readings in his edition of Clement. The contractions are numerous and at first sight perplexing. It systematically ignores the ι subscript or adscript with two exceptions, ii. § 1 τῆι θελήσει, ii. § 9 ἐν τῆι σαρκὶ ταύτῃ (sic); it generally omits before consonants the so-called ν ἐφελκυστικόν, though there are some exceptions (§ 27 λέληθεν τὴν, § 33 ἐστήρισεν καὶ, ἔπλασεν τῆς, § 49 ἔσχεν πρὸς, § 53 εἶπεν πρὸς, εἶπεν Κύριος, § 55 ἐξῆλθεν δι' ἀγάπην, ii. § 2 εἶπεν στεῖρα); and it writes οὕτω or οὕτως capriciously. It is written with a fair amount of care throughout, so far as regards errors of transcription. In this respect it contrasts favourably with A, which constantly betrays evidence of great negligence on the part of the scribe. But, though far more free from mere clerical errors, yet in all points which vitally affect the trustworthiness of a MS, it must certainly yield the palm to the Alexandrian. The scribe of A may be careless, but he is guileless also. On the other hand the text of C shows manifest traces of critical revision, as will appear in the sequel.

But notwithstanding this fact, which detracts somewhat from its weight, it still has considerable value as an authority. More especially it is *independent* of A; for it preserves the correct reading in some instances, where A is manifestly wrong. I pass over examples of slight errors where one scribe might blunder and another might correct his blunder (e.g. § 1 ξένοις A, ξένης C; § 2 ἐστερνισμένοι A, ἐνεστερνισμένοι C; § 3 ἀπεγαλάκτισεν A, ἀπελάκτισεν C; § 25 διανεύει A, διανύει C; § 35 φιλοξενίαν A, ἀφιλοξενίαν C). These are very numerous, but they prove nothing. Other instances however place the fact of its independence beyond the reach of doubt: e.g. § 2 μετ' ἐλέους (μετελαιουσ) A, which is read μετὰ δέους in C, where no divination could have restored the right reading; § 3 κατὰ τὰς ἐπιθυμίας αὐτοῦ τῆς πονηρᾶς A, where critics with one accord have substituted τὰς πονηράς for τῆς πονηρᾶς without misgiving, thus mending the text by the alteration of a single letter, but where the reading of C shows that the words τῆς καρδίας have dropped out in A after ἐπιθυμίας; § 21 διὰ τῆς φωνῆς A, where C has διὰ τῆς σιγῆς, as the sense demands and as the passage is quoted by Clement of Alexandria; § 34 προτρέπεται (προτρεπετε) οὖν ἡμᾶς ἐξ ὅλης τῆς καρδίας ἐπ' αὐτῷ μὴ ἀργοὺς μήτε παρειμένους εἶναι ἐπὶ πᾶν ἔργον ἀγαθόν, where some critics have corrected ἐπ' αὐτῷ in various ways, while others, like myself, have preferred to retain it and put a slightly strained meaning on it, but where C solves the difficulty at once by inserting πιστεύοντας after ἡμᾶς and thus furnishing a government for ἐπ' αὐτῷ; § 37, where ενεικτικωσ, or whatever may be the reading of A, could not have suggested ἐκτικῶς which appears in C. It follows from these facts (and they do not stand alone) that C is not a lineal descendant of A, and that the text which they have in common must be traced back to an archetype older than the 5th century, to which A itself belongs.

On the other hand, the *critical revision*, to which I have already referred, as distinguishing the text of C when compared with that of A, and thus rendering it less trustworthy, betrays itself in many ways.

(1) C exhibits *harmonistic* readings in the quotations. Thus in § 4 it has τῷ Κυρίῳ for τῷ Θεῷ in Gen. iv. 3 in accordance with the LXX; and again ἄρχοντα καὶ δικαστὴν for κριτὴν ἢ δικαστὴν in Exod. ii. 14, also in accordance with the LXX (comp. also Acts vii. 27). In § 13 it gives τοὺς λόγους for τὰ λόγια in Is. lxvi. 2 in conformity with the LXX. In § 22 again it has τὸν ἐλπίζοντα for τοὺς ἐλπίζοντας in Ps. xxxii. 10 after

the LXX. In § 33, having before spoken of justification by faith and not by works, Clement writes τί οὖν ποιήσωμεν, ἀδελφοί; ἀργήσωμεν ἀπὸ τῆς ἀγαθοποιΐας; as read in A: but this sentiment is obviously suggested by Rom. vi. 1 sq, τί οὖν ἐροῦμεν; ἐπιμένωμεν τῇ ἁμαρτίᾳ κ.τ.λ., and accordingly C substitutes τί οὖν ἐροῦμεν for τί οὖν ποιήσωμεν. In § 34 Clement quotes loosely from Is. vi. 3 πᾶσα ἡ κτίσις, but C substitutes πᾶσα ἡ γῆ in accordance with the LXX and Hebrew. Later in this chapter again Clement gives (with some variations) the same quotation which occurs in 1 Cor. ii. 9, and C alters it to bring it into closer conformity with S. Paul, inserting ἃ before ὀφθαλμὸς and substituting τοῖς ἀγαπῶσιν for τοῖς ὑπομένουσιν, though we see plainly from the beginning of the next chapter that Clement quoted it with τοῖς ὑπομένουσιν. In § 35, in a quotation from Ps. l. 16 sq., C substitutes διὰ στόματος for ἐπὶ στόματος so as to conform to the LXX. In § 36, where A reads ὄνομα κεκληρονόμηκεν, C has κεκληρονόμηκεν ὄνομα with Heb. i. 4. In § 47 for αὐτοῦ τε καὶ Κηφᾶ τε καὶ Ἀπολλώ, C substitutes ἑαυτοῦ καὶ Ἀπολλὼ καὶ Κηφᾶ, which is the order in 1 Cor. i. 12. Though A itself is not entirely free from such harmonistic changes, they are far less frequent than in C.

(2) Other changes are obviously made from *dogmatic* motives. Thus in ii. § 9 we read Χριστὸς ὁ Κύριος ὁ σώσας ἡμᾶς, ὢν μὲν τὸ πρῶτον πνεῦμα, ἐγένετο σάρξ κ.τ.λ. This mode of speaking, as I have pointed out in my notes, is not uncommon in the second and third centuries; but to the more dogmatic precision of a later age it gave offence, as seeming to confound the Second and Third Persons of the Holy Trinity. Accordingly C substitutes λόγος for πνεῦμα, 'Jesus Christ, being first Word, became flesh,' thus bringing the statement into accordance with the language of S. John. Again, in § 30 of the genuine epistle, τοῖς κατηραμένοις ὑπὸ τοῦ Θεοῦ, the words ὑπὸ τοῦ Θεοῦ are omitted in C, as I suppose, because the scribe felt a repugnance to ascribing a curse to God; though possibly they were struck out as superfluous, since they occur just below in the parallel clause τοῖς ηὐλογημένοις ὑπὸ τοῦ Θεοῦ. Again in § 12 Ῥαὰβ ἡ πόρνη, C reads Ῥαὰβ ἡ ἐπιλεγομένη πόρνη, the qualifying word being inserted doubtless to save the character of one who holds a prominent place in the Scriptures. Under this head also I am disposed to classify the various reading in § 2, τοῖς ἐφοδίοις τοῦ Θεοῦ ἀρκούμενοι, where C reads τοῦ Χριστοῦ for τοῦ Θεοῦ; but this is a difficult question, and I reserve the discussion of it till the proper place. In § 14 too the substitution of αἱρέσεις for ἔριν is probably due to an orthodox desire to give definiteness to Clement's condemnation of the factious spirit.

(3) But more numerous are the *grammatical* and *rhetorical* changes, i.e. those which aim at greater correctness or elegance of diction. These are of various kinds. (*a*) The most common perhaps is the substitution of a more appropriate tense, or what seemed so, for a less appropriate: e.g. § 1 βλασφημεῖσθαι for βλασφημηθῆναι; § 7 ἱκετεύοντες for ἱκετεύσαντες; § 12 λελάληκας for ἐλάλησας, ἐγενήθη for γέγονεν; § 17 ἀτενίσας for ἀτενίζων; § 20 προσφεύγοντας for προσπεφευγότας; § 21 ἀναιρεῖ for ἀνελεῖ; § 25 τελευτήσαντος for τετελευτηκότος, πληρουμένου for πεπληρωμένου; § 35 ὑποπίπτει for ὑπέπιπτεν; § 40 προσταγεῖσι for προστεταγμένοις; § 44 ἐστὶν for ἔσται, πολιτευσαμένους for πολιτευομένους; § 49 δέδωκεν for ἔδωκεν; § 51 στασιασάντων for στασιαζόντων; § 53 ἀναβάντος for ἀναβαί[νοντος]; ii. § 4 ὁμολογήσωμεν for ὁμολογῶμεν; ii. § 7 φθείρων for φθείρας; ii. § 8 ποιήσῃ for ποιῇ and βοηθεῖ for βοηθήσει. (*b*) The omission, addition, or alteration of connecting particles, for the sake of greater perspicuity or ease: e.g. § 8 γὰρ omitted; § 12 ὅτι... καὶ inserted; § 16 δὲ omitted; § 17 ἔτι δὲ omitted, and again δὲ inserted; § 30 τε...καὶ inserted; § 33 δὲ substituted for οὖν; § 65 καὶ omitted before δι' αὐτοῦ; ii. § 2 δὲ omitted; ii. § 3 οὖν omitted; ii. § 7 οὖν omitted; ii. § 10 δὲ substituted for γάρ. (*c*) The substitution of a more obvious preposition for a less obvious: e.g. § 4 ἀπό for ὑπό (twice), § 9 ἐν τῇ λειτουργίᾳ for διὰ τῆς λειτουργίας, § 11 εἰς αὐτὸν for ἐπ' αὐτόν, § 44 περὶ τοῦ ὀνόματος for ἐπὶ τοῦ ὀνόματος. (*d*) An aiming at greater force by the use of superlatives: § 2 σεβασμιωτάτῃ for σεβασμίῳ, § 33 παμμεγεθέστατον for παμμέγεθες. (*e*) The omission of apparently superfluous words: e.g. § 1 ἀδελφοί, ὑμῶν; § 4 οὕτως; § 7 εἰς (after διέλθωμεν); § 8 γὰρ (after ζῶ); § 11 τοῦτο; § 15 ἀπό; § 19 τὰς...γενεάς (τοὺς being substituted); § 21 ἡμῶν; § 30 ἀπό; § 38 [ἤτω] καί (if this mode of supplying the lacuna in A be correct), where the meaning of the words was not obvious; § 40 ὁ before τόπος; § 41 μόνῃ; § 44 ἄνδρες (with the insertion of τινες in the preceding clause); ii. § 7 αὐτῶν; ii. § 8 ἐν before ταῖς χερσίν (with other manipulations in the passage which slightly alter the sense); ii. § 8 μετανοίας: and (though much less frequently) the insertion of a word; e.g. § 14 τὸν before ἀσεβῆ; § 33 ἀγαθοῖς (but conversely ἀγαθῆς is absent from C but present in A in § 30); ii. § 1 τοῦ before μὴ ὄντος; ii. § 8 ἔτι. (*f*) Alterations for the sake of an easier grammatical construction or a more obvious sense: e.g. § 2 τῶν πλησίον for τοῖς πλησίον; § 4 τὸ πρόσωπον for τῷ προσώπῳ; § 15 ἔψεξαν αὐτὸν for ἐψεύσαντο αὐτόν; § 20 ἐπ' αὐτῆς for ἐπ' αὐτήν; ii. § 3 τῆς ἀληθείας boldly substituted for ἡ πρὸς αὐτόν on account of the awkwardness; ii. § 8 ἀπολάβητε for ἀπολάβωμεν. (*g*) The substitution of orthographical or grammatical forms of words, either more classical or more usual in the transcriber's own age: e.g.

§ 6 ὀστῶν for ὀστέων, § 15 εὐλόγουν for εὐλογοῦσαν, § 38 εἰσήλθομεν for εἰσήλθαμεν, § 57 προείλοντο for προείλαντο, §§ 4, 6 ζῆλον for ζῆλος, § 13 τύφον for τύφος, ἐλεεῖτε for ἐλεᾶτε, § 20 ὑγίειαν for ὑγείαν, § 33 ἀγάλλεται for ἀγαλλιᾶται, § 37 χρᾶται for χρῆται (but conversely, ii. § 6 χρῆσθαι for χρᾶσθαι), § 39 ἐναντίον for ἔναντι, § 40 ὑπερτάτῃ for ὑπερτάτῳ, § 50 ταμιεῖα for ταμεῖα (ταμια), § 53 Μωσῇ for Μωϋσῇ (and similarly elsewhere), § 65 ἐπιπόθητον for ἐπιποθήτην, ii. § 2 ἐκκακῶμεν for ἐγκακῶμεν, ii. § 5 ἀποκτένοντας (sic) for ἀποκτέννοντας, ii. § 7 πείσεται for παθεῖται, ii. § 12 δύο for δυσί, δήλη for δῆλος. So too ἐξερρίζωσε, ἐρρύσατο, φυλλορροεῖ, for ἐξερίζωσε, ἐρύσατο, φυλλοροεῖ; πρᾶος, πραότης, for πραΰς, πραΰτης; etc. And again C has commonly ἑαυτοῦ etc. for αὐτοῦ etc., where it is a reflexive pronoun. In many such cases it is difficult to pronounce what form Clement himself would have used; but the general tendency of the later MS is obvious, and the scribe of A, being nearer to the age of Clement than the scribe of C by about six centuries, has in all doubtful cases a prior claim to attention. (*h*) One other class of variations is numerous; where there is an exchange of simple and compound verbs, or of different compounds of the same verb. In several cases C is obviously wrong; e.g. § 20 παραβάσεως for παρεκβάσεως, μεταδιδόασιν for μεταπαραδιδόασιν; while other cases do not speak for themselves, e.g. § 7 ἐπήνεγκε for ὑπήνεγκεν, § 12 ἐκκρεμάσῃ for κρεμάσῃ, § 16 ἀπελθόντες for ἐλθόντες, § 25 ἐγγεννᾶται for γεννᾶται, § 37 τελοῦσι for ἐπιτελοῦσιν, § 43 ἠκολούθησαν for ἐπηκολούθησαν, § 55 ἐξέδωκαν for παρέδωκαν, ii. § 1 ἀπολαβεῖν for λαβεῖν, ii. § 12 ἐρωτηθεὶς for ἐπερωτηθείς, but the presumption is in favour of the MS which is found correct in the crucial instances. (*i*) Again there are a few instances where C substitutes the active voice for the middle; § 24 ἐπιδείκνυσι for ἐπιδείκνυται, § 43 ἐπέδειξε for ἐπεδείξατο, in both which the middle seems the more correct. In § 8 C has ἀφέλετε for ἀφέλεσθε, but here the active appears in Is. i. 16, the passage which Clement quotes. Conversely in § 38, ἐντρεπέσθω the reading of C must be substituted for the solœcistic ἐντρεπέτω which stands in A.

In some passages, where none of these motives can be assigned, the variations are greater, and a deliberate change must have been made on the one side or the other. In these cases there is frequently little or no ground for a decision between the two readings from internal evidence; e.g. § 1 περιστάσεις for περιπτώσεις, § 5 ἔριν for φθόνον (where however ἔριν may be suspected as an alteration made to conform to the expression ζῆλον καὶ ἔριν just below), § 6 κατέσκαψε for κατέστρεψεν, § 8 ψυχῆς for καρδίας, § 28 βλαβεράς for μιαράς, § 35 πονηρίαν for ἀνομίαν, § 51 ἄνθρωπον for θεράποντα, § 55 ὑπομνήματα for ὑποδείγματα. But elsewhere the judgment must be given against C; e.g. § 32 τάξει for δόξῃ, § 33 προετοιμάσας for προδημιουργήσας, § 41 προσευχῶν for εὐχῶν, § 47 ἀγάπης for ἀγωγῆς (possibly an accidental change), § 53 δεσπότης for θεράπων, § 56 Κύριος for δίκαιος, ii. § 1 πονηροὶ for πηροί, ii. § 10 ἀνάπαυσιν, ἀνάπαυσις, for ἀπόλαυσιν, ἀπόλαυσις: while in no such instance is A clearly in the wrong; for I do not regard § 41 εὐχαριστείτω A, εὐαρεστείτω C, as an exception. And generally of the variations it may be said that (setting aside mere clerical errors, accidental transpositions, and the like) in nine cases out of ten, which are at all determinable, the palm must be awarded to A[1].

The above account of the relation of C to A has received confirmation from two different quarters.

(i) The Syriac Version, discovered since it was written, bears strong testimony in its favour. We shall see in the sequel that in nearly every case which is indeterminable from internal evidence this version throws its weight into the scale of A.

(ii) The readings of C in other parts besides the Clementine Epistles have since been collated and they furnish an additional confirmation of my views. Thus we are now able to compare its readings in the Ignatian Epistles with the normal text as found in other MSS; and they exhibit just these same features of a literary revision which we have discovered in the case of the Clementine Epistles (see *Ign. and Polyc.* I. p. 110 sq).

It will be unnecessary to give examples of the usual clerical errors, such as omission from homœoteleuton, dropping of letters, and so forth. Of these C has not more than its proper share. Generally it may be said that this MS errs in the way of omission rather than of insertion. One class of omissions is characteristic and deliberate. The scribe becomes impatient of copying out a long quotation, and abridges it, sometimes giving only the beginning or the beginning and end, and sometimes mutilating it in other ways (see §§ 18, 22, 27, 35, 52). A characteristic feature of this MS also is the substitution of ὑμεῖς, ὑμῶν, etc., for ἡμεῖς, ἡμῶν, etc. I say characteristic; because, though the confusion of the first and second persons plural of the personal pronoun is a very common phenomenon in most MSS owing to itacism, yet

[1] This estimate of the relative value of the two MSS agrees substantially with those of Harnack (*Theolog. Literaturz.*, Feb. 19, 1876, p. 99), of Gebhardt (ed. 2, p. xv), and of Funk (*Patr. Apost.* I. p. xxxv, II. p. xxx). Hilgenfeld takes a different view, assigning the superiority to C (ed. 2, p. xx; comp. *Zeitschr. f. Wiss. Theol.* XX. p. 549 sq.).

in this particular case it is far too frequent and too one-sided to be the result of accident. The motive is obvious. When read aloud, the appeals in the letter gain in directness by the substitution of the second person.

Instances will be given in the notes which show how at some stage in its pedigree the readings of C have been influenced by the uncial characters of a previous MS from which it was derived: see §§ 2, 21, 32, 40, 43.

From the list of contents given above (p. 122) it will have appeared that the importance of this MS does not end with Clement's Epistles. All the interesting matter however has now been published. The various readings in the Epistle of Barnabas were communicated to Hilgenfeld for his second edition (1877) and have been incorporated by later editors of this epistle. The very important Διδαχὴ τῶν δώδεκα Ἀποστόλων was given to the world by Bryennios himself (Constantinople, 1883); in which volume also he gives the various readings in the Σύνοψις for the portion which was published by Montfaucon (see above p. 122, note 1) and supplies the missing end. Lastly, for the Ignatian Epistles Bryennios supplied collations of this MS to Funk (*Patr. Apost.* II. p. xxix sq) and to myself (*Ign. and Polyc.* I. p. 110).

In addition to the absolute gain of this discovery in itself, the appearance of the volume which I have been discussing is a happy augury for the future in two respects.

In the first place, when a MS of this vast importance has been for generations unnoticed in a place so public as the official library of a great Oriental prelate, a hope of future discoveries in the domain of early Christian literature is opened out, in which the most sanguine would not have ventured to indulge before.

Secondly, it is a most cheering sign of the revival of intellectual life in the Oriental Church, when in this unexpected quarter an editor steps forward, furnished with all the appliances of Western learning, and claims recognition from educated Christendom as a citizen in the great commonwealth of literature.

3. *Syriac Version.*

A few months after the results of this important discovery were given to the world, a second authority for the complete text of the two epistles came unexpectedly to light.

The sale catalogue of the MSS belonging to the late Oriental scholar M. Jules Mohl of Paris contained the following entry.

'1796. Manuscript syriaque sur parchemin, contenant le N. T. (moins l'Apocalypse) d'apres la traduction revue par Thomas d'Héraclée. ...Entre l'épître de S. Jude et l'épître de S. Paul aux Romains, se trouve intercalée une traduction syriaque des deux épîtres de S. Clément de Rome aux Corinthiens.'

It was the only Syriac MS in M. Mohl's collection.

The Syndicate of the Cambridge University Library, when they gave a commission for its purchase, were not sanguine enough to suppose that the entry in the catalogue would prove correct. The spurious Epistles on Virginity are found in a copy of the Syriac New Testament immediately after the Epistle of S. Jude taken from the Philoxenian version; and it was therefore concluded that the two epistles in question would prove to be these. It seemed incredible that such a treasure as a Syriac version of the Epistles to the Corinthians, forming part of a well-known collection, should have escaped the notice of all Oriental scholars in France. It was therefore a very pleasant surprise to Mr R. L. Bensly, into whose hands the MS first came after its purchase, to discover that they were indeed the Epistles to the Corinthians. He at once announced this fact in a notice sent simultaneously to the Academy and the Athenæum (June 17, 1876), and began without delay to prepare for the publication of this version.

To Mr Bensly's volume, which, I trust, will appear no long time hence, I must refer my readers for a fuller account of this unique MS and the version which it contains. It will be sufficient here to give those facts which are important for my purpose.

The class mark is now *Add. MSS* 1700 in the Cambridge University Library. The MS is parchment, 9½ inches by 6½, written in a current hand; each page being divided into two columns of from 37 to 39 lines. It contains the Harclean recension of the Philoxenian version of the New Testament; but, like some other MSS of this recension, without the asterisks, obeli, and marginal readings. The books are arranged as follows:

1. The Four Gospels. These are followed by a history of the Passion compiled from the four Evangelists.

2. The Acts and Catholic Epistles, followed by the Epistles of S. Clement to the Corinthians.

3. The Epistles of S. Paul, including the Epistle to the Hebrews, which stands last.

At the beginning of the volume are three tables of lessons, one for each of these three divisions.

Quite independently of the Clementine Epistles, this volume has the highest interest; for it is the only known copy which contains the whole of the Philoxenian (Harclean) version, so that the last two chapters of the Epistle to the Hebrews, with the colophon following them, appear here for the first time.

At the end of the fourth Gospel is the well-known subscription, giving the date of the Philoxenian version A.D. 508, and of the Harclean recension A.D. 616; the latter is stated to be based in this part of the work on three MSS (see White's *Sacr. Evang. Vers. Syr. Philox.* pp. 561 sq, 644 sq, 647, 649 sq; Adler *Nov. Test. Vers. Syr.* p. 45 sq; *Catal. Codd. MSS Orient. Brit. Mus.* I. p. 27, no. xix, ed. Forshall). The history of the Passion, which follows, was compiled for lectionary purposes. A similar compilation is found in other MSS (see White l. c. p. 645, Adler l. c. p. 63; so too Harclean Gospels, *Add. MSS* 1903, in Cambr. Univ. Libr.).

In the second division the colophon which follows the Epistle of S. Jude is substantially the same with that of the Oxford MS given by White (*Act. Apost. et Epist.* I. p. 274). The Catholic Epistles are followed immediately on the same page by the Epistles of Clement, the Epistle of S. Jude with its colophon ending one column, and the First Epistle of Clement beginning the next. This latter is headed:

ܐܓܪܬܐ ܩܬܘܠܝܩܐ ܕܩܠܝܡܝܣ ܬܠܡܝܕܐ
ܕܦܛܪܘܣ ܫܠܝܚܐ ܠܘܬ ܥܕܬܐ ܕܩܘܪܝܢܬܝܐ.

The Catholic Epistle of Clement the disciple of Peter the Apostle to the Church of the Corinthians.

At the close is written:

ܫܠܡܬ ܐܓܪܬܐ ܩܕܡܝܬܐ ܕܩܠܝܡܝܣ ܀ ܕܐܬܟܬܒܬ
ܡܢܗ ܠܘܬ ܩܘܪܝܢܬܝܐ ܡܢ ܪܗܘܡܐ.

Here endeth the First Epistle of Clement, that was written by him to the Corinthians from Rome.

Then follows:

ܕܝܠܗ ܕܗ ܕܝܠܗ ܐܓܪܬܐ ܕܬܪܬܝܢ ܠܘܬ ܩܘܪܝܢܬܝܐ.

Of the same the Second Epistle to the Corinthians.

At the close of the Second Epistle is

ܫܠܡܬ ܐܓܪܬܐ ܕܬܪܬܝܢ ܕܩܠܝܡܝܣ : ܕܠܘܬ ܩܘܪܢܬܝܐ.

Here endeth the Second Epistle of Clement to the Corinthians.

This subscription with its illumination ends the first column of a page; and the second commences with the introductory matter (the capitulations) to the Epistle to the Romans.

At the close of the Epistle to the Hebrews, and occupying the first column of the last page in the volume, is the following statement:

ܐܬܟܬܶܒ ܟܬܒܐ ܗܢܐ ܕܦܘܠܘܣ ܫܠܝܚܐ
ܘܐܬܦܚܸܡ. ܡܢ ܨܚܚܐ ܗܿܘ ܕܟܬܝܒ ܗܘܐ ܒܡܒܘܓ
ܡܕܝܢܬܐ: ܗܿܘ ܕܐܦ ܗܿܘ ܐܬܦܚܸܡ ܗܘܐ ܡܢ
ܨܚܚܐ ܕܐܝܬ[ܘܗܝ] ܗܘܐ ܒܩܣܪܝܐ ܡܕܝܢܬܐ
ܕܦܠܣܛܝܢܐ: ܒܝܬ ܟܬ̈ܒܐ ܕܩܕܝܫܐ ܦܡܦܝܠܘܣ:
ܕܟܬܝܒ ܗܘܐ ܒܟܬܒܬ ܐܝܕܗ. ⁘

This book of Paul the Apostle was written and collated from that copy which was written in the city of Mabug (Hierapolis); which also had been collated with (from) a copy that was in Cæsarea a city of Palestine in the library of the holy Pamphilus, and was written in his own handwriting, etc.

After this follows another colophon, which occupies the last column in the MS, and begins as follows:

ܫܠܡ ܕܝܢ ܗܟܢܐ ܐܦ ܥܠ ܫܘܡܠܝܐ ܕܟܬܒܐ ܗܢܐ
ܦܠܓܐ ܬܢܝܢܐ ܕܐܘܢܓܠܝܘܢ: ܘܕܦܪܟܣܝܣ ܕܫܠܝ̈ܚܐ
ܘܩܪ̈ܝܢܐ: ܘܐܓܪ̈ܬܐ ܬܪ̈ܬܝܢ ܕܩܠܝܡܝܣ: ܥܡ ܡܠܘܫܘܬܐ
ܕܦܘܠܘܣ ܫܠܝܚܐ: ܐܝܟ ܬܘܪ̈ܓܡܐ ܕܐܬܦܫܩܐ
ܚܘܠܡ̈ܐ. ܒܫܢܬܐ ܗܿܝ ܕܐܠܦ ܘܐܪܒܥܡܐܐ
ܘܬܡܢܝܢ ܘܚܕܐ ܕܝܘ̈ܢܝܐ. ܒܡܕܝܢܬܐ ܕܡܒܘܓ
ܠܢܘܟܪܝܐ ܗܿܝ ܕܒܫܢܬ ܫܬܡܐܐ. ܕܒܚܠܦܘܪܐ ܩܕܝܫܐ
ܕܐܦܪܗܝܡ ܡܕܝܢܬܐ ܡܒܘܪܟܬܐ. ⁘ ܐܬܟܬܒ ܕܝܢ

ܒܚܦܝܛܘ̄ ܪܒܬܐ ܘܪܚܡܬܐ ܠܐ ܡܬܟܠܝܢܝܬܐ:
ܘܚܡܝܡܘܬ ܗܝܡܢܘܬܐ ܡܫܬܒܚܢܝܬܐ ܡܢ ܢܦܩܬܐ
ܕܪܒܢ ܒܐܣܝܠ ܕܝܪܝܐ ܢܟܦܐ ܘܩܫܝܫܐ ܙܗܝܐ. ܕܡܬܩܪܐ
ܒܪ ܡܝܟܐܝܠ ܕܡܢ ܐܘܪܗܝ ܡܕܝܢܬܐ. ܐܝܟܢܐ
ܕܢܗܘܐ ܠܗ ܠܗܓܝܢܐ ܘܗܪܓܐ ܪܘܚܢܝܐ ܘܡܘܬܪܢܐ
ܕܢܦܫܐ ܘܕܦܓܪܐ. ܟܬܒܗ ܕܝܢ ܣܗܕܐ ܒܨܝܪܐ
ܒܕܝܪܝܐ ܕܗܢܘܢ ܕܐܘܪܗܝ ⁘

Now this life-giving book of the Gospel and of the Acts of the Holy Apostles[1]*, and the two Epistles of Clement, together with the teaching of Paul the Apostle, according to the correction of Thomas of Heraclea, received its end and completion in the year one thousand four hundred and eighty one of the Greeks in the little convent of Mar Saliba, which is in the abode of the monks on the Holy Mountain of the Blessed City of Edessa. And it was written with great diligence and irrepressible love and laudable fervour of faith and at the cost of Rabban Basil the chaste monk and pious presbyter, who is called Bar Michael, from the city of Edessa, so that he might have it for study and spiritual meditation and profit both of soul and of body. And it was written by Sahda the meanest of the monks of the same Edessa.*

The remainder of this colophon, which closes the volume, is unimportant. The year 1481 of the era of the Seleucidae corresponds to A.D. 1170.

On the last page of each quire, and on the first page of the following quire, but not elsewhere, it is customary in this MS to give in the upper margin the title of the book for the time being. This heading, in the case of the First Epistle of Clement, is

ܐܓܪܬܐ ܩܕܡܝܬܐ ܕܩܠܝܡܝܣ ܠܘܬ ܩܘܪܝܢܬܝܐ.

The First Epistle of Clement to the Corinthians.

In the case of the Second Epistle no occasion for any such heading arises.

[1] Under the title 'Acts' the writer here evidently includes the Catholic Epistles. At the beginning and end of the table of lessons for the second division it is used as a designation for the whole division, comprising the Clementine as well as the Catholic Epistles.

The Epistles of Clement are divided into lessons continuously with the Acts and Catholic Epistles, which constitute the former part of the same division. They are as follows:

94. 26th Sunday after the Resurrection; Inscr. Ἡ ἐκκλησία κ.τ.λ.
95. 27th Sunday after the Resurrection; § 10 Ἀβραάμ ὁ φίλος κ.τ.λ.
96. 34th Sunday after the Resurrection; § 16 Ταπεινοφρονούντων γὰρ κ.τ.λ.
97. 35th Sunday after the Resurrection; § 16 Ὁρᾶτε, ἄνδρες ἀγαπητοί κ.τ.λ.
98. 36th Sunday after the Resurrection; § 19 Τῶν τοσούτων οὖν κ.τ.λ.
99. 37th Sunday after the Resurrection; § 21 Τὸν Κύριον Ἰησοῦν κ.τ.λ.
100. The Funeral of the Dead; § 26 Μέγα καὶ θαυμαστὸν κ.τ.λ.
101. 38th Sunday after the Resurrection; § 30 Ἁγίου [Ἁγία] οὖν μερὶς κ.τ.λ.
102. 39th Sunday after the Resurrection; § 33 Τί οὖν ποιήσωμεν κ.τ.λ.
103. 28th Sunday after the Resurrection; § 50 Αἱ γενεαὶ πᾶσαι κ.τ.λ.
104. 29th Sunday after the Resurrection; § 52 Ἀπροσδεής, ἀδελφοί, κ.τ.λ.
105. 30th Sunday after the Resurrection; § 56 Βλέπετε, ἀγαπητοί κ.τ.λ.
106. 31st Sunday after the Resurrection; § 59 Ἐὰν δέ τινες κ.τ.λ.
107. 32nd Sunday after the Resurrection; § 62 Περὶ μὲν τῶν ἀνηκότων κ.τ.λ.
108. The Mother of God; ii. § 1 Ἀδελφοί, οὕτως κ.τ.λ.
109. 33rd Sunday after the Resurrection; ii. § 5 Ὅθεν, ἀδελφοί, κ.τ.λ.
110. 25th Sunday after the Resurrection; ii. § 19 Ὥστε, ἀδελφοὶ καὶ ἀδελφαί, κ.τ.λ.

These rubrics, with the exception of the numbers (94, 95, etc.), are imbedded in the text[1], and therefore cannot be a later addition. The numbers themselves are in the margin, and written vertically.

I have been anxious to state carefully all the facts bearing on the relation of the Clementine Epistles to the Canonical Books of the New Testament in this MS, because some questions of importance are affected by them. As the result of these facts, it will be evident that, *so far as regards the scribe himself*, the Clementine Epistles are put on an absolute equality with the Canonical writings. Here for the first time they appear, not at the close of the volume, as in A, but with the Catholic Epistles—the position which is required on the supposition of perfect canonicity. Moreover no distinction is made between them and the Catholic

[1] With the exception of the last rubric, which is itself in the margin, having apparently been omitted accidentally.

Epistles, so far as regards the lectionary. Lastly, the final colophon renders it highly probable that the scribe himself supposed these epistles to have been translated with the rest of the New Testament under the direction of Philoxenus and revised by Thomas of Heraclea.

But at the same time it is no less clear that he was mistaken in this view. In the first place, while each of the three great divisions of the New Testament, the Gospels, the Acts and Catholic Epistles, and the Pauline Epistles, has its proper colophon in this MS, describing the circumstances of its translation and revision, the Clementine Epistles stand outside these notices, and are wholly unaccounted for. In the next place the translation itself betrays a different hand, as will appear when I come to state its characteristic features; for the Harcleo-Philoxenian version shows no tendency to that unrestrained indulgence in periphrasis and gloss which we find frequently in these Syriac Epistles of Clement. Thirdly, there is no indication in any other copies, that the Epistles of Clement formed a part of the Harcleo-Philoxenian version. The force of this consideration however is weakened by the paucity of evidence. While we possess not a few MSS of the Gospels according to this version, only one other copy of the Acts, Catholic Epistles, and Pauline Epistles is known to exist[1]. Lastly, the table of lessons, which is framed so as to include the Clementine Epistles, and which therefore has an intimate bearing on the question, seems to be unique. There is no lack of Syriac lectionaries and tables of lessons, whether connected with the Peshito or with the Philoxenian (Harclean) version, and not one, I believe, accords with the arrangement in our MS; though on this point it is necessary to speak with reserve, until all the MSS have been examined. These facts show that the Clementine Epistles must have been a later addition to the Harclean New Testament. What may have been their history I shall not venture to speculate, but leave the question to Bensly for further discussion. It is his opinion that they emanated from the school of Jacob of Edessa. I will only add that the Syriac quotations from these epistles found elsewhere (see below, pp. 180 sq, 182 sq) are quite independent of this version, and sometimes even imply a different Greek text. This fact

[1] This is the Ridley MS, from which White printed his text, now in the Library of New College, Oxford. It contains the Gospels, Acts, Catholic Epistles, and Pauline Epistles, as far as Heb. xi. 27. Separate books however and portions of books are found elsewhere; e.g. Acts i. 1—10 (*Catal. Cod. Syr. Bibl. Bodl.* no. 24, p. 79, Payne Smith); James, 2 Peter, 1 John (*Catal. of Syr. Manusc. in the Brit. Mus.* no. cxxi. p. 76, Wright); 2 Peter, 2, 3 John, Jude, in an Amsterdam MS; besides lessons scattered about in different lectionaries.

however does not help us much; for they occur in collections of extracts, which we should expect to be translated, wholly or in part, directly from the Greek.

As a rendering of the Greek, this version is (with notable exceptions which will be specified hereafter) conscientious and faithful. The translator has made it his business to reproduce every word of the original. Even the insignificant connecting particle τε is faithfully represented by ܕܝܢ. The several tenses too are carefully observed, so far as the language admitted: e.g. an imperfect is distinguished from a strictly past tense. To this accuracy however the capabilities of the Syriac language place a limit. Thus it has no means of distinguishing an aorist from a perfect (e.g. § 25 τελευτήσαντος or τετελευτηκότος, § 40 προστεταγμένοις or προσταγεῖσι), or a future tense from a conjunctive mood (e.g. § 16 τί ποιήσομεν or τί ποιήσωμεν). And again in the infinitive and conjunctive moods it is powerless to express the several tenses (e.g. § 1 βλασφημηθῆναι and βλασφημεῖσθαι, § 13 στηρίζωμεν and στηρίξωμεν).

So far it is trustworthy. But on the other hand, it has some characteristics which detract from its value as an authority for the Greek text, and for which allowance must be made.

(i) It has a tendency to run into paraphrase in the translation of individual words and expressions. This tendency most commonly takes the form of double renderings for a word, more especially in the case of compounds. The following are examples: § 1 περιπτώσεις *lapsus et damna*; § 6 παθοῦσαι *quum passi essent et sustinuissent*; § 15 μεθ' ὑποκρίσεως *cum assumptione personarum et illusione*; § 19 ἐπαναδράμωμεν *curramus denuo* (*et*) *revertamus*, ἀτενίσωμεν *videamus et contemplemur*; § 20 τῶν δεδογματισμένων ὑπ' αὐτοῦ *quae visa sunt Deo et decreta sunt ab illo*, παρεκβαίνει *exit aut transgreditur*, διέταξεν *mandavit et ordinavit*; § 25 παράδοξον *gloriosum et stupendum*, ἀνατρεφόμενος *nutritus et adultus*, γενναῖος *fortis et firmus*; § 27 ἀναζωπυρησάτω *inflammetur denuo et renovetur*; § 30 ὁμόνοιαν *consensum et paritatem animi*; § 34 παρειμένους *solutos et laxos*, κατανοήσωμεν *contemplemur et videamus*; § 44 ἐλλογίμων *peritorum et sapientium* (a misunderstanding of ἐλλόγιμος, which is repeated in § 62); § 50 φανερωθήσονται *revelabuntur et cognoscentur*; § 58 ὑπακούσωμεν *audiamus et respondeamus*; § 59 ἀρχεγόνον *caput* (*principium*) *et creatorem*; ii. § 2 ὁ λαὸς ἡμῶν *congregatio nostra et populus*, στηρίζειν *sustentaret et stabiliret*; § 4 ἀποβαλῶ *educam et projiciam foras*; § 11 ἀνόητοι *stulti et expertes mente*; § 13 μετανοήσαντες ἐκ ψυχῆς *revertentes et ex corde poenitentes* (comp. § 15), θαυμάζουσιν *obstupescunt et admirantur*; § 14 αὐθεντικὸν *ideam et veritatem*; § 18 τῶν εὐχαριστούντων *eorum qui confitentur et accipiunt gratiam* (*gratias agunt*);

§ 19 ἀγανακτῶμεν *cruciemur et murmuremus;* with many others. Sometimes however the love of paraphrase transgresses these limits and runs into great excesses: e.g. § 21 μὴ λιποτακτεῖν ἡμᾶς ἀπὸ τοῦ θελήματος αὐτοῦ *ne rebellantes et deserentes ordinem faciamus aliquid extra voluntatem ejus;* § 53 ἀνυπερβλήτου *exaltatam et super quam non est transire;* § 55 πολλοὶ βασιλεῖς καὶ ἡγούμενοι λοιμικοῦ τινὸς ἐνστάντος καιροῦ *multi reges et duces de principibus populorum siquando tempus afflictionis aut famis alicujus instaret populo;* ii. § 3 παρακούειν αὐτοῦ τῶν ἐντολῶν *negligemus et spernemus mandata ejus dum remisse agimus neque facimus ea* (comp. § 6, where ἐὰν παρακούσωμεν τῶν ἐντολῶν αὐτοῦ is translated *si avertimus auditum nostrum a mandatis ejus et spernimus ea*) with many other instances besides.

(ii) The characteristic which has been mentioned arose from the desire to do full justice to the Greek. The peculiarity of which I have now to speak is a concession to the demands of the Syriac. The translation not unfrequently transposes the order of words connected together: e.g. § 30 ταπεινοφροσύνη καὶ πραΰτης; § 36 ἄμωμον καὶ ὑπερτάτην, ἀσύνετος καὶ ἐσκοτωμένη. This transposition is most commonly found where the first word is incapable of a simple rendering in Syriac, so that several words are required in the translation, and it is advisable therefore to throw it to the end in order to avoid an ambiguous or confused syntax (the Syriac having no case-endings). Thus in the instances given ταπεινοφροσύνη is *humilitas cogitationis*, and ἄμωμος, ἀσύνετος, are respectively *quae sine labe, quae sine intellectu.* Where no such reason for a transposition exists, it may be inferred that the variation represents a different order in the Greek: e.g. § 12 ὁ τρόμος καὶ ὁ φόβος, § 18 τὰ χείλη...καὶ τὸ στόμα, ii. § 15 ἀγάπης καὶ πίστεως, ii. § 17 προσέχειν καὶ πιστεύειν. Sometimes this transposition occurs in conjunction with a double or periphrastic rendering, and a very considerable departure from the Greek is thus produced: e.g. § 19 ταῖς μεγαλοπρεπέσι καὶ ὑπερβαλλούσαις αὐτοῦ δωρεαῖς *donis ejus abundantibus et excelsis et magnis decore;* § 64 τὸ μεγαλοπρεπὲς καὶ ἅγιον ὄνομα αὐτοῦ *nomen ejus sanctum et decens in magnitudine et gloriosum.*

To the demands of the language also must be ascribed the constant repetition of the preposition before several connected nouns in the Syriac, where it occurs only before the first in the Greek. The absence of case-endings occasioned this repetition for the sake of distinctness.

In using the Syriac Version as an authority for the Greek text, these facts must be borne in mind. In recording its readings therefore all such variations as arise from the exigencies of translation or the peculiarities of this particular version will be passed over as valueless for my purpose. Nor again will it be necessary to mention cases where the divergence arises simply from the pointing of the Syriac, the form of the letters being the same: as e.g. the insertion or omission of the sign of the plural, *ribui*. A more remarkable example is § 39, where we have ܥܒܕ̈ܐ ἔργων in place of ܥܒ̣ܕ̈ܐ παίδων. Experience shows that even the best Syriac MSS cannot be trusted in the matter of pointing. In all cases where there is any degree of likelihood that the divergence in the Syriac represents a different reading, the variation will be mentioned, but not otherwise. Throughout the greater part of the epistles, where we have two distinct authorities (A and C) besides, these instances will be very rare. In the newly recovered portion on the other hand, where A fails us, they are necessarily more frequent; and here I have been careful to record any case which is at all doubtful.

Passing from the version itself to the Greek text, on which it was founded, we observe the following facts:

(i) It most frequently coincides with A, where A differs from C. The following are some of the more significant examples in the genuine Epistle: § 1 ἡμῖν...περιπτώσεις AS, καθ' ἡμῶν...περιστάσεις C; § 2 ὁσίας AS, θείας C; *ib.* μετ' ἐλεοῦς (ελαιους) AS, μετὰ δέους C; *ib.* σεβασμίῳ AS, σεβασμιωτάτῃ C; § 4 βασιλέως Ἰσραὴλ AS, om. C; § 5 φθόνον AS, ἔριν C; § 6 κατέστρεψεν AS, κατέσκαψε C; § 7 ἐν γὰρ AS, καὶ γὰρ ἐν C; § 8 ὑμῶν AS, τοῦ λαοῦ μου C; § 9 διὰ τῆς λειτουργίας AS, ἐν τῇ λειτουργίᾳ C; § 10 τῷ Θεῷ AS, om. C; § 13 ὡς κρίνετε κ.τ.λ., where AS preserve the same order of the clauses against C; § 14 ἔριν AS (so doubtless S originally, but it is made ἔρεις by the diacritic points), αἱρέσεις C; § 15 ἐψεύσαντο AS, ἔψεξαν C; § 19 τὰς πρὸ ἡμῶν γενεὰς βελτίους AS, τοὺς πρὸ ἡμῶν βελτίους C; § 23 πρῶτον μὲν φυλλοροεῖ AS, om. C; § 25 ἐπιπτὰς AS, om. C; § 28 μιαρὰς AS, βλαβερὰς C; *ib.* ἐκεῖ ἡ δεξιά σου AS, σὺ ἐκεῖ εἶ C; § 30 ἀπὸ τοῦ Θεοῦ AS, τοῦ Θεοῦ C; *ib.* ἀγαθῆς AS, om. C; *ib.* ὑπὸ τοῦ Θεοῦ AS, om. C; § 32 δόξῃ AS, τάξει C; § 33 ποιήσωμεν AS, ἐροῦμεν C; § 34 ἡ κτίσις AS, ἡ γῆ C; § 35 ὁ δημιουργὸς καὶ πατὴρ κ.τ.λ. AS, where C has a different order; *ib.* τὰ εὐάρεστα καὶ εὐπρόσδεκτα αὐτῷ AS, τὰ ἀγαθὰ καὶ εὐάρεστα αὐτῷ καὶ εὐπρόσδεκτα C; § 39 ἄφρονες καὶ ἀσύνετοι κ.τ.λ. AS, where C transposes and omits words; § 43 αὐτὰς AS, αὐτὸς C; § 47 αὐτοῦ [τε] καὶ Κηφᾶ κ.τ.λ., where the order of the names is the same in AS, but different in C; *ib.* μεμαρτυρημένοις...δεδοκιμασμένῳ παρ' αὐτοῖς AS, δεδοκιμασμένοις...μεμαρτυρημένῳ παρ' αὐτῶν C; *ib.* ἀγωγῆς AS, ἀγάπης C; § 51 θεράποντα τοῦ Θεοῦ AS, ἄνθρωπον τοῦ Θεοῦ C; *ib.* Αἰγύπτου AS, αὐτοῦ C; § 53 θεράπων AS, δεσπότης C; § 55 ὑποδείγματα AS, ὑπομνήματα C; § 56 δίκαιος AS, Κύριος C; § 65 καὶ δι' αὐτοῦ AS, δι' αὐτοῦ C. The so-called Second Epistle furnishes the following examples among others: § 1 πηροὶ AS, πονηροὶ C; § 3 καὶ οὐ προσκυνοῦμεν αὐτοῖς AS, om. C; *ib.* ἡ πρὸς αὐτὸν AS, for which C substitutes τῆς ἀληθείας; § 9 πνεῦμα AS, λόγος C (see p. 125); § 10 ἀπόλαυσιν, ἀπόλαυσις AS, ἀνάπαυσιν, ἀνάπαυσις C; § 11 μετὰ ταῦτα AS, εἶτα C.

(ii) On the other hand there are some passages, though comparatively few, in which S agrees with C against A. Examples of these are: § 2 τοῦ Χριστοῦ CS, τοῦ Θεοῦ A; § 3 τῆς καρδίας CS, om. A; § 4 ἄρχοντα καὶ δικαστὴν CS, κριτὴν ἢ δικαστὴν A; § 8 ψυχῆς CS, καρδίας A; § 12 ἡ ἐπιλεγομένη πόρνη CS, ἡ πόρνη A; *ib.* τὴν γῆν CS, τὴν [πό]λιν A; *ib.* ὅτι...καὶ CS, om. A; § 15 διὰ τοῦτο CS, om. A; § 21 σιγῆς CS, φωνῆς A; *ib.* ἀναιρεῖ CS, ἀνελεῖ A; § 22 τὸν δὲ ἐλπίζοντα CS, τοὺς δὲ ἐλ[πίζον]τας A; § 25 ἐγγεννᾶται CS, γεννᾶται A; § 33 προετοιμάσας CS, προδημιουργήσας A; § 34 πιστεύοντας CS, om. A; *ib.* ἃ ὀφθαλμὸς CS, ὀφθαλμὸς A; *ib.* Κύριος CS, om. A; *ib.* ἀγαπῶσιν CS, ὑπομένουσιν A; § 35 διὰ στόματος CS, ἐπὶ στόματος A; § 38 τημελείτω CS, where A has μητμμελειτω; *ib.* the words [ἤτω] καὶ omitted in CS, but found in A; § 40 δέδοται CS, δέδεται A; § 41 εὐαρεστείτω CS, εὐχαριστείτω A; § 51 Αἰγύπτῳ CS, γῇ Αἰγύ[πτου] A; § 56 ἔλαιον CS, ἔλεος (ελαιος) A. In the Second Epistle the examples of importance are very few: e.g. § 8 ποιήσῃ (ποιῇ) σκεῦος ταῖς χερσὶν αὐτοῦ καὶ διαστραφῇ CS, ποιῇ σκεῦος καὶ ἐν ταῖς χερσὶν αὐτοῦ διαστραφῇ A; *ib.* ἀπολάβητε CS, ἀπολάβωμεν A.

Of these readings, in which CS are arrayed together against A, it will be seen that some condemn themselves by their harmonistic tendency (§§ 4, 22, 34, 35); others are suspicious as doctrinal changes (§ 12 ἐπιλεγομένη); others are grammatical emendations of corrupt texts (§ 38), or substitutions of easier for harder expressions (§ 12 ὅτι...καὶ, § 21 ἀναιρεῖ); others are clerical errors, either certainly (§ 40) or probably (§ 41): while in the case of a few others it would be difficult from internal evidence to give the preference to one reading over the other (§§ 25, 33, 51). There are only three places, I think, in the above list, in which it can be said that CS are certainly right against A. In two of these (§§ 3, 34 πιστεύοντας) some words have been accidentally omitted in A; while the third (§ 21 σιγῆς for φωνῆς) admits no such explanation.

(iii) The independence of S, as a witness, will have appeared from the facts already stated. But it will be still more manifest from another class of examples, where S stands alone and either certainly or probably or possibly preserves the right reading, though in some cases at least no ingenuity of the transcriber could have supplied it. Such instances are: § 7 τῷ πατρὶ αὐτοῦ, where C has τῷ πατρὶ αὐτοῦ τῷ Θεῷ, and A apparently τῷ Θεῷ [καὶ πατρ]ὶ αὐτοῦ; § 15, where S supplies the words omitted by homœoteleuton in AC, but in a way which no editor has anticipated; § 18 ἐλαίῳ for ἐλέει (ελαιει), but this is perhaps a scribe's correction; § 22 πολλαὶ αἱ θλίψεις κ.τ.λ. supplied in S, but omitted by AC because two successive sentences begin with the same words: § 35 διὰ πίστεως, where A has πίστεως and C πιστῶς; § 36 εἰς τὸ φῶς, where AC insert θαυμαστὸν [αὐτοῦ] in accordance with 1 Pet. ii. 9; § 43 ὡσαύτως καὶ τὰς θύρας, where AC read ῥάβδους to the injury of the sense, and some editors emend ὡσαύτως ὡς καὶ τὰς ῥάβδους, still leaving a very awkward statement; § 46 πόλεμός (πόλεμοί) τε, where S adds καὶ μάχαι, an addition which the connecting particles seem to suggest, though it may have come from James iv. 1; *ib.* ἕνα τῶν ἐκλεκτῶν μου διαστρέψαι, where AC have ἕνα τῶν μικρῶν μου σκανδαλίσαι, though for reasons which are stated in my notes I cannot doubt that S preserves the original reading; § 48 ἵνα...ἐξομολογήσωμαι, where A has ἐξομολογήσωμαι (without ἵνα) and C ἐξομολογήσομαι; ii § 1 οἱ ἀκούοντες ὡς περὶ μικρῶν [ἁμαρτάνουσιν, καὶ ἡμεῖς] ἁμαρτάνομεν, where the words in brackets are omitted in AC owing to the same cause which has led to the omissions in §§ 15, 22; ii. § 3, where S alone omits ἐνώπιον τῶν ἀνθρώπων and μου, which are probably harmonistic additions in AC; ii § 7 θέωμεν, where AC have the corrupt θῶμεν. These facts show that we must go farther back than the common progenitor of A and C for the archetype of our three authorities.

But beside these independent readings S exhibits other peculiarities, which are not to its credit.

(i) The Greek text, from which the translation was made, must have been disfigured by not a few errors; e.g. § 2 ἑκόντες for ἄκοντες; § 8 εἰπὼν for εἶπον; § 9 τελείους for τελείως; § 11 κρίσιν (?) for κόλασιν; § 14 θεῖον (ΘΕΙΟΝ) for ὅσιον (ΟϹΙΟΝ); § 17 ἀτενίσω (?) for ἀτενίζων; § 20 δικαιώσει for διοικήσει, διὰ for δίχα, ἄνεμοί τε σταθμῶν (?) for ἀνέμων τε σταθμοὶ, συλλήψεις (?) for συνελεύσεις; § 21 θείως (ΘΕΙωϹ) for ὁσίως (ΟϹΙωϹ); § 24 κοιμᾶται νυκτὸς ἀνίσταται ἡμέρας (?) for κοιμᾶται ἡ νὺξ ἀνίσταται ἡ ἡμέρα, ξηρὰν διαλύεται for ξηρὰ καὶ γυμνὰ διαλύεται; § 33 ἐκοιμήθησαν for ἐκοσμήθησαν; § 35 ὑποπίπτοντα for ὑπέπιπτεν (ὑποπίπτει) πάντα, some letters having dropped out; § 36 διὰ τοῦτο for διὰ τούτου several times, θανάτου for τῆς ἀθανάτου (the τῆς having been absorbed in the termination of the preceding δεσπότης); § 37 ὕπαρχοι (?) for ἔπαρχοι; § 39 καθαιρέτης (?) for καθαρός, ἔπεσον αὐτοῦ for ἔπαισεν αὐτοὺς; § 40 ἰδίοις τόποις for ἴδιος[ὁ]τόπος; § 42 κενῶς for καινῶς; § 45 μιαρῶν, ἀδίκων, for μιαρὸν, ἄδικον; § 50 εἰ μὴ add. ἐν ἀγάπῃ from just below; § 51 δὲ ἑαυτῶν omitted, thus blending the two sentences together; § 59 ἀνθρώπων

($\overline{\alpha\nu\omega\nu}$) for ἐθνῶν, εὑρετὴν for εὐεργέτην, ἐπιστράφηθι for ἐπιφάνηθι, ἀσθενεῖς (?) for ἀσεβεῖς; § 60 χρηστὸς for πιστὸς; § 62 ἢ δι' ὧν for ἤδιον, ἔδει μέν for ἤδειμεν; ii. § 2 τὰ πρὸς inserted before τὰς προσευχὰς (ΤΑΠΡΟCΤΑCΠΡΟC-); § 5 παροιμίαν for παροικίαν, ποιῆσαν (?) for ποιήσαντας; § 6 οὗτοι for [οἱ τοι]οῦτοι [δίκαιοι], the letters in brackets having been omitted; § 9 ἦλθε (ἦλθε) for ἐλ[εύσεσ]θε, again by the dropping of some letters; § 10 προδότην for προοδοιπόρον, perhaps owing to a similar mutilation; § 11 πιστεύσωμεν διὰ τὸ δεῖν for δουλεύσωμεν διὰ τοῦ μή; § 16 πατέρα δεχόμενον for παραδεχόμενον ($\overline{\text{ΠΡΑ}}$ for ΠΑΡΑ-); § 17 προσευχόμενοι for προσερχόμενοι (?), εἰδότες for ἰδόντες; § 19 τρυφήσουσιν for τρυγήσουσιν. There are occasionally also omissions, owing to the recurrence of the same sequence of letters, homœoteleuton, etc.: e.g. § 12 καὶ ἐλπίζουσιν (?), § 14 οἱ δὲ παρανομοῦντες κ.τ.λ., § 58 καὶ προστάγματα, § 59 τοὺς ταπεινοὺς ἐλέησον, ii. 6 καὶ φθοράν; but this is not a common form of error in S.

(ii) Again S freely introduces glosses and explanations. These may have been derived from the Greek MS used, or they may have been introduced by the translator himself. They are numerous, and the following will serve as examples: § 10 τοὺς ἀστέρας, add. τοῦ οὐρανοῦ; § 19 τοῦ Θεοῦ for αὐτοῦ, God not having been mentioned before in the same sentence; § 25 τοῦ χρόνου, add. τῆς ζωῆς; *ib.* οἱ ἱερεῖς explained οἱ τῆς Αἰγύπτου; § 42 παραγγελίας οὖν λαβόντες, add. οἱ ἀπόστολοι; § 43 τῶν φυλῶν, add. πασῶν τοῦ Ἰσραήλ; § 44 τὴν ἀνάλυσιν, add. τὴν ἐνθένδε; § 51 φόβου, add. τοῦ Θεοῦ; § 62 τόπον, add. τῆς γραφῆς; § 63 μώμου, add. καὶ σκανδάλου; ii. § 6 ἀνάπαυσιν, add. τὴν ἐκεῖ; *ib.* τὸ βάπτισμα, add. ὃ ἐλάβομεν; § 8 βαλεῖν, expanded by an explanatory gloss; *ib.* ἐξομολογήσασθαι, add. περὶ τῶν ἁμαρτιῶν ἡμῶν; § 9 ἐκάλεσεν, add. ὢν ἐν τῇ σαρκί; § 12 ὑπό τινος, add. τῶν ἀποστόλων; § 13 τὸ ὄνομα, add. τοῦ Κυρίου in one place and τοῦ Χριστοῦ in another; § 14 ἐκ τῆς γραφῆς τῆς λεγούσης, altered into *ex iis de quibus scriptum est*; *ib.* τὰ βιβλία, add. τῶν προφητῶν; *ib.* ὁ Ἰησοῦς ἡμῶν, an explanatory clause added; § 17 ἔσονται, add. ἐν ἀγαλλιάσει; § 19 τὸν ἀναγινώσκοντα ἐν ὑμῖν, add. τὰ λόγια (or τοὺς λόγους) τοῦ Θεοῦ.

(iii) Again: we see the hand of an emender where the original text seemed unsatisfactory or had been already corrupted; e.g. § 14 ἐξεζήτησα τὸν τόπον κ.τ.λ., altered to agree with the LXX; § 16 τῆς μεγαλωσύνης omitted; *ib.* πάντας ἀνθρώπους substituted for τὸ εἶδος τῶν ἀνθρώπων, in accordance with another reading of the LXX; § 17 κακοῦ changed into πονηροῦ πράγματος, in accordance with the LXX; § 20 τὰ substituted for τοὺς...μάζους, the metaphor not being understood by or not pleasing the corrector; § 21 τοῦ φόβου omitted; § 30 Ἁγία substituted for Ἁγίου, the latter not being understood; § 33 κατὰ διάνοιαν omitted for the same reason; § 35 σε omitted, and τὰς ἁμαρτίας σου substituted, in accordance with a more intelligible but false text of the LXX; § 38 the omission of μὴ before τημελείτω, and of [ἤτω] καὶ before μὴ ἀλαζονευέσθω (see above, p. 126); § 40 the omission of ἐπιτελεῖσθαι καὶ (see p. 143); § 44 ἐπὶ δοκιμήν, an emendation of the corrupt ἐπιδομήν; § 45 τῶν μὴ ἀνηκόντων, the insertion of the negative (see the notes); *ib.* the insertion of ἀλλὰ before ὑπὸ παρανόμων and ὑπὸ τῶν μιαρὸν (μιαρῶν) κ.τ.λ., for the sake of symmetry; § 59 the alteration of pronouns and the insertion of words at the beginning of the prayer, so as to mend a mutilated text (see below, p. 143 sq); § 62 the omission of εἰς before ἐνάρετον βίον, and other changes, for the same reason; ii § 3 ἔπειτα δὲ ὅτι substituted for ἀλλὰ, to supply an antithesis to πρῶτον μέν; § 4 ἀγαπᾶν [τοὺς πλησίον ὡς] ἑαυτούς, the words in brackets being inserted because the reciprocal sense of ἑαυτούς was overlooked; § 12 αὐτοῦ for τοῦ Θεοῦ, because τοῦ Θεοῦ has occurred immediately before; § 13 the substitution of ἡμᾶς...λέγομεν for ὑμᾶς...βούλομαι, from not understanding that the words are put into the mouth of God Himself; § 14 the omission of ὅτι, to mend a mutilated text; § 17 the omission of ἐν τῷ Ἰησοῦ owing to its awkwardness.

There are also from time to time other insertions, omissions, and alterations in S, which cannot be classed under any of these heads. The doxologies more especially are tampered with.

In such cases, it is not always easy to say whether the emendation or gloss was due to the Syrian translator himself, or to some earlier Greek transcriber or reader. In one instance at all events the gloss distinctly proceeds from the Syrian translator or a Syrian scribe: § 1, where the Greek word στάσις is adopted with the explanation *hoc autem est tumultus*. This one example suggests that a Syrian hand may have been at work more largely elsewhere.

THE inferences which I draw from the above facts are the following:

(1) In A, C, S, we have three distinct authorities for the text. Each has its characteristic errors, and each preserves the genuine text in some passages, where the other two are corrupt.

(2) The stream must be traced back to a very remote antiquity before we arrive at the common progenitor of our three authorities. This follows from their mutual relations.

(3) Of our three authorities A (if we set aside merely clerical errors, in which it abounds) is by far the most trustworthy. The instances are very rare (probably not one in ten), where it stands alone against the combined force of CS. Even in these instances internal

considerations frequently show that its reading must be accepted notwithstanding.

Its vast superiority is further shown by the entire absence of what I may call *tertiary* readings, while both C and S furnish many examples of these. Such are the following. In § 8 (1) διελεγχθῶμεν, the original reading; (2) [δι]ελεχθῶμεν A, its corruption; (3) διαλεχθῶμεν CS, the corruption emended. In § 15 (1) Ἄλαλα κ.τ.λ. S, the full text; (2) some words omitted owing to homœoteleuton, A; (3) the grammar of the text thus mutilated is patched up in C by substituting γλῶσσα for γλῶσσαν, and making other changes. In § 21 (1) εἰς κρίμα πᾶσιν ἡμῖν A; (2) εἰς κρίματα σὺν ἡμῖν C, an accidental corruption; (3) εἰς κρίματα (or κρίμα) ἡμῖν S, the σὺν being discarded as superfluous. In § 30 (1) Ἁγίου οὖν μερὶς A; (2) Ἁγία οὖν μερὶς S, a corruption or emendation; (3) Ἅγια οὖν μέρη C, a still further corruption or emendation. In § 35 (1) the original reading διὰ πίστεως S; (2) πίστεως A, the preposition being accidentally dropped; (3) the emendation πιστῶς C. In § 38 (1) μὴ ἀτημελείτω, the original reading; (2) μὴ τημελείτω (written apparently μητμμελειτω) A, the α being accidentally dropped; (3) τημελείτω CS, the μὴ being omitted to restore the balance, because the words now gave the opposite sense to that which is required. In § 39 ἔπαισεν αὐτοὺς C, or ἔπεσεν αὐτούς, as by a common itacism it is written in A; (2) ἔπεσεν αὐτοῦ, the final σ being lost in the initial σ of the following σητός; (3) ἔπεσον αὐτοῦ S, a necessary emendation, since a plurality of persons is mentioned in the context. In § 40 (1) ἐπιμελῶς ἐπιτελεῖσθαι καὶ οὐκ εἰκῆ...γίνεσθαι, presumably the original text; (2) ἐπιτελεῖσθαι καὶ οὐκ εἰκῆ...γίνεσθαι AC, the word ἐπιμελῶς being accidentally omitted owing to the similar beginnings of successive words; (3) οὐκ εἰκῆ... γίνεσθαι S, the words ἐπιτελεῖσθαι καὶ being deliberately dropped, because they have now become meaningless. In § 44 (1) the original reading, presumably ἐπιμονήν; (2) the first corruption ἐπινομήν A; (3) the second corruption ἐπιδομήν C; (4) the correction ἐπὶ δοκιμήν S. In § 45 (1) the original reading τῶν μιαρὸν καὶ ἄδικον ζῆλον ἀνειληφότων C; (2) τῶν μιαρῶν καὶ ἄδικον ζῆλον ἀνειληφότων A, an accidental error; (3) τῶν μιαρῶν καὶ ἀδίκων ζῆλον ἀνειληφότων S, where the error is consistently followed up. In § 48 (1) ἵνα εἰσελθὼν...ἐξομολογήσωμαι S with Clem. Alex.; (2) εἰσελθὼν...ἐξομολογήσωμαι A, ἵνα being accidentally dropped; (3) εἰσελθὼν...ἐξομολογήσομαι C, an emendation suggested by the omission. In § 59, where A is wanting, (1) the original text, presumably ὀνόματος αὐτοῦ. [Δὸς ἡμῖν, Κύριε,] ἐλπίζειν ἐπὶ τὸ...ὄνομά σου κ.τ.λ.; (2) the words in brackets are dropped out and the connexion then becomes ἐκάλεσεν ἡμᾶς...εἰς ἐπίγνωσιν δόξης ὀνόματος αὐτοῦ, ἐλπίζειν ἐπὶ τὸ...ὄνομά σου, as in C, where the sudden transition from the third to the second person is not accounted for; (3) this is remedied in S by substituting αὐτοῦ for σου and making similar alterations for several lines, till at length by inserting the words '*we will say*' a transition to the second person is effected. In § 62 in like manner (1) the original text had presumably εἰς ἐνάρετον βίον...διευθύνειν [τὴν πορείαν αὐτῶν]; (2) the words in brackets were omitted, as in C; (3) a still further omission of εἰς was made, in order to supply an objective case to διευθύνειν, as in S. In ii. § 1 (1) ποῖον οὖν C; (2) ποιουν A, a corruption; (3) ποῖον S. In ii. § 14 (1) the original reading, presumably ὅτι τὰ βιβλία...τὴν ἐκκλησίαν οὐ νῦν εἶναι...[λέγουσιν, δῆλον]; (2) the words in brackets are accidentally omitted, as in C; (3) this necessitates further omission and insertion to set the grammar straight, as in S. In some of these examples my interpretation of the facts may be disputed; but the general inference, if I mistake not, is unquestionable.

The scribe of A was no mean penman, but he put no mind into his work. Hence in his case, we are spared that bane of ancient texts, the spurious criticism of transcribers. With the exception of one or two harmonistic changes in quotations, the single instance wearing the appearance of a deliberate alteration, which I have noticed in A, is τῆς φωνῆς for τῆς σιγῆς (§ 21); and even this might have been made almost mechanically, as the words τὸ ἐπιεικὲς τῆς γλώσσης occur immediately before.

(4) Of the two inferior authorities S is much more valuable than C for correcting A. While C alone corrects A in one passage only of any moment (§ 2 μετὰ δέους for μετ' ἐλέους), S alone corrects it in several. In itself S is both better and worse than C. It is made up of two elements, one very ancient and good, the other debased and probably recent; whereas C preserves a fairly uniform standard throughout.

(5) From the fact that A shares both genuine and corrupt readings with C, C with S, and S with A, which are not found in the third authority, it follows that one or more of our three authorities must give a mixed text. It cannot have been derived by simple transcription from the archetype in a direct line, but at some point or other a scribe must have introduced readings of collateral authorities, either from memory or by reference to MSS. This phenomenon we find on the largest scale in the Greek Testament; but, wherever it occurs, it implies a considerable circulation of the writing in question.

(6) We have now materials for restoring the original text of Clement much better than in the case of any ancient Greek author, except the writers of the New Testament. For instance the text of a great

part of Æschylus depends practically on one MS of the 10th or 11th century; i.e. on a single authority dating some fifteen centuries after the tragedies were written. The oldest extant authority for Clement on the other hand was written probably within three centuries and a half after the work itself; and we have besides two other independent authorities preserving more or less of an ancient text. The youngest of these is many centuries nearer to the author's date, than this single authority for the text of Æschylus. Thus the security which this combination gives for the correctness of the ultimate result is incomparably greater than in the example alleged. Where authorities are multiplied, variations will be multiplied also; but it is only so that the final result can be guaranteed.

(7) Looking at the dates and relations of our authorities we may be tolerably sure that, when we have reached their archetype, we have arrived at a text which dates not later, or not much later, than the close of the second century. On the other hand it can hardly have been much earlier. For the phenomena of the text are the same in both epistles; and it follows therefore, that in this archetypal MS the so-called Second Epistle must have been already attached to the genuine Epistle of Clement, though not necessarily ascribed to him.

(8) But, though thus early, it does not follow that this text was in all points correct. Some errors may have crept in already and existed in this archetype, though these would probably not be numerous; e.g. it is allowed that there is something wrong in ii. § 10 οὐκ ἔστιν εὑρεῖν ἄνθρωπον οἵτινες κ.τ.λ. Among such errors I should be disposed to place § 6 Δαναΐδες καὶ Δίρκαι, § 20 κρίματα, § 40 the omission of ἐπιμελῶς before ἐπιτελεῖσθαι, § 44 ἐπινομήν, and perhaps also § 48 the omission of ἤτω γοργὸς (since the passage is twice quoted with these words by Clement of Alexandria), together with a few other passages.

And it would seem also that this text had already undergone slight mutilations. At the end of the First Epistle we find at least three passages where the grammar is defective in C, and seems to require the insertion of some words; § 59 ὀνόματος αὐτοῦ...ἐλπίζειν ἐπὶ τὸ ἀρχέγονον κ.τ.λ., § 60 ἐν πίστει καὶ ἀληθείᾳ...ὑπηκόους γενομένους, § 62 δικαίως διευθύνειν...ἱκανῶς ἐπεστείλαμεν. Bryennios saw, as I think correctly, that in all these places this faulty grammar was due to accidental omissions. Subsequent editors have gone on another tack; they have attempted to justify the grammar, or to set it straight by emendations of individual words. But, to say nothing of the abrupt transitions which still remain in the text so amended, the fresh evidence of S distinctly confirms the view of Bryennios; for it shows that these same omissions occurred in a previous MS from which the text of S was derived, though in S itself the passages have undergone some manipulations. These lacunæ therefore must have existed in the common archetype of C and S. And I think that a highly probable explanation of them can be given. I find that the interval between the omissions § 59, § 60, is 35½ or 36 lines in Gebhardt (37½ in Hilgenfeld), while the interval between the omissions § 60, § 62 is 18 lines in Gebhardt (19 in Hilgenfeld). Thus the one interval is exactly twice the other. This points to the solution. The archetypal MS comprised from 17 to 18 lines of Gebhardt's text in a page. It was slightly frayed or mutilated at the bottom of some pages (though not all) towards the end of the epistle, so that words had disappeared or were illegible. Whether these same omissions occurred also in A, it is impossible to say; but, judging from the general relations of the three authorities and from another lacuna (ii. § 10 οὐκ ἔστιν εὑρεῖν ἄνθρωπον οἵτινες κ.τ.λ.) where the same words or letters are wanting in all alike, we may infer that they did so occur. Other lacunæ (e.g. ii. § 14 ἀλλὰ ἄνωθεν κ.τ.λ.) may perhaps be explained in a similar way.

Whether other *Manuscripts* of these Epistles may not yet be discovered, it is impossible to say. Tischendorf (p. xv) mentions an eager chase after a palimpsest reported to be at Ferrara, which turned out after all to be a copy of the legendary Life of Clement. The unwary may be deceived by seeing 'Clementis Epistolae Duae' entered in the Catalogues of MSS in some of the great libraries of Europe. These are the two spurious Latin Epistles to James. It should be added that a record is preserved of a copy of the Epistles to the Corinthians of a different character from our extant MSS. Photius (*Bibl.* 126; see below, p. 197) found these two Epistles of Clement bound up in one small volume (βιβλιδάριον) with the Epistle of Polycarp to the Philippians.

No other ancient *Version* of the Epistles of Clement is known to have existed besides the Syriac. I cannot find any indications that it was ever translated into Latin before the seventeenth century; and, if so, it must have been a sealed book to the Western Church. This supposition is consistent with all the known facts; for no direct quotation is found from it in any Latin writer who was unacquainted with Greek[1].

[1] A quotation or rather a paraphrastic abridgment of Clement's account of the institution of the ministry (§ 44) is given by one Joannes a Roman deacon, who may have written at the end of the sixth century, with the heading *In Epistola Sancti Clementis ad Corinthios* (*Spicil. Solesm.* I. p. 293). Pitra, the learned editor, suggests (pp. lvii, 293) that this John must have got the quotation from a

Latin translation of the epistle by Paulinus of Nola, adding 'A Paulino Nolano conditam fuisse Clementinam versionem tam Paulinus ipse (*Epist.* xlvi) quam Gennadius (*Catal.* xlviii) diserte testatur.' I do not understand the reference to Gennadius, who says nothing which could be construed into such a statement. The reference in the passage of Paulinus' own letter addressed to Rufinus (*Epist.* xlvi. § 2, p. 275) is obscure. He says that he has no opportunity of getting a more thorough knowledge of Greek, as Rufinus urges him; that, if he saw more of Rufinus, he might learn from him; and that in his translation of S. Clement he had guessed at the sense where he could not understand the words. His commentator Rosweyd supposes that he alludes to the *Recognitions*, and that Rufinus himself afterwards translated them, not being satisfied with his friend's attempt. It seems to me more probable that Paulinus had rendered only an extract or extracts from some Clementine writing for a special purpose; for he calls Greek an 'ignotus sermo' to himself, and with this little knowledge he would hardly have attempted a long translation. Among the extracts so translated may have been this very passage, which is quoted by Joannes in illustration of the narrative in Numbers xvi. But we do not even know whether the Clement meant by Paulinus is the Alexandrian or the Roman, and all speculation must therefore be vague. At all events the loose quotation of a single very prominent passage is not sufficient evidence of the existence of a Latin version.

4.

QUOTATIONS AND REFERENCES.

THE course which was adopted with Ignatius and Polycarp (*Ign. and Polyc.* I. p. 127 sq, p. 536 sq) is followed in the case of Clement also. All references however to the *Homilies* and *Recognitions*, with other writings of the Petro-Clementine cycle, are omitted here, unless they have some special interest as illustrating the traditions respecting Clement. In like manner I have excluded references to the *Apostolic Constitutions*, except when they claimed admission for the same reason. And generally only passages are given which refer either to the two 'Epistles to the Corinthians', or to the character and history of Clement himself.

I.

BARNABAS [C. A.D. ?].

The following resemblances to Clement may be noted in the Epistle bearing the name of Barnabas. In § 1 *βλέπω ἐν ὑμῖν ἐκκεχυμένον ἀπὸ τοῦ πλουσίου τῆς ἀγάπης Κυρίου πνεῦμα ἐφ' ὑμᾶς* the language recalls Clem. 46 *ἓν πνεῦμα τῆς χάριτος τὸ ἐκχυθὲν ἐφ' ὑμᾶς*, but 'the outpouring' of the Holy Spirit is a common expression (e.g. Acts ii. 17, 18, and esp. Tit. iii. 6, after Joel iii. 1). Again the words § 17 *ἐλπίζει μου ὁ νοῦς καὶ ἡ ψυχὴ τῇ ἐπιθυμίᾳ μου μὴ παραλελοιπέναι τι τῶν ἀνηκόντων εἰς σωτηρίαν* resemble Clement's exhortation to his readers (§ 45) to be *ζηλωταὶ περὶ τῶν ἀνηκόντων εἰς σωτηρίαν*, but the expression might have occurred to both writers independently. Again the language used in describing the appearance of the Lord to Moses on the Mount (Exod. xxxii. 7, Deut. ix. 12) by Barnabas §§ 4, 14, closely resembles that of Clement relating to the same occurrence (§ 53), more especially in the reduplication of the name Μωϋσῆ, Μωϋσῆ, which is not found in the O. T. in either account of the event, though it occurs elsewhere (Exod. iii. 4).

These are the most striking of several parallels which Hilgenfeld (*Clem. Rom. Epist.* p. xxiii sq, ed. 2) has collected to prove that Barnabas was acquainted with Clement. The parallels however, though they may suggest a presumption, cannot be considered decisive. The two writers, having occasion to discourse on the same topics, the evil times in which they live, the approaching end of the world, and the attitude of believers at this crisis, and to refer to the same passages in the O. T., would naturally use similar language. Even if the connexion were more firmly established, it would still remain a question whether Barnabas borrowed from Clement or conversely.

2.

IGNATIUS [c. A.D. 110].

Certain resemblances to Clement's language and sentiments may be pointed out; e.g. *Polyc.* 5 εἴ τις δύναται ἐν ἁγνείᾳ μένειν κ.τ.λ. to § 38 ὁ ἁγνὸς ἐν τῇ σαρκὶ [ἤτω] καὶ μὴ ἀλαζονευέσθω, or *Ephes.* 15 ἵνα...δι' ὧν σιγᾷ γινώσκηται to § 21 τὸ ἐπιεικὲς τῆς γλώσσης αὐτῶν διὰ τῆς σιγῆς φανερὸν ποιησάτωσαν, and again *ib.* οὐδὲν λανθάνει τὸν Κύριον ἀλλὰ καὶ τὰ κρυπτὰ ἡμῶν ἐγγὺς αὐτῷ ἐστίν to § 27 πάντα ἐγγὺς αὐτῷ ἐστίν...καὶ οὐδὲν λέληθεν τὴν βουλὴν αὐτοῦ. But more stress should perhaps be laid on the language which Ignatius addresses to the Roman Church (see esp. §§ 3, 4, with the notes, pp. 203, 209), and which seems to be a reference to Clement's Epistle. The evidence however falls far short of demonstration.

3.

POLYCARP [c. A.D. 110].

The following passages furnish ample proof that Clement's Epistle was in the hands of Polycarp.

POLYCARP.	CLEMENT.
Inscr. τῇ ἐκκλησίᾳ τοῦ Θεοῦ τῇ παροικούσῃ Φιλίππους	Inscr. τῇ ἐκκλησίᾳ τοῦ Θεοῦ τῇ παροικούσῃ Κόρινθον
ἔλεος ὑμῖν καὶ εἰρήνη παρὰ Θεοῦ παντοκράτορος καὶ Ἰησοῦ Χριστοῦ τοῦ σωτῆρος ἡμῶν πληθυνθείη	χάρις ὑμῖν καὶ εἰρήνη ἀπὸ παντοκράτορος Θεοῦ διὰ Ἰησοῦ Χριστοῦ πληθυνθείη
§ 1 ἁγιοπρεπέσιν δεσμοῖς	§ 13 ἁγιοπρεπέσι λόγοις
§ 1 τῶν ἀληθῶς ὑπὸ Θεοῦ καὶ τοῦ Κυρίου ἡμῶν ἐκλελεγμένων	§ 50 τοὺς ἐκλελεγμένους ὑπὸ τοῦ Θεοῦ διὰ Ἰησοῦ Χριστοῦ τοῦ Κυρίου ἡμῶν

Polycarp.	Clement.
§ 1 ἡ βεβαία τῆς πίστεως ὑμῶν ῥίζα ἐξ ἀρχαίων καταγγελλομένη χρόνων	§ 1 τίς...τὴν...βεβαίαν ὑμῶν πίστιν οὐκ ἐδοκίμασεν; comp. § 47 τὴν βεβαιοτάτην καὶ ἀρχαίαν Κορινθίων ἐκκλησίαν
§ 1 ἕως θανάτου καταντῆσαι	§ 5 ἕως θανάτου ἤθλησαν, comp. §§ 6, 63, καταντῆσαι ἐπὶ δρόμον (σκοπόν)
§ 2 ἐν φόβῳ καὶ ἀληθείᾳ	§ 19 ἐν φόβῳ καὶ ἀληθείᾳ
§ 2 ἀπολιπόντες κ.τ.λ., see below § 7	
§ 2 μνημονεύοντες δὲ ὧν εἶπεν ὁ Κύριος διδάσκων· μὴ κρίνετε, ἵνα μὴ κριθῆτε· ἀφίετε καὶ ἀφεθήσεται ὑμῖν· ἐλεᾶτε, ἵνα ἐλεηθῆτε· ᾧ μέτρῳ μετρεῖτε, ἀντιμετρηθήσεται ὑμῖν	§ 13 μεμνημένοι τῶν λόγων τοῦ Κυρίου Ἰησοῦ οὓς ἐλάλησεν διδάσκων ἐπιείκειαν καὶ μακροθυμίαν· ἐλεᾶτε ἵνα ἐλεηθῆτε· ἀφίετε, ἵνα ἀφεθῇ ὑμῖν.... ᾧ μέτρῳ μετρεῖτε, ἐν αὐτῷ μετρηθήσεται ὑμῖν
§ 3 τοῦ μακαρίου καὶ ἐνδόξου Παύλου ...ὃς καὶ ἀπὼν ὑμῖν ἔγραψεν ἐπιστολάς, εἰς ἃς κ.τ.λ.	§ 47 ἀναλάβετε τὴν ἐπιστολὴν τοῦ μακαρίου Παύλου τοῦ ἀποστόλου· τί πρῶτον...ἔγραψεν; ἐπ' ἀληθείας πνευματικῶς ἐπέστειλεν ὑμῖν κ.τ.λ.
§ 3 εἰς ἃς ἐὰν ἐγκύπτητε κ.τ.λ.	§ 45 ἐγκεκύφατε εἰς τὰς γραφὰς τὰς ἀληθεῖς, § 53 ἐγκεκύφατε εἰς τὰ λόγια τοῦ Θεοῦ, comp. §§ 40, 62
§ 4 ἔπειτα καὶ τὰς γυναῖκας ὑμῶν ἐν τῇ δοθείσῃ αὐταῖς πίστει καὶ ἀγάπῃ καὶ ἁγνείᾳ, στεργούσας τοὺς ἑαυτῶν ἄνδρας ἐν πάσῃ ἀληθείᾳ,	§ 1 γυναιξίν τε ἐν ἀμώμῳ καὶ σεμνῇ καὶ ἁγνῇ συνειδήσει πάντα ἐπιτελεῖν παρηγγέλλετε, στεργούσας καθηκόντως τοὺς ἄνδρας ἑαυτῶν κ.τ.λ.
καὶ ἀγαπώσας πάντας ἐξ ἴσου ἐν πάσῃ ἐγκρατείᾳ,	§ 21 τὰς γυναῖκας ἡμῶν...διορθωσώμεθα...τὴν ἀγάπην αὐτῶν...πᾶσιν τοῖς φοβουμένοις τὸν Θεὸν ὁσίως ἴσην παρεχέτωσαν
καὶ τὰ τέκνα παιδεύειν τὴν παιδείαν τοῦ φόβου τοῦ Θεοῦ	§ 21 τοὺς νέους παιδεύσωμεν τὴν παιδείαν τοῦ φόβου τοῦ Θεοῦ
§ 4 μακρὰν οὔσας πάσης διαβολῆς, καταλαλιᾶς, κ.τ.λ.	§ 30 ἀπὸ παντὸς ψιθυρισμοῦ καὶ καταλαλιᾶς πόρρω ἑαυτοὺς ποιοῦντες, comp. § 35
§ 4 πάντα μωμοσκοπεῖται,	§ 41 μωμοσκοπηθὲν τὸ προσφερόμενον
καὶ λέληθεν αὐτὸν οὐδὲν οὔτε λογισμῶν οὔτε ἐννοιῶν κ.τ.λ.	§ 21 καὶ ὅτι οὐδὲν λέληθεν αὐτὸν τῶν ἐννοιῶν ἡμῶν οὐδὲ τῶν διαλογισμῶν κ.τ.λ.
§ 5 ᾧ ἐὰν εὐαρεστήσωμεν...ἐὰν πολιτευσώμεθα ἀξίως αὐτοῦ	§ 21 ἐὰν μὴ ἀξίως αὐτοῦ πολιτευόμενοι τὰ καλὰ καὶ εὐάρεστα ἐνώπιον αὐτοῦ ποιῶμεν, comp. § 62 Θεῷ ὁσίως εὐαρεστεῖν
§ 5 ὑποτασσομένους τοῖς πρεσβυτέροις	§ 57 ὑποτάγητε τοῖς πρεσβυτέροις
§ 5 τὰς παρθένους ἐν ἀμώμῳ καὶ ἁγνῇ συνειδήσει περιπατεῖν	§ 1 γυναιξίν τε ἐν ἀμώμῳ καὶ σεμνῇ καὶ ἁγνῇ συνειδήσει πάντα ἐπιτελεῖν

POLYCARP.	CLEMENT.
§ 6 εὔσπλαγχνοι	§§ 29, 54, εὔσπλαγχνος, § 14 εὐσπλαγχνία
§ 6 ἐπισκεπτόμενοι πάντας ἀσθενεῖς, ἐπιστρέφοντες τὰ ἀποπεπλανημένα	§ 59 τοὺς πλανωμένους τοῦ λαοῦ σου ἐπίστρεψον, τοὺς ἀσθενεῖς ἴασαι
§ 6 ἀπεχόμενοι πάσης ὀργῆς, προσωποληψίας	§ 13 ἀποθέμενοι πᾶσαν ἀλαζονείαν...καὶ ὄργας, § 1 ἀπροσωπολήμπτως πάντα ἐποιεῖτε
§ 6 οἱ εὐαγγελισάμενοι ἡμᾶς ἀπόστολοι	§ 42 οἱ ἀπόστολοι ἡμῖν εὐηγγελίσθησαν
§ 6 ζηλωταὶ περὶ τὸ καλόν (on ἀνήκειν εἰς see § 13)	§ 45 ζηλωταὶ περὶ τῶν ἀνηκόντων εἰς σωτηρίαν
§ 7 διὸ ἀπολιπόντες τὴν ματαιότητα τῶν πολλῶν καὶ τὰς ψευδοδιδασκαλίας ἐπὶ τὸν ἐξ ἀρχῆς ἡμῖν παραδοθέντα λόγον ἐπιστρέψωμεν, comp. § 2 διὸ δουλεύσατε τῷ Θεῷ...ἀπολιπόντες τὴν κενὴν ματαιολογίαν κ.τ.λ.	§ 7 διὸ ἀπολίπωμεν τὰς κενὰς καὶ ματαίας φροντίδας καὶ ἔλθωμεν ἐπὶ τὸν εὐκλεῆ καὶ σεμνὸν τῆς παραδόσεως ἡμῶν κανόνα, § 9 διὸ ὑπακούσωμεν...καὶ ἐπιστρέψωμεν ἐπὶ τοὺς οἰκτιρμοὺς αὐτοῦ, ἀπολιπόντες τὴν ματαιοπονίαν, § 19 ἐπαναδράμωμεν ἐπὶ τὸν ἐξ ἀρχῆς παραδεδομένον ὑμῖν τῆς εἰρήνης σκοπόν
§ 7 προσκαρτεροῦντες νηστείαις, δεήσεσιν αἰτούμενοι τὸν παντεπόπτην Θεόν	§ 55 διὰ γὰρ τῆς νηστείας καὶ τῆς ταπεινώσεως αὐτῆς ἠξίωσεν τὸν παντεπόπτην δεσπότην, § 64 ὁ παντεπόπτης Θεός
§ 8 μιμηταὶ οὖν γενώμεθα τῆς ὑπομονῆς αὐτοῦ...τοῦτον γὰρ ἡμῖν τὸν ὑπόγραμμον ἔθηκε δι' ἑαυτοῦ, comp. § 10 'Domini exemplar sequimini'	§ 5 ὑπομονῆς γενόμενος μέγιστος ὑπόγραμμος (Christ himself is called our ὑπόγραμμος in §§ 16, 33)
§ 9 ἣν καὶ εἴδατε κατ' ὀφθαλμοὺς...καὶ ἐν αὐτῷ Παύλῳ καὶ τοῖς λοιποῖς ἀποστόλοις	§ 5 λάβωμεν πρὸ ὀφθαλμῶν ἡμῶν τοὺς ἀγαθοὺς ἀποστόλους
§ 9 οὗτοι πάντες οὐκ εἰς κενὸν ἔδραμον	§ 6 ἐπὶ τὸν τῆς πίστεως βέβαιον δρόμον κατήντησαν
§ 9 εἰς τὸν ὀφειλόμενον αὐτοῖς τόπον εἰσὶ παρὰ τῷ Κυρίῳ	§ 5 ἐπορεύθη εἰς τὸν ὀφειλόμενον τόπον τῆς δόξης
§ 10 fraternitatis amatores	§§ 47, 48, φιλαδελφία
§ 10 Omnes vobis invicem subjecti estote (see the note)	§ 38 ὑποτασσέσθω ἕκαστος τῷ πλησίον αὐτοῦ
§ 10 Dominus in vobis non blasphemetur. *Vae* autem *per quem nomen Domini blasphematur*	§ 47 ὥστε καὶ βλασφημίας ἐπιφέρεσθαι τῷ ὀνόματι Κυρίου διὰ τὴν ὑμετέραν ἀφροσύνην, ἑαυτοῖς δὲ κίνδυνον ἐπεξεργάζεσθαι, comp. § 1
§ 11 qui estis in principio epistulae ejus	§ 47 τί πρῶτον ὑμῖν ἐν ἀρχῇ τοῦ εὐαγγελίου ἔγραψεν;
§ 11 ut omnium vestrum corpus salvetis	§§ 37, 38, εἰς τὸ σώζεσθαι ὅλον τὸ σῶμα, Σωζέσθω οὖν ἡμῶν ὅλον τὸ σῶμα
§ 12 Confido enim vos bene exerci-	§ 62 σαφῶς ᾔδειμεν γράφειν ἡμᾶς

POLYCARP.	CLEMENT.
tatos esse in sacris literis	ἀνδράσι...ἐγκεκυφόσιν εἰς τὰ λόγια κ.τ.λ. (comp. § 53 καλῶς ἐπίστασθε τὰς ἱερὰς γραφὰς κ.τ.λ.)
§ 12 ipse sempiternus pontifex	§§ 36, 61, 64, Jesus Christ is called ἀρχιερεύς
§ 12 aedificet vos in fide et veritate, et in omni mansuetudine et sine iracundia et in patientia et in longanimitate et tolerantia et castitate,	§ 62 περὶ γὰρ πίστεως καὶ μετανοίας καὶ γνησίας ἀγάπης καὶ ἐγκρατείας καὶ σωφροσύνης καὶ ὑπομονῆς πάντα τόπον ἐψηλαφήσαμεν, ὑπομιμνήσκοντες δεῖν ὑμᾶς ἐν δικαιοσύνῃ καὶ ἀληθείᾳ καὶ μακροθυμίᾳ κ.τ.λ.
et det vobis sortem et partem inter sanctos suos et nobis vobiscum, et omnibus qui sunt sub caelo,	§ 59 αἰτησόμεθα...ὅπως τὸν ἀριθμὸν τὸν κατηριθμημένον τῶν ἐκλεκτῶν αὐτοῦ ἐν ὅλῳ τῷ κόσμῳ διαφυλάξῃ ἄθραυστον κ.τ.λ., § 65 ἡ χάρις...μεθ' ὑμῶν καὶ μετὰ πάντων πανταχῇ τῶν κεκλημένων ὑπὸ τοῦ Θεοῦ δι' αὐτοῦ, comp. §§ 42, 58
qui credituri sunt	§ 42 τῶν μελλόντων πιστεύειν.
§ 14 Haec vobis scripsi per Crescentem, quem in praesenti commendavi vobis et commendo, conversatus est enim nobiscum inculpabiliter.	§ 63 ἐπέμψαμεν δὲ ἄνδρας πιστοὺς καὶ σώφρονας, ἀπὸ νεότητος ἀναστραφέντας ἕως γήρους ἀμέμπτως ἐν ἡμῖν.

In compiling this table of parallel passages I have made great use of those drawn up by previous writers, Hefele, Zahn, Funk, and Harnack, more especially the last mentioned.

4.

HERMAS [c. A.D. ?].

Visio ii. 4. 3.

Γράψεις οὖν δύο βιβλιδάρια [v. l. βιβλαρίδια] καὶ πέμψεις ἓν Κλήμεντι καὶ ἓν Γραπτῇ. πέμψει οὖν Κλήμης εἰς τὰς ἔξω πόλεις, ἐκείνῳ γὰρ ἐπιτέτραπται· Γραπτὴ δὲ νουθετήσει τὰς χήρας καὶ τοὺς ὀρφανούς· σὺ δὲ ἀναγνώσῃ εἰς ταύτην τὴν πόλιν μετὰ τῶν πρεσβυτέρων τῶν προϊσταμένων τῆς ἐκκλησίας.

See also the notes on §§ 11, 21, 23, 39, 46, 56, 60, where we seem to discern echoes, though somewhat faint, of Clement's language. In the notes on the so-called 'Second Epistle,' §§ 1, 7, 9, 14, will be found some resemblances to this Clementine writing in Hermas, but here it may be a question to which author the priority must be assigned.

5.

SECOND CLEMENTINE EPISTLE [C. A.D. ?].

See the notes on §§ 15, 34, of the First Epistle and on § 11 of the Second.

6.

JUSTIN MARTYR [C. A.D. 150].

In *Dial.* 56 (p. 274) Justin uses the same combination of epithets as Clement (§ 43) in speaking of Moses, ὁ μακάριος [καὶ] πιστὸς θεράπων: and in *Dial.* 111 (p. 338) he in like manner with Clement (§ 12) uses Rahab's scarlet thread as a symbol of the blood of Christ. These resemblances suggest a presumption of acquaintance with Clement's Epistle, but not more.

7.

LETTER OF THE SMYRNÆANS [C. A.D. 156].

The obligations of the writers of this letter, giving an account of Polycarp's martyrdom, are best seen by comparing its beginning and end with the corresponding parts of Clement's Epistle, as I have done elsewhere (*Ign. and Polyc.* I. p. 610 sq).

8.

HEGESIPPUS [C. A.D. 170].

(i) Euseb. *H. E.* iv. 22.

Ὁ μὲν οὖν Ἡγήσιππος ἐν πέντε τοῖς εἰς ἡμᾶς ἐλθοῦσιν ὑπομνήμασι τῆς ἰδίας γνώμης πληρεστάτην μνήμην καταλέλοιπεν, ἐν οἷς δηλοῖ ὡς πλείστοις ἐπισκόποις συμμίξειεν, ἀποδημίαν στειλάμενος μέχρι Ῥώμης, καὶ ὡς ὅτι τὴν αὐτὴν παρὰ πάντων παρείληφε διδασκαλίαν. ἀκοῦσαί γέ τοι πάρεστι μετά τινα περὶ τῆς Κλήμεντος πρὸς Κορινθίους ἐπιστολῆς αὐτῷ εἰρημένα ἐπιλέγοντος ταῦτα·

καὶ ἐπέμενεν ἡ ἐκκλησία ἡ Κορινθίων ἐν τῷ ὀρθῷ λόγῳ μέχρι Πρίμου ἐπισκοπεύοντος ἐν Κορίνθῳ· οἷς συνέμιξα πλέων εἰς Ῥώμην, καὶ συνδιέτριψα τοῖς Κορινθίοις ἡμέρας ἱκανάς, ἐν αἷς συνανεπάημεν τῷ ὀρθῷ λόγῳ. γενόμενος δὲ ἐν Ῥώμῃ διαδοχὴν ἐποιησάμην μέχρις Ἀνικήτου, οὗ διάκονος ἦν Ἐλεύθερος· καὶ παρὰ Ἀνικήτου διαδέχεται Σωτήρ, μεθ᾽ ὃν Ἐλεύθερος. ἐν ἑκάστῃ δὲ διαδοχῇ καὶ ἐν ἑκάστῃ πόλει οὕτως ἔχει ὡς ὁ νόμος κηρύσσει καὶ οἱ προφῆται καὶ ὁ Κύριος.

I have had no misgiving in retaining the reading διαδοχήν; for (1) It alone has any authority, being read not only by all the Greek MSS, but by the very ancient and perhaps coeval Syriac Version (see Smith and Wace *Dict. of Christ. Ant.*, s. v. Eusebius, II. p. 326). On the other hand διατριβήν is not found in a single MS. It is a pure conjecture of Savile founded upon Rufinus. But the general looseness of Rufinus deprives his version of any critical weight, and his rendering of this very passage shows that he either misunderstands or despises the Greek, 'Cum autem venissem Romam permansi inibi donec Aniceto Soter et Soteri successit Eleutherus,' where not only this list of succession but all mention of the diaconate of Eleutherus has likewise disappeared. In the next sentence again he translates ἐν ἑκάστῃ διαδοχῇ 'in omnibus istis ordinationibus,' thus showing that he entirely misapprehends the gist of the passage. There is no adequate reason therefore for supposing that Rufinus read διατριβήν. (2) It is quite clear that Eusebius himself did not read διατριβήν, for he says elsewhere (iv. 11) that Hegesippus visited Rome in the time of Anicetus and remained there till the time of Eleutherus. (3) The context requires διαδοχὴν ἐποιησάμην, 'I drew up a list of (the episcopal) succession.' He says that originally his list had ended with the then bishop Anicetus, and accordingly he now supplements it with the names of the two bishops next in order, Soter and Eleutherus, thus bringing it down to the time when he writes these 'Memoirs.' It is therefore with some surprise that I find Harnack (Clem. Rom. *Prol.* p. xxviii, ed. 2) adopting διατριβὴν confidently and declaring that 'ne levissima quidem dubitatio relicta est.'

(ii) Euseb. *H. E.* iii. 16.

Καὶ ὅτι γε κατὰ τὸν δηλούμενον τὰ τῆς Κορινθίων κεκίνητο στάσεως, ἀξιόχρεως μάρτυς ὁ Ἡγήσιππος.

This statement is considered below, p. 165.

9.

DIONYSIUS OF CORINTH [c. A.D. 170].

Epist. ad Rom. (Euseb. *Hist. Eccl.* iv. 23).

Ἔτι τοῦ Διονυσίου καὶ πρὸς Ῥωμαίους ἐπιστολὴ φέρεται, ἐπισκόπῳ τῷ τότε Σωτῆρι προσφωνοῦσα. ἐξ ἧς οὐδὲν οἷον τὸ καὶ παραθέσθαι λέξεις, δι' ὧν τὸ μέχρι τοῦ καθ' ἡμᾶς διωγμοῦ φυλαχθὲν Ῥωμαίων ἔθος ἀποδεχόμενος ταῦτα γράφει·

ἐξ ἀρχῆς γὰρ ὑμῖν ἔθος ἐστὶ τοῦτο, πάντας μὲν ἀδελφοὺς ποικίλως εὐεργετεῖν, ἐκκλησίαις τε πολλαῖς ταῖς κατὰ πᾶσαν πόλιν ἐφόδια πέμπειν, ὧδε μὲν τὴν τῶν δεομένων πενίαν ἀναψύχοντας, ἐν μετάλλοις δὲ ἀδελφοῖς ὑπάρχουσιν ἐπιχορηγοῦντας· δι' ὧν πέμπετε ἀρχῆθεν ἐφοδίων, πατροπαράδοτον ἔθος Ῥωμαίων Ῥωμαῖοι διαφυλάττοντες, ὃ οὐ μόνον διατετήρηκεν ὁ μακάριος ὑμῶν ἐπίσκοπος Σωτήρ, ἀλλὰ καὶ ἐπηύξηκεν, ἐπιχορηγῶν μὲν τὴν διαπεμπομένην δαψίλειαν τὴν εἰς τοὺς ἁγίους, λόγοις δὲ μακαρίοις τοὺς ανιόντας ὡς τέκνα πατὴρ φιλόστοργος παρακαλῶν.

ἐν αὐτῇ δὲ ταύτῃ καὶ τῆς Κλήμεντος πρὸς Κορινθίους μέμνηται ἐπιστολῆς, δηλῶν ἀνέκαθεν ἐξ ἀρχαίου ἔθους ἐπὶ τῆς ἐκκλησίας τὴν ἀνάγνωσιν αὐτῆς ποιεῖσθαι. λέγει γοῦν·

τὴν σήμερον οὖν κυριακὴν ἁγίαν ἡμέραν διηγάγομεν, ἐν ᾗ ἀνέγνωμεν ὑμῶν τὴν ἐπιστολήν· ἣν ἕξομεν ἀεί ποτε ἀναγινώσκοντες νουθετεῖσθαι, ὡς καὶ τὴν προτέραν ἡμῖν διὰ Κλήμεντος γραφεῖσαν.

This letter was written in the lifetime of Soter, as appears not only from the expression of Eusebius *τῷ τότε*, but also from the perfect tenses of Dionysius himself, *διατετήρηκεν*, *ἐπηύξηκεν*. The epithet *μακάριος* in these times is frequently used of living persons; see the note on Clem. Rom. 47. The episcopate of Soter extends from about A.D. 166—174.

10.

THEOPHILUS OF ANTIOCH [C. A.D. 180].

The passage, *ad Autol.* i. 13, on the resurrection of the dead, may have been suggested by Clem. Rom. 23, 24; but no stress can be laid on the resemblances. See also the note on § 7, with the reference to *ad Autol.* iii. 19.

A resemblance to the Second Epistle (see the note on § 8) appears in *ad Autol.* ii. 26.

II.

IRENÆUS [C. A.D. 180].

Adv. Haereses iii. 3. 3.

Θεμελιώσαντες οὖν καὶ οἰκοδομήσαντες οἱ μακάριοι ἀπόστολοι τὴν ἐκκλησίαν, Λίνῳ τὴν τῆς ἐπισκοπῆς λειτουργίαν ἐνεχείρισαν. τούτου τοῦ Λίνου Παῦλος ἐν ταῖς πρὸς Τιμόθεον ἐπιστολαῖς μέμνηται. διαδέχεται δὲ αὐτὸν Ἀνέγκλητος. μετὰ τοῦτον δὲ τρίτῳ τόπῳ ἀπὸ τῶν ἀποστόλων τὴν ἐπισκοπὴν κληροῦται Κλήμης, ὁ καὶ ἑωρακὼς τοὺς μακαρίους ἀποστόλους καὶ συμβεβληκὼς αὐτοῖς, καὶ ἔτι ἔναυλον τὸ κήρυγμα τῶν ἀποστόλων καὶ τὴν παράδοσιν πρὸ ὀφθαλμῶν ἔχων, οὐ μόνος· ἔτι γὰρ πολλοὶ ὑπελείποντο τότε ὑπὸ τῶν ἀποστόλων δεδιδαγμένοι.

Ἐπὶ τούτου οὖν τοῦ Κλήμεντος στάσεως οὐκ ὀλίγης τοῖς ἐν Κορίνθῳ γενομένης ἀδελφοῖς ἐπέστειλεν ἡ ἐν Ῥώμῃ ἐκκλησία ἱκανωτάτην γραφὴν τοῖς Κορινθίοις, εἰς εἰρήνην συμβιβάζουσα αὐτούς, καὶ ἀνανεοῦσα τὴν πίστιν αὐτῶν, καὶ ἣν νεωστὶ ἀπὸ τῶν ἀποστόλων παράδοσιν εἰλήφει,

Fundantes igitur et instruentes beati apostoli ecclesiam Lino episcopatum administrandae ecclesiae tradiderunt. Hujus Lini Paulus in his quae sunt ad Timotheum epistolis meminit. Succedit autem ei Anacletus; post eum tertio loco ab apostolis episcopatum sortitur Clemens, qui et vidit ipsos apostolos et contulit cum eis, et quum adhuc insonantem praedicationem apostolorum et traditionem ante oculos haberet, non solus; adhuc enim multi supererant tunc ab apostolis docti.

Sub hoc igitur Clemente, dissensione non modica inter eos, qui Corinthi essent, fratres facta, scripsit quae est Romae ecclesia potentissimas litteras Corinthiis, ad pacem eos congregans et reparans fidem eorum et annuntians quam in recenti ab apostolis acceperat traditionem, annuntiantem unum Deum omnipotentem, factorem caeli et terrae, plasmatorem hominis, qui induxerit cataclysmum et advocaverit Abraham, qui eduxerit populum de terra Aegypti, qui collocutus sit Moysi, qui legem disposuerit et prophetas miserit, qui ignem praeparaverit diabolo et angelis ejus. Hunc patrem Domini nostri Jesu Christi ab ecclesiis annuntiari ex ipsa scriptura, qui velint, discere possunt, et apostolicam ecclesiae traditionem intelligere; quum sit vetustior epistola his qui nunc falso docent, et alterum Deum super Demiurgum et factorem horum omnium, quae sunt, commentiuntur.

τὸν δὲ Κλήμεντα τοῦτον διαδέχεται Εὐάρεστος.	Huic autem Clementi succedit Evaristus.

In the expression, ἀδελφοῖς ἐπέστειλεν...ἱκανωτάτην γραφὴν, Irenæus echoes the words of Clement himself, § 62 ἱκανῶς ἐπεστείλαμεν ὑμῖν, ἄνδρες ἀδελφοί.

Immediately before this passage Irenæus has spoken of 'maximae et antiquissimae et omnibus cognitae, a gloriosissimis duobus apostolis Petro et Paulo Romae fundatae et constitutae ecclesiae' (iii. 3. 2).

The Greek portions are preserved by Eusebius *H. E.* v. 6.

12.

CLEMENTINE HOMILIES AND RECOGNITIONS [c. A.D.?].

The writings of the Petro-Clementine cycle cannot be dated earlier than the latter half of the second century. The story which they tell, though a pure fiction in itself, became the source of a powerful and wide-spread tradition respecting Clement. As Clement is a chief actor in these writings and they are full of references to him, it would be impossible to give all the passages at length, as I have done in most other cases. The whole subject will be more fitly discussed elsewhere. I would only call attention to two main points in this Petro-Clementine story, as bearing directly on the critical investigations which have already engaged our attention and will occupy us again—the one affecting the natural, the other the spiritual parentage, of the hero, but both alike contradicting the notices of a more authentic tradition or the probable results of critical investigation.

(i) Clement is represented as a scion of the imperial family. His father, who bears the name Faustus in the *Homilies* and Faustinianus in the *Recognitions*, is a near relative of the emperor (*Hom.* xii. 8, xiv. 6, 10, *Recogn.* vii. 8, ix. 35). His mother Mattidia likewise is apparently represented as connected by blood with the emperor (*Hom.* xii. 8, but see *Recogn.* ix. 35). His two brothers are named, the one Faustinus, the other Faustinianus in the *Homilies* and Faustus in the *Recognitions*. It will thus be seen that the names are borrowed from the imperial families of Hadrian and the Antonines; though Clement is represented as a young man at the time of the crucifixion, and the emperor spoken of as his father's kinsman is therefore Tiberius.

(ii) Not only is Clement a direct disciple and constant follower of S. Peter so that he faithfully represents his teaching, but he is consecrated to the Roman episcopate directly by him. Thus Clement becomes to all intents and purposes his spiritual heir. This fact is emphasized and amplified in the 'Letter of Clement to James,' prefixed to the *Homilies*; in which Clement gives an account of S. Peter's last charge and of his own appointment and consecration as the Apostle's immediate successor.

These fictions are a striking testimony to the space occupied by Clement's personality in the early Church; but beyond this the indications of the use of Clement's genuine epistle are only slight. The language however, which is used of S. Peter in *Epist. Clem.* 1, seems certainly to be suggested by the description of S. Paul in the genuine Clement (§ 5, see the note on the passage); and the same chapter of this epistle (§ 5 τοὺς ἀγαθοὺς ἀποστόλους· Πέτρον ὃς κ.τ.λ.) furnishes an epithet which the Clementine romance (*Hom.* i. 16 ὁ ἀγαθὸς Πέτρος) applies to S. Peter. In the main body of the *Homilies* again there are passages which recall the genuine Epistle to the Corinthians: e.g. the description of the marvels of creation (*Hom.* iii. 35), which has several points of resemblance with the corresponding panegyric in Clem. Rom. 20, and the lesson derived from the different gradations in the Roman military and civil government (*Hom.* x. 14), which likewise has its counterpart in Clem. Rom. 37.

13.

Clement of Alexandria [c. A.D. 200].

(i) *Strom.* i. 7. 38 (p. 339).

Πολλῶν τοίνυν ἀνεῳγμένων πυλῶν ἐν δικαιοσύνῃ, αὕτη ἦν ἐν Χριστῷ, ἐν ᾗ μακάριοι πάντες οἱ εἰσελθόντες καὶ κατευθύνοντες τὴν πορείαν αὐτῶν ἐν ὁσιότητι *γνωστικῇ*. αὐτίκα ὁ Κλήμης ἐν τῇ πρὸς Κορινθίους ἐπιστολῇ κατὰ λέξιν φησὶ τὰς διαφορὰς ἐκτιθέμενος τῶν κατὰ τὴν ἐκκλησίαν δοκίμων· ἤτω τις πιστός, ἤτω δυνατός τις γνῶσιν ἐξειπεῖν, ἤτω σοφὸς ἐν διακρίσει λόγων, ἤτω γοργὸς ἐν ἔργοις (Clem. Rom. § 48).

(ii) *Strom.* iv. 6. 32, 33 (p. 577 sq).

Εἶδον γάρ, φησί, τὸν ἀσεβῆ ὑπερυψούμενον κ.τ.λ....οὐκ ἐπαιρομένων ἐπὶ τὸ ποίμνιον αὐτοῦ.

Use is here made of Clem. Rom. 14, 15, 16, though no obligation is acknowledged.

(iii) *Strom.* iv. 17—19. 105—121 (p. 609 sq).

Ναὶ μὴν ἐν τῇ πρὸς Κορινθίους ἐπιστολῇ ὁ ἀπόστολος Κλήμης καὶ αὐτὸς ἡμῖν τύπον τινὰ τοῦ γνωστικοῦ ὑπογράφων λέγει· τίς γὰρ παρεπιδημήσας πρὸς ὑμᾶς κ.τ.λ. (Clem. Rom. § 1).

In the passage which follows, Clement of Alexandria sometimes quotes *verbatim* from his namesake and sometimes abridges the matter. The passages in the Roman Clement of which he thus avails himself range over a great part of the epistle (§§ 1, 9, 17, 21, 22, 36, 38, 40, 41, 48, 49, 50, 51). Twice again he names his authority.

iv. 17. 112 (p. 613) ὅτι ὃ ἐν τῇ πρὸς Κορινθίους ἐπιστολῇ γέγραπται, διὰ Ἰησοῦ Χριστοῦ ἡ ἀσύνετος καὶ ἐσκοτισμένη διάνοια ἡμῶν ἀναθάλλει εἰς τὸ φῶς (Clem. Rom. § 36).

iv. 18. 113 (p. 613) ἡ σεμνὴ οὖν τῆς φιλανθρωπίας ἡμῶν καὶ ἁγνὴ ἀγωγὴ κατὰ τὸν Κλήμεντα τὸ κοινωφελὲς ζητεῖ (Clem. Rom. § 48).

(iv) *Strom.* v. 12. 81 (p. 693).

Ἀλλὰ κἂν τῇ πρὸς Κορινθίους Ῥωμαίων ἐπιστολῇ ὠκεανὸς ἀπέραντος ἀνθρώποις γέγραπται καὶ οἱ μετ᾽ αὐτὸν κόσμοι (Clem. Rom. § 20).

(v) *Strom.* vi. 8. 64 (p. 772).

Ἐξηγούμενος δὲ τὸ ῥητὸν τοῦ προφήτου Βαρνάβας ἐπιφέρει· πολλῶν πυλῶν ἀνεῳγυιῶν ἡ ἐν δικαιοσύνῃ αὕτη ἐστὶν ἡ ἐν Χριστῷ, ἐν ᾗ μακάριοι πάντες οἱ εἰσελθόντες (Clem. Rom. 48).

He wrongly attributes the words to Barnabas, though in a passage quoted above (*Strom.* i. 7. 38) he has correctly ascribed them to Clement. For a similar blunder see Hieron. *Adv. Pelag.* iii. 2 (*Op.* II. p. 783), where Jerome ascribes some words of Barnabas to Ignatius.

He continues the quotation a little lower down;

vi. 8. 65 (p. 777 sq) ἔστω τοίνυν πιστὸς ὁ τοιοῦτος, ἔστω δυνατὸς γνῶσιν ἐξειπεῖν, ἤτω σοφὸς ἐν διακρίσει λόγων, ἤτω γοργὸς ἐν ἔργοις, ἤτω ἁγνός. τοσούτῳ γὰρ μᾶλλον ταπεινοφρονεῖν ὀφείλει, ὅσῳ δοκεῖ μᾶλλον μείζων εἶναι, ὁ Κλήμης ἐν τῇ πρὸς Κορινθίους φησί (Clem. Rom. 48).

Other passages likewise in the Alexandrian Clement seem to betray the influence of his Roman namesake. Thus in the form and connexion of the quotations (Matt. xxvi. 24, xviii. 6) in *Strom.* iii. 18. 107 (p. 561) there is a close resemblance to Clem. Rom. 46 (see the note on the passage). Again *Strom.* iv. 22. 137 (p. 625) has a conflate quotation which must be attributed to Clem. Rom. 34 (see the note), while immediately below we meet with the same quotation ἃ ὀφθαλμὸς οὐκ εἶδεν κ.τ.λ. (though quoted more closely after S. Paul, 1 Cor. ii. 9) which appears in this same chapter (34) of the Roman Clement.

14.

Tertullian [c. A.D. 200].

De Praescr. Haeret. 32.

Hoc enim modo ecclesiae apostolicae census suos deferunt, sicut... Romanorum [ecclesia] Clementem a Petro ordinatum [refert].

The passage *de Resurr. Carn.* 12, 13, is a parallel to Clem. Rom. 24, 25, in the order of the argument and in the mention of the phœnix, though the subject is worked up with a fresh vigour and eloquence characteristic of Tertullian. The obligation however, though probable, is not certain. In *de Virg. Vel.* 13 'si adeo confertur continentiae virtus, quid gloriaris', there is a parallel to Clem. Rom. 38.

15.

Clementine Epistles to Virgins [c. A.D. ?].

These forgeries were doubtless instigated by the fame of Clement's genuine Epistle; but they show only very slight traces of its influence. The faint resemblances which have been discerned will be found in Beelen's Proleg. p. lx sq to his edition. In the heading of the epistle the MS describes Clement as 'disciple of Peter the Apostle.'

16.

HIPPOLYTUS [c. A.D. 210—230].

For a somewhat striking resemblance in thought and diction to the Second Clementine Epistle in a passage ascribed to this writer see the notes on §§ 17, 19, of that epistle.

17.

ORIGENES [† A.D. 253].

(i) *de Princip.* ii. 3. 6 (*Op.* I. p. 82).

Meminit sane Clemens apostolorum discipulus etiam eorum quos ἀντίχθονας Graeci nominarunt, atque alias partes orbis terrae ad quas neque nostrorum quisquam accedere potest neque ex illis qui ibi sunt quisquam transire ad nos; quos et ipsos mundos appellavit, cum ait, *Oceanus intransmeabilis est hominibus, et hi qui trans ipsum sunt mundi, qui his eisdem dominatoris Dei dispositionibus gubernantur* (Clem. Rom. 20).

This treatise of Origen is only extant in a translation of Rufinus.

(ii) *Select. in Ezech.* viii. 3 (*Op.* III. p. 422).

Φησὶ δὲ καὶ ὁ Κλήμης, ὠκεανὸς ἀπέρατος ἀνθρώποις καὶ οἱ μετ' αὐτὸν κόσμοι τοσαύταις διαταγαῖς τοῦ δεσπότου διοικοῦνται.

(iii) *In Joann.* vi. § 36 (*Op.* IV. p. 153).

Μεμαρτύρηται δὲ καὶ παρὰ τοῖς ἔθνεσιν, ὅτι πολλοί τινες λοιμικῶν ἐνσκηψάντων ἐν ταῖς ἑαυτῶν πατρίσι νοσημάτων ἑαυτοὺς σφάγια ὑπὲρ τοῦ κοινοῦ παραδεδώκασι. καὶ παραδέχεται ταῦθ' οὕτως γεγονέναι οὐκ ἀλόγως πιστεύσας ταῖς ἱστορίαις ὁ πιστὸς Κλήμης ὑπὸ Παύλου μαρτυρούμενος λέγοντος· μετὰ Κλήμεντος καὶ τῶν λοιπῶν συνεργῶν μου, ὧν τὰ ὀνόματα ἐν βίβλῳ ζωῆς.

(iv) *Hom. in Hebr.* (Euseb. *H. E.* vi. 25).

Τίς δὲ ὁ γράψας τὴν ἐπιστολὴν [τὴν πρὸς Ἑβραίους] τὸ μὲν ἀληθὲς Θεὸς οἶδεν, ἡ δὲ εἰς ἡμᾶς φθάσασα ἱστορία ὑπό τινων μὲν λεγόντων ὅτι Κλήμης ὁ γενόμενος ἐπίσκοπος Ῥωμαίων ἔγραψε τὴν ἐπιστολήν, ὑπό τινων δὲ ὅτι Λουκᾶς κ.τ.λ.

It is probable also that in other passages, as in the interpretation of the scarlet thread of Rahab (*In Jes. Hom.* iii. § 5, *Op.* II. p. 405; comp. Clem. Rom. 12) and in the allusion to the story of the phœnix (*c. Cels.* iv. 98, *Op.* I. p. 576; comp. Clem. Rom. 25) he may have had the language and thoughts of Clement in his mind.

18.

Dionysius of Alexandria [c. a.d. 260].

Epist. ad Hierac. (Euseb. *H. E.* vii. 21).

ὁ πολὺς καὶ ἀπέραντος ἀνθρώποις ὠκεανός, an expression borrowed from our Clement (§ 20); but he may have got it from Origen who in his extant works twice quotes the passage.

19.

Apostolical Constitutions [a.d. ?].

(i) vi. 8. 3.

Ὁ μέντοι Σίμων ἐμοὶ Πέτρῳ πρῶτον ἐν Καισαρείᾳ τῇ Στράτωνος, ἔνθα Κορνήλιος ὁ πιστὸς ἐπιστεύσεν ὢν ἐθνικὸς ἐπὶ τὸν Κύριον Ἰησοῦν δι' ἐμοῦ, συντυχών μοι ἐπειρᾶτο διαστρέφειν τὸν λόγον τοῦ Θεοῦ, συμπαρόντων μοι τῶν ἱερῶν τέκνων, Ζακχαίου τοῦ ποτε τελώνου καὶ Βαρνάβα, καὶ Νικήτου καὶ Ἀκύλα ἀδελφῶν Κλήμεντος τοῦ Ῥωμαίων ἐπισκόπου τε καὶ πολίτου, μαθητευθέντος δὲ καὶ Παύλῳ τῷ συναποστόλῳ ἡμῶν καὶ συνεργῷ ἐν τῷ εὐαγγελίῳ.

The allusions to Zacchæus and Barnabas, and to Clement's brothers Nicetes and Aquila, are explained by the story in the *Homilies* and *Recognitions.*

(ii) vi. 18. 5.

Καὶ ταῦτα κατὰ πόλιν πανταχοῦ εἰς ὅλην τὴν οἰκουμένην τοῦ κόσμου πεποιήκαμεν, καταλιπόντες ὑμῖν τοῖς ἐπισκόποις καὶ λοιποῖς ἱερεῦσι τήνδε τὴν καθολικὴν διδασκαλίαν...διαπεμψάμενοι διὰ τοῦ συλλειτουργοῦ ἡμῶν Κλήμεντος τοῦ πιστοτάτου καὶ ὁμοψύχου τέκνου ἡμῶν ἐν Κυρίῳ, ἅμα καὶ Βαρνάβᾳ καὶ Τιμοθέῳ κ.τ.λ.

(iii) vii. 46. 1.

Τῆς δὲ Ῥωμαίων ἐκκλησίας Λίνος μὲν ὁ Κλαυδίας πρῶτος ὑπὸ Παύλου, Κλήμης δὲ μετὰ τὸν Λίνου θάνατον ὑπ' ἐμοῦ Πέτρου δεύτερος κεχειροτόνηται [ἐπίσκοπος].

The name is generally accentuated Λῖνος by patristic editors, but this is clearly wrong. His namesake, the mythical poet and son of Apollo, always has the first syllable short in Greek and in Latin. Moreover the Pseudo-Tertullian (see below, p. 176) so scans the name of the pope. I have therefore written it Λίνος with the chief recent editors of the Greek Testament (Lachmann, Tischendorf, Westcott and Hort, but not Tregelles) in 2 Tim. iv. 21.

(iv) viii. 10. 2.

Ὑπὲρ τοῦ ἐπισκόπου ἡμῶν Κλήμεντος καὶ τῶν παροικιῶν αὐτοῦ δεηθῶμεν.

Besides the direct references to Clement which I have given, this work exhibits from time to time traces of the influence of Clement's Epistle. Thus the opening salutation χάρις ὑμῖν καὶ εἰρήνη ἀπὸ τοῦ παντοκράτορος Θεοῦ διὰ τοῦ κυρίου ἡμῶν Ἰ. Χ. πληθυνθείη is borrowed from Clement, while immediately below the word ἐνεστερνισμένοι (*Ap. Const.* i. 1) is doubtless suggested from Clem. Rom. 2. Again the account of the phœnix (*Ap. Const.* v. 7) betrays in its language the influence of Clement's description (§ 25). Again in describing the characteristics of a faithful ministry, the two writers use the terms ἀβάναυσος, ἀβαναύσως, respectively (*Ap. Const.* ii. 3, Clem. Rom. 44). Again in *Ap. Const.* ii. 27 (comp. vi. 3) the language respecting Dathan and Abiron resembles Clem. Rom. 51; and other examples might be produced, where the use made of O. T. quotations and incidents recalls the treatment of Clement. Again in *Ap. Const.* vi. 12 συζητοῦντες πρὸς τὸ κοινωφελές we are reminded of Clem. Rom. 48 ζητεῖν τὸ κοινωφελές, this word κοινωφελές not being common. The parallels to the eighth book of the *Constitutions* in the concluding prayer of Clement (§ 59 sq), which are given in my notes, are too numerous to be explained as the result of accident.

Some parallels also to the Second Clementine Epistle will be found; e.g. *Ap. Const.* ii. 8, comp. § 13; ii. 17, comp. § 14; iii. 7, comp. § 15; v. 6, comp. § 10.

20.

PETER OF ALEXANDRIA [C. A.D. 306].

De Poenitentia c. 9 (Routh's *Rel. Sacr.* IV. p. 34, ed. 2).

Οὕτως ὁ πρόκριτος τῶν ἀποστόλων Πέτρος πολλάκις συλληφθεὶς καὶ φυλακισθεὶς καὶ ἀτιμασθεὶς ὕστερον ἐν Ῥώμῃ ἐσταυρώθη. ὁμοίως καὶ ὁ περιβόητος Παῦλος πλεονάκις παραδοθεὶς καὶ ἕως θανάτου κινδυνεύσας πολλά τε ἀθλήσας καὶ καυχησάμενος ἐν πολλοῖς διωγμοῖς καὶ θλίψεσιν ἐν τῇ αὐτῇ πόλει καὶ αὐτὸς μαχαίρᾳ τὴν κεφαλὴν ἀπεκείρατο.

Evidently founded directly or indirectly on Clem. Rom. 5.

21.

EUSEBIUS OF CAESAREA [C. A.D. 310—325].

(i) *Chronicon* II. p. 160 (ed. Schoene).

Ann. Abrah.	Domit.	
2103	7	Romanorum ecclesiae episcopatum iii excepit Clemes annis ix.

The corresponding words in Syncellus are τῆς Ῥωμαίων ἐκκλησίας ἡγήσατο δ' Κλήμης ἔτη θ', Clement being thus made the fourth in order. In Jerome's recension this notice is assigned to the 12th year of Domitian.

(ii) *Historia Ecclesiastica.*

(*a*) *H. E.* iii. 4.

Ἀλλὰ καὶ ὁ Κλήμης τῆς Ῥωμαίων καὶ αὐτὸς ἐκκλησίας τρίτος ἐπίσκοπος καταστὰς Παύλου συνεργὸς καὶ συναθλητὴς γεγονέναι πρὸς αὐτοῦ μαρτυρεῖται.

By αὐτοῦ is meant τοῦ Παύλου, the reference being to Phil. iv. 3, as in the next extract.

(*b*) *H. E.* iii. 15, 16.

15. Δωδεκάτῳ δὲ ἔτει τῆς αὐτῆς ἡγεμονίας τῆς Ῥωμαίων ἐκκλησίας Ἀνέγκλητον ἔτεσιν ἐπισκοπεύσαντα δεκαδύο διαδέχεται Κλήμης· ὃν συνεργὸν ἑαυτοῦ γενέσθαι Φιλιππησίοις

ἐπιστέλλων ὁ ἀπόστολος διδάσκει λέγων· μετὰ καὶ Κλήμεντος καὶ τῶν λοιπῶν συνεργῶν μου, ὧν τὰ ὀνόματα ἐν βίβλῳ ζωῆς.

16. τούτου δὴ οὖν τοῦ Κλήμεντος ὁμολογουμένη μία ἐπιστολὴ φέρεται μεγάλη τε καὶ θαυμασία, ἣν ὡς ἀπὸ τῆς Ῥωμαίων ἐκκλησίας τῇ Κορινθίων διετυπώσατο, στάσεως τηνικάδε κατὰ τὴν Κόρινθον γενομένης. ταύτην δὲ καὶ ἐν πλείσταις ἐκκλησίαις ἐπὶ τοῦ κοινοῦ δεδημοσιευμένην πάλαι τε καὶ καθ' ἡμᾶς αὐτοὺς ἔγνωμεν. καὶ ὅτι γε κατὰ τὸν δηλούμενον τὰ τῆς Κορινθίων κεκίνητο στάσεως, ἀξιόχρεως μάρτυς ὁ Ἡγήσιππος.

In this last sentence Harnack (p. xxviii, ed. 2) suggests that with *κατὰ τὸν δηλούμενον* we may understand *καιρόν*, the time of Clement's episcopate being defined in the preceding chapter. But, as the word *καιρός* does not occur anywhere in the context, not even in the preceding chapter, this explanation is impossible. The word would have been expressed, if this had been the meaning, as e.g. iii. 28, 29, *κατὰ τοὺς δεδηλωμένους* (*δηλουμένους*) *χρόνους*. A person must be meant, and the choice must lie between Clement and Domitian. Lipsius (*de Clem. Rom.* p. 156) assumes the former and this is the general opinion. The nearer proximity of Clement's name favours it. But I see strong reasons for preferring Domitian. (1) The succession of the emperors is the backbone of the chronology in the *History* of Eusebius, and the synchronisms are frequently introduced with this preposition *κατά*, e.g. ii. 7, 18, *κατὰ Γάϊον*, ii. 8, 17, 18, *κατὰ Κλαύδιον* (comp. ii. 8 *καθ' ὅν*), ii. 25 *κατ' αὐτὸν* (i.e. *Νέρωνα*), iii. 32 *Μετὰ Νέρωνα καὶ Δομετιανόν, κατὰ τοῦτον οὗ νῦν τοὺς χρόνους ἐξετάζομεν κ.τ.λ.* (meaning 'Trajan,' whose name however is not mentioned till some time afterwards), v. 2 *κατὰ τὸν δεδηλωμένον αὐτοκράτορα*, v. 5 *κατὰ τοὺς δηλουμένους* (the emperors Verus and Marcus, about whom however Eusebius is hopelessly confused), etc. So again in iv. 14 *Ἐπὶ δὲ τῶν δηλουμένων* the reference seems to be to the Antonines. Elsewhere however this preposition *κατὰ* is certainly used of synchronisms with other persons besides the emperors, while in other passages again the reference may be doubtful; see iii. 18 *κατὰ τοὺς δηλουμένους* (comp. iv. 19), iv. 11, 16, v. 11, 22, vi. 23, vii. 11, etc. (2) It was hardly necessary to appeal to Hegesippus to show that the feuds at Corinth took place in the time of Clement, as this fact is patent enough from the epistle itself. (3) The expression *τὸν δηλούμενον* is better suited to a more distant reference, than to Clement himself who is the prominent and only person mentioned in this paragraph up to this point. In the two previous chapters (cc. 14, 15) and in the four succeeding chapters (cc. 17, 18, 19, 20) the narrative directly connects the events related with Domitian's reign. In this chapter alone the connexion is missing, unless it lies in *κατὰ τὸν δηλούμενον*.

(*c*) *H. E.* iii. 21.

Ἐν τούτῳ δὲ Ῥωμαίων εἰσέτι Κλήμης ἡγεῖτο, τρίτον καὶ αὐτὸς ἐπέχων τῶν τῇδε μετὰ Παῦλόν τε καὶ Πέτρον ἐπισκο-

πευσάντων βαθμόν· Λίνος δὲ ὁ πρῶτος ἦν, καὶ μετ' αὐτὸν Ἀνέγκλητος.

In the preceding sentence he has mentioned the accession of Cerdon third bishop of Alexandria in the first year of Trajan.

(*d*) *H. E.* iii. 34.

Τῶν δὲ ἐπὶ Ῥώμης ἐπισκόπων ἔτει τρίτῳ τῆς τοῦ προειρημένου βασιλέως [Τραϊανοῦ] ἀρχῆς Κλήμης Εὐαρέστῳ παραδοὺς τὴν λειτουργίαν ἀναλύει τὸν βίον, τὰ πάντα προστὰς ἔτη ἐννέα τῆς τοῦ θείου λόγου διδασκαλίας.

(*e*) *H. E.* iii. 37, 38.

37. Ἀδυνάτου δ' ὄντος ἡμῖν ἅπαντας ἐξ ὀνόματος ἀπαριθμεῖσθαι, ὅσοι ποτὲ κατὰ τὴν πρώτην τῶν ἀποστόλων διαδοχὴν ἐν ταῖς κατὰ τὴν οἰκουμένην ἐκκλησίαις γεγόνασι ποιμένες ἢ καὶ εὐαγγελισταί, τούτων εἰκότως ἐξ ὀνόματος γραφῇ μόνων τὴν μνήμην κατατεθείμεθα, ὧν ἔτι καὶ νῦν εἰς ἡμᾶς δι' ὑπομνημάτων τῆς ἀποστολικῆς διδασκαλίας ἡ παράδοσις φέρεται· ὥσπερ οὖν ἀμέλει τοῦ Ἰγνατίου ἐν αἷς κατελέξαμεν ἐπιστολαῖς, καὶ τοῦ Κλήμεντος ἐν τῇ ἀνωμολογημένῃ παρὰ πᾶσιν, ἣν ἐκ προσώπου τῆς Ῥωμαίων ἐκκλησίας τῇ Κορινθίων διετυπώσατο. ἐν ᾗ τῆς πρὸς Ἑβραίους πολλὰ νοήματα παραθείς, ἤδη δὲ καὶ αὐτολεξεὶ ῥητοῖς τισὶν ἐξ αὐτῆς χρησάμενος, σαφέστατα παρίστησιν ὅτι μὴ νέον ὑπάρχει τὸ σύγγραμμα. ὅθεν εἰκότως ἔδοξεν αὐτὸ τοῖς λοιποῖς ἐγκαταλεχθῆναι γράμμασι τοῦ ἀποστόλου. Ἑβραίοις γὰρ διὰ τῆς πατρίου γλώττης ἐγγράφως ὡμιληκότος τοῦ Παύλου, οἱ μὲν τὸν εὐαγγελιστὴν Λουκᾶν, οἱ δὲ τὸν Κλήμεντα τοῦτον αὐτὸν ἑρμηνεῦσαι λέγουσι τὴν γραφήν. ὃ καὶ μᾶλλον ἂν εἴη ἀληθές, τῷ τὸν ὅμοιον τῆς φράσεως χαρακτῆρα τήν τε τοῦ Κλήμεντος ἐπιστολὴν καὶ τὴν πρὸς Ἑβραίους ἀποσώζειν, καὶ τῷ μὴ πόρρω τὰ ἐν ἑκατέροις τοῖς συγγράμμασι νοήματα καθεστάναι.

38. Ἰστέον δ' ὡς καὶ δευτέρα τις εἶναι λέγεται τοῦ Κλήμεντος ἐπιστολή· οὐ μὴν ἔθ' ὁμοίως τῇ προτέρᾳ καὶ ταύτην γνώριμον ἐπιστάμεθα, ὅτι μηδὲ καὶ τοὺς ἀρχαίους

αὐτῇ κεχρημένους ἴσμεν. ἤδη δὲ καὶ ἕτερα πολυεπῆ καὶ μακρὰ συγγράμματα ὡς τοῦ αὐτοῦ ἐχθὲς καὶ πρώην τινὲς προήγαγον, Πέτρου δὴ καὶ Ἀπίωνος διαλόγους περιέχοντα· ὧν οὐδ' ὅλως μνήμη τις παρὰ τοῖς παλαιοῖς φέρεται. οὐδὲ γὰρ καθαρὸν τῆς ἀποστολικῆς ὀρθοδοξίας ἀποσώζει τὸν χαρακτῆρα. ἡ μὲν οὖν τοῦ Κλήμεντος ὁμολογουμένη γραφὴ πρόδηλος· εἴρηται δὲ καὶ τὰ Ἰγνατίου καὶ Πολυκάρπου.

(*f*) *H. E.* v. 11.

Ἀλεξανδρείας ἐγνωρίζετο Κλήμης ὁμώνυμος τῷ πάλαι τῆς Ῥωμαίων ἐκκλησίας ἡγησαμένῳ φοιτητῇ τῶν ἀποστόλων.

(*g*) *H. E.* vi. 13.

Κέχρηται δ' ἐν αὐτοῖς [τοῖς Στρωματεῦσι] καὶ ταῖς ἀπὸ τῶν ἀντιλεγομένων γραφῶν μαρτυρίαις, τῆς τε λεγομένης Σολομῶντος σοφίας καὶ τῆς Ἰησοῦ τοῦ Σιρὰχ καὶ τῆς πρὸς Ἑβραίους ἐπιστολῆς, τῆς τε Βαρνάβα καὶ Κλήμεντος καὶ Ἰούδα.

The subject of this sentence is Clement of Alexandria. See above, p. 158 sq.

The passages of Eusebius referring to Hegesippus, Dionysius of Corinth and Origen, in which Clement of Rome is mentioned, are given above, pp. 153 sq, 154 sq, 161 sq.

22.

Cyril of Jerusalem [c. A.D. 347].

Catecheses xviii. 8 (p. 288, ed. Touttée).

Ἤδει Θεὸς τῶν ἀνθρώπων τὴν ἀπιστίαν, καὶ ὄρνεον εἰς τοῦτο κατειργάσατο, φοίνικα οὕτω καλούμενον. τοῦτο, ὡς γράφει Κλήμης καὶ ἱστοροῦσι πλείονες, μονογενὲς ὑπάρχον, κατὰ τὴν Αἰγυπτίων χώραν ἐν περιόδοις πεντακοσίων ἐτῶν ἐρχόμενον δείκνυσι τὴν ἀνάστασιν· οὐκ ἐν ἐρήμοις τόποις, ἵνα μὴ ἀγνοηθῇ τὸ μυστήριον γινόμενον, ἀλλ' ἐν φανερᾷ πόλει παραγενόμενον, ἵνα ψηλαφηθῇ τὸ ἀπιστούμενον. σηκὸν γὰρ ἑαυτῷ ποιῆσαν ἐκ λιβάνου καὶ σμύρνης καὶ λοιπῶν ἀρωμάτων καὶ ἐν τῇ συμπληρώσει τῶν ἐτῶν εἰς τοῦτον εἰσελθὸν τελευτᾷ φανερῶς καὶ σήπεται· εἶτα ἐκ τῆς σαπείσης σαρκὸς τοῦ τελευτήσαντος σκώληξ τις γεννᾶται, καὶ οὗτος αὐξηθεὶς εἰς ὄρνεον μορφοῦται...εἶτα πτεροφυήσας ὁ προειρημένος φοῖνιξ καὶ τέλειος, οἷος ἦν ὁ πρότερος, φοῖνιξ γενόμενος ἀνίπταται τοιοῦτος εἰς ἀέρα οἷος καὶ ἐτετελευτήκει, σαφεστάτην νεκρῶν ἀνάστασιν ἀνθρώποις ἐπιδείξας. Θαυμαστὸν μὲν ὄρνεον ὁ φοῖνιξ κ.τ.λ. (Clem. Rom. 25, 26).

23.

LIBERIAN CHRONOGRAPHER [A.D. 354].

The passage is given in the next chapter.

24.

EPHRAEM SYRUS [† A.D. 373].

(i) *De Humilitate* 33 (*Op. Graec.* I. p. 309).

Ταῦτα δέ φημι...ἵνα ἡ προσφορὰ ὑμῶν εὐπρόσδεκτος ᾖ...περὶ δὲ τῆς φιλοξενίας οὐ χρείαν ἔχετε γράφεσθαι ὑμῖν· ἐπίστασθε γὰρ ὅτι ἡ φιλοξενία πολλῶν ἐστι μείζων ἀρετῶν· καὶ γὰρ ὁ πατριάρχης Ἀβραὰμ διὰ ταύτης ἀγγέλους ἐξένισε, καὶ ὁ δίκαιος Λὼτ διὰ τῆς φιλοξενίας οὐ συναπώλετο τῇ καταστροφῇ Σοδόμων· ὁμοίως δὲ καὶ Ῥαὰβ ἡ ἐπιλεγομένη πορνὴ διὰ τῆς φιλοξενίας οὐ συναπώλετο τοῖς ἀπειθήσασι, δεξαμένη τοὺς κατασκόπους ἐν εἰρήνῃ.

These are the same three examples of φιλοξενία, which we have in Clement (§§ 10, 11, 12), and the language is similar. For the opening sentence also comp. Clem. Rom. 40 τάς τε προσφορὰς καὶ λειτουργίας ἐπιτελεῖσθαι...ἵν' ὁσίως πάντα γινόμενα ἐν εὐδοκήσει εὐπρόσδεκτα εἴη τῷ θελήματι αὐτοῦ· οἱ οὖν προστεταγμένοις καιροῖς ποιοῦντες τὰς προσφορὰς αὐτῶν εὐπρόσδεκτοι κ.τ.λ., and *ib.* 53 Ἐπίστασθε γὰρ καὶ καλῶς ἐπίστασθε κ.τ.λ.

(ii) *De Virtutibus et Vitiis* 3 (*Op. Graec.* I. p. 3).

A description of charity certainly founded on 1 Cor. xiii, and possibly influenced by Clem. Rom. 49, 50. Cotelier says 'Ephraem Syrus...utriusque vestigiis insistit,' but I do not see any indisputable traces of obligations to Clement.

25.

BASIL OF CAESAREA [C. A.D. 375].

De Spirit. Sanct. 29 (III. p. 61 A).

Ἀλλὰ καὶ Κλήμης ἀρχαϊκώτερον, ζῇ, φησίν, ὁ Θεὸς καὶ ὁ Κύριος Ἰησοῦς Χριστὸς καὶ τὸ πνεῦμα τὸ ἅγιον (Clem. Rom. 58).

26.

EPIPHANIUS [C. A.D. 375].

(i) *Haeres.* xxvii. 6 (p. 107).

Ἐν Ῥώμῃ γὰρ γεγόνασι πρῶτοι Πέτρος καὶ Παῦλος ἀπόστολοι καὶ ἐπίσκοποι, εἶτα Λίνος, εἶτα Κλῆτος, εἶτα Κλήμης σύγχρονος ὢν Πέτρου καὶ Παύλου, οὗ ἐπιμνημονεύει Παῦλος ἐν τῇ πρὸς Ῥωμαίους ἐπιστολῇ. καὶ μηδεὶς θαυμαζέτω ὅτι πρὸ αὐτοῦ ἄλλοι τὴν ἐπισκοπὴν διεδέξαντο ἀπὸ τῶν ἀποστόλων, ὄντος τούτου συγχρόνου Πέτρου καὶ Παύλου· καὶ οὗτος γὰρ σύγχρονος γίνεται τῶν ἀποστόλων. εἴτ᾽ οὖν ἔτι περιόντων αὐτῶν ὑπὸ Πέτρου λαμβάνει τὴν χειροθεσίαν τῆς ἐπισκοπῆς καὶ παραιτησάμενος ἤργει (λέγει γὰρ ἐν μιᾷ τῶν ἐπιστολῶν αὐτοῦ, ἀναχωρῶ, ἄπειμι, εὐσταθείτω ὁ λαὸς τοῦ Θεοῦ, ηὕρομεν γὰρ ἔν τισιν ὑπομνηματισμοῖς τοῦτο ἐγκείμενον) ἤτοι μετὰ τὴν τῶν ἀποστόλων διαδοχὴν ὑπὸ τοῦ Κλήτου τοῦ ἐπισκόπου οὗτος καθίσταται, οὐ πάνυ σαφῶς ἴσμεν. πλὴν ἀλλὰ καὶ οὕτως ἠδύνατο ἔτι περιόντων τῶν ἀποστόλων, φημὶ δὲ τῶν περὶ Πέτρον καὶ Παῦλον, ἐπισκόπους ἄλλους καθίστασθαι, διὰ τὸ τοὺς ἀποστόλους πολλάκις ἐπὶ τὰς ἄλλας πατρίδας στέλλεσθαι τὴν πορείαν ἐπὶ τὸ τοῦ Χριστοῦ κήρυγμα, μὴ δύνασθαι δὲ τὴν τῶν Ῥωμαίων πόλιν ἄνευ ἐπισκόπου εἶναι. ὁ μὲν γὰρ Παῦλος ἐπὶ τὴν Σπανίαν ἀφικνεῖται, Πέτρος δὲ πολλάκις Πόντον τε καὶ Βιθυνίαν ἐπεσκέψατο. ἐνεχώρει δὲ μετὰ τὸ κατασταθῆναι Κλήμεντα καὶ παραιτήσασθαι (εἴ γε οὕτως ἐπράχθη, διανοοῦμαι γάρ, οὐχ ὁρίζομαι) ὕστερον μετὰ τὸ τετελευτηκέναι Λίνον καὶ Κλῆτον ἐπισκοπεύσαντας πρὸς δεκαδύο ἔτη ἕκαστον μετὰ τὴν τοῦ ἁγίου Πέτρου καὶ Παύλου τελευτὴν τὴν ἐπὶ τῷ δωδεκάτῳ ἔτει Νέρωνος γενομένην, τοῦτον αὖθις ἀναγκασθῆναι τὴν ἐπισκοπὴν κατασχεῖν. ὅμως ἡ τῶν ἐν Ῥώμῃ ἐπισκόπων διαδοχὴ ταύτην ἔχει τὴν ἀκολουθίαν· Πέτρος καὶ Παῦλος, Λίνος καὶ Κλῆτος, Κλήμης, Εὐάρεστος, Ἀλέξανδρος, Ξύστος, Τελεσφόρος, Ὑγῖνος, Πίος, Ἀνίκητος ὁ ἄνω ἐν τῷ καταλόγῳ προδεδηλωμένος.

(ii) *Haeres.* xxx. 15 (p. 139).

Χρῶνται δὲ καὶ ἄλλαις τισὶ βίβλοις δῆθεν ταῖς Περιόδοις καλουμέναις Πέτρου ταῖς διὰ Κλήμεντος γραφείσαις, νοθεύσαντες μὲν τὰ ἐν αὐταῖς, ὀλίγα δὲ ἀληθινὰ ἐάσαντες, ὡς αὐτὸς Κλήμης αὐτοὺς κατὰ πάντα ἐλέγχει ἀφ' ὧν ἔγραψεν ἐπιστολῶν ἐγκυκλίων τῶν ἐν ταῖς ἁγίαις ἐκκλησίαις ἀναγινωσκομένων, ὅτι ἄλλον ἔχει χαρακτῆρα ἡ αὐτοῦ πίστις καὶ ὁ λόγος παρὰ τὰ ὑπὸ τούτων εἰς ὄνομα αὐτοῦ ἐν ταῖς Περιόδοις νενοθευμένα. αὐτὸς γὰρ παρθενίαν διδάσκει, καὶ αὐτοὶ οὐ δέχονται· αὐτὸς γὰρ ἐγκωμιάζει Ἠλίαν καὶ Δαυὶδ καὶ Σαμψὼν καὶ πάντας τοὺς προφήτας, οὓς οὗτοι βδελύττονται. ἐν ταῖς οὖν Περιόδοις τὸ πᾶν εἰς ἑαυτοὺς μετήνεγκαν καταψευσάμενοι Πέτρου κατὰ πόλλους τρόπους, ὡς αὐτοῦ καθ' ἡμέραν βαπτιζομένου ἁγνισμοῦ ἕνεκεν, καθάπερ καὶ οὗτοι, ἐμψύχων τε τὸν αὐτὸν ἀπέχεσθαι καὶ κρεῶν, ὡς καὶ αὐτοί, καὶ πάσης ἄλλης ἐδωδῆς τῆς ἀπὸ σαρκῶν πεποιημένης λέγουσιν.

(iii) *Ancoratus* 84 (p. 89).

Περὶ δὲ τοῦ φοίνικος τοῦ Ἀραβικοῦ ὀρνέου περισσόν μοι τὸ λέγειν· ἤδη γὰρ εἰς ἀκοὴν ἀφῖκται πολλῶν πιστῶν τε καὶ ἀπίστων. ἡ δὲ κατ' αὐτὸν ὑπόθεσις τοιάδε φαίνεται· πεντακοσιοστὸν ἔτος διατελῶν, ἐπὰν γνοίη τὸν καιρὸν τῆς αὐτοῦ τελευτῆς ἐνστάντα, σηκὸν μὲν ἐργάζεται ἀρωμάτων καὶ φέρων ἔρχεται εἰς πόλιν τῶν Αἰγυπτίων Ἡλιούπολιν οὕτω καλουμένην κ.τ.λ.

In these sentences and in the account which follows (e.g. σκώληκα γεννᾷ, ὁ σκώληξ πτεροφυεῖ νεοττὸς γενόμενος) Epiphanius appears to be indebted to the language of Clement, though there is reason to believe that his knowledge was indirect. Several of his statements show that he had some other account before him.

27.

PSEUDO-IGNATIUS [c. A.D. 370?].

(i) *Ign. Mar.* 4.

Ἔτι οὔσης σοῦ ἐν τῇ Ῥώμῃ παρὰ τῷ μακαρίῳ πάπᾳ Ἀνεγκλήτῳ, ὃν διεδέξατο τὰ νῦν ὁ ἀξιομακάριστος Κλήμης ὁ Πέτρου καὶ Παύλου ἀκουστής.

Ἀνεγκλήτῳ is certainly the right reading here, though one authority has 'Cleto' and another Λίνῳ (see the notes on the passage).

(ii) *Trall.* 7.

Ὡς Στέφανος ὁ ἅγιος [ἐλειτούργησεν διάκονος] Ἰακώβῳ τῷ μακαρίῳ, καὶ Τιμόθεος καὶ Λίνος Παύλῳ, καὶ Ἀνέγκλητος καὶ Κλήμης Πέτρῳ.

(iii) *Philad.* 4.

Ὡς Εὐοδίου, ὡς Κλήμεντος, τῶν ἐν ἁγνείᾳ ἐξελθόντων τὸν βίον.

See the note on the passage.

28.

OPTATUS [c. A.D. 370].

De Schism. Donat. ii. 3 (p. 31).

Ergo cathedram unicam, quae est prima de dotibus, sedit prior Petrus, cui successit Linus; Lino successit Clemens, Clementi Anacletus, Anacleto Evaristus, Evaristo Sixtus, Sixto Telesphorus, Telesphoro Iginus, Igino Anicetus, Aniceto Pius, Pio Soter, Soteri Alexander, Alexandro Victor, etc.

29.

PHILASTRIUS [† c. A.D. 387].

De Haeres. 89.

Sunt alii quoque qui epistolam Pauli ad Hebraeos non adserunt esse ipsius, sed dicunt aut Barnabae esse apostoli aut Clementis de urbe Roma episcopi.

30.

AMBROSIUS [† A.D. 397].

Hexaem. v. 23 (*Op.* I. p. 110).

Phoenix quoque avis in locis Arabiae perhibetur degere, atque ea usque ad annos quingentos longaeva aetate procedere; quae cum sibi finem vitae adesse adverterit, facit sibi thecam de thure et myrrha et ceteris odoribus, in quam impleto vitae suae tempore intrat et moritur. De cujus humore carnis vermis exsurgit, paulatimque adolescit, ac processu statuti temporis induit alarum remigia, atque in superioris avis speciem formamque reparatur. Doceat igitur nos haec avis vel exemplo sui resurrectionem credere etc.

Here Ambrose follows Clement (§ 25) closely. In two other passages also (*In Psalm. cxviii Expos.* xix. § 13, I. p. 1212; *de Fide Resurr.* 59, II. p. 1149) he refers to the story of the phœnix, but does not adhere so closely to Clement. In the latter passage however he has some almost identical expressions, e.g. in the sentence 'cum sibi finem vitae adesse...cognoverit, thecam sibi de thure et myrrha et ceteris odoribus adornare, completoque...tempore intrare illo atque emori, ex cujus humore oriri vermem,' and again 'locorum incolae completum quingentorum annorum tempus intelligunt'; but he mentions Lycaonia instead of Heliopolis as the scene where the coffin is deposited.

The *Hexaemeron* seems to have been written in the later years of his life.

31.

HIERONYMUS [c. A.D. 375—410].

(i) *Chronicon* Domitian. 12.

Tertius Romanae ecclesiae episcopus praefuit Clemens ann. viiii.

See the next chapter, respecting Jerome's edition of the *Chronicon*.

(ii) *de Viris Illustribus* 15.

Clemens de quo apostolus Paulus ad Philippenses scribens ait, *cum Clemente et ceteris cooperatoribus meis, quorum nomina scripta sunt in libro vitae*, quartus post Petrum Romae episcopus, si quidem secundus Linus fuit, tertius Anacletus, tametsi plerique Latinorum secundum post apostolum Petrum putent fuisse Clementem. Scripsit ex persona ecclesiae Romanae ad ecclesiam Corinthiorum valde utilem epistulam et quae in nonnullis locis etiam publice legitur, quae mihi videtur characteri epistulae, quae sub Pauli nomine ad Hebraeos fertur, convenire; sed et multis de eadem epistula non solum sensibus, sed juxta verborum quoque ordinem abutitur; et omnino grandis in utraque similitudo est. Fertur et secunda ex ejus nomine epistula, quae a veteribus reprobatur, et disputatio Petri et Appionis longo sermone conscripta, quam Eusebius in tertio ecclesiasticae historiae volumine coarguit. Obiit tertio Trajani anno, et nominis ejus memoriam usque hodie Romae exstructa ecclesia custodit.

Compare also *de Vir. Ill.* 5 Epistula quae fertur ad Hebraeos...creditur...vel Barnabae juxta Tertullianum vel Lucae evangelistae juxta quosdam vel Clementis, Romanae postea ecclesiae episcopi, quem aiunt sententias Pauli proprio ordinasse et ornasse sermone, etc.

(iii) *Adv. Jovinianum* i. 12 (*Op.* II. p. 257).

Ad hos [i.e. eunuchos] et Clemens successor apostoli Petri, cujus Paulus apostolus meminit, scribit epistolas, omnemque fere sermonem suum de virginitatis puritate contexuit.

(iv) *Comm. in Isaiam* lii. 13 (*Op.* IV. p. 612).

De quo et Clemens vir apostolicus, qui post Petrum Romanam rexit ecclesiam, scribit ad Corinthios; *Sceptrum Dei Dominus Jesus Christus non venit in jactantia superbiae, quum possit omnia, sed in humilitate* (Clem. Rom. 16).

(v) *Comm. in Ephes.* ii. 2 (*Op.* VII. p. 571).

Ad mundos alios, de quibus et Clemens in epistola sua scribit, *Oceanus et mundi qui trans ipsum sunt* (Clem. Rom. 20).

(vi) *Comm. in Ephes.* iv. 1 (*Op.* VII. p. 606).

Cujus rei et Clemens ad Corinthios testis est scribens, *Vinculum caritatis Dei qui poterit enarrare?* (Clem. Rom. 49).

The dates of the several works here quoted are; (i) A.D. 378, (ii) A.D. 392, (iii) c. A.D. 393, (iv) A.D. 397—411, (v) (vi) c. A.D. 387.

32.

Macarius Magnes [c. A.D. 400].

Apocr. iv. 14 (p. 181, ed. Blondel).

The resemblances in this passage, which gives an account of the deaths of the two Apostles S. Peter and S. Paul, to the corresponding account in Clem. Rom. (§ 5) are pointed out in the notes.

On this writer see *Ign. and Polyc.* I. p. 546.

33.

Augustinus [c. A.D. 400].

Epist. liii. § 2 (*Op.* II. p. 120, ed. Bened.).

Petro enim successit Linus, Lino Clemens, Clementi Anencletus, Anencleto Evaristus, Evaristo Sixtus, Sixto Telesphorus, Telesphoro Iginus, Igino Anicetus, Aniceto Pius, Pio Soter, Soteri Alexander, Alexandro Victor, etc.

34.

Paulinus of Nola [before A.D. 410].

Epistola xlvi Ad Rufinum (*Patrol. Lat.* LXI. p. 397, Migne).

§ 2. Sane, quod admonere dignaris affectu illo, quo nos sicut te diligis, ut studium in Graecas litteras attentius sumam, libenter accipio; sed implere non valeo, nisi forte desideria mea adjuvet Dominus, ut diutius consortio tuo perfruar. Nam quomodo profectum capere potero sermonis ignoti, si desit a quo ignorata condiscam? Credo enim in translatione Clementis, praeter alias ingenii mei defectiones, hanc te potissimum imperitiae meae penuriam considerasse, quod aliqua in quibus intelligere vel exprimere verba non potui, sensu potius apprehenso, vel, ut verius dicam, opinata transtulerim. Quo magis egeo misericordia Dei, ut pleniorem mihi tui copiam tribuat etc.

35.

Rufinus [† A.D. 410].

(i) *Praefatio in Recognitiones.*

Quidam enim requirunt, quomodo cum Linus et Cletus in urbe Roma ante Clementem hunc fuerunt episcopi, ipse Clemens ad Jacobum scribens sibi dicat a Petro docendi cathedram traditam. Cujus rei hanc accepimus esse rationem, quod Linus et Cletus fuerunt quidem ante Clementem episcopi in urbe Roma, sed superstite Petro, videlicet ut illi episcopatus curam gererent, ipse vero apostolatus impleret officium, sicut invenitur etiam apud Caesaream fecisse, ubi cum ipse esset praesens, Zacchaeum tamen a se ordinatum habebat episcopum. Et hoc modo utrumque verum videbitur, ut et illi ante Clementem numerentur episcopi, et Clemens tamen post obitum Petri docendi susceperit sedem.

The allusion to the ordination of Zacchæus is explained by *Clem. Recogn.* iii. 65 sq (comp. *Clem. Hom.* iii. 63 sq).

(ii) *Hist. Eccl.* iii. 38.

Clemens tamen in epistola quam Corinthiis scribit, meminit epistolae Pauli ad Hebraeos, et utitur ejus testimoniis. Unde constat quod apostolus tanquam Hebraeis mittendam patrio eam sermone conscripserit et, ut quidam tradunt, Lucam evangelistam, alii hunc ipsum Clementem interpretatum esse. Quod et magis verum est; quia et stylus ipse epistolae Clementis cum hac concordat, et sensus nimirum utriusque scripturae plurimam similitudinem ferunt. Dicitur tamen esse et alia Clementis epistola, cujus nos notitiam non accepimus; etc.

It will be seen that the statements of Eusebius in this passage (see above, p. 166) have been manipulated in passing through the hands of Rufinus. The other passages referring to Clement, *H. E.* iii. 4, 14, 15, 16, 21, 34, 37, though loosely translated and frequently abridged, do not call for comment.

(iii) *De Adult. Libr. Orig.* (Origen. *Op.* IV. App. p. 50, De la Rue).

Clemens apostolorum discipulus, qui Romanae ecclesiae post apostolos et episcopus et martyr fuit, libros edidit qui Graece appellantur ἀναγνωρισμός, id est *Recognitio*, in quibus quum ex persona Petri apostoli doctrina quasi vere apostolica in quamplurimis exponatur, in aliquibus ita Eunomii dogma inseritur, ut nihil aliud nisi ipse Eunomius disputare credatur, Filium Dei creatum de nullis extantibus asseverans...Quid, quaeso, de his sentiendum est? Quod apostolicus vir, imo pene apostolus (nam ea scribit quae apostoli dicunt), cui Paulus apostolus testimonium dedit dicens, *Cum Clemente et ceteris adjutoribus meis, quorum nomina sunt in libro vitae*, scribebat hoc quod libris vitae contrarium est? An id potius credendum, quod perversi homines ad assertionem dogmatum suorum sub virorum sanctorum nomine, tanquam facilius credenda, interseruerint ea, quae illi nec sensisse nec scripsisse credendi sunt?

The passage is quoted by Jerome, but not *verbatim* throughout, *c. Rufin.* ii. 17 (Hieron. *Op.* II. p. 507 sq, Vallarsi).

The passage relating to the phœnix in Rufinus *In Symbol. Apost.* 11 bears no special resemblance to the corresponding passage in Clement.

36.

PSEUDO-TERTULLIAN [4th or 5th cent.?].

Adv. Marcionem iii. 276 (Tertull. *Op.* II. p. 792, ed. Oehler).

Hac cathedra, Petrus qua sederat ipse, locatum
Maxima Roma Linum primum considere jussit;
Post quem Cletus et ipse gregem suscepit ovilis.
Hujus Anacletus successor sorte locatus;
Quem sequitur Clemens; is apostolicis bene notus.
Euaristus ab hoc rexit sine crimine legem.

On the various opinions held respecting the date and authorship of this poem, see esp. Duchesne *Liber Pontificalis* p. xi. Recent opinion fluctuates between Victorinus Afer (c. A.D. 360) and Victor or Victorinus Massiliensis (c. A.D. 430—440). The former view is maintained in the monograph of Hückstädt (Leipzig, 1875); the latter by Oehler, the editor of Tertullian (*Op.* II. p. 781 sq).

37.

DIDYMUS OF ALEXANDRIA [before A.D. 392].

Expos. in Psalm. cxxxviii (*Patrol. Graec.* XXXIX. 1596, ed. Migne).

Εἰ γὰρ καὶ ὠκεανὸς ἀπέραντος, ἀλλ' οὖν καὶ οἱ μετ' αὐτὸν κόσμοι ταῖς τοῦ δεσπότου διαταγαῖς διϊθύνονται· πάντα γὰρ τὰ πρὸς αὐτοῦ γεγενημένα ὅποι ποτ' ἐστὶν ταγαῖς τῆς ἑαυτοῦ προνοίας διοικούμενα ἰθύνεται (1 Cor. 20).

This work of Didymus is mentioned by Jerome in his *Vir. Illustr.* 109. Didymus was still living, at the age of 83, when Jerome wrote (A.D. 392). As this commentary on the Psalms stands first in his list of Didymus' writings, we may suppose that it was written some years before.

38.

ZOSIMUS [A.D. 417].

Epistola ii. § 2 (*Patrol. Lat.* XX. p. 650, Migne).

Die cognitionis resedimus in sancti Clementis basilica, qui, imbutus beati Petri apostoli disciplinis, tali magistro veteres emendasset errores tantosque profectus habuisset, ut fidem quam didicerat et docuerat etiam martyrio consecraret; scilicet ut ad salutiferam castigationem tanti sacerdotis auctoritas praesenti cognitioni esset exemplo.

See Labb. *Conc.* III. p. 401 (ed. Coleti).

39.

PRAEDESTINATUS [C. A.D. 430].

(i) *De Haeresibus* Praef. p. 231 (ed. Oehler).

Clemens itaque Romanus episcopus, Petri discipulus, Christi dignissimus martyr, Simonis haeresim a Petro apostolo cum ipso Simone superatam edocuit.

(ii) *ib.* cap. 14.

Hunc [Marcum haereticum] sanctus Clemens, episcopus Romanus et dignissimus martyr, fixis et integris adsertionibus confutans et coram omni plebe in ecclesia detegens aeterna damnatione punivit, docens vere natum et passum Dominum nostrum Jesum Christum, nihil ab eo in phantasia factum commemorans etc.

40.

EUCHERIUS OF LUGDUNUM [A.D. 432].

Epist. Paraen. ad Valerian. (*Patrol. Lat.* L. p. 718, ed. Migne).

Clemens vetusta prosapia senatorum, atque etiam ex stirpe Caesarum, omni scientia refertus, omniumque liberalium artium peritissimus, ad hanc justorum viam transiit; itaque etiam in ea excellenter effloruit, ut principi quoque apostolorum successor exstiterit.

41.

SYNOD OF VAISON [A.D. 442].

Labb. *Conc.* IV. p. 717 (ed. Coleti).

Canon vi. Ex epistola S. Clementis utilia quaeque, praesenti tempore ecclesiis necessaria, sunt honorifice proferenda et cum reverentia ab omnibus fidelibus, ac praecipue clericis, percipienda. Ex quibus quod specialiter placuit propter venerandam antiquitatem statutis praesentibus roboramus, quod suprascriptus beatus martyr de beatissimi apostoli Petri institutione commemorat, dicens; *Quaedam autem ex vobis ipsis intelligere debetis, si qua sint quae propter insidias hominum malorum* etc.

The lengthy quotation which follows is taken from Rufinus' translation of the *Epistle of Clement to James* (§ 18), which we find in the original prefixed to the *Homilies.*

This canon however is absent from one MS and appears in a somewhat different form in another.

42.

PSEUDO-JUSTINUS [5th cent.?].

Respons. ad Orthodox. 74 (Justin. *Op.* III. p. 108, ed. 3, Otto, 1880).

Εἰ τῆς παρούσης καταστάσεως τὸ τέλος ἐστὶν ἡ διὰ τοῦ πυρὸς κρίσις τῶν ἀσεβῶν, καθά φασιν αἱ γραφαὶ προφητῶν τε καὶ ἀποστόλων, ἔτι δὲ καὶ τῆς Σιβύλλης, καθώς φησιν ὁ μακάριος Κλήμης ἐν τῇ πρὸς Κορινθίους ἐπιστολῇ κ.τ.λ.

The date of this treatise is uncertain, but it was unquestionably written after the Nicene age; see Fabric. *Bibl. Graec.* IV. p. 380 sq, VII. p. 65, ed. Harles.

On the strength of this passage in Pseudo-Justin, I in my first edition (1869) assigned this assumed mention of the fiery judgement and of the Sibyl by Clement to the lacuna which then existed in the genuine epistle after § 57. This course I justified as follows (p. 166 sq):

"If there were no independent reason for inserting this fragment in our epistle, we might hesitate; for (1) I have shown above (§ 47) that ἐν τῇ πρὸς Κορινθίους ἐπιστολῇ might mean the Second Epistle; and to the Second Epistle Ussher and others after him have referred it; (2) The suggestion of Cotelier (Jud. de Epist. II) that for καθώς φησιν we should read καὶ ὡς φησὶν, or better καὶ καθώς φησιν, would be very plausible. But Cotelier himself points out (l.c.) that the statement of the Pseudo-Justin is confirmed from another source. Irenæus (iii. 3. 3) describes this epistle of Clement as preserving the tradition recently received from the Apostles, 'annuntiantem unum Deum omnipotentem, factorem caeli et terrae, plasmatorem hominis, qui induxerit cataclysmum et advocaverit Abraham, qui eduxerit populum de terra Ægypti, qui collocutus sit Moysi, qui legem disposuerit et prophetas miserit, qui *ignem praeparaverit diabolo et angelis ejus*'. This description corresponds with the contents of our epistle, excepting the last clause which I have italicised; and the insertion of a statement so remarkable could not have been an accidental error on the part of Irenæus. Wotton indeed supposes that these words do not give the contents of Clement's epistle, but that Irenæus is describing in his own language the general substance of the Apostolic tradition. To this interpretation however the subjunctive *praeparaverit* is fatal, for it shows that the narrative is oblique and that Irenæus is speaking in the words of another."

"It seems then that Clement towards the close of the epistle dwelt upon the end of all things, the destruction of the world by fire. For such an allusion the threats taken from the Book of Proverbs (§ 57) would prepare the way; and it would form a fit termination to a letter of warning."

"And for this statement he appealed to the authority, not only of the Apostles and Prophets, but also of the Sibyl. There is no difficulty in this. The oldest Jewish Sibylline Oracle, of which a large part is preserved in the 3rd book of the extant Sibylline collection and in quotations of the early fathers, appears to have been written in the 2nd century B.C. by an Alexandrian Jew (see esp. Bleek in Schleiermacher's *Theolog. Zeitschr.* I. p. 120 sq, II. p. 172 sq; Ewald *Entstehung etc. der Sibyll. Bücher*, Göttingen 1858; and Alexandre *Oracula Sibyllina*, Paris 1841,

1856). It is quoted and accepted as a genuine oracle of the Sibyl by Josephus (*Ant.* i. 4. 3), in the early apocryphal *Praedicatio Petri et Pauli* (Clem. Alex. *Strom.* vi. 5, p. 761 sq), by the Christian fathers Melito (Cureton's *Spicil. Syr.* pp. 43, 86), Athenagoras (*Legat.* § 30), Theophilus (*ad Autol.* ii. 3, 9, 31, 36, 38), and Clement of Alexandria (very frequently), in the *Cohort. ad Graec.* ascribed to Justin (§ 37), and in a Peratic document quoted by Hippolytus (*Haer.* v. 16), besides allusions in Hermas (*Vis.* ii. 4) and in Justin (*Apol.* i. §§ 20, 44). Justin in the last passage (§ 44) says that the reading of the Sibylline oracles had been forbidden under penalty of death, but that the Christians nevertheless read them and induced others to read them; and Celsus tauntingly named the Christians Sibyllists (Orig. *c. Cels.* v. 61, I. p. 625; comp. vii. 56, I. p. 734). Clement therefore might very well have quoted the Sibyl as an authority."

"After the enforcement of monotheism and the condemnation of idolatry, the main point on which the Sibyllines dwelt was the destruction of the world by fire. To this end the authority of the Sibyl is quoted in Justin (*Apol.* i. 20), *Apost. Const.* (v. 7), Theophilus (ii. 38), Lactantius (*Div. Inst.* vii. 15 sq), and others. The impending destruction by fire is connected in these oracles with the past destruction by water, as in 2 Pet. iii. 6, 7, 10, 11, 12. The juxta-position of the two great catastrophes in Melito (Cureton's *Spicil. Syr.* pp. 50, 51) is derived from the Sibyllines, as the coincidence of language shows, and not from 2 Pet. iii. 6 sq, as Cureton (§ 95) supposes: see Westcott *Hist. of the Canon* p. 195, 2nd ed. I have pointed out above (§§ 7, 9) that Clement's language respecting the 'regeneration' by the flood and Noah's 'preaching of repentance' seems to be taken from the Sibylline Oracles, and this affords an additional presumption that he may have referred to the Sibyl as his authority for the ἐκπύρωσις and παλιγγενεσία at the end of all things. It is a slight confirmation too, that the word παντεπόπτης at the beginning of § 58 seems to be derived from Sibylline diction (see the note on § 55, where also it occurs). The passage of Theophilus (ii. 38) shows how it might occur to an early father to combine the testimonies of the Prophets and the Sibyl to the ἐκπύρωσις, just as a similar combination is found in the far-famed medieval hymn, 'Dies irae, dies illa, Solvet saeclum in favilla, Teste David cum Sibylla'; see the note in Trench's *Sacred Latin Poetry* p. 297. For the passages in the Sibyllines relating to the conflagration of the universe see Alexandre II. p. 518 sq."

These grounds on which in my first edition I gave a place to the quotation of the Pseudo-Justin in the lacuna of the genuine epistle seemed sufficient to justify its insertion there. Harnack indeed objected (ed. 1, pp. 155, 177) that the use of γραφαί, applied to Prophets and Apostles alike, would be an anachronism in the genuine Clement. I did not mean however that the Pseudo-Justin was giving the exact words of the author quoted, but, as Harnack himself says (*Zeitschr. f. Kirchengesch.* I. p. 273), a free paraphrase. The objection therefore was not, I think, valid.

Still constructive criticism has failed here, and Harnack's opinion has proved correct. We have every reason to believe that we now possess the genuine epistle complete, and the passage to which Pseudo-Justin refers is not found there. When the edition of Bryennios appeared, the solution became evident. The newly recovered ending of the so-called Second Epistle presents references to the destruction of the world by fire and to the punishment of the wicked (§ 16 ἔρχεται ἤδη ἡ ἡμέρα τῆς κρίσεως ὡς κλίβανος καιόμενος κ.τ.λ., § 17 τὴν ἡμέραν ἐκείνην λέγει τῆς κρίσεως ὅταν ὄψονται τοὺς ἐν ἡμῖν ἀσεβήσαντας...ὅπως κολάζονται δειναῖς βασάνοις πυρὶ ἀσβέστῳ) which satisfy the allusion of the Pseudo-Justin, as I pointed out in the *Academy* (May 20, 1876). Harnack and Funk also take the same view. But there is no mention of the Sibyl in these passages. How is this difficulty to be met? Harnack would treat the clause containing this mention as parenthetical in accordance with a suggestion of Hilgenfeld (*Nov. Test. extr. Can. Rec.* 1. p. xviii, note 1), and would read accordingly; εἰ τῆς παρούσης καταστάσεως τὸ τέλος ἐστὶν ἡ διὰ τοῦ πυρὸς κρίσις τῶν ἀσεβῶν (καθά φασιν αἱ γραφαὶ προφητῶν τε καὶ ἀποστόλων, ἔτι δὲ καὶ τῆς Σιβύλλης), καθώς φησιν ὁ μακάριος Κλήμης ἐν τῇ πρὸς Κορινθίους ἐπιστολῇ κ.τ.λ. But to this solution it appears to me that there are two grave objections. (1) The mode of expression is rendered very awkward by the suspension of the last clause, when καθὰ and καθὼς are no longer coordinated. (2) As the writer quotes not the exact words, but only the general sense, of the supposed Clement, he must quote him not for his language, but for his *authority*. But the form of the sentence so interpreted makes Clement's authority paramount and subordinates the Prophets and Apostles to it; 'If Clement is right in saying that the world will be judged by fire as we are told in the writings of the prophets and apostles'. This sense seems to me to be intolerable; and I must therefore fall back upon a suggestion which is given above (p. 178), that for καθὼς we should read καὶ καθώς. The omission of καὶ (which was frequently contracted into a single letter ϗ) before καθὼς would be an easy accident, and probably not a few instances could be produced; comp. e.g. Rom. iii. 8, 1 Joh. ii. 18, 27. The testimony of Clement then falls into its proper place, as subordinate to the scriptures of the Old and New Testament, and even to the writings of the Sibyl. For other instances of the insertion or omission of καὶ before words beginning with κα in our epistle see § 7 [καὶ] καταμάθωμεν, § 8 [καὶ] κάθαροι, § 53 [καὶ] καλῶς; comp. also Gal. iii. 29 [καὶ] κατ' ἐπαγγελίαν, Ign. *Ephes.* 1 [καὶ] κατὰ πίστιν.

Hilgenfeld in his second edition (1876) offers another solution (p. 77). He postulates a lacuna in the Second Epistle § 10, where he supposes the language (including the mention of the Sibyl), to which the Pseudo-Justin refers, to have occurred. Reasons are given in my note for rejecting this theory of a lacuna as unnecessary.

43.

TIMOTHEUS OF ALEXANDRIA [A.D. 457].

Testimonia Patrum.

ܕܩܠܝܡܝܣ ܐܦܣܩܘܦܐ ܕܪܗܘܡܐ ܡܢ ܐܓܪܬܐ ܩܕܡܝܬܐ
ܕܥܠ ܒܬܘܠܘܬܐ ܀

ܐܢܐ ܐܬܒܣܡܬ ܕܐܝܟܢ ܐܝܠܐ ܐܡܪܐ ܒܝܢܐ ܕܚܝܘܬܐ.
ܐܢܐ ܝܕܥ ܐܢܬ ܠܬܫܒܘܚܬܐ ܐܝܟܐ ܕܐܫܬܒܚܬ
ܒܬܘܠܘܬܐ. ܡܪܝܒܐ ܕܒܬܘܠܘܬܐ ܓܝܪ ܠܒܪ ܡܢ ܟܘܠ
ܡܫܝܚܐ ܐܠܗܐ ܡܠܬܐ. ܘܗܘ ܡܢ ܡܬܒܪܝܢ ܗܘܐ

ܒܬܘܠܘܬܐ܆ ܕܡܕܒܪܢܘܬܐ ܗܘܝܐ ܐܬܕܒܪ ܒܥܠܡܐ܂ ܒܗܕܐ
ܬܕܥ ܠܬܫܒܘܚܬܐ ܕܒܬܘܠܘܬܐ܂

ܕܝܠܗ ܕܝܢ ܕܗܘ ܡܢ ܫܘܪܝܐ ܕܐܓܪܬܐ ܕܬܠܬ܂

ܐܚܝ ܗܟܢܐ ܘܠܐ ܠܢ ܠܡܬܪܥܝܘ ܥܠ ܝܫܘܥ ܡܫܝܚܐ
ܐܝܟ ܕܥܠ ܐܠܗܐ܂ ܐܝܟ ܕܥܠ ܕܝܢܐ ܕܚܝܐ ܘܕܡܝܬܐ܂
ܘܠܐ ܘܙܕܩ ܠܢ ܕܙܥܘܪܬܐ ܢܬܪܥܐ ܥܠ ܦܘܪܩܢܐ ܕܝܠܢ܂
ܟܕ ܓܝܪ ܕܡܬܪܥܝܢ ܙܥܘܪܝܬܐ ܥܠܘܗܝ܆ ܙܥܘܪܝܬܐ ܐܦ
ܡܣܟܝܢ ܚܢܢ ܕܢܣܒ܂ ܘܟܕ ܫܡܥܝܢ ܐܝܟ ܕܥܠ ܙܥܘܪܝܬܐ
ܚܛܝܢ ܚܢܢ܂ ܟܕ ܠܐ ܝܕܥܝܢ ܚܢܢ ܡܢ ܐܝܟܐ ܐܬܩܪܝܢ܂ ܘܡܢ
ܡܢܘ ܘܠܐܝܢܐ ܐܬܪܐ܂ ܘܟܠܗܝܢ ܐܝܠܝܢ ܕܣܝܒܪ ܝܫܘܥ
ܡܫܝܚܐ ܕܢܚܫ ܡܛܠܬܢ...

ܕܝܠܗ ܕܝܢ ܕܝܠܗ܂

ܚܕ ܗܘ ܡܫܝܚܐ ܡܪܢ܆ ܗܘ ܕܦܪܩ ܠܢ܂ ܕܐܝܬܘܗܝ ܗܘܐ
ܠܘܩܕܡ ܪܘܚܐ܂ ܗܘܐ ܕܝܢ ܒܒܣܪܐ ܘܗܟܢܐ ܩܪܐ ܠܢ܂

Of Clement, bishop of Rome, from the First Epistle on Virginity.

Understandest thou then what honour chastity requires? Knowest thou then with what glory virginity has been glorified? The womb of the Virgin conceived our Lord Jesus Christ, God the Word; and when our Lord was made man by the Virgin, with this conduct did He conduct Himself in the world. By this thou mayest know the glory of virginity.

Of the same, from the beginning of the Third Epistle.

My brethren, thus it behoveth us to think concerning Jesus Christ, as concerning God, as concerning the Judge of the living and the dead. And it is not right for us to think small things concerning our salvation; for by thinking small things concerning it, we also expect to receive small things. And when we hear as concerning small things, we sin, in that we do not know from whence we are called, and by whom, and to what place, and all those things which Jesus Christ endured to suffer for our sakes (2 Cor. 1).

Of the same.

There is one Christ our Lord, who saved us, who was first spirit, became then in the flesh, and thus called us (2 Cor. 9).

These extracts are taken from Cureton (*Corp. Ign.* pp. 212, 244), who first published them. He transcribed them from the MS *Brit. Mus. Add.* 12156. The extracts from the Pseudo-Clement are on 69 b (Wright's *Catalogue* p. 644 sq.) and follow immediately on the passages from Ignatius and Polycarp which I have given elsewhere, *Ign. and Polyc.* I. pp. 167 sq, 547. For an account of this writer, and of the MS, see *ib.* p. 168.

The first passage is from the Pseudo-Clement *de Virgin.* i. 5, 6 (pp. 24, 26, ed. Beelen). It has been translated direct from the Greek, and has no connexion with the Syriac version of these epistles; see *Ign. and Polyc.* I. p. 193.

44.

EUTHALIUS [C. A.D. 460].

Argum. Epist. ad Hebr. (*Patrol. Graec.* LXXV. p. 776, ed. Migne).

Ἡ δὲ πρὸς Ἑβραίους ἐπιστολὴ δοκεῖ μὲν οὐκ εἶναι Παύλου διά τε τὸν χαρακτῆρα καὶ τὸ μὴ προγράφειν κ.τ.λ.... τοῦ μὲν οὖν ἀπηλλάχθαι τὸν χαρακτῆρα τῆς ἐπιστολῆς φανερὰ ἡ αἰτία· πρὸς γὰρ Ἑβραίους τῇ σφῶν διαλέκτῳ γραφεῖσα ὕστερον μεθερμηνευθῆναι λέγεται, ὡς μέν τινες, ὑπὸ Λουκᾶ, ὡς δὲ οἱ πολλοί, ὑπὸ Κλήμεντος· τοῦ γὰρ καὶ σώζει τὸν χαρακτῆρα.

45.

SEVERUS OF ANTIOCH [C. A.D. 513—518].

Adv. Joannem Grammaticum.

ܕܩܠܝܡܝܣ ܐܦܝܣܩܘܦܐ ܕܬܠܬܐ ܕܒܬܪ ܫܠܝ̈ܚܐ ܕܪ̈ܗܘܡܝܐ.

ܡܢ ܐܓܪܬܐ ܕܬܪ̈ܬܝܢ ܕܠܘܬ ܒܬܘ̈ܠܬܐ.

ܐܚ̈ܝ ܗܟܢܐ ܙܕܩ ܠܢ ܠܡܬܚܪܝܘ ܡܛܠ ܚܘܒ ܡܫܝܚܐ.

ܐܝܟ ܡܛܠ ܐܠܗܐ. ܐܝܟ ܡܛܠ ܕܒܢܝܐ ܕܐܢ̈ܫܐ ܘܕܓܒ̈ܪܬܐ.

ܘܠܐ ܙܕܩ ܠܢ ܕܢܬܘ̈ܪܬܐ ܠܡܬܚܪܝܘ ܡܛܠ ܦܘܪܢܣ. ܐܝܟܢܐ

ܓܝܪ ܕܡܬܚܪܝܢ ܠܚܘ̈ܪܬܐ ܡܛܠܬܗ: ܠܚܘ̈ܪܬܐ ܘܡܫܬܒܪܝܢ

ܠܡܩܒܠ. ܘܟܕ ܫܡܥܝܢ ܐܝܟ ܕܥܠ ܙܥܘܪ̈ܝܬܐ: ܚܛܝܢ.
ܕܠܐ ܝܕܥܝܢ ܡܢ ܐܝܟܐ ܐܬܩܪܝܢ: ܘܡܢ ܡܢܘ. ܘܠܐܝܟܐ
ܐܬܪܐ: ܘܟܡܐ ܣܝܒܪ ܝܫܘܥ. ܡܫܝܚܐ ܕܢܚܫ ܚܠܦܝܢ ܀

Of Clement, the third bishop of Rome after the Apostles, from the Second Epistle to the Corinthians.

My brethren, thus is it right for us to think concerning Jesus Christ, as concerning God, as concerning the Judge of the living and the dead, and it is not right for us to think small things concerning our salvation: for if we think small things concerning it, we hope also to receive small things. And when we hear as concerning small things, we sin, because we do not know from whence we are called, and by whom, and to what place; and how much Jesus Christ endured to suffer for us (2 Cor. 1).

This passage is taken from the MS *Brit. Mus. Add.* 12157, fol. 200 b, and follows immediately upon the extracts from Ignatius and Polycarp which I have given elsewhere (*Ign. and Polyc.* I. pp. 170 sq, 548). It is given by Cureton (*Corp. Ign.* p. 215), from whom I have taken it. A description of the MS and of this work of Severus will be found *Ign. and Polyc.* I. p. 174.

46.

Anonymous Syriac Writers [6th or 7th cent. ?].

(i) *Demonstrationes Patrum.*

ܡܛܠ ܓܝܪ ܩܕܝܫܐ ܩܠܝܡܝܣ ܐܦܝܣܩܘܦܐ ܕܪܗܘܡܐ
ܘܬܠܡܝܕܐ ܕܫ̈ܠܝܚܐ. ܒܐܓܪܬܐ ܕܠܘܬ ܩܘܪܢܬܝ̈ܐ ܗܟܢܐ ܡܠܦ.
ܡܢܘ ܗܟܝܠ ܐܝܬ ܒܟܘܢ ܕܚܝܠܬܢ. ܡܢܘ ܡܪܚܡܢ
ܘܡܠܐ ܚܘܒܐ ܢܐܡܪ ܕܐܢ ܡܛܠܬܝ ܗܘܐ ܙܘܥܐ
ܘܦܠܓܘܬܐ ܘܚܪܝܢܐ. ܐܙܠ ܐܢܐ ܠܐܬܪܐ ܕܨܒܝܢ ܐܢܬܘܢ.
ܘܥܒܕ ܐܢܐ ܡܕܡ ܕܡܬܦܩܕ ܡܢ ܣ̈ܓܝܐܐ. ܒܠܚܘܕ ܥܢܗ
ܕܡܫܝܚܐ ܬܫܬܠܡ ܥܡ ܩܫ̈ܝܫܐ ܕܡܩܝܡܝܢ ܥܠܝܗ̇ ܀

For the holy Clement, bishop of Rome and disciple of the Apostles, teacheth thus in his Epistle to the Corinthians;

Who therefore is there among you that is strong? Who compassionate and full of love? Let him say, If on my account there is disturbance and strife and schism, I go whithersoever ye desire and I do that which is commanded by many. Only let the flock of Christ have peace with the elders that are placed over it (1 Cor. 54).

This passage is taken from the Syriac MS *Brit. Mus. Add.* 14533, fol. 167 b (see Wright's *Catalogue* p. 974), ascribed by Wright to the 8th or 9th century. It contains collections of passages from the fathers directed against various heresies. This particular section is headed 'Charges brought by the followers of Paul [of Beth-Ukkāmē, patriarch of Antioch], with replies to them, and chapters against them' (fol. 172 a). The extract was copied for my first edition by Prof. Wright. It is translated in Cowper's *Syriac Miscell.* p. 56.

(ii) *Excerpta Patrum.*

ܕܛܘܒܢܐ ܩܠܝܡܝܣ ܪܘܡܝܐ ܕܐܦܝܣܩܘܦܐ ܕܪܗܘܡܐ
ܘܣܗܕܐ. ܗܘ ܕܐܦ ܫܠܝܚܐ ܦܘܠܘܣ ܟܕ ܟܬܒ ܠܘܬ
ܦܝܠܝܦܣܝܐ ܗܟܢܐ ܐܡܪ ܕܥܠܘܗܝ. ܥܡ ܩܠܝܡܝܣ ܘܫܪܟܐ
ܕܡܥܕܪܢܝ. ܗܠܝܢ ܕܫܡܗܝܗܘܢ ܒܟܬܒܐ ܕܚܝܐ. ܐܘܣܒܝܣ
ܕܝܢ ܡܦܫܩܢܐ ܐܡܪ ܥܠܘܗܝ ܒܡܟܬܒܢܘܬܐ ܕܬܠܬ ܕܬܫܥܝܬܐ
ܥܕܬܢܝܬܐ. ܗܢܘ ܗܘܐ ܐܦܣܩܘܦܐ ܡܢ ܒܬܪ ܐܢܩܠܛܘܣ.
ܗܘ ܕܒܬܪ ܠܝܢܘܣ. ܠܝܢܘܣ ܕܝܢ ܒܬܪ ܦܛܪܘܣ ܪܫܐ
ܕܫܠܝܚܐ ܗܘܐ ܐܦܣܩܘܦܐ ܕܪܗܘܡܐ. ܡܢ ܐܓܪܬܐ
ܕܬܪܬܝܢ ܕܠܘܬ ܩܘܪܢܬܝܐ. ܡܢ ܗܝ ܕܐܦ ܩܕܡܝܐ ܦܬܓܡܐ
ܘܐܡܪ: ܒܡܨܥܬܐ ܕܡܟܬܒܢܘܬܗ ܗܢܐ ܬܘܬܒܘܬܐ.
ܕܐܬܘܗܝ ܪܫܗ

ܐܝܟ ܗܢܐ ܙܕܩ ܠܝ ܕܢܬܒܥܐ ܡܛܠ ܚܘܒ ܡܫܝܚܐ.
ܐܝܟ ܕܡܛܠ ܐܠܗܐ. ܐܝܟ ܕܡܛܠ ܕܝܢܐ ܕܥܬܝܕ
ܘܕܬܚܝܬܐ.

ܘܠܐ ܢܐܡܪ ܐܢܫ ܡܢܟܘܢ ܕܗܢܐ ܒܣܪܐ ܠܐ ܡܬܕܝܢ
ܘܠܐ ܩܐܡ. ܕܥܘ ܒܡܢܐ ܐܬܦܪܩܬܘܢ. ܘܒܡܢܐ
ܚܙܝܬܘܢ. ܐܠܐ ܗܘ ܕܠܘ ܟܕ ܒܗܢܐ ܒܣܪܐ ܐܝܬܝܟܘܢ.

ܡܕܡ ܗܟܝܠ ܙܕܩ ܠܟܘܢ: ܕܐܝܟ ܗܝܟܠܐ ܕܐܠܗܐ
ܬܛܪܘܢ ܠܒܣܪܐ. ܐܝܟܢܐ ܓܝܪ ܕܟܕ ܐܬܩܪܝܬܘܢ ܒܒܣܪܐ
ܐܝܬܝܟܘܢ: ܗܟܢܐ ܘܒܒܣܪܐ ܗܢܐ ܬܐܬܘܢ. ܐܢ
ܗ̤ܘ ܕܡܫܝܚܐ ܡܪܢ ܗ̇ܘ ܕܦܪܩܢ ܠܢ: ܗ̇ܘ ܕܩܕܡܐܝܬ ܡ̣ܢ
ܐܝܬܘܗܝ. ܗܘܐ ܪܘܚܐ: ܗ̤ܘܐ ܒܣܪܐ ܘܗܟܢܐ ܩܪܟܘܢ:
ܗܟܢܐ ܘܐܦ ܚܢܢ: ܒܗ ܒܗܢܐ ܒܣܪܐ ܢܩܒܠܝܢ
ܐܓܪܐ ܀

Of the holy Clement, archbishop of Rome and martyr, concerning whom the Apostle Paul also, when writing to the Philippians, speaks thus: *With Clement and the rest of my helpers whose names are in the book of life.* But Eusebius of Cæsarea says respecting him, in the third book of his Ecclesiastical History, that he was bishop after Anencletus, who followed Linus: but Linus was bishop of Rome after Peter, the chief of the Apostles. From the Second Epistle to the Corinthians, from which also the holy Patriarch Severus adduces proofs in many of his writings; the beginning of which is, *My brethren, thus it is right for us to think concerning Jesus Christ, as concerning God, as concerning the Judge of the living and the dead* (2 Cor. 1).

And let no one of you say that this flesh is not judged nor riseth again. Know by what ye have been saved, and by what ye have seen, if it be not when ye are in this flesh. Therefore it is right for you that you should keep your flesh as the temple of God. For as ye were called when ye were in the flesh, so also in this flesh shall ye come. If it be that Christ our Lord, who saved us, who at first indeed was spirit, became flesh, and thus called you; so that we also in the same flesh receive the reward (2 Cor. 9).

This is taken from the MS *Brit. Mus. Add.* 17214, fol. 76 b (see Wright's *Catalogue*, p. 916), ascribed by Wright to the 7th century. The MS contains an Ignatian quotation also, and has been described by me in connexion therewith (*Ign. and Polyc.* I. p. 190).

These same two extracts from the Second Epistle are found likewise in *Brit. Mus. Add.* 14532, fol. 214 b (see Wright p. 966), *Brit. Mus. Add.* 14538, fol. 20 a (see Wright p. 1004), and *Brit. Mus. Add.* 17191, fol. 58 b (see Wright p. 1013), containing various collections of extracts, and ranging from the 8th to the 10th century. They were first published by Cureton in *Corp. Ign.* pp. 365, 364, and afterwards by myself in my first edition from a fresh collation made by Wright. An English version is given in Cowper's *Syr. Miscell.* p. 57. Quite recently they have been republished in *Anal. Spicil. Solesm.* IV. p. 1 sq (comp. p. 276), where the various readings of all the MSS are given.

47.

LIBER FELICIANUS [C. A.D. 530].

Liber Pontificalis I. p. 53, ed. Duchesne.

Clemens, natione Romanus, de regione Celiomonte, ex patre Faustino, sedit ann. viiii, m. ii, d. x. Fuit autem temporibus Galbae et Vespasiani, a consulatu Tragali et Italici usque ad Vespasiano viiii et Tito. Martyrio coronatur. Hic fecit vii regiones et dividit notariis fidelibus ecclesiae qui gesta martyrum sollicite et curiose unusquisque per regionem suam diligenter perquireret; et fecit duas epistolas. Hic fecit ordinationes iii per mens. Decemb. presb. x, diac. ii, episcopos per diversa loca v. Obiit martyr iii Trajani. Qui sepultus est in Grecias viiii Kal. Decemb. Et cessavit episcopatus d. xxi.

This is the earlier edition of the *Liber Pontificalis*. For the dates of the two editions see the next chapter.

48.

GREGORY OF TOURS [A.D. 576, 592].

(i) *Hist. Franc.* i. 25.

Tertius post Neronem persecutionem in Christianos Trajanus movet; sub quo beatus Clemens, tertius Romanae ecclesiae episcopus, passus est.

(ii) *De Glor. Mart.* i. 35.

Clemens martyr, ut in passione ejus legitur, anchora collo ejus suspensa in mare praecipitatus est. Nunc autem in die solemnitatis ejus recedit mare per tria millia, siccumque ingredientibus iter praebens, usque dum ad sepulcrum martyris pervenitur; ibique vota reddentes et orantes populi regrediuntur ad littus.

He then relates two miracles wrought by the presence of S. Clement. The first is the story (told in the Acts of Clement) of the child discovered sleeping by its mother after a whole year, during which it had lain on Clement's tomb beneath the waves. The second is the miraculous re-opening of a fertilizing spring of waters at Limoges by the presence of Clement's reliques, after having been long dried up.

(iii) *De Glor. Mart.* i. 56.

Eutropius quoque martyr Santonicae urbis a beato Clemente episcopo fertur directus in Gallias.

49.

GREGORY THE GREAT [A.D. 590].

Oratio ad Plebem (Gregor. Turon. *Hist. Franc.* x. 1, p. 482 sq.).

Omnes autem mulieres conjugatae ab ecclesia sancti martyris Clementis cum presbyteris regionis tertiae.

The posts assigned to these several litanies are differently given by Paulus Diaconus *Vit. Greg.* i. 42 (Greg. Magn. *Op.* xv. p. 284), and the Basilica of S. Clement is not there mentioned.

50.

JOANNES DIACONUS [A.D. 550—600?].

Expositum in Heptateuchum (*Spicil. Solesm.* I. p. 293).

In Epistola sancti Clementis ad Corinthios.

Sciebat Moyses quod virga Aaron floritura esset; sed ideo convocavit populum ut honorabilis Aaron inveniretur, et Deus glorificaretur a populis; ipse autem careret invidia...Hanc formam tenentes apostoli vel successores ejus, quos eligebant, cum consensu totius ecclesiae ordinabant praepositos (Clem. Rom. 43 sq).

A very loose quotation or rather paraphrase.

It must remain uncertain who this John the Roman deacon was. Several persons bore this name and description. Pitra (*Spicil. Solesm.* I. p. lv sq) has given some reasons (not however absolutely conclusive) for supposing that this work was written in the latter half of the sixth century.

On Pitra's inference drawn from this passage respecting a supposed Latin translation by Paulinus of Nola see above, p. 146 sq; and on his opinion with regard to the meaning of 'hanc formam,' see the note on ἐπινομήν, § 44.

51.

APOSTOLICAL CANONS [6TH CENT.?].

Canon 85 (76).

Ἡμέτερα δὲ [βιβλία], τουτέστι τῆς καινῆς διαθήκης· εὐαγγέλια τέσσαρα, Ματθαίου, Μάρκου, Λουκᾶ, Ἰωάννου· Παύλου ἐπιστολαὶ δεκατέσσαρες· Πέτρου ἐπιστολαὶ δύο· Ἰωάννου τρεῖς· Ἰακώβου μία· Ἰούδα μία. Κλήμεντος ἐπιστολαὶ δύο· καὶ αἱ διαταγαὶ ὑμῖν τοῖς ἐπισκόποις δι' ἐμοῦ Κλήμεντος ἐν ὀκτὼ βιβλίοις προσπεφωνημέναι, ἃς οὐ χρὴ δημοσιεύειν ἐπὶ πάντων διὰ τὰ ἐν αὐταῖς μυστικά· καὶ αἱ πράξεις ἡμῶν τῶν ἀποστόλων.

On this Apostolical Canon see Westcott *Canon* pp. 434, 534.

52.

STEPHANUS GOBARUS [c. A.D. 575—600?].

Photius *Bibliotheca* 232 (p. 291 B).

Ὅτι Ἱππόλυτος καὶ Εἰρηναῖος τὴν πρὸς Ἑβραίους ἐπιστολὴν Παύλου οὐκ ἐκείνου εἶναί φασι· Κλήμης μέντοι καὶ Εὐσέβιος καὶ πολὺς ἄλλος τῶν θεοφόρων πατέρων ὅμιλος ταῖς ἄλλαις συναριθμοῦσι ταύτην ἐπιστολαῖς, καί φασιν αὐτὴν ἐκ τῆς Ἑβραΐδος μεταφράσαι τὸν εἰρημένον Κλήμεντα.

There is apparently a confusion here between the two Clements, unless indeed the apparent error arises from the condensation in Photius' account. The words τὸν εἰρημένον Κλήμεντα can only refer to the Alexandrian Clement who is the Κλήμης in the previous part of this sentence, and has likewise been mentioned in the preceding sentence as Κλήμης ὁ στρωματεύς. On the other hand the Roman Clement is nowhere mentioned in the context. If Stephanus was guilty of this error, he must have confused himself with the statements in Euseb. *H. E.* iii. 37, vi. 14, 25. See also John of Damascus below, p. 194.

53.

LEONTIUS AND JOANNES [c. A.D. 600].

Sacrarum Rerum Lib. ii (*Cod. Vat. Graec.* 1553, fol. 22).

Τοῦ ἁγίου Κλήμεντος Ῥώμης ἐκ τῆς πρὸς Κορινθίους ἐπιστολῆς.

αὐτὸς γὰρ ὁ δημιουργὸς καὶ δεσπότης τῶν ἁπάντων ἐπὶ τοῖς ἔργοις αὐτοῦ ἀγάλλεται. τῷ γὰρ παμμεγεστάτῳ (*sic*) αὐτοῦ κράτει οὐρανοὺς ἐστήριξεν καὶ τῇ ἀκαταλήπτῳ αὐτοῦ συνέσει διεκόσμησεν αὐτούς· γῆν δὲ διεχώρισεν ἀπὸ τοῦ περιέχοντος αυτὴν ὕδατος καὶ ἔδρασεν (*sic*) ἐπὶ τὸν ἀσφαλῆ τοῦ ἰδίου θελήματος θεμέλιον· ἐπὶ τούτοις τὸν ἐξοτατον (*sic*) καὶ παμμεγέθη ἄνθρωπον ταῖς ἰδίαις αὐτοῦ καὶ ἀμώμοις χερσὶν ἔπλασεν τῆς ἑαυτοῦ εἰκόνος χαρακτῆρα· οὕτως γὰρ φησιν ὁ Θεός· Ποιήσωμεν ἄνθρωπον κατ' εἰκόνα καὶ καθ' ὁμοίωσιν ἡμετέραν· καὶ ἐποίησεν ὁ Θεὸς τὸν ἄνθρωπον, ἄρσεν καὶ θῆλυ ἐποίησεν αὐτούς· ταῦτα οὖν πάντα τελειώσας ἐπαίνεσεν (*sic*) αὐτὰ καὶ εὐλόγησεν καὶ εἶπεν Αὐξάνεσθε καὶ πληθύνεσθε (1 Cor. 33).

τοῦ αὐτοῦ ἐκ τῆς θ̄ ἐπιστολῆς.

ἵνα καὶ γενώμεθα βουληθέντος αὐτοῦ, οὐκ ὄντες πρὶν γενέσθαι, καὶ γενόμενοι ἀπολαύσωμεν τῶν δι' ἡμᾶς γενομένων. διὰ τοῦτό ἐσμεν ἄνθρωποι καὶ φρόνησιν ἔχομεν καὶ λόγον, παρ' αὐτοῦ λαβόντες.

Mai (*Script. Vet. Nov. Coll.* VII. p. 84) in his extracts from Leontii et Joannis *Rer. Sacr. Lib.* ii, after giving the second of these extracts *ἵνα καὶ γενώμεθα κ.τ.λ.*, says in a note, 'Et quidem in codice exstat locus ex 1 ad Cor. cap. 33, quem exscribere supersedeo' etc. This language led me (ed. 1, pp. 10, 109) without hesitation to ascribe the quotation from § 33 also to this work of Leontius and John, as Hilgenfeld had done before me. To this Harnack took exception (p. lxxiii), stating that the extract in question occurs 'in libro quodam *incerti auctoris* (sine jure conjecerunt Hilgf. et Lightf. in *Leontii et Joannis* Sacr. Rer. lib.).' He seems to have interpreted Mai's 'in codice' not, as it naturally would be interpreted, 'in *the* manuscript,' but 'in *a* manuscript.' Accordingly elsewhere (p. 117) he quotes Dressel's words, 'Melius profecto fuisset, si ipsum locum exscripsisset [Maius] aut Msti numerum indicasset; codicem adhuc quaero,' and adds, 'Virum summe reverendum Vercellone (†), qui rogatu Dresselii schedulas Angeli Maii summa cum diligentia perquisivit, nihil de hoc capite invenisse, Dresselius mecum Romae mens. April. ann. 1874 communicavit.' Not satisfied with this, I wrote to my very kind friend Signor Ignazio Guidi in Rome, asking him to look at the MS of Leontius and John and see if the extract were not there. There was some difficulty in discovering the MS, as it was brought to the Vatican from Grotta Ferrata after the alphabetical catalogue was far advanced, and is not included therein; but through the intervention of Prof. Cozza it was at length found. As I expected, the extract was there, and accordingly I gave it in my *Appendix* p. 426 from Guidi's transcript (A.D. 1877), as I give it now. Some years later (A.D. 1884) Pitra (*Anal. Spicil. Solesm.* II. p. xxi, p. 1) printed the extract, evidently believing that he was publishing it for the first time.

The second extract presents a difficulty. Whence is it taken? Misled by Mai's heading *τοῦ ἁγίου Κλήμεντος Ῥώμης ἐκ τῆς θ' ἐπιστολῆς*, I had suggested in my first edition (pp. 22, 213) that we should read ε for θ (5th for 9th). In this case the five epistles in the collection referred to might have been (1) The Epistle to James, (2) (3) The Two Epistles to Virgins, (4) (5) The Two Epistles to the Corinthians; and we might have expected to find it in the then lost end of the Second Epistle. It is not however found in this ending, which has since been recovered. It bears some resemblance indeed in sentiment to a passage in the First Epistle (§ 38); but the words are not sufficiently close to justify us in regarding it as a quotation from that passage. It will be seen however that the heading is not, as Mai gives it, *τοῦ ἁγίου Κλήμεντος Ῥώμης* but *τοῦ αὐτοῦ*. It is true that this follows immediately after a quotation from the genuine epistle headed 'Of Saint Clement of Rome from the Epistle to the Corinthians'; but the indirectness makes all the difference in the value of the attribution. These extracts for instance may have been taken from an earlier collection containing an intermediate passage from some other author, to whom, and not to Clement, τοῦ αὐτοῦ would then refer. It is probably therefore in some letter written by a later father that this quotation should be sought.

54.

DOROTHEUS ARCHIMANDRITA [c. A.D. 600].

Doctrin. 23 (*Patrol. Graec.* LXXXVIII. p. 1836, ed. Migne).

ὡς λέγει καὶ ὁ ἅγιος Κλήμης· κἂν μὴ στεφανῶταί τις, ἀλλὰ σπουδάσῃ μὴ μακρὰν εὑρεθῆναι τῶν στεφανουμένων (loosely quoted from 2 Cor. 7).

55.

CHRONICON PASCHALE [c. A.D. 630].

p. 467 (ed. Bonn.).

(i) Ἰνδ. β'. ι'. ὑπ. Λαβρίωνος καὶ Τραϊανοῦ.

Τῆς Ῥωμαίων ἐκκλησίας ἡγεῖται τρίτος Κλήμης ἔτη θ', ὃς καὶ ὑπὸ Παύλου τοῦ ἀποστόλου ἐν τῇ πρὸς Φιλιππησίους ἐπιστολῇ μνημονεύεται φήσαντος, μετὰ καὶ Κλήμεντος κ.τ.λ.

(ii) Ἰνδ. α'. ζ. ὑπ. Συριανοῦ τὸ β' καὶ Μαρκέλλου.

Ἐν τούτῳ τῷ χρόνῳ Κλήμης ὁ Ῥώμης ἐπίσκοπος τελευτᾷ.

The two years named are

A.D. 91, M'. Acilius Glabrio M. Ulpius Trajanus.	A.D. 104, Sex. Attius Suburanus II M. Asinius Marcellus.

See also *Ign. and Polyc.* I. p. 66.

56.

ISIDORUS OF SEVILLE [† A.D. 636].

Etymol. vi. 2 (*Op.* II. p. 234, ed. Migne).

Ad Hebraeos autem epistola plerisque Latinis ejus [Pauli] esse incerta est propter dissonantiam sermonis, eandemque alii Barnabam conscripsisse, alii a Clemente scriptam fuisse suspicantur.

He writes to the same effect again *De Offic.* i. 12 (*Op.* III. p. 749).

57.

MAXIMUS THE CONFESSOR [† A.D. 662].

(i) *Prolog. in Op. S. Dionys.* (Dionys. *Op.* II. p. 20, ed. Migne).

Καὶ μὴν οὔτε Πανταίνου τοὺς πόνους ἀνέγραψεν [Εὐσέβιος ὁ Παμφίλου] οὔτε τοῦ Ῥωμαίου Κλήμεντος, πλὴν δύο καὶ μόνων ἐπιστολῶν.

(ii) *Sermo* 49.

Κλήμεντος. ΤΟΣΟΥΤΌΝ ΤΙΣ ΜΑ͂ΛΛΟΝ ὈΦΕΊΛΕΙ ΚΑΤΑΦΡΟΝΕΙ͂Ν, ὍΣΟΝ ΔΟΚΕΙ͂ ΜΑ͂ΛΛΟΝ ΕἾΝΑΙ (1 Cor. 48).

58.

LIBER PONTIFICALIS [c. A.D. 687].

I. p. 118 (ed. Duchesne).

Hic (Petrus) ordinavit duos episcopos, Linum et Cletum, qui praesentaliter omne ministerium sacerdotale in urbe Roma populo vel supervenientium exhiberent; beatus autem Petrus ad orationem et praedicationem, populum erudiens, vacabat...Hic beatum Clementem episcopum consecravit, eique cathedram vel ecclesiam omnem disponendam commisit dicens; *Sicut mihi gubernandi tradita est a Domino meo Jesu Christo potestas ligandi solvendique, ita et tibi committo ut ordinans dispositores diversarum causarum, per quos actus ecclesiasticus profligetur, et tu minime in curis saeculi deditus repperiaris; sed solummodo ad orationem et praedicare populo vacare stude.*

This is a loose paraphrase of passages in the *Letter of Clement* prefixed to the *Clementine Homilies*, § 2—6.

I. p. 123.

Clemens, natione Romanus, de regione Celiomonte ex patre Faustino, sedit ann. VIIII, m. II, d. X. Fuit autem temporibus Galbae et Vespasiani, a consulatu Tragali et Italici usque ad Vespasiano VIIII et Tito. Hic dum multos libros zelo fidei Christianae religionis adscriberet, martyrio coronatur. Hic fecit VII regiones, dividit notariis fidelibus ecclesiae, qui gestas martyrum sollicite et curiose, unusquisque per regionem suam, diligenter perquireret. Hic fecit duas epistolas quae catholicae nominantur. Hic ex praecepto beati Petri suscepit ecclesiae pontificatum gubernandi, sicut ei fuerat a Domino Jesu Christo cathedra tradita vel commissa; tamen in epistola quae ad Jacobum scripta est, qualiter ei a beato Petro commissa est ecclesia repperies. Ideo propterea Linus et Cletus ante eum conscribuntur, eo quod ab ipso principe apostolorum ad ministerium episcopale exhibendum sunt episcopi ordinati. Hic fecit ordinationes duas per mens. decemb., presbiteros x, diaconos II, episcopos per diversa loca xv. Obiit martyr Traiano III: qui etiam sepultus est in Grecias VIII Kal. Decemb. Et cessavit episcopatus dies XXI.

This is from the later recension of the *Liber Pontificalis*. For the earlier see above, p. 186.

59.

EARLIER WESTERN MARTYROLOGIES. [A.D.?]

(i) *Kalendarium Carthaginiense.*

[ ] Kal. Dec. Sancti Clementis.

For the lacuna see above p. 99. This document probably belongs to the sixth century; see Egli *Martyrien u. Martyrologien* p. 50 (Zürich, 1887).

(ii) *Martyrologium Hieronymianum* (Hieron. *Op.* XI. p. 601, etc.).

ix Kal. Dec. [Nov. 23] Romae Maximi, Natalis S. Clementis episcopi et martyris.

Other Clements are mentioned xi Kal. Febr., Prid. Kal. Mai, xvii Kal. Jul., v Kal. Jul., xv Kal. Aug., viii Kal. Aug., v Id. Nov., xi Kal. Dec., and perhaps iv Non. Dec. (Clemeni). The one given on v Id. Nov. 'Romae, Natalis sanctorum Clementis, Symphronii' is the same who appears in the Liberian *Depositio;* and two or three others are mentioned as Romans.

For the papal lists embedded in this Martyrology see De Rossi *Rom. Sotterr.* I. p. 114, Duchesne *Lib. Pontif.* I. pp. xxxi note, lxx. On this particular notice, which is duplicated, see above, p. 99.

(iii) *Martyrologium Vetus Romanum* (*Patrol. Lat.* CXXIII. p. 175, ed. Migne).

ix Kal. Dec. [Nov. 23] Sancti Clementis episcopi.

On the date and value of these two Roman Martyrologies see *Ign. and Polyc.* I. p. 554.

60.

BEDA [† A.D. 735].

(i) *Histor. Eccles.* ii. 4 (*Patrol. Lat.* XCV. p. 87, Migne).

Exemplum sequebatur [Augustinus] primi pastoris ecclesiae, hoc est, beatissimi apostolorum principis Petri, qui fundata Romae ecclesia

Christi Clementem sibi adjutorem evangelizandi, simul et successorem consecrasse perhibetur.

(ii) *Vit. Abbat. Wiram.* 1 (*Patrol. Lat.* XCIV. p. 719).

Nam et beatissimum Petrum apostolum Romae pontifices sub se duos per ordinem ad regendam ecclesiam constituisse, causa instante necessaria, tradunt historiae.

Bede is here justifying Benedict Biscop in appointing Abbots of his two monasteries under himself by the precedent of S. Peter, who is stated (see above, p. 192) to have consecrated two suffragans, Linus and Cletus.

See Duchesne *Lib. Pontif.* I. pp. xxxiv, xxxv.

61.

JOHN OF DAMASCUS [before A.D. 754].

(i) *Sacra Parallela* (*Op.* II. p. 274 sq, ed. Lequien).

(A) *Parallela Vaticana.* α. viii. p. 310.

Αὐτὸς ὁ δημιουργὸς καὶ δεσπότης τῶν ἁπάντων ἐπὶ τοῖς ἔργοις αὐτοῦ ἀγάλλεται. τῷ γὰρ παμμεγεστάτῳ αὐτοῦ κράτει οὐρανοὺς ἐστήριξεν, καὶ τῇ ἀκαταλήπτῳ αὐτοῦ συνέσει διεκόσμησεν αὐτούς· γῆν δὲ ἐχώρισεν ἀπὸ τοῦ περιέχοντος αὐτὴν ὕδατος, καὶ ἥδρασεν ἐπὶ τὸν ἀσφαλῆ τοῦ ἰδίου θελήματος θεμέλιον· ἐπὶ τούτοις τὸν ἐξοχώτατον καὶ παμμεγέθη ἄνθρωπον ταῖς ἰδίαις αὐτοῦ καὶ ἀμώμοις χερσὶν ἔπλασεν τῆς ἑαυτοῦ εἰκόνος χαρακτῆρα. οὕτως γάρ φησιν ὁ Θεός· Ποιήσωμεν ἄνθρωπον κατ' εἰκόνα ἡμετέραν καὶ καθ' ὁμοίωσιν. καὶ ἐποίησεν ὁ Θεὸς τὸν ἄνθρωπον, ἄρσεν καὶ θῆλυ ἐποίησεν αὐτούς. ταῦτα οὖν πάντα τελειώσας, ἐποίησεν αὐτὰ καὶ ηὐλόγησε καὶ εἶπεν, Αὐξάνεσθε καὶ πληθύνεσθε (1 Cor. 33).

It will be seen by comparison of this passage with the quotation in Leontius and John (see above, p. 188 sq) that the two cannot be independent, but must have been derived from a common source or taken the one from the other.

(B) *Parallela Rupefucaldina.*

κ. xxiii. p. 783. τοῦ ἁγίου Κλήμεντος ἐπισκόπου Ῥώμης ἐκ τῆς β′ πρὸς Κορινθίους ἐπιστολῆς.

Μὴ ταρασσέτω τὴν καρδίαν ὑμῶν, ὅτι βλέπομεν τοὺς ἀδίκους πλουτοῦντας, καὶ στενοχωρουμένους τοὺς τοῦ Θεοῦ δούλους. οὐδεὶς γαρ τῶν δικαίων ταχὺν καρπὸν ἔλαβεν, ἀλλ' ἐκδέχεται αὐτόν. εἰ γὰρ τὸν μισθὸν τῶν δικαίων ὁ Θεὸς εὐθέως ἀπεδίδου, ἐμπορίαν ἠσκοῦμεν καὶ οὐκ εὐσέβειαν· ἐδοκοῦμεν γὰρ εἶναι δίκαιοι, οὐ διὰ τὸ εὐσεβὲς ἀλλὰ τὸ κερδαλέον διώκοντες (2 Cor. 20).

π. 31. p. 787. *τοῦ ἁγίου Κλήμεντος ἐκ τῆς πρὸς Κορινθίους ἐπιστολῆς β'.*

ὁ τῶν παρόντων αἰσθητικὸς συνίησιν ὡς οὔτε ἃ λογίζονταί τινες εἶναι τερπνὰ ξενὰ καὶ μακράν ἐστι τῶν ἀπεχθῶν, ἀλλὰ καὶ πλοῦτος πολλάκις μᾶλλον πενίας ἔθλιψε, καὶ ὑγεία πλέον ἠνίασε νόσου· καὶ καθόλου τῶν λυπηρῶν καὶ φευκτῶν πάντων ὑπόθεσις καὶ ὕλη ἡ τῶν ἀσπαστῶν καὶ κατ' εὐχὴν περιβολὴ γίνεται.

The last sentence *καὶ καθόλου κ.τ.λ.* will mean '*and, speaking generally, acquisition of things desirable and eagerly sought after turns out to be the foundation and material of everything that is painful and to be avoided.*' The expression *κατ' εὐχὴν* is common in Aristotle, e.g. *Polit.* ii. 6, iv. 1, 20, vii. 4, 5, where it stands for ideal perfection. Περιβολὴ must mean '*the surrounding or investiture with*,' and so here '*the acquisition of*'; comp. Xen. *Hell.* vii. 1. 40 (*τῆς ἀρχῆς*), Polyb. xvi. 20. 9, Porphyr. *Vit. Pyth.* 54 *τῇ τε τῶν φίλων περιβολῇ καὶ τῇ τοῦ πλούτου δυνάμει*, Aristid. *Or.* 14 (I. 208) *περιβολῇ τε ἀρχῆς καὶ ὄγκῳ πραγμάτων*; and the translation 'affluentia' (as if *ὑπερβολή*) appears to be wrong.

The source of this last quotation is not known. So long as the end of the Second Epistle was wanting, it was naturally assigned to this missing part. But this solution is excluded by the discovery of the lost end. There must therefore be an error in the heading. Probably the Pseudo-Damascene got his quotations from some earlier collection of extracts, perhaps the *Res Sacrae* of Leontius and John (for the titles of the subjects in their works were much the same as his, and they had the particular title under which these words are quoted, *περὶ τῶν προσκαίρων καὶ αἰωνίων*, in common with him; see Mai *Script. Vet. Nov. Coll.* VII. p. 80), and in transferring these extracts to his own volume displaced the reference to Clement, which belonged to some other passage in the same neighbourhood.

For the age of this John of Damascus and for the attribution of these collections of fragments to him, see *Ign. and Polyc.* I. p. 210. The second collection, the *Rupefucaldina*, is certainly earlier than John of Damascus.

(ii) *In Epistol. S. Pauli* (*Op.* II. p. 258).

Τὴν πρὸς Ἑβραίους ἐπιστολὴν ἱστορεῖ Κλήμης, οὗ μέμνηται Παῦλος, ὃς καὶ ἐπίσκοπος Ῥωμαίων ἐγένετο· ὡς Παύλου αὐτὴν Ἑβραίοις τῇ Ἑβραΐδι διαλέκτῳ συντάξαντος ἡρμηνεύθη, ὥς τινες, ὑπὸ Λουκᾶ τοῦ εὐαγγελίστου, ὡς δὲ ἄλλοι, ὑπὸ αὐτοῦ τοῦ Κλήμεντος.

See above, p. 188, for a similar confusion of the two Clements.

62.

GEORGIUS SYNCELLUS [c. A.D. 800].

Chronographia p. 651 (ed. Bonn.).

Κόσμου ἔτη ͵εφοζ´. τῆς θείας σαρκώσεως οζ´.

Τῆς Ῥωμαίων ἐκκλησίας ἡγήσατο δ´ Κλήμης ἔτη θ´.

Κόσμου ἔτη ͵εφοη´. τῆς θείας σαρκώσεως οη´.

Τούτου καὶ ὁ ἀπόστολος ἐν τῇ πρὸς Φιλιππησίους μέμνηται πρώτῃ ἐπιστολῇ εἰπών· μετὰ καὶ Κλήμεντος...βίβλῳ ζωῆς· τούτου ἐπιστολὴ μία γνησία Κορινθίοις φέρεται, ὡς ἀπὸ τῆς Ῥωμαίων ἐκκλησίας γραφεῖσα, στάσεως ἐν Κορίνθῳ συμβάσης τότε, ὡς μαρτυρεῖ Ἡγήσιππος· ἥτις καὶ ἐκκλησιάζεται.

The last sentence is translated by Anastasius Bibliothecarius, 'Hujus epistola fertur ad Corinthios missa quam tota recipit, ut Egesippus testatur, ecclesia' (*Hist. Eccl.* p. 17, Paris 1649), where the testimony of Hegesippus is transferred to the wrong point.

63.

THEODORUS STUDITA [† A.D. 826].

Catechesis Chronica 11 (*Patrol. Graec.* XCIX. p. 1701, Migne).

Οἱ γὰρ θεῖοι τότε τοῦ σωτῆρος ἀπόστολοι, ὡς εὕρομεν ἐν τοῖς θείοις συγγράμμασι Κλήμεντος τοῦ Ῥωμαίου, τρεῖς πλήρεις ἡμέρας τῷ τάφῳ [τῆς θεοτόκου] προσμένοντες ἦσαν, ἕως οὗ ὑπὸ θείου ἀγγέλου τὸ πᾶν ἐμυήθησαν.

See above, page 102.

64.

NICEPHORUS OF CONSTANTINOPLE [† A.D. 828].

Chronographica Brevis.

p. 1039. Οἱ ἐν Ῥώμῃ ἐπισκοπεύσαντες ἀπὸ Χριστοῦ καὶ τῶν ἀποστόλων.

α'. Πέτρος ὁ ἀπόστολος ἔτη β'.
β'. Λίνος ἔτη β'·
γ'. Ἀνέγκλητος ἔτη β'.
δ'. Κλήμης ἔτη θ'.
ε'. Εὐάρεστος ἔτη θ'.

p. 1060. Καὶ ὅσα τῆς νέας ἀπόκρυφα.

* * *

ϛ'. Κλήμεντος α', β' στίχοι ͵βχ'.

See *Ignat. and Polyc.* I. p. 213.

65.

GEORGIUS HAMARTOLUS [c. A.D. 850].

(i) *Chron.* i. 9 (*Patrol. Graec.* cx. p. 140, ed. Migne).

Περὶ οὗ [τοῦ Ἀβρὰμ] μέντοι καὶ Κλήμης ὁ Ῥωμαῖος καὶ σοφώτατος καὶ μαθητὴς Πέτρου τοῦ μεγάλου γνήσιος οὕτως ἔφη· λιμοῦ δὲ γενομένου καταλιπὼν Ἀβρὰμ τὴν Χαναναίαν γῆν εἰς Αἴγυπτον ἀπῄει κ.τ.λ.

Here follows a long passage giving an account of Abraham's conflict with Abimelech which is not found in any of the extant writings bearing the name of Clement of Rome, whether genuine or spurious.

(ii) *Chron.* iii. 117 (*ib.* p. 383 sq).

Ἀντετάσσετο δὲ τῷ ἀσεβεῖ Σίμωνι καὶ Κλήμης ὁ Ῥωμαῖος Πέτρου μαθητὴς λόγῳ πεπαιδευμένῳ ἄκρῳ [πεπαιδευμένος ἄκρως ?] Ἑλληνικῷ τε καὶ Ῥωμαϊκῷ.

This is a reference to the conflict with Simon Magus recounted in the *Homilies* and *Recognitions*, to which narrative there is a direct reference lower down, iii. 121 (p. 429) ἅτινα Κλήμης ὁ Ῥωμαῖος καὶ πάνσοφος μαθητὴς Πέτρου καὶ συνέκδημος ἐπεξεργαστικοτέρως διηγήσατο κ.τ.λ. Comp. ib. p. 437.

66.

Photius [c. A.D. 850].

Bibliotheca c. 113 (p. 90).

Οὗτός ἐστιν ὁ Κλήμης περὶ οὗ φησιν ὁ θεσπέσιος Παῦλος ἐν τῇ Φιλιππησίους ἐπιστολῇ, μετὰ καὶ Κλήμεντος καὶ τῶν λοιπῶν συνεργῶν μου, ὧν τὰ ὀνόματα ἐν βίβλῳ ζωῆς. οὗτος καὶ ἐπιστολὴν ἀξιόλογον πρὸς Κορινθίους γράφει, ἥτις παρὰ πολλοῖς ἀποδοχῆς ἠξιώθη ὡς καὶ δημοσίᾳ ἀναγινώσκεσθαι. ἡ δὲ λεγομένη δευτέρα πρὸς τοὺς αὐτοὺς ὡς νόθος ἀποδοκιμάζεται, ὥσπερ ὁ ἐπιγραφόμενος ἐπ' ὀνόματι αὐτοῦ Πέτρου καὶ Ἀππίωνος πολύστιχος διάλογος. τοῦτόν φασιν οἱ μὲν δεύτερον μετὰ Πέτρον Ῥώμης ἐπισκοπῆσαι, οἱ δὲ τέταρτον· Λίνον γὰρ καὶ Ἀνάκλητον [v. l. Ἀνέγκλητον] μεταξὺ αὐτοῦ καὶ Πέτρου Ῥώμης ἐπισκόπους διαγεγονέναι· τελευτῆσαι δὲ αὐτὸν τρίτῳ ἔτει Τραϊανοῦ.

In the preceding chapter Photius has given an account of the *Recognitions* and other works belonging to the Petro-Clementine cycle.

Bibliotheca 126 (p. 95).

Ἀνεγνώσθη βιβλιδάριον ἐν ᾧ Κλήμεντος ἐπιστολαὶ πρὸς Κορινθίους β' ἐνεφέροντο, ὧν ἡ πρώτη δι' αἰτίας αὐτοὺς ἄγει, στάσεσι καὶ ταραχαῖς καὶ σχίσματι τὴν πρέπουσαν αὐτοῖς εἰρήνην καὶ ὁμόνοιαν ἐμπολιτεύεσθαι λύσαντας, καὶ παραινεῖ παύσασθαι τοῦ κακοῦ. ἁπλοῦς δὲ κατὰ τὴν φράσιν καὶ σαφής ἐστι καὶ ἐγγὺς τοῦ ἐκκλησιαστικοῦ καὶ ἀπεριέργου χαρακτῆρος. αἰτιάσαιτο δ' ἄν τις αὐτὸν ἐν ταύταις ὅτι τε τοῦ Ὠκεανοῦ ἔξω κόσμους τινὰς ὑποτίθεται εἶναι, καὶ δεύτερον ἴσως ὅτι ὡς παναληθεστάτῳ τῷ κατὰ τὸν φοίνικα τὸ ὄρνεον ὑποδείγματι κέχρηται, καὶ τρίτον ὅτι ἀρχιερέα καὶ προστάτην τὸν Κύριον ἡμῶν Ἰησοῦν Χριστὸν ἐξονομάζων, οὐδὲ τὰς θεοπρεπεῖς καὶ ὑψηλοτέρας ἀφῆκε περὶ αὐτοῦ φωνάς· οὐ μὴν οὐδ' ἀπαρακαλύπτως αὐτὸν οὐδαμῇ ἐν τούτοις βλασφημεῖ. ἡ δὲ δευτέρα καὶ αὐτὴ νουθεσίαν καὶ παραίνεσιν κρείττονος εἰσάγει βίου, καὶ ἐν ἀρχῇ Θεὸν τὸν Χριστὸν κηρύσσει, πλὴν ὅτι ῥητά τινα ὡς ἀπὸ τῆς θείας γραφῆς ξενίζοντα παρεισάγει· ὧν οὐδ' ἡ πρώτη ἀπήλλακτο παντελῶς. καὶ ἑρμηνείας δὲ ῥητῶν τινων ἀλλοκότους ἔχει. ἄλλως δέ τε καὶ τὰ ἐν αὐταῖς νοήματα ἐρριμμένα πως καὶ οὐ συνεχῆ τὴν ἀκολουθίαν ὑπῆρχε φυλάττοντα. ἐν τῷ αὐτῷ δὲ βιβλιδαρίῳ ἀνεγνώσθη καὶ Πολυκάρπου Ἐπιστολὴ πρὸς Φιλιππησίους κ.τ.λ.

Amphiloch. 122 (I. p. 716 C, ed. Migne).

τὸν δὲ συγγραφέα τῶν Πράξεων οἱ μὲν Κλήμεντα λέγουσι τὸν Ῥώμης, ἄλλοι δὲ Βαρνάβαν, καὶ ἄλλοι Λουκᾶν τὸν εὐαγγελιστήν.

See above, p. 102.

67.

ANONYMOUS CHRONOGRAPHER [A.D. 853].

Script. Vet. Nov. Coll. I. ii. p. 1 sq, Mai.

Πατριάρχαι Ῥώμης.

͵εφνα' καὶ δ' ἔτους Κλαυδίου Ῥωμαίων βασιλέως, ἐν Ῥώμῃ ἐπεσκόπησεν πρῶτος

α'.	Πέτρος	ἔτη κβ'.
β'.	Λίνος	ἔτη ιβ', ἐπὶ Οὐεσπασιανοῦ· οὗ μέμνηται Παῦλος ἐν τῇ β' πρὸς Κορινθίους ἐπιστολῇ.
γ'.	Ἀνέγκλητος	ἔτη ιβ', ἐπὶ Τίτου.
δ'.	Κλήμης	ἔτη θ', ἐπὶ Τραϊανοῦ.
ε'.	Εὐάρεστος	ἔτη ι'.

This is professedly taken from the works of Eusebius; comp. Duchesne *Liber Pontificalis*, I. pp. xxi, 34, and see below, pp. 240, 243.

68.

ARSENIUS [A.D. ?].

De SS. Clemente et Petro Alex. (*Anal. Spicil. Solesm.* I. p. 314 sq).

Ἐκκλησίας ἄσειστοι καὶ θεῖοι πύργοι, εὐσεβείας ἔνθεοι στῦλοι, ὄντως κραταιοί, Κλήμης σὺν Πέτρῳ, πανεύφημοι, ὑμῶν πρεσβείαις φρουρεῖτε τοὺς ἅπαντας.

Ἀπεριτρέπτῳ καὶ στερρᾷ ἐν τῇ ὁμολογίᾳ οἱ λάμποντες ἐνθέως καὶ φανέντες ἀφράστως, σήμερον χαίρουσιν ὁμοῦ. Κλήμης, τὸ ὡραῖον κλῆμα ὄντως τοῦ Χριστοῦ τὸ τρέφον κόσμον βότρυσι· Πέτρος δὲ κ.τ.λ.

Ῥώμης βλαστὸς ὁ εὐκλεής, ὁ Κλήμης ὁ θεόφρων, ἐν γνώμῃ φιλοσόφῳ καὶ τρόποις φιλοθέοις ταύτην ἐκόσμησε φαιδρῶς· ἔδειξεν ἐν λόγοις τὸ ἀθάνατον ψυχῆς καὶ δόξῃ ταύτην ἔστιλψε· γέγονεν οὖν τῷ Πέτρῳ συνόμιλος, Παύλου κοινωνός τε, καὶ τῶν ἄμφω ἐν πόνοις συμμέτοχος γραφεὺς τε καὶ μύστης· διὸ καὶ σὺν αὐτοῖς ὑπάρχει Ῥωμαίων κλέος ἅμα καὶ φωστήρ, καὶ καταυγάζει ἐνθέοις εὐχαῖς τοὺς ψάλλοντας καὶ βοῶντας κ.τ.λ.

S. Peter of Alexandria is commemorated on the same day (Nov. 24) in the Greek Church. Hence the connexion of the two in this hymn.

69.

ANTONIUS MELISSA [C. A.D. 900?].

Loci Communes ii. 73 (*Patrol. Graec.* CXXXVI. p. 1180).

ΤΟϹΟΥ͂ΤΌΝ ΤΙϹ ΜᾶΛΛΟΝ ὀΦΕΊΛΕΙ ΤΑΠΕΙΝΟΦΡΟΝΕΙ͂Ν, ὅϹΟΝ ΔΟΚΕΙ͂ ΜᾶΛΛΟΝ ΕἾΝΑΙ (1 Cor. 48).

70.

MENAEA [A. D. ?].

Novemb. xxiv (p. 159 sq, Venet. 1877).

Θείας σε κλῆμα, μάρτυς, ἀμπέλου σέβω.

Βληθεὶς ὁ Κλήμης εἰς βύθον σὺν ἀγκύρᾳ
πρὸς Χριστὸν ἥκει ἄγκυραν τὴν ἐσχάτην.

The parentage of Clement and his connexion with S. Peter are recounted as in the Clementines. His banishment to Chersonese, the mode of his martyrdom, and the miracle of the sleeping child, are told as in his Acts of Martyrdom. The play upon κλῆμα is frequent, and he is celebrated as a branch of the true vine, as fertile in clusters, as distilling the wine of godliness, etc.

A large part of the hymn of Arsenius appears (p. 162), as quoted above.

The passage of ANASTASIUS OF SINAI to which Harnack refers (Proleg. xliv, ed. 2), ὁ δὲ ἱερὸς καὶ ἀποστολικὸς διδάσκαλος Κλήμης ἐν τῷ περὶ προνοίας καὶ δικαιοκρισίας κ.τ.λ., is not in the *Hodegus*, as he gives it, but in the *Quaestiones* (c. 96, p. 741, ed. Migne); and the person intended is the Alexandrian Clement. Fragments from this work περὶ προνοίας of the Alexandrian father appear elsewhere; see Dindorf's edition III. pp. 497, 509, 510. Again, it is a wrong inference (of Hilgenfeld p. xxxi, ed. 2, and others) that a passage in ANTIOCHUS OF PALESTINE (*Hom.* xliii, *Bibl. Vet. Patr.* I. p. 1097, Paris 1624) is founded on the language of Clement (§ 13), for the words of Antiochus are much nearer to the original LXX (1 Sam. ii. 10) than to Clement's quotation.

In the above collection of passages I have not aimed at giving any references beyond the tenth century. Such quotations however will be found from time to time in the notes, e.g. Nicon of Rhaethus in §§ 14, 46, ii. § 3. Nor again have I within this period attempted to give extracts from every papal list in which Clement's name appears, but have selected typical examples. More on this subject will appear in the next chapter. Nor are liturgical references, as a rule, included. Several of these will be found in the notes on the closing chapters (§ 59 sq) of the genuine epistle. I have also deliberately omitted the references in second-hand chronicles, such as Orosius, unless there was a special reason for their insertion. The rule, which I laid down for myself at the commencement (p. 148), of excluding passages which refer to the Petro-Clementine writings, the *Recognitions* and *Homilies* etc, has been adhered to, unless they contained some information or suggestion outside this range.

5.

EARLY ROMAN SUCCESSION.

IT will not be necessary here to give any account of the earlier writers who have contributed to the subject, such as Ciampini, Schelestrate, Bianchini, Pearson, and others. Their contributions are often highly valuable, but the information collected and the points established by them have been incorporated in the investigations of later writers, so that it will rarely be necessary to refer to their works. The tract of Pearson *De Serie et Successione Primorum Romae Episcoporum*, a posthumous and unfinished treatise, is reprinted in his *Minor Theological Works* II. p. 296 sq. The contributions of the other writers mentioned are mostly gathered together in Migne's *Patrol. Latin.* CXXVII, CXXVIII, containing Anastasius Bibliothecarius. The starting point of recent criticism was an admirable monograph by Mommsen (A. D. 1850) on the Liberian Catalogue, which will be described below (p. 246 sq). It was followed after some years by a tract by R. A. Lipsius *Die Papstverzeichnisse des Eusebios und der von ihm abhängigen Chronisten* (Kiel, 1868). This was the beginning of a series of highly valuable contributions to the subject from this writer, who has made it especially his own. A year later appeared a more comprehensive work from his pen, *Chronologie der Römischen Bischöfe bis zur Mitte des vierten Jahrhunderts* (Kiel, 1869). It called forth an important critique from Hort, *Academy* Sept. 15, 1871, p. 434 sq, which, though brief, was full of valuable suggestions. An able article by Salmon also on the *Chronology of Hippolytus* in *Hermathena* I. p. 82 sq deals largely with the conclusions of Mommsen and Lipsius on the Liberian Catalogue. A fresh impulse and a somewhat new direction was given to the subject by Harnack *Die Zeit des Ignatius u. die Chronologie der Antiochenischen Bischöfe* etc (1878); for, though his main point was the episcopal succession at Antioch, yet he treated the Antiochene list as organically connected with the Roman (see *Ignat. and Polyc.* II. p. 450 sq).

This was followed by three articles by Erbes in the *Jahrb. f. Protest. Theol.*, entitled *Flavius Clemens von Rom u. das älteste Papstverzeichniss* IV. p. 690 sq (1878), *Die Chronologie der Antiochenischen u. der Alexandrinischen Bischöfe nach den Quellen Eusebs* i, ii, v. p. 464 sq, 618 sq (1879). His own conclusions will hardly command assent, but he has struck out sparks and contributed some suggestions which others have taken up. Meanwhile Duchesne was busy with his labours on the *Liber Pontificalis*. His first work, *Étude sur le Liber Pontificalis* (Paris), appeared in A.D. 1877. After this Lipsius again took up the subject in three articles in the *Jahrb. f. Protest. Theol.*, entitled *Neue Studien zur Papstchronologie*. These were, (i) *Das Felicianische Papstbuch* v. p. 385 sq (1879); (ii. 1) *Die ältesten Papstverzeichnisse* VI. p. 78 sq (1880); (ii. 2) *Die Bischofslisten des Eusebius ib.* p. 233 sq. In these articles he not only reviews the positions of Harnack, Hort, Erbes, and Duchesne, but goes over the old ground and considerably modifies his former views. Altogether they form a highly important supplement to his previous work. Still later (1884, 1885, 1886) three parts of Duchesne's *Liber Pontificalis*, containing pp. i—cclxii, 1—536, and completing the first volume, have appeared. They embody and extend the results of his previous work. This edition, when completed, will be supreme in its own province, while for the early history of the popes it stands second only to the works of Lipsius among recent contributions to this branch of the subject. Other contributions, more especially those relating to the *Liber Pontificalis*, will be mentioned from time to time in their proper places.

I.

THE EARLIEST LISTS.

Within a few years of the middle of the second century, the Hebrew Christian HEGESIPPUS visited Rome. Anicetus was bishop, when he arrived. If Eusebius has rightly understood him, he remained there throughout the episcopate of Soter, and did not leave till the time of Eleutherus. If so, he must have resided in the metropolis some ten years at the least. Heresy, more especially Gnostic heresy, was rife at this epoch. The three great heresiarchs, Basilides, Valentinus, Marcion, all had founded powerful schools, destined to spread widely, where they had not spread already. Besides these more famous systems, there were numberless minor forms of spurious Christianity bidding for acceptance. During his sojourn in Rome, Hegesippus drew up a list of the Roman succession. His motive in doing so is apparent. At Corinth, which he had visited on his way, he was careful to note how the orthodox doctrine had been transmitted unimpaired from the first century to the age of Primus, who was bishop at the time of his visit. So in like manner in Rome he made it his object to ascertain the continuity of the doctrine from the beginning, as a refutation of all religious pretenders. The Roman succession was a guarantee of the unbroken transmission of the original faith. His 'Memoirs,' in which he refers to this fact and in which probably this papal list was incorporated, were written when Eleutherus was bishop, apparently after his return to Palestine, but the original list was compiled under Anicetus. 'When I went to Rome (*γενόμενος ἐν Ῥώμῃ*)', he says, 'I drew up a list of succession (*διαδοχὴν ἐποιησάμην*) as far as Anicetus, whose deacon Eleutherus (then) was. After Anicetus Soter succeeded, and after Soter Eleutherus[1]'. It may be freely conceded that at this epoch no strict record of its past history would be kept by the Roman Church; but the memory of living men would supply this defect to a very great extent. Less than a century had elapsed since the martyrdom of the two Apostles, and sixty years—a little more or less—since the death of Clement.

Of this earliest papal list we know nothing directly, except what may be inferred from the language of Hegesippus which I have quoted. But about the same time with him, or a few years later, a more famous person paid a visit to Rome. IRENÆUS, then a young man, appears to have spent some time in the metropolis. His great work on Heresies however appeared somewhat later. The particular passage with which we are directly concerned was written, as he himself tells us, under Eleutherus (c. A.D. 175—190). Like Hegesippus, he is desirous of showing that the heretical doctrine was a recent growth; like him, he appeals to the succession of the bishops from the Apostolic times, more especially of the Roman bishops, as a guarantee of the preservation of the primitive creed in the Church. Happily he has given us a complete list of the Roman bishops[2]. After stating that the Roman Church was founded by the Apostles Peter and Paul, he adds that they 'entrusted the office of the episcopate' (*τὴν τῆς ἐπισκοπῆς λειτουργίαν ἐνεχείρισαν*) to Linus, who is mentioned by Paul 'in the Epistles to Timothy', and that Linus was succeeded by Anencletus. 'After him', he continues, 'third in order (*τρίτῳ τόπῳ*) from the Apostles, Clement is appointed to the episcopate' (*τὴν ἐπισκοπὴν κλη-*

[1] Euseb. *H. E.* iv. 22. The passage is given in full above, p. 154. On the conjectural reading *διατριβήν* for *διαδοχήν*, see the note there.

[2] *Haer.* iii. 3. 3. The passage will be found at length above, p. 156.

ρουται). Of this Clement he speaks as having associated on intimate terms with the Apostles, and he proceeds to give an account of the Letter to the Corinthians. He then continues the catalogue as follows: Clement is succeeded by Euarestus, Euarestus by Alexander; then comes Xystus who is thus 'sixth from the Apostles'; after him Telesphorus, whose career was crowned by a glorious martyrdom (ἐνδόξως ἐμαρτύρησεν); then Hyginus, then Pius, then Anicetus, then Soter; lastly, 'the twelfth in order from the Apostles' (δωδεκάτῳ τόπῳ...ἀπὸ τῶν ἀποστόλων), Eleutherus who holds the office of the episcopate at the time of his writing these words (νῦν). In another passage, writing a few years later to remonstrate with Victor on the Paschal question, he enumerates this pope's predecessors in the reverse order—Soter, Anicetus, Pius, Hyginus, Telesphorus, Xystus (Euseb. *H. E.* v. 24). Probably he had mentioned Victor's immediate predecessor Eleutherus in the previous context which Eusebius does not quote. It will thus be seen that Irenæus in the passage quoted separates the apostolic founders of the Roman Church from the bishops, and begins the numbering of the latter with Linus. Accordingly elsewhere (iii. 4. 3) he describes Anicetus as the tenth bishop. But in two other places (*Haer.* i. 27. 1, iii. 4. 3), speaking of Cerdon, he says that this heretic appeared in Rome in the time of Hyginus, whom he describes as 'the ninth in the episcopal succession from the Apostles' (ἔνατον κλῆρον τῆς ἐπισκοπικῆς διαδοχῆς ἀπὸ τῶν ἀποστόλων ἔχοντος), 'the ninth bishop' (ὅς ἦν ἔνατος ἐπίσκοπος). Here therefore, if the readings be correct[1], either the apostolic founder or founders must have been included in the enumeration, so that Linus would be the second bishop, or there must be some accidental tripping in the number. In either case Irenæus is probably copying from some earlier writer, such as Justin Martyr or Hegesippus. At all events we can hardly suppose him to have deliberately adopted a different enumeration in the second of these passages, which occurs only a chapter later than his own complete catalogue of the Roman bishops. An alternative remains, that the catalogue which he followed in these passages made two persons, Cletus and Anacletus, out of one; but this solution seems quite un-

[1] In the first passage (i. 27. 1) the text of the old Latin translator has 'nonum', and this reading is confirmed by Cyprian (*Epist.* 74, ed. Hartel), and Eusebius (*H. E.* iv. 11), as well as by Epiphanius (*Haer.* xli. 1). Here then all the authorities are agreed. In the second passage (iii. 4. 3) the Greek is preserved only in Eusebius who has ἔνατος, but the Latin translation of Irenæus has 'octavus'. I am disposed to think that in both passages—in the latter certainly—the 'ninth' was a later emendation, so as to include the episcopate of Peter.

tenable, since no traces of this duplication are found till considerably more than a century and a half after his time, and it never appears in Greek writers.

Whether Irenæus directly copied the catalogue of Hegesippus, or whether he instituted independent enquiries, we cannot say; but it would be a tolerably safe inference from the facts to assume that the series was the same in both writers, as they must have derived their information about the same time and from the same sources. But an important question here arises: Did the catalogue of Hegesippus, like that of Irenæus, contain only the names of the bishops, or did it, like later lists, specify also the respective terms of office? Reasons will be given hereafter for the surmise that it included the years of the several episcopates as well as the names; but for the present I must leave the question unanswered.

From the age of Hegesippus and Irenæus it is only one step to the age of the chronographers. As the motive of the earliest episcopal catalogues had been apologetic, so also was the motive of the first Christian chronographies, though in a different way. Their aim was to show that the true religion, as taught to the Jews first and as perfected in Christianity, was older than the rival heathen systems. Even in the Apologists themselves we find chronographical sketches introduced with this purpose. Such are the discussions in Tatian (*ad Graec.* 39 sq), in Theophilus (*ad Autol.* iii. 21 sq), and in Clement of Alexandria (*Strom.* i. 21, p. 378 sq). This succession of Apologists conducts us to the threshold of the Chronographers properly so called, who flourished in the age of the spurious Antonines, Elagabalus and Alexander.

Among the earlier race of Chronographers proper, two names stand out in special prominence, JULIUS AFRICANUS and HIPPOLYTUS, strictly contemporary with each other but representing the East and the West respectively. The Chronography of Africanus was brought down to the 4th year of Elagabalus, A.D. 221; the similar work of Hippolytus ended with the 13th year of Alexander, A.D. 234. Africanus was a native of Emmaus or Nicopolis in Palestine; Hippolytus lived and wrote in the immediate neighbourhood of Rome. The portion of Africanus' work relating to the Christian period is stated to have been concise[1]; but there is some reason for surmising that he found a place for the episcopates of the great sees of Rome, Antioch, and Alexandria. To this point however I shall return hereafter. Of Hippolytus I shall have much to say presently, when it will appear that the succession

[1] Photius *Bibl.* 34 ἐπιτροχάδην δὲ διαλαμβάνει καὶ τὰ ἀπὸ Χριστοῦ κ.τ.λ.

of the Roman episcopate most probably formed part of his plan. How far this earlier race of chronographers was instrumental in transmitting the primitive lists to a later age and thus furnishing the elements of the Eusebian and other catalogues of the fourth and succeeding centuries, we shall be better able to judge, when we have considered these catalogues themselves.

2.

THE EUSEBIAN CATALOGUES.

The Eusebian lists of the popes are two in number. (A) The series which may be put together from the notices in the *Ecclesiastical History*; (B) The series which may be gathered from the *Chronicle*, where the names occur under the respective years of their accession, this latter list being represented by two versions, the *Armenian* and the *Hieronymian*, which differ widely from each other. These three catalogues will be found in parallel columns in the tables which stand below on pp. 208, 209. In all these Eusebian lists the order of the early Roman bishops is the same, and accords with the catalogue of Irenæus. The differences are in the dates of accession and in the terms of years.

(A) THE HISTORY.

The notices of the Roman succession, from which the table is compiled, will be found in *H. E.* iii. 2, 4, 13, 15, 21, 34, iv. 1, 4, 5, 10, 11, 19, 30, v. procem., 22, 28, vi. 21, 23, 29, 39, vii. 2, 5, 27, 30, 32. The last of these notices refers to Marcellinus, who became pope A.D. 296 and died A.D. 304. Of the accession of the four succeeding popes, Marcellus, Eusebius, Miltiades, Silvester (in whose time the work was published), he says nothing, though Miltiades is mentioned in a document which he inserts (*H. E.* x. 5). He probably ended with Marcellinus, because he had reached his own times (see *H. E.* vii. 32 Γαΐῳ τῷ καθ' ἡμᾶς). In iii. 2 Eusebius states that 'after the martyrdom of Paul and Peter Linus was the first appointed to the bishopric (πρῶτος κληροῦται τὴν ἐπισκοπήν) of the Church of the Romans.' In thus placing both the Apostles at the head of the Roman succession he is following the lead of Irenæus (iii. 3. 2); and so again elsewhere (iii. 21) he speaks still more definitely of Clement as holding the third place in succession of those who 'were bishops after Paul and Peter' (τρίτον καὶ αὐτὸς ἐπέχων τῶν τῇδε μετὰ Παῦλόν τε καὶ Πέτρον ἐπισκοπευσάντων βαθμόν). In both passages however he gives the precedence to S. Paul, thus reversing the order of Irenæus (*Haer.*

iii. 3. 2). In a third passage (iii. 4) Linus is described as the first bishop of Rome 'after Peter' (πρῶτος μετὰ Πέτρον τῆς Ῥωμαίων ἐκκλησίας τὴν ἐπισκοπὴν...κληρωθείς). In the numbering of the several bishops Eusebius always omits the Apostolic founder or founders from the reckoning.

The following (*H. E.* iv. 5) will serve as a sample of these notices of the Roman succession, though they appear in variously modified forms:

ἤδη δὲ δωδέκατον ἐχούσης ἔτος τῆς ἡγεμονίας Ἀδριανοῦ, Ξύστον δεκαέτη χρόνον ἀποπλήσαντα ἐπὶ τῆς Ῥωμαίων ἐπισκοπῆς ἕβδομος ἀπὸ τῶν ἀποστόλων διαδέχεται Τελεσφόρος.

In these notices Eusebius always gives the duration of the episcopate in years, except in the case of Fabianus, where apparently it is omitted by accident, and of Marcellinus, who is the last mentioned and died during the persecution of Diocletian. He has also given for the most part the regnal year of the emperor at the time of each bishop's accession. There are however exceptions to this rule even in the earlier part of the list (Linus, Pius, Anicetus), and in the latter part, from Pontianus onward, these imperial synchronisms almost entirely cease. I have supplied the years A.D., corresponding to these regnal years, using for this purpose the reckoning of the *Chronicle*. Of the stricter mode of calculating—by the anniversaries of the emperor's accession-day[1]—we need not take any account here.

(B) THE CHRONICLE.

The *Chronicle* consists of two parts[2]. The first, which sets forth the principles on which the work is constructed and gives an account of the dynasties of the most famous nations of the world, together with large extracts from previous writers, appears to have been called by Eusebius himself the 'Chronography' or 'Chronographies' (χρονογραφία, χρονογραφίαι), though this is not certain[3]. The second part, which is the Chronicle proper, he designates the 'Canon' or 'Canons' (κανών, κανόνες). Elsewhere he speaks of the 'Chronological Canons'

[1] The years however were not always calculated in the same way: see *Ign. and Polyc.* II. p. 397 sq.

[2] This bipartite division seems to have had precedents in earlier chronological works. The arguments however for attributing this arrangement to Africanus break down; see Gelzer *Sextus Julius Africanus* I. p. 30 sq.

[3] See *Chron.* I. pp. 6, 7, 78, 95, 119, 294 (Schoene). The inference however from these passages is uncertain. An equivalent suggested by I. p. 119, II. p. 4, is χρόνων ἀναγραφή (-φαί). Epiphan. *Mens. et Pond.* 24 writes ἐν χρονογραφίαις Εὐσεβίου καὶ τῶν ἄλλων χρονογράφων.

Order	Roman Bishops	Armenian Chronicon			Hieronymian Chronicon			Ecclesiastical History		
		Duration	*Accession* A.D.	*Imperial year*	*Duration*	*Accession* A.D.	*Imperial year*	*Duration*	*Accession* A.D.	*Imperial year*
	Petrus	xx	39	Gaius iii	xxv	42	Claudius ii			
1	Linus	xiiii	66	Nero xii	xi	68	Nero xiv	xii		
2	Anencletus	viii	79	Titus i	xii	80	Titus ii	xii	80	Titus ii
3	Clemens	viiii	87	Domitian vii	viiii	92	Domitian xii	viiii	92	Domitian xii
4	Euarestus	viii	94	Domitian xiiii	viiii	99	Trajan ii	viii	100	Trajan iii
5	Alexander	x	103	Trajan vi	x	109	Trajan xii	x	109	c. Trajan xii
6	Xystus	xi	114	Trajan xvii	x	119	Hadrian iii	x	119	Hadrian iii
7	Telesphorus	xi	124	Hadrian viii	xi	128	Hadrian xii	xi[th]	128	Hadrian xii
8	Hyginus	iiii	134	Hadrian xviii	iiii	138	Antoninus i	iiii	138	Antoninus i
9	Pius	xv	138	Antoninus i	xv	142	Antoninus v	xv[th]		
10	Anicetus	xi	152	Antoninus xv	xi	157	Antoninus xx	xi		
11	Soter	viii	164	Marcus iiii	viii	169	Marcus viiii	viii[th]	167, 168	Marcus vii, viii
12	Eleutherus	xv	173	Marcus xiii	xv	177	Marcus xvii	xiii	177	Marcus xvii
13	Victor	xii	186	Commodus vii	x	192	Severus i	x	189	Commodus x
14	Zephyrinus	xii	198	Severus vii		200	Severus viiii	xviii	200	c. Severus viiii
15	Callistus	viiii	211	Caracalla ii	v	219	Elagabalus ii	v	218	Elagabalus i
16	Urbanus		218	Elagabalus i	viiii	224	Alexander iii	viii		[acc. Alexandri]
17	Pontianus	viiii	228	Alexander vii	v	233	Alexander xii	vi		

Order	Roman Bishops	Armenian Chronicon			Hieronymian Chronicon			Ecclesiastical History		
		Duration	*Accession* A.D.	*Imperial year*	*Duration*	*Accession* A.D.	*Imperial year*	*Duration*	*Accession* A.D.	*Imperial year*
18	Anteros	*m.* i	238	Gordian i	*m.* i	238	Gordian i	*m.* i		Gordian
19	Fabianus	xiii	238	Gordian i	xiii	238	Gordian i			
20	Cornelius	iii	246	Philippus iii	ii	252	Gallus i	c. iii		Decius
21	Lucius	*m.* ii	250	Philippus vii	*m.* viii	253	Gallus ii	*m.* viii		
22	Stephanus	ii	250	Philippus vii	iii (ii)	253	Gallus ii	ii		
23	Xystus	xi	253	Gallus ii				xi		
24	Dionysius	xii	261	Gallienus viii	viiii	265	Gallienus xii	viiii		
25	Felix	xviiii	271	Aurelian i	v	277	Probus i	v		
26	Eutychianus	*m.* ii	278	Probus ii	*m.* viii	281	Probus v	c. *m.* x		
27	Gaius	xv	278	Probus ii	xv	281	Probus v	xv		
28	Marcellinus	...	...	...		296	Diocletian xii			
29	Eusebius	...	...	...	*m.* vii	304	Diocletian xx	...	...	...
30	Miltiades	...	...	...	iiii	304	Diocletian xx	...	...	...
31	Silvester	...	...	...	xxii	309	Constantine iv	...	...	...
32	Marcus	...	...	...	*m.* viii	330	Constantine xxv	...	...	...
33	Julius	...	...	...	xvi *m.* iiii	330	Constantine xxv	...	...	...
34	Liberius	...	...	...		348	Constantius xii	...	...	...
35	Damasus	...	...	...		361	Valentinian ii	...	...	...

(χρονικοὶ κανόνες)[1]. It is distinguished by this epithet from a wholly different work by him, which was likewise styled 'Canons', and in which his aim was to indicate the parallel passages in the several Gospels and thus to furnish materials for a harmony[2]. The second part alone of the Chronicle was translated by Jerome, and hence the first was a matter of conjecture until the discovery of the Armenian version. Scaliger (*Thesaurus Temporum*, Leyden 1606, Amsterdam 1658) endeavoured to reconstruct it from extracts and references in later writers; but the whole question was so shrouded in uncertainty, that Vallarsi could even treat this first part as a figment of Scaliger's brain (Hieron. *Op.* VIII. p. xviii sq). On the other hand Tillemont (*Mémoires* VII. p. 49), Fabricius (*Bibl. Graec.* VII. p. 338, ed. Harles), and others adopted Scaliger's twofold division. The discovery of the Armenian proved Scaliger to be right in the main point; though his

[1] *Ecl. Proph.* i. 1 ἰστέον δ' ὡς πρὸ τῆς παρούσης ὑποθέσεως χρονικοὺς συντάξαντες κανόνας, ἐπιτομήν τε τούτοις παντοδαπῆς ἱστορίας Ἑλλήνων τε καὶ βαρβάρων ἀντιπαραθέντες, τὴν Μωσέως καὶ τῶν ἐξ αὐτοῦ προφητῶν ἀρχαιότητα δι' αὐτῶν παρεστήσαμεν. In this passage the second part of the work alone is described, in which the short historical notices (ἐπιτομήν) are ranged side by side (ἀντιπαραθέντες) with the chronological tables (χρονικοὺς κανόνας). I mention this because in Smith and Wace *Dict. of Biogr.* s. v. 'Eusebius, Chronicle of,' I. p. 348, the latter clause (ἐπιτομήν τε κ.τ.λ.) is paraphrased 'to which is prefixed an epitome' etc, and taken to refer to the first part, though lower down (p. 352) it is correctly interpreted. See also *H. E.* i. 1, where speaking of the pains which he has bestowed in the *History* itself on the episcopal succession, Eusebius adds in reference to the *Chronicle*, ἤδη μὲν οὖν τούτων καὶ πρότερον ἐν οἷς διετυπωσάμην χρονικοῖς κανόσιν ἐπιτομὴν κατεστησάμην, πληρεστάτην δ' οὖν ὅμως αὐτῶν ἐπὶ τοῦ παρόντος ὡρμήθην τὴν ἀφήγησιν ποιήσασθαι, and comp. *Praep. Evang.* x. 9 (p. 484) ταῦτα μὲν οὖν ἐν τοῖς πονηθεῖσιν ἡμῖν χρονικοῖς κανόσιν οὕτως ἔχοντα συνέστη. In the preface to the first part (*Chron.* I. p. 6, Schoene), after giving the contents of this part he adds, 'Atque materias ex his omnibus mihi recolligens ad *chronicos* temporales *canones* me convertam, ac resumens jam inde ab initio etc', after which he describes the contents of the second part, and then (*ib.* p. 7) resumes, 'sed illius secundi posterior elaboratio est; nunc vero in proximo sermone, agedum chronographiam ab Chaldaeis de ipsorum majoribus relatam inspiciamus'. Again in his preface to the second part (II. p. 4, Schoene), he describes the first part thus, ἐν μὲν τῇ πρὸ ταύτης συντάξει ὕλας ἐκπορίζων ἐμαυτῷ χρόνων ἀναγραφὰς συνελεξάμην παντοίας, βασιλείας τε Χαλδαίων, Ἀσσυρίων κ.τ.λ.; and then he proceeds to describe the second, ἐν δὲ τῷ παρόντι ἐπὶ τὸ αὐτὸ τοὺς χρόνους συναγαγὼν καὶ ἀντιπαραθεὶς ἐκ παραλλήλου τὸν παρ' ἑκάστῳ ἔθνει τῶν ἐτῶν ἀριθμὸν χρονικοῦ κανόνος σύνταξιν ἐποιησάμην κ.τ.λ. (quoted by Syncellus I. p. 122 sq, ed. Bonn.). Syncellus himself speaking of the first part writes (p. 125) ἐν τῷ πρώτῳ λόγῳ. The second part is called ὁ κανών by him, even when he distinguishes it from the first (pp. 118, 122, 125, 311).

[2] See Smith and Wace *Dict. of Christ. Biogr.* s. v. 'Eusebius', I. p. 334, for a description of this work.

restoration of the missing first part, as might have been expected, was not altogether successful. What title Eusebius gave to the whole work, we are unable to say with certainty. In the Armenian the title is wanting. Jerome describes it (*Vir. Ill.* 81) as 'Chronicorum canonum omnimoda historia et eorum epitome', but here we may suspect some error in the text[1]. His own recension of the work he designates (*Vir. Ill.* 135) 'Chronicon omnimodae historiae'. Elsewhere he writes (*Epist.* lvii. 6, I. p. 309) 'Quum Eusebii Caesariensis Χρονικὸν in Latinum verterem', and in another place (*Comm. in Daniel.* ix. 24, *Op.* V. p. 688) 'in Chronico ejusdem Eusebii.' In another passage again (*Nom. Loc. Hebr.* praef., III. p. 121) he speaks of Eusebius as publishing 'Temporum canones quos nos Latina lingua edidimus', and just below he designates the work which he translated 'Temporum liber', while elsewhere again (*c. Rufin.* i. 11, *Op.* II. p. 466) he describes it as 'Digestio temporum'. Augustine (*Quaest. in Exod.* ii. 47, *Op.* III. p. 435) writes, 'Eusebius in historia sua Chronica', and elsewhere (*de Civ. Dei* xviii. 8, *Op.* VII. p. 493) 'Nostri [i.e. Christiani] qui Chronica scripserunt, prius Eusebius, post Hieronymus'. Again Paulinus, writing to Augustine (Aug. *Op.* II. p. 35) calls it 'de cunctis temporibus historia', and lower down 'historia temporum'. Judging from these and other references we may conclude that χρονικόν or χρονικά—more probably the latter—formed part of the primary title; while in a secondary or expanded heading παντοδαπὴ ἱστορία would probably have a place. It is called *Chronica* by Cassiodorius (*Inst. Div. Lit.* xvii) and by Syncellus (p. 73). In his *Comm. in Isaiam* xiii. 17 (*Op.* VI. p. 189) Eusebius himself refers to the work generally as χρονικὰ συγγράμματα. *Chronicon* or *Chronica* seems to be given generally in the MSS, as the title of Jerome's translation, and so Gennadius speaks of it in the continuation of the *Catalogus* (§ 1), 'Beatus Hieronymus in libro χρονικῶν[2]'.

[1] Sophronius translates Jerome's words, χρονικῶν κανόνων παντοδαπῆς ἱστορίας καὶ τούτων ἐπιτομή, thus changing the case; and this title is repeated after him by Suidas s. v. Εὐσέβιος (I. p. 649, ed. Bernhard).

The passages in the last note show that the expressions χρονικοὶ κανόνες, παντοδαπὴ ἱστορία, and ἐπιτομή, as used by Eusebius himself, refer especially to the second part; and if they entered into the general title of the whole work, they can only have done so because he regarded the first part as merely introductory. Probably however Jerome was contemplating only the second part, which he himself translated. Even then the reference of καὶ τούτων is unexplained. Possibly Jerome has abridged the language of Eusebius and thus destroyed the proper connexion of the words.

[2] In Latin we find *Chronicon* and *Chronicum*, besides the plural *Chronica*. The first may occasionally be a transcription of χρονικῶν, but sometimes it certainly represents χρονικόν, e.g. *Vir. Ill.* 135,

The original text of the *Chronicle* is not extant, though considerable extracts are found in later writers, especially Syncellus. It is preserved however in three versions, of which the first in most respects, though not altogether, preserves the work in its original form; the second has undergone a certain amount of revision; and the third is a mere abridgement. These are (1) the Armenian; (2) the Latin; (3) the Syriac.

(i) *Armenian Version.*

To the well known Armenian scholar, the Mechitarist monk Aucher, belongs the credit of rendering this version accessible to European scholars. Before the close of the eighteenth century he had made preparations for an edition, but owing to various causes its publication was delayed. Meanwhile another Mechitarist scholar Zohrab had surreptitiously obtained possession of some of Aucher's materials, and in conjunction with Mai ('conjunctis curis') published a translation with introduction, etc, at Milan in 1818. Immediately on its appearance Aucher pushed forward the completion of his own work, and two editions of it appeared at Venice in this same year 1818. The fame of Aucher suffered for a time from the disparagements of Niebuhr and others (see II. p. xlv sq, ed. Schoene), who upheld the rival edition of Zohrab notwithstanding the questionable circumstances of its publication, but has been fully vindicated by Petermann.

These two earlier editions have been superseded by the labours of Petermann, who has furnished a revised Latin translation, together with a careful introduction and critical notes for Schoene's edition of the *Chronicon* (vol. II, 1866; vol. I, 1875). This last is now the standard edition both for the Armenian and Hieronymian versions, and indeed generally for the materials connected with this work of Eusebius. The text of Petermann's translation is founded on two Armenian MSS. (i) The one, belonging to the Armenian patriarch, and having its home in his library at Jerusalem, though transferred for a time to Constantinople. It was written for the then catholicus, one Grigorius, whom Aucher identifies with Grigorius III (A.D. 1113—1166), but Petermann with Grigorius VII (A.D. 1294—1307). (ii) The other, brought to Venice from Tokat in Asia Minor, and written A.D. 1696, belonged to Minas, Archbishop of Amida (A.D. 1689—1701). The two MSS are closely allied, exhibiting

where it is an accusative. From the plural χρονικὰ comes the Latin feminine *Chronica, -ae*, just as from *βιβλία, -ων*, is derived the Latin *Biblia, -ae*. *Chronica, -ae*, appears frequently in later writers (e.g. Greg. Tur. *Hist. Franc.* i. 1).

the same errors and lacunæ. Petermann's description of them will be found in II. p. xlix sq, ed. Schoene.

This version is unanimously assigned by Armenian scholars to the fifth century (Aucher p. vi sq; Zohrab p. xi; Petermann II. p. liii). This was the great era of Armenian literature. More especially was it rich in translations. In the earlier part of the century the famous Mesrob, the inventor of the Armenian alphabet, sent scholars to collect MSS far and wide, more especially in Greece and Syria. The result was not only the Armenian version of the Bible but also a great number of Armenian translations of the Christian fathers and of profane writers (see Moses of Khoren *Hist. Arm.* iii. 60, Langlois' translation p. 167, and comp. Langlois *Historiens de l'Arménie* II. p. vii sq, Paris 1869, and Félix Nève *L'Arménie Chrétienne* etc, p. 19 sq, Louvain 1886, with the references there given). From this great outburst of literary activity this age was entitled 'the age of the interpreters'. The translation of the *Chronicle* is said to reflect in its language the characteristics of this golden era of Armenian literature.

But the emissaries of Mesrob, as we have seen, brought back manuscripts from Syria as well as from Greece. From which language then was the Armenian version of the *Chronicle* made? There is good evidence to show that the *Chronicle* was translated into Syriac at some time or other, and Armenian translations were not uncommonly made from this language. This was certainly the case, for instance, with the Ignatian Epistles, which were not translated directly from the Greek original but have passed through a Syriac medium (*Ign. and Polyc.* I. p. 86 sq).

Petermann shows beyond question that, while many errors in this version are due to a misunderstanding or misreading of the Greek, many others certainly arise from corruptions or ambiguities in the Syriac (II. p. liii sq). His own conclusions from these facts are, that there were two Armenian versions of the *Chronicle*, both made in the fifth century—the one from the original Greek, the other from the Syriac version; that in the turbulent ages which followed, manuscripts were mutilated and defaced; and that in the seventh or eighth century, when the troubles abated and literature revived, the extant Armenian version was patched together and compiled (consarcinatio, compilatio) from the two. I venture to offer a different solution. It seems to me more probable that the first portion was translated altogether from the Greek, but that for the second the translator had before him, besides the Greek text, either a Syriac version, whether complete or in epitome, or a previous Armenian version made from the Syriac. With many Armenians the Syriac language was almost like a second native tongue, and they would naturally work upon the Syriac by preference. This suggestion appears to me to be consistent with the facts as I understand them. For (1) The errors which can be distinctly traced to the Syriac are all in the second portion (II. p. liv sq). The few instances which Petermann alleges from the first (I. p. x) do not carry conviction; and indeed he himself only says 'ad textum originalem Syriacum referri *posse videntur*'. (2) The second portion is said to be so much inferior to the first, not only as a faithful translation, but as a literary composition, that Zohrab expresses grave doubts whether it was by the same hand as the other (p. xix), and Petermann allows 'stilum hujus partis libri varium ac diversum nominandum esse' (II. p. liii). (3) There is no evidence, so far as I am aware, that the first portion, as a whole, was ever translated into Syriac. (4) The references to the *Chronicle* in the earlier Armenian writers seem to be all taken from the first part. If this be so, the fact suggests an interval between the translations of the two parts; but it is immaterial to my main position. At the same time, I offer this suggestion with all the misgiving which must be felt by one who has only the very slightest knowledge of Armenian, and who moreover has not had the requisite time to submit this particular question to a minute investigation.

The suggested date of the Armenian version, the fifth century, is borne out by the fact that the work is quoted by a succession of Armenian writers from Moses of Khoren and Lazarus of Pharbi, who both wrote in the latter half of the fifth century (see Aucher p. viii, Zohrab p. xi). In the 12th century Samuel of Ania wrote a Chronicle which he carried down to A.D. 1179, according to his own reckoning, which differs somewhat from the vulgar era. The introductory portion and the chronicle itself from the Christian era to the vicennalia of Constantine are abridged mainly from the Armenian *Chronicle* of Eusebius. A Latin translation of this work is attached to Zohrab and Mai's edition of the *Chronicle* (Milan, 1818), and has been reprinted by Migne, Euseb. *Op.* I. p. 599 sq. It is valuable for our purpose, as showing the condition of the Armenian text of Eusebius when Samuel wrote.

The gain to our knowledge by the discovery of the Armenian version was made the subject of a treatise by Niebuhr *Historischer Gewinn aus der Armenischen Uebersetzung der Chronik des Eusebius* (Berlin, 1822), first published in the Proceedings of the Berlin Academy. The value of the discovery was very great indeed. The first part of the work, throwing much light on ancient history, was wholly unknown before, except by extracts in later writers, as it had not been translated by Jerome. In the second part the Armenian version enables us to separate the original work of Eusebius from Jerome's additions. Only in the portion with which we are more especially concerned, the series of popes, does it introduce fresh perplexities. Here it has been the source not of elucidation, but of confusion.

Though the MSS of the Armenian Chronicle are mutilated at the close, so that it ends with the 16th year of Diocletian, the work itself was carried down to the vicennalia of Constantine. This is mentioned in the first part as the terminus (I. p. 71, 131), and Simeon distinctly states that the Chronicle of Eusebius ended here (p. 42, Zohrab). So too Syncellus (pp. 64, 318). This is also the terminus of the Syriac epitome. On all grounds therefore it is clear that the copy from which the Armenian translator made his version corresponded in this respect with the copy which was used by Jerome.

The names of the bishops are given in this work under the several years of their accession. The number of each pope in the order of succession is generally, though not always, stated. The omissions occur in the cases of Linus, Victor, Callistus, and Stephanus. Thus Clemens is the 3rd, Euarestus the 4th, Alexander the 5th, and so forth, S. Peter being excluded in the numbering in this work, as in the *History*. At the same time the presidency of S. Peter in the Roman Church is recognized in some sense in the notice under Ann. Abr. 2055 (= A.D. 39), 'Petrus apostolus, cum primum Antiochenam ecclesiam fundasset, Romanorum urbem proficiscitur ibique evangelium praedicat et commoratur illic antistes ecclesiae annis viginti' (II. p. 150, Schoene). The original expression of Eusebius, here represented by 'antistes ecclesiae,' is probably preserved by Syncellus, ὁ δὲ αὐτὸς [Πέτρος] μετὰ τῆς ἐν Ἀντιοχείᾳ ἐκκλησίας καὶ τῆς ἐν Ῥώμῃ πρῶτος προέστη ἕως τελειώσεως αὐτοῦ. Thus he refrains from directly calling him bishop, though a founder of the Roman episcopate. At the accession of each bishop the term of office is likewise given, e.g.

'Romanorum ecclesiae episcopatum xiii excepit Eleutherius annis xv.'

As the terms frequently do not agree with the corresponding interval between one accession and the next, they both are recorded in the tables below. Eusebius himself in this part of the *Chronicle* gives the years of Abraham, the Olympiads, and the years of the Roman emperors, the first being the back-bone of his chronology. His Olympiads however are not true Olympiads, but Julian Leap-years. I have omitted them in my table; and for the years of Abraham I have substituted years A.D. for convenience of reference. In converting the years from the one era to the other, I have observed Gutschmid's rule (*De Temporum Notis quibus Eusebius utitur etc.* p. 27 sq, Kiliae 1868) of subtracting 2016 for the years from 2017—2209 inclusive, and 2018 afterwards to the end of the work. At the point indicated, the reign of Pertinax, Eusebius gets wrong in his imperial chronology; and hence arises the necessity of making a change here in the mode of reckoning.

Two or three very patent errors I have tacitly corrected in this list. (1) The name of Linus is entered twice; first under Nero xii, and then under Titus i. At the second occurrence it is obviously a transcriber's error, and I have accordingly substituted Anencletus, this being more probable than the alternative name Cletus for this same bishop[1]. (2) The proper names are much disfigured in the transmission from one language to another. I have restored the correct forms. (3) An Alexandrian bishop, Agrippinus, is by a blunder assigned to Rome, between Soter and Eleutherus. His name is omitted in my table. (4) The number of Urbanus is wanting. So too the name, and the name only, of Eutychianus has dropped out owing to a mutilation[2]. I have replaced the later omission, but not the former.

The Armenian version has lost a page at the end, and closes with the 16th year of Diocletian. The last bishop of Rome mentioned is Gaius, whom it assigns to the 2nd year of Probus (Ann. Abr. 2296), and to whom it gives 15 years of office. The accession of his successor Marcellinus ought therefore to have been recorded under the 8th year of Diocletian (Ann. Abr. 2311); but there is no mention of him[3]. Whether Eusebius in this work continued his notices of the papal succession beyond this point or not, we are unable to say with certainty. In the Ecclesiastical History, as we shall see, the last notice refers to the death of Gaius and accession of Marcellinus. This coincidence would rather suggest that his list ended at this point.

[1] Simeon, copying the Armenian *Chronicle*, gives the name 'Clemetus'. In the MS which he used therefore it was in the process of corruption, this being a confusion of Cletus (or Anencletus) and Clemens. We may suppose that Eusebius himself in his *Chronicle* used the same form Anencletus, which appears in his *History*, but the evidence is defective. In the Syriac authorities the name is wanting. In Jerome the MSS give variously 'Anacletus', 'Cletus', and 'Clemens', and one has 'Cletus qui et Anacletus'. In the *Vir. Ill.* 15 there is the same variation between 'Anacletus' and 'Cletus'.

[2] Agrippinus is rightly assigned to Alexandria in Samuel. The number of Urbanus is wanting, but the name Eutychianus appears in his text.

[3] Samuel has 'Marcellinus annis x,' under the 13th year of Diocletian.

(ii) *Hieronymian Version.*

The *Chronicle* of Eusebius ended, as we have seen, with the vicennalia of Constantine (A.D. 325). Jerome translated and continued it, so as to bring it down to date, the 14th year of Valentinian and Valens (A.D. 378). Accordingly the papal record is carried down to Damasus (A.D. 366–384), who was bishop when he wrote. Marcellus (A.D. 307) the immediate successor of Marcellinus is omitted. This omission may be due partly to the similarity of the names, partly to the fact that Marcellus only held office less than a year. One or other of the two names, Marcellinus and Marcellus, is frequently wanting in papal lists. The degree of change which Jerome introduced into the work of Eusebius will be a subject of discussion hereafter. As far as A.D. 180, the imperial chronology of Jerome's recension agrees with the Armenian, and the reduction of the years of Abraham to the reckoning A.D. is effected in the same way by subtracting 2016; but Jerome omits Pertinax and places the first year of Severus Ann. Abr. 2209 (not 2210), so that from this point onward we deduct not 2018 as with the Armenian, but only 2017, to find the corresponding A.D. It should be observed also that Jerome's Olympiads are one year later than the Armenian (Julian Leap-years), but one year earlier than the true Olympiads.

The Roman primacy of S. Peter, as we should have expected, appears more definitely in Jerome than in Eusebius himself. Of this Apostle Jerome says, 'Romam mittitur, ubi evangelium praedicans xxv annis ejusdem urbis episcopus perseverat.' Thus S. Peter is distinctly stated to be the first bishop of Rome. Yet in the subsequent notices Jerome preserves the mode of enumeration which he found in Eusebius, and by which S. Peter himself is separated from the rest; 'Post Petrum primus Romanam ecclesiam tenuit Linus,' 'Romanae ecclesiae secundus constituitur episcopus Anacletus,' etc.

The variations in the MSS of Jerome's version, so far as they affect the papal dates, are not very considerable. Collations of six MSS (ABPFRM) are given by Schoene. The number of accessions from Peter to Marcellianus (Marcellinus) inclusive is 29; and in only 12 of these is there any discrepancy. The variations are exhibited in the table which follows. The first column of numbers gives the years of Abraham as they appear in Schoene's edition; and the second records the divergences, as noted in his collations.

Euarestus	2115	A 2114
Alexander	2125	A 2126
Hyginus	2154	AF 2155
Anicetus	2173	A 2171 F 2169
Eleutherus	2193	A 2192
Zephyrinus	2217	A 2216
Callistus	2236	A 2235
Urbanus	2241	A 2240
Pontianus	2250	A 2248
Cornelius	2269	BPF 2268
Dionysius	2282	A 2281
Marcellianus	2313	B 2314

It will thus be seen that ten out of these twelve variations amount only to a single year, and that seven of the ten appear in one MS alone (A). The only wide variation is the date of Anicetus in F, and the character of the MS deprives it of any weight[1].

(iii) *Syriac Version.*

Several of the principal works of Eusebius were translated into Syriac either during the life-time of the author or soon after (see Smith and Wace *Dict. of Christ. Biogr.* s. v. 'Eusebius' II. pp. 310, 320, 326, 332, 344). Whether the *Chronicle* was among those translated at this early date or not, we cannot say; but as it is included among the works of Eusebius in the catalogue of Ebedjesu (Assemani *Bibl. Orient.* III. p. 18), we may assume the existence of some Syriac translation. Elsewhere (III. p. 168) Ebedjesu mentions Simeon of Garmai as having interpreted (פשק) it; and this cannot well refer to anything else but a translation. This Simeon appears to have lived about A.D. 600 (Assem. *ib.* III. p. 633). Again the Jacobite patriarch of Antioch, Michael the Great, who flourished towards the close of the twelfth century, compiled a Chronography partly based upon the work of Eusebius (Assem. *Bibl. Orient.* II. p. 313; comp. Greg. Barhebr. *Chron.* I. pp. 590—606, ed. Abbeloos and Lamy). The existence of a Syriac version may also be inferred independently from the Armenian,

[1] This MS is very wild in this neighbourhood, and ante-dates several events (even the death of Antoninus Pius) by three or four years. Its near coincidence therefore with the Armenian date (2168) for the accession of Anicetus must be regarded as a mere accident.

which bears evidence in the corruption of the proper names and other ways, as we have seen (p. 213), that it was translated, at least in part, from a pre-existing Syriac version. No such version however is now extant, and it is only found in epitome. Two of these abridgements have been published:

(1) The one is by Dionysius of Telmachar, who was Jacobite patriarch of Antioch from A.D. 818—845. The work which contains this epitome is a Chronicle in four parts, from the beginning of the world to A.D. 775. An account of the author will be found in Assem. *Bibl. Orient.* II. p. 344 sq, and of the work *ib.* II. p. 98 sq. The first part, which ends with Constantine, is taken from the *Chronicle* of Eusebius[1], but contains likewise passages here and there inserted from the *History*[2] as also from other writers, more especially from an Edessene chronicle. This first part has been published in the Syriac by Tullberg (*Dionysii Telmahharensis Chronici Liber Primus*, Upsal. 1850) from the only known MS, *Vat.* clxii, which is described in Assem. *Bibl. Orient.* II. p. 98 sq, and *Catal. MSS Bibl. Apost. Vat.* III. p. 328[3]. It has been translated recently by Siegfried and Gelzer *Eusebii Canonum Epitome ex Dionys. Telmah. Chron. petita* (Lips. 1884), where the chronologies of the Latin and Armenian versions are compared with it and the corresponding fragments from Greek writers are given. This work is criticized, with especial reference to these comparative chronologies, by A. von Gutschmid *Untersuchungen über die Syrische Epitome der Eusebischen Canones* (Stuttgart 1886).

(2) The second of these epitomes is contained in the MS *Brit. Mus. Add.* 14643, described in Wright's *Catal. of Syr. MSS* p. 1040 and in Land's *Anecd. Syr.* I. p. 39 sq, 165 sq. This MS contains, with other matter, a Chronicle followed by a list of the Caliphs, which latter *Liber Calipharum* is adopted by Land as the title of the whole. The Chronicle falls into two parts. The first, including the period from Abraham to Constantine, is taken from the *Chronicle* of Eusebius, with a few interpolations from other sources. This first part is translated by Roediger for Schoene's edition (II. p. 203 sq), and some extracts are

[1] Dionysius himself (*Bibl. Or.* II. p. 100) tells us that this first part is taken from Eusebius.

[2] The extracts from the *History* are taken from the extant Syriac version: see *Literar. Centralbl.* 1886, April 17, p. 589.

[3] Siegfried and Gelzer (p. v) state that of this work there are two editions, a larger and a smaller ('cujus chronici duplex circumfertur editio'). I gather however from the account of Assemani (*Bibl. Orient.* II. p. 98), that the larger work corresponded rather to the *History* than to the *Chronicle* of Eusebius. The published work is the shorter. It does not appear whether the larger is extant.

given in the original by him in his *Chrestom. Syr.* p. 105 sq, ed. 2. The second part, which is a continuation, is printed in full by Land *Anecd. Syr.* Appx. I. p. 1 sq, and translated by him *ib.* I. p. 105 sq. The latest incident mentioned in this second part falls in the year A.D. 636, which seems to have been the date of the compiler. The list of Caliphs is continued to A.D. 724. See Roediger in Schoene's *Chron.* II. p. lvii.

So far as I have observed, the Eusebian portion of both these works appears to have been taken from the same Syriac version. But it is difficult to compare the two, as the Syriac of the latter remains unpublished; and I desire therefore to speak with all reserve. Each contains events taken from the Eusebian *Chronicle* which are wanting in the other. On the whole the latter contains a larger number of events (at least for the portion with which we are directly concerned), but the former gives the events frequently in greater detail. The latter as a rule has no dates, whereas the former commonly, though not always, prefixes the year of Abraham. Both alike omit the *fila regnorum*—the parallel columns of dynasties—which are a characteristic feature of the *Chronicle*, as it left the hands of its author. The table on the opposite page exhibits the information supplied by both these abridgements. Owing to the absence of dates in Roediger's Epitome, it is only possible to define the limits of time by the dates of the notices immediately before and after an event. This is done in the table, the dates being supplied from the Hieronymian *Chronicle*.

A Syriac excerpt from the *Chronicle* of Eusebius, contained in the Bodleian MS *Arch.* c. 5, which was written A.D. 1195, is translated by P. J. Bruns in the *Repertorium f. Bibl. u. Morgenländ. Litteratur* XI. p. 273 (Leipzig 1782). The only notices however which it contains bearing on our subject are those relating to S. Peter and S. Paul in Rome; '[After the accession of Claudius] Peter, after he had established the Church at Antioch, presided over the Church at Rome twenty years...[Nero] stirred up a persecution against the Christians in which also the Apostles Peter and Paul lost their lives.' In Wright's *Catal. of Syr. MSS in the Brit. Mus.* p. 1041 sq, three other MSS are named, DCCCCXIV—DCCCCXVI, which contain epitomes or portions of epitomes of the *Chronicle* of Eusebius. It is possible that a careful examination of these would throw some light on the history of the Syriac version or versions; but I gather from the investigation of friends that, with the exception of the last, they do not contain any notices bearing directly on the papal succession. The papal list in this exceptional case is not Eusebian, and I shall therefore defer the consideration of it for the present.

SYRIAC CHRONICLE

ROMAN BISHOPS	Dionysius		Roediger		Remarks
	Ann. Abr.	Term	Ann. Abr.	Term	
Petrus				xxv	Peter's accession twice entered in R $205\frac{7}{8}$ and 2064. Martyrdom of Peter and Paul 2084. In D likewise the death of Peter and Paul entered twice, 2084 and 2083. The notices hereabouts are frequently transposed
Linus	2090	xii	2084	xii	
Anencletus					Absent from both lists
Clemens	2106	om.	$210\frac{8}{9}$	ix	
Evarestus			$211\frac{4}{6}$	viii	Absent from D
Alexander	2124	x			Absent from R
Xystus	[2134]	iii	$213\frac{4}{5}$	iii	Date in D, Hadr. iv
Telesphorus	2144	xx	$214\frac{0}{4}$	xx	
Hyginus	[2154]	iiii	$215\frac{4}{6}$	iiii	Date in D, Anton. i
Pius	om.	xv	$215\frac{6}{8}$	xv	
Anicetus	2172	xi	$21\frac{69}{76}$	xi	
Soter	2183	viii	$218\frac{3}{5}$	viii	A double notice of Soter in R
Eleutherus	2192	xv			Absent from R
Victor			2209	x	Absent from D
Zephyrinus	2215	om.	$221\frac{0}{8}$	xviii	
Callistus	2234	om.	$223\frac{5}{9}$	v	
Urbanus	2240	ix	$22\frac{39}{45}$	ix	
Pontianus	2246	v	$22\frac{47}{51}$	xv	
Anteros	2255	*m.* I	$22\frac{55}{61}$	*m.* I	
Fabianus	2255	xii	$22\frac{55}{61}$	xii	
Cornelius	2269	ii	2269	ii	
Lucius	om.	*m.* viii	$22\frac{69}{70}$	om.	
Stephanus	om.	iii	$22\frac{69}{70}$	iii	
Xystus II					Absent from both lists
Dionysius	2280	om.			Absent from R
Felix	2292	v	$229\frac{4}{5}$	v	Events at this point confused in both D and R
Eutychianus	2298	*m.* viii	$229\frac{7}{9}$	*m.* viii	Double entry in D of Eutychianus and Gaius (called Gaianus in the first passage) under 2273 and 2298. The term-numbers the same in both entries.
Gaius	om.	xv	om.	xv	
Marcellinus	2313	om.	$23\frac{06}{14}$	om.	

It will have appeared from the tables (p. 208 sq) that the Armenian and Hieronymian versions of the *Chronicle* differ widely from one another. It will be seen also that, while Jerome exhibits so many and great divergences from the Armenian, he is yet in substantial agreement with the notices of Eusebius in the *History*. What account shall we give of these phenomena?

The solution commonly, indeed almost universally, adopted is, that the Armenian version preserves the actual form of the work as it left the hands of Eusebius[1], and that Jerome deliberately altered the dates in the *Chronicle*, making use, for this purpose, either of the *History* itself or of some catalogue closely allied to that which Eusebius had used for the *History*. This opinion however is beset with difficulties of which the following are the chief.

(1) It assumes that in the interval between his writing the *Chronicle* and the *History* Eusebius possessed himself of a second list of the popes with term-numbers, more accurate than his previous list, and that he accordingly adopted it in his later work. But the two works must have been published within a few months of each other, as the *Chronicle* is carried down to the vicennalia of Constantine (A.D. 325) and the *History* was completed apparently before the death of Crispus (A.D. 326), so that he must have been at work upon them at the same time. Nor is this all. In the opening of the *History* Eusebius himself refers to the *Chronicle*. He is speaking more especially of these very episcopal successions; and he there tells us that he intends in the present work to handle at greater length these and other events which in the *Chronicle* he had set down briefly[2]. The spirit of these words, if not the direct letter, precludes anything like a systematic revision of the chronology of the principal see in Christendom.

(2) The part thus ascribed to Jerome is hardly consistent with what we know of him and his work. It is extremely improbable that he would have taken the trouble to readjust the papal chronology in the *Chronicle*. Indeed this assumption seems to be precluded by his own language. In his preface he seeks to magnify his own services. He tells us that he supplied several omissions, 'in Romana maxime

[1] It is assumed for instance by Gutschmid (*Untersuchungen* etc p. 32), where he is discussing the relative accuracy of the Latin, Syriac, and Armenian dates; 'Von diesen sind 16, welche die Antrittsjahre der römischen Bischöfe betreffen, ohne Weiteres der armenischen Recension gut zu schreiben; denn die lateinisch-syrische hat die Liste der Kirchengeschichte an die Stelle der ursprünglichen gesetzt.' The assumption amounts to a *petitio principii*.

[2] See the passage as quoted above, p. 210, note 1.

historia'. He states moreover that the first part, as far as the Taking of Troy, 'is a mere translation from the Greek'; that from the Taking of Troy to the xxth year of Constantine he had made several additions 'quae de Tranquillo et ceteris illustribus historicis curiosissime excerpsimus'; and that all after the xxth year of Constantine was 'entirely his own.' The sources of the incidents in Roman history, which he thus boasts of adding, have been investigated by Mommsen *Die Quellen des Hieronymus* p. 667 sq (appended to his monograph on the Chronographer of 354). If Jerome had revised the papal chronology at much trouble, he would hardly have refrained from boasting of the fact.

(3) We have not only to reckon with Jerome's Latin version, but likewise with the Syriac. Now confessedly the Syriac chronology, so far as regards the early Roman succession, is substantially the same as Jerome's, whereas it exhibits none of the main features which distinguish the Armenian. But the Syriac cannot have been indebted to the Latin. This is agreed on all sides. It is necessary therefore to suppose—an extremely improbable supposition—that a Syriac reviser quite independently made the same substitution of the papal dates from the *History*, which was made by Jerome. On the other hand, if the Armenian had retained the original text of Eusebius free from corruption or revision, we should expect to find in it a strong resemblance to the Syriac. The connexion of Armenian and Syrian Christianity was close. Even if there had been no evidence that the Armenian in this case was indebted to a previous Syriac version, they would at all events be made from a similar text. If the one was not the daughter of the other, they would be related as sisters.

(4) Lastly; Harnack (see above, p. 201), comparing the chronology of the Roman succession with that of the Antiochene, believed that he had discovered a certain schematism or artificial arrangement, by which the Antiochene accessions were placed systematically each at the same fixed interval—an exact Olympiad—after the corresponding Roman. In other words the Antiochene chronology was a purely fictitious chronology. This attributed to Eusebius a somewhat stupid and not very honest procedure. Moreover the theory required such a manipulation of the facts to support it, that it stood self-condemned, and has not found any favour with subsequent critics. But it has done good service in directing attention to the relation between the chronology of the Roman and Antiochene succession. Obviously they are too symmetrical to be independent. What then is the true account of their relation? Two independent answers have been given to this question.

Lipsius (*Jahrb. f. Protest. Theol.* VI. p. 233, 1880) observed that by substituting the dates of the Roman episcopate given in the *History* for those given in the Armenian *Chronicle*, we obtain synchronisms of these two sees, after making allowance for accidental errors. In other words the Antiochene bishops, who were known or believed to be contemporary with any given Roman bishops, were co-ordinated with them in some previous document used by Eusebius—this co-ordination not being intended in the first instance to imply that their actual accessions fell on the same year, but merely that they held the sees at the same time. Lipsius' substitution of synchronisms for Harnack's artificial intervals of Olympiads was obviously correct; for it suggested an intelligible mode of procedure. His explanation however had this weak point, that to produce the synchronisms he was obliged to take his data from two different documents—the Antiochene chronology from the *Chronicle* and the Roman chronology from the *History*. To this necessity he was driven by his fundamental position—that the Armenian preserves the original dates of the Roman episcopate as given by Eusebius in the *Chronicle*.

About the same time or somewhat earlier[1], but at all events quite independently, Hort (see *Ignat. and Polyc.* II. p. 461 sq) offered another solution much simpler, though traced on the same lines. He pointed out that the synchronisms between the Roman and Antiochene bishops would be found in the *Chronicle* itself, if only we adopted not the Armenian, but the Hieronymian dates for the accession of the Roman bishops, due allowance being made for accidental errors. The simplicity of this solution is its highest recommendation. But we only attain this result, on the hypothesis that Jerome gives the original Eusebian dates, and that the Armenian chronology of the Roman episcopate is the result of later corruption or revision or both.

The difficulty might be partially met by supposing that Eusebius issued two editions of his *Chronicle*. There is indeed some independent evidence for a twofold issue. The extant work, as we have seen, is carried down to the vicennalia of Constantine (A.D. 325). But Eusebius directly refers to the *Chronicle* in two earlier works, the *Eclogae Propheticae* i. 1 (p. 1 Gaisford) and the *Praeparatio Evangelica* x. 9. 11, both written during or immediately after the persecution[2]. There must

[1] My work containing Dr Hort's solution was not published till 1885, some years after the appearance of Lipsius' paper; but this portion had been passed through the press as early as the close of 1878 or the beginning of 1879.

[2] On the two editions of the *Chronicle* see *Ignat. and Polyc.* II. p. 465, Smith and Wace *Dict. of Christ. Biogr.* s. v. 'Eusebius of Caesarea,' II. p. 321 sq.

therefore have been a prior edition of the *Chronicle* published some years before. This hypothesis however will not help us out of our difficulty; for the Armenian, like the Hieronymian, is brought down to the vicennalia and therefore does not represent this earlier edition. We might indeed fall back upon the supposition that the Armenian version was founded on a text which was a mixture of the two (see above, p. 213). But even then we have not overcome the difficulties with which we are confronted under the three previous heads. Altogether this hypothesis seems inadequate to explain the phenomena. The later edition of the *Chronicle* appears to have been nothing more than the earlier continued down to date. We must look in a wholly different direction for an explanation of the divergences.

It must be evident that in a work like the *Chronicle* the liabilities to error are manifold, and no stress therefore can be laid on any ordinary divergences. These liabilities fall under three heads.

(1) There is first the mode of tabulating the events. The events themselves were recorded in the right and left hand margins, or in the central columns between the lines of dynasties, and perhaps occasionally at the foot margin. In the modern editions they are referred to their several years in the chronological tables, which form the central column of the page, by the same letters or numbers attached to the event and to the year; but in the ancient copies, whether of the Armenian or of the Latin, there appears to be no such safeguard. The possibilities of *displacement* in the course of transcription are thus manifold.

(2) But besides the possibilities of displacement, the *confusion* of similar numbers or letters representing numbers is a still more fertile source of error. If the work is in Latin, the numerals x, v, ii, are frequently confused, so that for instance 12 and 7 (xii, vii), 7 and 4 (vii, iiii), will be substituted the one for the other, or the stroke denoting a unit will be dropped or superadded and thus for example 9 and 8 will be interchanged (viiii, viii). If it is in Greek, the errors will be different, but not less considerable. The confusion of 5 and 9 (ε, ϑ)

In these passages I have spoken of the two editions as offering a possible solution of the papal dates in the Armenian and Hieronymian versions respectively. I am now convinced that the divergences cannot be so explained. As a caution, I may add that the words of Beda *De Temp. Rat.* lxvi (*Op.* I. p. 546) 'Juxta vero Chronica eadem quae ipse Eusebius de utraque editione, ut sibi videbatur, composuit' have nothing to do with two editions of the *Chronicle* itself, as would appear to be the view of Scaliger *Thes. Temp.* Animadv. p. 4, where however 'vera' is substituted for 'utraque'. Beda is speaking of the two chronological systems of the Hebrew and LXX respectively in the Old Testament.

of 8 and 13 (η, ιγ), may be expected. In this very Armenian *Chronicle* we find Felix credited with 19 years, whereas we know from other sources that he only held office 5 years. The error has probably arisen from the confusion of ετηε and ετηιθ, the ι being explicable either by a confusion of the eye or by the fact that iotas adscript were frequently added by scribes where they were out of place, as anyone may satisfy himself by a glance at the Hyperides papyri. But in the case before us, we are dealing not only with the Latin and Greek, but likewise with one and probably two Oriental languages besides; for the existing text of the Armenian *Chronicle*, as we have seen (see p. 213 sq), must have been rendered partly from the Syriac. An abundant crop of errors would be the consequence of this double transmission[1]. The havoc made in the proper names, which in the Armenian are sometimes scarcely distinguishable, shows how great was the probability of error, where (as in the numerals) the transcribers were not guided and controlled by the sense.

(3) But arising out of these errors, a third source of change is created—*emendation* for the sake of consistency. A substitution of a wrong figure in the term-numbers, or of a wrong date in the year of reference, would introduce a discrepancy between the stated duration of office and the interval allowed in the chronological table. The next transcriber, observing this, would be tempted to bring the two into exact or proximate conformity by an alteration in one or the other or both. This source of error, arising out of *emendation*, has been almost entirely overlooked by Lipsius. Thus when Hort urges that the 9 years ascribed in the *Chronicle* to Callistus, whose actual term was 5 years, arose out of a confusion of θ and ε, Lipsius (VI. p. 272) considers it sufficient to answer that the sum total of the years ascribed to the three pontificates of Victor, Zephyrinus, and Callistus, is the same in the different lists (10 + 18 + 5 = 33 in the *History* and Hieronymian *Chronicle*, 9 + 19 + 5 = 33 in the Liberian Catalogue, 12 + 12 + 9 = 33 in the Armenian), and that therefore the 9 years are required for Callistus in this last list to make up the requisite number, because only 24 years (instead of 28) have been assigned to Victor + Zephyrinus. But this offers no explanation, why 12 years should be assigned to both Victor and Zephyrinus respectively, instead of 9 or 10 to the former and 19 or 18 to the latter. The natural explanation begins at the other end. The confusion of θ and ε involved a loss of 4 years within the

[1] See for instance the examples given by Petermann (II. p. lii, ed. Schoene); 22 for 3, 21 for 43, 51 for 19, 11 for 55, etc. The height of the Colossus (Ann. Abr. 2091) is 107 feet in Jerome, 127 in Syncellus, 128 in the Armenian.

interval of the three pontificates. A readjustment, more or less arbitrary, of the lengths assigned to the other two pontificates became necessary; and hence the result.

Thus the chances of alteration are almost unlimited; and before we argue on the divergences in the papal notices, as if they had any real value, it becomes us to enquire whether the phenomena in other parts of the *Chronicle* will not furnish some lessons for our guidance.

(1) The earliest part of the work supplies us with the most valuable test, because we have Jerome's own statement to guide us here. He tells us explicitly, as we have seen, that in the period before the Taking of Troy his edition is 'a strict translation from the Greek' (pura Graeca translatio). Here therefore the Armenian and Hieronymian versions ought to coincide but for the corruptions and vagaries of scribes. Accordingly I have taken from this period three pages at random for investigation, pp. 26, 36, 38, of Schoene's edition. The numbers describe the divergence in years between the two versions. Where no sign is prefixed, the Hieronymian dates are later; where a *minus* sign precedes, they are earlier.

On p. 26 there are twelve events, though only ten notices in the Armenian; for the 6th and 8th notices contain two events each, which are given in separate notices in Jerome. Only three out of the twelve coincide, the divergences being as follows;

0, 4, 0, 4, 5, 18, 21, 9, 9, 21, 0, 8,

and in two of these three the character of the notices themselves is such as almost to preclude the possibility of error.

On p. 36 there are nine notices, and in only one is there a coincidence of date. The divergences are

2, 1, 3, 7, 4, 0, 6, 1, 3.

On p. 38, there are five notices, and only one coincidence. The numbers describing the divergences are as follows;

2, 0, −1, 5, 1, −1.

It is quite true that the events during this period are mainly legendary, and there is therefore no adequate reason in the first instance why they should have been attached to one year more than to another. But this does not affect the question of the relation between the chronologies of the two versions of Eusebius; since Eusebius (following those who preceded him) did so attach them.

(2) I will now take samples from a succeeding period, pp. 120, 128, 152.

The first sample (p. 120) refers to the period of the First Punic War. The statistics stand thus

5, −7, −3, 6, 6, 5, −5, 2, 0, 3, 0, 1, 2, 3, 0, 1, 3, 1,

where there are eighteen notices, and only three coincidences. Moreover the violence of the transition deserves to be noticed. In the two first notices the transition is not less than twelve years—from 5 years before to 7 years after the corresponding Hieronymian notice.

On p. 128, on which the first notice refers to the destruction of Carthage, the relations of the two chronologies are represented by the numbers

4, −1, 0, −5, 2, −4, 0, 1, −1, 0, −2, 1, 0,

where there are four coincidences in thirteen events. In the last notice but two (−2), the error is not with the Armenian, but with Jerome, as the central column shows.

For p. 152, which begins A.D. 40, the numbers are as follows;

0, −1, 4, 2, 2, 1, 0, 3, 3, 2, 2, 1, −1, 2, −1, 2, 2,

where there are only two coincidences in seventeen events. These two exceptions are the deaths of Gaius (Caligula) and of Agrippa, in which owing to the arrangement of the dynasties it was next to impossible for scribes to go wrong. This is the page which immediately follows the notice of S. Peter's founding the Antiochene and Roman Churches, here assigned to A.D. 39—a date to which much significance has been attached, as differing three years from the corresponding notice in Jerome's edition, A.D. 42.

In these comparisons I have given Schoene's text of the Hieronymian version. But exception has been taken to his readings by Gutschmid, who maintains that the MS P is the best single authority. For the first five of these six pages the substitution of P for Schoene would not make any material difference; but in the last P approximates much more closely to the Armenian. The record of the variations would then be

0, −1, 3, 2, 2, 0, 0, 0, 0, 2, 0, 1, 0, 2, 0, 2, 2.

A later investigation however will show that the dates in P, though nearer to the Armenian in this part, are generally farther from the true chronology.

(3) Another test of the accuracy of the Armenian dates is the agreement or disagreement of Eusebius with himself. In the first book

of his *Chronicle*, Eusebius gives an account of the principles of his work, with the successions of the several dynasties of the different kingdoms which make up the main column of the tables contained in the chronology proper, or 'Canon', which forms the second book. For the most part this account only affects this main column, and it is just here that we can not expect divergences. But occasionally he gives some event which has no place there, but is recorded only in the lateral notices. Such for instance is the rise of the false Philip, Andriscus, and the consequent subjugation of Macedonia by the Romans. The former of these two events is dated Ol. 157. 3, and the later Ol. 157. 4 in the first book (a passage of Porphyry there quoted), where the Armenian agrees with the Greek (I. p. 239, Schoene); but in the tables in the second book (II. p. 128, Schoene) the one is Ol. 158. 3 (Ann. Abr. 1870) and the other Ol. 158. 4 (Ann. Abr. 1871). In the Hieronymian version on the other hand the dates are Ol. 157. 1 (Ann. Abr. 1865) and Ol. 157. 3 (Ann. Abr. 1867). In this particular case however the different modes of reckoning the Olympiads (see p. 217) must be taken into account.

(4) Again, as a test of the relative and absolute trustworthiness of the dates furnished by the Armenian and Hieronymian versions, it is instructive to take some period, and compare the chronology of those events in secular history of which the date is ascertained independently. For this purpose I shall select the reigns of Gaius (Caligula), Claudius, and Nero, as synchronizing with the earliest history of the Church, where the variations of the versions of the *Chronicle* are most important. The table is given on the next page (p. 230). In the Hieronymian column the main date is Schoene's, while the second date in brackets [ ] is from the MS P, which has been singled out by Gutschmid as the best.

It will be seen from this table that the general tendency of the Armenian is to antedate for this period, whether we compare it with Jerome's version or with the true chronology. It appears also that, though P approaches more nearly than Schoene's text of Jerome to the Armenian, it generally diverges more from the correct dates.

The transpositions of events are numerous, as must have been evident from what has been said already about the divergences of dates[1]. Indeed this form of error would be a dangerous snare to transcribers owing to the uncertainty of reference. Of these transpositions we have an example in the martyrdom of S. Peter and the

[1] In some cases however these transpositions appear in Schoene's text, where the Armenian is not at fault. When dealing with events referred to the same year,

EVENTS	*Arm.*	*Hieron.*	*Correct*
Gaius marries the wife of Memmius	35	38	38, not before June
Pontius Pilate commits suicide	36	38	40?
Gaius sends his sisters into exile	37	39	39
Gaius liberates Agrippa	37	36	37, April
Command to Petronius to outrage the Jews	37	38	39
Attacks on the Jews at Alexandria	37	38	38
Death of Gaius	39	39	41, Jan. 24
Great famine	40	44 [43]	42, 43
Claudius triumphs over Britain	43	44 [43]	44
Death of Agrippa	43	43	44
Census held by Claudius	44	47 [44]	48
Riot of the Jews under Cumanus	45	47 [46]	not before 49
Famine in Rome	49	48 [49]	51
Felix sent to Judæa	50	49 [50]	52
Festus succeeds Felix	53	55	60?
Death of Agrippina	54	57	59, April 13
Albinus succeeds Festus	59	60	62
Florus succeeds Albinus	62	63	64
Great fire at Rome	62	63	64
Earthquake at Laodicea, etc.	62	63	60
Olympian games postponed	63	64	65
Death of Octavia	63	66	62, June 9
Nero crowned at the Olympia	64	65 [64]	67
Nero at the Isthmia, etc.	65	65	67

accession of Linus, which two events in the Armenian version (II. p. 156) are thus recorded;

> d. Romanae ecclesiae post Petrum episcopatum excepit Linus annis xiv,
>
> f. Nero super omnia delicta primus persecutiones in Christianos excitavit, sub quo Petrus et Paulus apostoli Romae martyrium passi sunt;

where they are placed in two successive years. In the Hieronymian version on the other hand they are in the reverse order and in the same year. The Syriac agrees with the Hieronymian, as does also

Schoene records first those on the left margin and then those on the right, regardless of their actual sequence. Thus on p. 152 there are two examples;

> a. Gaius a suis ministris occisus est,
>
> b. Et per totius orbis synagogas Judaeorum statuae et imagines necnon arae erigebantur.

So again

> o. Sub Felice procuratore Judaeae multi seductores etc.,
>
> p. Claudius Filicem procuratorem Judaeae mittit etc.

These examples are not the less instructive, because the transpositions are due here not to the casual inadvertence of a scribe, but to the deliberate arrangement of an editor.

Syncellus. As Linus is made by the tradition to succeed S. Peter in the episcopate, the Hieronymian must be the original order. Indeed this error would seem to have been introduced at a late date into the Armenian text, for the Armenian chronicler Samuel gives the order correctly.

This investigation, which may be carried much farther by any one who is curious on the subject, suggests two remarks.

(1) Where the comparison of the two versions in other parts of the work shows *divergences* of date to be the general rule, rather than the rare exception, it is lost labour to deal with these divergences as having a special value in the case of the papal succession. To postulate documents and to surmise traditions in order to account for each such divergence is to weave ropes of sand.

(2) As the divergences have no special value, so neither have the *coincidences*. If the view which this examination has suggested be correct, we should expect that here and there the two versions would coincide in a date. Such a coincidence is a strong assurance that we have at the particular point the correct text of Eusebius; but of the absolute value of the date so given it is no guarantee whatever. It expresses simply the opinion of Eusebius, and nothing more. To take a case in point; Lipsius assumes that because the *Chronicle* and the *History* (with which latter Jerome here, as generally, coincides) agree in giving the year 238 (Gordian i) for the accession of Fabianus, therefore it was a date fixed by tradition (*Chronologie* p. 10, *Jahrb. f. Prot. Theol.* VI. p. 273); though at the same time he allows that it is some two years later than the correct date. The necessity of this concession might well have led him to reconsider not only his opinion here, but his general principle of dealing with these divergences and coincidences.

The following negative results follow from this discussion. (1) There is no sufficient ground for assuming that Eusebius had different documents before him, or that he adopted a different treatment, as regards the papal chronology, in the two works, the *Chronicle* and the *Ecclesiastical History*. (2) There is no adequate reason for postulating two different recensions of the *Chronicle* by Eusebius himself. Even if (as we have seen to be probable) there were two separate issues at different dates, yet we are not entitled, so far as the evidence goes, to assume that the later issue was anything more than the earlier with a continuation down to the date of the later, the vicennalia. At all events this hypothesis will not assist us in the solution of our problem: for the other edition was much earlier than the Armenian, and cannot therefore have given a revised papal chronology. (3) We are not justified in going beyond Jerome's own statement, as regards the alterations which he himself introduced into the work of Eusebius. Least of all, does the evidence support the theory of a systematic readjustment of the early papal chronology, such as many writers have ascribed to him.

These authorities then represent the single judgment—not two separate and divergent judgments—of Eusebius alone; and our object must be to compare the expression of this judgment as given in the two works, the *Chronicle* and the *History* respectively. The real difficulty lies in ascertaining the original statement of the *Chronicle*, where the divergences are so great. In comparing the two main authorities—the Armenian and Hieronymian texts—we must remember that the errors, being clerical and literary, will not be all on the one side. As we should expect to find, considering the vicissitudes through which it has passed, the Armenian is by far the most frequent offender[1]; but occasionally Jerome's recension (or at least the existing text) is demonstrably wrong. As a general rule it is safe to adopt the statement of that authority which coincides with the *History*, but there may be exceptional cases. Very rarely shall we be justified in calling in some independent tradition or some known fact of contemporary history to arbitrate.

Lipsius starts from the opposite point of view to this. The discrepancies with him represent divergences in previous documents or divergent judgments of the same or different authorities. It is only the rare exception when he attributes them to the carelessness or the manipulation of scribes. As he has contributed more than any recent writer towards the understanding of the early papal chronology, it cannot be otherwise than profitable to state the conclusions to which he is led. Much light will be thrown on the questions which confront us, even where we are unable to accept his results.

His earlier view is contained in his *Chronologie* p. 8 sq. He there divides the whole list into two parts; (1) From Peter to Urbanus, (2) From Pontianus to Gaius. In the second part the Armenian and the *History* generally coincide, so far as regards the term-numbers; but in the first part there is much difference. The discrepancy however is chiefly at the beginning (Peter, Linus, Anencletus) and at the end

[1] Gutschmid's estimate (*Untersuchungen* p. 39 sq) is somewhat more favourable to the Armenian version. But to begin with (see above, p. 222, note 1), he *assumes* that its papal dates are correct.

(Victor, Zephyrinus, Callistus, Urbanus) of the series. In the intermediate part of the list—from Clement to Eleutherus—there is substantial agreement. Again, the two nearly coincide in the date of the death of Urbanus. It is true that in the *History* no imperial synchronism is given for this event; but his accession is there placed somewhere about the first year of Alexander, and 8 years are assigned to him, so that his death must on this reckoning fall within two years of Alexander vii, which is the date assigned to it in the Armenian. Again, while the numbers giving the duration of the several episcopates are different in the two lists (the Armenian and the *History*), the sum total of these from Peter to Urbanus inclusive coincides. It is indeed 191 years in the Armenian and only 189 in the *History*; but if in the case of Eleutherus we correct the error of Eusebius in assigning to him 13 years instead of 15, which appears in the other lists, the coincidence is exact. Thus then the tradition underlying the two catalogues of Eusebius (in the *Chronicle* and in the *History* respectively) agree in the names, the order, and the sum total of the years from Peter to Urbanus. As regards the discrepancies in the term-numbers, the early differences (Peter, Linus, Anencletus) are due not to different traditions, but to critical manipulation and adjustment; the differences in the intermediate portion—between Clement and Eleutherus—are insignificant and for critical purposes may be neglected; but the differences at the end of the list (Victor, Zephyrinus, Callistus) are so considerable as to point to a separate source of tradition.

The latter part of the catalogues yields different results. In this latter part both lists of Eusebius involve statements strangely at variance with trustworthy information derived from other sources. In order to explain these, it is necessary here by anticipation to speak of the Liberian Catalogue which emanated from the Roman Church and is incorporated by the Chronographer of 354. This catalogue gives not only years, but months and days also. In the comparative table however, which follows, I shall record only the years and months, omitting the days, as we are not concerned with them here. The complete document will be found below (p. 253 sq). It is clear from the comparison that Eusebius had before him for this period a similar list, but blurred and mutilated, so that he has confused months and years and produced a strangely incongruous result. In the table I have for the sake of convenience added the Hieronymian and Syriac lists also to those of the Armenian *Chronicle* and of the *History*, as I shall have to refer to them presently; and for the same reason the table is continued down to Liberius, with whom the Liberian Catalogue ends.

NAMES	LIBERIAN		H. E.	ARMEN.	SYRIAC	HIERON.
Pontianus	Ann. v,	m. ii	Ann. vi	Ann. viii	Ann. v.	Ann. v
Anteros		m. i	Mens. i	Mens. i	Mens. i	Mens. i
Fabianus	Ann. xiii,	m. i	Ann. xiii	Ann. xiii	Ann. xii	Ann. xiii
Cornelius	Ann. ii,	m. iii	Ann. iii	Ann. iii	Ann. ii	Ann. ii
Lucius	Ann. iii,	m. viii	Mens. viii	Mens. ii	Mens. viii	Mens. viii
Stephanus	Ann. iiii,	m. ii	Ann. ii	Ann. ii	Ann. iii	Ann. iii
Xystus	Ann. ii,	m. xi	Ann. xi	Ann. xi		
Dionysius	Ann. viii,	m. ii	Ann. viiii	Ann. xii		Ann. viiii
Felix	Ann. v,	m. xi	Ann. v	Ann. xix	Ann. v.	Ann. v
Eutychianus	Ann. viii,	m. xi	Mens. x	Mens. ii	Mens. viii	Mens. viii
Gaius	Ann. xii,	m. iiii	Ann. xv	Ann. xv	Ann. xv	Ann. xv
Marcellinus	Ann. viii,	m. iii				
Marcellus	Ann. i,	m. vii				(omitted)
Eusebius		m. iiii				Mens. vii
Miltiades	Ann. iii,	m. vi				Ann. iiii
Silvester	Ann. xxi,	m. xi				Ann. xxii
Marcus		m. viii				Mens. viii
Julius	Ann. xv,	m. i				A. xvi m. iiii
Liberius						

A glance at this table reveals the source of the errors in the Eusebian chronology during this period. For Cornelius, Stephanus, and Xystus, Eusebius sets down as years the numbers which in the original document represented months. For the intermediate name of Lucius he gives the months correctly as months but omits the iii years. The insertion of the iii years indeed is an error in the existing text of the Liberian document, for Lucius' episcopate lasted only viii months. In the case of Eutychianus also the years are omitted, but (looking at the diverse authorities) it may be a question here whether Eusebius treated the years as months (viii of the Hieronymian and Syriac lists) or kept the months as such (the x of the *History*, corrupted from xi). Lipsius adopts the latter alternative, as consonant with his general theory of the relation of the Hieronymian *Chronicle* to the Eusebian. For the rest, the xv of Gaius is a corruption of xii, which we find in the Liberian list and which is his correct term of office. Conversely the viiii for Dionysius gives the true number of years, so that in the viii of the present Liberian text a unit must have been dropped.

His inference from this investigation is as follows. The original list which was the foundation of the Eusebian catalogues ended with Eleutherus, at which point also the lists of Hegesippus (Eus. *H. E.* iv. 22) and Irenæus (*Haer.* iii. 3. 3) stopped. This original list was continued by various persons. When he compiled the *Chronicle*, Eusebius had one such list before him, carried down to the death of Gaius and accession of Marcellinus. When he wrote the *History*, he had obtained possession of another such list, carried down to the same point. These two lists were independent of each other for the first part—from Peter to Urbanus; but for the latter part—from Pontianus to Gaius—they were derived from the same source, and therefore are not to be regarded as separate authorities. This source was, as we have seen, a corrupt and mutilated copy of a list which was substantially the same as the Liberian Catalogue. Of the two lists which Eusebius had before him, that which he discovered after the compilation of the *Chronicle* was the more correct; and seeing this, he substituted its numbers in his *History*, in place of those previously adopted by him in the *Chronicle*.

Jerome, according to Lipsius, treated the *Chronicle* of Eusebius with a very free hand. For the imperial synchronisms and the term-numbers which he found there, he substituted those which appear in the *History*. He did not however derive them directly from the *History* but from a catalogue closely allied to that which Eusebius used for this work, yet presenting affinities with later Latin catalogues (e.g. the Felician), of which therefore it was presumably the parent. This catalogue had originally ended with Urbanus, but was continued to Marcellinus, and then again by another hand to Silvester. The document used for the continuation was closely allied to the Liberian Catalogue. It was not however the same document which had been used for the two Eusebian lists. It was blurred and mutilated, like the Eusebian document; for Jerome, like Eusebius, confuses years with months. But Jerome preserves the correct years both for Cornelius ii, where Eusebius substitutes the months iii, and for Stephanus iii, where Eusebius substitutes the months ii. Again for Eutychianus, Jerome transforms the years viii into months, whereas Eusebius omits the years altogether and gives only the months x. On the other hand it was more correct in some respects than our present Liberian text, for it preserved the correct number of years for Stephanus (iii, not iiii) and for Dionysius (viiii, not viii). In all this Lipsius sees evidence that Jerome had in his hands besides the works of Eusebius a catalogue of Roman origin likewise.

The real gain here, for which Lipsius deserves our thanks, is the explanation of the figures in Eusebius and Jerome for the period between Pontianus and Gaius. He has rightly discerned that the strange anomalies here arise from a mutilated and inaccurate transcript (in which years and months were confused) of the document embodied in the Liberian Catalogue. Erbes indeed has called this explanation in question (*Jahrb. f. Protest. Theol.* v. p. 640 sq); but he has been refuted by Lipsius (*ib.* VI. p. 283 sq), nor is his view at all likely to command assent. The relation between the Eusebian and Liberian lists is patent, when once pointed out. But our thanks are not the less due to the critic who placed in our hands the key which unlocks the secret.

The rest of this theorizing seems to me to be lost labour. So far as regards the Eusebian lists, the break which Lipsius finds between Urbanus and Pontianus is purely fictitious. When we come to consider the Liberian Catalogue, we shall find a line of demarcation at this point; but in Eusebius himself there is no indication of any difference of treatment or variation of authority. Again, I need say nothing of the different authorities which Eusebius is supposed to have employed in composing the *Chronicle* and the *History* respectively. At a later date, as we shall see presently, Lipsius himself abandoned this earlier view. For the rest, I have already stated at sufficient length what I consider to be the true principle of explanation as regards the discrepancies in the two works of Eusebius. But a few words may not be out of place to dispose of the *third* document, which Lipsius adds to the two Eusebian lists—the catalogue supposed to be used by Jerome. For the period, which is covered by Eusebius, I cannot see any evidence that Jerome travelled beyond Eusebius himself. The differences in the case of Cornelius ii (iii) and Stephanus iii (ii) are samples of the commonest type of clerical error. The number of months viii assigned to Eutychianus where the present text of Eusebius has x is quite as easily explained by a confusion of H or II and I, as by the hypothesis of Lipsius. On the other hand a very serious demand is made on our estimate of probabilities by Lipsius when he postulates two corrupt copies of the list between Pontianus and Gaius—one in the hands of Eusebius and the other in the hands of Jerome—both corrupt and mutilated in the same sort of way, so as to create a confusion of years and months, and yet not with the same mutilations, so that the results are different. For the concluding period from Marcellinus to Damasus, where he had no longer the guidance of Eusebius, I see no reason for supposing that Jerome had any list before him. The Liberian list at all events cannot have been his authority, for he diverges too widely from it. This period comprises eight names. One of these, Marcellus, Jerome omits altogether. For another, Marcellinus, he apparently gives a different form, Marcellianus. Of the names which he has, he gives no figures at all for two out of the seven, Marcellianus and Liberius. Of the remaining five, the figures for four—Eusebius, Miltiades, Silvester, Julius—are different. Thus in the whole list there is only one strict coincidence, in the case of Marcus, to whom viii months are assigned in both lists. But Marcus held the episcopate almost within his own lifetime; and the number here seems to be strictly correct. In a single instance only, that of Julius, does he give the months as well as the years; and though Julius likewise was his contemporary, his numbers seem in this case to be wrong. Altogether the phenomena suggest not transcription from a complete and definite list, but recourse to such fragmentary knowledge as he had ready at hand either in books or through personal enquiry or by direct knowledge of the facts.

I need not follow the earlier speculations of Lipsius any further. This line of treatment leads him to very complicated results, as may be seen from the genealogy of early papal lists which he gives, *Chronologie* p. 39 sq. His later theory involves the abandonment of these results to a considerable extent, while it tends to greater simplification. But he still fails to shake himself free from the preconceived opinion respecting the Armenian *Chronicle*, which fetters his critical movements and more or less affects his results.

His later investigations will be found in an article entitled *Die Bischofslisten des Eusebius* in *Neue Studien zur Papstchronologie* (*Jahrb. f. Protest. Theol.* VI. p. 233 sq, 1880). He now supposes that Eusebius had in his hands exactly the same documents, neither more nor fewer, when he wrote his two works, the *Chronicle* and the *History* (see pp. 241 sq, 245 sq, 266 sq, 274). These documents, so far as regards the earlier popes—from Peter to Urbanus—were two in number. (A) An Antiochene Chronicle which gave the accessions of the Roman bishops under the regnal years of the emperors, as we find them recorded in the *History*, and which likewise placed side by side the contemporaneous Roman, Antiochene, and Alexandrian bishops. (B) A Catalogue of the Roman bishops which gave simply the names and the duration of office in years. In his *History* Eusebius for the most part gave the statements of the two documents together, without any attempt to reconcile them where there was a discrepancy. In his *Chronicle* on the other hand he manipulated them, as the form of the work required him to do, in order to adapt them one to another and to preconceived chronological theories of his own. Of the documentary theory of Lipsius I shall have something to say hereafter. For the present we are only concerned with his attempt to explain the phenomena of the *Chronicle*, which may be summed up as follows.

The martyrdom of S. Peter was placed by A in A.D. 67, and the accession of Linus in A.D. 68. Thus reckoning 25 years backwards we arrive at A.D. 42 as the beginning of S. Peter's episcopate. On the other hand in B the martyrdom was placed in A.D. 64, the year of the fire at Rome and of the outbreak of the persecution, so that the accession of Linus would fall in A.D. 65. In the *Chronicle* Eusebius combines the two. While retaining A.D. 67 as the year of Peter's death with A, he adopts A.D. 65 as the year of Linus' accession from B. In A the episcopate of Linus extends over twelve years, A.D. 68—79. In B also his term of office is xii years, but Eusebius makes it xiv, so as to fill up two out of the three additional years which he has gained by ante-dating the accession of Linus. Thus the episcopate of Linus extends over A.D. 65—78. The term-number of the next bishop Anencletus is xii, and by adding on a single year Eusebius might have made all straight. Why he did not adopt this very obvious expedient, Lipsius does not explain. On the contrary, he supposes him to have perversely reduced Anencletus' term of office from xii to viii, thus increasing the number of superfluous years from one to five. But there is more than compensation for this excess at the other end of the list. Lipsius finds that the same year (Elagabalus i), which in the *History* is assigned to the accession of Callistus, appears in the *Chronicle* as the year of his death. This he supposes to be a blunder of Eusebius, though Eusebius is quite explicit on the subject in his *History*, on which he must have been engaged at the same time with his *Chronicle*. By this error a loss of 6 or 7 years is incurred at the end of the list. It is impossible therefore to allow Anencletus his full dozen of years, and he is curtailed accordingly. But again there are unexplained difficulties. Why should Anencletus especially be selected for this act of robbery, though so many episcopates have interposed? Why again should he be robbed of four years, and four only, when five were wanted? In the intermediate period the divergences vary on no intelligible principle; nor is it easy to see what explanation can be given of them, so long as Eusebius is held responsible for the Armenian numbers. Certainly Lipsius has failed altogether to explain them. The divergences expressed in years during this period (as will appear from the table printed above, p. 208) are represented by this series,

1, 5, 6, 6, 5, 4, 4, 4, 5, 4, 4, 3, 2, 7;

where the first and last are those of the accessions of Anencletus and Callistus respectively. To explain the curtailment of Anencletus by the blunder about Callistus, where there were twelve intervening episcopates to draw upon, where the divergences vary in this capricious way, and where the compensation might have been so much more easily obtained in the immediate neighbourhood of Callistus, is to make a demand upon the critical judgment which it will hesitate to meet.

It will have appeared that the two main pillars of this theory are *first* the speculation relating to the respective dates of the death of S. Peter and the accession of Linus, and *secondly* the supposed error of Eusebius in confusing the dates of the accession and death of Callistus. On the first point I have said something already (pp. 228, 231) and shall have to return to the subject at a later stage. The second may be briefly dismissed. This is not the only episcopate in which the accession of a pope in the Armenian synchronizes with his death in the Hieronymian or the *History*, or conversely. The tables given above (p. 208 sq) will show that the same phenomenon recurs in the case of Hyginus, when it falls in the first year of Antoninus, and of Stephanus, when it falls in the second year of Gallus. Are we to suppose that Eusebius was guilty of the same confusion in these two cases likewise? If this is so, why should the coincidence deserve special prominence in the case of Callistus, to the entire neglect of these two strictly analogous cases?

This account, however imperfect, of the earlier and later views of so able and accomplished a critic as Lipsius will not have been in vain, if it has shown the hopelessness of arriving at a solution, so long as the papal chronology of the *Chronicle*, as it left the hands of Eusebius, is sought in the Armenian version.

Indeed all the direct evidence tends in the opposite direction. We have seen already that we are not warranted by anything in Jerome's own language in supposing that he made such sweeping changes in the papal chronology as on this assumption would have been the case. Again, the Syriac epitome in its papal chronology, coincides with the Hieronymian version both in the term-numbers and in the dates of accession, proper allowance being made for occasional errors of transcription[1]. Yet it is very improbable, as Lipsius himself says (*Chronologie* p. 27), and as is allowed by Gutschmid (p. 26), that the Syrian epitomator should have made use of Jerome; and they can only offer the suggestion that this epitomator must have had possession of a list closely allied to that which was in Jerome's hands and altered his text accordingly, or that such a list must have been already incorporated into the text of the *Chronicle* which he had before him[2]. This theory in fact re-

[1] The only divergence of any importance is in the successive episcopates of Xystus and Telesphorus, which are 3+20=23 in the Syriac, whereas they are 11+11=22 in the Armenian and 10+11=21 in the Hieronymian (which accords with the *History*). This is an illustration of the procedure mentioned above (p. 226), whereby an error in one episcopate leads to a corresponding readjustment in the next, so that the total is the same or nearly the same.

[2] Gutschmid (l. c.) suggests that this revised edition of the *Chronicle* was the

quires us to postulate *three* separate persons manipulating the original chronology of the *Chronicle* independently, but in the same way; (1) Eusebius himself in his *History*, (2) Jerome in his Latin version, and (3) A Syriac translator or epitomator, or some previous person whose text he used.

A little more light is thrown upon this question by the later Greek and Oriental lists. The table on the next page exhibits the papal chronology of these lists compared with the Eusebian. On the left hand of the names are placed the Eusebian lists, as represented by the four different authorities, a, b, c, d. On the right are the later lists. A is taken from the 'Short Chronography' (*χρονογραφεῖον συντόμον*) which was compiled in the year 853 and professes to be derived 'from the works of Eusebius' (*ἐκ τῶν Εὐσεβίου τοῦ Παμφίλου πονημάτων*). It was first published by Mai (*Script. Vet. Nov. Coll.* I. i. p. 2 sq), and has been re-edited by Schoene (Euseb. *Chronicon* I. App. iv. p. 66 sq). The papal list (*πατριάρχαι Ῥώμης*) which it contains will be found in Duchesne *Lib. Pont.* I. p. 34 sq. The extract relating to Clement has been given above, p. 198. The list of bishops in this catalogue is continued to Paschal I (A.D. 817—824), but the term-numbers end with Pelagius I († A.D. 561), so that the document on which this part of the chronography was founded must belong to this epoch. B is from the *Chronographica Brevis* of Nicephorus, patriarch of Constantinople († A.D. 828), and will be found in de Boor's edition of his works, p. 121 (Leipzig, 1880). It is given also by Duchesne *Lib. Pontif.* I. p. 37 sq. The extract relating to Clement will be found above, p. 195. The term-numbers reach as far as Benedict I († A.D. 579), the names alone being continued down to Boniface IV (A.D. 608—615). C is gathered from the notices in Georgius Syncellus (see for example the notice given above, p. 195), who wrote about A.D. 800. The collective list, thus gathered together, may be seen in Lipsius *Chronol.* p. 30, or Duchesne *Lib. Pont.* I. p. 39. The last pope whose accession is recorded is Benedict I († A.D. 579). D is from the *Annales* of Eutychius (Saïd-Ebn-Batrik), which work is brought down to A.D. 937. He had a continuous catalogue of popes which ended with John IV (A.D. 640—642), the successor of Severus († A.D. 640). This work was first published under the title *Contextio Gemmarum sive Eutychii Patriarchae Alexandrini Annales* by Selden

work of Eusebius himself and that its home was Syria. To this I would reply (1) That, as I have already stated (p. 225), there is no notice of any such revision; and (2) That this view fails to explain the divergences in the two synchronous works, the *History* and the Armenian *Chronicle*.

EUSEBIAN LISTS				ROMAN BISHOPS	LATER GREEK AND ORIENTAL LISTS				
a. *Armenian*	*b.* *Hieronymian*	*c.* *Syriac*	*d.* *H. E.*		A. *Chronog.* 853	B. *Nicephorus*	C. *Georg. Syncell.*	D. *Eutychius*	E. *Elias Nisib.*
xx	xxv	xxv		Petrus	xxii	ii		xxii	xxviii
xiiii	xi	xii	xii	Linus	xii	xii	xviii	xii	xii
viii	xii		xii	Anencletus	xii	ii	ii	ii	viii
viiii	viiii	viiii	viiii	Clemens	viiii	viiii	viiii	viiii	viiii
viii	viiii	viii	viii	Euarestus	x	viiii	viiii	viii	viii
x	x	x	x	Alexander	xiii	xii	xii	x	x
xi	x	iii	x	Xystus	x	viiii	viiii	x	x
xi	xi	xx	xi	Telesphorus	xi	x	x	xi	xi
iiii	iiii	iiii	iiii	Hyginus	xiiii	iiii	iiii	iiii	iiii
xv	xv	xv	xv	Pius	xv	xv	xv	xv	xv
xi	xi	xi	xi	Anicetus	xi	xi	xi	xi	xi
viii	viii	viii	viii	Soter	viii	viiii	viiii	viii	viii
xv	xv	xv	xiii	Eleutherus	xiii	xv	v	xv	xv
xii	x	x	x	Victor	x	xii	xii	x	x
xii		xviii	xviii	Zephyrinus	xviiii	xviiii	xviiii	xviii	xviii
viiii	v	v	v	Callistus	viii	viii	viii	vi	v
	viiii	viiii	viii	Urbanus	vii	vii	vii	iiii	viii
viiii	v	v	vi	Pontianus	vii	iii	iii	v	v
m. i	m. i	m. i	m. i	Anteros	m. i	m. i	m. [ ]	xii	m. i
xiii	xiii	xii		Fabianus	x	xiii	xiii	xiii	xiii
iii	ii	ii	iii	Cornelius	iii	iii	ii	ii	ii
m. ii	m. viii	m. viii	m. viii	Lucius	viii	ii	ii	m. viii	viii
ii	iii	iii	ii	Stephanus	ii	viiii	ii	vi	ii
xi			xi	Xystus	xi	ii	viiii	viiii	xi
xii	viiii		viiii	Dionysius	viiii	viii	viii	viii	viiii
xviiii	v	v	v	Felix	v	v	v	v	v
m. ii	m. viii	m. viii	m. x	Eutychianus	m. x	m. viii	m. viii	viii	viii
xv	xv	xv	xv	Gaius	xv	xv	xv	xii	xii

and Pococke (Oxford 1658), and is reprinted in Migne's *Patrol. Graec.* CXXI. p. 892 sq. E is the *Chronography* of Elias of Nisibis, who wrote in the eleventh century. The autograph (in Syriac and Arabic) is in the British Museum (*Rich.* 7197, fol. 5 b). It is edited by Abbeloos and Lamy in Gregor. Barhebr. *Chronicon* I. p. 38 (Louvain 1872), but had been previously given in a German translation by Lipsius *Chronologie* p. 36 sq. from a transcript made by Sachau[1]. Elias gives a list of the 'patriarchs' of Rome from the time of the Apostles to the Council of Chalcedon (Leo I).

Of these five lists ABCD concur in writing 'Soterichus' (Σωτήριχος) for Soter; BD have Flavianus (Φλαυιανός) for Fabianus; and B has Antros (Ἄντρος) for Anteros. The names are occasionally so obscured in D, that they would scarcely be recognized except for their position, e.g. Aurianus, Bitianus, for Urbanus, Pontianus. Pontianus and Anteros are transposed in C, so that Anteros takes the precedence, as in the Felician list and in some copies of the *Liber Pontificalis*; but the note is added, 'Some say that Pontianus was bishop before Anteros' (τινὲς Ποντιανὸν πρὸ τοῦ Ἀντέρωτός φασιν ἐπισκοπῆσαι). The successor of Linus is Anencletus in ABC and Cletus in E. In D he appears as 'Dacletius,' and this probably represents 'Cletus,' the first syllable being the Arabic and Syriac prefix, just as Pius is written 'Dapius' in *Ancient Syriac Documents* p. 71 (ed. Cureton). While C assigns 19 years to Zephyrinus, he adds, 'but according to Eusebius 12 years' (κατὰ δὲ Εὐσέβιον ἔτη δώδεκα).

Comparing these lists together, we meet with frequent repetitions of the usual types of error; such as the omission or addition of letters, e.g. β′ for κβ′ or ιβ′ in Petrus (B) and Anencletus (BCD), ιδ′ for δ′ in Hyginus (A), etc. Again, other variations may be explained by a confusion of letters, such as H and I (Euarestus x for viii in A). Again, others are accounted for by accidental transpositions. The numbers of Stephanus and Xystus in B, as compared with C, exhibit this last source of error. If besides the confusions in the Greek notation we take into account the Syriac and Arabic, and if, moreover, we are allowed to suppose

[1] There are several discrepancies between these two transcriptions of the papal list; and Duchesne (*Lib. Pont.* I. p. 41) professing to derive his information from one or other of these sources adds fresh variations of his own. By the kindness of Mr E. Budge who consulted the MS for me I am able to give the correct numbers, where there are any discrepancies. For Euarestus the number is viii, not x; for Anteros, i *month*, not i *year*; for Fabianus xiii, not iii; for Lucius viii *years*, not viii *months*; for Marcellinus x *months*, not x *years*; for Miltiades viii, not xviii; for Damasus viii years.

that the lists in some cases passed through the medium of the Latin language, we have an explanation which might cover all the variations.

A comparison of the lists shows at once that ABC are not independent of one another. Not only have they the name Soterichus in common (a feature appearing likewise in D, as we have seen), but in the middle of the list (Zephyrinus 19, Callistus 8, Urbanus 7, and partly Pontianus 7) they have characteristic numbers in common, which do not appear in any of the Eusebian lists. For the rest the alliance of all the lists with the Eusebian will be obvious. As regards A, if we set aside the years of Peter which were a matter of speculation rather than of tradition, if we except likewise the four pontificates just mentioned, and if we correct the errors arising from the causes suggested in the last paragraph, we get a complete Eusebian list. Lipsius maintains that this Eusebian affinity is derived from the *History* not from the *Chronicle.* This may have been the case, but the evidence is not conclusive. His main argument is the number xiii (instead of xv) for Eleutherus, a peculiarity found in no other papal list. But the value of this coincidence is largely discounted by the following considerations. (1) In this chronographer's list Eleutherus is numbered the 13th bishop of Rome (S. Peter being counted in), so that there may be a confusion here between the term-number and the order of succession; (2) The sequence xiii, x, given for Eleutherus, Victor, here is the same sequence which is given a few lines above for Alexander, Xystus, so that the eye of the transcriber may have wandered; (3) Though the term-number in the Armenian *Chronicle* is 15, yet the *interval* is only 13 years. Lipsius' theory is that these three lists ABC were based on an independent catalogue; that this independent catalogue was followed more strictly by BC; but that in A it was corrected for the most part from the *History* of Eusebius, and to this limited extent A's list might be said to be derived 'from the works of Eusebius'. I would only remark in passing that these words implying indebtedness to Eusebius have no direct reference to the papal list, that they seem to refer more particularly to the general chronographical sketch which immediately follows them, and that many other parts of this chronographer's work were certainly not taken from Eusebius. For the rest, I agree so far with Lipsius, as to think it probable that the features, which are shared in common by these three authorities ABC and partly also by D, should be attributed to another separate list; but, whether this list was or was not *ultimately* derived from the Eusebian list in the *Chronicle*, where they travel over the same ground, is another question. The sources and affinities of these lists, when they leave Eusebius behind, will be a matter for investigation hereafter. It is clear that Syncellus had two authorities before him, at least for some points. His statements, respecting the years of Zephyrinus and the reversal of the order of Anteros and Pontianus, show this. In the former case he evidently adopts the number which he finds in the document common to ABC, while he gives as the alternative the number 12, which he ascribes to Eusebius and which is found only in the Armenian recension of the *Chronicle*. In the latter case, he himself adopts the order which places Anteros before Pontianus—an order which is wrong in itself and appears only in some Latin lists; but he mentions the other order as adopted by 'some persons,' so that he must have had both before him. In the fourth list, D, the affinities with the peculiarities of ABC are very slight. Indeed beyond the name Soterichus there is very little on which we can fasten, as suggesting an identity of source. The numbers are for the most part Eusebian. Where they diverge from Eusebius (e.g. in Urbanus, Anteros, Stephanus), they are generally unique. The only exception is the two consecutive numbers, 9, 8, for Xystus and Dionysius. In the last list E, there is no indication of the use of any other but Eusebian data for any of the popes before the persecution of Diocletian, except Gaius, the last of them, where for xv, which is given in all the Eusebian lists, E has xii, which was the correct number. All the other numbers are either Eusebian or obvious corruptions of such.

Two important considerations are suggested by an inspection of these lists.

(1) Of all ancient documents we should expect the *Chronicle* of Eusebius to be taken as the authority for later lists. It was the most famous and the most available source of information on this and similar points. To this source, rather than to the *History*, we should expect later compilers of chronographies and catalogues to turn for information. In the *Chronicle* the required facts are tabulated in proper sequence; in the *History* they must be sought out here and there with much pains, and pieced together. Yet in all these later Greek and Oriental catalogues there is no trace whatever of the adoption of the chronology of the Eusebian *Chronicle*, as a whole, if this chronology is correctly represented by the Armenian version. On the other hand if the *Chronicle*, as it left the hands of Eusebius, agreed substantially with the *History* in its papal chronology, and if therefore it is properly represented not by the Armenian, but by the Latin translation and the Syriac epitome, it has exerted its proper influence on subsequent lists. Moreover the phenomena are just what we might expect on this supposition.

The form which the *Chronicle* has assumed in the Armenian version was not the result of a single deliberate and systematic revision. It was rather the gradual accumulation of transcribers' errors in the course of transmission. On the former hypothesis we should expect the phenomena of the Armenian version to be reproduced whole, where they are reproduced at all, in later lists. Thus the assignment of xiv years to Linus and viii years to Anencletus (instead of xii to each) was, according to the view of Lipsius and others, a product of a single deliberate act; the two numbers hanging together. We should expect therefore, in the later catalogues, where we find the one, to find the other also. On the other hand, if the individual variations are the result of isolated errors, the one may easily be present where the other is absent. And this is exactly what we do find. Thus in E the Armenian figure viii is adopted for Anencletus, while the original xii for Linus remains untouched. The process of corruption was not completed, when Elias, or rather the previous authority whom Elias copied, took his list from Eusebius.

In the first instance then the divergences of the Armenian should probably be attributed to the errors and caprice of transcribers, with the compensations and corrections to which, as I have indicated above (p. 226), these errors may have given occasion. But the question still remains whether, over and above such isolated displacements, this form of the *Chronicle* may not have undergone a systematic critical revision, at least so far as regards the papal list, from some later hand. The one single reason for this surmise lies in the fact that the dates of the papal accessions are almost universally antedated, being on the average three or four years earlier in the Armenian than in the Hieronymian form or in the *History*. This fact suggests that some later critical reviser had a theory with respect to the commencement of the list, and pushed back the Eusebian dates accordingly throughout the whole line. On this point it is impossible to speak with confidence, until some further light is thrown on the subject.

(2) There is a singular agreement (after due allowance made for corruptions) in all the lists, more especially in the early part from Linus to Eleutherus. We must however set aside the years of Peter, which (as I have already stated) were a matter of critical inference and of arithmetical calculation based thereupon, and therefore vary in the different catalogues. For the rest, even where the discrepancies seem greatest, we often find that the total sum for two or three successive popes coincides. Thus for Alexander and Xystus we have $12 + 9 = 21$ in BC, but $10 + 11 = 21$ in the Armenian. So again for Victor, Zephyr-

inus, and Callistus, we have 10 + 18 + 5 = 33 in the *History* and in the Syriac *Chronicle* (presumably also in the Hieronymian), but 12 + 12 + 9 = 33 in the Armenian. Again for Urbanus and Pontianus we have 9 + 5 = 14 in the Hieronymian and Syriac *Chronicle*, but 8 + 6 = 14 in the *History*. These agreements in the total sum, where the items are different, may be explained by a tabular arrangement in a parent document, similar to that which we have in the Eusebian *Chronicle*. The limits kept their proper places, but the intermediate positions were displaced and readjusted in different ways.

We may then with tolerable confidence restore the Eusebian catalogue as follows:

1. Linus xii
2. Anencletus xii
3. Clemens viiii
4. Euarestus viii
5. Alexander x
6. Xystus x
7. Telesphorus xi
8. Hyginus iiii
9. Pius xv
10. Anicetus xi
11. Soter viii
12. Eleutherus xv
13. Victor x
14. Zephyrinus xviii
15. Callistus v
16. Urbanus viiii (viii)
17. Pontianus v (vi)
18. Anteros mens. i
19. Fabianus xiii
20. Cornelius ii (iii)
21. Lucius mens. viii
22. Stephanus iii (ii)
23. Xystus xi
24. Dionysius viiii
25. Felix v
26. Eutychianus mens. viii
27. Gaius xv,

where the figures in brackets show the less probable but still possible alternatives.

3.

THE LIBERIAN CATALOGUE.

This catalogue of the Roman bishops forms one of several tracts, chronological and topographical, which were gathered together and edited in the year 354[1]. It is sometimes called the *Liberian* from the pope whose name ends the list and in whose time therefore presumably it was drawn up, sometimes the *Philocalian* from Philocalus or Filocalus

[1] Mommsen (p. 607) remarks on the 'mere accident' that the older recension of the *Chronicon Paschale* ended with this same year (see Ducange II. p. 16, ed. Bonn.); but indeed the existence of this older recension has been questioned by Clinton (*Fast. Rom.* II. p. 209) for valid reasons.

whose name appears on the title page as the illuminator and who is supposed consequently to have been the editor of the collection, sometimes the *Bucherian* from the modern critic Bucher who first printed this Papal list in full and thus rendered it accessible to scholars (*de Doctrina Temporum Commentarius in Victorium Aquitanum*, Antwerp, 1633, 1644).

This collection of tracts is the subject of an admirable monograph by Th. Mommsen *Ueber den Chronographen vom Jahre* 354, published in the *Abhandlungen der philolog. histor. Classe der Königl. Sächs. Gesellschaft der Wissenschaften* I. p. 549 sq. (1850), in which a flood of light is thrown upon it by the sagacity and learning of this eminent scholar. Mommsen's labours have been supplemented (so far as regards the papal catalogue) by other scholars whose names have been mentioned already (p. 201), and among whom the chief place must be assigned to Lipsius.

The work is extant in two transcripts, each made from an earlier MS now lost, but known to critics since the revival of letters.

(1) *Bruxell.* 7542—7548, a transcript made by H. Rossweyde from an old MS, of which we hear as being at Luxembourg in 1560 and which was afterwards in the hands of Peiresc. This MS is stated by Peiresc to have been written in the viiith or ixth century. It contained elaborate illuminations, of which he made copies, now preserved in the Vatican Library (*Vatic.* 9135).

(2) *Vindobon.* 3416, a transcript in the Vienna Library made at the end of the xvth century from an older MS. Some fragments of a MS of the ixth century are still preserved at Berne (*Bernens.* 108), and in all probability these belong to the original from which *Vindobon.* 3416 was transcribed.

Full accounts of these manuscripts will be found in Mommsen p. 550 sq.; see also Duchesne *L. P.* I. p. vi.

The contents of the two manuscripts differ in some respects. The difference is exhibited in the following table:

Brussels MS.	*Vienna MS.*
	1. Title Leaf
	2. [wanting]
	3. Calendars
	Imperial Annals to A.D. 539
4. Consular Fasti from A.D. 205	4. Consular Fasti from the beginning
5. Paschal Tables	5. Paschal Tables

Brussels MS.	*Vienna MS.*
6. List of City Prefects	6. List of City Prefects
7. Commemoration Days (Depositio) of Bishops and Martyrs	7. Commemoration Days (Depositio) of Bishops and Martyrs
8. Catalogue of Roman Bishops	8. Catalogue of Roman Bishops
	Imperial Annals to A.D. 496
9. [wanting]	9. Chronicle of the World
10. [wanting]	10. Chronicle of the City
11. [wanting]	11. Regions of the City
1. Title Leaf	
2. Natales Caesarum	
3. Calendars (mutilated)	

The tracts are here arranged in the order in which they occur in the two MSS respectively. The numbers I have prefixed for convenience, so as to show the probable sequence in the original collection.

In the Brussels MS it is evident at once that the last leaves have been displaced, either in this MS itself or in the parent MS from which it was transcribed. Thus the tracts which I have numbered 1, 2, 3, should be transferred to the beginning. At the same time it is mutilated in what ought to be the middle part (3, 4), the Calendars (3) having gaps here and there, and the Consular Fasti (4) having lost the beginning, so that instead of commencing with Brutus and Collatinus (A.U.C. 245) they commence with Antoninus II and Geta (A.D. 205). Moreover this MS has lost the last three treatises (9) (10) (11) by mutilation; if indeed these formed part of the collection of A.D. 354 and were not added to it at a later date.

On the other hand the Vienna MS contains two tracts (those which I have printed in Italics and have not numbered), which are wanting in the Brussels MS, and which can have been no part of the original collection, as is shown clearly by the date to which they are brought down. These two sets of Imperial Annals are copied from two separate MSS of one and the same work, both more or less mutilated. In some parts (B.C. 47—A.D. 45, A.D. 77—A.D. 387) they overlap each other, so that we have the same matter twice over; while elsewhere (A.D. 404—A.D. 437) there is a gap which neither supplies (see Mommsen p. 656 sq).

As a set-off against these additions, this manuscript omits the 'Natales Caesarum' (2), probably because they have a place elsewhere in the Calendar, and the repetition would seem unmeaning.

The Berne MS (see above, p. 247) contains only the end of the

Calendar (3) and the beginning of the Consular Fasti (4) as far as A.D. 254.

The collection then consisted originally of the following parts.

1. *Title Leaf*, which bears the inscription, FVRIVS . DIONYSIVS FILOCALVS . TITVLAVIT. This Filocalus[1] was a famous calligrapher, whose name is found in connexion with the inscriptions set up by Pope Damasus (A.D. 366–384) in the catacombs: see De Rossi *Rom. Sotterr.* I. p. 118 sq, II. p. 196 sq, *Bull. di Archeol. Crist.* 1877, p. 18 sq, 1884, 1885, p. 20 sq. He was therefore the author of the titles and illustrations and may have been also the editor of the work. The work is dedicated to one Valentinus, as appears from the words VALENTINE . LEGE . FELICITER, and other sentences on this title leaf. The identity of this person is doubtful, as several bearing the name are known to have lived about this time.

2. *Natales Caesarum*, i.e. the Commemoration Days of those emperors who had been deified and of those who were still living. This is closely connected with the Calendars which follow.

3. *Calendars.* Internal evidence shows that these Calendars were constructed between A.D. 340 and A.D. 350.

4. *Consular Fasti*, being a list of consuls from the beginning down to A.D. 354.

5. *Paschal Tables*, for a hundred years from A.D. 312. As far as A.D. 342, the Easter Days actually celebrated at Rome are given. From A.D. 343 onward the Easters are calculated according to the cycle then in use in Rome.

6. *City Prefects*, a list giving the names for every year from A.D. 254 to A.D. 354.

7. *Depositio Episcoporum*, giving the commemoration days of the Roman Bishops, as follows:

vi	Kal. Januarias	Dionisi, in Calisti	[A.D. 268]
iii	Kal. Januar.	Felicis, in Calisti	[A.D. 274]
Prid.	Kal. Januar.	Silvestri, in Priscillae	[A.D. 335]
iiii	Idus Januarias	Miltiades, in Calisti	[A.D. 314]
xviii	Kal. Feb.	Marcellini, in Priscillae	[A.D. 304]
iii	Non. Mar.	Luci, in Calisto	[A.D. 254]
x	Kal. Mai.	Gai, in Calisto	[A.D. 296]
iiii	Non. Augustas	Steffani, in Calisti	[A.D. 257]
vi	Kal. Octob.	Eusebii, in Calisti	[A.D. 309?]
vi	Idus Decemb.	Eutichiani, in Calisti	[A.D. 283]

[1] So he appears always to write his own name, not Philocalus.

Non. Octob.	Marci, in Balbinae	[A.D. 336]
Prid. Idus Apr.	Juli, in via Aurelia miliario iii, in Calisti	[A.D. 352]

The dates of the years are added here for convenience of reference. It will thus be seen that chronologically the list begins with Lucius [A.D. 254], and ends with Julius [A.D. 352] the immediate predecessor of Liberius. The last two names however are a later addition. This appears from the fact that the days of their depositions are no longer given, as in the other cases, in the order of the calendar. The last name on the original list therefore was that of Silvester, who died on the last day of A.D. 335. Moreover this list must have been taken from an earlier list, where the names were arranged not according to the days in the calendar, but according to the year of their death. In this way the omission of Marcellus, the successor of Marcellinus, is accounted for. In the Roman calendar Marcellus was celebrated on xvii Kal. Feb., and Marcellinus on vi Kal. Mai, so that the record would run

Marcellini,	vi Kal. Mai	in Priscillae
Marcelli,	xvii Kal. Feb.	in Priscillae

In our Liberian *Depositio* the two lines are blended, the eye of the transcriber having strayed from the one to the other[1]. Lastly; this *Depositio* is complete within its own limits, Lucius to Julius, with the single exception of Xystus II († A.D. 258). He is omitted probably because his name occurs in the document which follows, and which is headed

Item Depositio Martirum. With two exceptions ('viii Kl. Janu. Natus Christus in Betleem Judae,' and 'viii Kl. Martias, Natale Petri de catedra') this list gives only the days of martyrs. All these martyrs are Roman with the exception of

Non. Martias, Perpetuae et Felicitatis, Africae
xviii Kl. Octob. Cypriani, Africae. Romae celebratur in Calisti

The places where the commemorations are held, and where presumably the martyrs were buried, are given in every case. In two or

[1] This is substantially the solution of Mommsen (p. 631); but he has stated it in such a way as to expose himself to the objection urged by Lipsius (*Chronol.* p. 72), who pronounces this solution impossible on the ground that in our *Depositio* the names are not in alphabetical sequence, but in the order of the calendar. We have only to suppose a previous document, as I have done, and the difficulty is met. Lipsius himself (pp. 72, 242) makes a twofold postulate; (1) that Marcellinus was at first omitted altogether, and (2) that a transcriber has substituted his name for Marcellus. For the view of De Rossi see *Rom. Sott.* II. p. ix sq.

three instances the dates of the deaths are marked by the consulships. The only popes mentioned (besides S. Peter) are

viii Idus Aug.	Xysti in Calisti
Idus Aug.	Ypoliti in Tiburtina et Pontiani in Calisti
Pri. Idus Octob.	Calisti in via Aurelia, miliario iii.

In the entry

v Idus Nov. Clementis Semproniani Claudi Nicostrati in comitatum

some other Clement must be intended[1].

8. *Catalogue of Roman Bishops* (as given below, p. 253 sq), ending with Liberius, who was still living. His accession is A.D. 352.

9. *Chronicle of the World*, brought down to the consulship of Optatus and Paulinus A.D. 334; of which I shall have something to say presently.

10. *Chronicle of the City*, with the heading 'Item origo gentis Romanorum ex quo primum in Italia regnare coeperunt.' It ends with the death of the emperor Licinius (A.D. 324), and may therefore have been drawn up in the same year as the last (A.D. 334), with which apparently it is connected.

11. *Description of the Regions of the City*. It is without any heading here, but is found elsewhere with the title *Notitia Regionum*. It was compiled after the dedication of the Horse of Constantine (A.D. 334) and before the erection of the great obelisk in the Circus Maximus by Constantius (A.D. 357). Mommsen supposes it to have been compiled in the same year as (9) and (10), A.D. 334. If so however, it has

[1] The other names here associated with Clement belong to the five Dalmatian stone-cutters of Diocletian (Sempronianus or Symphorianus, Claudius, Castorius, Nicostratus, and Simplicius) who were put to death by the tyrant (see Mason's *Diocletian* p. 259 sq). Their cultus was early introduced into Rome, where it was closely connected both in the locality and in the time of celebration with that of the 'Quatuor coronati,' the four Roman martyrs, who were at first anonymous but afterwards had the names Severus, Severianus, Carpophorus, Victorianus, bestowed upon them. From this connexion much confusion has arisen. On the whole subject see especially Hunziker, Wattenbach, Benndorf, and Büdinger, in Büdinger *Untersuch. z. Röm. Kaisergesch.* III. p. 3 sq, 321 sq, 339 sq, 357 sq, and De Rossi *Bull. di Archeol. Crist.* 1879, p. 45 sq, with their references. De Rossi (p. 75) regards 'Clementis' here as either corrupt or belonging to an unknown person. The Hieronymian Martyrology contains a double entry of these martyrs.

vi Id. Nov. Romae natalis sanctorum Simplicii, Sympronii, Claudii, Custori, Nicostrati.

v Id. Nov. Romae natalis sanctorum Clementis, Symphronii.

The last would seem to be derived from this Liberian *Depositio*. See also above, pp. 99, 192.

been touched up afterwards, as in one place Constantine is called 'Divus', and he only died in A.D. 337.

It may be a question whether these three last pieces (9, 10, 11) were incorporated in the original collection of A.D. 354, as they seem to have been compiled twenty years earlier; or whether they were appended at a later date in some MS which was an ancestor of the Vienna transcript. The former is the view of Mommsen (p. 609) and of Duchesne (p. vii); and all the indications point that way. The list of the emperors in (10) is required for the completeness of the work; and (9) is intimately connected with (8), as will be seen presently. They have evidently undergone some modifications since they were compiled in A.D. 334, as the example already given of Divus applied to Constantine shows, and this revision should probably be ascribed to the Chronographer of A.D. 354. At the same time he has not taken the pains to bring them strictly down to date, probably because it was unimportant for his purpose to do so.

Of this compilation made by the Chronographer of A.D. 354, Mommsen has edited all the parts in his monograph, except (1) (2) (3), i.e. the Calendars with the Title Leaf and the Natales Caesarum prefixed, and (11) the Notitia Regionum. The first group however (1) (2) (3) is published by Mommsen elsewhere, *Corp. Inscr. Lat.* I. p. 332—356; and the last tract (11) has been edited by Preller *Die Regionen der Stadt Rom* (Jena 1846) and by H. Jordan *Forma Urbis Romae Regionum xiii* (Berlin 1874) p. 47 sq (see likewise Becker and Marquardt *Röm. Alterth.* I. p. 709 sq).

The Liberian Catalogue is printed by Mommsen (p. 634) with a collation of various readings. The lacunæ are supplied by him from the later documents derived from this catalogue—the different editions of the *Liber Pontificalis.* Where I have departed from Mommsen's text, the fact is stated in my notes. In these notes FK denotes respectively the Felician and Cononian abridgements of the assumed earlier form (c. A.D. 530) of the *Liber Pontificalis*, while P is used to designate the later form (A.D. 687) of this work. BV are the Brussels and Vienna MSS of the Liberian Catalogue itself. When I speak of 'the Fasti,' I mean the Consular Fasti included in the collection of the Chronographer of A.D. 354. In preparing this text of the Liberian Catalogue, I have consulted those of Lipsius (*Chronologie* p. 265) and of Duchesne (*Lib. Pont.* I. p. 1 sq.), comparing them with Mommsen. Only those various readings are here given which have some interest, and I have not aimed at a complete list. The dates of the different consulships are added in brackets for convenience. This papal list has no special heading in the MSS.

IMPERANTE TIBERIO CAESARE PASSUS EST DOMINUS NOSTER IESUS CHRISTUS DUOBUS GEMINIS CONS. [A.D. 29] viii KL. APR., ET POST ASCENSUM EIUS BEATISSIMUS PETRUS EPISCOPATUM SUSCEPIT. EX QUO TEMPORE PER SUCCESSIONEM DISPOSITUM, QUIS EPISCOPUS, QUOT ANNIS PREFUIT, VEL QUO IMPERANTE.

PETRUS, ann. xxv, mens. uno, d. viiii. Fuit temporibus Tiberii Caesaris et Gai et Tiberi Claudi et Neronis, a cons. Minuci[1] et Longini [A.D. 30] usque Nerine et Vero [A.D. 55]. Passus autem cum Paulo die iii Kl. Iulias, cons. s̄s̄, imperante Nerone.

LINUS, ann. xii, m. iiii, d. xii. Fuit temporibus Neronis, a consulatu Saturnini et Scipionis [A.D. 56] usque Capitone et Rufo [A.D. 67].

CLEMENS, ann. ix, m. xi, dies xii. Fuit temporibus Galbae et Vespasiani, a cons. Tracali et Italici [A.D. 68] usque Vespasiano vi et Tito[2] [A.D. 76].

CLETUS, ann. vi, m. duo, dies x. Fuit temporibus Vespasiani et Titi et initio Domitiani, a cons. Vespasiano viii et Domitiano v [A.D. 77][3] usque Domitiano ix et Rufo [A.D. 83].

ANACLETUS[4], ann. xii, m. x, d. iii. Fuit temporibus Domitiani, a cons. Domitiano x et Sabino [A.D. 84] usque Domitiano xvii et Clemente [A.D. 95].

ARISTUS, annos xiii, m. vii, d. duos. Fuit temporibus novissimis Domitiani et Nervae et Trajani, a cons. Valentis et Veri [A.D. 96] usque Gallo et Bradua [A.D. 108].

ALEXANDER, ann. viii[5], m. ii, d. uno. Fuit temporibus Trajani, a cons. Palmae et Tulli [A.D. 109] usque Veliano[6] et Vetere [A.D. 116].

SIXTUS[7], ann. x, m. iii, d. xxi. Fuit temporibus Adriani, a cons. Nigri et Aproniani [A.D. 117] usque Vero iii et Ambibulo [A.D. 126].

TELESFORUS, annos xi, m. iii, d. iii. Fuit temporibus Antonini Macrini[8],

[1] 'Minuci,' a corruption of 'Vinicii.' Again just below 'Nerine (Nervae in V) et Vero' should be 'Nerone et Vetere.' All these are correct in the Fasti.

[2] This should be 'Vespasiano vii et Tito v,' as in the Fasti.

[3] The consuls of this year are 'Vespasiano viii, Tito vi', but the Fasti give 'Domitiano v', as here; see Klein *Fast. Consul.* p. 45.

[4] So B. Mommsen has 'Anaclitus' with VFK.

[5] For Mommsen's vii (with V) I have substituted viii with B, which has 'annis octo.' This is also required by the interval of the consulates.

[6] The true name is Aeliano, as in the Fasti.

[7] So the MSS here; but FK have Xystus (Xistus). See also below, p. 256, note 3.

[8] For 'Macrini', FKP read 'et Marci.' Probably therefore 'Macrini' is an error

a cons. Titiani et Gallicani [A.D. 127] usque Caesare et Balbino[1] [A.D. 137].

HIGINUS, ann. xii, m. iii, d. vi. Fuit temporibus Veri *et Marci, a cons. Magni*[2] *et Camerini* [A.D. 138] *usque Orfito et Prisco* [A.D. 149].

ANICETUS, ann. iiii, m. iiii, d. iii[3]. *Fuit temporibus Veri*[4] *et Marci* a cons. Gallicani et Veteris [A.D. 150] usque Presente et Rufino [A.D. 153].

PIUS, ann. xx, m. iiii, d. xxi. Fuit temporibus Antonini Pii, a cons. Clari et Severi [A.D. 146] usque duobus Augustis [A.D. 161]. Sub hujus episcopatu frater ejus Ermes librum scripsit, in quo mandatum continetur, quod ei praecepit angelus, cum venit ad illum in habitu pastoris.

SOTER, ann. ix, m. iii, d. ii. Fuit temporibus *Severi, a cons. Rustici et Aquilini* [A.D. 162] *usque Cethego et Claro* [A.D. 170].

ELEUTHERUS, ann. xv, m. vi, d. v[5]. *Fuit temporibus* Antonini et Comodi, a cons. Veri[6] et Hereniani [A.D. 171] usque Paterno et Bradua [A.D. 185].

VICTOR, ann. ix, m. ii, d. x. Fuit temporibus *Caesaris*[7], *a cons. Commodi ii et Glabrionis* [A.D. 186] *usque Laterano et Rufino* [A.D. 197].

of a transcriber whose eye has wandered lower down.

[1] Mommsen has 'Albino' with V. I have substituted the correct name 'Balbino,' which appears in B.

[2] This consul's true name is 'Nigri,' as it appears in the Fasti; but 'Magni' is found in FKP.

[3] This lacuna in the MSS is supplied by Mommsen from F. He however omits the numbers of the years, months, and days, of Anicetus, inasmuch as F derives these numbers from another source and is not to be followed on this point. The years which I have inserted are those properly belonging to Hyginus, in accordance with the rule of displacement which is given below, p. 271 sq. The months and days are those assigned in F to Pius, according to another rule of displacement likewise indicated below, p. 267 sq. See also the next note but one. Lipsius (*Jahrb. f. Prot. Theol.* VI. p. 89) treats these numbers as I have done.

[4] So it is read in KP, but Mommsen has *Severi* with F.

[5] The numbers for Eleutherus and Zephyrinus I have filled in after Lipsius (*Chronologie* p. 63, *Jahrb. f. Prot. Theol.* VI. p. 89) from those MSS of the *Liber Pontificalis* which have been corrected throughout from the Liberian Catalogue; see below, p. 282. Though the numbers for Anicetus were supplied from other authorities, the result would have been just the same, if I had taken these MSS of the *Liber Pontificalis* as my guide; and this is a proof of the justice of the principle.

[6] This consul's name is not Veri, but Severi. It is rightly given in the Fasti.

[7] The lacuna is filled in mainly from FP. The general name 'Caesar' for a particular emperor or emperors is strange, but occurs in all the three authorities FKP. The true consulship of A.D. 186 is 'Commodi v Glabrionis ii,' but it is given as here in FP, and K has a corruption of the same. Here therefore the ii of Commodus is a corruption of v,

Zephyrinus, ann. xix, m. vii, d. x. Fuit temporibus Severi et Antonini, a cons. Saturnini et Galli [A.D. 198] usque Presente et Extricato [A.D. 217].

Callistus[1], ann. v, m. ii, d. x. Fuit temporibus Macrini et Eliogabali, a cons. Antonini et Adventi [A.D. 218] usque Antonino iii et Alexandro [A.D. 222].

Urbanus, ann. viii, mens. xi, d. xii. Fuit temporibus Alexandri, a cons. Maximi et Eliani [A.D. 223] usque Agricola et Clementino [A.D. 230].

Pontianus, ann. v, m. ii, d. vii. Fuit temporibus Alexandri, a cons. Pompeiani et Pelignian [A.D. 231]. Eo tempore Pontianus episcopus et Yppolitus presbyter exoles sunt deportati in Sardinia, in insula nociva, Severo et Quintiano[2] cons. [A.D. 235]. In eadem insula discinctus est iiii Kl. Octobr., et loco ejus ordinatus est Antheros xi Kl. Dec. cons. s̅s̅. [A.D. 235].

Antheros, m. uno, dies x. Dormit iii Non. Jan. Maximo[3] et Africano cons. [A.D. 236].

Fabius, ann. xiiii, m. i, d. x. Fuit temporibus Maximi et Cordiani et Filippi, a cons. Maximini[4] et Africani [A.D. 236] usque Decio ii et Grato [A.D. 250]. Passus xii Kl. Feb. Hic regiones divisit diaconibus et multas fabricas per cimiteria fieri jussit. Post passionem ejus Moyses et Maximus presbyteri et Nicostratus diaconus comprehensi sunt et in carcerem sunt missi. Eo tempore supervenit Novatus ex Africa et separavit de ecclesia Novatianum et quosdam confessores, postquam Moyses in carcere defunctus est, qui fuit ibi m. xi, d. xi.

Cornelius, ann. ii, m. iii, d. x, a consul. Decio iiii et Decio ii[5] [A.D. 251] usque Gallo et Volusiano [A.D. 252]. Sub episcopatu ejus Novatus extra ecclesiam ordinavit Novatianum in urbe Roma et Nicostratum in Africa. Hoc facto confessores, qui se separaverunt a Cornelio,

which is correctly given in the Fasti, where however the ii of Glabrio is omitted as here. At the end of the lacuna, FKP transpose the names, 'Antonini et Severi,' but the order 'Severi et Antonini' which must have stood in our text is the correct one, as Caracalla is intended by Antoninus.

[1] So in B, but Mommsen has Calixtus with V.

[2] So B. Mommsen has 'Quintino' with V.

[3] Maximino should be written for Maximo here; and Maximini for 'Maximi' two lines below. The consul of A.D. 236 was the emperor Maximinus himself.

[4] Maximini, as B; but Mommsen's text has Maximiani with V.

[5] The consuls of A.D. 251 were Decius iii and Decius Caes.; those of A.D. 252, Gallus ii and Volusianus; those of A.D. 253, Volusianus ii and Maximus. They are all rightly given in the Fasti.

cum Maximo presbytero, qui cum Moyse fuit, ad ecclesiam sunt reversi. Post hoc Centumcelis expulsi. Ibi cum gloria dormicionem accepit.

LUCIUS, ann. iii, m. viii, d. x. Fuit temporibus *Galli et Volusiani, a cons.*[1] Galli et Volusiani [A.D. 252] usque Valeriano iii et Gallieno ii [A.D. 255]. Hic exul fuit, et postea nutu Dei incolumis ad ecclesiam reversus est. *Dormit*[2] iii Non. Mar. cons. ss.

STEFFANUS, ann. iiii, m. ii, d. xxi. Fuit temporibus Valeriani et Gallieni, a cons. Volusiani et Maximi [A.D. 253] usque Valeriano iii et Gallieno ii [A.D. 255].

XYSTUS[3], ann. ii, m. xi, d. vi.[4] Coepit a cons. Maximi et Glabrionis [A.D. 256] usque Tusco et Basso [A.D. 258] et passus est viii Id. Aug., *et presbyteri praefuerunt*[5] a cons. Tusci et Bassi [A.D. 258] usque in diem xii Kl. Aug. Aemiliano et Basso cons. [A.D. 259].

DIONISIUS, ann. viii, m. ii, d. iiii. Fuit temporibus Gallieni, ex die xi Kl. Aug. Aemiliano et Basso cons. [A.D. 259] usque in diem vii Kl. Jan. cons. Claudi et Paterni [A.D. 269].

FELIX, ann. v, m. xi, d. xxv. Fuit temporibus Claudi et Aureliani, a cons. Claudi et Paterni [A.D. 269] usque ad consulatum Aureliano ii et Capitolino [A.D. 274].

EUTYCHIANUS, ann. viii, m. xi, d. iii. Fuit temporibus Aureliani, a cons. Aureliano iii et Marcellino [A.D. 275] usque in diem vii[6] Idus Dec. Caro ii et Carino cons. [A.D. 283].

GAIUS, ann. xii, m. iiii, d. vii. Fuit temporibus Cari et Carini, ex die xvi Kal.[7] Jan. cons. Carino ii[8] et Carino [A.D. 283] usque in x Kl. Mai Diocletiano vi et Constantio ii [A.D. 296].

MARCELLINUS, ann. viii, m. iii, d. xxv. Fuit temporibus Diocletiani et Maximiani, ex die prid. Kl. Iulias a cons. Diocletiano vi et Constantio ii [A.D. 296] usque in cons. Diocletiano viiii et

[1] These words *Galli et Volusiani a cons.* are wanting in our MSS and in FKP. They are absent also in the texts of Mommsen, Lipsius, and Duchesne. The insertion is needed for symmetry with the other entries, and the omission by scribes is easily explained by the repetition of the names.

[2] *Dormit* is supplied by Mommsen, being absent from the MSS.

[3] So VF, but B has Sixtus; see above, p. 253, note 7.

[4] F inserts here, 'Fuit temporibus Valeriani et Decii,' but it should be 'Valeriani et Gallieni.' It is wanting in K.

[5] These three words are inserted from F, where however they are displaced.

[6] So too Lipsius and Duchesne read vii with B; Mommsen has iiii with V. The *Depos. Episc.* (see above, p. 249) has vi Idus.

[7] For xvi Kal., B has vii Kal., and F xv Kal.

[8] It should be Caro ii, as correctly given above.

Maximiano viii [A.D. 304]. Quo tempore fuit persecutio et cessavit episcopatus, ann. vii, m. vi, d. xxv.

MARCELLUS, annum unum, m. vii[1], d. xx. Fuit temporibus Maxenti, a cons. x et Maximiano[2] [A.D. 308] usque post consulatum x et septimum [A.D. 309].

EUSEBIUS, m. iiii, d. xvi; a xiiii Kl. Maias usque in diem xvi Kl. Sept.

MILTIADES, ann. iii, m. vi, d. viii[3]; ex die vi Nonas Julias a consulatu Maximiano[4] viii solo, quod fuit mense Sep. Volusiano et Rufino [A.D. 311], usque in iii Id. Januarias Volusiano[5] et Anniano coss. [A.D. 314].

SILVESTER, ann. xxi, m. xi. Fuit temporibus Constantini, a consulatu Volusiani et Anniani [A.D. 314] ex die prid. Kl. Feb. usque in diem Kl. Jan. Constancio et Albino coss. [A.D. 335].

MARCUS, mens. viii, dies xx. Et hic fuit temporibus Constantini, Nepotiano et Facundo coss. [A.D. 336] ex die xv Kl. Feb. usque in diem Non. Octob. coss. s̄s̄.

IULIUS, ann. xv, m. i, d. xi. Fuit temporibus Constantini, a consulatu Feliciani et Titiani [A.D. 337] ex die viii Id. Feb. in diem pridie Idus Apr. Constancio v et Constancio Caes. [A.D. 352]. Hic multas fabricas fecit: basilicam in via Portese miliario iii; basilicam in via Flaminia mil. ii, quae appellatur Valentini; basilicam Iuliam, quae est regione vii juxta forum divi Trajani; basilicam trans Tiberim regione xiiii juxta Calistum[6]; basilicam in via Aurelia mil. iii ad Callistum.

[1] So BP, and it explains the iiii of other catalogues; but Mommsen has vi with V. Duchesne reads vi tacitly, not mentioning a v. l.; Lipsius rightly adopts vii, *Chronol.* pp. 136, 248, 264.

[2] In A.D. 308 the consuls were Maximianus x, Galerius vii; but Galerius bore the name Maximianus also. In the Fasti the year is designated as here 'Decies, et Maximiano vii.' The following year also appears in the Fasti as 'Post consul. x et septimum' in accordance with the designation here.

[3] So V, but B has ix.

[4] Mommsen has 'Maximiniano,' obviously a printer's error. In the consular Fasti attached to this Chronography (Mommsen p. 623) this year is designated 'Maximiano solo.' In the list of City Prefects (*ib.* p. 628) it is marked by the note 'Consules quos jusserint DD. NN. AVG. *Ex mense Septembris factum est* Rufino et Eusebio.' Mommsen in his note here says it should be 'Volusiano Rufino et Eusebio'; see also De Rossi *Rom. Sott.* II. p. vii. The name of the City Prefect given for the preceding year is 'Rufius Volusianus.' See also Tillemont *Empereurs* IV. p. 630 sq, on the various discrepancies in the authorities for this year's consulate. The Maximianus here meant is Galerius. He issued the edict putting an end to the persecution on April 30, and died a few days afterwards. See Clinton *Fast. Rom.* I. p. 358, II. p. 82.

[5] This should be Volusiano ii, but the ii is omitted in the Fasti also. So again three lines below.

[6] V has 'Calixtum' here, and 'Callistinu' just below. The readings in the text are those of B.

LIBERIUS, in diem coss. [A.D. 352].	Fuit temporibus Constanti, ex die xi Cal. Iun. a consulatu Constantio v et Constantio Caes.

Of the other treatises in this collection the only one which claims our special attention is the *Chronicle of the World*, as being closely connected with this Papal Catalogue with which alone we are directly concerned. This connexion is traced with great sagacity by Mommsen p. 585 sq; see also Duchesne *Lib. Pont.* I. p. ix sq.

It has been mentioned already that this *Chronicle of the World*, as it stands in our collection, is brought down to the year 334. After the table of contents and the preface follows the heading

Incipit chronica Horosii
Liber generationis mundi

Plainly the ascription to Orosius is wrong, for he did not flourish till a century later. His name was doubtless prefixed to this anonymous work, as that of a well known chronographer.

But this same Chronicle is extant elsewhere in a different recension, under the title 'Liber Generationis.' In this latter form and under this title, it is prefixed to the work of the so called Fredegar (A.D. 641), and is likewise found separate in two MSS in the Middlehill collection, no 1895 of the 8th or 9th cent., and no 12266 of the 10th. The former has been long known; the latter was brought to light a short time ago by Mommsen (*Hermes* XXI. p. 142 sq). Though this second MS bears evidence that it is derived from an earlier MS written A.D. 359, and though it contains other matter of the highest interest, which Mommsen has recently made the subject of a valuable paper on Latin Stichometry (l. c.), yet for our particular subject it is of inferior value to the other, and contributes nothing new.

When we compare the two forms together, it becomes evident at once that they are two independent Latin translations of a Greek original. A comparison of an extract from the table of contents will best show this;

(A) *Liber Generationis*	(B) *Chronographer of* 354
Declaratio gentium quae ex quibus factae sunt;	Manifestationes gentium, que gentes ex quibus nate sunt;
Et quas singuli terras et civitates sortiti sunt;	Et quas singuli eorum provincias et civitates habitaverunt;
Quantae insulae clarae;	Quot insule manifeste;
Qui ex quibus gentibus transmigraverunt.	Qui ex quibus gentibus advene facti sunt.

Again A has 'bellorum commissiones,' where B has 'civitatum conventiones,' a various reading πολέμων συστάσεις for πόλεων συστάσεις (see Mommsen p. 593).

The recension A however is not brought down to the year 334, but terminates with the 13th year of Alexander Severus, which is mentioned more than once, e.g. 'a passione usque ad hunc annum, qui est xiii imperii Alexandri annus,' and accordingly the catalogue of the emperors ends with 'Alexander annis xiii, diebus ix.' It seems therefore to have been compiled in the year of Alexander's death A.D. 234, so that it is just a century older than the recension incorporated by our chronographer. At all events it must date from some time during the reign of his successor Maximinus. All these references to the 13th year of Alexander are omitted in B.

Who then is the author of this Chronicle in its earlier form as represented by A? The so called Fredegar (Canisius *Lect. Antiq.* II. p. 218, ed. Basnage, 1725) names as the sources of his work, 'Beati Hieronymi, Idatii, et cujusdam sapientis seu Isidori, imoque et Gregorii chronicas.' As the 2nd, 3rd, and 4th books are taken from Jerome, Idatius, and Gregory, it follows that this 'quidam sapiens seu Isidorus' is given as his authority for the first. The form of expression moreover shows that he was not acquainted with the name of the author of this Chronicle, but conjectured that it might be Isidore. He was evidently catching at the first straw which came in his way, Isidore being a well known chronographer. The ascription to Isidore however would involve a greater anachronism even than the ascription to Orosius. Ducange (*Chron. Pasch.* II. p. 23 sq, ed. Bonn.) first suggested the true author, Hippolytus of Portus. In the catalogue of this father's works, inscribed on his chair, is one entitled ΧΡΟΝΙΚΩΝ. In another of his works, the *Paschal Tables*, which are given in full there, the Easter Days are noted from A.D. 222—237. Thus the time of the compilation of this Chronicle of the World would fit in exactly with its Hippolytean authorship. Moreover the statements in this *Liber Generationis* harmonize with the very scanty notices elsewhere referring to the chronology of Hippolytus[1]. There can hardly be any doubt therefore that it is a translation of the ΧΡΟΝΙΚΑ of Hippolytus. Basnage indeed (Canisius *Lect. Ant.* II. p. 148) ascribed it to Africanus; but Africanus wrote some years too early, under Elagabalus (A.D. 221).

[1] See on this subject (in addition to the remarks of Mommsen) Salmon l. c. p. 93 sq, *Dict. of Christ. Biogr.* I. p. 506 sq, III. p. 92, Krusch *Neues Archiv* VII. p. 456 sq (1882), Gelzer *Sex. Julius Africanus* ii. p. 1 sq (1885).

There is good reason however for believing that Hippolytus appended to his *Chronica* a list of the Roman bishops. At the close of the table of contents in recension A we have

Nomina episcoporum[1] Romae et quis quot annis praefuit.

No catalogue of the Roman bishops however follows, either in Fredegar or in the Middlehill MS. In Fredegar it was doubtless omitted because he gives elsewhere a more complete list carried down to pope Theodore (A.D. 642—649); and the Middlehill MS is imperfect at the end, so that it is impossible to say whether the catalogue appeared there originally or not. On the other hand in recension B (the form of this chronicle given by the Chronographer of 354) neither the table of contents nor the body of the work bears any traces of this catalogue. What account can be given of the omission? For an answer to this question we must turn to the catalogue of Roman bishops given in another place by this chronographer.

This catalogue, which is printed above (p. 253 sq), comprises the series of the Roman bishops from S. Peter to Liberius. The length of office is given in each case in years, months, and days. The beginnings and ends of the several episcopates are indicated by the consulships of the several years. The names of the emperors who reigned during their several tenures of office are given. Occasional notes also are added, recording events of importance in the history of the Roman Church.

This description applies to the whole series. But the catalogue is not homogeneous throughout. There is a marked break at Pontianus (A.D. 231—235). During the earlier period up to this point the consulships are reckoned as if the several episcopates began and ended with the beginning and ending of a year. In other words the consulate for the accession of any one bishop is the consulate for the year next following the consulate for the death of his immediate predecessor. Thus the reckoning of the consulates is inconsistent with the corresponding durations of office, where not whole years only, but the additional months and days are given. In the latter part of the list from the death of Pontianus onward the consulships are given on a more rational principle. The explanation of this fact seems to be that the editor who added the consulships found no dates in this earlier part—from S. Peter to Pontianus—to guide him, whereas for the later popes—from Pontianus onward—there were already in the document,

[1] On the reading see Duchesne *Lib. Pont.* I. p. iii, Mommsen *Hermes* XXI. p. 144. The table of contents is abridged in the recently discovered Middlehill MS (no 12266), and this thesis is wanting.

if not occasional consulships, at least dates which served to determine the consulships, ready to hand. At all events it suggests that the earlier parts had a separate origin from the later. Moreover there is in the earlier part an exceptional absence of those notices of remarkable events which after Pontianus are given with frequency. From Peter to Pontianus two such incidents only are recorded—the day of S. Peter's crucifixion, and the authorship of the Shepherd of Hermas.

This point however at which we find a break in our catalogue is just the date when Hippolytus wrote his *Chronicle*; and to this, as we have seen, he appears to have attached a list of the Roman bishops. We are thus led to the conclusion that we have here the list of Hippolytus himself, detached from its former connexion, altered in some respects, and completed (as the Chronicle itself is completed) to bring it down to date. We are confirmed in this opinion by finding that the first notice in the supplementary portion, added to this presumably Hippolytean list, contains a notice of Hippolytus himself; 'Eo tempore Pontianus episcopus et Yppolitus presbyter exoles sunt deportati in Sardinia, in insula nociva, Severo et Quintiano cons.' [A.D. 235]. It would naturally occur to the continuator to add this memorandum respecting the author of the list which he took as his basis.

The original list of Hippolytus however did not contain all the matter which appears in the later recension. The heading of Hippolytus' list was, as we have seen (p. 260), 'Nomina episcoporum Romae et quis quotannis praefuit.' The heading in our chronographer is 'Per successionem dispositum, quis episcopus, quot annis prefuit, *vel quo imperante*.' The addition of the words which I have italicized indicates that the synchronisms of the emperors were an addition of a later editor. This view is borne out, as we shall see (p. 265 sq), by the chronological confusion which they involve, and which would have been hardly possible, if they had formed part of the original document. Again the consulships, as we have seen, form another of these later additions. Lastly; the months and days were most probably a third such addition. The words of the heading 'quot annis' suggest that only the years were given by Hippolytus himself. Moreover the fact already mentioned, that the consulships take no account of the months and days, seems to show that these were added after the addition of the consulships either by the same person or by some later editor. The authorship of the notes may be doubtful, but there is much to be said for the opinion that these were from the pen of Hippolytus himself. The notice respecting the Shepherd of Hermas seems intended to discredit the pretensions of that work to a place in the Canon and therefore would probably be written at a time when such pretensions were still more or less seriously entertained[1]. With the possible exception of these notes the Catalogue of Hippolytus seems to have contained nothing but a list of the bishops in succession with the durations of their respective episcopates given in years only.

But there is a difficulty attending the ascription of this list to Hippolytus. The author of the *Philosophumena*, who is now generally allowed to have been Hippolytus, speaks of Callistus in language which seems inconsistent with his recognition in this list as a genuine pope. Even Zephyrinus, the predecessor of Callistus, is described in terms which do not harmonize with the respect due to so high an office. Accordingly Döllinger, who maintains that Hippolytus was the first antipope, feels himself constrained to reject the Hippolytean authorship of this papal list[2]. Hort also (*Academy*, Sept. 15, 1871, p. 436), partly I suppose for this same reason, would ascribe the original list from S. Peter to Pontianus, not to Hippolytus himself, but to some contemporary writer. If however there be any force in this objection it may easily be met by supposing that this part of the catalogue was altered subsequently, so as to conform to the recognized opinion of the Roman Church respecting its episcopal succession, by one of the later editors, say the next continuator, who carried the list down to Lucius (A.D. 255) and who seems to have been the author of the note respecting the fate of 'Hippolytus the presbyter.' If indeed Hippolytus, the author of the *Philosophumena*, was in any sense an antipope, as there are some grounds for surmising, the designation 'presbyter' applied to him by the continuator of his work, as contrasted with 'episcopus' applied to Pontianus, may be regarded as an indirect protest against these assumptions. It would not surprise us to find that the earliest antipope was coeval with the earliest Western papal catalogue. A dispute respecting the succession would naturally stimulate enquiry and lead to the formation of rival lists. We have at least one clear example of this phenomenon in the later history of the papacy. At the close of the fifth century the Roman Church was distracted by a contest between Symmachus and

[1] The motive would be the same as with the author of the *Muratorian Canon*, who has a precisely similar note (p. 58, ed. Tregelles). Salmon indeed (p. 122 sq) is disposed to identify this anonymous author with Hippolytus.

[2] *Hippolytus u. Kallistus* p. 67 sq. He argues that Hippolytus cannot have been guilty of two such great blunders as (1) to make two persons out of Cletus or Anacletus, and (2) to transpose the names of Pius and Anicetus. I agree with him so far as to regard these errors as almost inconceivable in one occupying the position of Hippolytus; but I have endeavoured to show lower down that they are both the work of some later editor.

Laurentius for the papacy. Symmachus finally prevailed by the interposition of Theodoric. The first known edition of the *Liber Pontificalis* was the offspring of this age. It takes the side of the recognized pope Symmachus. But there is also extant the concluding fragment of another similar document, dating from this same epoch, which as distinctly ranges itself with his antagonist Laurentius in this dispute. Unfortunately it is only a fragment, and we are not able to say whether they were two entirely different documents, or whether they were substantially the same document with two different endings—the divergence beginning with the outbreak of the feud. If this latter hypothesis be true, we have a parallel to the suggested double form of the Hippolytean catalogue[1].

But the break already discussed is not the only indication of different authorships in this list. For the papacies from Pontianus [A.D. 231—235] to Lucius [A.D. 253] the notices of contemporary events affecting the Roman Church are incomparably fuller than for the preceding or the succeeding times. Moreover the dates for this period are strictly correct, due allowance being made for errors of transcription. Thus the first continuator of the Hippolytean list seems to have written under the successor of Lucius and to have described the events of the twenty intervening years from personal knowledge, possibly having access also to official documents. This second break was first pointed out, I believe, by Lipsius (*Chronologie* p. 42 sq; comp. *Jahrb. f. Protest. Theol.* VI. p. 82 sq); and it has been accepted by Hort (*Academy* l. c. p. 435), Duchesne (*Lib. Pont.* I. p. ix), and others.

But again; there are indications of a third break towards the end of the catalogue. After an entire absence of historical notes from Lucius onwards, an elaborate notice—the most elaborate in the whole document—is appended to the name of Julius [A.D. 337—352] the immediate predecessor of Liberius, containing an enumeration of the churches built by him. It is an obvious and reasonable inference that this notice was the work of a contemporary, and presumably therefore of the Liberian editor himself, whether Filocalus or another. The immediate predecessor of Julius is Marcus who was bishop less than a year and of whom probably there would be nothing to record. Thus we are carried back to Silvester, the predecessor of Marcus, who died on Dec. 31, 335. But we have seen above (p. 249 sq) that the *Depositio*

[1] There is another difficulty in supposing this Catalogue in its present form to be the product of Hippolytus. If Gelzer be right (*Africanus* ii. pp. 19, 21), Hippolytus placed the Crucifixion A.D. 28, whereas our author dates it (see p. 253) A.D. 29. See however Salmon p. 96, and *Dict. of Christ. Biogr.* I. p. 507.

Episcoporum was originally carried down to this same pope's death, and that the subsequent names were added afterwards. We have seen likewise that three other documents (9) (10) (11), incorporated (as would appear) by the Liberian editor, belong to this same date, having been compiled in A.D. 334 or a year or two later. The *Depositio* therefore would appear to have belonged to this same group, which was synchronous with the second editor of the Hippolytean Chronicle, who brought it down to the death of Silvester.

It follows from this investigation that in order to arrive at the Hippolytean nucleus in the first portion of the Catalogue—from S. Peter to Pontianus—we shall have to eliminate any matter added by three successive editors or continuators; (1) The continuator who added the portion from Pontianus to Lucius (supposing that this part was added on to the original document in the age of Lucius and did not—as is quite possible—remain a separate document till the time of the next editor); (2) The continuator who carried the record on from Lucius to Silvester or (if we take the alternative hypothesis in the last sentence) who carried it on from Pontianus to Silvester, incorporating a separate document for the period from Pontianus to Lucius; (3) The final editor who added the last three names, thus carrying it on from A.D. 334 to A.D. 354. For this purpose it will be convenient to treat the matter under four several heads.

(1) In separating the earlier part of the list—from S. Peter to Pontianus—into its component elements, our attention is first directed to the *consulships.* The dates obtained from these consular names are exhibited in the table on the next page.

It appears from this table that the consulships are a later addition, and the *modus operandi* of the editor to whom they are due betrays itself. He takes only complete years, disregarding the months and days, either because they were not in the list before him or because, being there, they seemed unworthy of notice. He also treats the episcopates as all beginning on Jan. 1 and ending on Dec. 31. Moreover having a fixed date (A.D. 29) for the Crucifixion at the top of the list, and a fixed date (A.D. 235) for the death of Pontianus at the bottom, he works downwards from Peter to Anicetus, arriving at A.D. 153 for Anicetus' death, and works upward from Pontianus to Pius, arriving at A.D. 146 for Pius' accession. But, inasmuch as he makes Pius the successor of Anicetus, this last date ought according to his reckoning to be A.D. 154. Thus he overlaps himself by eight years. The names of the consuls (making allowance for errors of transcription) are the same as in the *Consular Fasti* included by the Chronographer of 354 in his work (see above, pp. 247, 249), and apparently were taken from this document. This will have been evident from the coincidences which are given in my notes (p. 253 sq).

Bishops	Duration			Consulates
	ann.	mens.	dies	A. D.
Petrus	xxv.	i.	ix	30—55
Linus	xii.	iiii.	xii	56—67
Clemens	ix.	xi.	xii	68—76
Cletus	vi.	ii.	x	77—83
Anacletus	xii.	x.	iii	84—95
Aristus	xiii.	vii.	ii	96—108
Alexander	viii.	ii.	i	109—116
Xystus	x.	iii.	xxi	117—126
Telesphorus	xi.	iii.	iii	127—137
Hyginus	xii.	iii.	vi	[138—149]
[Anicetus]	[	....	]	150—153
Pius	xx.	iiii.	xxi	146—161
Soter	ix.	iii.	ii	[162—170]
[Eleutherus]	[		]	171—185
Victor	ix.	ii.	x	[186—197]
[Zephyrinus]	[		]	198—217
Callistus	v.	ii.	x	218—222
Urbanus	viii.	xi.	xii	223—230
Pontianus	v.	ii.	vii	231—235

Nevertheless these consular dates have a value, as enabling us to correct the numbers of the years, where they have been corrupted by transcription, and to restore the original text of the Chronographer of 354. Thus for S. Peter these consular dates give xxvi instead of xxv, for Cletus vii instead of vi, for Pius xvi instead of xx, for Victor xii instead of ix. The corruption in this last case is not easily explicable; yet the consular dates are clear, and moreover the result derives some support from the Eusebian lists. In other cases, where the text is mutilated, they enable us to replace the missing numbers, e.g. iv for Anicetus, xv for Eleutherus, xx for Zephyrinus.

(2) The *imperial synchronisms* for the most part accord with the consulates. During the time of the Antonines however, at which point the confusion in the chronology reaches its climax, they do not agree, while they are inconsistent among themselves, as the following table will show;

BISHOPS	CONSULATES	IMPERIAL SYNCHRONISMS	
Xystus	A.D. 117—126	Hadrianus	A. D. 118—138
Telesphorus	127—137	{Antoninus Marcus	138—161 161—180
Hyginus	138—149	{Verus Marcus	161—169 161—180
Anicetus	150—153	{Verus Marcus	161—169 161—180
Pius	146—161	Antoninus Pius	138—161
Soter	162—170	Verus	161—169
Eleutherus	171—185	{Antoninus Commodus	161—180 180—192

It is unnecessary for my purpose to attempt to explain the blunders and inconsistencies in these synchronisms. Clearly they cannot have been the work of Hippolytus.

(3) I have already stated (p. 261) that *the weeks and days* can have formed no part of the original document. But whence they came, and what is their value, is a matter for consideration. Besides this Liberian Catalogue, they appear likewise in two other authorities.

(i) A series of papal catalogues dating from the age of Felix III († A.D. 492) and Hormisdas († A.D. 523) onward, all founded on a common original, which presumably belonged to the age of Leo the Great (A.D. 440—461). An account will be given of these lower down.

(ii) The Felician Book, which is the oldest form of the *Liber Pontificalis*, dating about A.D. 530, and of which likewise I shall have occasion to speak hereafter. The two main authorities employed in this Felician Book, so far as regards the dates and numbers, are; (α) The Liberian Catalogue itself, and (β) The Papal Catalogue which has just been mentioned, and which for convenience I shall call the *Leonine*.

For the earliest bishops the Leonine list has the order of Eusebius—Petrus, Linus, Cletus (or Anacletus), Clemens, Euarestus—without the duplication of Cletus and Anacletus. On the other hand in the Felician Book the series runs; Petrus, Linus, Cletus, Clemens, Anacletus, Euarestus, thus duplicating Cletus and Anacletus with the Liberian Catalogue, yet not agreeing with this authority in placing Clemens immediately after Linus but retaining him in his proper traditional place as the fourth in order or 'the third after Peter', so that he stands between Cletus and Anacletus.

The following table then will exhibit the relations between the lists. In the Liberian Catalogue, for Anicetus, Eleutherus, and Zephyrinus, where there are lacunæ in the extant MSS, I have supplied the missing numbers from certain MSS of the *Liber Pontificalis*, which show that their figures have been revised throughout by those of the Liberian Catalogue[1]. The numbers of years, months, and days, in the Felician Book are obviously taken from the Leonine Catalogue, though they do not always exactly coincide, the stream of transmission having been corrupted in both cases by clerical errors of the usual type. Having regard to the manifest connexion between the Liberian numbers on the one hand and the Leonine and Felician on the other, I have felt justified, where there are variations, in adopting the reading which brings the Liberian figures into closer accord with the other authorities, and conversely. The variations however are few and unimportant.

LIBERIAN				*LEONINE AND FELICIAN*			
NAMES	*Ann.*	*Mens.*	*Dies*	*Ann.*	*Mens.*	*Dies*	NAMES
1. Petrus	xxv.	i.	viiii	xxv.	ii.	iii	1. Petrus
2. Linus	xii.	iiii.	xii	xi.	iii.	xii	2. Linus
3. Clemens	viiii.	xi.	xii	xii.	i.	xi	3. Cletus
4. Cletus	vi.	ii.	x	viiii.	ii.	x	4. Clemens
				xii.	x.	iii	Anacletus
5. Anacletus	xii.	x.	iii	viiii.	x.	ii	5. Euarestus
6. (Eu)arestus	xiii.	vii.	ii	x.	vii.	ii	6. Alexander
7. Alexander	viii.	ii.	i	x.	ii.	i	7. Xystus
8. Xystus	x.	iii.	xxi	xi.	iii.	xxi	8. Telesphorus
9. Telesphorus	xi.	iii.	iii	iiii.	iii.	iiii	9. Hyginus
10. Hyginus	xii.	iii.	vi	xi.	iiii.	iii	10. Anicetus
11. [Anicetus	iiii.	iiii.	iii]	xviiii.	iiii.	iii	11. Pius
12. Pius	xx.	iiii.	xxi	viii.	vi.	xxi	12. Soter
13. Soter	viiii.	iii.	ii	xv.	iii.	ii	13. Eleutherus
14. [Eleutherus	xv.	vi.	v]				
15. Victor	viiii.	ii.	x	x.	ii.	x	14. Victor
16. [Zephyrinus	xviiii.	vii.	x]	xviii(viii).	vii.	x	15. Zephyrinus
17. Callistus	v.	ii.	x	v.	ii.	x	16. Callistus
18. Urbanus	viii.	xi.	xii	viiii(iiii).	x.	xii	17. Urbanus

In comparing the two tables it will be remembered that for the present we are concerned only with the months and days. The relation of the years depends on a wholly different principle, which will be investigated hereafter. As regards the months and days, it will be seen that there is a wide divergence in the case of S. Peter. A

[1] See above, p. 254, note 5, and below, p. 282.

possible explanation of this is given by Duchesne (*Lib. Pont.* I. p. xx). Both lists take the traditional day of his martyrdom (June 29) as the close of his episcopate; but it is calculated in the one as commencing from the Crucifixion, in the other from the Day of Pentecost. We thus get

From March 25 (Crucifixion) to June 29; m. iii. d. iiii,
,, May 15 (Pentecost) ,, ,, m. i. d. xiiii;

numbers which closely resemble the figures in the two tables respectively, and from which they would be derived by easy corruptions. From this point onward, taking the Leonine list which omits Anacletus (whose name accordingly I have not numbered), we see at a glance that for twelve episcopates—from Linus to Soter in the Liberian list—the same numbers for the months and days (making allowance for corruptions) are assigned to the bishops who occupy the same position in the series, whether they are different persons or not. The only case about which there can be any doubt is the third name in the list (Clemens in the Liberian, Cletus in the Leonine), but even here the discrepancy may easily be explained by the dropping of letters (xi into i, or ια′ into α′). From this point onward we have obviously an identical list, though occasionally in the present texts a v has been split up in ii (e.g. vi and iii for the days of the 10th bishop) or conversely (e.g. iiii and vi for the months of the 12th bishop), or a unit has been dropped; but even such divergences are rarer than might have been expected. This mechanical transference of the figures from the one list to the other, irrespective of the persons, has had a curious result. Inasmuch as there is one name more, Anacletus, in the Liberian list than in the Leonine, from this point onward for nine episcopates the figures of any one bishop in the Liberian list are those of the next bishop in the Leonine. The displacement continues as far as Soter and Eleutherus. With Victor the irregularity is set straight, and from this point onward the same bishop has the same numbers in both lists. It should be added that when the Felician editor, taking as his basis the Leonine list, inserted the name Anacletus from the Liberian Catalogue, he naturally assigned to him the numbers which were affixed to his name in that catalogue, so that in the Felician series the same numbers occur twice in succession—first for Anacletus and then for Euarestus—

mens. x. dies iii (ii).

But which was the original position of these figures for the months and days—the Liberian or the Leonine? There is nothing in the lists which decides this question. Nor do the numbers themselves indicate what was their earliest position. They seem to have been an arbitrary invention, based on no historical or traditional data. They do not bear any relation to the days on which the several bishops were commemorated in later ages. The reasons for attributing the priority to the one assignment rather than to the other must be sought elsewhere. Nor are such reasons wanting. On the following grounds I venture to think that these numbers were due to the Liberian Catalogue in the first instance, and that consequently they occupy their original position in this list.

(1) The Liberian Catalogue is a century and a half or two centuries older than the Felician and Hormisdan lists, in which the other attribution first appears. There are indeed grounds for believing that these Felician and Hormisdan lists had a progenitor in the age of Leo I, but even this is a century later than the Liberian Catalogue. On the other hand we find no trace whatever of these months and days before the Liberian Catalogue. Even Jerome who wrote about a quarter of a century later betrays no knowledge of them.

(2) The history of the Liberian list explains how their origination may have been suggested to the compiler. In the later continuation to the list from Pontianus onward, the months and days, as well as the years, were given; and the Liberian chronicler would thus be tempted to supply them for the earlier names, from Peter to Urbanus, so that his list might be symmetrical throughout.

(3) The present text of the Liberian Catalogue explains the procedure of the Leonine editor, on the supposition that this latter was the plagiarist, but not conversely. The name of Eleutherus is omitted. Now, if we suppose this same lacuna to have existed in the copy which fell into the hands of the Leonine editor, everything becomes plain. There would then be 13 names with numbers for months and days in the Liberian list, and 13 names without such numbers in the Leonine—before Victor, who would be the 14th in both lists. What more simple course then than that the Leonine editor should take the 13 numbers of the other list and apply them in regular order to the 13 names in his own? In this way the numbers in both lists would first coincide in Victor, as we find to be actually the case.

It will thus be seen that, except so far as they throw any light on the genealogy of the different papal lists, these numbers for the months and days from S. Peter to Urbanus are valueless, and may be neglected. From Pontianus onward the case is different. Here we are face to face with contemporary history; and for this reason the separation between the years on the one hand and the months and days on the other will no longer hold. The consideration of this period therefore must be deferred, till the years likewise can be taken into account.

(4) The *names*, and the *years* assigned to the names, still remain to be considered. They cannot be investigated apart, as each assists in explaining the other.

Confining ourselves however for the moment to the names, we find that the peculiarities in this Liberian or Hippolytean catalogue, by which it is distinguished from other early lists, are three;

(i) Clement is placed immediately after Linus, thus holding the second place in the list (not reckoning the Apostles), whereas in the other early catalogues he stands third, Cletus or Anacletus or Anencletus being interposed.

(ii) For the one bishop, Cletus or Anacletus (Anencletus), we have two separate names Cletus and Anacletus, treated as two distinct persons, each with his separate term of office in years, months, and days.

(iii) Whereas in the other lists Pius precedes Anicetus, the two are here transposed so that Anicetus is made the earlier.

On this last point the Liberian Catalogue is demonstrably wrong. Hegesippus and Irenæus were contemporaries of Anicetus. The former visited Rome during his tenure of the episcopate; the latter resided there, if not at this same time, yet only a few years later. Both these writers are explicit on the subject. Hegesippus tells us distinctly that Anicetus was succeeded by Soter and Soter by Eleutherus (Euseb. *H. E.* iv. 22). Irenæus in three different passages testifies to this same sequence—in two places in his extant work *On Heresies* (iii. 3. 3, iii. 4. 3) of which this portion at all events was written under Eleutherus, and in a third passage in his Letter on the Paschal controversy of which Eusebius preserves a fragment (*H. E.* v. 24) and which was addressed to Pope Victor from ten to twenty years later. But it is difficult to suppose that Hippolytus can have been guilty of so great an error respecting events which occurred almost within the range of his own life-time, and on a subject about which he took special pains to inform himself. Nor indeed do modern critics, as a rule, father this error upon him.

Again; the second divergence from the normal type—the separation of Cletus and Anencletus (or Anacletus, as it is written in the Liberian Catalogue and generally in Latin writers) into two distinct persons—cannot with any degree of probability be charged to Hippolytus. An anonymous writer quoted by Eusebius (*H. E.* v. 28), the author of the *Little Labyrinth*, who was a Roman presbyter in the time of Zephyrinus, speaks of Victor as the 13th Roman bishop after Peter (τρισκαιδέκατος ἀπὸ Πέτρου ἐν Ῥώμῃ ἐπίσκοπος). But, if the two names, Cletus and Anencletus, be taken to designate two different persons, Victor would be not the 13th, but the 14th after Peter. This writer was certainly contemporary with Hippolytus and thus expresses the mind of the Roman Church in his age. But we may go farther than this. Very cogent reasons exist for identifying this anonymous author with Hippolytus himself. With this fact before us, it is difficult to suppose that Hippolytus could have adopted the duplication which appears in this Liberian Catalogue; and indeed Lipsius rightly, as I believe, postpones this divergence from the common tradition to the latest stage in the growth of this document[1].

But, if this be so, what sufficient ground is there for charging Hippolytus with the remaining discrepancy, the transposition of the names Cletus and Clemens, so as to place Clement the earlier? This transposition would easily be made, as the names begin with the same letters, Κλῆτος, Κλήμης. The following hypothesis will, I think, explain all the facts, while it is not improbable in itself.

The original list of Hippolytus contained only the names of the bishops and their durations of office. The names were the same, and in the same order, as in Eusebius. The durations of office also were the same, allowance being made for slight discrepancies owing to transcription or other causes. Thus, from Linus to Eleutherus inclusive, there would be twelve names with the corresponding term-numbers. Now it was pointed out by Hort (*Academy*, Sept. 15, 1871, p. 436), with the concurrence of Lipsius (*Jahrb. f. Prot. Theol.* vi. p. 86, 1880), that from Euarestus to Pius the term-numerals in the Liberian Catalogue are one behind those of the Eusebian lists, so that there has been a displacement. This will appear from the following table;

[1] *Jahrb. f. Prot. Theol.* vi. pp. 96, 100, 104, 107 sq, 112 sq, 116 (comp. *Chronologie* pp. 61, 66). His explanation of this doubling of Cletus (Anacletus) I am unable to accept. It will be considered hereafter. On the other hand Hort (*Academy* l. c.) regards this as one of the earliest stages in the corruption of the list (see Lipsius *Jahrb. f. Prot. Theol.* vi. p. 97); and Salmon (p. 114 sq) attributes it to Hippolytus himself. So too Erbes (*Jahrb. f. Prot. Theol.* iv. p. 732 sq) supposes the insertion of Anacletus to have preceded and to have occasioned the omission of Anicetus. He is controverted by Lipsius (*ib.* p. 98 sq).

LIBERIAN		*EUSEBIAN*				
NAMES	*Duration*	*Duration*				NAMES
		H. E.	*Arm.*	*Hieron.*	*Syr.*	
Petrus	xxvi [xxv]		xx	xxv		Petrus
Linus	xii	xii	xiiii	xi	xii	Linus
Clemens	viiii	xii	viii	xii		Anencletus
Cletus	vii [vi]	viiii	viiii	viiii	viiii	Clemens
Anacletus	xii					
Euarestus	xiii	viii	viii	viiii	viii	Euarestus
Alexander	viii	x	x	x	x	Alexander
Sixtus	x	x	xi	x	iii	Xystus
Telesphorus	xi	xi	xi	xi	xx	Telesphorus
Hyginus	xii	iiii	iiii	iiii	iiii	Hyginus
Anicetus	iiii [ ]	xv	xv	xv	xv	Pius
Pius	xvi [xx]	xi	xi	xi	xi	Anicetus
Soter	viii	viii	viii	viii	viii	Soter
Eleutherus	xv [ ]	xiii	xv	xv	xv	Eleutherus

In the Liberian list the numbers are here given as corrected by the consulates. The accompanying numbers in brackets are those which stand in the present text, when there is any difference, and are presumably errors of transcription. It will be remembered that in the cases of Anicetus and Eleutherus, where the empty brackets [ ] are added, the term-numerals are missing and the duration of office is learnt from the accompanying consulates alone.

This comparison of the two catalogues, the Eusebian and the Liberian, suggests a solution. The πρώταρχος ἄτη, the initial mischief, in this tragedy of blunders, was the omission of the line containing the name and number of Anicetus in a parent document of the Liberian Catalogue. The number (xi) was thus finally lost to this list; but the name, being missed, was replaced in the margin, opposite to Pius. In the next transcription it was inserted in the text, but erroneously before Pius.

At the same, or on a subsequent transcription, the name Clemens, with its accompanying number, was accidentally omitted after Cletus, owing to the identity of the initial letters, just as it is omitted in the papal list in *Ancient Syriac Documents* p. 71 (ed. Cureton), doubtless from the same cause. The names from Petrus to Soter were thus reduced to twelve; and the term-numbers likewise were twelve. Accordingly the twelve numbers were attached mechanically to the twelve names. Or the omission of Clemens may have been due to another cause. Just as we saw (p. 264 sq) that the editor who added the consulates began at the top and bottom of the list of names, so here, having a list ot twelve numbers, he may have filled in the corresponding names similarly. The consequence would be the extrusion of one of the names, inasmuch as the names were one in excess of the term-numbers. On either supposition, when the omission was discovered, the name with its well known term-number would be supplied in the margin, 'Clemens viiii'. At the next transcription it would naturally find a place in the text; but a similar blunder to that which caused the transposition of Pius and Anicetus befel here also, and the insertion was made before instead of after Cletus.

The doubling of the person, Cletus and Anencletus, comes in at a later stage. A reader missing in this list the name Anencletus, with which he was familiar, places it in the margin, 'Anencletus xii'. He fails to perceive that this same person occurs already under the name 'Cletus vii' (the number xii having been already corrupted into vii). Or he may have intended his marginal note to be a *correction* of 'Cletus vii', but the next transcriber treats it as an addition and inserts it accordingly in the body of the list.

Supposing the first blunder, respecting Anicetus, to have been already made and to have produced its consequences, the subsequent errors with their causes will be exhibited in the process of formation in the following table;

	Petrus	xxv	
	Linus	xii	
Clemens viiii	Cletus	vii	Anencletus xii
	Euarestus	xiii	
	Alexander	viii	
	Xystus	x	
	Telesphorus	xi	
	Hyginus	xii	
	Anicetus	iiii	
	Pius	xvi	
	Soter	viii	
	Eleutherus	xv	

The numbers here are the same as in the Eusebian list (see above, p. 246), making allowance for the displacements as already explained and for the omission or addition of a stroke (e.g. x or xi, xi or xii, xv or xvi), with the exception of those attached to Cletus and Euarestus. The vii for xii of Cletus is a common type of clerical error. The xiii for Euarestus may in like manner have been a corruption of viii which is the Eusebian number, or it may have arisen from a confusion between ιΓ and ΙΙ (Η), when the catalogue was still in its original Greek dress, or it may have been the result of literary manipulation for a purpose which will be explained hereafter.

This hypothesis supposes that the three errors occurred in the following order: (1) The transposition of Pius and Anicetus; then, simultaneously with or soon after this, (2) The displacement of Clemens; and lastly, at a later date, (3) The doubling of the one person, Cletus or Anencletus. This order entirely accords with the external evidence. The transposition of Pius and Anicetus, though the most demonstrably false, is the most widely diffused, of the three errors, being found not only in the African fathers, Optatus (c. A.D. 370) and Augustine (c. A.D. 400), but also in many papal lists of the succeeding centuries. The displacement of Clemens again is found in these African fathers, and in others[1]. Yet it was obviously unknown to Jerome; for in his *Catalogus* (A.D. 392) he mentions, as an alternative to the common tradition which gave the order Linus, Anacletus, Clemens, only the belief of 'plerique Romanorum' which placed Clemens immediately after S. Peter and before Linus. Nor again was Rufinus acquainted with it; for he constructs an elaborate theory to explain how Clement, though coming after Linus and Cletus in the episcopal series, was yet ordained directly by S. Peter himself. Both these fathers therefore were acquainted with the fiction of the Clementines, but both were ignorant of the Liberian order[2]. Thus the evidence, so far as regards the fourth century, is confined to the two African fathers alone[3]. These however are not two authorities but one. It seems highly probable that Augustine took his list directly from Optatus, seeing that he uses the facts for the same purpose of confuting the Donatists and that he gives the list in precisely the same form, 'Petro successit Linus, Lino [successit] Clemens, etc.'[4] If not, he must have transcribed it from the same or a closely allied copy, as the two exhibit the same errors lower down in the series. Both omit

[1] See e.g. *Vit. xiii Apost.* (*Zeitschr. f. Wiss. Theol.* XXIX. p. 445) ὁ Πέτρος Κλήμεντα τὸν μαθητὴν αὐτοῦ ἐπίσκοπον Ῥώμης κεχειροτόνηκε, τοῦ Λίνου πρὸς Κύριον ἐκδημήσαντος.

[2] The passages of Jerome and Rufinus are given above, p. 173, p. 174 sq.

[3] The notice in *Apost. Const.* vii. 46. 1 will be considered lower down.

[4] The fact that the present text of Optatus has lower down 'Felici Marcellinus, Marcellino Eusebius', thus omitting three names, while Augustine has the series complete at this point 'Felici Eutychianus, Eutychiano Gaius, Gaio Marcellinus, Marcellino Marcellus, Marcello Eusebius', is no objection to this hypothesis. Such omissions are a common form of error with transcribers, and even in Augustine's text here many MSS omit 'Marcellinus, Marcellino'.

Eleutherus, and both displace Alexander by six steps, substituting him for Eleutherus. They have also other peculiarities in common. But while they give the order Linus, Clemens, Anencletus, with the Liberian Catalogue, they are free from the error of duplicating Cletus or Anacletus, which is found in this document. Thus they seem to have got hold of a copy of this papal catalogue before it received its last touches from the late editor to whom this duplication is due. The earliest instance of this duplication outside the Liberian Catalogue appears in the poem *Against Marcion*[1], but this was almost certainly written later than the date of our chronographer and probably in the next century. This anonymous verse-writer however gives the names in a different order, Linus, Cletus, Anacletus, Clemens.

For the earlier part therefore, from Linus to Eleutherus, the Western list which was the original basis of the Liberian Catalogue appears to have been identical with the Eastern list which was in the hands of Eusebius, except perhaps in the name of Linus' successor, which seems to have been Cletus not Anencletus. In other respects the variations are due to later corruptions or manipulations. The next five episcopates however, which carry us to the accession of Pontianus, present somewhat greater difficulties. The numbers in the different lists are as follows;

NAMES	*EUSEBIAN*				*LIBERIAN*	
	Armen.	*Hieron.*	*Syriac*	*H. E.*	*Numbers*	*Intervals*
Victor	xii	x	x	x	viiii	xii
Zephyrinus	xii	om	xviii	xviii	[xviiii]	xx
Callistus	viiii	v	v	v	v	v
Urbanus	om	viiii	viiii	viii	viii	viii
Pontianus	viiii	v	v	vi	v	v

The intervals, as well as the term-numbers, are given in the case of the Liberian list, because in this case they seem to have been calculated from some earlier form of the list itself (see above, p. 265). The number for Zephyrinus has disappeared; but the reason for restoring it xviiii (otherwise xix)[2] is explained above (p. 254, note 5). In the Armenian

[1] *Adv. Marc.* iii. 276 sq. The passage is quoted above, p. 176.

[2] I have most frequently written xviiii rather than xix (as also viiii rather than

Chronicle the number for Urbanus is omitted, but the corresponding interval is x. In the same way in the Hieronymian the number of Zephyrinus is wanting, but the interval is xix.

It will be seen that the great discrepancies are in the Armenian; but they may be practically disregarded. The initial error is the corruption of the number for Callistus ϴ for ϵ (9 for 5), and this has led to the readjustment of the neighbouring numbers as explained above (p. 226). This corruption must have been found likewise in the text of the Eusebian *Chronicle* which was in the hands of Syncellus, for he mentions Eusebius as assigning 12 years to Zephyrinus (see above, p. 242). But, after the Armenian is set aside, the question will still remain whether the discrepancies in the other lists in the case of Victor and Zephyrinus are not best explained by supposing that the original list was continued by different hands.

But there are certain phenomena in this Liberian Catalogue on which Lipsius lays great stress (*Jahrb. f. Prot. Theol.* VI. p. 103 sq), and which seem to militate against the solution here offered. At all events they might suggest that the list in its present form was not so entirely the result of accidental errors, but was manipulated by a literary reviser with a distinct purpose. The Crucifixion is dated by the consulate of the 'two Gemini', i.e. A.D. 29, and the death of Urbanus is placed in A.D. 230, this last being apparently the correct date. There is thus an interval of 201 years between the two events. But if (omitting the months and days) we add up the term-numbers for the years of the successive episcopates from Peter to Urbanus inclusive, we get 207 or 208 years, according as we assign 6 or 7 years to Cletus. No deduction however is here made for the duplication of Cletus or Anencletus. As I have already stated (p. 271), I agree with Lipsius in thinking that this duplication took place at one of the latest stages in the growth of the document. He himself assigns it to the last stage of all, ascribing it to the Chronographer of 354, whom he calls Philocalus. But here our divergence begins. In the solution which I have offered, the late intruder is 'Anencletus xii'; and if we deduct these twelve years from the total of 207 or 208, we get a remainder of 195 or 196 years, which diverges widely from the 201 years of the historic interval. Lipsius however chooses the other alternative and regards Cletus as the late insertion; nor would it be difficult to modify my own solution so as to admit this alternative. Not very consistently

ix) to show the relation to other lists; but as a fact the MSS of the Liberian Catalogue always have ix, xix.

with himself Lipsius assigns 7 years to Cletus, following in this instance alone the interval (vii), and rejecting the term-numeral (vi)[1]. Here I believe that he is right and that the vi of our MSS is a clerical error; for not only is vii an obvious corruption of xii the proper term-number for this bishop, but it is found in the Cononian abridgment of the *Liber Pontificalis* in which the figures elsewhere are corrected by the Liberian Catalogue. The difference of vi or vii however does not affect the question before us, for whether we deduct 6 from 207 or 7 from 208, we get the result 201 years, as the total of the term-numbers, and this total exactly coincides with the historic space.

If instead of the term-numbers, we take the intervals as determined by the consulates, and add them up, the result is slightly different. The addition gives 209 years in all; and by striking out Cletus, to whom 7 years are here assigned, we reduce the sum to 202, or one year more than the total of the term-numbers and than the actual period comprised within the limits. The same fact may be expressed in another way. Whereas only 7 years are assigned to Cletus, the consulates overlap each other by 8 years[2]; so that, after casting out Cletus, a superfluous year remains.

A comparison of the term-numbers and the intervals leads to the following result. While the individual term-numbers and the individual intervals differ from each other in four several cases not counting Cletus (25 and 26 for Peter, 20 and 16 for Pius, 9 and 12 for Victor, 19 and 20 for Zephyrinus), yet the variations compensate for each other in such a way, that there is only a difference of a unit in the two totals. The effect of these variations is represented thus; $1 - 4 + 3 + 1 = 1$.

Of Lipsius' theory as a whole I shall have occasion to speak immediately. It seems to me to be burdened with difficulties. But it is entitled to the support, whether great or small, which it derives from the coincidence between the whole historic period and the total of the term-numbers. His contention is, I presume, that the Hippolytean chronicler intended to cover the whole space from the Crucifixion to the death of Urbanus, and that he manipulated the numbers accordingly. Yet I fail to find where he explains how this manipulation was brought about. His discussion, as I read it, seems to come to this; that, while each individual anomaly may be explained as an accidental

[1] See *Jahrb. f. Prot. Theol.* VI. p. 101 'The total of the consulates reckoned up shows that ann. vi is a simple clerical error for ann. vii.'

[2] In his earlier work (*Chronologie* pp. 53, 57, etc) Lipsius speaks of this as 7 years. He corrects himself in his later work (*Jahrb. f. Prot. Theol.* VI. p. 100).

error, as for instance the xiii years of Euarestus (Aristus) as a corruption of the viii assigned to him elsewhere, the numbers attached to Alexander, Xystus, etc, as owing to an accidental displacement (see above, p. 271 sq), and so forth, yet the sum total of these accidental items somehow or other betrays a deliberate design. If deliberate purpose were at work anywhere, a place could best be found for it in the substitution of xx for xv (or xvi) in the case of Pius[1], or in the addition of a unit in some instances where the Liberian number is one higher than the corresponding Eusebian number. But he does not, so far as I have noticed, explain himself clearly; and in all these cases the divergences may be easily accounted for by clerical errors. Moreover a chronicler of any discernment would not have desired to fill up the whole space. Such a person would see that the incidents in the Acts, in which S. Peter bears a prominent part, must have occupied a considerable time, to say nothing of the traditional Antiochene episcopate, which he might or might not accept, so that it was necessary to leave an interval, if only of a few years, after the Crucifixion, before the Apostle became, as he is assumed to have become, the head of the Roman Church[2]. On the whole therefore I am disposed to regard the coincidence at which Lipsius arrives, as accidental. Nor under the circumstances is such a result surprising. From the very nature of the case we should expect the total of the term-numbers in such a list as this to be within a few years of the historic period, in the way either of excess or of defect; so that a very little critical adjustment, such as Lipsius applies, might produce exact agreement.

Still Lipsius may be right in his contention that the numbers have been manipulated so as to cover the whole interval from the Crucifixion. It is not here that I find the really serious objections to his theory. Such a manipulation is as consistent with my explanation as with his. Only it must have come at a late stage in the genesis of the existing Liberian document. It would only be necessary in this case to suppose that one of the later editors increased the term-numbers by a unit here and there (Telesphorus, Hyginus, Pius), so as to bridge over an

[1] In his earlier work (*Chronologie* pp. 58, 64 sq) Lipsius explained this xx as iiii + xvi the numbers for Hyginus and Pius added together, and he founded thereupon a somewhat elaborate pedigree of documents. This solution was accepted by Erbes (*Jahrb. f. Prot. Theol.* IV. p. 741 sq), but Lipsius has himself withdrawn it since (*ib.* VI. p. 104).

[2] In his *Chronologie* p. 67 Lipsius himself contemplates Hippolytus as placing the beginning of Peter's episcopate in the 3rd year after the Passion.

interval of three or four years, by which the total of the term-numbers fell short of the historical space. This is a simple and natural proceeding in itself, and it is suggested by a comparison of the Liberian numbers with the Eusebian.

The hypothesis which I have put forward above (p. 272 sq) to explain the peculiar features of the Liberian Catalogue seems to me to give an intelligible account of their origin. I do not venture to say that it is the only reasonable explanation which could be offered; but, if I mistake not, it takes the right direction, as well in ascribing the peculiarities of this list largely to the blundering of transcribers, as also in postponing these errors to the later stages in the development of the document. On the other hand Lipsius takes another view (*Jahrb. f. Prot. Theol.* VI. p. 100 sq, 1880)[1]. He credits the Chronicler of the year 234, or in other words Hippolytus himself (see esp. pp. 107, 111, 116), with all the principal blunders in the order of the names and in the numbers of the years[2], except the insertion of 'Cletus vii.' His theory is that the Liberian Chronicler had two wholly independent lists before him. The one was the list of the Chronicler of 234, which had the order Linus, Clemens, Anencletus, which transposed Pius and Anicetus, which displaced the years so as to push them one lower down in the manner described above (p. 271 sq), and which, partly owing to this displacement and partly from other causes, incorporated such errors as ascribing xiii years to Euarestus, iiii to Anicetus, xx to Pius, and the like. This list gave the years only. It was manipulated, as we have seen, so as to cover the whole space from the Crucifixion, the first episcopate being placed in the following year. The second list, which was combined, or at least partially combined, with it by the Liberian Chronographer, was widely different. It had the order Linus, Cletus, Clemens; and it assigned vii years instead of xii to Cletus. The numbers for the years were (with the exception just named) the same, or substantially the same, as in the *History* of Eusebius, and from these numbers the intervals in the Liberian Catalogue, as reckoned by the consulates, were taken. Hence their want of agreement with the term-numbers to which they are attached. But besides the years, this document had likewise the months and days, as we find them at a

[1] I am only dealing here with his later view. His earlier theory (*Chronologie* pp. 43, 52 sq, 63 sq) is in some respects preferable, though too elaborate.

[2] Elsewhere however (VI. p. 274) he offers as an alternative the postponement of these blunders to the next editor of the Hippolytean list under Stephanus (A.D. 253).

much later date in the Leonine and Felician lists; and these months and days the Liberian Chronographer adopted, but with the displacement which has been described above (p. 267 sq). On this hypothesis the original attribution of the months and days is not that of the Liberian Catalogue, as I have maintained above (p. 269), but that of the Felician and Leonine lists. The following table will, I believe, fairly express Lipsius' theory of the two documents. It is right however to add that he speaks with some diffidence about the numbers in his second list; nor indeed does he express himself with absolute confidence as to the existence of any such list, though he considers it to offer the most probable explanation of the phenomena.

HIPPOLYTEAN	*NAMES*	*SECOND LIST*		
xxv	Petrus	xxv.	i.	viiii (xiiii).
xii	Linus	xii.	iiii.	xii.
(wanting)	Cletus	vii.	xi.	xii.
viiii	Clemens	viiii.	ii.	x.
xii	Anencletus		(wanting)	
xiii	Euarestus	viii.	x.	ii.
viii	Alexander	x.	vii.	ii.
x	Xystus	x.	ii.	i.
xi	Telesphorus	xi.	iii.	xxi.
xii	Hyginus	iiii.	iii.	iii.
iiii	Anicetus / Pius	xvi.	iiii.	vi.
xx	Pius / Anicetus	xi.	iiii.	iii.
viiii	Soter	viiii.	vii (iii).	xxi.
xv	Eleutherus	xv.	iii (vi).	ii (v).
viiii	Victor	xii.	ii.	x.
xviiii	Zephyrinus	xviiii.	vii.	x.
v	Callistus	v.	ii.	xi.
viii	Urbanus	viiii.	xi.	xii.

This theory appears to me to be complicated and improbable. In the first place, it gives no adequate account of the particular blunders in the Hippolytean list, not to mention the fundamental improbability which has been urged already, that errors of such magnitude should be found at this early date. Secondly; there is the assumption that the months and days for the earlier bishops were already tabulated, and that the tabulation of the Leonine and Felician lists represents their original place, though all the probabilities point to the opposite conclusion (see p. 269). Lastly; there is the strange mode of procedure thus ascribed to the Liberian Chronographer. He is represented as attaching to one list the intervals which belong to another. He does this notwithstanding that his second list contains different names from the first and in a different order. He executes his task in a perfectly arbitrary way, sometimes calculating these intervals from his second list, but frequently abandoning it and basing his calculations on the term-numerals of the first. He gives himself the trouble of going through the successive consulates for more than 200 years in order to note these intervals. He is nothing daunted by finding that all this trouble leads him only into hopeless confusion; that in individual cases the result is flagrant contradiction between the intervals and the term-numbers, and that for the whole list he has doubled back upon himself and reckoned in the same eight years twice over, thus computing 209 years within limits which comprised only 201. This elaborate piece of stupidity is hardly conceivable in any man. On the other hand the solution which I have suggested involves no such improbabilities. The Liberian Chronographer on this hypothesis has before him a very corrupt list with term-numbers. He begins to compute the chronology, reckoning back from a fixed date by means of a list of the Consular Fasti which he has before him. When he has got some way, he is arrested in his calculation, seized perhaps by a misgiving that he is exhausting the number of years at his disposal too quickly. He then begins at the other end and works downward as before he had worked upward. At the meeting point he finds that he has overlapped himself by 8 years. But he has no data before him which will enable him to correct the chronological error. He therefore leaves this slovenly piece of workmanship to take care of itself. This is no doubt a careless and not very conscientious proceeding; but it is at least intelligible according to human motives of action.

On the whole therefore I am disposed to believe that, except for trivial inaccuracies in his arithmetic, the Liberian editor's intervals as designated by the consulships agreed with the corresponding term-numbers, as he found them in his text, and that where at present they diverge widely, this divergence is due to the corruptions of later transcribers. The trifling numerical inaccuracies, which I thus contemplate, would be exemplified by the case of Pius where the interval included by the consulates is xvi years, but where not improbably the term-number in his text was xv, this being the number in the Eusebian Catalogues, and likewise better explaining the corruption xx, which we find in the existing text. So again in the case of Zephyrinus, the interval included by the consulates is xx. Here there is a lacuna and the term-number is wanting. Yet I am disposed to think that Lipsius is right in giving xix for the term-number, though it does not exactly correspond with the interval. It is the number found in those MSS of the *Liber Pontificalis* in which the figures have been corrected throughout after the Liberian Catalogue (see pp. 254, 267) and, as otherwise written (xviiii = xix), it explains most of the variations in the term-number assigned to this pope in other papal lists, xviii, xvii, viii (though not the xii of the Armenian *Chronicle*, of which another explanation may be given). If this were so, the twenty consulates may not have been due to the bad arithmetic of the chronographer, but he may have found the corruption xx already in his text, though the original number was xix.

If indeed there were any adequate reason for supposing that the Liberian Chronographer had a second list before him, we should naturally ascribe to it the intervals, where these differ from the term-numbers. But in this case it would be much simpler to postulate a list of a very different kind from that which Lipsius imagines. We might then suppose that our chronographer had in his hands, not two wholly different lists, but two copies (A, B) of the same list[1], containing the same names and in the same order, and differing only in the numbers assigned to four or (including Cletus) five episcopates during the period under review. From A he took the term-numbers, while from B he derived the intervals, calculating them, or finding them already calculated, by the consulates from its term-numbers. The list, of which these were copies, might then be ascribed to the chronographer who edited the Hippolytean Chronicle some twenty years earlier (see p. 263 sq), and the divergences would be mainly accidental corruptions on one side or the other. This hypothesis would involve far fewer difficulties than that of Lipsius; and it may possibly be correct. But, if the coincidence which has been pointed out above (p. 277) be disallowed, no adequate reason for postulating a second list remains.

Salmon goes even farther than Lipsius, though in much the same direction. He not only ascribes the order and the term-numerals, as we find them in the Liberian Catalogue, to Hippolytus himself, but he makes him responsible likewise for the duplication of Cletus and Anacletus. He supposes the date for the Crucifixion 'duobus Geminis' (A.D. 29) to have been the invention of Hippolytus himself, so that the treatise of Tertullian in which it is found[2] must have been written later

[1] Lipsius himself in his earlier view (*Chronologie* p. 66) supposes that the Chronographer of 354 had before him two copies of the Hippolytean list.

[2] *Adv. Jud.* 8 'sub Tiberio Caesare, coss. Rubellio Gemino et Rufio Gemino, mense Martio, temporibus paschae, die viii Kalendarum Aprilium, die prima azymorum.'

than Hippolytus' chronological works. The twenty-five years of Peter he likewise ascribes to Hippolytus. Given the date of the Passion as A.D. 29, this term of 25 years followed as a consequence of his desire to harmonize the two facts, (1) that tradition made Linus the first of the Roman bishops and assigned 12 years to him, and (2) that the Clementine story represented Clement as having been ordained bishop by S. Peter himself. But this could only be done by placing the episcopate of Linus in S. Peter's lifetime and by transposing the names of Cletus and Clement. If then S. Peter was martyred in A.D. 67 and room is found for the twelve years of Linus before his martyrdom, Linus' accession must be dated as early as A.D. 55. Neglecting the parts of years, this would leave 25 years from the Crucifixion to the accession of the first bishop after Peter. But by this process the different dates have been pushed 12 years earlier, and a gap would be created in consequence. Hippolytus then, finding Cletus in one list and Anacletus in another, and having left 'a space in his chronology large enough to admit of both bishops, convinced himself that the two were distinct.' By this compensation the date of accession of the next bishop Euarestus (or Aristus) does not differ very seriously from that which Eusebius and Jerome assign to it. On this hypothesis the reckoning of the 25 years back from the martyrdom of Peter, as Eusebius and Jerome reckon them, arose out of a misapprehension. They adopted the 25 years as computed by Hippolytus, but they overlooked the grounds of his computation and took a different starting-point.

This ingenious theory seems to me to be untenable. I may here waive the question whether the date 'duobus Geminis' was Hippolytus' invention or not. Neither is it necessary to enquire whether we owe to him the 25 years of Peter; for it might have been adopted as a convenient round number, and not as exactly spanning a chronological gap. The objections to the theory lie outside these two questions. In the first place it takes no account of the list as a whole. As Lipsius pointed out, if both names Cletus and Anacletus are retained, the sum total of the several episcopates exceeds by 8 years the available chronological space[1], even if we omit the reckoning of the months and days which would add on several years more to the total. What moreover are we to say of the displacement and confusion of the term-numerals, as described above (p. 271 sq)? What account

[1] Salmon must have overlooked this fact when he writes (p. 115); 'Since both Cletus and Anacletus are required in order to fill out the time in the Hippolytine chronology, I think it to be without reason that Lipsius has suggested that this duplication may have arisen through transcribers' error.'

again shall we give of the transposition of Pius and Anicetus? But besides all this, how shall we explain the fact, to which I have already referred, that apparently Hippolytus himself (Euseb. *H.E.* v. 28) reckons Victor as the thirteenth bishop from Peter, whereas the duplication of Cletus and Anacletus would make him the fourteenth? To this objection Salmon can only give the following answer; 'The mode of counting Sixtus 6th, Eleutherus 12th, from the apostles, etc, must have been too well established in the time of Hippolytus for him to think of changing it; but as he believed the second bishop, Clement, in his series to have been in immediate contact with the apostles, Hippolytus could without inconsistency express the distance of each bishop from the apostles according to the received number' (p. 115). This explanation strikes me as too clever to be true[1].

But whether my solution is or is not preferable to its rivals, whether I am right or wrong in postponing the characteristic corruptions in the Liberian Catalogue to its later stages and thus saving the credit of Hippolytus or his contemporary, the historical result is the same. All these solutions alike go to establish one fact. The original list, from which the Liberian Catalogue was ultimately derived, was essentially the same in the order of the names and in the terms of office, with the list which is embodied in the *Chronicle* of Eusebius as represented by the Hieronymian version, and in the *Church History* of this same writer. Indeed, it would be a distinct gain, if Lipsius and others who throw back the corruptions in this list to the age of Hippolytus could establish their case; for testimony would thus be furnished to the great antiquity of a document which at this early age had been so largely corrupted.

The later part of this Catalogue—from Pontianus to Liberius—has no direct bearing on the earliest bishops, with whom alone we are immediately concerned; but indirectly it is important, as throwing some light on the pedigree and affinities of the several papal lists. We are now on historical ground, and the months and days must henceforth be treated in connexion with the years. Hitherto the Liberian Catalogue has been found far inferior to the Eusebian lists. For the chronology of the period at which we have now arrived it is quite the most important document. Though it still contains several errors of transcription, these will not give any serious trouble, as they can generally

[1] In Smith and Wace *Dict. of Christ. Biogr.* IV. p. 98 *s. v.* 'Hippolytus Romanus,' he meets the difficulty in another way, by assigning the work which is quoted by Eusebius to Gaius the Roman presbyter, and not to Hippolytus.

DURATION OF EPISCOPATES FROM PONTIANUS TO LIBERIUS.

Names	*Hieron.*	*Liberian List*			*Leonine List*			*Lib. Pont.*			*Actual Term*			*Limits*
Pontianus	v	v.	ii.	vii	vii.	x.	xxii	viiii.	v.	ii	v.	ii.	vii	21 Jul. 230—28 Sep. 235
Anteros	m. i		i.	x [xii]		i.	xviiii	xii.	i.	xii		i.	xii	21 Nov. 235— 3 Jan. 236
Fabianus	xiii	xiiii.	i [,,]	x	xiiii.	ii.	x	xiiii.	i [xi].	xi	xiiii.	,,	x	10 Jan. 236—20 Jan. 250
Cornelius	ii	ii.	iii.	x	ii.	iii.	x	ii.	ii.	iii	ii.	iii.	x	Mar. 251— June 253
Lucius	m. viii	iii.	viii.	x	iiii.	viii.	x	iii.	iii.	iii		viii.	x	25 June 253— 5 Mar. 254
Stephanus	iii	iiii [iii].	ii.	xxi	vi.	v.	v	vi [vii].	v.	ii	iii.	ii.	xxi	12 May 254— 2 Aug. 257
Xystus II	[xi]	ii.	xi.	vi	i.	x.	xxvi	i.	x.	xxiii		xi.	vi	24 Aug. 257— 6 Aug. 258
Dionysius	viiii	viii [viiii].	ii [v].	iiii	viii.	v.	iiii	vi.	ii.	iiii	viiii.	v.	iiii	22 Jul. 259—26 Dec. 268
Felix	v	v.	xi.	xxv	iiii.	i.	xxv	iiii.	iii.	xxv	v.	xi.	xxv	5 Jan. 269—30 Dec. 274
Eutychianus	m. viii	viii.	xi.	iii	i.	i.	i	i.	i.	i	viii.	xi.	iii	4 Jan. 275— 7 Dec. 283
Gaius	xv	xii.	iiii.	vii	xi.	iiii.	xii	xi.	iiii.	xii	xii.	iiii.	vii	17 Dec. 283—22 Apr. 296
Marcellinus	[viii]	viii.	iii.	xxv		om.		viii.	iiii.	xvi	viii.	iii.	xxv	30 June 296—25 Oct. 304
Marcellus	om.	i.	vii.	xx	i.	iiii.	xvi	iiii[v].	,, [vii].	,, [xxi]	i.	vii.	xx	[?] — [?]
Eusebius	m. vii		iiii.	xvi [,,]		vi.	iii	vi.	i.	iii		iiii.	,,	18 Apr. 310—17 Aug. 310
Miltiades	iiii	iii.	vi.	viii	iiii.	,,	,,	iiii.	vii [,,].	viii [,,]	ii.	vi.	viii	2 Jul. 311—10 Jan. 314
Silvester	xxii	xxi.	xi.	,,	xxiii.	x.	xi	xxiii.	x.	xi	xxi.	xi.	,,	31 Jan. 314—31 Dec. 335
Marcus	m. viii		viii.	xx	ii.	,,	xx	ii.	,, [viii].	,, [xx]		viii.	xx	18 Jan. 336— 7 Oct. 336
Julius	xvi. m. iiii	xv.	i [ii].	xi [vi]	xv.	ii.	vii	xv.	i [ii].	,, [vi]	xv.	ii.	vi	6 Feb. 337—12 Apr. 352
Liberius			,,		vi.	iiii.	viii	vi.	iii.	iiii	xiiii.	iiii	vii	17 May 352—24 Sep. 366

be corrected by external authorities. For the purposes of reference I have given on the preceding page a comparative table of the principal Latin lists for this period. In the first column, containing the list of the Hieronymian *Chronicle*, I have, in those cases where there are no term-numbers (Xystus II and Marcellinus), placed in brackets the figures taken from the allied Eusebian lists (pp. 209, 221). In the second column, in the Liberian Catalogue (which I shall call L) the alternative numbers enclosed in brackets give the intervals as calculated from the days of consecration and death, wherever these intervals differ from the term-numbers. The third column gives the Leonine list. It should be stated however that the MSS here fall into two classes, giving different figures in several cases (see below, p. 318). I have only recorded the figures of the first; those of the second, where they differ from the first, are generally identical with those of the *Liber Pontificalis*. In the fourth column, assigned to the *Liber Pontificalis* (which I shall henceforth designate *LP*), the precedence is given to the earlier edition as represented by the Felician Book (F), and where there is any difference of reading, the figures in brackets are those of the later edition (P) or of some MSS of this later edition. The fifth and sixth columns give the actual duration of office of the respective bishops, with the dates of the commencement and close of their respective episcopates, the notices being sufficient (with a few exceptions) to determine these with a reasonable degree of probability. The amount of uncertainty existing in any individual case may be gathered from the investigation which follows.

For the first name in the list, PONTIANUS, the days of the commencement and termination of his episcopate are given. The limits thus fixed agree exactly with the term-numbers. The divergence of the numbers in *LP*, viiii. v. ii, is easily explicable. There has been a displacement; the years viiii are borrowed from the previous bishop Urbanus (viii or viiii), and the months and days, v. ii, are the years and months of Pontianus himself shifted from their proper places. The close of Pontianus' episcopate (Sept. 28, A.D. 235) was not his death, but his resignation or deprivation, for this must be the meaning of the Liberian notice 'discinctus est[1].' The bearing of this notice,

[1] So *Epist. Synod. Sardic.* (Labb. *Conc.* II. p. 741, ed. Coleti) 'ut Julium urbis Romae et Osium ceterosque supra commemoratos discingeret atque damnaret', Greg. Turon. *Hist. Franc.* v. 28 'ab episcopatu discincti' [v. l. 'dejecti']. Hence, when said of a cleric, it is equivalent to 'unfrock.' So again it is used of 'cashiering' a soldier, e.g. Vulcat. Gall. *Vit. Avid. Cass.* 6 'ut si quis cinctus inveniretur apud Daphnen, discinctus rediret.' There can, I think, be no doubt

which connects his 'divestiture' with the name of Hippolytus, I have considered already (p. 262) and shall have to return to the subject again. Whatever may be its meaning, we cannot doubt that it states a historical fact. The *LP* records of Pontianus, 'defunctus est iii (iiii) Kal. Nov.', thus professing to give the date of his death; but this seems to be merely a corruption of the Liberian notice, as several modern critics have seen (e.g. Tillemont *H.E.* III. p. 693, Mommsen *l. c.* p. 635, Lipsius *Chron.* p. 195), and is therefore valueless. This same work also states that his body was brought from Sardinia to Rome by Fabianus, which is highly probable. In the Liberian *Depos. Mart.* (see above, p. 251) his deposition is dated on the same day with that of Hippolytus, Aug. 13 (Id. Aug.). This must have happened on one of the following years, A.D. 236 or 237. De Rossi (*R.S.* II. p. 77), accepting the date of the *LP*, places his death on Oct. 30, A.D. 236, and therefore necessarily postpones his deposition till A.D. 237. He calls attention to the fact that an imperial rescript was necessary before removing the body of one who had died in exile (*Digest* xlviii. 24. 2).

For ANTEROS the present text of L gives m. i. d. x; but its own limits require m. i. d. xii. As i. xii is read in *LP*, it must have stood originally in the text of L. Thus the death of Anteros took place Jan. 3, A.D. 236, whereas the deposition of his predecessor cannot date till Aug. 13 of the same year at the earliest. The circumstance that Anteros was buried in the Cemetery of Callistus before Pontianus and that the translation of Pontianus to this cemetery took place under Fabianus the successor of Anteros, would explain the fact that in some papal lists (notably in F) the order is Anteros, Pontianus, Fabianus—Anteros being placed before Pontianus. This explanation is suggested by De Rossi (*Rom. Sott.* II. p. 75) and adopted by Lipsius, Duchesne, and others.

For the next bishop FABIANUS the term in L is xiiii. i. x. Yet his predecessor's death is dated Jan. 3, and his own death Jan. 21 (xii Kal. Feb.). Thus there is no room for the one month, and it should probably be obliterated. It may have been inserted to fill the vacant space; or the m. i. d. x may have been a mechanical reproduction of the figures assigned to the previous pope Anteros in L. The m. xi. d. xi, which we find in some copies of the *LP*, is doubtless taken from the notice of the imprisonment of Moyses in the same paragraph of L which contains the account of Fabianus. As Fabianus perished in the Decian persecution, and therefore in A.D. 250, the xiiii

about the meaning. Yet some writers (e.g. Tillemont III. p. 693) treat it as equivalent to 'defunctus est.'

years of the other catalogues must be correct, rather than the xiii of Jerome, who indeed himself gives xiiii as the interval.

With CORNELIUS we arrive at the period of the Cyprianic correspondence, which now accompanies us through several pontificates, thus affording means of testing and correcting the numbers in L. After the martyrdom of Fabianus the see remained vacant for more than a year[1]. The election of Cornelius as bishop cannot be placed before February or March 251, nor can it have occurred later, as it was known in Carthage about April[2]. All this appears from the notices in the Cyprianic letters combined with the statement respecting the schism of Novatus and the captivity of Moyses in L (Cyprian *Epist.* 37, 43 sq; comp. Cornelius in Euseb. *H. E.* vi. 43). All the Latin lists give two years to Cornelius as against three which appears in the *History* of Eusebius and in some other Greek lists (see p. 241). For the months and days L has m. iii. d. x, and the Leonine list agrees herewith. The figures in *LP* (ii. ii. iii) are a displacement of those given by L (ii. iii. x), similar to the displacement which we noticed in the case of Pontianus, so that the years and months of L become the months and days of *LP*. If we calculate our m. iii. d. x from the beginning of March, we shall arrive at the middle of June for the death of Cornelius[3], which took place according to L at Centumcellae (Civita Vecchia); see above, p. 256. This agrees with the time of the consecration of his successor, as established on independent data.

To LUCIUS, his successor, L assigns ann. iii. m. viii. d. x. It will be shown presently that the years should be omitted. The m. viii. d. x appear likewise in the Leonine list, and Jerome gives viii months to this pope. On the other hand *LP* has iii. iii. iii, where the months and days are a mere repetition of the figure for the years, or they may have been handed down from his predecessor Cornelius, whose numbers in

[1] The notices of the length of the vacancies in *LP* are purely fictitious, and may be dismissed from our consideration; see Duchesne *Lib. Pont.* I. p. clx. The authentic sources of information here are L and the Cyprianic letters.

[2] The dates are established by Lipsius *Chronol.* p. 200 sq. Duchesne's chronology (*Lib. Pont.* I. p. ccxlviii) agrees.

[3] The older critics, following the *LP* which founds its statements on the spurious *Acta Cornelii* (Schelestrate *Antiq. Eccl. Illustr.* I. p. 188 sq) and represents Cornelius as martyred at Rome (thus directly contradicting the contemporary testimony incorporated in L, which places his death at Civita Vecchia), adopted xviii Kal. Oct. (Sept. 14) as the date of his death. Reckoning backward from this date, and deducting m. iii. d. x, they arrived at June 4, as the day of his accession; e.g. Pearson *Ann. Cypr.* A.D. 251 § 6, A.D. 252 § 13; Tillemont *H. E.* III. pp. 431, 735. This introduces confusion into the chronology of Cyprian. Sept. 14 was probably the date of the translation of his body to Rome.

LP are, as we have seen, ii. ii. iii. At all events m. viii. d. x was the original tradition. Allowing a reasonable number of days for the vacancy and calculating from the middle of June (the date established for the death of his predecessor), we shall arrive at the beginning of March for the death of Lucius. This agrees with the notice in the Liberian *Depos. Episc.* (see above, p. 249), which places his death on iii Non. Mart. (March 5). But the three years in L cannot have had a place in the contemporary document, and must have been introduced in the course of transmission before it reached the hands of the Liberian editor. Eusebius had 8 months only for his term of office, as is explicitly stated in the *H. E.* vii. 3 (μησὶν οὐδ' ὅλοις ὀκτὼ), and as we find in the Hieronymian *Chronicle.* This is undoubtedly correct. Cyprian's correspondence contains only one letter to Lucius (*Epist.* 61), in which he says that, having recently congratulated him at once on his 'ordination' and on his 'confession,' he now congratulates him on his return from exile. The banishment and return of Lucius therefore, which are recorded in L (see above, p. 256), must have taken place immediately after his accession. Moreover, when the Synod of Carthage assembled, which was held not later than A.D. 255, Stephanus had already been bishop some time (Cyprian *Epist.* 68). Thus the death of Lucius falls in A.D. 254. Yet the editor who inserted the consular reckoning must have found the three years already in his text; for three consulates—the same three [A.D. 253—255] which are assigned to his successor—are given to him.

To Stephanus, the successor of Lucius, the present text of L assigns ann. iiii. m. ii. d. xxi, but inasmuch as the consulates only include three years, and as iii is the number in the Leonine list and in the *LP*, this was doubtless the original reading of L also. It stands likewise in the present text of Jerome, but as Eusebius has ii, it might be thought that iii was an accidental alteration of a transcriber, who thus blundered into the correct number. The *Depos. Episc.* (see p. 249) gives iiii Non. Aug. (Aug. 2) for the deposition of Stephanus, and this must belong to the year 257, if he were more than three years in office. If therefore, reckoning backward, we deduct iii. ii. xxi from 2 Aug. 257, we arrive at 12 May 254 for the day of his accession. This would leave two months and a few days for the vacancy of the see after the death of Lucius.

His successor Xystus has ann. ii. m. xi. d. vi assigned to him, and here again the two years were evidently in the text of the editor who inserted the consulates [A.D. 256—258]. But, if our reckoning hitherto has been correct, so long a term of office is impossible. We know that

Xystus was martyred on 6 Aug. 258 (viii Id. Aug., Tusco et Basso coss.); see the Liberian *Depos. Mart.* above, p. 251, Cyprian *Epist.* 80, Pontius *Vit. Cypr.* 14, *Act. Procons.* 2. The two years therefore must be struck out[1]. They may possibly have arisen out of the statement that he was the second of his name, thus 'Xystus ii. m. xi. d. vi.' At all events the absence of any number for the years in the original document will explain the fact that in the Eusebian lists he is credited with eleven years, the number for the months being taken to supply the missing number for the years. If then m. xi. d. vi be assigned to Xystus, he will have been consecrated about 31 Aug. 257, thus leaving nearly a month for the vacancy of the see after the death of his predecessor. The *Acta Stephani* however (*Act. SS. Bolland.* August. T. I. p. 144) give viiii Kal. Sept. (Aug. 24) as the date of Xystus' consecration, which would require d. xii or xiii. The figures in the Leonine list and in the *LP* give some countenance to such an alteration in L. Otherwise these Acts, being a later production, are not worthy of credit. The consular date for the death of Xystus (A.D. 258) is again correct, all the intervening consular dates since the accession of Cornelius having been wrong. The bearing of the dates established for these two last popes, Stephanus and Xystus II, on the chronology of Cyprian and of Dionysius of Alexandria is traced by Lipsius *Chronologie* p. 215 sq, but I am not concerned with it here. After the martyrdom of Xystus the see was vacant for nearly a year, as we learn from L, during which 'presbyteri praefuerunt.'

DIONYSIUS, the successor of Xystus, is stated in L to have commenced his episcopate on 22 July (xi Kal. Aug.) and ended it on Dec. 26 (vii Kal. Jan.). For this latter day however the *Depos. Episc.* (see p. 249) gives Dec. 27 (vi Kal. Jan.). Inconsistently with these notices the present text of L assigns to him ann. viii. m. ii. d. iiii. Here it is clear that for the months instead of ii we should read v, as in the Leonine list, by which change the notices are reduced to harmony. For the years there can be little doubt that viii should be changed into viiii, this being likewise the number in the *History* of Eusebius (vii. 30) and in the Hieronymian *Chronicle*. It is required moreover to fill up the space of time. The interval indeed, as given by the consulates, is ten years [A.D. 259—269]; but without doubt the editor who supplied these consulates has been misled by the date vii (vi) Kal. Jan. (Dec. 26 or 27), and given the consuls who entered upon their office on these

[1] The necessity of rejecting the years and retaining only the months and days in the case of Xystus was seen already by the older critics; e.g. Pearson *Ann. Cypr.* A.D. 258, § 5, Tillemont *Mémoires* III. p. 35.

Kalends, whereas the year 268 had still four or five days to run at the time of this pope's death. So long an episcopate as ten years is inconsistent with the space required by the bishops who follow. For the history of the controversy respecting Paul of Samosata, in its bearing on the papal chronology at this time, I must be content to refer to Lipsius *Chronol.* p. 226 sq.

For the three bishops next in order, FELIX, EUTYCHIANUS, and GAIUS, the term-numbers in L seem to be strictly correct. The consulates also are correctly filled in. Here we have not only the term-numbers but also the days of consecration and of death for Gaius[1] and the day of death for Eutychianus. Moreover the Liberian *Depos. Episc.* (see p. 249) gives the close of all the three episcopates. The harmony of all these notices one with another, and the intrinsic probability of the results arrived at from their combination, are a guarantee of the historical truth of this portion of the chronology. The results are exhibited in the table on p. 285. The divergences from L in the other lists offer a few points for notice. The variations of the Leonine list and of *LP* for Felix are difficult to account for. I can only explain them by some confusion of the transcriber's eye with the numbers for Marcellinus three lines lower down. A glance at the table will show my meaning. In the case of Eutychianus the divergences are interesting. The confusion of years with months, by which 8 months are assigned to this pope in the Eusebian lists, has been already explained (p. 234). The figures in the Leonine list and in *LP*, ann. i. m. i. d. i, are a transcriber's way of filling up the gaps where the numbers were left blank. The reason of this blank may have been, as Duchesne (*Lib. Pont.* I. p. xviii) suggests, that some editor finding a wide divergence between the Eusebian and Liberian numbers, omitted them altogether in despair. For Gaius the Eusebian number xv (for xii) is an example of a very common type of clerical error. In L the number of days assigned to him, vii, which should be iiii, is another illustration of the same.

The next group of four bishops, Marcellinus, Marcellus, Eusebius, and Miltiades, presents greater difficulties. If this period had stood alone, we should have had some hesitation about relying on the Liberian figures. But for the periods immediately preceding and succeeding they are found to be most excellent guides. The term-

[1] Fragments of the inscription on the actual tombstone of Gaius have been found. With the aid of the Liberian record De Rossi (see *Rom. Sott.* III. p. 115, *Bull. di Archeol. Crist.* 1876, p. 87) has pieced them together and restored the whole inscription; ΓΑΙΟΥ. ΕΠΙϹΚ. ΚΑΤ. ΠΡΟ. Ι. ΚΑΛ. ΜΑΙΩΝ, where ΚΑΤ stands for *κατάθεσις* = *depositio*; see above pp. 249, 256.

numbers indeed are very liable to clerical errors, but after due allowance made for such they have proved trustworthy. On the other hand in the consulates from A.D. 258 onward this list is never once convicted of error, if we except the date for the death of Dionysius where there is a slight miscalculation of a few days (see above, p. 290 sq).

The space covered by these four episcopates with the intervening vacancies comprises 17½ years, from 30 June 296 to 31 Jan. 314. The term-numbers in L are

Marcellinus	viii.	iii.	xxv
Marcellus	i.	vii.	xx
Eusebius		iiii.	xvi
Miltiades	iii.	vi.	viii
Total	xiii.	x.	ix,

so that only ann. iii. m. vii. d. xxi are left for all the vacancies. But L after the notice of the death of Marcellinus writes, 'Quo tempore fuit persecutio et cessavit episcopatus ann. vii. m. vi. d. xxv.' As this term largely exceeds all the available space, De Rossi suggested that the expression 'cessavit episcopatus' does not here signify the vacancy of the see, but the non-recognition of it by the Roman government, when the 'loci ecclesiastici' were under confiscation[1]. This however is a wholly unnatural sense to ascribe to the words. No one appears to have noticed the relation of these figures, vii. vi. xxv, to the term-numbers for this pope, viii. iii. xxv, of which they are apparently a corruption or a correction. The original figures therefore for the vacancy, if they ever existed, have disappeared; and the existing figures have no value, except so far as they may enable us to verify or correct the term-numbers.

The two successive popes, Marcellinus and Marcellus, owing to the similarity of their names and to their immediate proximity, are frequently confused; and sometimes the one is entirely absorbed and lost in the other. Thus Jerome recognises only Marcellinus (Marcellianus), while the Leonine lists know only Marcellus. So again with the later Greek and Oriental lists. The Chronographer of 354, Syncellus, and Eutychius, have Marcellus alone; whereas Nicephorus and Elias admit Marcellinus (Marcellianus) only. No safe in-

[1] *Rom. Sotterr.* II. p. vii; see also Duchesne *Lib. Pont.* I. p. ccl. Lipsius (*Chronol.* p. 249 sq) suggests that some words have dropped out and that the text stood originally thus;

quo tempore fuit persecutio
ann. vii. m. vi. d. xxv.
et cessavit episcopatus
ann. ii. m. vi. d. xxvii.

ference can be drawn respecting Eusebius. In the *History* he does not trace the papal succession beyond the accession of Marcellinus. The Armenian Version of the *Chronicle* is mutilated at the end, but it passes the year at which the accession of Marcellinus should be recorded, and there is no mention of him (see above, p. 216). Of the mention of Marcellinus and the omission of Marcellus in the Liberian *Depositio* I shall have to speak presently.

A dark and mysterious story has fastened upon the memory of MARCELLINUS, not unconnected with our present subject. About a century after his death, a Donatist bishop Petilianus attacked his fair fame, representing him as having, with his presbyters Miltiades, Marcellus, and Silvester, delivered up the sacred books and offered incense during the persecution[1]. By the presbyters thus named as implicated with him the accuser doubtless intended the three successors of Marcellinus in the papal chair. Indeed Augustine expressly states this of Miltiades, about whom there might have been some doubt. Thus the whole Roman episcopate was in a manner blackened by this charge. The charge however is not recommended either by the form of the accusation or by the person of the accuser. The selection of the names of Marcellinus' three colleagues in guilt betrays the wholesale character of fiction; while the blind recklessness of the Donatists in charging Catholic bishops as 'traditores' and 'thurificati' bids us pause before crediting their assertions in this particular instance. Moreover in the Conference of Carthage, held A.D. 411, the Donatists produced certain documents which seemed to prove that two persons, Straton and Cassianus, who were deacons under Miltiades, had fallen away during the persecution, but they adduced nothing affecting the character of Miltiades himself, while Marcellinus, Marcellus, and Silvester, are not even named[2]. If therefore the matter had rested at this point, we might have dismissed the charge without a misgiving. The *LP* however in its notice of this pope endorses it, but gives the sequel. He appears here as an anticipation of Cranmer alike in his fall and in his recantation. A great persecution, we are told, was raging. Within thirty days sixteen or seventeen thousand persons of both sexes were crowned with martyrdom. Marcellinus was bidden to offer sacrifice and yielded. Within a few days he was seized with remorse, led away penitent, and beheaded by Diocletian. The bodies of the holy martyrs

[1] The authorities on this subject are Augustin. *Contra Litteras Petiliani* ii. 202 sq (*Op.* IX. p. 275 sq), where the words of Petilianus are quoted, *De Unico Baptismo* 27 (*Op.* IX. p. 541 sq).

[2] Augustin. *Brev. Coll.* 34—36 (*Op.* IX. p. 574 sq).

lay in the streets twenty days by the emperor's orders. Then Marcellus the presbyter took up the body of Marcellinus with the others and 'buried it on the Salarian Way in the Cemetery of Priscilla, in a chamber that can be seen to this day, as he himself had ordered when penitent, while he was being dragged to execution, in a crypt near the body of the holy Crescentio, on the 6th of the Kalends of May.' With these facts before us we cannot, with Milman (*Latin Christianity* I. p. 53), peremptorily dismiss 'the apostacy of Marcellinus' as 'a late and discarded fable adopted as favouring Roman supremacy.' In the earlier form of the story at all events the motive of supporting the ascendancy of the Roman see is nowhere apparent. Even in the account of the *LP*, which I have just given, and which seems to have been taken from a spurious *Passio Marcellini* no longer extant (see Duchesne *Lib. Pont.* I. pp. lxxiv, xcix), there are no traces of any such motive. It appears first in the Acts of the spurious Council of Sinuessa[1], where Marcellinus is represented as judging and condemning himself, because only a superior can be a judge and the Roman see has no superior: 'Jam audi, pontifex, et judica causam tuam, quoniam ex ore tuo justificaberis, et ex ore tuo condemnaberis.' But these Acts are obviously an afterthought. They presuppose the fact of his lapse and make capital out of it. The character of the pope is sacrificed to the authority of the papacy. On the whole the charge is not sufficiently well supported to deserve credit. At all events there is no reason for thinking that the omission of Marcellinus from some of the papal lists, notably the Leonine, is owing to this slur on his character, as Duchesne supposes (*Lib. Pont.* I. p. lxxi sq); for the confusion with Marcellus is sufficient to explain the omission of either name, and Marcellus is more often extruded than Marcellinus. Thus Marcellus is omitted even by Jerome, and his numbering of the bishops shows that the omission was not accidental. It should be added that the story of the apostasy does not seem to have been known in the East; for Eusebius speaks of Marcellinus as having been 'overtaken' by the persecution (*H. E.* vii. 32 ὃν...ὁ διωγμὸς κατείληφε), and Theodoret even describes him as 'having borne a distinguished part' at this crisis (*H. E.* i. 2 τὸν ἐν τῷ διωγμῷ διαπρέψαντα). This last expression at all events can only be intended as eulogistic. It is right however to mention that Theodoret knows nothing of Marcellus or

[1] Labb. *Conc.* I. p. 955 sq (ed. Coleti); see Baronius *Annal.* s. ann. 303 § lxxxix sq. Baronius is greatly exercised with the question and blows hot and cold by turns. He scandalizes Tillemont (*H. E.* v. p. 613 sq) by this levity when dealing with a question of such moment as the faith of a sovereign pontiff.

indeed of Eusebius, but mentions Miltiades as if he were the immediate successor of Marcellinus.

The term-numbers assigned to Marcellinus are viii. iii. xxv. The year of his death then is A.D. 304, both as calculated from these term-numbers and as given by the consulates. This comparatively long term of office agrees with the notices of Eusebius[1] and Theodoret already quoted, which represent him as still living when the persecution began (23 Feb., 303). If the figures for the months and days are correct, he must have died on Oct. 25. But this does not agree with his commemoration, as given by any authority. The present text of the Liberian *Depositio* (see p. 249) places it on xviii Kal. Feb., but this, as we have seen (p. 250), is probably a confusion with his successor Marcellus. All the other ancient authorities give his commemoration day in April. It is vi Kal. Mai (April 26) in the *Old Roman Martyrology*, vii Kal. Mai (April 25) in the *Liber Pontificalis* (FKP), and xii Kal. Mai (April 20) in the *Hieronymian Martyrology*. The vi and xii seem to be different corruptions of the vii, so that April 25 was probably the original day. This would exactly suit the number of days xxv, but would require a considerable change in the years and months, vii. viiii for viii. iii; but it is not profitable to speculate any further in conjectural emendation. We may perhaps accept the term-numbers provisionally as correct and suppose that owing to the troubles of the times there was a long interval between the death (25 Oct., 304), and the deposition proper (25 April, 305), just as we have seen in the earlier case of Cornelius (p. 288). The dates thus provisionally accepted would not be inconsistent with the story of his lapse and martyrdom. We might then suppose him to have been imprisoned after the Second Edict (about March A.D. 303) which especially aimed at the imprisonment of the clergy but avoided the shedding of blood[2], to have lapsed after the Third Edict, which was an amnesty issued at the vicennalia (21 Dec. A.D. 303) and offered release *even* to the clergy, *provided they would sacrifice*[3], and to have suffered martyrdom after the Fourth Edict, which was promulgated in Rome by Maximian (30 April, 304). The judicial slaughters perpetrated in consequence extended over many months.

[1] I do not understand what Lipsius (*Chronol.* p. 242) means, when he says that 'the 8 years are established by the reckoning of Eusebius in the *Chronicon.*' Marcellinus is not mentioned in the Armenian version, which alone Lipsius accepts as representing the original work of Eusebius; but as xv years are there assigned to his predecessor Gaius, and as the accession of Gaius is placed in 278, the accession of Marcellinus ought to fall in 293.

[2] See Mason's *Persecution of Diocletian*, p. 103 sq.

[3] Mason, p. 206.

Marcellinus was the first pope for some generations who was not buried in the Cemetery of Callistus. By his own directions, we are told, he was laid in the Cemetery of Priscilla. From the language which the *LP* uses in making this statement, Lipsius (*Chronol.* p. 246) infers that this is represented as a penitential act, as if he deemed himself unworthy of lying with his predecessors in the papal vault, and he himself supposes Marcellinus to have been excluded by reason of his lapse. This is not a very probable account of the fact. It is simpler with De Rossi (*Rom. Sott.* II. p. 105) to suppose that the well-known Cemetery of Callistus had been confiscated at the outbreak of the persecution and not yet restored, and that therefore he had to choose some new place of sepulture.

The two next episcopates were days of trouble for the Roman Church. The epitaphs of Damasus on both Marcellus and Eusebius are extant (*Rom. Sott.* II. pp. 195 sq, 204 sq). He tells us that the efforts of these two prelates to enforce penitential discipline on the lapsed led to strife and bloodshed; that the Church was rent asunder by feuds; that Marcellus was driven into banishment by the tyrant instigated by one of the offenders; and that Eusebius died an exile and a martyr in Sicily. The word 'martyr' ought not probably to be interpreted here in its stricter sense. In the *Hieronymian Martyrology* he is called a 'confessor.'

For these two prelates the Liberian Catalogue is very deficient. While the term-numbers are recorded for both, the consulates only, without the days of accession and death, are given for Marcellus, and the days of accession and death alone, without the consulates, for Eusebius.

The term-numbers for MARCELLUS are ann. i. m. vii. d. xx. It has been pointed out above (p. 257), that the proper number for the months is vii, as Lipsius correctly reads, not vi, as Mommsen gives it. If however the Martyrologies are right, the 'depositio,' and presumably the death, of this pope fell on Jan. 15 or one of the succeeding days (p. 250). If therefore the death took place so early as January and the year was 309, as the consulate gives it, the accession must belong not to the year 308, as represented by the consulate, but to the preceding year 307. There are three ways out of this difficulty: (1) We may with Lipsius (*Chronol.* p. 248 sq, 264) suppose a mistake in the consulate and may substitute 307 for 308 as the year of his accession. (2) We may with Duchesne cut out the one year, in which case his episcopate will extend from 26 May 308 to 15 Jan. 309. This is no violent procedure, since transcribers were fond of inserting a unit where they found a blank[1]. I should prefer this solution to that of Lipsius, seeing that the consulates have in this part of the list proved our safest guides. (3) We may leave both the term-numbers and the consulates intact, and we may suppose that the *depositio* here, as in the case of Cornelius and probably also of Marcellinus, is the anniversary not of his death, but of his translation to the Cemetery of Priscilla. He may have died in exile; and in these times of trouble, when the Church was assailed by persecution from without and torn asunder by internal strife, a long interval might have elapsed before his body was laid peacefully in a Roman Cemetery. In the Leonine list there has been a misplacement of the months and days, so that those of Eusebius have been transferred to Marcellus, and those of Miltiades to Eusebius. Miltiades himself has lost his own months and days in consequence.

With EUSEBIUS, the successor of Marcellus, the difficulties of reconciling the different statements are still greater. The beginning and end of his episcopate are given as xiiii Kal. Mai (April 18) and xvi Kal. Sept. (August 17), a period of exactly 4 months. The term-numbers however give 4 months and 16 days. The 'd. xvi' therefore must be struck out. It may have crept in accidentally from 'diem xvi Kal. Sept.' in the context. But another difficulty remains. In the Liberian *Depositio* his day is given as vi Kal. Oct. (Sept. 26); and so too the *Hieronymian Martyrology* on this day, 'Romae Via Appia in coemeterio Calesti (Callisti) depositio S. Eusebii episcopi et confessoris.' But we know that Eusebius died in exile, and his remains would have to be brought to Rome. This latter therefore is the day of his translation. The seven months assigned to this bishop by Jerome are an evident corruption, the iiii becoming vii by a common form of error. The variations in the other lists also are explicable. The numbers in the Leonine list are perhaps borrowed from Miltiades by a displacement; those of the *LP* are a variation of the Leonine[2]. But the year still remains unsettled. No consulates are given to determine it. The alternative lies between 309 and 310, as will be seen presently.

The term-numbers for MILTIADES are ann. iii. m. vi. d. viii (viiii). The beginning of his episcopate is given as vi Non. Jul. (July 2), the end as iii Id. Jan. (Jan. 11). Moreover the latter date accords substantially with the *Depositio*, which has iiii Id. Jan. (Jan. 10), so that there is an error of a single day only in the one place or the other. Miltiades survived the edict of Milan, when more settled times arrived. Hence there is no interval between the death and the 'depositio', as in

[1] See the note on p. 291.

[2] Lipsius gives another explanation, *Jahrb. f. Prot. Theol.* VI. p. 93 sq.

the case of the preceding bishops. So far, well and good. But the three years present a difficulty. If the consulates are correctly given (A.D. 311—314), they can only be reconciled with the months and days by writing ii for iii. This is Duchesne's solution (*Lib. Pont.* I. p. ccxlix); and as the consulates elsewhere have been found trustworthy, perhaps it is the more probable alternative. Otherwise we should be obliged with Lipsius to suppose an error in the consulate for the accession (A.D. 311), and to place it in the previous year. It must be confessed however that the iiii years of Jerome and others are favourable to the larger number iii in this list. Unfortunately external events connected with this episcopate do not assist us in determining this point. A letter from Constantine to Miltiades is extant (Euseb. *H. E.* x. 5), in which the emperor directs him to summon a synod at Rome to adjudicate on the Donatist question. The synod met on the 2nd of October 313[1], under the presidency of Miltiades. On the other hand the synodal letter of the Council of Arles, dated the 1st of August 314, is addressed to his successor Silvester[2]. Thus external history furnishes a signal verification of the Liberian chronology so far as regards the close of this episcopate. Of the beginning it has nothing to say.

We may now return to Eusebius. The death of his predecessor has been placed in January 309, the accession of his successor in July 311. He himself held the episcopate for four months, from April 18 to August 17. The year 311 is thus excluded from the competition; and the alternative

[1] Optat. *De Schism. Donat.* i. 23 (p. 23, Dupin) 'Convenerunt in domum Faustae in Laterano, Constantino quater et Licinio ter consulibus, sexto Nonas Octobris die...Cum consedissent Miltiades episcopus urbis Romae etc.,' Augustin. *Post Collat.* 56 (*Op.* IX. p. 614) 'Melchiades judicavit Constantino ter et Licinio iterum consulibus, sexto Nonas Octobres,' *Epist.* 88 (*Op.* II. p. 214) 'Domino nostro Constantino Augusto tertium cos.,' where the same year is intended. The consuls of this year were 'Constantinus III, Licinius III,' as appears from a letter of Constantine on the subject in *Cod. Theodos.* xvi. ii. 1 (VI. p. 22, ed. Gothofred) so that the 'quater' of Optatus and the 'iterum' of Augustine, at least of their present texts, must be corrected. Constantine and Licinius were consuls together for the second time in A.D. 312, for the third time in A.D. 313, and for the fourth time in A.D. 315.

The form Melciades or Melchiades is a corruption of Miltiades, arising out of careless Latin pronunciation or transcription, more especially the latter, for the interchange of C and T is a very common occurrence. In the printed texts of Augustine the name is commonly written Melchiades, though the best MSS seem to support the correct form Miltiades. The Greek Μελχιάδης can only have been derived from a corrupt Latin source. In the different MSS of the *LP* (see Duchesne I. p. 168), we have the forms Miltiades, Myltiades, Meltiades, Meletiades, Melciades, Melchiades, etc.

[2] Labb. *Conc.* I. p. 1445 sq (ed. Coleti); see Hefele *Conciliengesch.* I. p. 172 sq.

remains of 309 or 310. We have no data for deciding between these two years.

The next three popes in succession, SILVESTER, MARCUS, and JULIUS, present no difficulty. We have evidently a strictly contemporary record here. The beginnings and the ends of all the three episcopates are carefully recorded. The beginnings are all found to coincide with Sundays in accordance with the rule followed from the time of Miltiades. The ends are given likewise in the *Depos. Episc.* (see p. 249 sq); and the dates agree exactly with those of our Papal Catalogue, with one slight exception. In the Papal Catalogue for the death of Silvester, instead of 'Kl. Jan.', we should read 'Pr. Kl. Jan.'[1] For (1) It is so in the *Depos. Episc.*; (2) It is required to make the reckoning of the xi months; (3) It is required likewise by the consulates; for if he had died, not on Dec. 31, but on Jan. 1, the consuls would not have been those of A.D. 335, but those of A.D. 336. The xxii years assigned to this pope by Jerome are a round number for the exact xxi years, xi months. For Julius it seems necessary that we should correct m. i. d. xi into m. ii. d. vi, for these latter numbers are not only required by the interval, but are reproduced (with slight errors of transcription) in the Leonine Catalogue and in *LP*. The term assigned to him by Jerome, ann. xvi. m. iiii, is not easily explained and must be an error, though Jerome was probably born some years before his accession. These three episcopates then occupy the period from 31 Jan. 314 to 12 Apr. 352. The limits of each severally are exhibited in the table above, p. 285.

The accession of the next bishop, LIBERIUS, during whose episcopate this Catalogue was drawn up, is given as xi Kal. Jun. (May 22). This day however was not a Sunday in the year 352. An easy correction (comp. *Ign. and Polyc.* I. p. 666) would be xi Kal. Jul. (June 21), which would meet the requirement respecting the day of the week. This correction was suggested by Pagi and is accepted as probable by Lipsius (*Chron.* pp. 262, 264). Another solution however is proposed by Duchesne (*Lib. Pont.* I. p. cxl). The *Hieronymian Martyrology* gives the commemoration 'Liberii episcopi' under two several dates, xvi Kal. Jun. (May 17) and viiii Kal. Oct. (Sept. 23). In the latter case the entry is, 'Romae, depositio sancti Liberii episcopi.' It would seem therefore that the former is the date of his accession, and that we have here an instance of confusion, which we find elsewhere in this Martyrology, between the days of accession and of death. In this year May 17 was a Sunday. The *Libellus Precum* praef. c. 1 (Migne's *Patrol. Lat.* XIII.

[1] We have a similar omission of the letters 'pr.' in the date of the accession of Marcellinus in FP, which have 'Kal. Jul.' for 'pr. Kal. Jul.'

p. 81) of Faustus and Marcellus against Damasus places the death of Liberius 'octavo Kalendas Octobris' (Sept. 24), and this (viii, not viiii) is probably correct. The term-numbers for the months and days of this pope would then be m. iiii. d. vii, and this (making allowance for slight errors) accords with the Leonine figures m. iiii. d. viii and with those of the *LP* m. iii. d. iiii (where iiii is a corruption of vii). We may therefore adopt May 17 as the probable day of his accession. The figures for the years of Liberius in the later Latin lists are wide of the mark.

Having gone through the whole of the Liberian Catalogue and tested the amount of credibility which attaches to its several parts, we are now in a position to state some conclusions as to its origin and growth. It should be premised however that these conclusions must be regarded as in some points tentative. Whether we shall ever arrive at results which will command a general assent, must depend on new discoveries. Criticism has been working earnestly on this Catalogue for a long time and has almost exhausted its resources. We need fresh documentary evidence before we can hope for a final solution.

(1) The ground-work of this Catalogue was a list drawn up under Pontianus A.D. 230–235. There is a fair degree of probability that Hippolytus was its author. If not, it must have been the work of some contemporary. It contained nothing besides a list of names with the years of office, except perhaps the note relating to Hermas. This chronographer of the Hippolytean age however was not dependent on oral tradition. He had before him an earlier list of the papal succession. Of the prior document or documents which he used I shall have occasion to speak hereafter.

(2) A list was drawn up under Stephanus (A.D. 254–257) of the pontificates from Pontianus to Lucius inclusive (five episcopates). It contained the names of the popes in succession; the terms of office expressed in months, years, and days; and the dates of the close of each episcopate with the manner of death or other cause of the vacancy ('discinctus', 'dormit', 'passus', 'cum gloria dormicionem accepit', 'dormit'). It moreover gave certain historical notices, affecting more especially the government and governors of the Church. Thus it recorded the deportation of Pontianus together with Hippolytus to Sardinia; the Novatian schism under Fabius [Fabianus] and Cornelius; and the banishment and restoration of Lucius. It contained likewise one notice of episcopal administration, which is somewhat different from the rest and which served as a pattern for the later fictions of the *Liber Pontificalis*. We are told of Fabianus that he divided out the

city among the deacons and that he was the author of many erections in the cemeteries.

The compiler of this portion, which comprises about twenty years, writing under Stephanus, was contemporary with the events recorded. Whether he derived his information from official archives or from private knowledge, we cannot say. Though not homogeneous with the work of the Hippolytean chronicler, it may possibly have been compiled as a continuation of this work. This relation would explain how the second list begins at the same point at which the first ends. But with the banishment and resignation of Pontianus a new epoch in the history of the papacy commenced, and this fact alone would be enough to suggest the drawing up of a new record.

(3) We have seen that these first and second portions (A.D. 29–234, and A.D. 234–254), though not homogeneous the one with the other, were yet homogeneous each in itself. This is not the case with the portion comprising the third period, from A.D. 254—336. There is much variety of treatment in the different parts. For the half century from Stephanus to Marcellinus (A.D. 254–304) the irregularity is the greatest. Sometimes the days both of accession and of death are given, sometimes the one or the other, and sometimes neither. For the remaining portion, from Marcellus to Marcus (A.D. 308–336), the treatment is more even, and both days are regularly given. The want of homogeneity in this third portion of the Catalogue may suggest that it was not the work of one hand; but that the previous list from Peter to Stephanus received supplements from time to time from different persons, the latter and homogeneous part being the work of the Chronographer of 336.

(4) During this period, while it was receiving supplements from time to time, copies of the list were multiplied by transcription, and it was seriously corrupted in the process. Hence the transpositions of Cletus and Clemens, and of Pius and Anicetus, as well as the displacement of the figures for the years through several papacies (see above, p. 270 sq), in the former part of the list. Hence likewise the insertion of three years for Lucius and of two years for Xystus II, with other less flagrant errors, in the latter part. A very inaccurate and blurred copy also fell into the hands of Eusebius, though corrupt in a different way and much purer for the earlier episcopates than the Liberian copy.

(5) The Chronographer of 336 seems to have inserted Anacletus, if indeed his name had not been already inserted in the process of transmission. He also added the consulates. They agree very exactly with the names in the Consular Fasti which form part of his collection (see p. 248, p. 253 sq). But he encountered great difficulties in carrying

out this task, owing to the gross corruptions which had already crept into the text. He had certain fixed dates, as for instance the Crucifixion (A.D. 29), the exile and deposition of Pontianus (A.D. 235), the martyrdom of Fabianus (A.D. 250), the martyrdom of Xystus II (A.D. 258), and probably some later events also. In some of these cases (e.g. the exile of Pontianus, and the martyrdom of Xystus II) he probably found the consulates already in the text[1]; at all events they were well known dates. Having the Consular Fasti before him, he filled in the years by the aid of the term-numbers, working backwards or forwards, as the case might be, from the fixed dates. In the earlier part of the list, as far as Urbanus inclusive, there were as yet no figures for months and days. Accordingly he treats the years as whole years in the manner described above (p. 264). In the latter part however he found not only the duration of office in months and days as well as years, but also in many cases the actual day of the year on which the episcopate began or ended. The same consulate therefore, which ends one episcopate, is properly made to commence the next, except where, as in the cases of Felix and of Silvester[2], a pope died at the very close of a year, so that his successor's consecration necessarily fell in the next. But this mode of working backwards and forwards from fixed dates, though the only course open to our chronographer, had its inconveniences. It is like boring a tunnel underground, beginning at both ends. There is danger that the two may not meet but overlap each other. This mishap befel our chronographer in two instances. (i) In the first (Hippolytean) part of the list he began with the Crucifixion at one end and with the deposition of Pontianus at the other; but owing to the corruptions in his list the aggregate of the term-numbers was far in excess of the historic space, and accordingly at the middle of this period (Anicetus, Pius) he overlaps himself by eight years (see above, p. 264). (ii) Again in the second (Stephanic) part, having to fill the space between the martyrdom of Fabianus and that of Xystus II, which were fixed dates, and beginning in like manner at both ends, he overlaps himself by three years. Here again the sum of the term-numbers (owing to corruptions) exceeded the available historic space by this period. In the last part of the list, where he was dealing with contemporary history, he had

[1] The names given to the consuls are so obvious during the period from Pontianus to Marcellinus, as well as in some other parts, that their accordance with the Consular Fasti of our chronographer in any particular instance is no presumption that they were derived thence.

[2] This was likewise the case with Dionysius, but by a slight error our chronographer places his decease in the wrong consulate (see above, p. 290).

accurate information, even if he did not find the consulates already recorded in most instances. His real difficulty would naturally be in the earlier episcopates of this portion; and it was the greater, because the see was frequently vacant for a long time owing to the troubles, and the episcopates therefore were not chronologically continuous, so that the thread of his reckoning was snapped. Hence no consulates are assigned to Eusebius (A.D. 309 or 310). This omission is unique in the whole list. Probably our chronographer was in the same perplexity as ourselves, having no means of determining the exact year.

This chronographer is probably responsible for the imperial synchronisms also.

(6) The document received its final touches from the Chronographer of 354. He continued it from the point where his predecessor had dropped it, adding the notices of the episcopate of Julius and of the accession of Liberius, in whose time he wrote. He also inserted the months and days for the earlier part—from Peter to Pontianus—where hitherto only years had been given, thus making the record symmetrical throughout. My reason for assigning this last-mentioned insertion to the latest stage in the growth of the document will have appeared already. From what has been said, it will be evident that the months and days cannot have had any place there when the consulates were added.

(7) To the carelessness of later transcribers must be attributed such errors as the omission of Anicetus, Eleutherus, and Zephyrinus; or again the corruption of the numbers, where these differ from the intervals as determined by the consulates.

4.

THE LIBER PONTIFICALIS.

It will not be necessary to enter into a detailed account of the history and contents of this work (which I shall continue to designate *LP*). We are only concerned with it here, so far as it throws back any light on the early papal lists. A short summary therefore will suffice.

The preface to the work consists of two letters, one purporting to be written by Jerome to pope Damasus requesting him to compile a history of the see from the episcopacy of S. Peter to his own time; the other a reply from Damasus complying with this request and forwarding to him such particulars as he could discover ('quod gestum potuimus repperire').

The body of the work comprises accounts of the several popes in order, brief in the earlier part, but increasing in length as time advances. The earlier lives contain notices of their parentage and country, of the date of their accession and length of their pontificate, of their chief episcopal acts, especially their ordinations, and of the day and place of their 'depositio'.

Owing to the forged letters prefixed to the work, the earlier lives as far as Damasus were supposed to have been written by him, and in the thirteenth century and later, we find such designations as *Chronica Damasi* or *Damasus de Gestis Pontificum* given to it (see Duchesne *Lib. Pont.* I. p. xxxiii sq). The subsequent lives Panvinio (in Platina *de Vit. Pont. Roman.* p. 9, Cologne 1600) without any authority whatever ascribed to Anastasius the Librarian. This date was obviously far too late; for Anastasius flourished in the latter half of the ninth century, and the *LP* is frequently quoted by much earlier writers. Yet Bellarmin accepted this attribution, and to Anastasius the work is ascribed in the editio princeps (Mogunt. 1602). Baronius (s. ann. 867 § cxxxix) so far modifies this opinion as to hold that Anastasius was the author, only as having collected together lives written by others before him. Somewhat later (A.D. 1687) Pearson arrived at a substantially correct view of the history of the *LP* (*Minor Works* II. p. 416 sq). He saw that it must have been written as early as the sixth century and have been interpolated before the age of Anastasius. After him Schelestrate (*Antiq. Eccles. Illustr.* I. p. 375 sq, Romae 1692) dealt the death-blow to the Anastasian authorship, and his verdict was adopted by Bianchini. Bianchini however unfortunately retained the name of Anastasius in the title of his edition; and in our own age it is still included among the works of Anastasius in Migne's *Patrol. Latin.* CXXVII, CXXVIII.

The materials accumulated by later research have contributed to a more definite solution of the problem. It is now ascertained that there were two distinct editions of the work, the one traced back to the earlier years of the sixth century, the other to the close of the seventh.

1. The earlier of these editions has not reached us in its completeness, but is preserved in two abridgments.

The first of these (F), the *Felician*, closes with the life of Felix IV († A.D. 530), though followed in the MSS by a bare list of the succeeding popes as far as Pelagius II († A.D. 590). It was evidently made during the short pontificate of Felix' successor, Boniface II (A.D. 530—532). In two out of the three MSS in which it is preserved (*Paris.* 1451, *Vatic.*

Regin. 1127) it is prefixed to a collection of Canons. In the third (*Bernens.* 225) it breaks off suddenly in the middle of a line in the life of Liberius and is followed by Jerome's treatise *de Viris Illustribus* (see Lipsius *Chronologie* p. 279). There is good reason for supposing that this abridgment was originally made to accompany the collection of Canons, which shows by its contents that it was drawn up in the 6th century and in Gaul (see Duchesne *Étude* p. 6 sq, *Lib. Pont.* I. p. xlix sq), though its connexion with these Canons is questioned by Lipsius (*Jahrb. f. Protest. Theol.* v. p. 397). This abridgment is quoted by Gregory of Tours.

The second (K), the *Cononian*[1], is a later abridgment of the same work, but is continued as far as Conon († A.D. 687). In the extant MSS however there are lists of the popes carrying the series much lower down. The lives from Felix IV († A.D. 530) to Conon, which are wanting in F, are taken from the common (later) edition of the *LP*, but not without abridgment.

Of these two abridgments of the earlier edition of the *LP*, F adheres for the most part rigidly to the text, omitting but not changing words; while on the other hand K occasionally gives the substance in different language. Duchesne (*Lib. Pont.* I. p. 47 sq) has restored this primitive edition of the *LP* from these two abridgments with the aid of the later recension.

This opinion, that F and K represent an older text of the *LP* than the so-called Anastasian work, but in an abridged form, has been put forward with great ability and clearness by Duchesne (*Étude* p. 6 sq, *Lib. Pont.* I. p. lvii sq). It is also shared by Lipsius (*Chronol.* p. 80 sq, *Das Felicianische Papstbuch* in *Jarhb. f. Prot. Theol.* v. p. 385 sq, esp. p. 425 sq), and will probably meet with general acceptance. On the other hand Waitz (*Neues Archiv* IV. p. 217 sq, IX. p. 459 sq, X. p. 453 sq, XI. p. 217 sq) regards them as abridged from a later altered and somewhat corrupt text of the Anastasian work; and he seems to have found an adherent, at least to some extent, in Harnack (*Theolog. Literaturz.* 1886, no. 11, p. 244 sq). For Duchesne's replies to the criticisms of Waitz see *Revue des Questions Historiques* XXVI. p. 493 sq (1879), XXIX. p. 246 sq (1881), *Mélanges d'Archéologie* etc. II. p. 277 sq, IV. p. 232 sq, VI. p. 275 sq. Waitz is also answered by Lipsius, though more briefly, in the notes to his paper in *Jahrb. f. Prot. Theol.* v.

[1] Care must be taken not to confuse two different works: (1) The Cononian *abridgment* of the earlier or Felician edition of the *LP*, of which I am speaking here; and (2) The later or Cononian *edition* (not abridgment) of the *LP*, of which an account will be given presently (p. 307 sq).

p. 387 sq. The paper itself had been written before Waitz published his views.

The earlier edition then of the *LP* was brought down to the death of Felix IV (A.D. 530). Whatever may be thought of the particular texts of F and K, this fact seems to be established. The lives of the popes at this epoch bear evidence that they were written by a contemporary or contemporaries. It is Duchesne's opinion that the book, which is thus abridged in F and K, was compiled originally under Hormisdas (A.D. 514—523), the successor of Symmachus, and continued by contemporary hands to the death of Felix (*Lib. Pont.* I. p. xlviii). Lipsius (*Jahrb. f. Prot. Theol.* V. p. 395 sq) would place its compilation a few years earlier, in the age of Gelasius († A.D. 496) or Anastasius II († A.D. 498), the immediate predecessors of Symmachus. Among other reasons he is desirous of giving sufficient room for the corruptions in the text, as they appear in FK. I need not stop to discuss these divergent views. The difference is not great; nor has the question any bearing on the earlier history of the papacy, with which alone we are directly concerned, whatever may be its interest for the events of the close of the 5th and commencement of the 6th century.

This period was marked by the contention between Symmachus and Laurentius for the papacy. Symmachus was the chosen of the Roman party; Laurentius of the Byzantine. The feud was at length brought to an end by the intervention of King Theodoric. Symmachus was established on the papal throne, while Laurentius was consoled with the Campanian bishopric of Nuceria. Such an epoch would direct attention to the previous history of the Roman see, and call forth publications favourable to either side. The *LP*, of which (as we have seen) the earlier edition belongs to this epoch, advocates strongly the cause of Symmachus. But there is likewise extant in a Veronese MS a fragment of what was apparently a papal history, containing the few closing lines of a life of Anastasius II († A.D. 498) followed by a life of Symmachus, in which this latter pope is severely handled and the cause of the antipope Laurentius advocated. As the life of Symmachus is followed by a mere list of names and terms of office (in years, months, and days) for the succeeding popes, the work itself was evidently written during this pontificate. Indeed, since it mentions the schism which arose upon the 'henoticon' of Zeno as still existing, it must date before A.D. 519, and therefore within four or five years of the death of Symmachus (Duchesne *Lib. Pont.* I. p. xxx). Here then we have two contemporary papal histories written from diametrically opposite points of view. Unfortunately the *Laurentian* history is only a fragment, and we do not know what preceded it. But it is at least a plausible conjecture that the two histories had the same, or substantially the same, matter in common till towards the close of the fifth century, and that here they diverged, each building upon a common foundation the last storey of contemporary history according to his own prejudices and in his own party interests[1]. Attention has been called already (p. 262 sq) to this phenomenon, as illustrating what may have occurred at an earlier date, in the age of Hippolytus. The Laurentian fragment is given in full by Duchesne (*Lib. Pont.* I. p. 43 sq).

2. The later edition of the *Liber Pontificalis* can be traced as far back as Conon († A.D. 687). Of this we have direct manuscript evidence. The Neapolitan MS, to which attention was called by Pertz, and of which I shall have to speak presently, contains this recension. From the handwriting it appears to belong to the end of the 8th century and not later; and originally it must have comprised biographies of the popes down to Conon. It is true that in its present state, owing to the mutilation of the MS, it breaks off in the middle of the life of Anastasius II (A.D. 496—498), but prefixed to the work is a list of the popes as far as Conon. Moreover the biographies at this epoch, both before and after Conon, in this recension were evidently written by contemporaries. Thus in the life of Leo II († A.D. 683) the Sixth Ecumenical Council is mentioned as having been held 'lately' (*Lib. Pont.* I. p. 359, ed. Duchesne). The age of Conon therefore is the latest possible date for this recension. Hence it is sometimes called the 'Cononian' edition. But there is every reason for supposing that it belongs to a much earlier date and was added to from time to time. The evidence in favour of its earlier origin derived from the history of the text will be mentioned shortly. For this and for other reasons Duchesne (*Lib. Pont.* I. p. ccxxx sq) would place it as early as the middle of the 6th century, the age of Vigilius (A.D. 537—555). His arguments do not seem to me conclusive; but the term 'Cononian,' as applied to this recension of the *LP*, is certainly misleading, as it suggests a date which is much too late, and it has the further disadvantage of creating a confusion with a wholly different form of this work (see p. 305, note 1).

A full account of the MSS of this 'second edition' of the *LP* will be

[1] If however the calculations of Duchesne (*Lib. Pont.* I. p. xxxi) as to the contents of the missing portion be correct, the earlier lives must have been very much briefer even than those of the Felician abridgment.

found in Duchesne (*Lib. Pont.* I. p. clxiv sq; comp. *Étude* p. 46 sq). If we confine our attention to the portion from S. Peter to Felix IV, they fall into two main classes.

(A) The chief representative of the first class is the *Lucca* MS, no. 490, in the Chapter Library of that city. The volume contains various works in different hands of the 8th or beginning of the 9th century. The *LP* in this MS consists of two parts, (1) the first reaching as far as Constantine († A.D. 712) in one handwriting, and (2) the second with a different numbering of the sheets in a different hand, from Gregory II to Hadrian I (A.D. 715—758). Each part presumably was written about the date at which it closes. At the end of the first part is a notice, *Hūc usque cxxviiii anni sunt quod Longobardi venerunt et vii menses.* The point of time from which the 129 years should be reckoned is a little uncertain[1].

(B) The most ancient representative of the other class is the *Neapolitanus* iv. A. 5, already mentioned (p. 307), which must have been written before the close of the 7th century. It bears the inscription *Liber S. Columbani* and most probably therefore belonged originally to the Monastery of Bobbio. For the reasons which have been already stated, we may fairly conclude that it was carried down to Conon († A.D. 687). Attention was first called to the exceptional importance of this MS for the history of the *LP* by Pertz (*Archiv* v. p. 70 sq, 1824).

Though this MS is some years earlier than the Lucca MS, and perhaps coeval with the completion of this second recension of the *LP*, yet the type of text B is certainly inferior to the type of text A, and exhibits both corruptions and additions from which the latter is free. This point seems to be made quite clear by Duchesne (*Lib. Pont.* I. p. ccvii sq, comp. *Étude* p. 40 sq), and Lipsius (*Jahrb. f. Prot. Theol.* v. p. 389) acquiesces. On the other hand Waitz (*Neues Archiv* IV. p. 225 sq, and elsewhere) maintains the priority of the text B against Duchesne.

But the fact, that in a MS coeval or nearly so with Conon the text is already corrupt, shows that this recension of the *LP* had already had a continuous history at this epoch, though the age of Conon is the earliest at which we have direct evidence of its existence. It was not a

[1] In his *Étude* p. 47 Duchesne dates the Lombard invasion A.D. 568; so that, adding 129 years, we arrive at 697, not 715, as the date intended. He therefore supposes this reckoning, A.D. 697, to give the date of 'the original of the Lucca MS.' In his later work (*Lib. Pont.* I. p. clxv) he assumes the Lucca MS to have been written not earlier than the accession of pope Constantine (A.D. 708), in which case the date (not earlier than 708 − 129 = 579) will refer to the Lombard invasion of the particular country 'where the MS was in the 8th century.'

cast as of molten metal, but a growth as of a tree. The text of this recension must have existed already in two distinct types before the later lives ending with Conon were attached to it. It is altogether beside my purpose to pursue this question further. Those who are anxious to follow up the subject will do well to consult Duchesne's own account of the relations of the MSS and the growth of the text[1]. But indeed, notwithstanding the great care and ability of his work, it were too sanguine to hope that the last word had been spoken on a question so intricate and thorny.

So far as regards the earlier popes, our interest in the *LP* ends with these two editions or recensions. With the continuations which from time to time were attached to the work, or with the modifications which affect the later portions, we have no concern. A full account of these will be found in Duchesne (*Lib. Pont.* I. ccxxx sq; comp. *Étude* p. 199 sq).

For the early centuries the differences between the two editions of the *LP* are for the most part inconsiderable. It is only when we have advanced well into the 4th century, that they assume a greater prominence. One group of insertions however which appears in the later edition—perhaps the most striking during this early period—affects the first four lives and therefore has a direct bearing on our subject. In the biography of S. Peter a paragraph is inserted, explaining how Linus and Cletus were appointed during the Apostle's life-time to act as suffragans[2], that he might not be cumbered with business which would interfere with his preaching. It then goes on to speak of his disputes with Simon Magus—all this being preparatory to the succeeding notice[3], which represents S. Peter as ordaining Clement to be his immediate successor, and committing to him the care of the Church (in language borrowed from the Clementine *Letter to James*), charging him at the same time to appoint others to relieve him of ecclesiastical business, that he may devote himself to prayer and to preaching. Accordingly in the lives of Linus and of Cletus, where these two bishops are represented as performing certain episcopal acts, this later edition inserts the words 'ex praecepto beati Petri,' which are wanting in the earlier, thus representing them as only carrying out the directions of a living superior. The same idea again is insisted upon in the life of Clement, where he is said to have

[1] *Lib. Pont.* I. pp. xlix sq, clxiv sq; see also *Mélanges d'Archéologie* VI. p. 275 sq, which contains a summary of Duchesne's views on this subject.

[2] See above, p. 191 sq.

[3] See above, pp. 186, 191, where the forms of the life of Clement in the earlier and later editions of the *LP* are given.

undertaken the pontificate of the Church 'ex praecepto beati Petri,' this being the last occasion on which the phrase is used. Here the Epistle of Clement to James, which had been indirectly quoted in a previous life, is mentioned by name; and the explanation is given that the names of Linus and Cletus stand before Clement on the roll ('ante eum conscribuntur'), as having been ordained bishops by Peter under the circumstances described. This, it will be remembered, is a suggestion of Epiphanius, who is followed by Rufinus[1], to reconcile the discrepancies of order in the different papal lists. It should be added that no attempt is made to rectify the chronology, so as to bring it into harmony with this theory. Though Clement is represented as consecrated by S. Peter himself, he is stated nevertheless to have held the episcopate nine years, and to have died in the third year of Trajan.

The other changes in these earlier lives likewise betray a later date. Thus Anicetus and Soter are said in the Felician edition to be buried 'juxta corpus beati Petri,' i.e. in the Vatican, which we learn from other authorities to have been the case; but in this second edition their place of sepulture is given as the Cemetery of Callistus, though this cemetery did not exist in their time. Again Anicetus and Eutychianus are made martyrs, though the earlier edition knows nothing of this; while Gaius, from being a simple confessor, is promoted to the higher honour of martyrdom. The most significant indication of a later date however occurs in the notice of the Paschal dispute in the life of Victor (Duchesne *Lib. Pont.* I. pp. lxiii, ccxxxi, 138). In the earlier edition, as Duchesne points out, the language is 'inspired by the *Liber Paschalis* of Victorius of Aquitaine, published in 457'; whereas in the later the editor has in view the system of Dionysius Exiguus, which was given to the world in 525.

But the question of real interest for our immediate purpose has reference to the earlier authorities on which the *Liber Pontificalis* is founded. These are twofold.

(1) The *Liberian Catalogue.* The whole of this Catalogue is incorporated in the *LP.* This is done without any intelligence or appreciation, and often with very incongruous results. This fact furnishes one of the strongest evidences that F and K are abridgments. The quotations from the Liberian Catalogue, which appear in full in the later edition of the *LP*, are found in these authorities in a mutilated form. Yet it is almost inconceivable that the later editor, finding these

[1] See above, pp. 169 sq, 174 sq, where the passages of Epiphanius and Rufinus are quoted.

broken fragments in the earlier edition, should have taken the trouble to gather the corresponding pieces from the original document and fit them together, thus restoring the quotations to their pristine condition. We are therefore driven to the only remaining conclusion that at one time they were complete in the earlier edition, as they still are in the later, and that they suffered mutilation by the abridgment of the former. The example which Duchesne gives (I. p. xlii) from the life of Fabianus is a good illustration.

(2) The *Leonine Catalogue.* Though this document is no longer extant, its existence must be postulated in order to explain the pedigree of later authorities. A considerable number of papal lists are found, giving the years, months, and days, of the several pontificates, and all obviously derived from one parent. The principal of these are given by Duchesne (*Lib. Pont.* I. p. 12 sq; comp. p. xiv—xxv); see also *Anal. Noviss. Spicil. Solesm.* I. p. 315 sq, where there is a list of these and other papal catalogues (p. 332 sq). A collation of several will be found in Lipsius *Chronol.* p. 128 sq. The oldest date from the age of Felix III († A.D. 492) and Hormisdas († A.D. 523). This fact points to about the middle of the 5th century, or a little after, as the lowest possible date of the parent list.

But in the year 447 a book on the Paschal Cycle was published and dedicated to Leo the Great. Only a few fragments remain, which have been edited by Mommsen (*Die Zeitzer Ostertafel vom Jahre 447* p. 537 sq, in the *Abhandl. der Acad. der Wiss. zu Berlin* 1862). This Easter Table derives its name from Zeitz in Saxony, in the library of which place it was found. Happily a portion of the prologue has been preserved, in which the author thus describes the appendix to his work;

'Huic autem collectioni paschalium dierum, non solum seriem consulum conexuimus, sed etiam annos apostolicae sedis antistitum et aetates regni principum Romanorum diligentissima adnotatione subdidimus (p. 541).'

An account of this work will be found in Krusch *Der 84jährige Ostercyclus u. seine Quellen* p. 116 sq. The papal list which accompanied it has unfortunately perished. But was it not the lost parent which has left this numerous progeny of catalogues behind? I need not stop to enquire whether there is any probability in Duchesne's conjecture (*Lib. Pont.* I. p. xiv), that the author of this Cycle was none other than the chronographer Prosper himself. Whoever he may have been, there are good reasons for thinking that its calculations were adopted for the regulation of Easter by the Roman authorities (see Krusch p. 124 sq).

At all events it was brought prominently before the notice of the Roman Church; and the papal list accompanying it would thus obtain a notoriety which would lead to its frequent transcription.

Great stress is laid by Lipsius on other documentary evidence which he finds, that the episcopate of Leo the Great marked a distinct stage in the fabric of this pontifical chronicle (*Chronologie* p. 126; comp. *Jahrb. f. Prot. Theol.* v. pp. 450, 456 sq). At the end of the life of Xystus III, the immediate predecessor of Leo, some MSS (see Duchesne *Lib. Pont.* I. p. 235) of the *LP* have the notice, 'A morte Silvestri usque ad hunc primum Leonem sunt anni xcviiii. m. v. d. xxvi.' But the value of this argument is materially diminished by the fact that there is no trace of this note in the earlier edition of the *LP*, and that it is not found in the oldest and best MSS even of the later. Moreover, as Duchesne has pointed out (*Étude* p. 134), in these same MSS, which single out the epoch of Leo I, a similar notice occurs at the close of the Life of Pelagius II, the immediate predecessor of Gregory the Great, 'A morte sancti Silvestri usque ad hunc primum Gregorium fuerunt anni ccxlvi' (*Lib. Pont.* I. p. 309). It would seem therefore that the author of this note desired to emphasize the great epochs in the history of the papacy, marked by the three most famous popes of the period, Silvester, Leo, and Gregory, and that he reckoned up the intervals accordingly.

This Leonine Catalogue, if we may now assume its existence, seems to have been published simultaneously, or almost simultaneously, in Greek. The conspicuous part taken by Leo the Great in the controversies which culminated in the Council of Chalcedon brought the Roman pontificate prominently before the Eastern Church at this epoch, and would naturally excite an interest in the papal succession. At all events in some extant Latin catalogues we find traces of a Greek parentage. Thus in the *Corbie* MS (now *Paris.* 12097), the name Osus (Ὅσιος) appears instead of Pius; and elsewhere the forms seem to be influenced by a Greek original, though Lipsius has pressed this point too far (*Chronol.* p. 134, *Jahrb. f. Prot. Theol.* v. p. 453).

At an earlier stage in this investigation (p. 240 sq) attention was directed to certain Greek and Oriental Catalogues (ABCDE) of the Roman bishops, which were subsequent to the age of Leo. One of these, the list of Elias of Nisibis (E), actually ends with this pontificate. Another, that of 'the Short Chronography' (A), contains imperial synchronisms which break off with Leo (Lipsius *Chronol.* p. 28, *Jahrb. f. Prot. Theol.* v. p. 455). It is not unnatural therefore that we should look to the Leonine Catalogue as the source of their inspiration, and should expect to find strong coincidences with the Latin Catalogues of the 5th and subsequent centuries, betokening affinity of origin. This expectation is not disappointed. It is not however in the early part of the list that we trace any close resemblances. During the period which elapsed before the great persecution, the Eusebian numbers prevail. It is only here and there that we see, or imagine we see, the influence of the Leonine list. The resemblances and differences for this earlier epoch will be seen from a comparison of the Greek and Oriental Catalogues on p. 241 with the Leonine list in the table on p. 316. But from Marcellinus onward, where the Eusebian lists cease, the Leonine numbers dominate. The table which follows will make this point clear. It is carried down to Xystus III, the immediate predecessor of Leo.

NAMES	*AC*	*B*	*D*	*E*	*LEONINE*	*CORRECT*
					ann. mens.	ann. mens.
Marcellinus	*om.*	2	*om.*	10 m.	*om.*	8 . 3
Marcellus	2	*om.*	2	*om.*	1 . 4	0 . 7
Eusebius	1	1	6	*om.*	0 . 6	0 . 4
Miltiades	4	4	4	8	4 . 0	2 . 6
Silvester	28	28	28	18	23 . 10	21 . 11
Marcus	2	12	2	2	2 . 0	0 . 8
Julius	15	15	15	15	15 . 2	15 . 2
Liberius	6	6	6	7	6 . 4	14 . 4
Felix	1	1	*om.*	3	,, ,,	,, ,,
Damasus	28	*om.*	28	8	18 . 3	18 . 2
Siricius	15	15	12	15	15 . 0	15 . 0
Anastasius	3	3	3	3	3 . 0	2 . 0
Innocentius	15	15	15	16	15 . 2	15 . 2
Zosimus	8	8	1	2	7 (1) . 9 (3)	1 . 9
Bonifacius	4	4	3	3	3 . 8	3 . 8
Celestinus	10	21	10	10	9 . 10	9 . 10
Xystus III.	8	8	8	9	8 . 0	8 . 0

The documents designated by the letters A, B, C, D, E, are explained above (p. 240 sq). Of these the first and third (A, C) coincide exactly for this period, and are therefore included in one column. The Leonine list gives months and days, as well as years. I have recorded the years and months, but not the days, for a reason which will appear presently. Inasmuch as coincidence in the numbers is no evidence of identity of origin, where these numbers represent historical facts, I have added the correct terms of office, as tabulated by Duchesne[1] (*Lib. Pont.* I. p. cclxi), giving however only the years and months and omitting the days. The common origin of the Leonine and of the Greek and Oriental lists will be manifest in the numbers assigned to Eusebius, Miltiades, Marcus, Liberius, Anastasius, and Zosimus, where the Leonine numbers are more or less wide of the truth. In other cases also the affinity appears, when the Roman numerals are used and allowance is made for the accidental addition or omission or interchange of a figure, e.g. Silvester xxviii or xviii compared with xxiii (or xxiiii), Damasus xxviii or viii compared with xviii, Siricius (in D) xii for xv (the same interchange which has been noticed above in the case of Gaius). It will be seen that several of the figures in E are greater by a unit than in the other lists, and this phenomenon may be explained in the same way. The 8 assigned to Miltiades in E must arise out of a confusion with his successor Silvester; and the 21 given to Celestinus in B is perhaps to be explained similarly, as the figure belonging to Leo who stands next but one below him in this list and whose term of office it correctly gives, though it might possibly be accounted for as a confusion of the years and months (ix. x) in the Leonine list. As regards the mode of dealing with the months, I note the following rule observed by the compiler of the Greek table, in which they are omitted. Where the number for the months was 6 or over in the Leonine list, the next higher whole number of years was taken. Thus we have 1 for Eusebius, 8 for Zosimus, 4 for Bonifacius, 10 for Celestinus. As the figures at present stand, Marcellus would be the the only distinct exception to this rule; but there is good independent reason for thinking that the figures for his months and years were originally ann. i. m. vii, and that by a common type of error they were corrupted into ann. i. m. iiii (see above, p. 257). It is obvious that Marcellinus and Marcellus are fused into one person in these catalogues, and that the figures properly belonging to the latter are assigned to this conjoint person.

It should be added that, if we make allowance for accidental blunders and omissions, these Greek and Oriental lists all agree with the Leonine Catalogue as regards the names and order of the popes. The main points of agreement between the two, where divergence is found in

[1] The calculations of Lipsius (*Chronologie* p. 264) comprise only the early part of this period as far as Julius inclusive. His results differ from those of Duchesne in assigning 1 yr. 7 m. (instead of 7 months only) to Marcellus, and 3 yrs. 6 m. (instead of 2 yrs. 6 m.) to Miltiades. See above, p. 296 sq, where reasons are given for preferring the one reckoning to the other. In *Lib. Pont.* I. p. xx Duchesne by an accident assigns 5 months instead of 4 to Liberius.

other lists, are as follows; (1) The order at the commencement of the series is Peter, Linus, Cletus (or Anacletus), Clemens; (2) Cletus is not treated as a different person from Anacletus, though in some of these lists he is called Cletus, in others Anacletus (Anencletus); (3) The correct order, Pius, Anicetus, is retained; (4) The correct order, Pontianus, Anteros, is also retained; (5) Marcellinus and Marcellus are fused, as I have already explained; (6) A place is given to Felix II, the antipope in the time of Liberius. There is indeed one exception to this agreement. In C, the list of Syncellus, Anteros is placed before Pontianus (see p. 242). So far as our knowledge goes, he cannot have got this transposition from the Leonine Catalogue. All the extant Leonine lists give the correct order. It is found however in the earlier (Felician) edition of the *LP*, and this may have been the source from which directly or indirectly he derived it.

I may remark also, before leaving this subject, that the table (p. 313) shows the figures for the pontificates immediately preceding Leo to be strictly accurate; and this is additional evidence in favour of the Leonine date for the compilation of the list.

There seems then to be sufficient evidence for postulating such a Leonine Catalogue which was the parent on the one hand of the Latin lists of the 5th and following centuries, and on the other of the Greek and Oriental lists, at least from the point where Eusebius ceases. Its existence was affirmed first, I believe, by Bianchini (II. p. lxx sq), who however diminishes the value of his suggestion by finding this Leonine list in the frescoes of S. Paul (see below, p. 318 sq); and it assumes a special prominence in the investigations of Lipsius, who invests it with the highest significance (*Chronologie* pp. 28, 38, 76, 86, 92, 94, 114—117, 126—141, 143; comp. *Jahrb. f. Prot. Theol.* v. p. 449 sq). On the other hand Duchesne in his earlier work (*Étude* p. 133) was disposed to deny such a catalogue altogether. He even says (p. 213) that he considers it 'almost certain' that the catalogues of the age of Hormisdas 'have been extracted from the *Liber Pontificalis*.' But in his later book, the edition of the *LP*, his antagonism to the view of Lipsius is considerably modified; and at least for the period between Siricius and Xystus III, he is prepared to admit a common origin of the Latin and Greek lists and to place the parent document of these two families in the age of Leo the Great (*Lib. Pont.* I. pp. xxi sq, lxix).

But admitting the fact of such a Leonine Catalogue, two important questions arise; *First*, What did it contain? and *Secondly*, On what authorities was it founded?

NAMES	*Hieron.*	*Liberian List*			*Leonine List*			*Liber Pontificalis*			*Frescoes of S. Paul*		
Petrus	xxv	xxvi [xxv].	i.	viiii	xxv.	ii.	iii	xxv.	ii.	iii	xxv.	ii.	viiii
Linus	xi	xii.	iiii.	xii	xi.	iii.	xii	xi.	iii.	xii	?	iii.	xii
Cletus	xii	vii [vi].	ii.	x	xii.	i.	ii	xii.	i.	xi	xii.	?	xi
Clemens	viiii	viiii.	xi.	xii	viiii.	i [ii].	x	viiii.	ii.	x	viiii.	ii.	x
Anacletus	wanting	xii.	x.	iii		wanting		xii. viiii.	x. ii.	iii [F] x [P]	xii.	x.	vii
Evarestus	viiii	xiii.	vii.	ii	viiii.	x.	ii	viiii.	x.	ii	?	vii.	ii
Alexander	x	viii.	ii.	i	xii [x].	vii.	ii	x.	vii.	ii	x.	vii.	iii
Xystus	x	x.	iii.	xxi	x.	ii.	i	x.	ii.	i	?	iii.	xxi
Telesphorus	xi	xi.	iii.	iii	xi.	i [iii].	xxi	xi.	iii.	xxi	xi.	ii.	xxii
Hyginus	iiii	xii.	iii.	vi	iiii.	iii.	iiii	iiii.	iii.	iiii	iiii.	iii.	viii
Anicetus	xi	iiii [ ].			xi.	iiii.	iii	xi.	iiii.	iii	viii.	iii.	iii
Pius	xv	xvi [xx].	iiii.	xxi	xviii.	iiii.	xi [iii]	xviiii.	iiii.	iii	xi.	iiii.	xxi
Soter	viii	viiii.	iii.	ii	viiii.	ii [vi].	xxi	viiii.	vi.	xxi	viiii.	iii.	xxi
Eleutherus	xv	xv.			xv.	iii.	ii	xv.	iii.	ii	xv.	iiii.	v
Victor	x	xii [viii].	ii.	x	xv [x].	iii [ii].	ii	x.	ii.	x	x.	ii.	x
Zephyrinus	[xviii]	xx [ ].			xviii [viii].	vi [vii].	x	viii.	vii.	x	xvii.	ii.	x
Callistus	v	v.	ii.	x	v.	x [ii].	x	vi.	ii.	x	v.	ii.	x
Urbanus	viiii	viii.	xi.	xii	viiii [iiii].	i [x].	ii [xii]	iiii.	x.	xii	viii.	xi.	xii
Pontianus	v	v.	ii.	vii	vii [viiii].	x [v].	xxii [ii]	viiii.	v.	ii	…………		
Anteros	m. i		i.	x	[xii].	i.	xviiii [xii]	xii.	i.	xii	…………		
Fabianus	xiii	xiiii.	i.	x	xiiii.	ii.	x	xiiii.	i.	xi	xiii.	i.	x
Cornelius	ii	ii.	iii.	x	ii.	iii.	x	ii.	ii.	iii	iii.	,,	x
Lucius	m. viii	iii.	viii.	x	iii [iiii].	viii.	x	iii.	iii.	iii	iii.	iii.	iii
Stephanus	iii	iiii.	ii.	xxi	vi.	v.	v	vi [vii].	v.	ii	iiii.	ii.	xv
Xystus II	[xi]	ii.	xi.	vi	i.	x.	xxvi	i.	x.	xxiii	ii.	xi.	vi
Dionysius	viiii	viii.	ii.	iiii	viii.	v.	iiii	vi.	ii.	iiii	ii.	iii.	vii
Felix	v	v.	xi.	xxv	iiii.	i.	xxv	iiii.	iii.	xxv	ii.	x.	
Eutychianus	m. viii	viii.	xi.	iii	i.	i.	i	i.	i.	i	viii.	x.	iii
Gaius	xv	xii.	iiii.	vii	xi.	iiii.	xii	xi.	iiii.	xii	xi.	iiii.	viiii

(1) The first question is answered by Lipsius in a way which would greatly enhance the value of the document, if we could accept his answer. He supposes it to have marked a distinct stage in the growth of the *LP*. On his showing it was not a mere catalogue of names and figures, but contained divers facts or fictions relative to the popes. In other words it was a series of short biographies and thus, in point of contents, it would stand somewhere midway between the Liberian Catalogue (A.D. 354) and the Felician Book (A.D. 530), where also it stood in point of date (c. A.D. 440). In short he makes it responsible, so far as regards the earlier popes, for almost all the statements in the *LP* which were not taken from the Liberian Catalogue. More especially he urges that the notices of the depositions of the several bishops, introduced with the words 'qui sepultus est,' were derived from this document; so that in several instances (Fabianus, Lucius, Dionysius, Eutychianus, Gaius, Silvester, Marcus), where the Liberian Catalogue likewise preserved a notice of the deposition, the statement is doubled, the one being sometimes in accordance with the other, sometimes at variance (see *Chronologie* p. 114, *Jahrb. f. Prot. Theol.* v. p. 458 sq). For all this there is absolutely no evidence. It is indeed extremely probable that the compiler of the *LP* had before him a list of depositions which was tolerably continuous; and that he inserted this into his book, as he inserted those of the Liberian Catalogue, regardless of repetitions or contradictions; but there is no ground whatever for supposing that these notices were interwoven so as to form part of the Leonine papal list containing the names and terms of office. So far as the evidence goes, the Leonine Catalogue was a simple list with term-numbers, like the Latin lists derived from it.

(2) But, if so, on what previous documents was it founded? Does it furnish independent testimony to the early papal chronology, or is it altogether derived from sources otherwise known to us? I believe Duchesne to be right in supposing that for the period till the middle of the 4th century the sources of the Leonine list were two and two only; (i) The notices in the Hieronymian *Chronicle*, and (ii) The Liberian Catalogue; to which perhaps we should add the earlier document (see p. 300 sq) incorporated by the Liberian editor (see *Étude* p. 134 sq, *Lib. Pont.* I. p. xvi sq). For the period between Peter and Urban the numbers of the years coincide with those of Jerome, as the table given above (p. 316) shows, and as Lipsius himself allows (*Jahrb. f. Prot. Theol.* v. p. 450). On the other hand the months and days are taken from the Liberian Catalogue, but with the displacement explained above on p. 267 sq.

It should be added that the MSS of the Leonine lists, as Duchesne has pointed out (*Lib. Pont.* I. p. lxxix), fall into two classes with distinctive variations in the figures. The one type (A) can be traced as far back as A.D. 523; whereas the other (B) is only extant in lists carried down to the age of Gregory the Great (A.D. 590—604) or later. Yet the readings of B appear most commonly in the *LP.* They are also not unfrequently closer to the readings in the sources from which the Leonine Catalogue was derived, the Hieronymian Chronicle and the Liberian Catalogue; and in such cases they are presumably the original readings. In my table (p. 316), where there was any variation worth recording, I have given the preference to what was apparently the original reading, and placed the variation in brackets after it.

No account of the *Liber Pontificalis* would be complete which omitted to mention the evidence of monumental records closely connected with it. The ancient basilicas of S. Peter and S. Paul at Rome had two sets of portraits of the popes painted in fresco round the church. The more ancient was above the cornice of the entablature over the arcade of the nave; the more modern was immediately above the capitals of the columns. The later is known to have been executed in both these churches by order of Pope Nicolas III (A.D. 1277—1280), who also decorated S. John Lateran with a similar set of portraits. The upper series was much more ancient.

Of the upper series in S. Peter's we have no information which is of any value for our present purpose; but there is every reason to believe that in both churches the names and term-numbers for the several popes who had a place in the earlier series were copied in the later. The lower series in S. Peter's commenced with Pius, then came Soter, Eleutherus, Victor, Zephyrinus, Callistus, Urbanus, Anteros, Pontianus, Fabianus, etc. It included both Marcellinus and Marcellus; and it recognized likewise Felix II, the opponent of Liberius (see Müntz's *Recherches sur L'Œuvre Archéologique de J. Grimaldi*, p. 249, included in the same volume with Duchesne's *Étude*).

Of the papal frescoes in S. Paul's we have fuller information. This basilica was burnt down in 1823[1], when the greater part perished, but the South wall containing the earlier popes was left standing. The portraits were carefully preserved, as far as possible; but no attention

[1] Lipsius (*Chronologie* p. 86) writes as if he were unaware that this basilica had perished in the fire and been rebuilt. His description of the order of the medallions on the North wall seems to be founded on a misconception.

was paid to the inscriptions. In the earlier part of the 18th century however they had been copied with great care by Bianchini and are included in his edition (A.D. 1724) of 'Anastasius' (II. p. lxxxii sq). Somewhat later, when Benedict XIV undertook the restoration of these frescoes, Marangoni published an elaborate work giving the portraits and inscriptions (*Chronologia Romanorum Pontificum superstes in pariete australi Basilicae S. Pauli* etc, Romae 1751); but it is disfigured by great carelessness, so that Bianchini remains our chief authority on the subject. Besides these, there is extant a MS in the library of the Barberini Palace at Rome (*Cod.* xlix. 15, 16) containing coloured copies of the portraits, executed by order of Card. Barberini (A.D. 1634), with notes relating to their respective positions and to the inscriptions accompanying them. Using all these sources of information, Duchesne (*Lib. Pont.* I. p. lxxxi sq) has given a table of the numbers with a full collation of the different authorities.

The more ancient series began at the East end of the South wall and then passed round the West wall and along the North side to the East end near the high altar. The portraits were medallions grouped two and two, each pair occupying the spaces corresponding to the intercolumniations; and between the medallions were the inscriptions giving the respective names and terms of office in years, months, and days. Of the portion of the series on the Western wall no trace is preserved. For the North wall our information is very fragmentary, but we know that here the portraits were jumbled together without any regard to chronological order. In some cases the same pope was introduced a second time. Among the portraits on this wall was the antipope Laurentius who for several years (A.D. 501—506) contested the possession of the see with Symmachus. The South wall comprised 42 portraits, from S. Peter to Innocent I inclusive. The order of the immediate successors of S. Peter was Linus, Cletus, Clemens, Anacletus. Pius was correctly placed before Anicetus, but on the other hand Anteros preceded Pontianus as in the *Liber Felicianus* and in Syncellus. This last point seems to have been satisfactorily established by Duchesne (*Lib. Pont.* I p. xxviii sq), though Bianchini and Marangoni read it otherwise, and they have been followed by subsequent writers (e.g. Lipsius *Chronologie* p. 87). Both Marcellinus and Marcellus were included, and a place was accorded to Felix II. In this way Innocent became the 42nd in the series. Thus in every respect, except the inversion of the order of Pius and Anicetus, the series on the South wall corresponded with the earlier edition of the *LP* as represented by the *Felicianus*. Of the number of years, months, and days, ascribed to the successive popes in these frescoes, I shall have occasion to speak presently.

Bianchini (p. lxx) supposed that portraits and inscriptions alike belonged to the age of Leo the Great (A.D. 440—461), and accordingly he attached the highest value to them. This view however seems untenable. It is stated indeed that Leo 'renovated' the basilica of S. Paul after it had been set on fire by lightning ('post ignem divinum'), and extant inscriptions show that his work of restoration was very considerable (Duchesne *Lib. Pont.* I. p. 240). But there is no evidence that he placed the portraits in the church. The heads which once decorated the South wall are purely conventional. This applies equally to Innocent I († A.D. 417), as to the earlier heads. At what point in the series there was any attempt at portraiture we cannot say, as the succeeding popes for some decades after this time are wanting. But Laurentius is certainly a portrait; nor indeed would a place have been assigned to him in the series after the schism was ended and Symmachus recognized as pope. We must suppose therefore that this particular portrait was painted while he and his party had possession of most of the Roman basilicas, though not of S. Peter's (*Lib. Pont.* I. p. 46). If so, the series must have existed before his time. As regards the portraits, De Rossi (*Bull. di Archeol. Crist.* 1870, p. 122 sq) judges that they belong rather to the middle than to the end of the 5th century; and, if so, they may have been part of Leo's work. But it does not follow that the inscriptions were contemporary with the portraits. Duchesne lays great stress on the inversion, Anteros, Pontianus, which was his own discovery, and concludes from this inversion that the inscriptions must have been later than the *LP*, and therefore not earlier than the 6th century. He urges that the source of the inversion is the recension of the *LP* which is represented by the *Felicianus*. His explanation of the error seems highly probable. An account of it has been given already (p. 287). Yet it would be possible to explain the inversion in another way. The manner in which the inscriptions were linked together two and two in the frescoes of S. Paul would render such a transposition easy on the part of the painter, and as a matter of fact we know that Anteros and Pontianus did form such a couple (Duchesne *Lib. Pont.* I. p. xxviii sq). It is conceivable therefore that the frescoes may themselves have been the source of the inversion; and, if so, they would have been prior to the *Liber Pontificalis*.

After tracing, however briefly, the history and relations of the *Liber Pontificalis*, it remains for us to add a few words respecting *first* the names and order of the bishops, and *secondly* the term-numbers assigned to them severally, in the two recensions of this document.

(1) In the names of the earliest bishops the Liberian Catalogue is followed in both recensions of the *LP.* Not only the duplication of Cletus or Anencletus, but the order of the names, is taken from this document—Petrus, Linus, Cletus, Clemens, Anacletus. Again the transposition which places Anicetus before Pius is adopted in the earlier recension (FK) from the Liberian list, but in this instance the correct order is restored in the later (P). Again the transposition lower down in the list, by which Anteros is made to precede Pontianus, was adopted by the editor of the earlier recension, who not improbably originated it. It still stands in the abridgment F, but the true order has been substituted not only in the later recension P, but also in the other abridgment K of the earlier. This transposition has been already discussed, pp. 287, 320. Marcellinus and Marcellus are properly distinguished in both recensions. The antipope Felix II, who contested the see with Liberius, has also a place after Liberius in both recensions. It is no part of my plan to pursue the list lower down.

(2) The figures for the terms of office—the years, months, and days—in both recensions of the *LP* are taken directly from the Leonine Catalogue, as a glance at the tables (pp. 285, 316) will show. But as Anacletus was wanting in the Leonine list, his term-number could not be supplied thence. For this reason he seems to have remained for a time without any term-number. Afterwards it was supplied in two different ways. In MSS of the earlier edition, as represented by F, the numbers for Anacletus in the Liberian Catalogue were borrowed; but in the later edition (P) the numbers for Clemens, the pope next above him, were adopted, so that they occur twice. The relations of the figures assigned in these lists to Marcellinus and Marcellus have been already discussed (p. 291 sq).

It will be remembered that the Leonine figures are not a mere copy of the Liberian. They are combined with the Hieronymian, and they have been seriously displaced (see above, p. 267). Thus the result is something very different from the Liberian original, especially in the earlier part where the displacement is chiefly active. Hence the wide divergence from the Liberian Catalogue in the *LP*, which copies the Leonine numbers.

But certain MSS of the *LP* (*Guelpherbytan. Lat.* 10, 11, *Bernens. Lat.* 408, and others[1]) betray the hand of a reviser who has somewhat

[1] See especially Duchesne *Lib. Pont.* I. p. lxxxviii sq; comp. Lipsius *Chronologie* p. 63, *Jahrb. f. Prot. Theol.* V. p. 451, VI. p. 89, and see above, p. 254, note 5.

capriciously substituted the figures of the Liberian list here and there, but not throughout, for the original figures of the *LP.* This revised series of figures corresponds with that of the frescoes in S. Paul's, which must have been taken from it, unless indeed the revision had its origin in the frescoes, and the figures in these MSS of the *LP* were copied thence. In the table (p. 316) I have taken this revised list from the frescoes rather than from any MS. The differences are unimportant.

But besides these MSS of the later recension of the *LP*, the second abridgment, the Cononian, of the earlier edition, has likewise been revised as regards the figures and from the same source, the Liberian Catalogue. This revision however is less complete even than the last. As nothing depends on the figures of this Cononian abridgment, I have not thought it necessary to record them in the table. Those who are curious will find them in Duchesne (*Lib. Pont.* I. p. lxxxi sq).

At an earlier point (p. 220) I mentioned a papal list contained in a Syriac MS, but deferred the consideration of it. This MS, *Brit. Mus. Add.* 14642, is described in Wright's *Catalogue* p. 1041, where it is numbered DCCCCXVI[1]. It is a palimpsest, the vellum being made up of portions of several Greek MSS. The upper writing is Syriac, in a hand or hands of the 10th century, containing 'part of a chronicle, chiefly ecclesiastical, compiled from the similar works of Eusebius, fol. 1 b, Andronicus, foll. 1 b, 15 a, and others, and continued to A. Gr. 1108, A.D. 797, fol. 36 a. The later additions, foll. 36 b—39 a, bring the history down to A. Gr. 1122, A.D. 811 (*Catalogue* l. c.).'

Of Andronicus I know nothing, except that he is one of the authors quoted by Gregory Barhebræus[2]; that Elias of Nisibis in an unpublished work speaks of him as the author of a *Canones Annorum*, i.e. a Chronography, which is cited as the authority for events at least as late as A.D. 335, and states that he lived in the age of Justinian (A.D. 527—565)[3]; and that he is quoted by Jacob of Edessa and by Jacob's contemporary and correspondent John the Stylite[4] about A.D. 715, so that he

[1] I owe the particulars which are not found in Wright's *Catalogue*—more especially the account of the papal list—to the kindness of Dr Wright and Dr Bezold, who examined the MS and extracted the matter which was of importance for my immediate purpose.

[2] See Greg. Barhebr. *Chron. Eccles.* I. p. 5, ed. Abbeloos and Lamy; comp. Assem. *Bibl. Orient.* III. pp. 310, 313.

[3] Forshall *Catal. Cod. Orient. qui in Musæo Britannico asservantur* I. p. 86, a reference which I owe to Abbeloos and Lamy (l. c.).

[4] Wright's *Catalogue* pp. 598, 988. A tract on the 'Names of the Nations which arose after the Confusion of Tongues' is ascribed to Andronicus, *ib.* p. 1066. It was not improbably connected with his Chronography.

SYRIAC CATALOGUE. Brit. Mus. Add. 14642									
Order	NAMES	DURATION			Order	NAMES	DURATION	
1	Petrus	xx.	ii.	iii	31	Miltiades	iiii	
2	Linus	xi.	?		32	Silvester	xxiiii.	x
3	Anacletus	xii.	i		33	Marcus	ii	
4	Clemens	viiii			34	Julius	[x]v.	ii
5	Euarestus	viii.	x		34	Liberius	vi.	iii
6	Alexander	x.	vii		35	Felix	no figures	
7	Xystus	x.	ii		36	Damasus	xv.	?
8	Telesphorus	xi			37	Siricius	xv	
9	Hyginus	?	iii		38	Innocentius	[	]
10	Pius	xviiii.	iiii			*A lacuna in the MS*		
11	Anicetus	xi.	iiii					
12	Soter	viiii.	?		[ ]	Leo	xxii.	i
13	Eleutherus	xiii			44	Hilarius	vi.	iii
14	Victor	x.	vi		45	Simplicius	xvi	
15	Zephyrinus	xviii.	vii		46	Felix	viii.	xi
16	Callistus	v.	ii		47	Gelasius	iiii.	viii
17	Urbanus	[	]		48	Anastasius	viiii.	xi
	A lacuna in the MS				49	Symmachus	viii	
					50	Hormisdas	no figures	
[ ]	Dionysius	ix.	ii			Johannes	,,	
26	Felix	v.	iii			Bonifatius	,,	
27	Eutychianus	i				Johannes	,,	
28	Gaius	xv.	vii			Agapetus	,,	
29	Marcellinus	xvii(?).	iiii			Silverius	,,	
30	Eusebius	vi.	i(?)			Vigilius	,,	

must have flourished before the last date at all events. These facts point to the familiar use of his work among the Syrian Christians.

No authority is given for the papal list. This was drawn up in part, either mediately or immediately, from the *History* of Eusebius. So much is evident from the fact that our chronicler dates the accessions of the several popes by the regnal years of the emperors, as far as Eusebius dates them, and no farther; that in these notices he most frequently adopts the very language of Eusebius; and that the numbers of the years are in some cases characteristic of the *History*, e.g. xiii for Eleutherus and xv for Gaius. But he must have used some other authority also, since he gives not only the years but the months for most of the popes, and in the case of S. Peter the days likewise. Moreover he carries the catalogue much lower down. The last pope whose term of office he gives is Symmachus († A.D. 514), and the last pope whom he numbers is his successor Hormisdas (†A.D. 523); but the names of the six succeeding popes are added, ending with Vigilius (A.D. 537—555). These are introduced with the words, 'But the high-priests that were in the days of Justinian in Rome (were) John, and after him Bonifatius,' etc. These facts would seem to show that the papal list, which was used by our chronicler, had been drawn up in the time of Hormisdas and that the author in whom he found it had supplemented it with the names (and nothing more) of the subsequent popes whose accessions fell in the reign of Justinian and who were his own contemporaries. This author therefore may well have been Andronicus. It will be remembered that the age of Hormisdas is (roughly speaking) the date of the oldest extant papal lists which represent the Leonine Catalogue (see above, p. 311). It was also an age in which the Eastern Christians would be especially interested in the Roman succession, inasmuch as at this time the popes were interfering actively in the affairs of the East, and the feud between the rival popes Symmachus and Laurentius (see above, pp. 262 sq, 306 sq) had brought the matter prominently before them.

To a catalogue of this family the author seems to be indebted for the months during the period comprised in the *History* of Eusebius, and for both the years and months afterwards. Where the MSS of the Leonine Catalogue vary, his figures agree generally with the readings of Class B (see above, p. 318). Like the Leonine lists he includes Felix the antipope in the time of Liberius (without however giving his term of office); but as he repeats the number 34 twice (for Julius and Liberius), Damasus becomes the 36th in order, just as he would have been, if Felix had not been inserted. Both the numbers giving the order of the popes and the numbers giving the terms of office are in red ink—the former above the names, the latter in the line with the rest of the text. During the Eusebian period he has added the months which he found in the Leonine Catalogue to the years which he found in Eusebius; but he has not done his work completely, and in some cases the months are omitted, e.g. Clement and Eleutherus. The Leonine list which he used (directly or indirectly) was in Latin. The form 'Anacletus' points to a Latin source, and the corruptions in the numbers tell the same tale. Thus he gives vi for iii to Victor, and vii for iiii to Gaius, and in other cases a unit has been dropped or added.

As this is the only Eastern catalogue, so far as I am aware, which has the months as well as the years, I have given a fuller account of it than its intrinsic value deserves. Indications indeed have been found (see above, p. 313 sq) that lists with the months were not unknown in the East, though the months themselves are not recorded. For convenience I have arranged it in a tabular form (see p. 323), and I have omitted the regnal years, where given, as these coincide exactly with the *History* of Eusebius. All irrelevant matter which intervenes between the notices of the several popes is necessarily excluded.

5.

THE HISTORICAL RESULTS.

In the previous investigations the genealogy of the different papal lists has been traced, so far as it was necessary for my purpose. Incidentally also something has been said about the bearing of these documents on history; and more especially for the period from Pontianus to Liberius the historical gains have been gathered together and appraised (p. 284 sq). It remains for us now to concentrate our attention on the earlier period, and to gauge the value of the chronological data furnished by these lists.

It has been seen that the earliest Eastern and Western lists, though at first sight diverging in many respects, may yet be traced back to one and the same original—the same not only in the order of the names, but likewise in the terms of years assigned to the several episcopates.

Omitting the xxv years assigned to S. Peter, which I purpose considering at a later point, the list (as far as Eleutherus) runs as follows;

1.	Linus	xii	7.	Telesphorus	xi [xii]
2.	Anencletus	xii	8.	Hyginus	iiii
3.	Clemens	ix	9.	Pius	xv [xvi]
4.	Euarestus	viii	10.	Anicetus	xi [ ]
5.	Alexander	x	11.	Soter	viii
6.	Xystus	x [xi]	12.	Eleutherus	xv,

where the main figures represent the Eastern list, and the secondary figures in brackets the possible variations in the Western. The empty bracket attached to Anicetus denotes that his number in the Western list has been lost beyond recovery. In the three other cases—Xystus, Telesphorus, and Pius—the Western list, at the earliest point to which we can trace it back, differs by a unit from the Eastern. It is a probable supposition however that the units in these cases were either errors introduced in the course of transcription, or manipulations in order to fill up the historical space, as explained above (pp. 273, 278).

The only other point, which may raise a question, is the xv years assigned to Eleutherus in the Eastern list. Though the Armenian, Hieronymian, and Syriac versions of the *Chronicle* all agree in xv, and though this is the number likewise in the early Western list incorporated in the Liberian Catalogue, yet in the *History*, as read in the existing text, Eusebius distinctly assigns to him xiii years. With this weight of evidence for xv, we can only conclude that the xiii is either a slip of Eusebius himself or an error of some early transcriber. The present text of Eusebius (*H. E.* v. 22) runs, 'Now in the tenth year of the reign of Commodus, after administering the office of the episcopate thirteen years, Eleutherus is succeeded by Victor (Δεκάτῳ γε μὴν τῆς Κομόδου βασιλείας ἔτει δέκα πρὸς τρισὶν ἔτεσι τὴν ἐπισκοπὴν λελειτουργηκότα Ἐλεύθερον διαδέχεται Βίκτωρ); in which year (*or* at which time) also (ἐν ᾧ καὶ), Julianus having completed his tenth year, Demetrius takes in hand the administration of the dioceses of Alexandria (τῶν κατ' Ἀλεξάνδρειαν παροικιῶν).' The form of the sentence, combined with other facts, suggests that through the carelessness of Eusebius or of some later scribe the γ of the ιγ' (or ι πρὸς γ) may have been transferred to the wrong place. Not only is Victor the 13th bishop according to Eusebius' own reckoning in the *Chronicle*[1], but the death of Eleutherus

[1] The number xiii is distinctly given to Victor in the Hieronymian version. In the Armenian there is some confusion at this point. Soter is numbered as the xith and Zephyrinus as the xivth, so that Eleutherus should be the xiith and Victor the xiiith. But by an error the Alexandrian bishop Agrippinus is designated 'Romanorum ecclesiae episcopus xii,' and consequently Eleutherus is counted the xiiith. When the transcriber arrived at Victor, he found that he had no num-

and accession of Victor according to that same reckoning falls in A.D. 192, which was the 13th year of Commodus (who died on the last day of the year), though Eusebius himself there reckons it the first of his successor Pertinax[1]. There were thus many possibilities of confusion[2]. The versions confirm the existing text in the main and thus seem to show that Eusebius himself was the offender, rather than a later transcriber[3].

But what is the historical value of this list of names with the term-numbers annexed? Can we ascertain the authority on which it rests, or at all events the date at which it was compiled?

We have seen (p. 203) that the list of names is found in a work of Irenæus, written during the episcopate of Eleutherus, whose date may be placed provisionally about A.D. 175—190. A few years earlier however, under Anicetus (about A.D. 155—165), a catalogue was drawn up by Hegesippus then sojourning in Rome, though not published till the time of Eleutherus. Is this catalogue irretrievably lost, or can we recover it in any later writer[4]?

Attention has been called already (p. 202 sq) to the motives which

ber left for him, and consequently he is unnumbered. The enumeration in the Armenian chronicler Samuel is correct, thus showing that the errors in the existing Armenian text of Eusebius are later than his date (see above, p. 214). In the Syriac, Soter is xith and Zephyrinus is xivth, but the numbers of Eleutherus and Victor are not preserved in either epitome of this version (see p. 221).

[1] Strangely enough in the account of Eleutherus in Syncellus (p. 667) the number 13 appears in the context twice over, but in different connexions from these: 'Ρωμαίων ιγ' ἐπίσκοπος 'Ελευθέριος ἔτη ε' 'Αντιοχείας ἕβδομος ἐπίσκοπος Μάξιμος ἔτη ιγ', where the enumeration of Eleutherus as the 13th includes S. Peter, and where ε' is an error for ιε'.

[2] See also above, p. 243. The fact there stated that, though the number for Eleutherus in the *Chronicle* is xv, the interval is only xiii, may suggest another explanation of Eusebius' statement in the *History*; viz. that in this instance he deserted the document which contained the term-numbers and followed the document which gave the intervals: see below, p. 334 sq.

[3] Rufinus renders the passage; 'Igitur sub ejusdem Commodi principatu Eleuthero in urbe Roma tredecim annos sacerdotio functo Victor succedit; sed et Juliano apud Alexandriam post decem annos defuncto Demetrius substituitur', where the xiii is retained, though the rendering possibly betrays a consciousness that there was something wrong, and that the accessions of Eleutherus of Rome and Demetrius of Alexandria did not both fall in the same year, the tenth of Commodus. In the Syriac translation of the *History* (yet unpublished) the reading accords exactly with the existing Greek text, as I have ascertained.

[4] The opinion here maintained that the catalogue of Hegesippus is preserved in Epiphanius, was first put forward by me in the *Academy*, May 21, 1887, p. 362 sq. It is accepted by Salmon *Infallibility of the Church* p. 353 sq.

prompted Hegesippus to undertake this task and to the language in which he describes it; but my present purpose requires me to dwell at greater length on his statement.

Eusebius (*H. E.* iv. 22) records that Hegesippus 'after certain statements respecting the Epistle of Clement to the Corinthians, proceeded as follows (ἐπιλέγοντος ταῦτα)';

> 'And the Church of the Corinthians continued in the orthodox doctrine till the episcopate of Primus. Their acquaintance I made (οἷς συνέμιξα) on my journey to Rome, when I stayed with the Corinthians a considerable time (ἡμέρας ἱκανάς), during which we refreshed one another (συνανεπάημεν) with the orthodox doctrine. And after I went to Rome, I drew up a list of succession[1] as far as Anicetus, whose deacon Eleutherus (then) was. After Anicetus Soter succeeded, and after Soter Eleutherus. But in every succession and in every city they adhered to the teaching of the Law and the Prophets and the Lord.'

It will be observed that Hegesippus is here dealing with heresies and that the catalogue of the Roman bishops, as I have already explained (p. 203), was drawn up as a practical refutation of these. It should be noted likewise that this catalogue is mentioned in immediate connexion with Clement's Epistle and with the dissensions in the Corinthian Church which called it forth. We may infer then that the catalogue was included somewhere in these *Memoirs*, and not improbably in the context of the passage which Eusebius quotes.

Now Epiphanius (*Haer.* xxvii. 6) devotes a long paragraph to the early history of the Roman bishops, in which he introduces a list of succession. It has been strangely neglected by writers on the subject. Even Lipsius barely mentions it once or twice casually, and (so far as I remember) never discusses it. Yet a catalogue of this early date (c. A.D. 375), which is plainly independent of the Eusebian lists, deserves more than a mere passing mention.

Epiphanius has been speaking of Carpocrates and his school, and as connected therewith he mentions one Marcellina, a lady heretic, who taught in Rome in the time of Anicetus[2]. His opening words are sufficiently curious to deserve quoting;

[1] It has been contended that the words διαδοχὴν ἐποιησάμην cannot have this meaning, and that we should read διατριβὴν for διαδοχήν. I have already disposed of this alternative reading, which is purely conjectural; see above, p. 154. As regards the interpretation given to διαδοχὴν ποιεῖσθαι, it is sufficient to quote *H. E.* v. 5 οὗτος [Εἰρηναῖος] τῶν ἐπὶ Ῥώμης τὴν διαδοχὴν ἐπισκόπων ἐν τρίτῃ συντάξει τῶν πρὸς τὰς αἱρέσεις παραθέμενος κ.τ.λ.

[2] See *Ignat. and Polyc.* I. p. 436.

'A certain Marcellina who had been led into error by them [the disciples of Carpocrates] paid us a visit some time ago (ἦλθεν δὲ εἰς ἡμᾶς ἤδη πως Μαρκελλίνα τις)[1]. She was the ruin of a great number of persons in the time of Anicetus bishop of Rome who succeeded Pius and his predecessors[2].

He then commences a list of the Roman episcopate, in which he places 'first Peter and Paul, apostles and bishops, then Linus, then Cletus, then Clemens, who was a contemporary of Peter and Paul.' This leads him to explain how Clement, though a contemporary, was not next in succession after the apostles. He suggests that, though consecrated to the episcopate by the apostles who still survived, Clement may have waived his claims in favour of others for the sake of peace, as 'he himself says in one of his letters, *I withdraw, I will depart, let the people of God remain at peace* (εὐσταθείτω)[3]; for I have found this,' adds Epiphanius, 'in certain Memoirs (ἔν τισιν ὑπομνηματισμοῖς).' Then, after other alternative solutions of the difficulty, Epiphanius continues;

'But possibly after Clement was appointed and had waived his claims (if indeed it did so happen, for I only surmise it, I do not affirm it), subsequently after the death of Linus and Cletus, when they had held the bishopric twelve years each after the death of saint Peter and Paul, which happened in the twelfth year of Nero, he [Clement] was again obliged to take the bishopric. Howbeit the succession of the bishops in Rome is as follows; Peter and Paul, Linus and Cletus, Clement, Euarestus, Alexander, Xystus, Telesphorus, Pius, Anicetus, who has been mentioned above in the catalogue (ὁ ἄνω ἐν τῷ καταλόγῳ προδεδηλωμένος)',

after which he resumes his account of Marcellina. Have we not here the lost list of Hegesippus? My reasons for thinking so are as follows;

(i) It is evident that Epiphanius does not quote the passage of Clement's Epistle from the Epistle itself. His own language shows this. Nor does he elsewhere betray any direct knowledge of it[4].

[1] In *Haer.* xxviii. 6 we have the expressions τι παραδόσεως πρᾶγμα ἦλθεν εἰς ἡμᾶς and ἡ παράδοσις ἡ ἐλθοῦσα εἰς ἡμᾶς, 'reached our times, reached our ears,' and in the passage before us it might occur to some one to read πῶς and translate 'The tradition has reached our times how one Marcellina etc.' The harshness of this rendering however is a sufficient condemnation. The expression in the text might possibly indeed mean 'survived to our own times' (see Euseb. *H. E.* iv. 22 quoted below, p. 330, note 1); but nothing would be gained by this.

[2] The passage which follows will be found quoted at length above, p. 169 sq.

[3] The passage is in Clem. Rom. 54, but it is very loosely quoted.

[4] See the next chapter.

Whence then did he obtain it? He himself answers this question. He found it 'in certain Memoirs (ἔν τισιν ὑπομνηματισμοῖς).' I had thought at one time that by this expression he meant some collection of excerpts, but I now see a more probable explanation. Eusebius not only designates the work of Hegesippus ὑπομνήματα in two other passages[1], but he uses the corresponding verb ὑπομνηματίζεσθαι of the writer[2], perhaps quoting his own expression. Were not these then the very ὑπομνηματισμοί in which Epiphanius read the words of Clement?

(ii) Another passage of Epiphanius, a few pages lower down (*Haer.* xxix. 4, p. 119), where the same word is used, affords a strong confirmation of this view. He is there discussing the Nazoræans, and refuting their views respecting the parentage of Jesus. This leads him to speak of James the Lord's brother and to explain that he was a son of Joseph by another wife, not by Mary; and he proceeds,

> 'For he was Joseph's eldest born (πρωτότοκος τῷ Ἰωσήφ) and consecrated [as such]. Moreover we have found that he exercised a priestly office (ἱερατεύσαντα) according to the old priesthood. Wherefore it was permitted to him to enter once a year into the holy of holies, as the law enjoined the high-priests in accordance with the Scriptures. For so it is recorded concerning him by many before us, Eusebius and Clement *and others*. Nay he was allowed to wear the (high-priest's) mitre (τὸ πέταλον) on his head, as the afore-mentioned trustworthy persons have testified, *in the Memoirs written by them* (ἐν τοῖς ὑπ' αὐτῶν ὑπομνηματισμοῖς)',

where I have underlined the words to which I desire to direct attention.

Whom else can Epiphanius have had mainly in view in these 'others' who wrote 'Memoirs,' but Hegesippus? Hegesippus is quoted by Eusebius for several of the facts here mentioned respecting James the Lord's brother. He is quoted likewise by him for information respecting the kindred of Joseph (*H. E.* iii. 11, iv. 22)[3]. Moreover it

[1] *H. E.* ii. 23 ἐν τῷ πέμπτῳ αὐτοῦ ὑπομνήματι, iv. 22 ἐν πέντε τοῖς εἰς ἡμᾶς ἐλθοῦσιν ὑπομνήμασι. The word ὑπομνήματα however is used very comprehensively.

[2] *H. E.* iv. 8 τὴν ἀπλανῆ παράδοσιν τοῦ ἀποστολικοῦ κηρύγματος ἁπλουστάτῃ συντάξει γραφῆς ὑπομνηματισάμενος.

[3] It may be suspected likewise that in another passage also, *Haer.* lxxviii. 7 sq, where Epiphanius is discussing the relationship of the Lord's brethren, he is indebted to Hegesippus for some of his statements. On some points indeed, though the ultimate source of the information was Hegesippus, he might have derived it through the medium of Eusebius, e.g. when he mentions that Clopas was the brother of Joseph (p. 1039; comp. Eus. *H. E.* iii. 11, 32, iv. 22), but in the same context he gives many particulars besides—whether true or false—which are not found in Eusebius.

should be noted that the fragmentary remains of Hegesippus show a strong affinity to Epiphanius in his account of the heretical sects among the Jews and Judaic Christians (Euseb. *H. E.* iii. 20, 32, iv. 22). I may add also that in an extant fragment of Hegesippus the Carpocratians are mentioned together with other Gnostic sects (Euseb. *H. E.* iv. 22). Nor is it perhaps altogether beside the question to call attention to the fact that Hegesippus made use of 'the Gospel according to the Hebrews' (Euseb. *H. E.* iv. 22), while Epiphanius in this immediate neighbourhood several times mentions this Gospel (xxix. 9, xxx. 3, 6, 13, 14).

(iii) Hegesippus certainly dwelt at some length on Clement's letter and on the feuds at Corinth which called it forth. Eusebius refers to his testimony respecting the Epistle of Clement, not only in the passage quoted, but in another place also (*H. E.* iii. 16). Moreover the mention of Clement's letter occurred in the same context with the mention of the Roman succession, just as it occurs in Epiphanius. It should be added that the discussion of Clement's position is quite out of place in Epiphanius[1], where its introduction can best be explained on the supposition that Clement occupied a large space in the authority which lay before him. Nothing in his own context suggests this long digression.

(iv) Hegesippus tells us that his catalogue was in the first instance brought down to Anicetus, and the list in Epiphanius stops at this same episcopate. On the other hand the catalogue of Irenæus reaches as far as Eleutherus. The value of this coincidence might indeed be thought to be diminished by the fact that Epiphanius has been speaking just before of Marcellina, who taught in Rome in the time of Anicetus. But this fact only strengthens the coincidence. For

(v) We may reasonably surmise that this very notice of Marcellina was taken from Hegesippus, and that in its original context in the elder writer it elicited the reference to the Roman succession, just as it does in Epiphanius. It is difficult to assign any probable sense to the opening sentence of the whole paragraph Ἦλθεν δὲ εἰς ἡμᾶς κ.τ.λ., 'A certain Marcellina paid us a visit etc.', so long as Epiphanius is supposed to be speaking in his own person. The expression gives some trouble to Lipsius, who contemplates the possibility of its being taken verbatim from the *Syntagma* of Hippolytus[2]. What if it were taken verbatim

[1] Lipsius *Quellenkritik des Epiphanios* p. 114 'Die lange Exposition über die Reihenfolge der römischen Bischöfe und über Clemens und Cletus insbesondere ist natürlich *ein hier ziemlich unpassendes Einschiebsel* des Epiphanios selbst.'

[2] Lipsius l. c. p. 114, note 3.

from the *Memoirs* of Hegesippus? This would explain everything. A portion of the context indeed, relating to the Carpocratians and Marcellina, so closely resembles the language of Irenæus, that it cannot be independent of this father's account. If therefore my hypothesis be true, either Irenæus must have borrowed from Hegesippus, or Epiphanius must have been indebted partly to Hegesippus and partly to Irenæus, besides using the *Syntagma* of Hippolytus. But I see no difficulty in either supposition.

(vi) At another point at all events Epiphanius is detected transferring the language of a previous authority verbatim into his account, without modifying it so as to adapt it to his own context. He refers back to 'the catalogue' in which the name of Anicetus had been mentioned already (ὁ ἄνω ἐν τῷ καταλόγῳ δεδηλωμένος). But no catalogue has been given previously. Is not this then a careless insertion of the very words of Hegesippus, in forgetfulness that his own manipulation and transposition of the matter borrowed from Hegesippus had made them no longer appropriate?

This result throws light upon another point. The name of Linus' successor in Irenæus and Eusebius is Anencletus, but Epiphanius calls him Cletus. This alone shows that Epiphanius cannot have borrowed his list from either of these authors. Yet the form Cletus must have appeared in some early list, inasmuch as it is found in several catalogues of the fourth and fifth centuries. In the West it is the most frequent form. It appears in the Latin Canon of the Mass; it has a place side by side with Anacletus in the Liberian document and in lists derived therefrom, as well as in the anonymous poem 'Against Marcion'; it is the form commonly found in the Leonine catalogues; and it occurs in Rufinus. From a survey of the existing MSS we might be led to suppose that Jerome had substituted it for Anencletus in the *Chronicle* of Eusebius[1], but this would probably be a wrong inference; for in the *Catalogus* (c. 15) he apparently writes Anencletus, though here again there is a various reading. Even Optatus and Augustine have Anencletus (Anacletus). In the East the form Cletus is less frequent; but it

[1] See above p. 216. Duchesne (*Lib. Pont.* I. p. lxx) writes, 'Il faut remarquer que saint Jérôme emploie tantôt l'un des deux noms, tantôt l'autre.' This is true of Jerome's transcribers, but there is (so far as I know) no evidence that Jerome himself used the two names indifferently. In the only two passages where he has occasion to mention this person, he is copying Eusebius, and where the evidence of the MSS is conflicting, we may suppose that he followed his authority and wrote 'Anencletus'; especially as 'Cletus' was the more familiar form with Latin scribes and therefore likely to be substituted by them.

appears, as we have seen, in Epiphanius and is found likewise in *Ancient Syriac Documents* p. 71. In the list of Hegesippus, who had relations with both East and West, we seem to have found the root, from which this form was propagated.

Moreover, if Epiphanius did thus derive his list from Hegesippus, one highly important result follows. Epiphanius gives the durations of office of Linus and Cletus respectively as twelve years each. The catalogue therefore which he used had not only the names of the bishops but the term-numbers also. He might indeed have gathered the numbers from different parts of the *History* (iii. 13, 15) or of the *Chronicle* of Eusebius. This however is improbable in itself, and the fact that Eusebius gives the name Anencletus, not Cletus, makes it doubly so. But, if Hegesippus was the authority for these term-numbers, the tradition is carried back at least to Eleutherus, under whom he published his 'Memoirs,' if not to Anicetus, under whom he first drew up the list.

We are now in a position to consider the theory of Lipsius, which has been mentioned already (p. 237); and we shall find reason for agreeing with him in the broad results, though unable to follow him always in the reasons which he alleges or in the inferences which he draws. The two documents which he supposes Eusebius to have employed in matters relating to the Roman episcopate were as follows:

(1) The one was a simple list of the Roman bishops, giving the lengths of their several episcopates in years. This list he supposes to have been drawn up under Victor, the immediate successor of Eleutherus, and therefore in the last decade of the second century. Though I am unable to adopt his arguments for this particular date, I have no fault to find with his conclusion, having myself in the previous investigation arrived at substantially the same result, though by a wholly different path. Speaking generally, we may say that a catalogue which was the progenitor alike of the Eusebian and the Liberian lists cannot well be dated later than the close of the second century. If indeed it were possible to accept his position that Hippolytus writing about A.D. 235 or, if not Hippolytus himself, a subsequent redactor editing the Hippolytean work some twenty years later, had already in his hands a grossly corrupt copy of this original list—the order of the names being in some cases transposed, and the term-numbers not only corrupted in themselves but shifted through a considerable part of the list—this fact alone would be powerful evidence of

its early date. But for reasons which have been explained above (p. 270 sq) I cannot claim the support of this argument.

(2) The other document, which Lipsius in common with other recent writers has postulated as necessary to explain the phenomena of the Eusebian lists, is of a different kind. Like the former, with which it was nearly contemporaneous, it emanated from Antioch; but it was a Chronicle, not a Catalogue. The main reasons for postulating such a second document are twofold.

(i) It is plain that Eusebius had before him some work in which the early Antiochene episcopates were co-ordinated with those of Rome and Alexandria with which they were, or were supposed to be, synchronous (see above, p. 223 sq). While he had in his hands a list of the Roman bishops with term-numbers—which we have just been considering—and another list of the Alexandrian bishops likewise with term-numbers—with which we are not directly concerned here—he had no such list of the early Antiochene bishops giving the corresponding information. In the *Chronicle* and in the *History* alike he is silent about the duration of office in the case of the Antiochene bishops. Yet in the *History* he mentions their several episcopates in connexion with the contemporary Roman (and Alexandrian) bishops; and in the *Chronicle* he sets them down under the same or the neighbouring year. In this latter work he was constrained by the exigencies of the case to give definiteness to information which, as he found it, was indefinite[1].

(ii) The imperial synchronisms likewise seem to require such a document. The beginnings of the Roman episcopates, as defined by the regnal years of the emperors, are given in the *History* by direct statement and in the *Chronicle* by tabulation. Thus we get the intervals between any two successive accessions, and these ought to correspond exactly to the numbers which give the durations of the several episcopates. This however is not the case; and the conclusion seems to be that the two were drawn from different documents. Moreover these intervals as recorded in the *Chronicle*, where they differ from the term-numbers in that same work, agree so closely with the intervals in the *History* (reasonable allowance being made for errors of transcription) as to suggest that in both works the imperial synchronisms which give these intervals were derived from the same authority. The following table exhibits for comparison the numbers in the two works from the accession of Linus to the accession of Eleutherus. This is a convenient

[1] In the *History* we have such language as 'Then also flourished' (iv. 20 τηνικαῦτα καὶ...ἐγνωρίζετο), or 'in whose time flourished' (v. 22 καθ' οὓς...ἐγνωρίζετο), or other equally vague expressions.

period for our purpose, because it ends with the same year (A. D. 177) in both works. Beyond this point comparison becomes difficult owing to the confusion introduced by the twofold error of Eusebius, the one relating to the imperial chronology at the death of Commodus (see above, p. 216) and the other affecting the length of office of the bishop Eleutherus (see above, p. 326). For the *Chronicle* I have taken the Hieronymian version and rejected the Armenian for reasons which have been already given. The numbers in brackets are the corrections which it seems necessary to make of errors due either to Jerome himself or to some early transcriber. The fuller facts will be found in the tables given above, pp. 208, 209.

BISHOPS	*CHRONICLE*		*HISTORY*	
	Duration	*Interval*	*Duration*	*Interval*
Linus	xi [xii]	12	xii	
Anencletus	xii	12	xii	12
Clemens	viiii	7 [8]	viiii	8
Euarestus	viiii [viii]	10 [9]	viii	9
Alexander	x	10	x	10
Xystus	x	9	x	9
Telesphorus	xi	10	xi	10
Hyginus	iiii	4	iiii	—
Pius	xv	15	xv	—
Anicetus	xi	12 [11]	xi	—
Soter	viii	8 [9]	viii	9

In the column containing the term-numbers or durations of office in the *Chronicle*, as represented by Jerome's text, two corrections should be made. To Linus should be assigned xii instead of xi years, since xii appears in the Syriac version (see above, p. 221) and is the traditional number for this bishop; and for Euarestus we must substitute viii for viiii, this correction again being supported by the Syriac version. So corrected, the term-numbers in the *Chronicle* agree exactly with the term-numbers in the *History*. In the intervals of the *Chronicle* again two corrections must be made. The accession of Euarestus must be brought one year lower down, and the accession of Soter pushed one year higher up. Thus the intervals for Clemens and Euarestus become 8 and 9 instead of 7 and 10; and the intervals for Anicetus and Soter become 11 and 9 instead of 12 and 8. For the former correction there is no authority (the intervals in the Syriac Version not being preserved), but it has this recommendation at least, that the discrepancy between the term-numbers and the intervals is lessened; the latter correction is supported by the Syriac version, which in this case preserves the intervals, giving 11 to Anicetus and 9 to Soter. Thus after making these corrections there are 5 names (Clemens, Euarestus, Xystus, Telesphorus, Soter), for which the intervals differ from the term-numbers (though only by a unit); and in all these cases the *Chronicle* and the *History* are in exact accordance with one another. The value of this fact indeed is not great, where the induction is so slender; but it serves to confirm the inference already drawn from other considerations, that, besides the episcopal list with term-numbers, Eusebius made use of a second document, and that this document gave the imperial years of the episcopal accessions, as well as the synchronisms of the Antiochene see.

What then was the date and country of this second document? Erbes (*Jahrb. f. Protest. Theol.* v. p. 474 sq, 1879) assigns it to Antioch and to the year A.D. 192 (or 193). Lipsius likewise assigns it to this same place and date (*ib.* VI. pp. 241 sq, 245 sq, 254 sq, 260, 266 sq, 274, 277, 1880). At the same time he believes that Eusebius did not use the original document directly, but only through the medium of a later chronicler of the year 218 or thereabouts (*ib.* pp. 254, 274), and that this later chronicler was probably Africanus. It may be a question however whether there is sufficient ground for postulating any document of the year 192, as the facts seem to be fully satisfied by supposing that the Chronicle of Africanus himself was the original of the imperial dates and of the episcopal synchronisms.

The document seems to have been Antiochene, or at least Syrian, if the calculations of Gutschmid be accepted as correct. He has pointed out (*De temporum notis* etc. p. 8 sq) that the regnal years of the earlier emperors in Eusebius' *Chronicle* are Antiochene years, which began on the first of October, and that each Antiochene year is coordinated with the year of Abraham which began on the preceding Jan. 1, the years of Abraham being in fact Julian years. Thus for instance the date of Trajan's accession was Jan. 25, A.D. 98, but it is set down to A.D. 97 (=Ann. Abr. 2114) because the corresponding Antiochene year was Oct. 1, A.D. 97—Oct 1, A.D. 98.

This holds good of all the emperors up to a certain point, with the exception of Nerva, whose accession (xiv Kal. Oct. = Sept. 18), falling at the close of one Antiochene year has been transferred by a very natural error (xiv Oct. for xiv Kal. Oct.) to the next[1].

To this argument Lipsius (*ib.* VI. p. 241) adds another indication of Antiochene origin. The Antiochene episcopates, as far as Zebennus (6th or 7th year of Alexander) inclusive, are attached not to the years of Abraham (the left-hand margin) but to the imperial years (the right-hand margin). This is perhaps significant; but it might be largely due to the fact that, as the Antiochene episcopates were for the earlier period treated as synchronistic with the Roman, the right-hand margin was already in most cases preoccupied by the Roman episcopates.

A glance at the tables on p. 208 sq will show that the imperial synchronisms, as given in the *History*, are fairly continuous till the accession of Alexander (A.D. 222), and that after this point they cease. It would seem therefore that his document failed him here. This however was just the point down to which Africanus brought his Chronicle (A.D. 221, the last year of Elagabalus).

In the absence of any direct evidence therefore, everything points to the Chronicle of Africanus as the document containing the imperial years, which was used by Eusebius for these papal lists. Gutschmid however (l.c. p. 10 sq) considers that Eusebius' earliest authority ended at A.D. 192, and in this he is followed by Erbes and Lipsius, as we have seen. The grounds are threefold, (1) That the Antiochene years cease at this point, and Alexandrian years take their place; (2) That there is a break in the imperial chronology at this same point, as explained above, Eusebius being led astray by the confusion which followed on the death of Commodus (see above, pp. 216, 217); (3) That at this same point also the historical notices suddenly diminish in frequency, 'argumentorum ubertas subito exarescit.' To these three indications which he draws from Gutschmid, Erbes adds another, (4) That the synchronisms between the Antiochene and Roman bishops likewise cease here.

(1) As regards the first point, I cannot see that Gutschmid has brought any evidence of a change of reckoning from Antiochene to Alexandrian years, though he himself assumes this change in his treat-

[1] Gutschmid's calculations are here accepted, though not without misgiving; but I had no right to challenge the work of a chronological expert without devoting more time to these investigations than I have been able to give. As regards the result, I see no reason to doubt the Antiochene origin of the document.

ment. There is not a single accession of a Roman emperor from A.D. 192 to A.D. 221, or till some time later, which can serve as a test[1]. The Antiochene year began on the 1st of October; the Alexandrian year on the 29th of August. To test such a change therefore we require an accession which took place between the end of August and the end of September. But none such is forthcoming.

(2) The error in the imperial chronology does not in any way suggest a transition from one authority to another at this point. It is only one of three places within a little more than half a century (A.D. 192—243), where Eusebius reckons a year too much, as Gutschmid's table (p. 12) shows. In this particular instance Africanus had been guilty of the same error, if Gelzer (*Sext. Julius Africanus* I. p. 279) is right; and he may have led Eusebius astray.

(3) Nor again does it seem to me that much weight can be attached to the sudden paucity of the historical notices. Fluctuations are very common in other parts of this Chronicle, both before and after this point. There are indeed periods of four or five years immediately after which are bare of incidents; but these are equalled and even exceeded elsewhere during the imperial age (e.g. Ann. Abr. 1975—1982). On the whole the disparity is not so great, as to justify the postulate of different documents.

(4) The synchronisms of the Antiochene bishops with the Roman, both in the *History* and in the *Chronicle*, end with Eleutherus and Maximinus[2] (A.D. 177), or at all events with their successors Serapion and Victor. After this point the accessions to the two sees are independent of each other. This however is what we should expect in an author of the age of Julius Africanus. For the earlier bishops of Antioch, having no definite information, he could only give rough approximations; but when he arrived at those who were his own contemporaries he was able to assign them to definite years.

It seems therefore that the arguments adduced in support of an earlier chronicle (A.D. 192), which was afterwards incorporated and carried down to A.D. 221, all break down. Still, though severally weak and inadequate, they may be thought to have a cumulative force and so to justify the conclusion. But if Africanus really had such a document in his hands, may it not have been the work of Bruttius, whom

[1] The dates of the emperors' deaths are as follows: Commodus, Dec. 31, 192; Pertinax, March 28, 193; Julianus, June 1, 193; Severus, Feb. 4, 211; Caracalla, April 8, 217; Macrinus, June 11, 218; Elagabalus, March 11, 222; Alexander, Feb. 10, 235.

[2] See the table in *Ignat. and Polyc.* II. p. 464.

we have already seen good reason to regard as a Christian chronographer (p. 48), and whose chronicle we have on independent grounds supposed to have been known to Africanus?

We have thus arrived at the same result with Harnack, viz. that the symmetrical relations of the early bishops of Rome and Antioch, which appear in the *Chronicle* of Eusebius, were probably derived from Julius Africanus. But the way by which we have reached it has been quite different. Supposing that the Armenian version represented the original papal chronology of the Eusebian *Chronicle*, Harnack found that the early Antiochene bishops were placed about 4 years after the corresponding Roman bishops severally, and he explained this by the fact that Africanus arranged his Chronicle by Olympiads. Rejecting the papal chronology of the Armenian version, as a later revision, we ourselves have rejected the Olympiad-theory with it. The regularity of the intervals (not always 4 years however, but sometimes 3, sometimes 5) is due to the fact that the reviser of the Armenian recension (for reasons of his own) pushed back the earlier papal chronology a few years, and thus from actual synchronisms produced equal intervals. On the other hand we have found that the phenomena of the episcopal synchronisms and of the regnal years in the *History* and the *Chronicle* of Eusebius suggest a chronological document of the age and country of Africanus, and therefore presumably the work of Africanus itself, as their source. Of the manner in which Africanus may have recorded the episcopal synchronisms we can form some idea from the practice of Syncellus.

But, if this papal chronology, as determined by the regnal years of the several accessions, proceeded from Africanus or a contemporary, what weight shall we attribute to it? Has it an independent value? or was it calculated from a list containing the term-numbers, such as we have seen existing before the close of the second century, and such as I have attributed to Hegesippus? The latter seems to me the probable alternative. The discrepancies between term-numbers and the intervals are comparatively slight, never varying by more than a unit, so that the latter may easily have been derived from the former by a backward reckoning, with possibly here and there some fixed date as a guide. As Hegesippus was a Palestinian Christian, his work would probably be in the hands of Africanus, who was himself a native of Emmaus.

If so, we must fall back upon the simple catalogue of names with the accompanying term-numbers, as our sole authority for the chronology of the early bishops. But, if this catalogue dates from the pontificate of Eleutherus or at the latest of Victor for its publication, and probably from that of Anicetus for its compilation, it will have the highest value. By its aid therefore we may restore the chronology of the Roman episcopate by working backward from some fixed date, with results which will be approximately true. But in using the list for this purpose the following considerations must be borne in mind.

(1) As we have no ground for assuming that, when first drawn up, it was founded on any contemporary written documents, we can only treat it as giving the best tradition which was accessible to its author, though perhaps in some cases he may have been guided by contemporary records. Its value therefore will increase, as we approach his own time. As regards the first century this will not be great; but from the beginning of the second century onward it will claim the highest deference. Of the xxv years of Peter I need say nothing here, except that there is no ground for supposing that it formed any part of the original list. Whether it was first introduced by Hippolytus, or by Eusebius, or by some third person, and on what grounds (whether of tradition or of criticism) it was so introduced, I will leave for discussion at a later point. Adequate reasons will then be produced to show that it is wholly unhistorical. To the two next in succession, Linus and Cletus (or Anencletus), twelve years each are assigned. The symmetry of the numbers suggests that, where no direct information was attainable, the author of the list divided the vacant space—a rough quarter of a century—between them. As regards the names, I see no reason to question that they not only represent historical persons, but that they were bishops in the sense of monarchical rulers of the Roman Church, though their monarchy may have been much less autocratic than the episcopate even of the succeeding century. With Clement we seem to emerge into the dawn of history. He at all events has a historical record independently of the catalogue. Let me add also that I see no sufficient ground for placing the daybreak of the papal chronology at the epoch of Xystus, whose episcopate may be dated roughly at A.D. 115—125. Those who take up this position[1] have no other reason for their opinion than that Irenæus, writing to Victor in the last decade of the century and speaking of the Roman usage as regards Easter, appeals to the practice of 'the elders who before Soter presided over the Church' of Rome, 'Anicetus and Pius, Hyginus and Telesphorus and Xystus[2]'; but this has reference solely to the Paschal

[1] So Lipsius *Chronol.* 169, 263, *Jahrb. f. Prot. Theol.* VI. p. 119.

[2] Euseb. *H. E.* v. 24.

question, in which case he does not go beyond living memory in support of his contention. It does not in any sense mark a period.

(2) The original list gives whole years only; for the months and days are a much later addition and were unknown to Eusebius. How then were these whole years calculated? Was the whole number next below the actual term of office taken, so that the fractions of years however great were entirely neglected? If so, we might on a rough average estimate add 6 months for every episcopate, so that the period from Linus to Eleutherus inclusive, comprising twelve episcopates, might be reckoned as six years longer than the addition of the term-numbers makes it. Or was the whole number nearest to the actual term of office, whether greater or less, taken? Or was sometimes one course and sometimes another adopted? As these questions cannot be answered, a large margin of uncertainty must remain.

(3) But we must reckon likewise with another element of uncertainty. In times of persecution more especially there was frequently an interregnum between the end of one episcopate and the beginning of another. Thus there was an interval of a year after the martyrdom of Xystus I, and apparently one of several years after the death of Marcellinus. The same probably occurred more than once during the earlier period, with which we are concerned. It is not probable, for example, that when Telesphorus was martyred, his successor would be installed in office immediately.

(4) Since for all these reasons the chronological results derived from the list can only be regarded as approximately true for the second century, it follows that, if we are able to ascertain any dates in the history of the papacy independently on highly probable grounds, and if the dates so ascertained are at variance with the results derived from the papal lists, the latter must yield to the former. On the other hand, if these independent dates agree with the chronology as derived from the episcopal catalogue, this agreement is an important verification of its trustworthiness. In other words the independent dates must be used to test the accuracy of the chronology of the papal list, and *not conversely*[1].

i. One such independent date (within narrow limits) is furnished by the account of the earlier life of Callistus, as related in Hippolytus (*Haer.* ix. 11 sq)[2]. Callistus was condemned by Fuscianus the City Prefect[3], and transported to Sardinia to work there in the mines. After

[1] This caution applies especially to the treatment of the date of Polycarp's death by Lipsius.

[2] See Lipsius *Chronol.* p. 172 sq.

[3] Capitolin. *Pertinax* 4, Dion Cass. lxxiv. 4.

a time (μετὰ χρόνον) he was released through the influence of Marcia with the emperor Commodus, much to the displeasure of bishop Victor. Now Fuscianus held the consulship for the second time in A.D. 188, and would not be appointed to the City prefecture till after the expiration of his tenure of office or, in other words, not till A.D. 189[1]. On the other hand Commodus was assassinated on the last day of A.D. 192. Between these limits therefore (A.D. 189—192) the condemnation, exile, and pardon of Callistus must have taken place, and Victor must have been in office before the termination of the period, probably some time before.

ii. Again; we are informed on the best authority that Polycarp visited Rome to confer with Anicetus, who was then bishop[2], and that the visit was paid at Eastertide. But recent criticism has shown, on evidence which must be regarded as almost, if not quite decisive, that Polycarp was martyred A.D. 155, in February[3]. Therefore the latest possible date for the accession of Anicetus is the beginning of A.D. 154.

iii. Again; the date of Clement's Epistle is fixed with a fair degree of certainty at A.D. 95 or 96, as it was written during, or immediately after the persecution under Domitian. This year therefore must fall within the episcopate of Clement.

To ascertain how far the chronology of the papal list satisfies these three tests, we will take as the earliest fixed date the resignation or deprivation of Pontianus, assuming that the consulships 'Severo et Quintiano' [A.D. 235] in the Liberian list (see above, p. 255) formed part of the original document, and are therefore historical. But, if exception be taken to this assumption, we have only to advance to the martyrdom of Fabianus, who certainly suffered under Decius [A.D. 250]; and, as the notices of time between Pontianus and Fabianus are very definite even to the days of the month, we reckon back from this and arrive independently at the same date, A.D. 235, for the close of Pontianus' episcopate. Taking this then as our fixed date, we have the following figures:

From accession of Linus to accession of Clement

12 + 12 = 24 years

[1] See Borghesi *Œuvres* VIII. p. 535, IX. p. 322 sq, De Rossi *Bull. di Archeol. Crist.* IV. p. 4 sq. He was succeeded in the prefecture by Pertinax during the life-time of Commodus. The changes in the prefectures were very rapid at this time; Lamprid. *Commod.* 14.

[2] Irenæus in Euseb. *H. E.* V. 24.

[3] See the chapter on the 'Date of the Martyrdom' in *Ignat. and Polyc.* vol. I.

From accession of Clement to accession of Anicetus

9 + 8 + 10 + 10 + 11 + 4 + 15 = 67 years

From accession of Anicetus to accession of Victor

11 + 8 + 15 = 34 „

From accession of Victor to resignation of Pontianus

10(9) + 18(19) + 5 + 9(8) + 5(6) = 46—48 „

so that the accession of Victor would be placed A.D. 187—189, the accession of Anicetus A.D. 153—155, and the accession of Clement A.D. 86—88, without making allowance for the treatment of months and days or for possible interregna[1].

Having thus tested the list at three different points, from external chronology, we have in all cases obtained confirmation of its trustworthiness as affording a rough approximation; but at the same time these tests strengthen the suspicion which the probabilities of the case suggest, that the numbers in the earlier part of the list are less true to fact than the later.

The term of office assigned to Clement with exceptional unanimity in the lists earlier and late is nine years. His death is assigned by Eusebius to the third year of Trajan[2]. This result may have been attained by Eusebius himself or by some previous writer by calculation from the term-numbers, thus following the same process which I have followed. If so, it has no independent value. But it may possibly represent a separate tradition. If we accept it, the episcopate of Clement will extend over the last nine years of the century (A.D. 92—100). This reckoning is some four years at least later than the approximation at which we have arrived from our backward reckoning of the episcopal catalogue as a whole; but, as we have seen, the character of this catalogue does not justify us in expecting that by this path we should arrive any nearer to the correct date.

Before leaving the subject of Clement's episcopate, a few words more will be necessary as to the different places which he occupies in the various lists. The only position which has any historical value, as resting on a definite tradition, is, as we have seen, that which places

[1] It will be seen that by this reckoning the whole period from the accession of Linus to the deprivation or resignation of Pontianus [A.D. 235] is 161—163 years. The accession of Linus would thus be placed A.D. 62—64. This is probably a few years too early, but this point will be discussed when I speak of S. Peter in Rome.

[2] Euseb. *H. E.* iii. 34, Hieron. *Vir. Ill.* 15; see above, pp. 166, 173.

him after Linus and Anencletus, and thus reckons him *third* after the Apostles. The Eastern romance of the Clementines however made him the immediate successor of S. Peter and so *first* on the list (see above, p. 158). This story was so flattering to the corporate pride of the Roman Christians in the unique position which it assigned to Clement, that it rapidly spread and largely influenced popular opinion in Rome. Whether Tertullian when he states (see above, p. 160) that the Roman Church recorded Clement to have been ordained by S. Peter, and himself therefore presumably regards Clement as the Apostle's next successor in the episcopate, was influenced directly or indirectly by the Clementine fiction, or whether it was his own independent inference drawn from the fact that Clement had been a hearer of S. Peter, we have no means of determining. The *second* position, which Clement occupies in many Western lists, where he is the immediate successor of Linus, apparently originated in a blunder (see p. 272 sq). It does not satisfy the Clementine story and seems to have been quite independent of its influence. Though this same position is likewise given to him by the writer of the *Apostolic Constitutions* (vii. 46), it is not probable (considering the date and country of this writer) that he derives it from these Western lists. He states that 'Linus was appointed first by Paul, and then Clemens the second, after Linus' death, by Peter.' This seems to be an independent attempt to combine the story of the Clementines, which was obviously familiar to him, with the established tradition that Linus was the earliest bishop of Rome after the Apostles, which he may have learnt from Irenæus or Hegesippus or from common report.

The whole episcopal list from the age of the Apostles to the age of Constantine falls into three parts: (1) From Linus to Eleutherus; (2) From Victor to Pontianus; (3) From Anteros onwards. For the *first* of these periods it has been shown that the catalogues of Eusebius and the Easterns were founded on one and the same traditional list (committed to writing) with the Western catalogues (see p. 275 sq). For the *third* period it has appeared that Eusebius used a written document which contained substantially the same record of numbers with the Western lists, though it was mutilated and misread by him (see p. 233 sq). But, inasmuch as this record of numbers was, so far as we can discern, strictly historical, and inasmuch as the Roman Church at this age would probably preserve archives in some form or another, this coincidence is no ground for supposing that he had before him the same literary document. Indeed, considering the phenomena of the different lists and the circumstances of the case, this is hardly probable.

The Western document which is incorporated in the Liberian Catalogue would not probably be accessible to Eusebius, and indeed it contains facts of which he betrays no knowledge. For the *second* and intermediate period—from Victor to Pontianus inclusive—it is difficult to form any definite conclusion as to the relations between the Eastern and Western lists (see above, p. 275 sq). On the whole they would seem to be independent. The Eastern lists so far agree with the Western, that they may be regarded as substantially historical, while they exhibit differences which point to a distinct source of information.

6.

THE LETTER OF THE ROMANS

TO

THE CORINTHIANS.

THE following eight points relating to the Epistle to the Corinthians, which bears the name of Clement, will be considered in this chapter: (1) The date; (2) The authorship; (3) The genuineness and integrity; (4) The ecclesiastical authority; (5) The purport and contents; (6) The liturgical ending; (7) The doctrine; (8) The printed text and editions.

1. *The date.*

Common opinion places the date of this document about the close of the reign of Domitian or immediately after (A.D. 95, 96). This view, which was put forward by Patrick Young the first editor (A.D. 1633), has commended itself to critics of divers schools, and has now become so general that it may be regarded as the received opinion. On the other hand some writers of consideration, such as Grotius (Cotel. *Patr. Apost.* I. p. 133 sq, ed. Cleric. 1724), Grabe (*Spicil. SS. Patr.* I. p. 254 sq, ed. 2), and Wotton (S. Clem. Rom. *Epist.* p. cciii sq, 1718) with others, and in more recent times Uhlhorn (*Zeitsch. f. Hist. Theol.* 1851, p. 322; but retracted, *ib.* 1866, p. 33), Hefele (*Patr. Apost.* p. xxxiv sq, ed. 3), and Wieseler (*Untersuch. über die Hebr.* p. 339, 1861; *Jahrb. f. Deutsche Theol.* 1877, p. 383 sq; *Zur Gesch. d. Neutest. Schrift etc* p. 48 sq, 1880), with one or two besides, assign it to the close of Nero's reign (A.D. 64—68); while a few extreme critics of our own age such as Schwegler (*Nachapost. Zeitalter* II. p. 125 sq, 1846), Volkmar (*Theol. Jahrb.* 1856, p. 362 sq; 1857, p. 441 sq; *Einl. in die Apokr.* I. I. p. 28 sq, and elsewhere; see my note on § 55), and after Volkmar, Baur (*Dogmengesch.* p. 82, 1858; *Vorles. über Neutest. Theol.* p. 41 sq, 1864), Keim (*Gesch. Jesu von Nazara* I. p. 147 sq, 1867), and one or two others, have placed it as late as the reign of Trajan or of Hadrian or even later. But the two minorities, even when added together, are not comparable, either in weight or in numbers, to the vast majority in favour of the intermediate date.

The *external* testimony is altogether favourable to the received view, as against the earlier and later dates. The notices of HEGESIPPUS and IRENÆUS alike point to this intermediate epoch. They had both visited Rome, where apparently they had resided a considerable time, when the memory of Clement was still fresh. The former tells us explicitly that he arrived in the metropolis during the episcopate of Anicetus (c. A.D. 154—167) and did not leave till Eleutherus the next but one in succession occupied the episcopal throne (c. A.D. 175), so that he must have been there eight or ten years. We must confess indeed that the account which Eusebius[1] gives of the language of Hegesippus, referring to Clement, is not altogether free from ambiguity. If the words 'in his time' (κατὰ τοῦτον) refer to Domitian, as I have contended above (p. 165), then we have the direct statement of this writer in support of the received date; but, even if they do not, Hegesippus at all events expressed himself in such a way as to lead Eusebius to this conclusion, and indeed the fragments preserved by this historian make the same impression on ourselves. Moreover, Hegesippus drew up a list of the bishops of Rome in order of succession; and there is every reason to believe that he placed Clemens where Irenæus placed him, in the last decade of the first century. The testimony of Irenæus himself[2] is quite explicit on this point. He too gives a succession of the Roman bishops—perhaps not independent of Hegesippus—in which he places Clement third in order. The founders of the Roman Church are 'the glorious Apostles Peter and Paul.' They committed it to the charge of Linus, who is mentioned in the Epistles to Timothy (2 Tim. iv. 21). The next in succession to Linus was Anencletus. After Anencletus followed Clemens, 'who also had seen the blessed Apostles and conversed with them and had the preaching of the Apostles still ringing in his ears and their tradition before his eyes.' 'Nor was he alone in this,' continues Irenæus, 'for many still remained at that time who had been taught by the Apostles.' 'In the time (i.e. during the episcopate) of this Clement a feud of no small magnitude arose among the brethren in Corinth, and the Church in Rome sent a very sufficient (ἱκανωτάτην) letter to the Corinthians, striving to bring

[1] *H. E.* iii. 16, quoted above p. 153 sq. On the chronology of Hegesippus see esp. pp. 154, 203, 328.

[2] *Haer.* iii. 3. 3, given at length above, p. 156 sq; see also p. 203 sq.

them to peace and quickening their faith and declaring the tradition which they had so lately (νεωστὶ) received from the Apostles'; after which follows a brief summary of the contents of our epistle, concluding 'This Clement was succeeded by Euarestus.' It is evident that the position of Clement in the succession, and the relations of Clement himself and his contemporaries to the Apostles, as here described, are equally inconsistent with a date so early as Nero, or so late as Hadrian.

Besides this more direct external testimony, which consists in historical statement, we have the evidence drawn from the influence of this epistle, as shown in subsequent writers. It is undeniable that the Epistle of POLYCARP is pervaded through and through with indications of a knowledge of Clement's letter (see above, p. 149 sq). But, if the Epistle of Polycarp was written about A.D. 110, or soon after, the inference in favour of an earlier date than Hadrian is irresistible. If the genuineness and integrity of Polycarp's Epistle be accepted (and I have shown, if I mistake not, elsewhere[1], that doubts respecting these points are unreasonably sceptical) Polycarp wrote while the martyrdom of Ignatius was recent, and before the news of his death had reached Smyrna, though the martyrdom itself was foreseen. Some passages in IGNATIUS himself also seem to reflect Clement's language (see p. 149); and more especially his references to the past history of the Romans (*Rom.* 3, 4) seem to me to be best explained by the fact of Clement's letter[2]. But not much stress can be laid on these. Nor can I see any force in the parallels adduced by Hilgenfeld to show that the author of the Epistle of BARNABAS was acquainted with Clement's language (see above, p. 148 sq). On the other hand, the allusion in HERMAS (*Vis.* ii. 4. 3) seems to be an obvious recognition of the existence of this letter; 'Thou shalt write two copies (βιβλιδάρια) and shalt send one to Clement...and Clement shall send it to the foreign cities...for this duty is committed to him (ἐκείνῳ γὰρ ἐπιτέτραπται),' where Clement is represented as the writer's contemporary who held a high office which constituted him, as we might say, foreign secretary of the Roman Church. If our Clement be meant, this notice is at all events inconsistent with the early date assigned to the epistle, the close of Nero's reign; but the passage is not without its difficulties and will be considered presently (p. 359 sq).

The *internal* evidence in favour of the intermediate date—the reign

[1] See *Ign. and Polyc.* I. p. 562 sq, ed. 1 (p. 579 sq, ed. 2).

[2] *Ign. and Polyc.* I. p. 357 sq, ed. 1 (p. 371 sq, ed. 2); II. pp. 203, 209; see also above, p. 71.

of Domitian, or immediately after his death—is still stronger than the external.

(i) The *personal notices* more especially point this way. Of the delegates who are sent by the Roman Church, as the bearers of the letter, the writer or writers say, 'we send you faithful and prudent men, who have conducted themselves blamelessly among us *from youth to old age*, and they shall be witnesses between you and us' (c. 63). Here the words which I have italicized are unintelligible on the supposition of the early date. If the epistle was written about A.D. 68 or earlier, how could it be said of any Roman Christian that he had lived from youth to old age in the Church of Christ, seeing that the first Apostle visited Rome about A.D. 60, and that two years earlier when writing to the Roman Church, while recognizing the existence of a Christian congregation, he speaks throughout as though this were practically a virgin soil in which he was called to sow the seed of the Gospel? The chronology of these delegates' lives as suggested by their names, Claudius and Valerius, I have pointed out already (see above, p. 27 sq). Again, when we turn to the notice of the feuds at Corinth, we have still more decisive evidence in favour of the intermediate date as against the earlier and later alike. The Apostles, we are there told (c. 44), having complete foreknowledge of the strife that would arise concerning the office of bishop (or presbyter), appointed the persons aforesaid (their contemporaries) and made provision that 'if they should die, other approved persons should succeed to their ministration.' 'Those therefore,' the letter continues, 'who were appointed by them (the Apostles) or afterward by other men of repute with the consent of the whole Church and have ministered unblameably...and for long years (πολλοῖς χρόνοις) have borne a good report with all men—these persons we consider to be unjustly deposed from their ministration.' If we remember that the first point of time, when the narrative in the Acts will permit us to place the appointment of a regular ministry at Corinth, is about A.D. 52, and that the language here points to a long succession and not a few changes in the presbyterate, we feel instinctively that the sixteen years which elapsed to A.D. 68 are not enough to satisfy the requirements of the passage. On the other hand we cannot suppose that not a few of those who had been ordained by the Apostles S. Paul or S. Peter, being then no longer young men, as their appointment to the presbyterate suggests, should have survived to A.D. 120 or later, in other words, 50 or 60 years after the death of these Apostles. At the same time I cannot lay stress, as some have done, on the fact that the Church of Corinth (§ 47) is called 'ancient' or 'primitive' (ἀρχαία), though I can scarcely believe that a community not yet twenty years old would be so designated, and the analogies brought to support this view seem to me to be fallacious[1].

(ii) The notices of the *persecutions* point the same way. All the early Church writers speak of the first persecution under Nero and the second under Domitian. This is the case not only with Eusebius, who had the great mass of the earliest Christian literature before him, but with Melito, Tertullian, and Lactantius (see above p. 104 sq). The only exception to this universal belief is Hilary, who mentions Vespasian as a persecutor of the Church. If his language be not founded altogether on a misapprehension, it must refer to some local troubles in Gaul. But on this subject I have already spoken[2]. We may safely assume then from the universal silence, that during the intermediate reigns between Nero and Domitian no assault was made on the Christians of the metropolis which deserved to be dignified by the name of a persecution. Nor indeed did the third persecution, under Trajan, so far as we know, touch the Roman Church. It was fierce enough in some parts of Asia Minor and the East, but the evidence of any martyrdoms in Rome is confined to spurious Acts and other equally untrustworthy documents[3].

Now the letter to the Corinthians speaks of two persecutions. In the fifth and following chapters we have an unmistakeable reference to the troubles of Nero's reign. The sufferers are there described as 'the athletes who lived very near to the present day' (τοὺς ἔγγιστα γενο-

[1] Grabe (*Spicil. Patr.* I p. 256), followed by Hefele (*Patr. Apost.* p. xxxvi, ed. 3), argues that because S. Paul (*Phil.* iv. 15) uses ἐν ἀρχῇ τοῦ εὐαγγελίου of the Philippian Church which was some nine years old [say rather 'eleven' or 'twelve'], Clement could *a fortiori* use the same expression of the Corinthian Church which at the supposed date (the close of Nero's reign) was from fifteen to eighteen years old. This is true, but not to the point. Grabe himself explains the words to mean '*prima Evangelii*, vel simpliciter in orbe vel in specie apud ipsos praedicati, *tempora*'; and plainly both S. Paul and Clement use them in the latter sense 'when the Gospel was *first preached to you*'. Strangely enough he goes on to argue after Dodwell, that those churches could be called ἀρχαῖαι which were converted ἐν ἀρχῇ τοῦ εὐαγγελίου, thus assuming the former sense to be Clement's. It stands to reason that, a person writing A.D. 64 (or at the outside A.D. 68) could hardly call a community 'ancient' or 'primitive' which came into existence after considerably more than half of the whole period of the Church's history had passed. Nor again is Wieseler justified (*Jahrb. f. Deutsch. Theol.* XXII. p. 387) in citing Acts xv. 7 as a parallel, for S. Peter, speaking of the conversion of Cornelius or possibly some earlier event, could well describe the epoch as ἀφ' ἡμερῶν ἀρχαίων even in A.D. 51; since on any showing it belonged to the beginnings of the spread of the Gospel. In Acts xxi. 16 ἀρχαῖος μαθητής is 'a primitive disciple', i.e. an early convert to the Gospel.

[2] See above, p. 81, and comp. *Ign. and Polyc.* I. p. 15.

[3] See *Ign. and Polyc.* I. p. 52 sq.

μένους ἀθλητάς), and again as 'the noble examples belonging to our own generation' (τῆς γενεᾶς ἡμῶν τὰ γενναῖα ὑποδείγματα). This is the sort of language which we Englishmen to-day (1889) might use of the heroes of the Crimea (1854) or of the Indian Mutiny (1857). It implies a certain lapse of time, and yet the persons so designated could well be called contemporaries of the writer. The letter then describes the principal figures among the martyrs: 'Let us set before our eyes the good Apostles,' where the epithet (as I have elsewhere stated, p. 73) seems to imply personal acquaintance. These are the Apostles S. Peter and S. Paul, whose martyrdom is distinctly mentioned. Gathered round these, as the central figures, was 'a great multitude of the elect' who after suffering cruel tortures were put to death, and thus 'set a glorious example among ourselves (ὑπόδειγμα κάλλιστον ἐγένοντο ἐν ἡμῖν).' The paragraph ends with the warning, 'Jealousy and strife overthrew great cities and rooted out great nations.' In this last sentence some have seen a special reference to the Jewish war and the destruction of Jerusalem (A. D. 79). Bearing in mind the language in which Josephus on the one hand, and Hegesippus[1] on the other, describe the causes of the Jewish war, we cannot consider this allusion altogether fanciful.

Universal tradition speaks of S. Peter and S. Paul as suffering under Nero in consequence of the general assault on the Christians. Whether they were martyred at the same time with the great bulk of the sufferers in the year of the fire (A. D. 64), or whether they were isolated victims of the spent wave of the persecution (A. D. 67 or 68), we need not stop to enquire. The allusion in the letter would be satisfied by either.

On the other hand the letter speaks of a persecution, which was now raging or had been raging very recently, when it was written. This is separated chronologically from the persecution under Nero by the significant language (c. 7) which follows immediately after the account of these earlier troubles; 'These things, beloved, we write, not only to warn you but *to remind ourselves, for we are in the same lists and the same contest awaits us*,' which awaited these earlier sufferers. In the commencement of the letter (c. 1) an apology is offered by the Romans for the long delay in writing to the Corinthians on the ground that they had been prevented from attending to the matter by the 'sudden and successive troubles' which had befallen them.

It should be remembered also, that the language used in each case is, as I have already observed (p. 81), especially appropriate to the particular persecution. Nero's attack was a savage onslaught, regardless

[1] For Josephus, see *Bell. Jud.* v. 1 sq, vi. 1 and *passim*: for Hegesippus, see Eus. *H. E.* ii. 23 καὶ εὐθὺς Οὐεσπασιανὸς πολιορκεῖ αὐτούς, with the context.

alike of sex and age, a war of extermination: Domitian's consisted of short, sharp, intermittent assaults, striking down now one and now another, not perhaps deserving the name of a general persecution, but only the more harassing from its very caprice.

Here then we have the two persecutions; and the letter was written either during the continuance of the second or immediately after its cessation—in the last year of Domitian or the first of Nerva (A.D. 95 or A.D. 96). The alternative depends largely on the reading, γενομένας or γινομένας. On the whole γενομένας should probably be retained, as the better supported, and this points to the time when by the accession of Nerva the Christians breathed more freely again[1].

(iii) Of the notices of *Church government* we may say generally, that they savour of the first rather than the second century. We find ἐπίσκοπος still used as a synonyme for πρεσβύτερος, as it is in the New Testament[2]; though in the first or second decade of the succeeding century in the Epistles of Ignatius the two words are employed to designate two distinct offices of the ministry, so that in Asia Minor, and apparently in wide regions besides, the office of the episcopate proper was definitely established and recognized. Moreover in the account of the feuds at Corinth no mention is made of any single presiding ruler of the Church, and we must suppose either that there was a vacancy in the bishopric at this time, or that the bishop's office had not yet assumed at Corinth the prominence which we find a few years later in Asia Minor. It should be remembered that when the letter was written the last of the twelve Apostles, if the best ancient tradition may be credited, was still living, the centre of a body of Christian disciples, at Ephesus.

Of the Christian ministry at Rome I have already spoken (p. 68 sq). Not only have we no traces of a bishop of bishops, but even the very existence of a bishop of Rome itself could nowhere be gathered from this letter. Authority indeed is claimed for the utterances of the letter in no faltering tone, but it is the authority of the brotherhood declaring the mind of Christ by the Spirit, not the authority of one man, whether bishop or pope. The individual is studiously suppressed. This however was apparently the practice of the Roman Church for some generations, the letter of bishop Soter to Corinth (c. A.D. 170) being apparently cast in the same mould. It seems to have been retained

[1] On the various readings see above, p. 58, and the note on the passage.

[2] See *Philippians* p. 95 sq; comp. *Ign. and Polyc.* I. p. 375 sq, ed. 1 (p. 389 sq, ed. 2).

still later, when Victor wrote at the close of the century[1]. This feature therefore does not assist us to decide between the rival dates, but is consistent with a later epoch than either.

(iv) One important test of date in early Christian writings lies in the *Biblical quotations*—both the form and the substance. Now the quotations from the Gospels in this letter exhibit a very early type. They are not verbal; they are fused; and they are not prefaced by 'It is written (γέγραπται)' or 'The Scripture saith' (ἡ γραφὴ λέγει) or the like, but a more archaic form of citation is used, 'The Lord spake' (ὁ Κύριος εἶπεν), or some similar expression. Of the Canonical writings of the New Testament, besides the definite reference to S. Paul's First Epistle to the Corinthians (A.D. 57), where not only the main purport of the epistle is described but the Apostle's name is directly mentioned, we seem to have sufficiently definite traces of the influence of several other Pauline Epistles, of the Epistle of S. James, and of the First Epistle of S. Peter, while the expressions taken from the Epistle to the Hebrews are numerous and undeniable (e.g. § 36). Now this last mentioned epistle seems to have been written, so far as we can discern from internal evidence, whether by Apollos or by Barnabas or by some other disciple or companion of the Apostle, soon after the Apostle's death and when Timothy, of whom we last read as about to join the Apostle in Rome (2 Tim. iv. 9) and who apparently had shared his master's captivity, had been again set free (Heb. xiii. 23). If the letter to the Corinthians were written in Nero's reign (A.D. 64–68), these quotations would be highly improbable, if not altogether impossible.

One argument however has been alleged in favour of the early date—the reign of Nero—which at first sight has some value. The present tense is used of the sacrifices and the temple-worship at Jerusalem, as if the catastrophe under Vespasian and Titus had not yet overtaken the holy city (§ 41). However specious, this argument is found to be altogether delusive. Parallel instances will be adduced in the notes on this passage, which show conclusively that this mode of speaking was common long after the destruction of the temple and the cessation of the sacrifices, so that no argument respecting date can be founded on it.

But Volkmar, who adopts the latest date—the reign of Hadrian—finds his chief argument in one of the references to a quasi-scriptural

[1] Victor did not indeed suppress his own name, but he wrote on behalf of the Church, for Polycrates in replying uses the plural (Eus. *H. E.* v. 24 ὑμεῖς ἠξιώσατε); see Salmon *Infallibility of the Church* p. 374.

book in the letter (see above, p. 346). In the 55th chapter there is a direct reference to the apocryphal book of Judith. This book he assigns to the reign of Hadrian; and in this he has been followed by Baur and a few others. It may however be said with confidence that the arguments which place the Epistle of Clement in the first century are a hundred-fold stronger than those which place the book of Judith in the second; so that any uncertainty in the date of the latter must be decided by the date of the former and not conversely.

The story which forms the plot of the Book of Judith runs as follows.

It is the twelfth year of the reign of Nebuchadnezzar the Assyrian king whose capital is the great city Nineveh. The king of the Medians at that time is Arphaxad, whose seat of government is Ecbatana. Nebuchadnezzar makes war against Arphaxad in the great plain of Rhagau, and the people of the East, dwelling in the mountain region and on the banks of the Euphrates, Tigris, and Hydaspes, are arrayed under him[1]. He likewise summons to his standard the Persians and the nations of the West, of Cilicia and Syria and Palestine, Galilee and Samaria and Judæa, and the Egyptians, as far as the Æthiopian frontier. They however refuse to obey the summons. Then in the fifteenth year he marches against Arphaxad and takes Ecbatana. The whole country is subjugated, and Arphaxad is slain.

Afterwards in the sixteenth year he determines to avenge himself on the rebel nations of the West. For this purpose he sends an army under Olophernes his chief captain, which carries everything before it. Of the offending nations some are subdued by force; others surrender voluntarily. Having thus made a clean sweep of everything which stood in his way, he meets the Israelites at Bethulia and calls on them to surrender. While he is encamped there, an Israelite widow, Judith by name, gains access to his tent, ingratiates herself with him, and kills him in his sleep, cutting off his head and carrying it away as a trophy. The next day the Assyrians retire in dismay, and Israel is saved. The story ends with a psalm of thanksgiving, wherein Judith celebrates the deliverance which God has wrought by her hand.

This romance founded on the history of the past was evidently written to inspire the patriotism or stimulate the courage of the Israelite people, when they were passing through some great crisis. Critics have

[1] The reference of πρὸς αὐτόν (i. 6) is evidently to Nebuchadnezzar, not to Arphaxad, as Volkmar takes it; see Hilgenfeld *Zeitschr. f. Wiss. Theol.* 1858 p. 273, Lipsius *ib.* 1859, p. 49. Thus Volkmar transfers these nations to the side of the enemy.

generally supposed that it was suggested by the trouble which overwhelmed them under Antiochus Epiphanes. At all events it has usually been ascribed to some date long before the Christian era. Volkmar however, following in the footsteps of Hitzig[1], gives an entirely different account of its origin.

Nebuchadnezzar is Trajan the monarch of the world. His capital 'the great city Nineveh' is none other than the great city Rome, or (as on second thoughts he considers preferable) the great city Antioch, which the Roman emperor made his head-quarters during his expeditions in the East. Arphaxad is the Parthian king, who was defeated by Trajan. But who are the counterparts of the two principal figures in the story, Olophernes and Judith?

The history of Trajan's campaigns in the East I have had occasion to discuss, though not in full, when treating of the Acts of Martyrdom of Ignatius[2]. In his 17th year Trajan starts for the East, and winters at Antioch. This is the winter A.D. 113, 114. The campaigns in the East occupy the next three years A.D. 114, 115, 116, the 18th, 19th, and 20th of Trajan. He overruns Armenia and deposes the Armenian king; marches into Mesopotamia; receives the submission of Augarus (Abgar) of Edessa and other petty kings; takes Nisibis and Batnæ; crosses the Tigris; reduces the whole of Adiabene; advances to Babylon, where he stays awhile; enters Ctesiphon; and proceeds thence to the Persian Gulf. Meanwhile, during this journey to the Eastern Ocean, tidings reach him that the reduced provinces have revolted behind his back. Accordingly he sends his generals to quell the revolt. Among these the most famous name is Lusius Quietus, who recovers Nisibis and sets fire to Edessa. Trajan now gives a king to the Parthians, as the easiest solution of the difficulty. Not long after this his health begins to fail. Meanwhile there is an uprising of the Jews in Cyrene, Egypt, and Cyprus. Lusius is despatched to the scenes of the revolt, and puts down the insurrection. Owing to his increasing malady, Trajan now sets out on his return to Italy, leaving Hadrian in command of the army in Syria; but he dies on the way at Selinus in Cilicia. The date of his death is August 11, A.D. 117, in the 20th year of his reign. Hadrian is proclaimed emperor by the army and succeeds him. Soon after Hadrian's accession, Lusius Quietus is recalled from Mauretania, where he is residing at the time, as governor of the province, and is put to death on his way home by order of the Senate. Hadrian in his autobiography stated that Lusius, as well as other generals who were

[1] See *Ueber Johannes Marcus etc.* p. 165, 1843.

[2] *Ign. and Polyc.* II. p. 390 sq, ed. 1 (p. 391 sq, ed. 2).

put to death about the same time, was not executed with his consent. But the odium which his supposed participation in these murders brought upon him, obliged him to return to Rome to dispel the suspicions[1].

This then is Volkmar's solution. Olophernes, Nebuchadnezzar's chief-captain, is none other than Lusius Quietus, Trajan's general, who thus paid the penalty of death for his persecution of the Jews. Judith represents the Jewish people who are the instruments of his punishment. The war which is represented in the Book of Judith is none other than the *Polemos-shel-Quitos* (פולמים של קיטום) or 'War against Quietus,' of which we read in rabbinical writers. Volkmar goes beyond this; he can tell us the exact year and day of the publication of the book. It was written soon after Trajan's death, on the first celebration of the 'Day of Trajan' (יום טוריינוס), the 12th of Adar A.D. 118, which day the Jews kept annually in commemoration of their deliverance from Trajan[2].

I shall not attempt to dissect this theory in detail, for it would be mere waste of time to do so. Those who wish to see it torn into shreds have only to consult the criticisms of Hilgenfeld (*Zeitschr. f. Wiss. Theol.* 1858, p. 270 sq; comp. *ib.* 1861, p. 338 sq) and of Lipsius (*Zeitschr. f. Wiss. Theol.* 1859, p. 39 sq), who have shown that neither the dates nor the localities nor the incidents will admit it. I would only remark that no Jew could be expected to interpret an enigma so studiously veiled. On the main point it is sufficient to say that there is no evidence that the Jews in Palestine revolted against Trajan, or that Quietus conducted any operations against them. Indeed the silence of history is fatal to this supposition. We may allow that there is much probability in the conjecture, not unsupported[3], which substitutes 'Quietus' for 'Titus' (קיטום for טיטום) in the rabbinical notices; but this does not help the theory, for the scene of the war is not thereby brought into Palestine. On the other hand the 'Day of Trajan' is highly problematical. If the name be really Trajanus and not, as some suppose, Tyrannius[4], we are still as

[1] For the account of this incident see Spartian *Hadr.* 7; comp. Dion Cass. lxix. 2.

[2] See Volkmar *Einl. in die Apokr.* I. i. p. 83 sq.

[3] See Volkmar l. c. p. 85; Lipsius *Zeitschr. f. Wiss. Theol.* 1859, p. 97 sq.

[4] So Lipsius l. c. p. 105 sq. This is the proconsul Rufus under Hadrian, his nomen being variously written Tyrannius, etc. (see Buxtorf s. v. טורנוס). Volkmar's own view is developed, l. c. p. 90 sq. Derenbourg (*L'histoire et la géographie de la Palestine* p. 408, note 2) considers that all the different ways in which the name is spelt in Hebrew, point to *Trajanus* rather than to *Tyrannus* or *Turnus*; but he altogether repudiates the inferences of Volkmar as contradicted by the silence of history.

far as ever from finding any support for Volkmar's theory in Jewish legend[1]. There is nothing to show even then that it has any reference to the Jews in the mother country or to a war waged against them—of which authentic history is profoundly silent—but the allusions would be easily explained by the uprisings and conflicts either in the farther east or in Cyprus and Africa, whether under Trajan himself or (by a slight chronological confusion) under his successor[2].

And after all, what resemblance does the fate of Olophernes bear to the fate of Quietus, except that both die violent deaths? But the one dies by the dagger of an enemy, the other by the hand of his countrymen; the one is stealthily assassinated, the other judicially murdered; the one is killed while holding command under his sovereign, the other after deposition from his office; the one in the camp amidst the turmoil of war, the other in the progress of a homeward journey. Nor indeed does the analogy hold in the most vital points. If Nebuchadnezzar is Trajan, and Olophernes is Quietus, then Quietus ought to have perished under Trajan; but it is quite certain that he was put to death under Trajan's successor Hadrian. If our romancer's purpose had been to put his Israelite fellow-countrymen on the wrong scent, and thus defeat his own object, he could not have done this more effectively than by trailing this story of Olophernes across their path, when he wanted to remind them of Quietus. Who would be so insane?

Ingenuity often wears the mask of criticism, but it is not unfrequently the caricature of criticism. Ingenuity is not necessarily divination; it is not wholesome self-restraint, is not the sober weighing of probabilities, is not the careful consideration of evidence. Criticism is all these, which are wanting to its spurious counterfeit. Yet Volkmar has succeeded in carrying two or three notable writers with him. '[Volkmari] sententiam...Baurio placuisse semper admiratus sum,' says Hilgenfeld (*Clem. Rom. Ep.* p. xxxviii, ed. 2). But why should he have wondered? No man has shown himself more ready to adopt the wildest speculations, if they fell in with his own preconceived theories, than Baur, especially in his later days—speculations which in not a few cases have been falsified by direct evidence since discovered. Nothing has exercised a more baneful influence on criticism in the country of critics than the fascination of his name. While he has struck out some lines which have stimulated thought, and thus have not been unfruitful in valu-

[1] On the Judith-legend in Jewish sources see the researches of Jellinek in an article of Lipsius *Jüdische Quellen zur Judithsage*, *Zeitschr. f. Wiss. Theol.* x. p. 337 sq (1867).

[2] See especially Derenbourg l. c. p. 409 sq.

able results, the glamour of his genius has on the whole exercised a fatal effect on the progress of a sober and discriminating study of the early records of Christianity[1].

2. *The authorship.*

Closely connected with the question of the date of this epistle is the question of the authorship. Is it rightly ascribed to Clement, or is the common designation at fault? This is not a very momentous question. The historical value of the document will remain for the most part unaffected, now that we have ascertained that it was written during the last decade of the first century and with the authority of the Roman Church, whoever may have been the actual author.

Confessedly the letter nowhere claims to have been written by Clement. Confessedly also it is sent in the name of a community, not of an individual. It is the Epistle of the Romans, not of Clement. Moreover the language of the three earliest writers who mention it by name is not free from obscurity, when they describe the connexion of Clement with it. These are Hegesippus, Dionysius of Corinth, and Irenæus, whose language is given in full above (pp. 153 sq, 154 sq, 156) and whose testimony I have had occasion to discuss in the last section. Respecting HEGESIPPUS, who gathered his information at Rome in the time of Anicetus, we are not directly informed that he named Clement as the author. Eusebius indeed prefaces his quotations by stating that he 'makes some remarks relating to the Epistle of Clement to the Corinthians', but he does not give any words of Hegesippus himself, testifying to Clement's authorship. Again, DIONYSIUS OF CORINTH, the next in order, who wrote to the Romans in the time of Soter (c. A.D. 170) the successor of Anicetus, is stated by Eusebius to make mention of the letter of Clement to the Corinthians (τῆς Κλήμεντος πρὸς Κορινθίους ἐπιστολῆς); but he fortunately proceeds to quote the very words. From these it appears that Dionysius does not speak so definitely, but says, 'the letter which was written to us (the Corinthians) διὰ Κλήμεντος' (p. 155). This is a warning to us not to assign too much weight to the language of Eusebius in the former case. The assumption of Clement's authorship may have been a mere inference—albeit a probable inference—of Eusebius in the case of Hegesippus, as it certainly was in the case of Dionysius. The preposition here used, 'through' or

[1] As these sheets are being passed through the press, I hear of a recent book entitled *Les Emprunts d'Homère au Livre de Judith* by the Abbé Fourrière. This is out-heroding Herod. Volkmar is beaten on his own ground.

'by the hands of' (διὰ), may mean any one of three things—either the author or the amanuensis or the bearer of the letter[1]; and we can only judge in any individual instance from the context or the probabilities of the case, which of these three meanings it has. Again our third witness, IRENÆUS, who wrote under the episcopate of Eleutherus (c. A.D. 175—190) the successor of Soter, though his information was probably obtained much earlier, connects the epistle with Clement's name, but does not directly ascribe it to him; 'In the time of this Clement the Church in Rome wrote, etc' (p. 156).

Only a few years later (c. A.D. 200) we meet with the first distinct statement of its Clementine authorship. CLEMENT OF ALEXANDRIA four times at least ascribes it to his namesake, 'The Apostle Clement in the Epistle to the Corinthians' or some similar phrase; yet he also occasionally suppresses the name of the personal author and says, 'It is written in the Epistle of the Romans to the Corinthians', or words to this effect (see above p. 158 sq). And from this time this letter is persistently assigned to Clement as its author, as for instance by ORIGEN and EUSEBIUS and CYRIL OF JERUSALEM and BASIL OF CÆSAREA (pp. 161, 165, 167, 169)—not to mention later writers.

But many years before the earliest of the above-named writers flourished, Clement of Rome is regarded as an author; and the language used of him is only explained by the existence of such a letter commonly attributed to him. In the Shepherd of Hermas which, even if we adopt the latest possible date, must have been written before the middle of the second century, Hermas is reminded that the duty of communicating with foreign Churches appertains to Clement, and he is accordingly commanded to discharge this same function in the case of the divine message imparted to Hermas. But here we are met with a great difficulty. As Hermas is stated in an ancient tradition to have written this work during the episcopate of his brother Pius (c. A.D. 140—155), it is urged that the Clement here mentioned cannot have been the same with the illustrious bishop of Rome[2]. Thus the notice in the Shepherd gives us another Roman Clement, who flourished about half a century

[1] See *Ign. and Polyc.* II. p. 233, II. pp. 933, 982 ed. 1 (III. pp. 349, 398, ed. 2).

[2] Harnack Prol. p. lxxiv, *Z. f. K.* I. p. 363 sq. See also his remarks in the *Theolog. Literaturz.* Feb. 3, 1877, p. 55 sq. The distinction of this Clement, mentioned by Hermas, from the famous Roman bishop is maintained also by G. Heyne (*Quo tempore Hermae Pastor scriptus sit*, 1872, p. 15 sq) quoted in Harnack, and by Skworzow (*Patrol. Unters.* p. 54 sq): see also Donaldson *Apostolical Fathers* p. 330, ed. 2. Wieseler (*zur Gesch. d. Neutest. Schrift.* p. 166, 1880), if I understand him rightly, supposes the name to be a pseudonym for bishop Pius himself who was Clement's successor.

later than his more famous namesake, and to this second Clement some have ascribed the so-called Second Epistle to the Corinthians. Yet notwithstanding the chronological difficulty, it is not easy to resist the conviction that the famous bishop of Rome himself was intended by the author of the Shepherd. The function assigned to him of communicating with foreign cities is especially appropriate to one who was known as the author and transmitter of the epistle written in the name of the Roman Church to the Corinthians. Nor, if we remember the obscurity which shrouds the authorship and date of the Shepherd, is the chronological difficulty serious. The Shepherd indeed is stated by our earliest authority, the Muratorian Fragmentist, to have been written *during* the episcopate of Pius[1]. But, considering that we only possess this testimony in a very blundering Latin translation, it may reasonably be questioned whether the Greek original stated as much definitely. Again, it is quite possible that, though the book may have been published as late as A.D. 140, yet the epoch of the supposed revelation was placed at a much earlier period in the writer's life, while the Roman bishop was still living. For, though the latest date mentioned by any authority for the death of the Roman bishop is A.D. 100 or 101, yet no overwhelming weight can be attached to any testimony which we possess on this point, and we might suppose Clement to have lived several years after the close of the century, if independent facts had seemed to require it. Even if this explanation of the chronological difficulty should fail, the possibility still remains that Hermas is a *nom de plume* assumed by the brother of Pius for the purposes of dramatic fiction, and that the epoch of this fiction is placed by him half a century or so before he wrote, and while Clement the bishop was still living. In this case he may have had in his mind the Hermas mentioned by S. Paul among the Roman Christians. On the whole however it seems probable that, like Dante's relation to Beatrice in the Commedia, the fiction of the Shepherd is founded on the actual circumstances of the writer's own life.

[1] The words in the *Muratorian Canon* are, 'Pastorem vero nuperrime temporibus nostris in urbe Roma Hermas conscripsit sedente cathedram urbis Romae ecclesiae Pio episcopo fratre ejus' (see Westcott *Canon* pp. 519, 530, ed. 4), when some obvious errors of orthography and transcription are corrected. Considering the blunders of which this translation elsewhere is guilty, the probability is that the translator would not carefully distinguish between the absence and presence of the article, e.g. between ἐπικαθημένου and τοῦ ἐπικαθημένου: see *Philippians* p. 166 sq. There is no reason to suppose that the notice in the *Liberian Chronicle* 'Sub huius [Pii] episcopatu frater eius Ermes librum scripsit etc.' is independent of this notice in the *Muratorian Canon*; see above, I. pp. 256, 261, 262, 300.

Moreover the general belief in the age succeeding the date of this epistle is testified by another fact. Whatever theory may be held respecting the dates and mutual relations of the Clementine *Homilies* and *Recognitions*, the original romance which was the basis of both cannot well be placed later than the middle of the second century; for, though originally written in Syria or Palestine (as its substance bears evidence), it had circulated so as to influence public opinion largely in the West before the time of Tertullian. Yet the position assigned in this romance to Clement is inexplicable, except on the supposition that he was known in the Church at large as an expositor of the Apostolic doctrine, whether by authorship or by preaching or both.

To these considerations should be added the negative argument that it is difficult to conceive anyone else as the author; and that, if this letter be not ascribed to our Clement, then the most important document outside the Canon in the generation next succeeding the Apostles must remain anonymous.

3. *The genuineness and integrity.*

The *genuineness* may be regarded as already established by the investigations respecting the date and authorship. Few writings of antiquity are guaranteed by so many and various testimonies. There is the fact that it was read weekly in the Church of Corinth to which it was addressed, and that this example was followed afterwards by other Churches. There are the direct testimonies of Hegesippus and Dionysius and Irenæus. The two former of these were in a specially favourable position for ascertaining the facts—the first, Hegesippus, having visited Corinth and Rome in succession about half a century after Clement's death, staying at the one place 'a considerable time' (ἡμέρας ἱκανάς) and at the other for many years; the second, Dionysius, having heard it read Sunday by Sunday in the Church and bearing witness to this fact when writing to the Romans on the receipt of a later letter from them, which he promises to treat in the same way. There are the numerous expressions derived from it in the Epistle of Polycarp written only a few years later; and the frequent quotations and references in Clement of Alexandria, who flourished at the end of the century. In these two cases the quotations and allusions are taken from all parts of the epistle, so that they guarantee not only the existence of the letter, not only its general aim and purport, but also the identity of form. There is lastly the circumstance that its genuineness was never questioned by any individual critic of repute or by any Church for more than seventeen centuries, from the reign of Domitian or Nerva to the reign of Victoria. I pass by one or two writers of the 17th century and the beginning of the 18th, whose method deprives them of any weight as authorities, and whose opinions it would be waste of time to discuss or even to record[1].

It does not follow that those who place it so late as the reign of Hadrian question its genuineness, though there is a tendency among some of these critics to depreciate its value; and indeed generally their language on this point is far from explicit. The genuineness of a document implies that it is what it professes to be; but this letter neither professes to have been written under Domitian nor claims Clement as its author. These are, as we have seen, critical results derived from an investigation of its contents, though confirmed by a universal tradition. The conclusion is only the more convincing, because it does not depend on any direct statement in the letter itself. Indeed the mere fact of its reticence is a strong additional mark of genuineness, where all the other features point the same way—whether we adopt the earlier date or the later, whether we ascribe it to our own Clement or to another. We have shown indeed that the later date (the age of Hadrian) is untenable; but in neither case can it be called a forgery. We may therefore consider its genuineness as practically unassailed[2].

[1] See Lipsius *de Clem. Ep. ad Cor.* p. 3; Harnack p. xlix.

[2] The one undoubted exception to this universal recognition of its early date, with which I am acquainted, in recent times is the *Peregrinus Proteus* of the Rev. J. M. Cotterill (Edinburgh, 1879). His theory is that the two Epistles of Clement to the Corinthians together with a group of other writings (p. 298), among which are the *Epistle to Diognetus*, the *De Morte Peregrini* ascribed to Lucian, and the *Ecclesiastical History* bearing the name of Nicephorus Callistus (c. A.D. 1330), were forged at the revival of learning by the same hand or hands. The great French scholar, H. Estienne or Stephanus (A.D. 1528—1598), was 'an accessory after the fact, possibly one of the principals' (p. 320; comp. pp. 8 sq, 182 sq). The origin of these frauds is not earlier than the fifteenth century (p. 293), and they are ultimately connected with the person who passes under the name of Nicephorus Callistus (pp. 279, 287, 288, 293, 316). Of course the forger or forgers introduced into them the passages in ancient writers where they quote from or refer to Clement's Epistles, those of his namesake Clement of Alexandria for instance. But his or their knowledge or memory was defective. Hence the difficulty of identifying the allusions in one or two instances (see above, pp. 178, 194). We are not told however how they got hold of the references which are only known to us from Syriac extracts discovered in our own time (see above, p. 180

But while the genuineness of the letter as a whole is unimpeachable, the *integrity* of parts has been questioned at rare intervals and on different grounds, though in every case subjective and arbitrary. Soon after its first appearance in print (A.D. 1633), a French advocate, Hieron. Bignon, expressed his misgivings to Grotius, that in style and contents there were some things unworthy of the disciple of an Apostle. More especially he fastened on the story of the phœnix, as Photius (*Bibl.* 126; see above, p. 197) had attacked it before him. As a matter of fact, this is one of the best authenticated passages in Clement; and indeed we may well excuse a simple Christian for a credulity of which not a few among his highly educated heathen contemporaries were guilty (see the note on § 25). Again soon after, an Englishman, E. Bernard, suggested that some later impostor had foisted into the text of the Roman Clement some fragments of the Alexandrian who quoted him. This was hardly worth refutation, but it was refuted by Wotton.

In subsequent times assaults have been made on its integrity by two Church historians of note, Mosheim (*De Reb. Christ.* p. 156 sq, and elsewhere) condemned § 40 sq and other parts, as he imagined he discerned an interruption of the argument, besides their hierarchical tendency; but to say nothing else quotations from these condemned parts are found in ancient fathers as early as Origen. Still later Neander attacked the passage, § 40 sq, on the ground of its sacerdotalism[1]. But this attack had no other basis than the writer's own subjectivity; and notwithstanding his great name, it has fallen into merited oblivion.

sq, 182 sq). It follows from this theory that the existing authorities for these epistles, the two Greek MSS and the Syriac Version, cannot be earlier than the 15th century (p. 318 sq, p. 325 sq). They 'must have been written by the same man, or at least have been the offspring of one and the same mind' (p. 327). It will be time enough to discuss this theory when any jury of critics, or any single competent critic conversant with MSS, can be got to declare that the Alexandrian MS is from eight to ten centuries younger than has been hitherto supposed (see above, p. 117), to say nothing of the other Greek MS and the Syriac version. It should be added that he considers that the forger was given to joking (pp. 114, 153, 293, 306, 307, 311, 316). The First Epistle of Clement has always struck me as one of the most serious writings with which I am acquainted; but if I have been so utterly deceived, I despair of discriminating between what is playful and what is serious, and a misgiving seizes me lest the criticisms of *Peregrinus Proteus* may be after all an elaborate joke. We live in strange times, when we are asked to believe that Shakespeare was written by Bacon, and Tacitus by a scholar of the renaissance. For a parallel to these contemporary phenomena in earlier days, see above, p. 75.

[1] *Church History* I. p. 272 note (Bohn's trans.). Milman (*Hist. of Christianity* III. p. 259) likewise says that it is 'rejected by all judicious and impartial scholars'; see *Philippians* p. 250, note 1.

Again recently Jacobi (*Theol. Stud. u. Krit.* 1876, iv. p. 710 sq) doubts whether the liturgical portion at the close was any part of Clement's original letter, and suggests that it was inserted afterwards at Corinth. This theory seems to me impossible for many reasons.

(1) In the first place it is contained in both our authorities CS, and obviously was contained in A, before the missing leaf disappeared, as the space shows (see Harnack *Theolog. Literaturz.* Feb. 19, 1876). The combination of these three authorities points to a very early date (see above p. 145). Moreover the writer of the last two books of the *Apostolical Constitutions* obviously borrows indifferently from this prayer and from other parts of Clement's Epistle; and though he might have been indebted to two different sources for his obligations, the probability is that he derived them from the same.

(2) The expedient which Jacobi ascribes to the Corinthians would be extremely clumsy. He supposes that the reading of the letter in the Corinthian Church was followed by congregational prayer, and that, as Clement states it to be the intention of the Romans, if their appeal to the Corinthians should be disregarded, to betake themselves to prayer on behalf of Christendom generally (§ 59), it occurred to the Church at Corinth to interpolate their own form of prayer in the epistle at this point. When we remember that this prayer of Clement is followed immediately by special directions relating to individual persons who are mentioned by name, nothing could well be more incongruous than the gratuitous insertion of a liturgical service here.

(3) Jacobi remarks on the affinity to the type of prayer in the Greek Church. I have shown that the resemblances to pre-existing Jewish prayers are at least as great. Indeed the language is just what we might expect from a writer in the age of Clement, when the liturgy of the Synagogue was developing into the liturgy of the Church.

(4) Jacobi does not conceal a difficulty which occurs to him in the fact that, together with ἀρχιερεύς, the very unusual title προστάτης, 'Guardian' or 'Patron', which is given to our Lord in this prayer (§ 61), is found twice in other parts of the epistle, §§ 36, 64; but he thinks this may have been adopted into the Corinthian form of prayer from Clement. If this had been the only coincidence, his explanation might possibly have been admitted. But in fact this prayer is interpenetrated with the language and thoughts of Clement, so far as the subject allowed and the frequent adoption of Old Testament phrases left room for them. Thus in § 59 for ἐλπίζειν ἐπὶ see §§ 11, 12; again ἀνοίξας τοὺς ὀφθαλμοὺς τῆς καρδίας ἡμῶν has a close parallel in § 36; εὐεργέτην applied to God is matched by εὐεργετεῖν, εὐεργεσία, in the same

connexion §§ 19, 20, 21, 38; with the whole expression *εὐεργέτην πνευμάτων καὶ Θεὸν πάσης σαρκὸς...τὸν ἐπόπτην ἀνθρωπίνων ἔργων*, compare § 58 *ὁ παντεπόπτης Θεὸς καὶ δεσπότης τῶν πνευμάτων καὶ Κύριος πάσης σαρκός*; for *βοηθὸς* see § 36; for *κτίστης*, §§ 19, 62; for *ἐκλέγεσθαι*, §§ 43, 64, and the use of *ἐκλεκτὸς* elsewhere in this epistle; for *ἀγαπῶντάς σε*, § 29; for *διὰ* I. X. *τοῦ ἠγαπημένου παιδός σου*, § 59 *διὰ τοῦ ἠγαπημένου παιδὸς αὐτοῦ* I. X. in the same connexion; for *ἀξιοῦμεν* of prayer to God, §§ 51, 53, and with an accusative case, as here, § 55; for *δεσπότης* applied to God, the rest of the epistle *passim*. In § 60, for *ἀέναος* see § 20; for *ὁ πιστὸς κ.τ.λ.* compare a very similar expression § 27 *τῷ πιστῷ ἐν ταῖς ἐπαγγελίαις καὶ τῷ δικαίῳ ἐν τοῖς κρίμασιν*; for *θαυμαστός*, §§ 26, 35, [36], 43, 50; for *ἑδράζειν* of God's creative agency, § 33; for the repetition of the article *τὰς ἀνομίας καὶ τὰς ἀδικίας κ.τ.λ.*, the rest of the epistle *passim*, and for the connexion of the two words, § 35; for *παραπτώματα*, §§ 2, 51, 56 (comp. *παράπτωσις* § 59); for *πλημμελείας*, § 41; for *κατεύθυνον κ.τ.λ.*, § 48 *κατευθύνοντες τὴν πορείαν αὐτῶν ἐν ὁσιότητι καὶ δικαιοσύνῃ*; for *πορεύεσθαι ἐν*, § 3 (comp. § 4); for *τὰ καλὰ καὶ εὐάρεστα ἐνώπιον* (comp. § 61) see § 21, where the identical phrase appears, and compare also §§ 7, 35, 49; for the combination *ὁμόνοιαν καὶ εἰρήνην* (comp. § 61) see §§ 20 (twice), 63, 65; for *καθὼς ἔδωκας τοῖς πατράσιν ἡμῶν* compare § 62 *καθὼς καὶ οἱ προδεδηλωμένοι πατέρες ἡμῶν κ.τ.λ.* (see the whole context, and comp. § 30); for *ὁσίως* (omitted however in C), §§ 6, 21 (twice), 26, 40, 44, 62; for *ὑπηκόους*, §§ 10, 13, 14; for *παντοκράτωρ*, inscr., §§ 2, 32, 62; for *πανάρετος*, §§ 1, 2, 45, 57; for *ἡγούμενοι*, §§ 3, 5, 32, 37, 51, 55. In § 61 for *μεγαλοπρεπὴς* (comp. *μεγαλοπρεπεία* in § 60) see §§ 1, 9, 19, 45, 64; for *ἀνεκδιήγητος*, §§ 20, 49; for *ὑπὸ σοῦ* .. *δεδομένην* (see also twice below), § 58 *ὑπὸ τοῦ Θεοῦ δεδομένα*; for *δόξαν καὶ τιμήν*, § 45 (see below, and comp. § 59); for *ὑποτάσσεσθαι*, §§ 1, 2, 20, 34, 38, 57; for *εὐστάθειαν*, § 65; for *ἀπροσκόπως*, § 20; for *βασιλεῦ τῶν αἰώνων*, see § 35 *πατὴρ τῶν αἰώνων*, § 55 *Θεὸς τῶν αἰώνων*; for *ὑπαρχόντων*, this epistle *passim*, where it occurs with more than average frequency; for *διευθύνειν*, §§ 20, 62, and for *διέπειν...εὐσεβῶς*, § 62 *εὐσεβῶς καὶ δικαίως διευθύνειν*; for *ἵλεως*, § 2; for *ἐξομολογεῖσθαι*, §§ 51, 52; for *μεγαλωσύνη*, §§ 16, 27, 36, 58, and more especially joined with *δόξα* in doxologies, as here, §§ 20, 64, comp. § 65; and for *εἰς τοὺς αἰῶνας τῶν αἰώνων* see the conclusion of Clement's doxologies generally.

Thus the linguistic argument is as strong as it well could be against Jacobi's theory.

4. *The ecclesiastical authority.*

We have seen that the genuine Epistle of Clement to the Corinthians was widely known and highly esteemed from the earliest date. But a wholly different question arises when we come to discuss its claims to canonicity. There is no evidence that any respectable writer during the early centuries ever placed it in the same category, or invested it with the same authority, as the canonical books of Scripture. Thus DIONYSIUS OF CORINTH (c. A.D. 170), who first mentions its being publicly read in Church, speaks of it in language which forbids us to regard him as claiming for it any such character (see above, p. 154). Thus again IRENÆUS (p. 156) assigns to it the highest importance; but this importance consists in its recording the *traditional interpretation* of the Apostolic teaching which prevailed in the great Church of Rome from the earliest times. In no sense does he regard it in itself as a primary source of truth. His notice is unintentionally a protest against any claims to canonicity, for he is obviously unaware of any such claims. If he designates it γραφή, he uses the term in its ordinary untechnical sense as 'a writing,' and he attaches to it an epithet 'a most adequate' or 'sufficient writing' (ἱκανωτάτην γραφὴν), which would be inappropriate of 'Scripture' properly so-called. In short he adduces it as expressing the mind of the Church of Rome, the depositary of the tradition of S. Peter and S. Paul, just as he adduces the Epistle of Polycarp in the same context as expressing the mind of the Churches of Smyrna and Ephesus, the depositary of the teaching of S. John, respecting the tenour of the Apostolic teaching in the next age to the Apostles themselves. In the case of Polycarp's Epistle also he uses precisely the same expression (ἔστι δὲ ἐπιστολὴ Πολυκάρπου πρὸς Φιλιππησίους γεγραμμένη ἱκανωτάτη) 'most adequate' or 'sufficient[1].' In both cases he describes not the *source* but the *channel* of the Apostolic tradition, though the channel at the point where the stream issues from its sources. Again CLEMENT OF ALEXANDRIA, though he quotes it frequently and with great respect, nowhere treats it as Scripture. He cites 'the Apostle Clement' indeed, as he cites 'the Apostle Barnabas,' one of whose interpretations he nevertheless criticizes and condemns with a freedom which he would not have allowed himself in dealing with writings regarded by him as strictly canonical[2]. Moreover, though he commented on several of the dis-

[1] Iren. iii. 3, 4, comp. Euseb. *H. E.* v. 6.

[2] See Clem. Alex. *Paed.* ii. 10 (pp. 220, 221, Potter), where he sets aside the in-

puted books of Scripture in his *Hypotyposeis*, he left the Epistle of Clement unnoticed[1]. Again ORIGEN quotes several passages from this Apostolic father, and holds his testimony in honour, as his master Clement had done. Yet he does not go so far as his predecessor and designate him 'the Apostle Clement,' but prefers using such expressions as 'Clement the disciple of Apostles' or 'the faithful Clement to whom Paul bears testimony' (see above, p. 161 sq).

We have now arrived at the age of Eusebius and found absolutely no evidence that the epistle was regarded as canonical. The language of EUSEBIUS himself is highly significant and points in the same direction. It is remarkable that while he calls Clement's Epistle 'great and marvellous,' while he distinguishes it from the spurious second Clementine Epistle as having the testimony of antiquity to its genuineness, while he speaks of its being read publicly 'in very many churches,' yet in the two passages where he discusses the Canon of Scripture (*H. E.* iii. 3, and iii. 24, 25) and distinguishes the acknowledged from the disputed and spurious books, he does not even mention it, though in the first passage he refers to the Acts of Peter, the Gospel according to Peter, the Preaching of Peter, and the Apocalypse of Peter, as also the Acts of Paul and the Shepherd of Hermas, and in the latter to the three last-mentioned works again, together with the Epistle of Barnabas, the Teaching of the Apostles, the Gospel according to Hebrews, the Gospels of Peter, of Thomas, and of Matthias, and the Acts of Andrew, of John, and of 'the other Apostles,' besides the ἀντιλεγόμενα of our present Canon. Here is a large and comprehensive catalogue of apocryphal or doubtful Scriptures; and its comprehensiveness gives a special significance to the omission of Clement's Epistle. Only at a later point (*H. E.* vi. 13), having occasion to mention the wide learning displayed by the Alexandrian Clement in the *Stromateis*, he says that he quotes not only the canonical Scriptures but also profane writers 'Greek and barbarian', and 'employs likewise the evidence which is obtained from the disputed writings (ταῖς ἀπὸ τῶν ἀντιλεγομένων γραφῶν μαρτυρίαις), the Wisdom of Solomon, as it is entitled, and the Wisdom of Jesus the Son of Sirach and the Epistle to the Hebrews besides those of Barnabas and Clement and Jude', referring also to many and various writers such as Tatian and Cassianus, Philo and Aristobulus, etc. Yet in the very next chapter (vi. 14) he records that this same Clement in his other great work, the *Hypotyposeis*, comments on 'all the canonical

terpretation of Barnab. 10 respecting certain animals pronounced unclean by the Mosaic law, though he does not actually mention his name.

[1] See Euseb. *H. E.* vi. 14.

Scriptures (πάσης τῆς ἐνδιαθήκου γραφῆς), not even omitting the disputed books (μηδὲ τὰς ἀντιλεγομένας παρελθών), that is to say, Jude and the rest of the Catholic Epistles and the Epistle of Barnabas and the Apocalypse which bears the name of Peter'. It is clear from these several passages placed side by side, that the claims of Clement's Epistle to a place among the canonical Scriptures were not seriously entertained in the age of Eusebius, since he himself hardly allows it a place even among the ἀντιλεγόμενα, and this only incidentally.

The same negative inference may be drawn from the Canon of ATHANASIUS (*Epist. Fest.* 39, I. p. 767) who, after giving a list of the veritable Scriptures, at the close expressly excludes the *Teaching of the Apostles* ascribed to our Clement, and the *Shepherd of Hermas*, but does not mention our Epistle to the Corinthians.

This accords likewise with the testimony of other fathers of this and succeeding ages. Thus Clement is quoted by name by CYRIL OF JERUSALEM (c. A.D. 347; see above p. 167), by BASIL THE GREAT (c. A.D. 375; p. 169), by EPIPHANIUS (c. A.D. 375; p. 169), by JEROME (c. A.D. 375—410; p. 172 sq), by RUFINUS († A.D. 410; p. 174 sq), by TIMOTHEUS OF ALEXANDRIA (A.D. 457), by SEVERUS OF ANTIOCH (c. A.D. 513—518; p. 182 sq), and others, yet there is not the slightest inkling in any of these that they regarded Clement's Epistle as having more authority than any other very ancient patristic authority; and in most cases their mode of reference is distinctly inconsistent with the recognition of any claims to canonicity.

The first apparent exception to this universal testimony is found in the 85th of the *Apostolical Canons* attached to the *Apostolic Constitutions*, and these Canons may belong to the 6th century (see above, p. 187). It is sufficient to say here that this document has no authority, even if it were free from interpolations. The grave suspicions, and more than suspicions, which rest on the genuineness of this particular clause will be fully considered below (p. 373 sq).

About the same time, or somewhat earlier, the Two Epistles of Clement appear at the end of the New Testament in the Alexandrine MS (A). What may be the significance of this juxtaposition I shall investigate presently (p. 370 sq).

Of the later fathers it may be said generally, that their testimony concurs with the earlier. They betray no suspicion of the canonicity of either or both the 'Epistles of Clement to the Corinthians.' Any one who will read through the testimonies of these later writers as given above (p. 188 sq) may convince himself of this. The silence of some is not less eloquent than the repudiation by others.

Altogether a review of these facts leads irresistibly to the conclusion that the Epistle of Clement had not the same quasi-canonical place which was given to the Shepherd of Hermas in the West, and to the Epistle of Barnabas in Alexandria and some Eastern churches. Indeed the evidence in the two cases differs in one all-important point. Whereas the testimony in the case of Clement—if it deserves the name of testimony—first appears many centuries after the writer's age, the testimony in those of Barnabas and Hermas is confined to the earliest times, and is then sifted and put aside.

In the Latin Church indeed there could be no question of canonicity; for the Epistle of Clement was practically unknown, except to the learned few, if as there is the strongest reason for believing, it was never translated into the vernacular language. Thus, if it had been generally known in the West, it could hardly have failed to be included in the very miscellaneous and comprehensive list of apocryphal works condemned in the later forms of the so-called Gelasian decree[1], which seems to have been republished at intervals with additions (A.D. 500—700), though issued originally without the list of apocrypha by Gelasius himself (A.D. 492—496).

We are now in a position to trace with a high degree of probability the several stages which our epistle passed, in its futile struggle to attain full canonicity.

(1) The genuine Epistle of Clement was read from time to time on Sundays in the Church of Corinth to which it was addressed. Our information on this point relates to about A.D. 170. The practice however seems to have prevailed from the date when it was first received (see above, p. 154 sq). But this reading did not imply canonicity. On the contrary, Dionysius bishop of Corinth, to whom we are indebted for the information, tells us at the same time that his church purposes doing the same thing with a second letter of the Roman Church, which was written under bishop Soter his own contemporary, and which the Corinthians had just received when he wrote[2].

(2) This practice was extended from the Church of Corinth to other Christian communities. Eusebius in the first half of the fourth century speaks of the epistle as 'having been publicly read *in very many churches* both formerly and in his own time' (*H. E.* iii. 16 ἐν πλείσταις ἐκκλησίαις ἐπὶ τοῦ κοινοῦ δεδημοσιευμένην πάλαι τε καὶ καθ' ἡμᾶς αὐτούς).

[1] On the Gelasian decree see Credner *Zur Gesch. d. Kanons* p. 151 sq; Westcott *Canon* pp. 449, 563.

[2] For the reasons for assuming that this letter was written while Soter was still living see above pp. 72, 155.

Somewhat later (c. A.D. 375) Epiphanius (*Haer.* xxx. 15; see above p. 170) speaks to the same effect of 'encyclical letters' written by Clement, 'which are read in the holy churches (τῶν ἐν ταῖς ἁγίαις ἐκκλησίαις ἀναγινωσκομένων).' It will be shown presently (p. 409) from his language, that he was unacquainted with the genuine epistle to the Corinthians, and that he is here speaking of the spurious Clementine Epistles to Virgins; but he doubtless transferred to these the statement which Eusebius made respecting the genuine epistle.

Later still Jerome (A.D. 378) says in his *Vir. Illustr.* 15; 'Scripsit [Clemens] ex persona ecclesiae Romanae ad ecclesiam Corinthiorum valde utilem epistulam et *quae in nonnullis locis etiam publice legitur*' (see p. 173). But, as Jerome copies Eusebius almost verbatim in the context, and as it is very questionable whether he had read Clement's genuine epistle (see below, p. 410), we may reasonably suspect that he follows the same leading here also. If so the statement of Jerome adds nothing to the testimony of Eusebius on this point. It will be observed however that Jerome substitutes *some* (nonnullis) for *very many* (πλείσταις) which stands in Eusebius. This points to a diminution of area in the interval, at least so far as the knowledge of Jerome extends.

The reference of Photius quoted below (p. 375) shows that at the close of the ninth century, when he wrote, this practice of reading Clement's Epistle had long ceased, at least in those churches to which his knowledge extended.

(3) For convenience of reading, it would be attached to MSS of the New Testament. But, so far as our evidence goes, this was not done until two things had first happened. (*a*) On the one hand, the Canon of the New Testament had for the most part assumed a definite form in the MSS, beginning with the Gospels and ending with the Apocalypse. (*b*) On the other hand, the so-called Second Epistle of Clement had become inseparably attached to the genuine letter, so that the two formed one body. Hence, when we find our epistle included in the same volume with the New Testament, it carries the Second Epistle with it, and the two form a sort of *appendix* to the Canon. This is the case with the Alexandrian MS in the middle of the fifth century, where they stand after the Apocalypse, i.e. after the proper close of the sacred volume. They thus occupy the same position which in the earlier Sinaitic MS is occupied by other apocryphal matter, the Epistle of Barnabas and the Shepherd of Hermas, while the Second Epistle is followed immediately by the spurious Psalms of Solomon; whereas the proper place for an epistle of Clement, if regarded as strictly canonical, would have been with the Apostolic Epistles and

before the Apocalypse. When moreover it is remembered that in this MS even Christian hymns are appended to the Psalms of David in the Old Testament for ecclesiastical purposes, it will be evident that no canonical authority is implied by the fact that these two epistles are added to the sacred volume.

If we were disposed to speculate on the church to whose instrumentality this step in advance was mainly due we should name without much hesitation Alexandria[1]. The MS which thus connects them as an appendix to the New Testament is Alexandrian. If we should venture a step further, and specify an individual as chiefly responsible in this movement, our eyes would naturally turn to Clement, who was a great traveller, whose writings are steeped through and through with the influence of his Roman namesake, and who occupied a position of the highest influence as master of the catechetical school in Alexandria. Eusebius informs us that the public reading of Clement's genuine epistle had spread from Corinth to other churches. Alexandria would from its position and its thirst for knowledge be among the first to take up this practice. But bound up in the same volume which contained the genuine Epistle of the Roman Clement was another document likewise which had its birth in that city, addressed like the former to the Corinthians—not however another letter written to Corinth by a foreign church, but a sermon preached in Corinth by a native presbyter[2]. To the Corinthians it would have a special value; at all events its juxtaposition with Clement's famous letter to their church would be natural enough. Such a volume we may suppose was brought from Corinth to Alexandria; and the introduction of Clement's Epistle for occasional reading in the Alexandrian Church began. The phenomena of the Alexandrian MS would follow naturally.

(4) It was an easy stage from this to include them among the

[1] Zahn, *Geschichte des Neutest. Kanons* I. p. 351 sq, insists with great force on the influence of Alexandria in the diffusion of the two Clementine Epistles (the genuine letter and the homily which accompanies it). But he uses some arguments in which I am unable to follow him. Thus he assigns the Syriac translation to Alexandria (p. 352), but the facts seem to point another way (see above, p. 135). Thus again he credits Clement of Alexandria with a knowledge of the 'Second Epistle of Clement' (p. 358). I think it highly probable that this father was not unacquainted with it, though he certainly did not ascribe it to his namesake; but the resemblances which Zahn quotes (e.g. *Quis div. salv.* 3. 32 πλεῦσον with 2 Clem. 7 καταπλεύσωμεν) are too feeble to bear the weight of the conclusion which he builds upon them.

[2] It will be shown in the introduction to the 'Second Epistle' that it was a homily and that Corinth was probably its birthplace.

Books of the New Testament, and thus to confer upon them a patent of canonicity. Uncritical transcribers and others would take this step without reflexion. This is done by the scribe of A in his table of contents (see above, p. 117 sq).

It is interesting to observe, though the fact seems to have been overlooked, that the treatment in the Alexandrian MS exactly accords with the language of the 85th Apostolical Canon as read in the Coptic Churches. The Books of the New Testament are there given as 'The Four Gospels......the Acts of us the Apostles; the two Epistles of Peter; the three of John; the Epistle of James, with that of Judas; the fourteen Epistles of Paul; the Apocalypse of John; the two Epistles of Clement which ye shall read aloud[1].' Here the several divisions of the New Testament occur in the same order as in A, though the Catholic Epistles are transposed among themselves[2]; moreover

[1] The Coptic form of the Apostolical Canons is preserved in both the great dialects of the Egyptian language.

(1) The Thebaic is found in a MS acquired not many years ago by the British Museum, *Orient.* 1320. I gave a full account of this MS which was before unknown in my *Appendix* (1875) to Clement, p. 466 sq, to which I may refer those who are interested in the subject. It throws another ray of light on the dark question of the history of the *Apostolical Constitutions*. More recently it has been printed *in extenso* by Lagarde *Aegyptiaca* p. 207 sq (Gottingae 1883). Its date is Ann. Diocl. 722 = A.D. 1006.

(2) The Memphitic is published by Tattam in the volume entitled '*The Apostolic Constitutions or Canons of the Apostles in Coptic*,' London 1848. It was not made however directly from the Greek, but is a very recent and somewhat barbarous translation from the previously existing Thebaic Version. This Memphitic version is stated in a colophon in the MS to have been translated from the language of Upper Egypt (the Thebaic), and a very recent date is given, Ann. Diocl. 1520 = A.D. 1804.

The concluding words of the clause quoted stand in the Thebaic ⲧⲥⲛⲧⲉⲛ̇ⲉ̇ⲡⲓⲥⲧⲟⲗⲏⲛ̇ⲕⲗⲏⲙⲏⲥ · ⲉⲧⲉⲧⲛⲉⲟ̇ϣⲟⲩϩⲓⲃⲟⲗ, which I have translated in the text; in the Memphitic, as given by Tattam (p. 211), ϯⲃ̄ϯ ⲛ̇ⲉ̇ⲡⲓⲥⲧⲟⲗⲏ ⲛ̇ⲁⲕⲗⲏⲙⲏⲥ ⲉ̇ⲧⲉⲧⲉⲛⲟϣⲟⲩ ϩⲓ ⲉ̇ⲃⲟⲗ, which he renders 'the two Epistles of Clemens which you read out of,' but this is surely wrong.

In the Arabic Version of this canon, Brit. Mus. *Add.* 7211, fol. 22 b (dated A.D. 1682), in like manner the 14 Epistles of S. Paul are followed by the Revelation, and the Revelation by the 'Two Epistles of Clement, and they are one book.' After this comes the clause about the Apostolic Constitutions, substantially the same as in the Greek canon. This is an Egyptian MS. In the Carshunic MS, *Add.* 7207, fol. 27 b (A.D. 1730), which is of Syrian origin, the Apocalypse is omitted, so that the Epistles of Clement are mentioned immediately after the 14 Epistles of St Paul. Here again follows a clause relating to the eight books of the Apostolic Constitutions.

[2] The order of the Catholic Epistles among themselves is the same also in the Greek 85th canon. It may have been determined either by the relative importance of the Apostles themselves, or by the fact that the Epistles of S. James and

the Clementine Epistles are placed after the Apocalypse, as in that MS; and, as a reason for adding them, it is stated that they were to be read publicly[1].

(5) Their canonicity being assumed, it remained to give practical effect to this view, and to place them in a position consistent with it. In other words, they must be transferred from the appendix to the body of the New Testament. The only known document, which has actually taken this step is our Syriac version, where they are attached to the Catholic Epistles. The date of this MS (A.D. 1170) throws some light on the matter.

It has been observed above (p. 366 sq), that the general silence about the Epistles of S. Clement in the older discussions on the Canon of Scripture seems to show that their claims to canonicity were not considered serious enough to demand refutation. In the 85th and last of the Apostolical Canons however the case is different. If the existing Greek text of this canon may be trusted, this document not only admits them to a place among the Scriptures, but ranges them with the Catholic Epistles. The list of the New Testament writings runs as follows; 'Four Gospels,......; of Paul fourteen Epistles; of Peter two Epistles; of John three; of James one; of Jude one; of Clement two Epistles; and the Constitutions (διαταγαὶ) addressed to you the bishops through me Clement in eight books, which ought not to be published to all (ἃς οὐ χρὴ δημοσιεύειν ἐπὶ πάντων), owing to the mystical teaching in them (διὰ τὰ ἐν αὐταῖς μυστικά); and the Acts of us the Apostles[2].' Some doubt however may reasonably be entertained whether the words Κλήμεντος ἐπιστολαὶ δύο are not a later interpolation. In the first place, the form is somewhat suspicious. As these Clementine letters range with the Catholic Epistles, we should not expect a repetition of ἐπιστολαί; and, as Clement is the reputed author of the Canons, we should expect ἐμοῦ Κλήμεντος, so that the obvious form would be 'Of me Clement two[3].' On this point however I should not lay any stress, if the

S. Jude were accepted as canonical, in the church from which the list emanated, at a later date than 1 Peter and 1 John.

[1] The clause about reading aloud seems to refer solely to the Epistles of Clement. At least this restriction is suggested by the connexion, as well as by comparison with a somewhat similar clause relating to Ecclesiasticus, which closes the list of the Old Testament writings. But on this point there must remain some uncertainty.

[2] Ueltzen *Const. Apost.* p. 253.

[3] Beveridge (*Synod.* II. ii. p. 40) remarks on the difference between the mention of Clement in the two cases. He argues from it that different persons are meant.

In the Syriac copy, Brit. Mus. *Add.* 14,526 fol. 9 a (a MS of the VIIth cent., and probably written soon after A.D. 641; see Wright's *Catalogue* p. 1033) it is 'of me Clement two Epistles.' In another external evidence had been satisfactory. But the subsequent history of this canon tends to increase our suspicions. The Trullan Council (A.D. 692) in its 2nd canon adopts 'the 85 Canons handed down to us in the name of the holy and glorious Apostles,' adding however this caution; 'But seeing that in these canons it hath been commanded that we should receive the Constitutions (διατάξεις) of the same holy Apostles, (written) by the hand of Clement, in which certain spurious matter that is alien to godliness hath been interpolated long ago by the heterodox to the injury of the Church, thus obscuring for us the goodly beauty of the divine ordinances, we have suitably rejected such Constitutions, having regard to the edification and safety of the most Christian flock, etc.[1]' Here no mention is made of the Epistles of Clement; and therefore, if the Trullan fathers found them in their copy of the 85th Apostolical Canon, they deliberately adopted them as part of the canonical Scriptures. The Canons of this Trullan Council were signed by the four great patriarchs of the East. The Council itself was and is regarded by the Eastern Church as a General Council[2]. From this time forward therefore the Epistles of Clement would become an authoritative part of the New Testament for the Christians of the East. How comes it then, that not a single MS of the Greek Testament among many hundreds written after this date includes them in the sacred volume? But this is not all. About the middle of the eighth century John of Damascus gives a list of the New Testament Scriptures (*de Fid. Orthod.* iv. 17, *Op.* I. p. 284, Lequien). It ends: 'Of Paul the Apostle fourteen Epistles; the Apocalypse of John the Evangelist; the Canons of the Holy Apostles by the hand of Clement'

Syriac copy, *Add.* 12,155, fol. 205 b (apparently of the VIII th cent.; *ib.* pp. 921, 949) the scribe has first written 'of me Clement,' and has corrected it 'of him Clement' (ܠܝ altered into ܠܗ). This seems to be a different translation from the former. The canon in question is the 81st in the former, the 79th in the latter. A third Syriac MS *Add.* 14,527 (about the XI th cent.; *ib.* p. 1036) follows the last as corrected and reads 'of him Clement.' I owe these facts to the kindness of Prof. Wright, who also investigated the readings of the Æthiopic, Carshunic, and Arabic MSS for me, as given elsewhere in my notes, pp. 372, 376. In the Syriac MS from which Lagarde has published his text (*Rel. Jur. Eccl. Ant. Syr.* 1856 p. ܣ) the form exactly follows the Greek, 'Of Clement two Epistles.'

[1] Bevereg. *Synod.* I. p. 158.

[2] The Trullan or Quinisextine Council was commonly called the 'Sixth' Council by the Greeks, being regarded as a supplement to that Council; Hefele *Conciliengeschichte* III. p. 299. The 7th General Council (the Second of Nicæa, A.D. 787) adopted both the Apostolical Canons themselves and the Canons of the Trullan Council as a whole (see Hefele *ib.* p. 443); and thus they were doubly confirmed as the law of the Greek Church.

(κανόνες τῶν ἁγίων ἀποστόλων διὰ Κλήμεντος). Here is no mention of Clement's Epistles. But one MS, Reg. 2428, which exhibits interpolations elsewhere, inserts a mention of them, reading the last sentence κανόνες τῶν ἁγίων ἀποστόλων καὶ ἐπιστολαὶ δύο διὰ Κλήμεντος, where the very form of the expression betrays the insertion. This interpolation is significant; for it shows that there was a disposition in some quarters to introduce these epistles into the Canon, and that ancient documents were tampered with accordingly[1]. Again, in the Stichometria attached to the *Chronographia* of Nicephorus patriarch of Constantinople († A.D. 828), though itself perhaps of an older date, the Epistles of Clement are not placed among the undoubted Scriptures, nor even among the disputed books of the Canon, among which the Epistle of Barnabas and the Gospel of the Hebrews have a place, but are thrown into the Apocrypha[2]. Again, a little later we have the testimony of another patriarch of Constantinople, the great Photius, who died towards the close of the ninth century. In his edition of the *Nomocanon*[3] (Tit. iii. cap. ii, *Op.* IV. p. 1049 sq, ed. Migne) he mentions the 85th Apostolical Canon as an authority on the subject of which it treats. Yet elsewhere he not only betrays no suspicion that these Clementine Epistles are canonical, but speaks in a manner quite inexplicable on this hypothesis. In one passage of his *Bibliotheca* (Cod. 113) he incidentally repeats the statement of Eusebius (without however mentioning his name), that the First Epistle was at one time 'considered worthy of acceptance among many, so as even to be read in public' (παρὰ πολλοῖς ἀποδοχῆς ἠξιώθη ὡς καὶ δημοσίᾳ ἀναγινώσκεσθαι), whereas 'the so-called Second Epistle is rejected as spurious' (ὡς νόθος ἀποδοκιμάζεται). In another (Cod. 126) he records reading the two epistles, apparently for the first time; he treats them exactly in the same way as the other books of which he gives an account; he criticizes them freely; he censures the First, not only for its faulty cosmography, but also for its defective statements respecting the Person of Christ; he complains of the Second, that the thoughts are tumbled together without any continuity; and he blames both in different degrees for quoting apocryphal sayings

[1] Harnack (*Praef.* xli, ed. 2) seems disposed to accept καὶ ἐπιστολαὶ δύο as part of the genuine text, though he speaks hesitatingly. But seeing that this MS stands alone and that it is, as Lequien says, 'interpolatus varie' in other parts, the spuriousness of these words can hardly be considered doubtful.

[2] Westcott *Canon* p. 552 sq (ed. 4), Credner *Zur Gesch. des Kanons* p. 97 sq.

[3] On the relation of the *Nomocanon* of Photius to earlier works of the same name, see Hergenröther *Photius* III. p. 92 sq.

'as if from the Divine Scripture.' Moreover, his copy of these Clementine Epistles was not attached to the New Testament, but (as he himself tells us), was bound up in a little volume with the Epistle of Polycarp[1].

For these reasons it may be questioned whether the Clementine Epistles were included in the Greek catalogue of the 85th Apostolic Canon, as ratified by the Trullan Council[2], though they are found in

[1] It is true that the procedure of the Trullan Council in this respect was very loose. It confirmed at the same time the Canons of the Councils of Laodicea and Carthage, though the Canons of Carthage contained a list of the Canonical books not identical with the list in the Apostolical Canons, and this may also have been the case with the Laodicean Canons (see Westcott *Canon* p. 434, ed. 4). But these Canons were confirmed *en bloc* along with those of other Councils and individual fathers; and no indication is given that their catalogues of Scriptural books came under review. On the other hand not only are the Apostolical Canons placed in the forefront and stamped with a very emphatic approval, but their list of Scriptural books is made the subject of a special comment, so that its contents could not have been overlooked. The difficulty however is not so much that the Trullan Council should have adopted these Clementine Epistles into their Canon carelessly, as that (if they had done this) the fact should have been ignored for several centuries.

[2] This inference will seem the more probable, when it is remembered that the list of the New Testament writings in the 85th Apostolical Canon occurs in several other forms, in which the Clementine Epistles are differently dealt with.

(i) The Egyptian form has been given already (p. 372). Here the Apocalypse is inserted, and the two Clementine Epistles are thrown to the end. No mention is made of the Apostolic Constitutions.

(ii) Harnack (praef. p. xlii, ed. 2) has given another form of this Greek list which was copied by Gebhardt from a Moscow MS of the 15th century, Bibl. S. Synod. cxlix, fol. 160 b, where the New Testament writings are enumerated as follows; *τῆς δὲ καινῆς διαθήκης βιβλία δ΄. ἐπιστολαὶ Πέτρου β΄. Ἰωάννου τρεῖς. Ἰακώβου Ἰούδα μία. Κλήμεντος α΄. Παύλου ἐπιστολαὶ ιδ΄.* The context shows decisively that this Moscow list is taken from the 85th Apostolical Canon. The word *εὐαγγελία* seems to have been left out after *βιβλία* by homœoteleuton; and Acts is perhaps omitted from carelessness owing to its position at the end of the list in the Canon itself. The omission of the Second Clementine Epistle is the remarkable feature here.

(iii) The three *Æthiopic* MSS, Brit. Mus. *Orient.* 481 (XVII th cent.), *Orient.* 796 (about A.D. 1740), *Orient.* 793 (about the same date as the last), after the Apocalypse, name the eight books of the Ordinances of Clement (i.e. the Apostolic Constitutions) and do not mention the Epistles of Clement at all. On the other hand the Æthiopic text of the Canons as printed by W. Fell (*Canones Apostolorum Æthiopice* p. 46, Lips. 1871) repeats the list as it stands in the Coptic (see above, p. 372), ending 'Abukalamsis, i.e. visio Ioannis, duae Epistolae Clementis'; and the Æthiopic MS Brit. Mus. *Orient.* 794 (XV th cent.) ends similarly, though the number of Clement's Epistles is not mentioned. Again the independent list in the MS *Add.* 16,205, (described by Dillmann *Catal. Cod. Æthiop. Brit. Mus.* p. 40), has them, but in a different position, ending '...Epistola Iudae, Clementis Epistolae 2, Apocalypsis, Pauli

Syriac copies of an earlier date. But in the 12th century the case is different. At this date, and afterwards, the Greek canonists no longer pass them over in silence. Alexius Aristenus, œconomus of the Great Church at Constantinople (c. A.D. 1160), repeats this list of the 85th Canon, expressly naming 'the two Epistles of Clement,' and mentioning the rejection of the Constitutions by the Trullan Council (*Bevereg. Synod.* I. p. 53); and more than a century and a half later, Matthæus Blastaris (c. A.D. 1335, *Syntagma* B. 11) interprets the second Trullan Canon as including the Clementine Epistles in the same condemnation with the Constitutions[1]. This is certainly not the case; but it shows to what straits a writer was driven, when he felt obliged to account for the conflict between the current text of the 85th Apostolical Canon and the universal practice of his church.

It will thus be seen that the only author who distinctly accepts the two Clementine Epistles as canonical is Alexius Aristenus. His work was written within a few years of the date of our MS (A.D. 1170), and its authority stood very high. It would perhaps be over bold to assume that the influence of Aristenus was felt in a Syrian monastery at Edessa; but at all events the coincidence of date is striking, and seems to show a tendency to the undue exaltation of these Clementine Epistles in the latter half of the twelfth century. There is no reason however for thinking that our MS represents more than the practice of a very restricted locality, or perhaps of a single monastery. Several other Syriac MSS, either of the Gospels or of Evangelistaries, are in existence, dating not many years before or after this, and written (in some instances) on this same Mountain of Edessa[2]; and on examina-

14.' In other independent lists, *Add.* 16,188 (described by Dillmann l.c. p. 4) and *Orient.* 829, the Epistles of Clement are omitted. On the Æthiopic recensions of the *Apostolic Canons*, and on different Æthiopic lists of the Biblical books, see Dillmann in Ewald's *Jahrbücher*, 1852, p. 144 sq.

An account of Arabic and Carshunic MSS is given above, p. 372.

Generally it may be said that this canon is altered freely so as to adapt it to the usage of particular churches. Still the normal Greek form is the best supported, as being confirmed by the Syriac MSS, which are the most ancient of all.

[1] Bevereg. *Synod.* II. ii. p. 56 ἃς δὲ προστίθησι διὰ τοῦ Κλήμεντος δύο ἐπιστολὰς καὶ τὰς πονηθείσας τούτῳ διατάξεις τῶν ἀποστόλων ὕστερον ὁ τῆς συνόδου δεύτερος κανὼν διέγραψεν, ὡς πολὺ τὸ νόθον πρὸς τὴν αἱρετικὴν καὶ παρέγγραπτον δεξαμένας.

[2] The Paris MS described by Adler (*Nov. Test. Vers. Syr.* p. 58), of which the date is A.D. 1192 (not 1212, as wrongly given by Adler), and the place 'Coenobium Deiparae, cui cognomen est Hospitium, in monte sancto Edessae,' was written at the same monastery a little more than twenty years after; see *Catalogue des Manuscrits Orientaux de la Bibliothèque Impériale* (*Fonds Syriaque*)

tion of these it may possibly be found that a comparison of the tables of lessons throws some light on the position ascribed by our manuscript to the Clementine Epistles.

5. *The purport and contents.*

Mention has been made already of the circumstances under which the letter was written (p. 82 sq). Its character and contents are determined by the nature of the feuds in the Corinthian Church which called it forth. What these dissensions were—so far as our information goes—I have briefly stated (see above, p. 82). It does not seem to me that anything is gained by going behind our information, and speculating in detail on the supposed heresy which lurks under these party-strifes. We have first to answer the question whether there was any such heresy. Beyond the revived scepticism about the resurrection, which prevailed in S. Paul's days (p. 82), I fail to discover any traces of heretical doctrine at Corinth refuted in Clement's Epistle. Indeed very few of those who have made a special study of the epistle declare themselves able to discern more than this.

The following is an analysis of the letter:

'THE CHURCH OF ROME TO THE CHURCH OF CORINTH. Greeting in Christ Jesus.'

'We regret that domestic troubles have prevented our writing before: we deplore the feuds which have gained ground among you; for your present unhappy state reminds us by contrast of the past, when such breaches of brotherly love were unknown among you, and your exemplary concord and charity were known far and wide (§§ 1, 2). Now all is changed. Like Jeshurun of old, you have waxed fat and kicked. Envy is your ruling passion (§ 3). Envy, which led Cain to slay his brother; which sent Jacob into exile; which persecuted Joseph; which compelled Moses to flee; which drove Aaron and Miriam out of the camp; which threw Dathan and Abiram alive into the pit; which incited Saul against David (§ 4); which in these latest days, after inflicting countless sufferings on the Apostles Peter and Paul, brought them to a martyr's death (§ 5); which has caused numberless woes to women and girls, has separated wives from their husbands, has destroyed whole cities and nations (§ 6). We and you alike need this warning. Let us therefore repent, as men repented at the preaching

p. 20, no. 54. See also this same catalogue p. 19, no. 52, for a somewhat similar MS written at a neighbouring monastery on the same 'Holy Mountain of Edessa' a few years earlier (A.D. 1165).

of Noah, at the preaching of Jonah (§ 7). The Holy Spirit, speaking by the prophets, again and again calls to repentance (§ 8). Let us not turn a deaf ear to the summons; let us supplicate God's mercy; let us follow the example of Enoch who was translated, of Noah who was saved from the flood (§ 9), of Abraham whose faith was rewarded by repeated blessings and by the gift of a son (§ 10). Call to mind the example of Lot whose hospitality saved him from the fate of Sodom, when even his wife perished (§ 11); of Rahab whose faith and protection of the spies rescued her from the general destruction (§ 12). Pride and passion must be laid aside; mercy and gentleness cherished; for the promises in the Scriptures are reserved for the merciful and gentle (§§ 13, 14). We must not call down denunciations upon our heads, like the Israelites of old (§ 15): but rather take for our pattern the lowliness of Christ as portrayed by the Evangelical Prophet and by the Psalmist (§ 16); and copy also the humility of the ancient worthies, Elijah, Elisha, Ezekiel, Abraham, and Job; of Moses the most highly favoured and yet the meekest of men (§ 17); of David the man after God's heart, who nevertheless humbled himself in the dust (§ 18). Nay, let us have before our eyes the long-suffering of God Himself, the Lord of the Universe, whose mind can be read in His works (§ 19). Harmony prevails in heaven and earth and ocean; day and night succeed each other in regular order; the seasons follow in due course; all created things perform their functions peacefully (§ 20). Let us therefore act as becomes servants of this beneficent Master. He is near at hand, and will punish all unruliness and self-seeking. In all relations of life behave soberly. Instruct your wives in gentleness, and your children in humility (§ 21). For the Holy Spirit in the Scriptures commends the humble and simple-hearted, but condemns the stubborn and double-tongued. The Lord will come quickly (§§ 22, 23).'

'All nature bears witness to the resurrection; the dawn of day; the growth of the seedling (§ 24); above all the wonderful bird of Arabia (§ 25). So too God Himself declares in the Scriptures (§ 26). He has sworn, and He can and will bring it to pass (§ 27).'

'Let us therefore cleanse our lives, since before Him is no concealment (§ 28). Let us approach Him in purity, and make our election sure (§ 29). As His children, we must avoid all lust, contention, self-will, and pride (§ 30). Look at the example of the patriarchs, Abraham, Isaac, and Jacob (§ 31). See how the promise was granted to their faith, that in them all the nations of the earth should be blessed (§ 32). To their *faith;* but we must not therefore be slack in works. The Creator Himself rejoices in His works, and we are created in His image. All righteous men have been rich in good works (§ 33). If we would win the reward, we must not be slothful but ever diligent, as the angels in heaven are diligent (§ 34). And how glorious is the hope held out to us! Well may we strive earnestly to attain this bright promise: well may we school ourselves to lay aside all bitterness and strife, which, as the Scriptures teach us, are hateful in God's sight (§ 35). Nor shall we be unaided in the struggle. Christ our High-Priest is mightier than the angels, and by Him we are ushered into the presence of God (§ 36).'

'Subordination of rank and distinction of office are the necessary conditions of life. Look at the manifold gradations of order in an army, at the diverse functions of the members in the human body (§ 37). We likewise are one body in Christ, and members in particular (§ 38). They are fools and mad, who thirst for power; men whom the Scriptures condemn in no measured terms (§ 39). Are not the ordinances of the Mosaic law—where the places, the seasons, the persons, are all prescribed—a sign that God will have all things done decently and in order (§§ 40, 41)? The Apostles were sent by Jesus Christ, as Jesus Christ was sent by the Father. They appointed presbyters in all churches, as the prophet had foretold (§ 42). Herein they followed the precedent of Moses. You will remember how the murmuring against Aaron was quelled by the budding of Aaron's rod (§ 43). In like manner the Apostles, to avoid dissension, made provision for the regular succession of the ministry. Ye did wrongly therefore to thrust out presbyters who had been duly appointed according to this Apostolic order, and had discharged their office faithfully (§ 44). It is an untold thing, that God's servants should thus cast out God's messengers. It was by the enemies of God that Daniel and the three children were persecuted of old (§ 45). There is one body and one Spirit. Whence then these dissensions (§ 46)? Did not the Apostle himself rebuke you for this same fault? And yet you had the excuse then, which you have not now, that they whom you constituted your leaders—Cephas and Paul and Apollos—were Apostles and Apostolic men (§ 47). Away with these feuds. Reconcile yourselves to God by humility and righteousness in Christ (§ 48). Love is all-powerful, love is beyond praise, love is acceptable to God. Seek love before all things, and ye shall be blessed indeed; for so the Scriptures declare (§§ 49, 50). Ask pardon for your offences, and do not harden your hearts like Pharaoh. Else, like Pharaoh, ye will also perish (§ 51). God asks nothing from us, but contrition and prayer and praise (§ 52). Moses spent forty days and nights in prayer, entreating God that he himself might be blotted out and the people spared (§ 53). Let the same spirit be in you. Let those who are the causes of dissension sacrifice themselves and retire, that strife may cease (§ 54). Nay, have not heathen kings and rulers been ready to offer themselves up for the common weal? Even women have perilled their lives, like men, for the public good. So did Judith; so also did Esther (§ 55). Let us intercede for one another; let us admonish one another (§ 56). And you especially, who were the first to stir up this feud, be the first to repent. Remember the stern threats, which the Scriptures pronounce against the stubborn and impenitent (§ 57).'

'Let us therefore render obedience that we may escape His threatened punishment. They that fulfil His commandments shall most assuredly be saved among the elect (§ 58). We have warned the guilty and thus we have absolved ourselves from blame. We will pray to God therefore that He will keep His elect intact.

'Open our eyes, O Lord, that we may know Thee and feel Thine omnipresence. Help all those who need help. Teach the nations the knowledge of Thy Son Jesus Christ (§ 59). O Lord, our Creator, pity and forgive us; purify and enlighten us; give peace to us and to all men (§ 60). Thou hast given authority to our earthly rulers, that we may submit to them as holding their office from Thee. Give them health and peace and security; direct their counsels that they rule religiously and peacefully. Through Jesus Christ, our High-Priest, we pour out our hearts to Thee (§ 61).'

'Enough has been said by us concerning a godly and virtuous life. We have spoken of faith and repentance; we have exhorted you to love and peace; and we have done this the more gladly, as speaking to faithful men who have studied the oracles of God (§ 62). We are bound to follow the great examples of the past, and to render obedience to our spiritual leaders. Ye will give us great joy therefore, if ye listen to our words and cease from your strife. Along with this letter we have, as a token of our care for you, sent faithful and wise men to be witnesses between you and us (§ 63).'

'Finally, may He grant all graces and blessings to them that call upon His name, through Jesus Christ our High-Priest (§ 64).'

'Ephebus and Bito and Fortunatus are the bearers of this letter.'

'Despatch them speedily, that they may return with the glad tidings of your peace and concord.'

'The grace of our Lord Jesus Christ be with you and with all men (§ 65).'

6. *The liturgical ending.*

When the closing chapters, which had disappeared with the loss of a leaf in the Alexandrian manuscript, were again brought to light by the discovery of fresh documents, we could not fail to be struck by the *liturgical* character of this newly-recovered portion. The whole epistle may be said to lead up to the long prayer or litany, if we may so call it, which forms a fit close to its lessons of forbearance and love. Attention is directed to it at the outset in a few emphatic words: 'We will ask with fervency of prayer and supplication that the Creator of the universe may guard intact the number of His elect that is numbered throughout the whole world, through His beloved Son Jesus Christ' (§ 59). The prayer itself extends to a great length, occupying some seventy lines of an ordinary octavo page. Moreover it bears all the marks of a careful composition. Not only are the balance and rhythm of the clauses carefully studied, but almost every other expression is selected and adapted from different parts of the Old Testament.

This prayer or litany begins with an elaborate invocation of God arranged for the most part in antithetical sentences. Then comes a special intercession for the afflicted, the lowly, the fallen, the needy, the wanderers, the hungry, the prisoners, and so forth. After this follows a general confession of sins and prayer for forgiveness and help. This last opens with an address, evincing the same deep sense of the glories of Creation which is one of the most striking characteristics in the earlier part of the epistle: 'Thou through Thine operations didst make manifest the everlasting fabric of the world, etc.' (§ 60). It closes, as the occasion suggests, with a prayer for unity: 'Give concord and peace to us and to all that dwell on the earth, as Thou gavest to our fathers, etc.' After this stands the intercession for rulers, to which I desire to direct special attention. The whole closes with a doxology.

One striking feature in this litany, and indeed throughout the whole epistle, especially arrests our attention—the attitude maintained towards the Roman government. The close connexion, not only of Christianity, but (as it would appear) of the bearers and the writer of the letter, with the imperial household has been dwelt upon already at length (pp. 27 sq, 60 sq), and seems to explain the singular reserve maintained throughout this epistle. The persecuted and the persecutor met face to face, as it were; they mixed together in the common affairs of life; they even lived under the same roof. Thus the utmost caution was needed, that collisions might not be provoked. We can well understand therefore with what feelings one who thus carried his life in his hand would pen the opening words of the letter, where he excuses the tardiness of the Roman Church in writing to their Corinthian brethren by a reference to 'the sudden and repeated calamities and reverses' under which they had suffered (§ 1). Not a word is said about the nature of these calamities; not a word here or elsewhere about their authors. There is no indication that the fears of the Roman Christians had ceased. On the contrary, after referring to the victims of the Neronian persecution, it is said significantly, 'We are in the same lists, and the same struggle awaits us' (§ 7). The death of the tyrant may have brought a respite and a hope, but the future was still uncertain. At all events the letter can hardly have been penned before the two most illustrious members of the Church, the patron and patroness of the writer (if my hypothesis be correct), had paid the one by his death, the other by her banishment, the penalty of their adherence to the faith of Christ; for these seem to have been among the earliest victims of the emperor's wrath. Not long after the execution of Flavius Clemens and the banishment of Domitilla the tyrant was slain. The chief assassin is agreed on all hands to have been Stephanus, the steward of Domitilla[1]. Thus the household of this earliest of Christian princes must have contained within its walls strange diversities of character. No greater contrast can be conceived to the ferocity and passion of these bloody scenes which accompanied the death of Domitian, than the singular gentleness and forbearance which distinguishes this letter throughout. The fierceness of a Stephanus is the dark background which throws into relief the self-restraint of a Clement. In no respect is the ἐπιείκεια, to which beyond anything else it owes its lofty moral elevation[2], more conspicuous than in the attitude of these Roman Christians towards their secular rulers, whom at this time they had little cause to love. In the prayer for princes and governors, which appears in the liturgical ending, this sentiment finds its noblest expression: 'Guide our steps to walk in holiness and righteousness and singleness of heart, and to do such things as are good and well-pleasing in Thy sight, and in the sight of our rulers.' 'Give concord and peace to us and to all that dwell on the earth...that we may be saved, while we render obedience to Thine almighty and most excellent Name, and to our rulers and governors upon the earth. Thou, O Lord and Master, hast given them the power of sovereignty through Thine

[1] See above, p. 40.

[2] See above, p. 97.

excellent and unspeakable might, that we, knowing the glory and honour which Thou hast given them, may submit ourselves unto them, in nothing resisting Thy will. Grant unto them therefore, O Lord, health, peace, concord, stability, that they may administer the government which Thou hast given them without failure. For Thou, O heavenly Master, King of the ages, givest to the sons of men glory and honour and power over all things that are upon the earth. Do Thou, Lord, direct their counsel according to that which is good and well-pleasing in Thy sight, that, administering in peace and gentleness, with godliness, the power which Thou hast given them, they may obtain Thy favour' (§§ 60, 61). When we remember that this prayer issued from the fiery furnace of persecution after the recent experience of a cruel and capricious tyrant like Domitian, it will appear truly sublime—sublime in its utterances, and still more sublime in its silence. Who would have grudged the Church of Rome her primacy, if she had always spoken thus?

Christianity is adverse to political tyranny, as it is to all breaches of the law of love. But it was no purpose of the Gospel to crush the evil by violence and rebellion. Just in the same way, though slavery is abhorrent to its inherent principles, we nowhere find that it encourages any rising of slaves against their masters. On the contrary, it inculcates obedience as a service rendered not to human masters but to God Himself (Ephes. vi. 5 sq, Col. iv. 22 sq). Its business was not to overthrow social and political institutions directly; but it provided a solvent which in the one case, as in the other, did the work slowly but surely. A loyal submission to the sovereign powers is enforced in the strongest terms as a religious duty by the Apostles S. Paul and S. Peter, when the supreme earthly ruler was none other than the arch-tyrant Nero himself (Rom. xiii. 1 sq, 1 Pet. ii. 13 sq)—Nero, whose savagery was soon to cost them both their lives. So here again, the noble prayer for temporal sovereigns is heard from a scholar of the two Apostles at the second great crisis of the Church when the Christians are just emerging from the ruthless assaults of a 'second Nero,' more capricious but hardly less inhuman than the first.

It is impossible not to be struck with the resemblances in this passage to portions of the earliest known liturgies[1]. Not only is there a general

[1] A very convenient collection of these services is Hammond's *Liturgies Eastern and Western* Oxford 1878, and to this work I shall generally refer, thus saving my readers the trouble of turning to the large works of Assemani, Martene, Goar, Renaudot, Mabillon, Muratori, and others. The foundations of a more thorough and critical study of the liturgies (in their earlier and later forms) are laid in Swain-

coincidence in the objects of the several petitions, but it has also individual phrases, and in one instance a whole cluster of petitions[1], in common with one or other of these. Moreover, this litany in S. Clement's Epistle begins with the declaration, 'We will ask with fervency of prayer and supplication (ἐκτενῆ τὴν δέησιν καὶ ἱκεσίαν ποιούμενοι)'; and the expression reminds us that this very word, ἡ ἐκτενής, was the designation given to a corresponding portion in the Greek ritual, owing to its peculiar fervency[2]. We remember also that the name of S. Clement is especially connected with a liturgy incorporated in the closing books of the Apostolic Constitutions, and the circumstance may point to some true tradition of his handiwork in the ritual of the Church. Moreover, this liturgy in the Constitutions, together with the occasional services which accompany it, has so many phrases in common with the prayer in S. Clement's Epistle, that the resemblances cannot be accidental. But no stress can be laid on this last fact, seeing that the writers alike of the earlier and later books of the Apostolic Constitutions obviously had Clement's Epistle in their hands.

What then shall we say of this litany? Has S. Clement here introduced into his epistle a portion of a fixed form of words then in use in the Roman Church? Have the extant liturgies borrowed directly from this epistle, or do they owe this resemblance to some common type of liturgy, founded (as we may suppose) on the prayers of the Synagogue, and so anterior even to Clement's Epistle itself? The origin of the earliest extant liturgies is a question of high importance; and with the increased interest which the subject has aroused in England of late years, it may be hoped that a solution of the problems connected with it will be seriously undertaken; but no satisfactory result will be attained, unless it is approached in a thoroughly critical spirit and without the design of supporting foregone conclusions. Leaving this question to others for discussion, I can only state the inference which this prayer of S. Clement, considered in the light of probabilities, suggests to my own mind. There was at this time no authoritative

son's *Greek Liturgies*, Cambridge, 1884, an invaluable work for the history of the growth of the text. But only a beginning has thus been made; as the libraries of the East doubtless contain unsuspected treasures in this department of ecclesiastical literature.

[1] See the parallel from *Liturg. D. Marc.* p. 185 (Hammond; see also Swainson, p. 48) in the note on § 59 τοὺς ἐν θλίψει κ.τ.λ.

[2] See e.g. *Apost. Const.* vii. 6—10, where the deacon invites the congregation again and again to pray ἐκτενῶς, ἔτι ἐκτενῶς, ἔτι ἐκτενέστερον; but it is common in the liturgies generally.

written liturgy in use in the Church of Rome, but the prayers were modified at the discretion of the officiating minister. Under the dictation of habit and experience however these prayers were gradually assuming a fixed form. A more or less definite order in the petitions, a greater or less constancy in the individual expressions, was already perceptible. As the chief pastor of the Roman Church would be the main instrument in thus moulding the liturgy, the prayers, without actually being written down, would assume in his mind a fixity as time went on. When therefore at the close of his epistle he asks his readers to fall on their knees and lay down their jealousies and disputes at the footstool of grace, his language naturally runs into those antithetical forms and measured cadences which his ministrations in the Church had rendered habitual with him when dealing with such a subject. This explanation seems to suit the facts. The prayer is not given as a quotation from an acknowledged document, but as an immediate outpouring of the heart; and yet it has all the appearance of a fixed form. This solution accords moreover with the notices which we find elsewhere respecting the liturgy of the early Church, which seem to point to forms of prayer more or less fluctuating, even at a later date than this[1].

Nor is it alone in the concluding prayer that the liturgical character of Clement's language asserts itself. The litany at the close is only the climax of the epistle, which may be regarded as one long psalm of praise and thanksgiving on the glories of nature and of grace. Before the discovery of the lost ending, discerning critics had pointed out the resemblances of language and of thought to the early liturgies even in

[1] Justin *Apol.* i. 67 (p. 98) *καὶ ὁ προεστὼς εὐχὰς ὁμοίως καὶ εὐχαριστίας, ὅση δύναμις αὐτῷ, ἀναπέμπει.* We cannot indeed be certain from the expression *ὅση δύναμις* itself that Justin is referring to unwritten forms of prayer, for it might express merely the fervency and strength of enunciation; though in the passage quoted by Bingham (*Christ. Ant.* xiii. 5. 5) from Greg. Naz. *Orat.* iv. § 12 (I. p. 83) *φέρε, ὅση δύναμις, ἀγνισάμενοι καὶ σώματα καὶ ψυχὰς καὶ μίαν ἀναλαβόντες φωνὴν κ.τ.λ.*, the *ὅση δύναμις* has a much wider reference than to the actual singing of the Song of Moses, as he takes it. But in connexion with its context here, it certainly suggests that the language and thoughts of the prayers were dependent on the person himself; as e.g. in *Apol.* i. 55 (p. 90) *διὰ λόγου καὶ σχήματος τοῦ φαινομένου, ὅση δύναμις, προτρεψάμενοι ὑμᾶς κ.τ.λ.* (comp. i. 13, p. 60). This is forty or fifty years after the date of Clement's letter. In illustration of *ὅση δύναμις* Otto refers to Tertullian's phrase (*Apol.* 39), 'Ut quisque...*de proprio ingenio* potest, provocatur in medium Deo canere,' quoting it however incorrectly. The force of *ὅση δύναμις* may be estimated from its occurrences in Orig. *c. Cels.* v. 1, 51, 53, 58, viii. 35.

the then extant portions of the epistle[1]. At an early stage, before he enters upon the main subject of the letter—the feuds in the Corinthian Church—the writer places himself and his readers in an attitude of prayer, as the fittest appeal to their hearts and consciences. He invites his correspondents (§ 29) to 'approach God in holiness of soul, raising pure and undefiled hands to Him.' He reminds them that they are an elect and holy people. As the special inheritance of a Holy One (§ 30 *Ἁγίου οὖν μερὶς ὑπάρχοντες*), they are bound to do the things pertaining to holiness (*ποιήσωμεν τὰ τοῦ ἁγιασμοῦ*). This mode of expression is essentially liturgical[2]. Again, they are bidden to attach themselves to the blessing of God (§ 31 *κολληθῶμεν τῇ εὐλογίᾳ αὐτοῦ*) and to recognize the magnificence of the gifts given by Him (§ 32 *μεγαλεῖα τῶν ὑπ' αὐτοῦ δεδομένων δωρεῶν*). The greatness of God's gifts reminds him of their proper counterpart—our ministrations due to Him by the law of reciprocity. These were rendered under the Old Covenant by the levitical hierarchy; they culminate under the New in Jesus Christ (§ 32). We must be prompt to render with fervency (*ἐκτενείας*) and zeal every good service. We are made in God's own likeness, and are consequently the heirs of His blessing (§ 33). Our ministrations on earth are the copy and counterpart of the angelic ministrations in heaven. Only the eye and ear of faith are needed (§ 34 *κατανοήσωμεν τὸ πᾶν πλῆθος τῶν ἀγγέλων αὐτοῦ*) to recall the sight and sound of these celestial choirs—the ten thousand times ten thousands of angels crying 'thrice holy' to the Lord of hosts—'all creation is full of His glory.' Here again we are brought face to face with a leading feature of ancient liturgical service, the 'ter sanctus' as the ideal of our human ministrations[3]. Whether the peculiar combination of Dan. vii. 10 with

[1] See especially Probst *Liturgie der drei ersten Jahrhunderte* p. 41 sq, the section on *Der Brief des Clemens u. die Liturgie überhaupt.*

[2] See *Lit. D. Jacob.* p. 322 (Swainson) *φύλαξον ἡμᾶς, ἀγαθέ, ἐν ἁγιασμῷ, ἵνα ἄξιοι γενόμενοι τοῦ παναγίου σου πνεύματος εὕρωμεν μερίδα καὶ κληρονομίαν μετὰ πάντων τῶν ἁγίων κ.τ.λ.*, slightly different in its later forms.

[3] The first direct reference to this hymn of the heavenly hosts, as forming part of the eucharistic service, appears in Cyril. Hieros. *Catech. Mystag.* v. 5 (p. 327) *μετὰ ταῦτα μνημονεύομεν οὐρανοῦ καὶ γῆς καὶ θαλάσσης, ἡλίου καὶ σελήνης, ἄστρων, καὶ πάσης τῆς κτίσεως λογικῆς τε καὶ ἀλόγου, ὁρατῆς τε καὶ ἀοράτου· ἀγγέλων, ἀρχαγγέλων, δυνάμεων, κυριοτήτων, ἀρχῶν, ἐξουσιῶν, θρόνων, τῶν χερουβὶμ τῶν πολυπροσώπων· δυνάμει λέγοντες τὸ τοῦ Δαυίδ, Μεγαλύνατε τὸν Κύριον σὺν ἐμοί· μνημονεύομεν δὲ τῶν σεραφίμ, ἃ ἐν πνεύματι ἁγίῳ ἐθεάσατο Ἡσαΐας παρεστηκότα κύκλῳ τοῦ θρόνου τοῦ Θεοῦ, καὶ ταῖς μὲν δυσὶ πτέρυξι κατακαλύπτοντα τὸ πρόσωπον ταῖς δὲ δυσὶ τοὺς πόδας καὶ ταῖς δυσὶ πετόμενα, καὶ λεγόμενα* ἅγιος, ἅγιος, ἅγιος κύριος σαβαώθ· *διὰ τοῦτο γὰρ τὴν παραδοθεῖσαν ἡμῖν θεολογίαν ταύτην λέγομεν, ὅπως κοινωνοὶ τῆς ὑμνῳδίας ταῖς ὑπερκοσμίοις γενώμεθα στρατιαῖς.* Thus

Is. vi. 3 in describing the praises of the heavenly hosts was borrowed directly from a liturgical form familiar to Clement, I need not stop to enquire, though this seems not improbable[1]. After thus ushering us

we can trace it back distinctly to the first part of the fourth century; but there is every reason to believe that this was one of the primitive elements in the liturgical service, dating from the time when this service took a definite shape. It appears in the earliest extant forms of the Liturgy of S. James, i.e. of Palestine and Syria (Swainson p. 268 sq), as Cyril's account would lead us to expect, and of the Liturgy of S. Mark, i.e. of Alexandria (Swainson p. 48 sq). It is found likewise in the Clementine Liturgy of the *Apost. Const.* viii. 12 § 13, which is probably based on the oldest usage known in the middle of the third century, even though itself probably the compilation of a private individual, rather than the authoritative document of a church. It has a place not only in the Syriac Liturgy of S. James (Hammond p. 69) as might have been anticipated, but also in the Nestorian Liturgies of Eastern Syria and Persia, e.g. that of SS. Adæus and Maris (Hammond p. 273). I need scarcely add that it is not wanting in the Roman and Western Liturgies (Hammond p. 324). If therefore there be any first or second century nucleus in the existing liturgies, we may reasonably infer that this triumphal hymn formed part of this nucleus.

[1] The kernel of this hymn is the 'ter sanctus,' as sung by the seraphs in Isaiah vi. 3 ἅγιος, ἅγιος, ἅγιος Κύριος Σαβαώθ, but the words are introduced by various descriptions of the angelic hosts and followed up by various supplements.

(1) As regards the introductory preface, the passage in Cyril of Jerusalem already quoted furnishes a common normal type. It agrees substantially with the Liturgy of S. James and with the Clementine Liturgy (*Apost. Const.* viii. 12). But this is already a considerably developed form. A simpler and very obvious preface would be the adoption of the words from Dan. vii. 10 'Thousands of thousands stood by Him, and myriads of myriads ministered unto Him.' From the passage of the genuine Clement (§ 34), with which we are directly concerned, we may infer that, when the liturgical service was taking shape under his hands, this form of preface prevailed; for he combines Dan. vii. 10 with Is. vi. 3 under one quotation λέγει ἡ γραφή. There are some traces of the survival of this preface in the Liturgy of S. Mark p. 185 (Hammond), σοὶ παραστήκουσι χίλιαι χιλιάδες καὶ μύριαι μυριάδες ἁγίων ἀγγέλων καὶ ἀρχαγγέλων στρατιαί (comp. Swainson p. 48 sq), where it retains its proper place; and in the Liturgy of S. James p. 47 (Hammond) ᾧ παρεστήκασι χίλιαι χιλιάδες καὶ μύριαι μυριάδες ἁγίων ἀγγέλων καὶ ἀρχαγγέλων στρατιαί (comp. Swainson p. 304 sq), where it preserves the same form but occupies a place in the Preface to the Lord's Prayer. This latter is probably a displacement; for in the Syriac Liturgy of Adæus and Maris (p. 273 Hammond) it still occupies what was presumably its primitive place. See also the Coptic and Æthiopic Liturgies pp. 218, 221, 257 (Hammond). In *Apost. Const.* viii. 12 a *reminiscence* of Dan. vii. 10 (ἅμα χιλίαις χιλιάσιν ἀρχαγγέλων καὶ μυρίαις μυριάσιν ἀγγέλων) forms part of the preface to the 'ter sanctus' of Is. vi. 3.

(2) As regards the conclusion, it should be observed that the quotation of Clement preserves the original expression of Isaiah πλήρης πᾶσα ἡ γῆ τῆς δόξης αὐτοῦ (substituting however κτίσις for γῆ), whereas in *all* liturgies without exception (so far as I have noticed) it runs 'heaven and earth are full (πλήρης ὁ οὐρανὸς καὶ ἡ γῆ)

into the immediate presence-chamber of the Almighty, he follows up this eucharistic reference by a direct practical precept bearing on congregational worship; 'Let us then'—not less than the angels—'gathered together (συναχθέντες) in concord with a lively conscience (ἐν συνειδήσει) cry unto Him fervently (ἐκτενῶς) as with one mouth, that we may be found partakers of His great and glorious promises,' where almost every individual expression recalls the liturgical forms—the σύναξις as the recognized designation of the congregation gathered together for this purpose, the συνείδησις which plays so prominent a part in the attitude of the worshipper[1], the ἐκτενῶς which describes the intensity of the prayers offered. Then again; after this direct precept follows another liturgical reference, hardly less characteristic than the former; 'Eye hath not seen nor ear heard.' What may be the original source of this quotation, either as given by S. Paul (1 Cor. ii. 9) or by S. Clement here (§ 34) or in the so-called Second Epistle which bears Clement's name (ii. § 11), we have no definite information; but that (in

etc.,' and sometimes with other amplifications. A favorite addition is the 'Ωσαννὰ ἐν τοῖς ὑψίστοις κ.τ.λ. (from Matt. xxi. 9).

Thus the reference in Clement seems in both respects to exhibit an incipient form of the liturgical use of the 'ter sanctus' of Isaiah.

The caution should be added that the word 'trisagion,' as technically used, does not refer to the 'thrice holy' of Isaiah, which is called 'the triumphal hymn' (ὕμνος ἐπινίκιος), but to another form of words (ἅγιος ὁ Θεός, ἅγιος ἰσχυρός, ἅγιος ἀθάνατος, κ.τ.λ.) which is known to have been introduced into the liturgy later. The eucharistic hymns which have a place in the liturgies are distinguished in Hammond's glossary, p. 380 sq. For this reason, though the term 'trisagion' would be most appropriate in itself and indeed occurs in the liturgies themselves, when referring to the seraphs' hymn of Isaiah (e.g. *Lit. D. Marc.* p. 185 Hammond, τὸν ἐπινίκιον καὶ τρισάγιον ὕμνον; comp. Swainson p. 48 sq), yet owing to its ambiguity it is better avoided, and I have used the Latin term 'ter sanctus' instead, as free from any objection. Probst constantly calls it 'trisagion.'

[1] For the place which 'conscience' plays in the liturgical services, comp. Probst l. c. p. 42 sq. On the necessity of a pure conscience in the orientation of the soul for effective prayer and praise see Clem. Alex. *Strom.* vi. 14 (p. 797 Potter). The phrases καθαρὰ καρδία, καθαρὸν συνειδός, καθαρὰ (or ἀγαθὴ) συνείδησις, and the like, are frequent in the liturgies. See also especially the passage in Iren. *Haer.* iv. 4 'non sacrificia sanctificant hominem, non enim indiget sacrificio Deus; sed conscientia eius qui offert sanctificat sacrificium, pura existens' with the whole context, where this father speaks of the oblations of the Church and uses illustrations—more especially the contrast of the offerings of Cain and Abel —which recall the liturgical spirit of the Roman Clement. For Clement himself see esp. § 41 εὐχαριστείτω Θεῷ ἐν ἀγαθῇ συνειδήσει ὑπάρχων, μὴ παρεκβαίνων τὸν ὡρισμένον τῆς λειτουργίας αὐτοῦ κανόνα, and § 45 τῶν ἐν καθαρᾷ συνειδήσει λατρευόντων, compared with Ign. *Trall.* 7 ὁ χωρὶς ἐπισκόπου καὶ πρεσβυτερίου καὶ διακόνων πράσσων τι οὗτος οὐ καθαρός ἐστιν τῇ συνειδήσει, in all which passages it has a reference to the services of the Church.

some form or other) it found a place in early liturgical services the available evidence seems to show[1].

[1] Over-sanguine liturgiologists have given a ready explanation of the quotation in S. Paul, 1 Cor. ii. 9 καθὼς γέγραπται, Ἃ ὀφθαλμὸς οὐκ εἶδεν καὶ οὖς οὐκ ἤκουσεν καὶ ἐπὶ καρδίαν ἀνθρώπου οὐκ ἀνέβη ὅσα ἡτοίμασεν ὁ Θεὸς τοῖς ἀγαπῶσιν αὐτόν. They have supposed the Apostle to be quoting from some liturgical form with which he was acquainted, and hence they have inferred the very early origin of the liturgies, at least in their nucleus—a too hasty inference not warranted by the facts of the case. This view, which is eagerly maintained by Neale (*Essays on Liturgiology* p. 414 sq), is properly repudiated by Hammond *Liturgies Eastern and Western* p. x, note). In my note on § 34, where Clement quotes the same words with modifications, I have stated the probability that the passage is not a strict quotation, but a loose reference giving the substance of Is. lxiv. 4 combined with Is. lxv. 16, 17. At all events neither Origen nor Jerome was aware that S. Paul derived it from any liturgical source; for the former ascribes it to the apocryphal *Apocalypse of Isaiah*, and the latter explains the reference from the Canonical Isaiah, as I have done.

The fact however remains that the same quotation is found in some liturgies and that Clement's context encourages us to trace a liturgical connexion. What then shall we say? Textual criticism will help us to give a right answer, or at least warn us against giving a wrong answer, because it is the first which suggests itself. The quotation occurs in two forms; (1) The *Pauline*, of which the characteristic feature is τοῖς ἀγαπῶσιν αὐτόν, 1 Cor. ii. 9: (2) The *Clementine*, which on the contrary has τοῖς ὑπομένουσιν αὐτόν, suggested by Is. lxiv. 4. This is the form also which evidently underlies the same quotation in *Martyr. Polyc.* 2, as appears from the context τὰ τηρούμενα τοῖς ὑπομείνασιν ἀγαθά. But the writer of this account of Polycarp's death was certainly acquainted with and borrowed elsewhere from Clement's Epistle (see above, p. 153). Though two of our extant authorities for Clement's text (CS) conspire in substituting τοῖς ἀγαπῶσιν in Clement's text, the oldest and best of all is unquestionably right in reading τοῖς ὑπομένουσιν, as the context of Clement plainly shows (see the note on the passage).

Among the extant Greek liturgies which have any pretentions to be considered early, it occurs, so far as I have observed, twice; (*a*) In the Greek Liturgy of S. James (Hammond, p. 42), where it is part of the Great Oblation, τὰ ἐπουράνια καὶ αἰώνιά σου δωρήματα ἃ ὀφθαλμὸς κ.τ.λ., but it is wanting in the corresponding Syriac form (Hammond, p. 70) and would seem therefore to be a later addition; (*b*) In the Liturgy of S. Mark (Hammond, p. 183) τὰ τῶν ἐπαγγελιῶν σου ἀγαθὰ ἃ ὀφθαλμὸς κ.τ.λ., where it appears in a different place, in the Diptychs for the Dead. In both these passages it has the Pauline τοῖς ἀγαπῶσιν, not the Clementine τοῖς ὑπομένουσιν. The obvious inference is that the liturgical quotation was derived directly from S. Paul, and not conversely. This is also the case apparently with all the quotations of the passage from the close of the second century onward (e.g. Clem. Alex. *Protr.* 10, p. 76; Pseudoclem. *de Virg.* i. 9). See the references gathered together in Resch's *Agrapha* pp. 102, 281 (Gebhardt u. Harnack's *Texte u. Untersuchungen* v. Hft. 4, 1889).

Still the phenomenon in S. Clement suggests that in one form or other it had a place in early liturgical services, for indeed its liturgical appropriateness would suggest its introduction: and, considering its connexion as quoted by Clement here,

After this liturgical climax, the writer not unnaturally speaks of the marvellous *gifts* of God, more especially His moral and spiritual gifts—life in immortality, splendour in righteousness, and the like (§ 35). Their magnitude and beauty are beyond all human language. Of these proffered bounties (τῶν ἐπηγγελμένων δωρεῶν) we must strain every nerve to partake. Accordingly we approach God with the sacrifice of praise (θυσία αἰνέσεως). This is the *way*, of which the Psalmist speaks l(xlix). 23—the way of salvation. Along this way we proceed, under the guidance of our great High-priest who presents our offerings (§ 36). Thus all human life, as truly conceived, and as interpreted by the Church of Christ, is a great eucharistic service. It is not difficult to see how this one idea pervades all Clement's thoughts. Indeed the proper understanding of the structure of the epistle is lost, if this key be mislaid. Our true relation to God is a constant interchange—God's magnificent gifts realized by us, our reciprocal offerings, however unworthy, presented to and accepted by Him. The eucharistic celebration of the Church is the outward embodiment and expression of this all-pervading lesson. The eucharistic elements, the bread and wine—and, still more comprehensively, the tithes and first fruits and other offerings in kind, which in the early Church had a definite place amidst the eucharistic offerings—are only a part of the great sacramental system. All things spiritual and material, all things above and below, the kingdom of nature and the kingdom of grace, fall within its scope. Heaven and earth alike are full of God's glory; and shall they not be full of human thanksgiving also? This idea underlies the earliest liturgical forms; it underlies, or rather it absorbs, Clement's conception. There is no narrow ritual and no cramping dogma here. The conception is wide and comprehensive, as earth and sea and sky are wide and comprehensive. It inspires, explains, justifies, vivifies, the sacramental principle.

it is probable that he himself so used it. But on the other hand I see no reason on second thoughts to abandon the explanation of the origin of the quotation in S. Paul, as given in my notes (§ 34), viz. that it was intended by the Apostle as a reference to Isaiah (the words ὅσα ἡτοίμασεν ὁ Θεὸς τοῖς ἀγαπῶσιν αὐτὸν being his own comment or paraphrase) and that S. Clement mixed up the Apostolic quotation with the prophet's own words, substituting τοῖς ὑπομένουσιν for τοῖς ἀγαπῶσιν and thus returning more closely to the original. With our existing data, until some fresh discovery throws more light on the difficulty, we may accept this explanation provisionally. I do not see any force in the arguments by which Resch (whose volume appeared after my note on § 34 was written) strives to show (p. 154 sq) that S. Paul quoted a saying of Christ from some written evangelical document.

In this way Clement prepares the minds of his hearers for the lessons and rebukes which follow (§ 37). The ordination service was apparently closely connected with the eucharistic service in the early Church[1]. The ordained ministers were set apart especially to present the offerings of the people. Church order—which is the counterpart to the natural order, to the political order—requires that this special work shall be duly performed (§ 37 sq). The presbyters at Corinth had fulfilled their appointed task faithfully. They had been blameless in their ministrations. Not once nor twice only (§ 44) is this *blamelessness* of conduct, which doubtless had formed part of their ordination charge[2], emphasized by Clement (λειτουργήσαντας ἀμέμπτως, τοὺς ἀμέμπτως καὶ ὁσίως προσενεγκόντας τὰ δῶρα τῆς ἐπισκοπῆς, τῆς ἀμέμπτως αὐτοῖς τετιμημένης λειτουργίας). The deposition of these faithful ministers therefore was a shocking irregularity. It was a violation of the eternal order: it was a blow struck at the root of first principles; it was a confusion of all things human and divine.

This analysis will show that the liturgical close of the epistle is the proper sequel to what precedes. The whole letter is a great eucharistic psalm which gathers about its main practical aim—the restoration of order at Corinth.

Moreover the true apprehension of this idea has an important bearing on the attacks made on the integrity of the epistle. The portions hastily condemned as 'sacerdotal' or 'hierarchical' by otherwise intelligent and note-worthy critics are found to be not only no late irrelevant and incongruous interpolations, but belong to the very essence and kernel of the original writing. To excise these by the critical scalpel is to tear out its heart and drain its very life-blood.

The earliest services of the Christian Church, so far as they were grafted on the worship of the Jews, would be indebted to the Synagogue rather than to the Temple. Recent archæological discoveries, more

[1] See Probst *Sakramente u. Sakramentalien* p. 398 sq. So *Clem. Recogn.* xvi. 15 'et eucharistiam frangens cum eis, Maronem...constituit eis episcopum et duodecim cum eo presbyteros, simulque diaconos ordinat' (comp. *Clem. Hom.* xi. 36).

[2] The word in S. Paul (1 Tim. iii. 2; comp. v. 7, vi. 14) describing this qualification of the ministry is the synonyme ἀνεπίληπτος, and this word is emphasized in the Pionian *Life of Polycarp* 23, which throws some light on the consecration of a bishop in early times. For ἄμεμπτος see *Apost. Const.* viii. 4 ἐν πᾶσιν ἄμεμπτον, 5 ἀμέμπτως λειτουργοῦντα, ἀμέμπτως ἀνεγκλήτως προσφέροντα, 17 λειτουργήσαντα τὴν ἐγχειρισθεῖσαν αὐτῷ διακονίαν ἀτρέπτως ἀμέμπτως ἀνεγκλήτως μείζονος ἀξιωθῆναι βαθμοῦ, of qualifications for the ministry; comp. ii. 26.

especially in Galilee and in Eastern Palestine, have enlarged our ideas on this subject. The number, the capacity, and even (in some cases) the magnificence of the synagogues are attested by their ruins[1]. What we find at such Jewish centres as Capernaum would certainly not be wanting in the mighty cities of the world like Alexandria and Rome. The ritual would bear some proportion to the buildings; and thus the early Christian congregations would find in their Jewish surroundings ample precedent for any ritual developement which for some generations they could desire or compass. Again as regards the substance of public worship, they would naturally build upon the lines traced by their Jewish predecessors[2]. The common prayer, the lessons from the Law, the lessons from the Prophets, the chanting of the Psalms or of hymns, the exposition or homily, all were there ready for adoption. The eucharistic celebration—the commemoration of and participation in the Lord's Passion—was the new and vivifying principle, the centre round which these adopted elements ranged themselves, being modified as the circumstances suggested. The earliest account of the Christian eucharist, as given by Justin Martyr, shows that this is no merely conjectural view of the genesis of the Christian celebration[3].

The investigation of the prayers of the Synagogue, which I have suggested above, as in part a source of Clement's language, would be impossible without a special knowledge which I cannot command. I must therefore leave it to others. I would only offer the following, as a slight contribution to the subject.

Among the prayers which are acknowledged to be the most ancient is the form called either absolutely *Tephillah* 'The Prayer' (תפלה) or (from the number of the benedictions) *Shemoneh Esreh* 'The Eighteen' (שמונה עשרה). They are traditionally ascribed by the Jews to the Great Synagogue; but this tradition is of course valueless, except as implying a relative antiquity. They are mentioned in the Mishna *Berachoth* iv. 3, where certain precepts respecting them are ascribed to Rabban Gamaliel, Rabbi Joshua, and Rabbi Akiba; while from another passage, *Rosh-ha-Shanah* iv. 5, it appears that they then existed in substantially the same form as at present. Thus their high

[1] For an excellent and succinct account of the synagogue—the buildings and the worship—see Schürer *Geschichte des Jüdischen Volkes* II. p. 369 sq (ed. 2, 1886).

[2] See the Abbé L. Duchesne's *Origines du Culte Chrétien* p. 45 sq (1889). His plan does not permit him to do more than give a very brief sketch of the transition from the Synagogue to the Church; but his caution and moderation contrast favourably with the reckless assumptions of some writers on liturgiology.

[3] *Apol.* i. 65—67 (p. 97—99).

antiquity seems certain; so that the older parts (for they have grown by accretion) were probably in existence in the age of our Lord and the Apostles, and indeed some competent critics have assigned to them a much earlier date than this. Of these eighteen benedictions the first three and the last three are by common consent allowed to be the oldest. On the date and prevalence of the *Shemoneh Esreh*, see Zunz *Gottesdienstliche Vorträge* p. 366 sq, Herzfeld *Geschichte des Volkes Jisrael* II. p. 200 sq, Ginsburg in Kitto's *Cyclop. of Bibl. Lit.* (ed. Alexander) s. v. *Synagogue*, Schürer *Geschichte des Jüdischen Volkes* II. pp. 377 sq, 384 sq (ed. 2, 1886).

I have selected for comparison the first two and the last two; and they are here written out in full with the parallel passages from Clement opposite to them, so as to convey an adequate idea of the amount of resemblance. The third is too short to afford any material for comparison; while the sixteenth, referring to the temple-service, is too purely Jewish, and indeed appears to have been interpolated after the destruction of the second temple. The parallels which are taken from other parts of S. Clement's Epistle are put in brackets.

1. Blessed art Thou, O Lord our God, and the God of our fathers, the God of Abraham, the God of Isaac, and the God of Jacob, the God great and powerful and terrible, God Most High, who bestowest Thy benefits graciously, the Possessor of the Universe, who rememberest the good deeds of the fathers and sendest a redeemer unto their sons' sons for Thy Name's Sake in love. Our King, our Helper and Saviour and Shield, blessed art Thou, O Lord, the Shield of Abraham.	[ὁ πατὴρ ἡμῶν Ἀβραὰμ § 31.] θαυμαστὸς ἐν ἰσχύϊ καὶ μεγαλοπρεπείᾳ § 60. τὸν μόνον ὕψιστον § 59. μόνον εὐεργέτην κ.τ.λ. *ib.* [ὁ οἰκτίρμων κατὰ πάντα καὶ εὐεργετικὸς πατὴρ § 23]. σύ, Κύριε, τὴν οἰκουμένην ἔκτισας § 60. [δεσπότης τῶν ἁπάντων §§ 8, 20, 33, 52]. καθὼς ἔδωκας τοῖς πατράσιν ἡμῶν, ἐπικαλουμένων σε αὐτῶν ὁσίως κ.τ.λ. § 60. [καθὼς καὶ οἱ προδεδηλωμένοι πατέρες ἡμῶν εὐηρέστησαν § 62]. βασιλεῦ τῶν αἰώνων § 61. ἀξιοῦμέν σε, δέσποτα, βοηθὸν γενέσθαι καὶ ἀντιλήπτορα[1] ἡμῶν § 59.
2. Thou art mighty for ever, O Lord; Thou bringest the dead to life, Thou art mighty to save. Thou sustainest the living by Thy mercy, Thou bringest the dead to	ὁ μόνος δυνατὸς ποιῆσαι ταῦτα § 61. τὸν τῶν ἀπηλπισμένων σωτῆρα § 59. ὁ ἀγαθὸς...ἐλεῆμον καὶ οἰκτίρμον § 60.

[1] The word מגן 'shield' is translated by ἀντιλήπτωρ in the LXX of Ps. cxix (cxviii). 114, from which Clement here borrows his expression.

life by Thy great compassion, Thou supportest them that fall, and healest the sick, and loosest them that are in bonds, and makest	τοὺς πεπτωκότας ἔγειρον...τοὺς ἀσεβεῖς (ἀσθενεῖς) ἴασαι...λύτρωσαι τοὺς δεσμίους ἡμῶν, ἐξανάστησον τοὺς ἀσθενοῦντας § 59.
good Thy faithfulness to them that sleep in the dust. Who is like	πιστὸς ἐν τοῖς πεποιθόσιν ἐπὶ σέ § 60
unto Thee, O Lord of might? and who can be compared unto	τοῦ...ἀνεκδιηγήτου κράτους σου § 61.
Thee, O King, who killest and makest alive, and causest salvation to shoot forth? And Thou art faithful to bring the dead to life. Blessed art Thou, O Lord, who bringest the dead to life.	τὸν ἀποκτείνοντα καὶ ζῆν ποιοῦντα § 59.
17. We confess unto Thee	σοὶ ἐξομολογούμεθα § 61.
that Thou art He, the Lord our God and the God of our fathers	ὅτι σὺ εἶ ὁ Θεὸς μόνος § 59.
for ever and ever, the Rock of our life, the Shield of our salvation,	εἰς τὸ σκεπασθῆναι τῇ χειρί σου κ.τ.λ. § 60.
Thou art He from generation to generation. We will thank Thee and declare Thy praise. Blessed	ὁ πιστὸς ἐν πάσαις ταῖς γενεαῖς § 60.
art Thou, O Lord; Goodness is Thy Name, and to Thee it is meet to give thanks.	τῷ παναρέτῳ ὀνόματί σου § 60.
18. Grant peace, goodness and blessing, grace and mercy and	δός, Κύριε, ὑγίειαν, εἰρήνην, ὁμόνοιαν, εὐστάθειαν § 61.
compassion, unto us and to all Thy people Israel.	δὸς ὁμόνοιαν καὶ εἰρήνην ἡμῖν τε καὶ πᾶσιν τοῖς κατοικοῦσιν κ.τ.λ. § 60.
Bless us, O our Father, all together with the light of Thy countenance.	ἐπίφανον τὸ πρόσωπόν σου ἐφ' ἡμᾶς εἰς ἀγαθὰ ἐν εἰρήνῃ § 60.
Thou hast given unto us, O Lord our God, the law of life, and loving-kindness and righteousness and blessing and compassion and life	[δῴη πίστιν, φόβον, εἰρήνην, ὑπομόνην, μακροθυμίαν, ἐγκράτειαν, ἁγνείαν καὶ σωφροσύνην § 64].
and peace. And may it seem good in Thy sight to bless Thy people	καλὸν καὶ εὐάρεστον ἐνώπιόν σου § 61.
Israel at all times and at every	ἡμεῖς λαός σου § 59.
moment with Thy peace. Blessed art Thou, O Lord, who blessest Thy people Israel with peace.	[ὁ ἐκλεξάμενος...ἡμᾶς...εἰς λαὸν περιούσιον § 58].

These parallels are, I think, highly suggestive, and some others might be gathered from other parts of the *Shemoneh Esreh*. The resemblance however is perhaps greater in the general tenour of the thoughts and cast of the sentences than in the individual expressions. At the same time it is instructive to observe what topics are rejected as too purely Jewish, and what others are introduced to give expression to Christian ideas.

One point we must not overlook. The resemblances between this liturgical portion and the rest of the letter, as already shown (p. 386 sq), are so strong that we cannot divorce this portion from Clement's handiwork. To what extent his language in the rest of the epistle was influenced by the prayers with which he was familiar, and to what extent he himself infused his own modes of expression into liturgical forms which he adapted from Jewish sources, it is vain to speculate.

7. *The doctrine.*

It is not my intention to discuss at length the theological opinions, or to put together the doctrinal system, of Clement of Rome from the notices in this epistle. Before doing so we should be obliged to enquire whether it is worth our while to pursue that which must necessarily elude our search. Christianity was not a philosophy with Clement; it consisted of truths which should inspire the conscience and mould the life: but we are not led by his language and sentiments to believe that he put these truths in their relations to one another, and viewed them as a connected whole. In short there is no *dogmatic system* in Clement.

This, which might be regarded from one point of view as a defect in our epistle, really constitutes its highest value. Irenæus[1] singles out Clement's letter as transmitting in its fulness the Christianity taught by the Apostles, more especially by S. Peter and S. Paul. It exhibits the belief of his church as to the true interpretation of the Apostolic records. It draws with no faltering hand the main lines of the faith, as contrasted with the aberrations of heretical, and more especially dualistic, theologies. The character of all the heretical systems was their one-sidedness. They severed the continuity of God's dispensation by divorcing the Old Testament from the New. They saw one aspect of the manifold Gospel to the exclusion of others. They grasped the teaching—or a part of the teaching—of one single Apostle, and neglected the rest. It was the special privilege of the early Roman

[1] *Haer.* iii. 3. 3, quoted above, p. 156.

Church that it had felt the personal influence of both the leading Apostles S. Paul and S. Peter—who approached Christianity from opposite sides—the Apostle of the Gentiles and the Apostle of the Circumcision (Gal. ii. 7). Comprehensiveness therefore was its heritage, and for some three centuries or more it preserved this heritage comparatively intact. Comprehensiveness was especially impersonated in Clement, its earliest and chief representative.

Of this comprehensiveness I have already spoken (p. 95 sq), and it is hardly necessary to add anything here. A writer in the early days of Christianity is best judged doctrinally by the Apostolic books which he reads and absorbs. No one satisfies this test so well as Clement. A writer who shows that he is imbued with the Epistles to the Romans, Corinthians, and Ephesians, not to mention several minor letters of S. Paul, with the First Epistle of S. Peter and the Epistle of S. James, and (along with these) the Epistle to the Hebrews, cannot well have forgotten anything which was essential to the completeness of the Gospel. Attention has been called above (p. 96) more especially to his co-ordination of S. Paul and S. James. Yet from a strictly dogmatical point of view this co-ordination is his weakness. Though he emphasizes faith with fond reiteration, he does not realize its doctrinal significance according to the teaching of S. Paul, as the primary condition of acceptance with God, the mainspring of the Christian life. Thus for instance we cannot imagine S. Paul placing together 'faith and hospitality,' as Clement does twice (§§ 9, 10, διὰ πίστιν καὶ φιλοξενίαν). 'Hospitality' was a virtue of the highest order, when roads were insecure and inns were few[1]. The members of the Christian brotherhood more especially stood in need of it, for they were in a very literal sense 'strangers' and 'sojourners' in the world. A place like Corinth too, which stood on the great way of transit between the East and the West, would be the most suitable scene for its exercise. But high as it stood as a Christian virtue, it would not have been thus placed by the Apostle side by side with 'faith' as a ground of favour with God. To co-ordinate 'faith' and 'hospitality' is to co-ordinate the root of the plant with one of the flowers. Nor again can we suppose that S. Paul could or would have written such a sentence as § 30 ἔργοις δικαιούμενοι καὶ μὴ λόγοις. Good words are demanded of the Christian as well as good works. But neither the one nor the other 'justifies' in S. Paul's sense of justification. Yet we may well forgive Clement's imperfect appreciation of S. Paul's teaching of 'faith' and 'justification,' seeing

[1] We read that Melito wrote a treatise on φιλοξενία (Euseb. *H. E.* iv. 26).

that it has been so commonly misunderstood and limited in later ages, though in a different way, by those who cling to it most tenaciously. On the other hand there are passages in Clement such as § 22 *ταῦτα πάντα βεβαιοῖ ἡ ἐν Χριστῷ πίστις* with its context, or again § 31 *δικαιοσύνην καὶ ἀλήθειαν διὰ πίστεως ποιήσας*, which show that practically he has caught the spirit of the Pauline teaching, whatever may be the defect in the dogmatic statement.

Again; we are led to ask, what is the opinion of this writer respecting the doctrines of the Atonement and the Mediation of Christ? Here we have a ready answer. Without going into detail we may say that one who is so thoroughly imbued with the language and sentiments of the Epistle to the Hebrews cannot have been blind to the Apostolic teaching on these points. Accordingly he speaks of Jesus Christ not once nor twice only as our High-Priest, and in some passages with other additions which testify to the completeness of his conceptions on this point (§ 36 *τὸν ἀρχιερέα τῶν προσφορῶν ἡμῶν, τὸν προστάτην καὶ βοηθὸν τῆς ἀσθενείας ἡμῶν*, § 61 *τοῦ ἀρχιερέως καὶ προστάτου τῶν ψυχῶν ἡμῶν*, § 64 *τοῦ ἀρχιερέως καὶ προστάτου ἡμῶν*), where the word *προστάτης* 'patron' or 'guardian' is his own supplement to the image borrowed from the Epistle to the Hebrews and serves to enforce the idea more strongly. So the repeated mention of 'the blood of Christ' (§§ 7, 12, 21, 49, 55), with the references to 'ransom,' 'deliverance,' and the like, in the several contexts, tells its own tale. Again the constant recurrence of the preposition *διὰ* denoting the mediatorial channel, 'through Jesus Christ' (see esp. § 36, where *διὰ τούτου* recurs five times), varied with the twin expression 'in Jesus Christ,' sufficiently reveals the mind of the writer. Indeed the occurrence of the expression *διὰ Ἰησοῦ Χριστοῦ* twice within the three or four lines in the opening salutation strikes the key-note of the epistle[1]. To Clement, as to all devout Christians in all ages, Jesus Christ is not a dead man, whose memory is reverently cherished or whose precepts are carefully observed, but an ever living, ever active Presence, who enters into all the vicissitudes of their being. Nor again can we doubt from the manner in which he adopts the language of the Epistle to the Hebrews (§ 36), that he believed in the

[1] In speaking of this subject we should distinguish between the Logos-doctrine and the Logos-terminology. Thus it seems to me to be a mistake in Dorner (*Person Christi* I. 1. pp. 101, 356, Eng. trans.) and others to maintain that Clement uses *λόγος* in its theological sense on the strength of such passages as § 27 *ἐν λόγῳ τῆς μεγαλωσύνης αὐτοῦ κ.τ.λ.* But for the reason given in the text (in which I find that I have been anticipated by Dorner) we can hardly deny his recognition of the *doctrine*, though we may see grave reasons for questioning his use of the *term*. See the note on § 27.

pre-existence of Christ. This indeed is clearly implied in § 16 οὐκ ἦλθεν ἐν κόμπῳ κ.τ.λ. Of His resurrection he speaks explicitly (§ 24), not only as raised from the dead Himself but also (in S. Paul's language) as having been made 'the first-fruit' of the general resurrection.

From the discussion of Clement's Christology we turn naturally to the doctrine of the Holy Trinity. The genuineness of the words (§ 58) relating to this subject and quoted by S. Basil (see above, p. 169) was questioned by many. The absence of the passage from the Alexandrian MS afforded an excuse for these doubts. The hesitation was due chiefly to the assumption that this very definite form of words involved an anachronism; and it was partially justified by the fact that several spurious writings bearing the name of Clement were undoubtedly in circulation in the fourth century when Basil wrote. Those however who gave it a place in the lacuna at the close of the epistle, as I had ventured to do in my first edition, have been justified by the discovery of the Constantinople manuscript and of the Syriac version. It is thus shown to be genuine; and though, as S. Basil says, it is expressed ἀρχαϊκώτερον, i.e. 'with a more primitive simplicity,' than the doctrinal statements of the fourth century, yet it is much more significant in its context than the detached quotation in this father would have led us to suppose. 'As God liveth,' writes Clement, 'and Jesus Christ liveth, and the Holy Ghost, (who are) the faith and the hope of the elect, so surely etc.,' where the three sacred Names are co-ordinated as in the baptismal formula (Matt. xxviii. 19). The points to be observed here are twofold. *First*; for the common adjuration in the Old Testament, 'as the Lord (Jehovah) liveth,' we find here substituted an expression which recognizes the Holy Trinity. *Secondly*; this Trinity is declared to be the object or the foundation of the Christian's faith and hope. With this passage also may be compared the words in § 46 'Have we not one God and one Christ and one Spirit of grace which was poured out upon us?'

On the other hand our recently discovered authorities throw considerable doubt on the reading in an earlier passage of the epistle (§ 2), where the Divinity of Christ is indirectly stated in language almost patripassian, of which very early patristic writings furnish not a few examples. Where Clement speaks of 'His sufferings' (τὰ παθήματα αὐτοῦ), the two new authorities agree in substituting 'Christ' (τοῦ Χριστοῦ), as the person to whom the pronoun refers, in the place of 'God' (τοῦ Θεοῦ) which stands in the Alexandrian MS. This various reading will be discussed in the note on the passage, where the reasons will be given which have led me to retain τοῦ Θεοῦ as on the whole the more probable reading.

Those who are desirous of pursuing this subject further, may consult Ekker *de Clem. Rom. Prior. ad Cor. Ep.* p. 75 sq (1854); Lipsius *de Clem. Rom. Ep. Prior. Disq.* p. 16 sq (1855); Hilgenfeld *Apost. Väter* p. 85 sq (1853); Gundert *Zeitschr. f. Luther. Theol. u. Kirche* XIV. p. 638 sq, XV. pp. 29 sq, 450 sq, 1854, 1855; Dorner *Person Christi* I. i. p. 96 sq (Eng. trans. 1861); Ritschl *Entst. d. Altkathol. Kirche* p. 274 sq (ed. 2, 1857); Ewald *Gesch. des Volkes Isr.* VII. p. 266 sq (1859); Reuss *Théologie Chrétienne* II. p. 318 sq (ed. 2, 1860); Thiersch *Kirche im Apost. Zeitalter* p. 247 sq (1850); Westcott *Hist. of Canon* p. 24 sq (ed. 4, 1875); Uhlhorn *Herzog's Real-Encyclopädie* s. v. Clemens von Rom (ed. 2, 1878); Donaldson *Apostolical Fathers* p. 153 sq (ed. 2, 1874); Renan *Les Évangiles* p. 318 sq (1877); Wieseler *Jahrb. f. Deutsch. Theol.* XXII. p. 373 sq (1877); Sprinzl *Theol. d. Apost. Väter* pp. 57, 81, 105, 113, 127 sq, etc. (1880); Lechler *Apost. u. Nachapost. Zeitalter* p. 593 sq (ed. 3, 1885); Pfleiderer *Paulinism* II. p. 135 sq (Eng. trans. 1877), *Urchristenthum*, p. 640 sq (1887); and others.

8. *The printed text and editions.*

The history of the printed text has been almost exhausted in the account of the documents (p. 116 sq). For nearly two centuries and a half from the first publication of the epistle (A.D. 1633) to the appearance of Bryennios' edition (A.D. 1875), the only improvements which were possible in the text consisted in the more careful deciphering of the manuscript which is much blurred and mutilated, the more skilful dealing with the lacunæ, and the more judicious use of the extraneous aid to be obtained from the LXX and the quotations in the fathers.

The list of editions which seemed to me to deserve notice as having advanced in any appreciable degree the criticism or the exegesis of the epistle by original contributions, when my own first edition appeared, is here repeated. The asterisks mark those works which may be regarded as the most important. As I am dealing here solely with Clement, I have not so distinguished such works as Dressel's, whose additions to our knowledge—not inconsiderable in themselves—are restricted to the other Apostolic Fathers.

*1633 Oxon. *Clementis ad Corinthios Epistola Prior;* PATRICIUS JUNIUS (P. Young). The 'editio princeps.' After the 1st

Epistle is added *Fragmentum Epistolae Secundae ex eodem MS*, but it is not named on the title-page.

1637 Oxon. A second edition of the same.

1654 Helmest. *Clementis ad Corinthios Epistola Prior;* J. J. MADER: taken from Young's edition. Some introductory matter is prefixed, and the 2nd Epistle is added as in Young.

1669 Oxon. *S. Patris et Martyris Clementis ad Corinthios Epistola;* J. FELL (the name however is not given). The 2nd Epistle is wanting.

1677 Oxon. A 2nd edition of the same. *Clementis ad Corinthios Epistola II* is added, but not named on the title page. The name of the editor is still suppressed.

*1672 Paris. *SS. Patrum qui temporibus Apostolicis floruerunt etc. Opera* etc.; J. B. COTELERIUS (Cotelier).

1698 Antverp. The same: 'recensuit J. CLERICUS' (Leclerc).

1724 Amstelaed. Another edition of Cotelier by Leclerc. The notes of W. Burton and J. Davies are here printed with others, some of them for the first time.

1687 Londini. *S. Clementis Epistolae duae ad Corinthios* etc.; P. COLOMESIUS (Colomiès).

1695 Londini. The same; 'editio novissima, prioribus longe auctior.'

1699 Lipsiae. *Bibliotheca Patrum Apostolicorum Graeco-Latina;* L. T. ITTIGIUS.

*1718 Cantabr. *Sancti Clementis Romani ad Corinthios Epistolae duae;* H. WOTTON. See above, p. 118. This edition contains notes by J. Bois, Canon of Ely, not before edited.

1721 Paris. *Epistolae Romanorum Pontificum* etc.; P. COUSTANT.

1796 Gotting. The same, re-edited by C. T. G. SCHOENEMANN.

1742 Basil. *Epistolae Sanctorum Patrum Apostolicorum* etc.; J. L. FREY.

1746 Londini. *SS. Patrum Apostolicorum* etc. *Opera Genuina* etc.; R. RUSSEL.

1765 Venet. *Bibliotheca Veterum Patrum* etc. (I. p. 3 sq); A. GALLANDIUS. The editor has availed himself of a treatise by A. Birr, *Animadversiones in B. Clementis Epistolas*, Basil. 1744.

1839 Tubing. *Patrum Apostolicorum Opera;* C. J. HEFELE. The 4th ed. appeared in 1855.

*1840 Oxon. *S. Clementis Romani, S. Ignatii, S. Polycarpi, Patrum Apostolicorum, quae supersunt;* GUL. JACOBSON. See above, p. 118. The 4th edition appeared in 1863.

1857 Lipsiae. *Patrum Apostolicorum Opera;* A. R. M. DRESSEL. The so-called 2nd edition (1863) is a mere reissue, with the addition of a collation of the Sinaitic text of Barnabas and Hermas.

*1866 Lipsiae. *Clementis Romani Epistulae* etc.; A. HILGENFELD. It forms the first part of the *Novum Testamentum extra Canonem Receptum.*

Further details about editions and translations will be found in Fabricius *Bibl. Græc.* IV. p. 829 sq (ed. Harles), and Jacobson's *Patres Apostolici* p. lxiv sq.

The more recent editions, which it would be impertinent, if it were possible, to separate one from another by any special marks of distinction, are the following,

1. *Appendix Codicum Celeberrimorum Sinaitici Vaticani.* ÆN. F. CONST. TISCHENDORF. Lipsiae 1867.

In this work the editor gives a 'facsimile' of the Epistles of Clement. It has been described already, p. 119.

2. *S. Clement of Rome. The Two Epistles to the Corinthians. A revised text with Introduction and Notes.* J. B. LIGHTFOOT, D.D. 8vo. London and Cambridge 1869.

The efforts made by the editor to secure a more careful collation of the readings of the Alexandrian MS are described above, p. 119 sq. The introduction and notes will approve or condemn themselves.

3. *Clementis Romani ad Corinthios Epistula. Insunt et altera quam ferunt Clementis Epistula et Fragmenta.* Ed. J. C. M. LAURENT, 8vo. Lipsiae 1870.

The editor had already distinguished himself in this field by one or two admirable conjectures, § 38 ἔστω, § 45 ἔγγραφοι (*Zur Kritik des Clemens von Rom*, in *Zeitschr. f. Luther. Theol. u. Kirche* XXIV. p. 416 sq, 1863). This edition is furnished with prolegomena and notes, but the text is perhaps the most important part. The editor has made use of Tischendorf's earlier text and of the first photograph (A. D. 1856; see above, p. 118); but he was not acquainted with my edition which had then but recently appeared.

4. *Clementis Romani Epistulae. Ad ipsius Codicis Alexandrini fidem ac modum repetitis curis, edidit* CONST. DE TISCHENDORF, 4to. Lipsiae 1873.

In his prolegomena and commentarius the editor discusses the points in which he differs from myself with regard to the readings of the Alexandrian MS. The significance of this edition has been discussed by me already (p. 119).

5. *Barnabae Epistula Graece et Latine, Clementis Romani Epistulae. Recensuerunt atque illustraverunt, etc.*, OSCAR DE GEBHARDT *Estonus*, ADOLFUS HARNACK *Livonus*. Lipsiae, 1875. This forms the first fasciculus of a new *Patrum Apostolicorum Opera*, which is called *Editio post Dresselianam alteram tertia*, but is in fact a new work from beginning to end.

The joint editors of this valuable edition have divided their work so that the text and apparatus criticus with those portions of the prolegomena which refer to this department are assigned to Gebhardt, while Harnack takes the exegetical notes and the parts of the prolegomena which refer to date, authorship, reception, etc. The text is constructed with sobriety and judgment; and in other respects the work is a useful and important contribution to early patristic literature.

6. Τοῦ ἐν ἁγίοις πατρὸς ἡμῶν Κλήμεντος ἐπισκόπου Ῥώμης αἱ δύο πρὸς Κορινθίους ἐπιστολαί κ.τ.λ. ΦΙΛ. ΒΡΥΕΝΝΙΟΣ. Ἐν Κωνσταντινουπόλει 1875.

The title of this work is given in full above, p. 121. It marks the commencement of a new era in the history of the text and literature, being founded on a hitherto unknown MS which supplies all the lacunæ of A, thus furnishing us for the first time with the Two Epistles of Clement complete. The new MS has been already described at length (l. c.).

It will be remembered that the learned editor had not seen any of the editions published in western Europe, later than Hilgenfeld's (1866). He was therefore unacquainted with the most recent and accurate collations of the Alexandrian MS, and not unfrequently misstates its readings accordingly; but he gives the readings of the new MS with praiseworthy accuracy. Occasionally, but very rarely, he has allowed a variation to escape him, as the photograph of this MS, which I hope to give at the end of this volume, will show. These lapses however are mostly corrected in his edition (1883) of the *Didache* ργ´. His edition of Clement is furnished with elaborate and learned prolegomena and with a continuous commentary. In the newly recovered portion of the genuine epistle more especially he has collected the Biblical references, which are very numerous here, with great care; and in this respect his diligence has left only gleanings for subsequent editors. Altogether the execution of this work is highly creditable to the editor, allowance being made for the difficulties which attend an editio princeps.

7. *Clementis Romani Epistulae. Edidit, Commentario critico et adnotationibus instruxit, etc.* AD. HILGENFELD. ed. 2. Lipsiae 1876.

In this new edition of the work described above (p. 402) Hilgenfeld has availed himself of the discovery of Bryennios and revised the whole work, so as to bring it down to date.

8. *Clementis Romani ad Corinthios quae dicuntur Epistulae. Textum ad fidem codicum et Alexandrini et Constantinopolitani nuper inventi recensuerunt et illustraverunt* O. DE GEBHARDT, AD. HARNACK. Ed. 2. Lipsiae 1876.

These editors also have largely revised their earlier edition, greatly improving it and making such additions and alterations as were suggested by the recent discovery.

9. *S. Clement of Rome. An Appendix containing the newly recovered portions.* With introductions, notes, and translations. J. B. LIGHTFOOT D.D. London 1877.

This work gave to the world for the first time the readings of a recently discovered Syriac version which is described above, p. 129 sq. In this the editor had the invaluable assistance of Bensly. The newly recovered portions were edited with textual and exegetical notes; the relations of the three documents were discussed at length; fresh introductory matter was added; a complete translation of the two Epistles was given; and in the Addenda the various readings exhibited by the two new authorities were recorded, while a few additions were made to the exegetical notes. The greater part of this *Appendix* is worked into my present (second) edition of Clement.

10. *Opera Patrum Apostolicorum. Textum recensuit, Adnotationibus criticis, exegeticis, historicis illustravit, Versionem Latinam, prolegomena, indices addidit* FR. XAV. FUNK. Tubingae, Vol. I. 1878, Vol. II. 1881.

Though this is called 'editio post Hegelianam quartam quinta,' it is in fact a new work. The Two Epistles to the Corinthians are contained in the first volume; some pseudo-Clementine literature in the second. The editor had the advantage of writing after both the additional documents (the Constantinopolitan MS and the Syriac version) had been published. The introductions are satisfactory; the notes, exegetical and critical, though slight, are good as far as they go; and the whole edition is marked by moderation and common sense.

The two photographic reproductions of the Codex Alexandrinus are not included in this list, but are described above, pp. 118, 119.

The edition of *Clemens Romanus* in Migne's *Patrologia Graeca* I. II, though excluded from the above list as being a mere reprint of other men's labours, deserves to be mentioned as containing all the Clementine works, genuine and spurious, in a convenient form for reference.

The literature connected with and illustrative of the Epistles to the Corinthians is manifold and various—more especially since the discovery of the additional documents. A list is given in Gebhardt and Harnack, p. xviii sq, ed. 2, and another in Richardson's *Bibliographical Synopsis* (*Antenicene Fathers*) p. 1 sq (1887). Completeness in such a case is unattainable, but these lists approach as near to it as we have any right to expect.

THE LETTERS ASCRIBED TO S. CLEMENT.

Of the works falsely ascribed to Clement of Rome something has been said already (p. 99 sq). With the rest of the Clementine literature we are not concerned here; but a short account of the *Letters* will not be out of place, since the notices and references to them are sometimes perplexing. The extant letters, which bear the name of this father, are nine in number.

1. *The First Epistle to the Corinthians*, a genuine work, to which this introduction refers and of which the text is given in my second volume. I cannot find any indications that it was ever translated into Latin before the seventeenth century; and, if so, it must have been a sealed book to the Western Church (see above, p. 146 sq). This supposition is consistent with the facts already brought forward; for no direct quotation from it is found in any Latin father who was unacquainted with Greek. When the Church of Rome ceased to be Greek and became Latin, it was cut off perforce from its earliest literature. The one genuine writing of the only illustrious representative of the early Roman Church was thus forgotten by his spiritual descendants, and its place supplied by forgeries written in Latin or translated from spurious Greek originals. In the same way the genuine Epistles of Ignatius were supplanted first by spurious and interpolated Greek letters, and ultimately by a wretched and transparent Latin forgery, containing a correspondence with the Virgin, by which chiefly or solely this father was known in the Western Church for some generations.

2. *The Second Epistle to the Corinthians*, a very early work, perhaps written before the middle of the second century, but neither an Epistle nor written by Clement. It also is printed in my second volume, and its date and character will be discussed in a special introduction. I need only say here that it early obtained a place after the genuine Epistle, though not without being questioned, as appears from the notice of Eusebius (*H. E.* iii. 38) and from its position in the Alexandrian MS.

These two generally went together and had the widest circulation in the Greek Church to very late times.

3, 4. *The Two Epistles on Virginity*, extant only in Syriac. They were first published, as an appendix to his Greek Testament, by J. J. Wetstein (Lugd. Bat. 1752), who maintained their genuineness. They have found champions also in their two latest editors, Villecourt (Paris 1853) whose preface and translation are reprinted with the text in Migne's *Patrologia* I. p. 350 sq, and Beelen (Louvain 1856) whose edition is in all respects the most complete: and other Roman Catholic divines have in like manner held them to be genuine. A Latin translation, derived mainly from Beelen, is assigned a place in the 2nd volume of Funk's *Patres Apostolici*, but he does not defend their genuineness. The lame arguments urged in many cases by their impugners have given to their advocates almost the appearance of a victory; but weighty objections against them still remain, unanswered and unanswerable. To say nothing of the style, which differs from that of the true Clement, the manner and frequency of the quotations from the New Testament, and the picture presented of the life and development of the Church, do not accord with the genuine epistle and point to a later age. For these reasons the Epistles to Virgins can hardly have been written before the middle of the second century. At the same time they bear the stamp of high antiquity, and in the opinion of some competent writers (e.g. Westcott *Canon* p. 162, Hefele in *Wetzer u. Welte's Kirchen-Lexicon* II. p. 586) cannot be placed much later than this date. Neander (*Church History* I. p. 408, Bohn's transl.) places them 'in the last times of the second or in the third century'. As they seem to have emanated from Syria, and the Syrian Church changed less rapidly than the Greek or the Western, it is safer to relax the limits of the possible date to the third century.

The MS which contains them is now in the Library of the Seminary of the Remonstrants at Amsterdam (no. 184) and is fully described by Beelen. It forms the latter part of what was once a complete copy of the Syriac New Testament, but of which the early part containing the Gospels is lost. It bears the date 1781 (i.e. A.D. 1470), and was brought to Europe from Aleppo in the last century. 'The first 17 quires are lost,' says Prof. Gwynn[1], 'with three leaves of the 18th, as appears from the numbering. The extant quires are of ten leaves each; and therefore, if the lost quires were so likewise, the first 173 leaves are wanting. The Gospels would fill, I calculate, little more than 130; so that the lost quires must have contained other matter—capitulations,

[1] In a written memorandum, which he has communicated to me. Prof. Gwynn has himself examined the manuscript and thus enabled me to correct the account given in my first edition.

no doubt, and perhaps lection-tables—possibly the Apocalypse, placed after S. John's Gospel, as in Lord Crawford's Syriac MS no. 2. But the subscription describes its contents as only the Gospels, the Acts, and the Pauline Epistles.' It includes other books of the New Testament besides those which have a place in the Peshito Canon. After the books comprised in this Canon, of which the Epistle to the Hebrews stands last, the scribe has added a doxology and a long account of himself and the circumstances under which the MS was written. Then follow in the same handwriting 2 Peter, 2, 3 John, and Jude, 'secundum versionem Philoxenianam,' says Beelen (p. x). 'He may possibly mean by these words,' writes Prof. Gwynn, 'to designate the version commonly known as the Pococke text which in the Paris and London Polyglots, and in all ordinary modern printed editions, appears as part of the Syriac New Testament and which many believe to be the *original* Philoxenian version of A.D. 508. If so, he is right; for these epistles are given in that version, not in the version which was printed by White and designated by him (as it has been commonly, though inexactly, designated since) the Philoxenian—more correctly the Harclean or Harcleo-Philoxenian, the revision published by Thomas of Harkel A.D. 616. The scribe however of this MS (or of the MS whence he copied these four Epistles) must have had a Harclean copy at hand. For (1) alternative renderings are in the margin in four places (2 Pet. iii. 5, 10; 2 Joh. 8; 3 Joh. 7), all borrowed from the Harclean; and (2) in one place (Jude 7) a Harclean rendering has been substituted in the text, which I believe no extant Greek MS countenances. Wetstein notes this as a variant, but was not aware that it was Harclean.'

Immediately after the Epistle of S. Jude there follow in succession '*The First Epistle of the blessed Clement, the disciple of Peter the Apostle*,' and '*The Second Epistle of the same Clement*.' Thus the two Epistles on Virginity hold the same position in this late Syrian copy which is held by the two Epistles to the Corinthians in the Alexandrian MS. This is possibly due to a mistake. A Syrian transcriber, finding the 'Two Epistles of Clement' mentioned at the end of some list of canonical books, might suppose that the two letters with which alone he was acquainted were meant, and thus assign to them this quasi-canonical position in his MS.

Though the fact has been questioned, there can be no reasonable doubt that these two epistles were known to EPIPHANIUS and accepted by him as genuine. Arguing against those heretics who received the Itinerary of Peter as a genuine writing of Clement (*Haer.* xxx. 15, p. 139), he urges that 'Clement himself refutes them on all points from the encyclical letters which he wrote and which are read in the holy churches (ἀφ' ὧν ἔγραψεν ἐπιστολῶν ἐγκυκλίων τῶν ἐν ταῖς ἁγίαις ἐκκλησίαις ἀναγινωσκομένων); for his faith and discourse have a different stamp from the spurious matter fathered upon his name by these persons in the Itinerary: he himself teaches virginity, and they do not admit it; he himself praises Elias and David and Samson and all the prophets, whom these men abominate.' This is an exact description in all respects of the Epistles to Virgins; while on the other hand the letters to the Corinthians (not to mention that they could not properly be called 'encyclical') contain no special praise of virginity (for the passages § 38 ὁ ἁγνὸς κ.τ.λ. and § 48 ἤτω ἁγνὸς κ.τ.λ. are not exceptions) but speak of the duties of married life (§ 1, 21), and make no mention at all of Samson. Indeed it appears highly probable that Epiphanius had no acquaintance with the Epistles to the Corinthians. He once alludes to the genuine letter, but not as though he himself had seen it. 'Clement,' he writes (*Haer.* xxvii. 6, p. 107; see above, p. 169), 'in one of his epistles says, Ἀναχωρῶ, ἄπειμι, ἐνσταθήτω (l. εὐσταθείτω) ὁ λαὸς τοῦ Θεοῦ, giving this advice to certain persons: for I have found this noted down in certain Memoirs (ηὕρομεν γὰρ ἔν τισιν ὑπομνηματισμοῖς τοῦτο ἐγκείμενον).' This is doubtless meant for a passage in the genuine epistle (§ 54). But the quotation is loose, and the reference vague. Moreover Epiphanius states that he got it at second hand. I have already given (p. 328 sq) what seems to me a highly probable explanation of these ὑπομνηματισμοί, which he mentions as the source of his information.

To JEROME also these epistles were known. He must be referring to them when he writes (*adv. Jovin.* i. 12, II. p. 257), 'Ad hos (i.e. eunuchos) et Clemens successor apostoli Petri, cujus Paulus apostolus meminit, scribit epistolas, *omnemque fere sermonem suum de virginitatis puritate contexit.*' This reference again seems to me unquestionable. Not only is the description perfectly appropriate as referring to the Epistles addressed to Virgins, but it is wholly inapplicable as applied to any other epistles—genuine or spurious—known to have borne the name of Clement. Throughout this treatise indeed Jerome betrays a knowledge of these Clementine Epistles to Virgins, though he only refers to them this once. The parallels are too close to allow any other inference, unless we should suppose that both Jerome and the spurious Clement borrowed from some one and the same earlier work—a solution which is excluded by the one direct reference[1]. On the other hand it is

[1] These parallels, which had been overlooked by preceding writers (myself included), are pointed out in Cotterill's *Modern Criticism and Clement's Epistles*

strange that in his Catalogue of Christian writers (§ 15) he mentions only the two Epistles to the Corinthians. Here indeed, as in other parts of this treatise, he copies Eusebius implicitly; but as he proffers his own opinion ('quae *mihi* videtur') of the resemblance between the First Epistle of Clement and the Epistle to the Hebrews (though even this opinion exactly coincides with the statement of Eusebius), and as moreover in several other passages he quotes from the genuine letter (*in Is.* lii. 13, IV. p. 612; *ad Ephes.* ii. 2, VII. p. 571; *ad Ephes.* iv. 1, VII. p. 606), we may give him the benefit of the doubt and suppose that he had himself read it[1]. The quotations, if they had stood alone, he might have borrowed from earlier commentators.

Epiphanius was intimately connected with Syria and Palestine, and Jerome spent some time there. Both these fathers therefore would have means of acquainting themselves with books circulated in these churches. As regards the latter, we must suppose that he first became acquainted with the Epistles to Virgins in the not very long interval between the publication of the Catalogue and of the work against Jovinianus; and, as this interval was spent at Bethlehem, the supposition is reasonable[2]. The alternative is, that in writing against

to Virgins p. 29 sq (Edinburgh, 1884). He himself takes up the strange and untenable position, that the author of these Clementine Epistles borrows from Jerome, and not conversely — notwithstanding Jerome's own reference.

[1] I have no pretensions to that accurate knowledge of S. Jerome's works which Mr Cotterill considers it a disgrace not to possess; but I think I know enough to say that—especially in his controversial writings—he is not a writer to whom I should look for strict accuracy and frankness. Cotterill's main argument depends on Jerome's possession of these two qualities in the highest degree: yet with strange inconsistency he argues (p. 25) that 'quae *mihi* videtur' means nothing at all when Jerome says of a work, which (on Mr Cotterill's own showing) he had never seen, that it 'appears to him' to resemble the Epistle to the Hebrews 'non solum sensibus sed juxta verborum quoque ordinem' etc. This would naturally be taken to imply *personal* knowledge, more especially as the position of the words suggests a contrast to the notice (in the next clause) of the 'Disputatio Petri et Appionis,' of which he says 'Eusebius...coarguit,' thus quoting the authority of *another*. Nevertheless I feel very far from certain that Jerome had himself read or seen the epistle.

[2] 'We must now pass on,' writes Mr Cotterill (p. 31), 'to *Ep.* xxii written to Eustochium specially upon the subject of virginity. This letter was written before the Catalogue, and is referred to in it § 135. If it be found that—if the epistles were in existence—Jerome used them in this letter, Dr Lightfoot's theory that he had no knowledge of them until after writing the Catalogue will be effectually disposed of. A single passage will amply suffice etc.' He then quotes from § 7 sq of the Second Epistle, and shows the close resemblance to Jerome *Epist.* xxii § 11, 12 (p. 95), 'ad Eustochium.' Again after this he sums up; 'This theory being

Jovinianus he for polemical purposes assumed the genuineness of these Clementine letters, which he had silently ignored a year or two before.

now effectually disposed of, the difficulty which it was intended to meet comes back with full force. If Jerome knew the epistles at all, he knew them all through his life' (p. 34). Now I believe with Mr Cotterill that (the resemblances being so close) the two passages cannot be independent; but though I am sorry to mar the exultation of his triumph, I venture to submit that my theory—on which however I lay no stress and which I am prepared to resign if any better can be found, or if it can be proved to be wrong, though it seems to me to be the most probable explanation consistent with Jerome's perfect straightforwardness—is not yet 'effectually disposed of.' I would only make two remarks in reply:

(1) From what private source is the information drawn that the *Letter to Eustochium* was written after the *Catalogus?* The Letter to Eustochium is assigned by Vallarsi on excellent grounds to the year A.D. 384; the *Catalogus* was certainly circulated some years before this (the date assigned is A.D. 378; see above, p. 173), and is referred to by Jerome himself at an earlier date (e.g. *adv. Jovinian.* ii. 26, II. p. 279). But the last chapter (§ 135), to which Mr Cotterill refers, was as certainly added to the *Catalogus* at some later revision or republication, as Jerome gives the date 'praesentem annum, id est, Theodosii principis decimum quartum' [A.D. 392], in the beginning of the same chapter *about ten lines before the mention of the Epistle to Eustochium.* These dates might have been learnt easily from Vallarsi's edition which (if we may judge by the paging) Mr Cotterill himself used; see also Clinton *Fasti Romani* I. p. 527. Truly an unkind but not unrighteous nemesis betrayed our merciless censor at the very moment when he was hurling his severest reproaches at others into this cruel pitfall which lay before his very eyes. Like star-gazing Thales of old, our stern mentor, falling into the well which lies at his feet, may well provoke a smile in us mere household drudges of criticism (*θεραπαινὶς αποσκῶψαι λέγεται, ὡς τὰ μὲν ἐν οὐρανῷ προθυμοῖτο εἰδέναι τὰ δὲ ἔμπροσθεν αὐτοῦ καὶ παρὰ πόδας λανθάνοι αὐτόν*).

(2) The spurious Clement, warning his readers of the danger of falling away from chastity, speaks of those 'qui *lumbos suos* volunt *succingere* veraciter,' as the passage is printed in the Latin version of Beelen and Funk, followed in two places by Cotterill (pp. 32, 40). In none of these critics is there any indication of the true source of the quotation. Beelen (p. 96) says distinctly that it is an allusion to Luke xii. 35 (xii. 95, as he prints incorrectly) *ἔστωσαν ὑμῶν αἱ ὀσφύες περιεζωσμέναι.* Cotterill twice alludes to the 'succingere veraciter' (pp. 33, 35), and says (I know not why) that it 'suggests that he [the spurious Clement] was the copyist.' The real source of the quotation is not Luke xii. 35, but Ephes. vi. 14 *περιζωσάμενοι τὴν ὀσφὺν ὑμῶν ἐν ἀληθείᾳ.* The Syriac has not *veraciter*, as it is loosely translated by Beelen, but *in veritate*, as it is correctly given by Wetstein, though in his edition a misprint in the Syriac context entirely obliterates the reference to Ephes. vi. 14. The rendering of Villecourt (Clem. Rom. I. p. 438, ed. Migne) is quite wild and substitutes a paraphrase 'qui immaculatos se custodire volunt.' The original Greek expression is happily preserved in Antiochus *Hom.* xvii p. 1052 *τοῖς θέλουσιν ἐν ἀληθείᾳ τὴν ὀσφὺν περιζώσασθαι*, quoted by Cotterill himself (p. 40). Jerome amplifies this interpretation of 'girding the loins,' dwelling especially on Job xl. 16 (xl. 11),

Besides the references in Epiphanius and Jerome, the 'First Epistle on Virginity' is quoted also by TIMOTHEUS OF ALEXANDRIA (A.D. 457) in his work against the Council of Chalcedon, of which parts are preserved in a Syriac translation (see above, p. 181). But it would appear that these epistles were not known or not commonly known westward of these regions. Even Eusebius betrays no knowledge of them. The fact which Epiphanius mentions, that they were read in the churches, is noteworthy, if true. In this case the reading would probably be confined to a few congregations in Syria and Palestine. But it is probable that he carelessly repeats a notice which he had read elsewhere and which in his original authority referred not to these, but to the two Epistles to the Corinthians. The existing Syriac text is doubtless a translation from a Greek original, as the phenomena of the letters themselves suggest (see Beelen p. lxiii), and as the references in these fathers seem to require. The quotation in Timotheus of Alexandria is evidently an independent translation from the Greek.

A later writer also, ANTIOCHUS THE MONK [c. A.D. 620], quotes very largely from these *Epistles on Virginity*, though without mentioning them or their supposed author by name. This is his common practice in dealing with early writers, as we find in the case of Ignatius, from

and Job xxxviii. 3. Cotterill says (p. 35) that 'the line which Jerome takes as to *girding the loins* is strictly his own,' and refers to *In Jerem.* i. 17, [IV.] p. 842, *In Ephes.* vi. 14, [VII.] p. 678. To these references I would add *In Ezech.* xvi. 4 (V. p. 145). When I read these words, I felt tolerably sure that this interpretation, which indeed is not uncommon in patristic writings, would be found at all events as early as Origen; and I was not disappointed. In his work *In Levit. Hom.* iv § 6 (II. p. 202, Delarue), speaking of the dress of the priest in offering the burnt offering (Lev. vi. 8 sq), he writes 'Hoc est quod Dominus in Evangeliis praecipit ut *sint lumbi vestri praecincti etc.*' (Luke xii. 35), and he explains 'femoralibus utitur qui luxuriam fluxae libidinis cingulo restrinxerit castitatis; ante omnia enim sacerdos qui divinis assistit altaribus castitate debet accingi.' Again in another extant work of Origen, *In Ezech. Hom.* vi § 4 (III. p. 378), we have the source whence the corresponding passage in Jerome is taken. In fact Jerome copies from his predecessors not only the interpretation of 'girding the loins', which he would find alike in the spurious Clement and in Origen, but most of the illustrations likewise. But, as I cannot suppose that Mr Cotterill lays down for others a more stringent literary rule than he carries out himself, I must believe that he read the whole of Jerome's *Commentary on the Ephesians* to which he refers, and there found in the preface that Jerome expresses frankly his obligations to Origen's three books (no longer extant) on this same epistle (VII. p. 543, Vallarsi); and it is a matter of regret that he did not follow in the track thus suggested to him and search in this father's extant works before he made the assertion which I have been discussing. By this precaution he would have saved himself from this second pitfall.

whom he borrows numerous extracts without acknowledgment, while only on one occasion, I believe, mentioning his name (see *Ignat. and Polyc.* I. p. 197 sq, ed. 1 p. 205 sq, ed. 2.) In the case of the spurious Clement he does not in a single instance mention the source of the quotations incorporated in his text, just as he borrows numerous passages from Hermas without any indication of their authorship. They are so numerous however in our pseudo-Clement, that we are able to restore

[1] To Cotterill (p. 37 sq) the credit is due of pointing out the passages which the spurious Clement has in common with Antiochus, though overlooked not only by outsiders like myself, but by all the editors and commentators of the epistles themselves from Wetstein downward. The severe scolding which we get is a small price to pay for the information. It costs me the less to make this acknowledgment of gratitude, because I feel confident that in the main point of difference between us the opinion of posterity will not be on his side. But it is somewhat sad that so much diligence and research, which might do excellent service in other fields, has been expended on the maintenance of a view which plain testimony, plainly interpreted, shows to be impossible. Here again, as in the case of the Epistles to the Corinthians (see above, p. 362, note 2), he reverses the true order, making Antiochus the original and the author of these epistles the plagiarist. Indeed to maintain his cart-before-the-horse theory he uses some curious arguments; e.g. he finds (p. 46) in the fact that the pseudo-Clement (*Ep.* i § 2) uses the words *oboediunt illi qui dixit* (as it is rendered by Funk), whereas Antiochus (*Hom.* 98) has ἀκούει τοῦ λέγοντος, a confirmation of his view, arguing as follows; 'The point of our writer's prefatory remark lies in the word obey. Here again, as so often, a weaker word ἀκούει is used by Antiochus.' If from Funk's translation (which follows Beelen) he had turned to Wetstein's, he would have found *audiunt eum qui dixit*, and if from the translations he had turned to the Syriac itself (Beelen, p. 7), he would have discovered that the ordinary Shemitic word שמע (Hebrew, as well as Syriac) for 'to hear' was used. So much for the 'weaker word.' It is quite pardonable not to know Syriac; but I will leave my readers to form their own opinion of this criticism from the pen of one who lays down such stringent rules for others. To most minds indeed the very parallels which Mr Cotterill gathers together between the pseudo-Clement and Antiochus (p. 115 sq), to prove the priority of the latter, will suggest a wholly different conclusion. Is it not a striking fact that in five several places at least (pp. 115, 116, 117, 123, 124), where Ignatian texts are incorporated in Antiochus in the midst of matter which runs parallel with the pseudo-Clement, these texts are wanting in the pseudo-Clement? How could a later writer, impersonating Clement, have avoided all these pitfalls, adopting the matter before and after from Antiochus and rejecting these texts, *though there is no indication in Antiochus that they are quotations?* The same question may be asked also of the quotation from Dionysius the Areopagite (*Cael. Hier.* iii. 2) in Hom. 122 (comp. *Ep. ad Virg.* i. 13; see Cotterill pp. 73, 122).

As bearing on this question I may call attention to Cotterill's remark (p. 89 sq). 'In *Hom.* 112 Antiochus has καὶ τῆς ἁγνείας τὸν πολύμοχθον καὶ πολύμισθον πλοῦτον. It seems impossible not to suppose that Antiochus has in view Ignat. *ad Polyc.* 1

large fragments of the original Greek text from which the Syriac was translated. These plagiarisms are most extensive in *Hom.* 17, 18, 21, 99, 111, 112, 122, 130, but they occur elsewhere.

The writing or writings of Clement mentioned in Ebed-Jesu's Catalogue (Assemani *Bibl. Orient.* III. p. 13) may be these epistles, but the allusion is more probably to the Apostolic Constitutions.

These *Epistles on Virginity* may have been suggested by the fame of Clement as the writer of the Epistle to the Corinthians; but the traces which they contain of any knowledge of this letter are few and disputable. Their contents are described without exaggeration by Jerome, as quoted above (p. 160), and need not occupy us here.

5. *The Epistle to James the Lord's brother*, giving an account of S. Clement's appointment by S. Peter as his successor in the see of Rome, and containing also the Apostle's directions relating to the functions of church-officers and the general administration of the Church. Whether this letter was originally prefixed to the Homilies or to the Recognitions or to some other work of the Petro-Clementine cycle different from either, is still a moot question. Under any circumstances its date can hardly be earlier than the middle of the second century or much later than the beginning of the third. In the original Greek it is now found prefixed to the Homilies in the MSS, and may be read conveniently in the editions of this work (e.g. Dressel

ὅπου γὰρ πλείων κόπος πολὺ καὶ τὸ κέρδος [the correct text is ὅπου πλείων κόπος, πολὺ κέρδος] our writer's version of Antiochus is *virginitatis quae ut res est magni laboris, ita et magnam quoque habet mercedem* (*Ep.* i. 5). Our writer seems more nearly to have approached Ignatius.' If instead of trusting the translation of Beelen and Funk he had consulted the Syriac, he would have found that it runs 'virginitatis cujus magnus labor et magna merces,' the closest rendering which the genius of the Syriac language allows of πολύμοχθος καὶ πολύμισθος. As my notes on the passage of Ignatius show, and as appears from Mr Cotterill's own illustrations, the idea, which is a very obvious one, was probably embodied in 'some ancient γνώμη,' to use his own language. At all events such parallels are much nearer to the words of Ignatius than the πολύμοχθος καὶ πολύμισθος of the pseudo-Clement.

These examples must suffice. I should have much more to say on this subject, if it were not waste of time for myself and my readers to dwell so long on a subject which is only remotely connected with the Epistles to the Corinthians. No one would lay much stress on the coincidences between the true Clement and the *Epistles on Virginity* (see above, p. 160), even though they seem to show a knowledge of the genuine work on the part of the author of the spurious. Nor again is it a matter of real moment for my purpose, whether the Epistles on Virginity were written in the latter half of the first century or the first half of the fourth—the latest date at which the direct evidence will allow us to place them.

or Lagarde). About the end of the fourth century it was translated into Latin by Rufinus. In the preface to the Recognitions, which he afterwards translated, he mentions this fact, and excuses himself from again reproducing it partly on this ground. Not unnaturally his translation of the one came to be attached to his translation of the other: and the letter is often found in the MSS prefixed or affixed to the larger work. In one of the two earliest known MSS of the Recognitions (*Vercell.* I. clviii), belonging to the sixth or seventh century, the letter follows the main work. Notwithstanding its questionable doctrine, this epistle is quoted as genuine by the synod of Vaison (see above, p. 177) held A.D. 442, and is cited occasionally by popes and synods from this time onward.

Besides many important questions relating to the early history of Christianity which are connected with this letter, it is interesting also as having been made the starting point of the most momentous and gigantic of mediæval forgeries, the Isidorian Decretals. In its first form, as left by Rufinus, the Latin ends 'sub eo titulo quem ipse (i.e. Petrus) praecepit affigi, id est Clementis Itinerarium Praedicationis Petri[1]; sed et nunc jam exponere quae praecepit incipiam,' in accordance with the Greek. But when incorporated in the false Decretals, where it stands at the head of the pontifical letters, it is extended to more than twice its original length by some additional instructions of S. Peter for which the words 'exponere quae praecepit incipiam' furnish the occasion, and ends 'regni ejus mereamur esse consortes.' In this longer form it may be read conveniently in Mansi *Concilia* I. p. 91 (Flor. 1759), or in Migne's *Patrol. Graec.* I. p. 463, where all the Decretal letters bearing the name of Clement are printed, or in the *Decretales Pseudo-Isidorianae* p. 30 sq (ed. Hinschius).

6. *A Second Epistle to James*, relating to the administration of the eucharist, to church furniture, etc. The date of this forgery is uncertain, but it is evidently much later than the former. It would form a very obvious sequel to the earlier letter which spoke of ecclesiastical

[1] As this title is sometimes read 'Clementis Itinerarium non Praedicationis Petri' (so Cotelier *Patr. Ap.* I. p. 620), and as arguments respecting the letter have been built upon this fact (*e.g.* Uhlhorn *Homil. u. Recogn.* p. 82, Hilgenfeld *Nov. Test. extr. Can. Rec.* IV. p. 53), I may say that of some 30 MSS which I have examined, only one (*Brussels* 5220, 10th cent.) has the negative; that it is absent in the oldest of all (*Vercelli* I. clviii); and that it must therefore be regarded as a mere interpolation, whether by accident or from design. In the Brussels MS the epistle occurs as one of the Decretal letters; but even in such copies I have not elsewhere found the negative.

officers, and was doubtless suggested by it. As no Greek original is known to exist, and it appears to have been written in Latin, its date must at all events be after Rufinus' translation of the First Letter to James, *i.e.* not before the beginning of the fifth century.

This letter is generally found in company with the preceding, and sometimes the two are attached to copies of the Recognitions, but this only occurs in comparatively late MSS. Like the First Epistle to James, this also was incorporated in the false Decretals, forming the second in the series of pontifical letters; and for this purpose it appears to have been interpolated and enlarged in a similar manner[1]. In its shorter form it begins 'Clemens Jacobo carissimo,' and ends 'damnationem accipiet (*or* acquiret)': in its longer form the opening generally runs 'Clemens Romanae ecclesiae praesul,' and the ending is 'reverentissime frater [Amen].' The two forms will be found in Mansi *Conc.* I. pp. 126, 158.

When attached to the Recognitions, the two letters to James have almost universally the shorter form, as might be expected. Among a large number of MSS of the Recognitions which I have examined, I have only found one exception, *Turin* D. III. 17 (cod. CC, Passini), where they are so attached in the longer form, though probably other examples exist.

The MSS of these two epistles, both separate from and attached to the Recognitions, are very numerous; and in the Latin Church after the age of S. Jerome, when the 'Two Epistles of Clement' are mentioned, we may generally assume that the reference is to these. Such, I can hardly doubt, is the case in the 'Liber Pontificalis,' where in the notice of Clement it is said in the earlier edition (A.D. 530—532; see

[1] The sources of these false Decretals are investigated by Knust *de Fontibus et Consilio Pseudoisid. Coll.*, Göttingen 1832. For the literature of the subject generally see Migne's *Patrol. Lat.* CXXX. p. xxiv, Rosshirt *Zu den Kirchenr. Quellen* etc. p. 39. The very thorough and excellent edition of the *Decretales Pseudo-Isidorianae* (Lips. 1863) by P. Hinschius appeared after my first edition. It contains not only a revised text and *apparatus criticus*, but a preface in which all questions relating to date, place, authorship, and sources, are fully discussed. Rosshirt (p. 47) states that the *two* letters to James were translated from the Greek by Rufinus. This is a mistake. In some MSS indeed the 2nd Epistle is stated to have been translated by him, but then the same statement is likewise made of one or more of the remaining three included in the false Decretals. It must therefore be regarded either as a device of the forger aiming at verisimilitude, or as an error of some transcriber carrying on the statement from the 1st Epistle to those following. Internal probability and external evidence alike are unfavourable to the supposition that Rufinus translated the second letter.

above, p. 304) 'Fecit duas epistolas' (*Liber Pontificalis* I. p. 53, Duchesne), which in the later edition (not after A.D. 687; see above, p. 307) is expanded into 'Hic fecit duas epistolas quae canonicae (v.l. catholicae)[1] nominantur' (*Lib. Pont.* I. p. 123). This last expression it should be added, occurs of the two Epistles of S. Peter in the Life of the Apostle himself in both editions (pp. 51, 118)[2]. Indeed the editor of the later recension quotes the Epistle to James in the Life of Peter (p. 118) and refers to it distinctly again ('in epistola quae ad Jacobum scripta est qualiter ei a beato Petro commissa est ecclesia') in the Life of Clement (p. 123); and the earlier recension at all events shows a knowledge of the writings of this pseudo-Clementine cycle by describing Clement as 'ex patre Faustino' (p. 53). Nor does this view present any chronological difficulty. Lipsius indeed raises the objection[3] that 'the original edition of the *Liber Pontificalis* was probably borrowed from a more ancient source,' which he has 'succeeded in discovering in the *Catalogus Leoninus* of the year 440.' He therefore concludes that my explanation of the two Epistles of Clement mentioned in the *Liber Pontificalis* 'will scarcely bear examination.' I have already discussed (p. 311 sq) this Leonine Catalogue and acknowledged the great service which Lipsius has rendered to the pedigree of the papal lists by supplying this missing link; but I have there pointed out (p. 317) that there is no reason for supposing that this Catalogue contained anything more than the names and the terms of office, and no evidence at all to show that it comprised short biographies. The earlier recension of the *Liber Pontificalis* therefore is the first place (so far as our present knowledge goes) where the notice 'fecit duas epistolas' occurs. At this late date there is no difficulty in supposing that 'the Second Epistle to James' was in circulation. It is actually found in

[1] If the reading 'canonicae' be correct (and it is much less likely to have been substituted for 'catholicae' than the converse) this is decisive; for the two letters to James are strictly 'canonicae' in the technical sense, i.e. they contain ecclesiastical canons and directions. But even 'catholicae' is more appropriate to these than to the Epistles to the Corinthians, for they are addressed to the 'bishop of bishops' and are of Church-wide application, whereas the Corinthian letters deal with the internal feuds of a single community.

[2] Duchesne in his excellent edition gives in the Life of Peter 'canonicae' in the text and 'catholicae' as a variant in the notes in the earlier recension; 'catholicae' in the text and 'canonicae' among the variants in the Life of Peter (p. 118), and 'catholicae' *both* in the text and as a variant in the notes in the Life of Clement (p. 123). There is obviously a misprint somewhere, but I do not know how to correct it; for he comments on 'catholicae' in his exegetical notes on Clement.

[3] In a review of my first edition *Academy*, July 9, 1870; repeated again *Jenaer Literaturzeitung*, Jan. 13, 1877.

its original and shorter form in collections of Canons, belonging to the seventh century[1]. As the 'First Epistle to James' had been in circulation in Rufinus' translation considerably more than a century before the *Liber Pontificalis* in its older form appeared, there was ample time for the 'Second Epistle to James,' entitled *de Sacramentis conservandis*, to take its place by the side of the earlier letter and gain currency with it. The alternative would be to suppose that the author of this earlier recension of the *Liber Pontificalis* borrowed the notice of the Two Epistles of Clement from Jerome's *Catalogue*[2] without attaching any meaning to it. At all events I cannot doubt that to the redactor of the later recension of the *Liber Pontificalis* the 'Two Epistles which are called canonical' (or 'catholic')[3] meant the letters addressed to James. Indeed this later editor not only mentions shortly afterwards Clement's letter to James relating to his appointment to the Roman see, but actually quotes it in the previous Life of Peter (p. 118); and there is no reason for supposing that he intended to distinguish this from the two letters already mentioned (as Cotelier and others think). Moreover the two letters to James are distinctly named in another similar and apparently not independent notice in the Lives of the Roman pontiffs ascribed to Liutprand (Migne *Patrol. Lat.* CXXIX. p. 1153), 'Hic scripsit duas epistolas Jacobo Hierosolymorum episcopo, quae catholicae nominantur.' Anastasius Bibliothecarius indeed (*c.* A.D. 872) refers to the genuine Epistle to the Corinthians, but he must not be taken as representing the Latin Church; for he does not speak from personal knowledge, but translates, or rather mistranslates, a passage of Georgius Syncellus. The words of Georgius are τούτου ἐπιστολὴ μία γνησία Κορινθίοις φέρεται, ὡς ἀπὸ τῆς Ῥωμαίων ἐκκλησίας γραφεῖσα, στάσεως ἐν Κορίνθῳ συμβάσης τότε, ὡς μαρτυρεῖ Ἡγήσιππος, ἥτις καὶ ἐκκλησιάζεται (*Chronogr.* I. p. 651, ed. Dind.). Anastasius writes 'Hujus epistola fertur ad Corinthios missa, quam tota recipit, ut Egesippus testatur, ecclesia' (*Hist. Eccl.* p. 17, Paris 1649), where the testimony of Hegesippus is transferred to the wrong point. So little was known of the genuine epistle even by the ablest mediæval writers of the Latin Church, that in the thirteenth century S. Thomas Aquinas speaks of some Antenicene writers having attributed the Epistle to the He-

[1] See Hinschius p. lxxxi; comp. Leon. Magn. *Op.* III. pp. 630, 674, by the brothers Ballerini.

[2] This is Duchesne's opinion (I. p. 123). Yet of this Second Epistle to James he says that it 'paraît avoir été fabriquée vers le commencement du vime siècle.'

[3] Duchesne supposes that this addition 'quae catholicae (or 'canonicae') nominantur' is repeated 'assez mal à propos' from the notice of S. Peter.

brews to Clement the pope, because 'ipse scripsit *Atheniensibus* quasi per omnia secundum stilum istum' (*prol. ad Hebr.*), and the error has misled others (see above, p. 102, note).

The false Decretals made their appearance in the east of France, and the date of the forgery may be fixed within very narrow limits about the middle of the ninth century[1]. The oldest extant MSS belong to this same century. The writer enlarged the two existing Latin letters (5 and 6) in the manner already described, and raised the whole number to five by forging three additional letters.

These three Clementine forgeries of the ninth century are:

7. A letter headed, 'Clemens urbis Romae episcopus omnibus coepiscopis presbyteris diaconibus ac reliquis clericis et cunctis principibus majoribus minoribusve, etc.'

8. Another beginning, 'Clemens Romanae urbis episcopus carissimis fratribus Julio et Juliano ac reliquis consodalibus nostris gentibusque quae circa vos sunt.'

9. A third, 'Dilectissimis fratribus et condiscipulis Hierosolymis cum carissimo fratre Jacobo coepiscopo habitantibus Clemens episcopus.'

These three letters require no comment.

If the above account be correct, it follows that the 'two letters of Clement' would be differently understood in different branches of the Church. To the Greek they would suggest the two Epistles to the Corinthians; to the Latin the two addressed to James; and to the Syrian probably the two in praise of virginity[2]. It is stated likewise by Abulbarcatus (as represented by Assemani, *Bibl. Orient.* III. p. 14), that the Coptic Church also received two epistles of Clement. These might have been either those to the Corinthians or those to Virgins. The great estimation in which the former were held at Alexandria, as appears from the Alexandrian MS and the quotations of the Alexandrian fathers, would promote their circulation among the native Egyptian

[1] The history of the appearance and reception of these false Decretals is given fully by Gfrörer *Gesch. der Ost- u. West-fränk. Carolinger* I. p. 71 sq, and by Hinschius *l.c.* p. clxxxiii sq. See also Milman's *Latin Christianity* II. p. 303 sq.

[2] This sentence is left as it stood in the first edition; but with regard to the Syrian Church we cannot now speak without some qualification. The recent discovery of a Syriac translation, probably belonging to the age of Jacob of Edessa (see above, p. 135), of the Epistles to the Corinthians, shows that after that time at all events the 'Two Epistles might have an alternative meaning to a Syrian writer.

Christians. On the other hand the high value which was attached to celibacy in Egypt would make the Epistles on Virginity very acceptable to this church. It has been seen (p. 181) that both sets of epistles were known to and quoted by Timotheus patriarch of Alexandria (A.D. 457).

But the above list of nine letters probably does not comprise all which at one time or other were circulated in the name of Clement. At the beginning of the seventh century Maximus the Confessor, who (as we have seen) quotes the genuine epistle, speaking of the omissions of Eusebius, complains that he has mentioned only two epistles of this apostolic father (*prol. ad Dionys. Areop.* οὔτε Πανταίνου τοὺς πόνους ἀνέγραψεν, οὔτε τοῦ Ῥωμαίου Κλήμεντος, πλὴν δύο καὶ μόνων ἐπιστολῶν, i.e. no other works besides his epistles, and only two of these). And about the same time in the *Sacr. Rer. Lib. II* of Leontius and John (see above, p. 189) the writers, after quoting a passage from the genuine First Epistle to the Corinthians, give another quotation headed 'From the *ninth* Epistle of the same writer' (τοῦ αὐτοῦ ἐκ τῆς θ′ ἐπιστολῆς, where Hilgenfeld's conjecture of θείας for θ′ is improbable). As not more than five of the extant epistles, including the two addressed to Virgins, can ever have existed in Greek, and the passage is not found in any of these, we must assume several lost Clementine letters, unless there be some error in the ascription to Clement (see p. 189). Again Timotheus of Alexandria, who before has quoted 'the First Epistle on Virginity,' immediately afterwards cites the opening of our Second Epistle to the Corinthians as 'Of the same Clement from the beginning of the *Third* Epistle' (see above, p. 181 sq). This shows that the epistles were differently arranged in different collections. The Epistle of Clement, to which Dionysius Barsalibi alludes as written against those who reject matrimony (so he is reported by Assemani, *Bibl. Orient.* II. p. 158), may have been one of these lost letters; but as the First Epistle to James urges very strongly the importance of early marriages (§ 7), I am disposed to think that he referred to this. This opinion is confirmed by the language of Epiphanius quoted above, p. 409.

AN AUTOTYPE

OF THE

CONSTANTINOPLE MANUSCRIPT.

IN an earlier part of this volume (p. 121 sq) a full account is given of the only authority which contains the Greek text of the Two Epistles of S. Clement complete.

It is there and throughout these volumes called the Constantinopolitan MS, because its abode at the time was the Library of the Patriarch of Jerusalem in Fanar at Constantinople; but it has since been restored to its proper and permanent home, the Library of the Holy Sepulchre of the Patriarch at Jerusalem.

Though it was collated with praiseworthy care by the first editor, Bryennios, infallible accuracy is beyond human reach; and this authority for the text of the earliest Apostolic Father is unique. I thought therefore that I should be doing a service to patristic literature, if once for all I gave to the public an absolute reproduction of this manuscript, by which they might test the labours of others and myself.

This autotype is the result. My gratitude is due to the Patriarch of Jerusalem in so kindly allowing it to be taken; and also to the Very Rev. C. R. Hale, Dean of Davenport, Iowa U. S., and to the American Consul at Jerusalem, Mr Gillman, through whose joint services the whole matter was negotiated and arranged.

This facsimile will explain itself. In accordance with the table of contents (see above, p. 122), the first page contains the conclusion of the Epistle of Barnabas, which immediately precedes the Epistles of S. Clement, and the last page commences the Didache. Between the two is a list of the Old Testament Scriptures. The Didache has been published in facsimile by Prof. Rendel Harris. The autotype of the Clementine Epistles occupies 50 pages or 25 leaves in all.

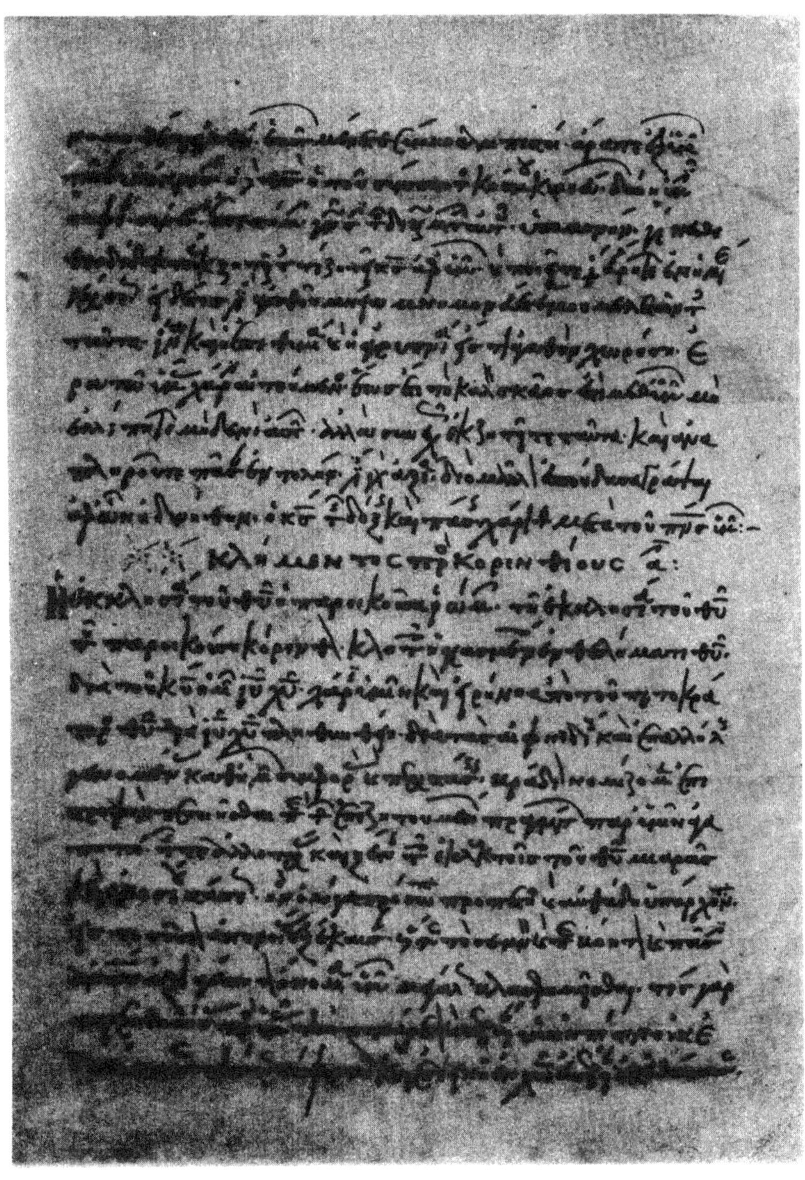

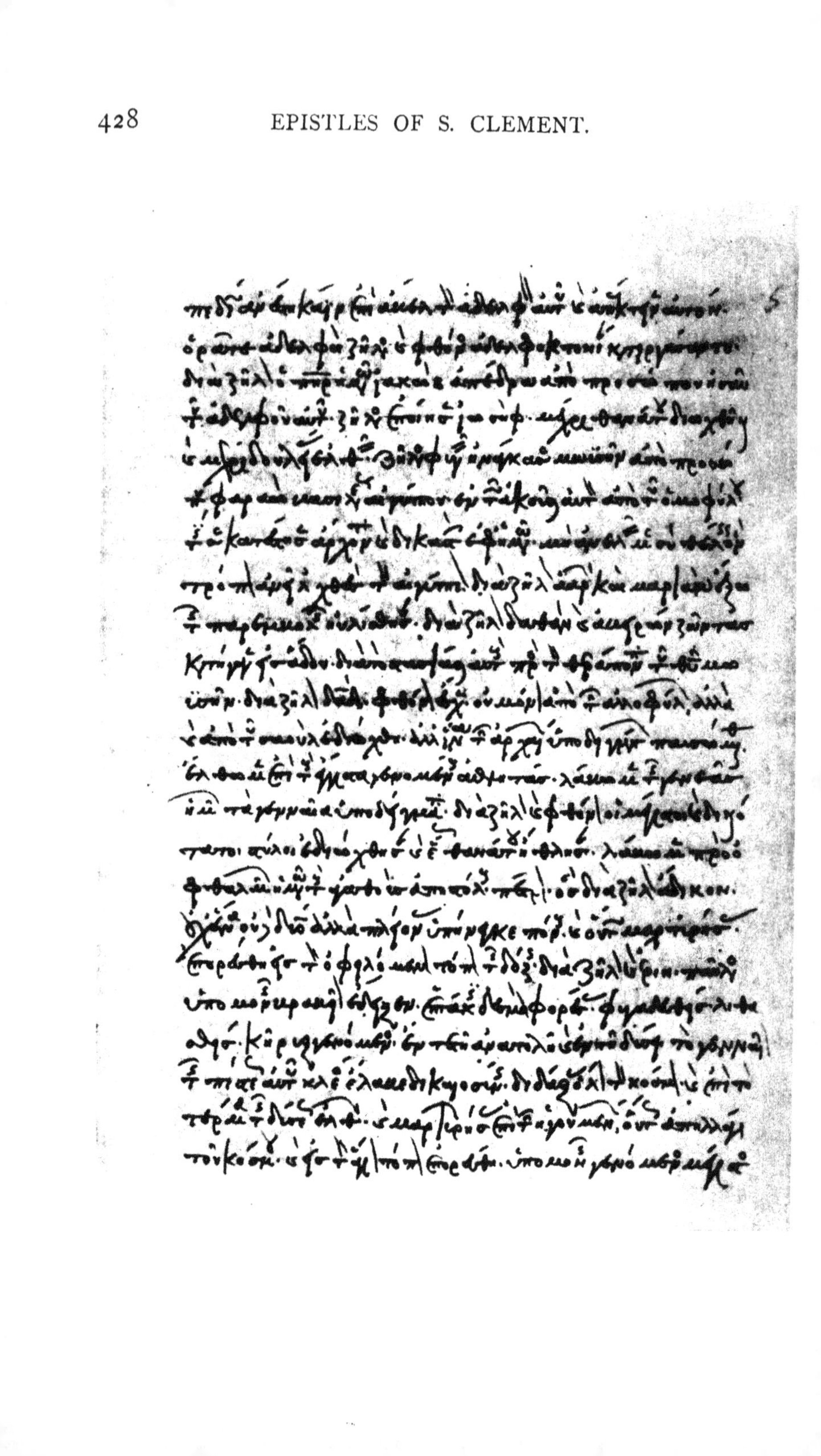

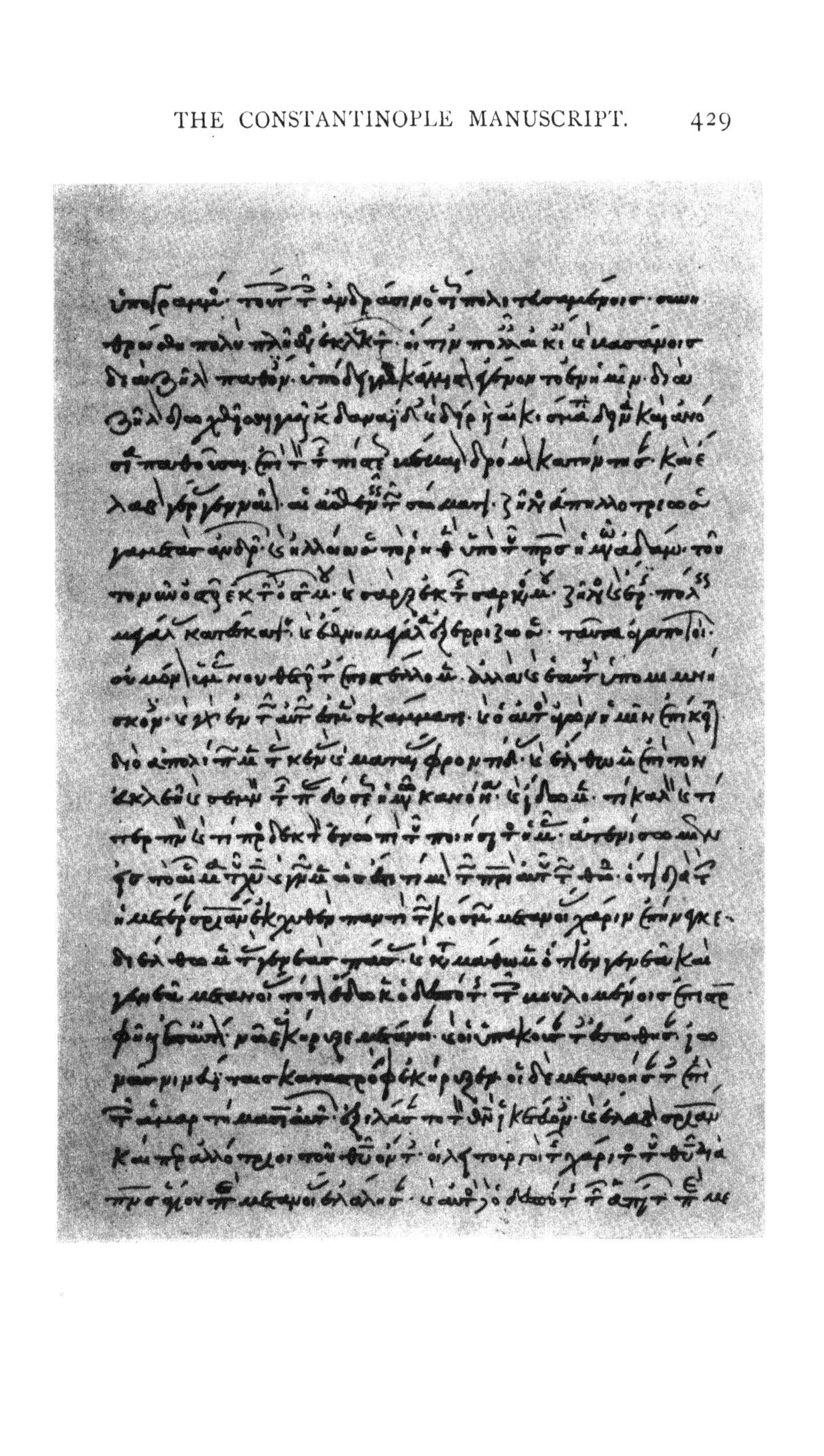

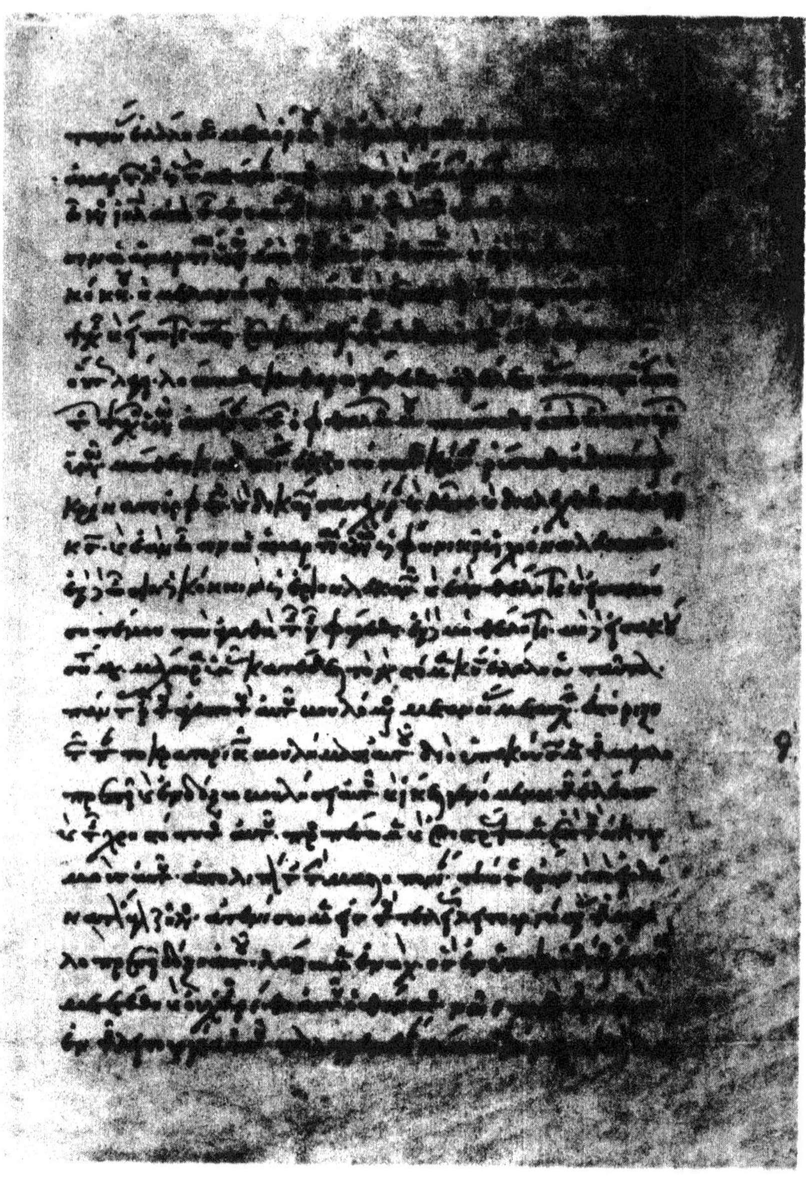

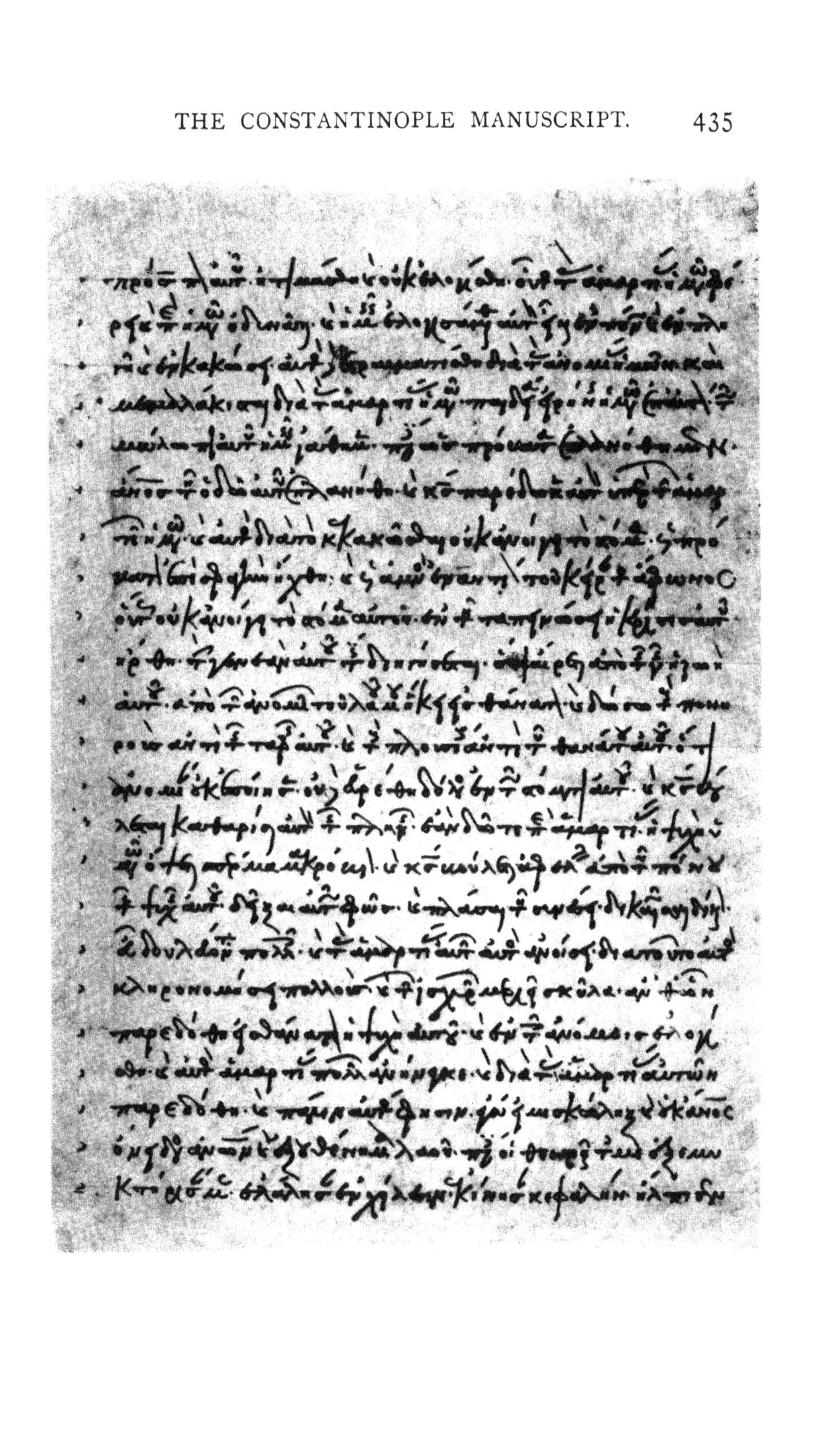

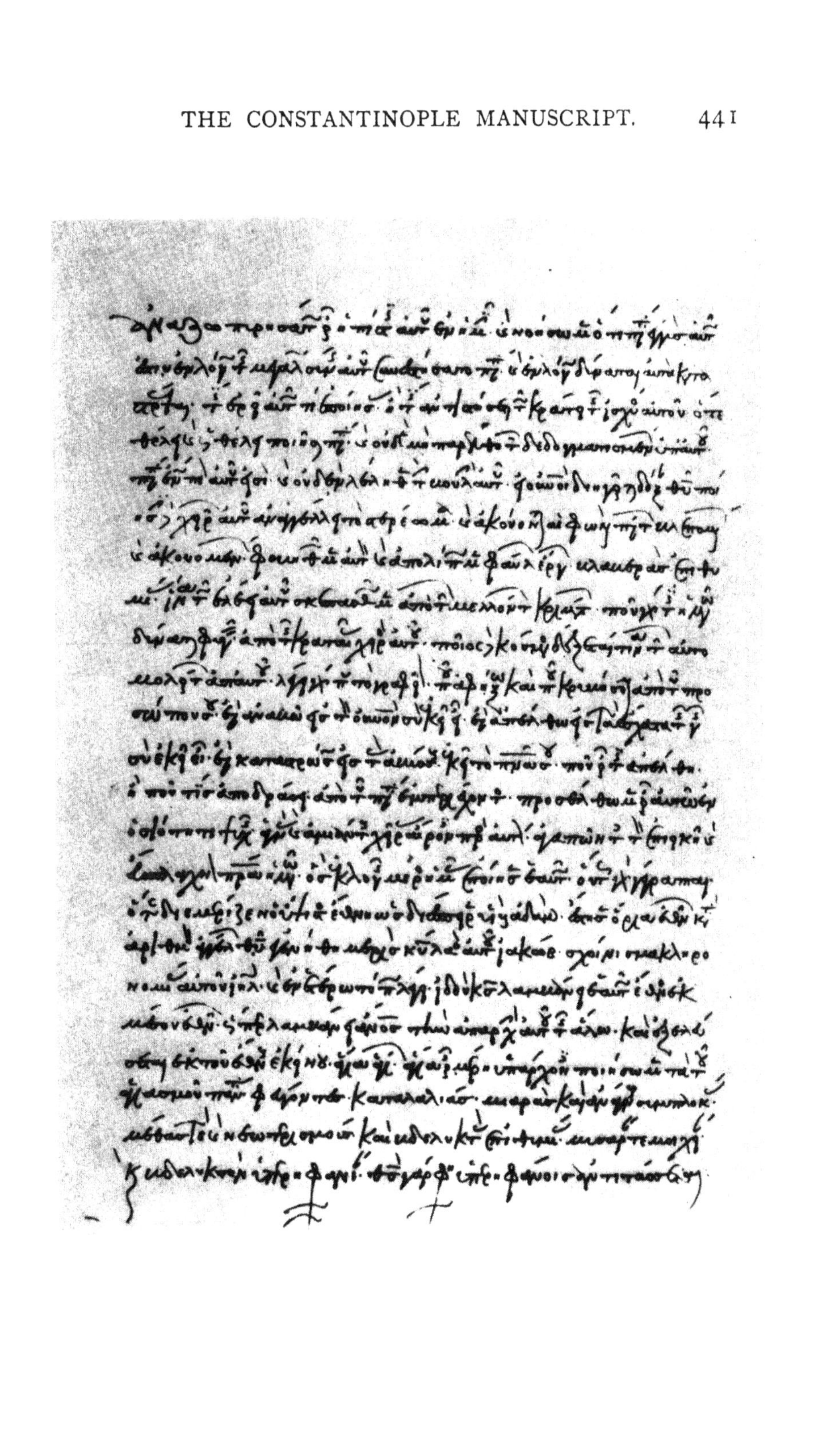

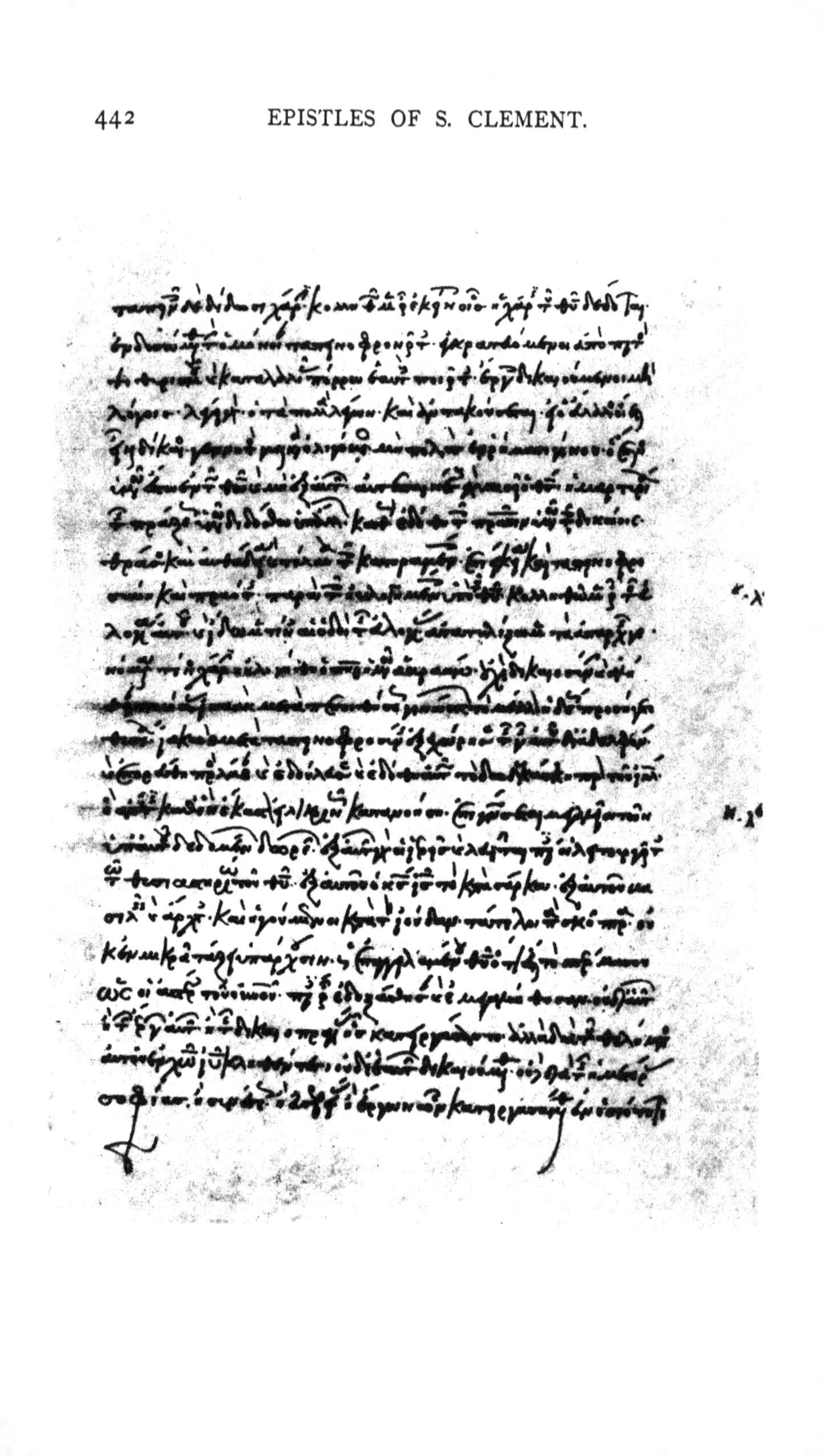

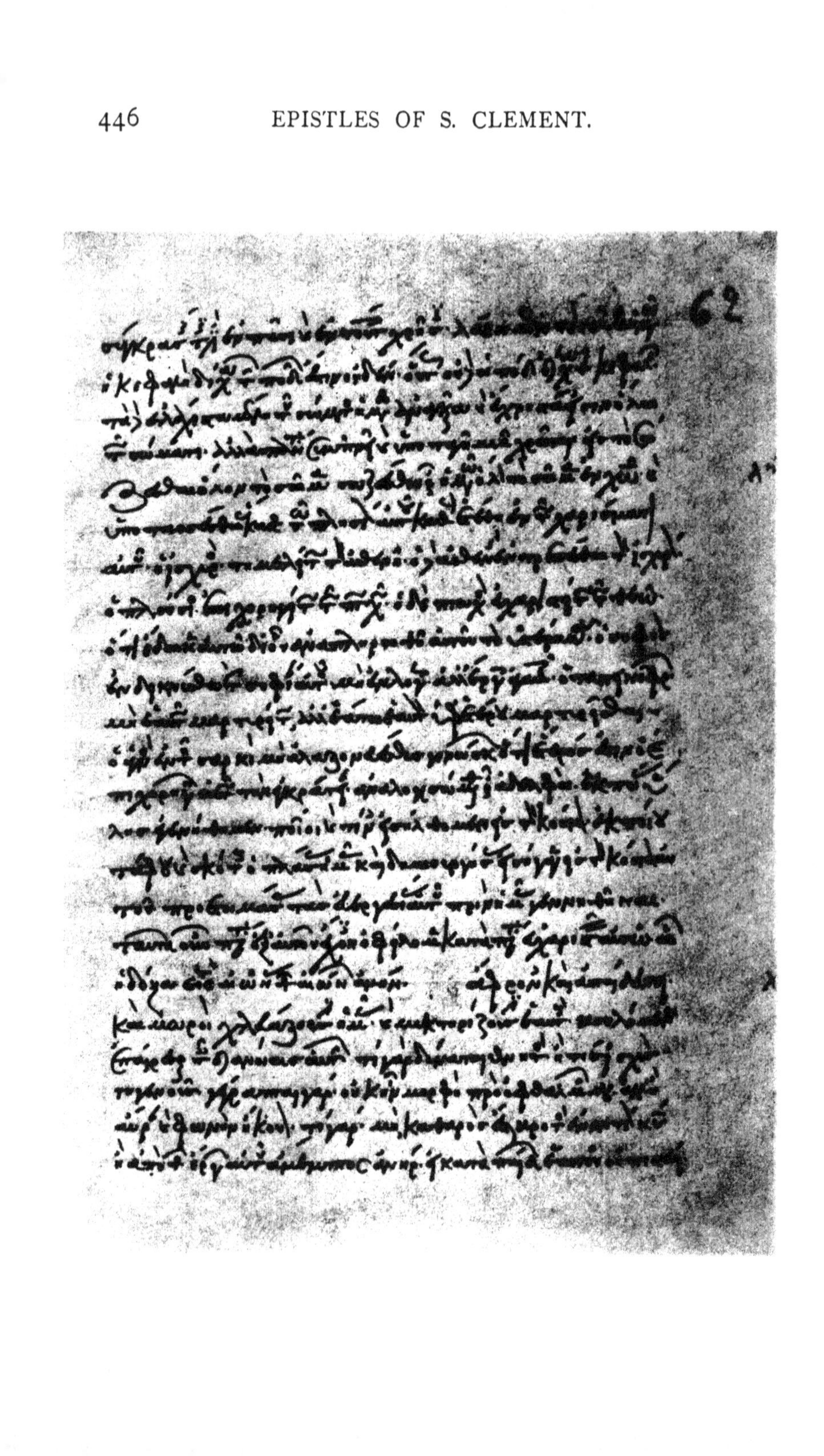

62

χ̅ῶ̅ ἀγωγῆς. ἀκούεσθαι τὴν βεβαιοτάτην καὶ ἀρχαίαν Κορινθίων ἐκ- 65
κλησίαν δι' ἓν ἢ δύο πρόσωπα στασιάζειν πρὸς τοὺς πρεσβυ-
τέρους. καὶ αὕτη ἡ ἀκοὴ οὐ μόνον εἰς ἡμᾶς ἐχώρησεν· ἀλλὰ καὶ εἰς τοὺς
ἑτεροκλινεῖς ὑπάρχοντας ἀφ' ἡμῶν· ὥστε καὶ βλασφημίας ἐπιφέρεσθαι
τῷ ὀνόματι κυρίου διὰ τὴν ὑμετέραν ἀφροσύνην. ἑαυτοῖς δὲ
κίνδυνον ἐπεξεργάζεσθαι. ἐξάρωμεν οὖν τοῦτο ἐν τάχει. καὶ προσ- ε.
πέσωμεν τῷ δεσπότῃ. καὶ κλαύσωμεν ἱκετεύοντες αὐτόν. ὅπως ἵλεως γενόμενος ἐπικαταλλαγῇ ἡμῖν. καὶ ἐπὶ τὴν σεμνὴν τῆς φιλαδελφίας ἡ-
μῶν ἁγνὴν ἀγωγὴν ἀποκαταστήσῃ ἡμᾶς. πύλη γὰρ δικαιοσύνης ἀνεῳ-
γυῖα εἰς ζωὴν αὕτη. καθὼς γέγραπται· ἀνοίξατέ μοι πύλας
δικαιοσύνης. ἵνα εἰσελθὼν ἐν αὐταῖς ἐξομολογήσωμαι τῷ κυρίῳ. αὕτη ἡ
πύλη τοῦ κυρίου· δίκαιοι εἰσελεύσονται ἐν αὐτῇ. πολλῶν οὖν πυλῶν ἀνεῳγυιῶν. ἡ ἐν δικαιοσύνῃ αὕτη ἐστὶν ἡ ἐν Χριστῷ. ἐν ᾗ μακάριοι πάντες οἱ εἰσελθόντες καὶ κατευθύνοντες τὴν πορείαν αὐτῶν ἐν ὁ-
σιότητι καὶ δικαιοσύνῃ. ἀταράχως πάντα ἐπιτελοῦντες. ἤτω
τις πιστός. ἤτω δυνατὸς γνῶσιν ἐξειπεῖν. ἤτω σοφὸς ἐν διακρίσει
λόγων. ἤτω ἁγνὸς ἐν ἔργοις· τοσούτῳ μᾶλλον ταπεινοφρονεῖν
ὀφείλει. ὅσῳ δοκεῖ μᾶλλον μείζων εἶναι. καὶ ζητεῖν τὸ κοινωφελὲς πᾶ-
σι. καὶ μὴ τὸ ἑαυτοῦ. ὁ ἔχων ἀγάπην ἐν Χριστῷ ποιησάτω τὰ τοῦ Χριστοῦ μ
παραγγέλματα. τὸν δεσμὸν τῆς ἀγάπης τοῦ θεοῦ τίς δύναται ἐξηγή-
σασθαι. τὸ μεγαλεῖον τῆς καλλονῆς αὐτοῦ. τίς ἀρκετὸς ἐξειπεῖν. τὸ
ὕψος εἰς ὃ ἀνάγει ἡ ἀγάπη ἀνεκδιήγητόν ἐστιν. ἀγάπη κολλᾷ ἡμᾶς
τῷ θεῷ. ἀγάπη καλύπτει πλῆθος ἁμαρτιῶν. ἀγάπη πάντα ἀνέ-

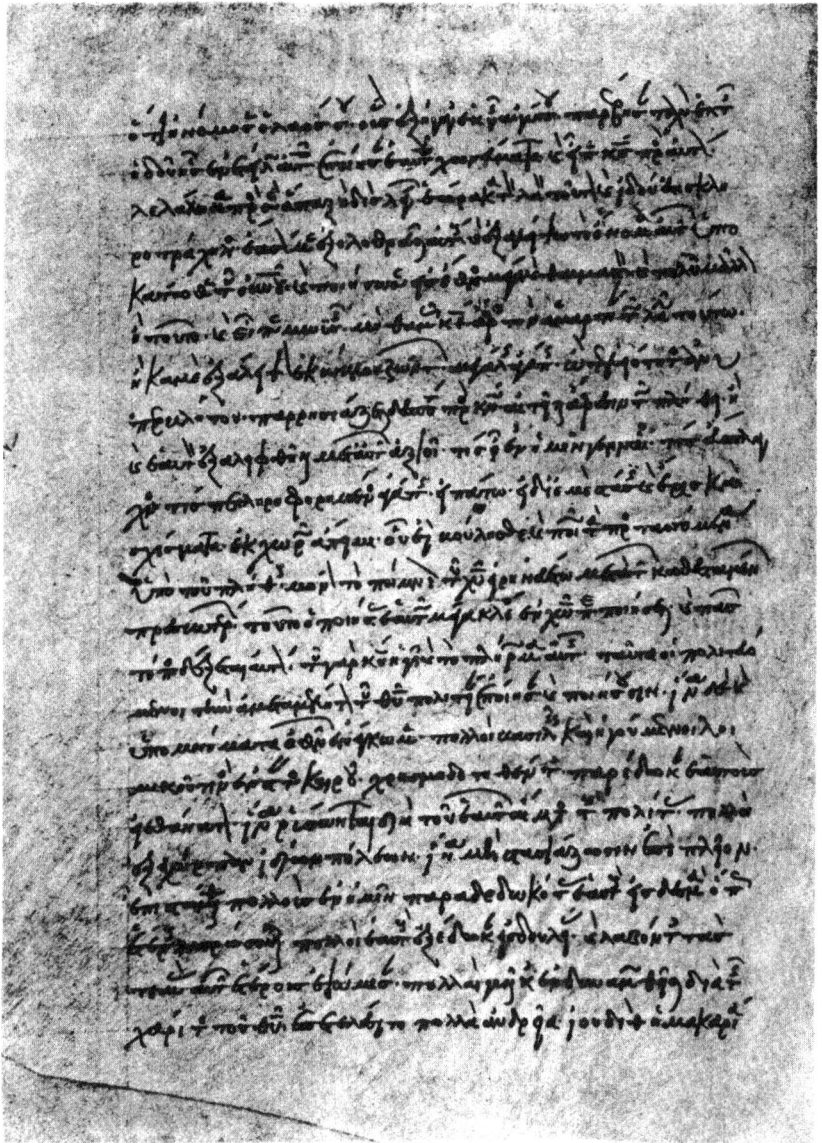

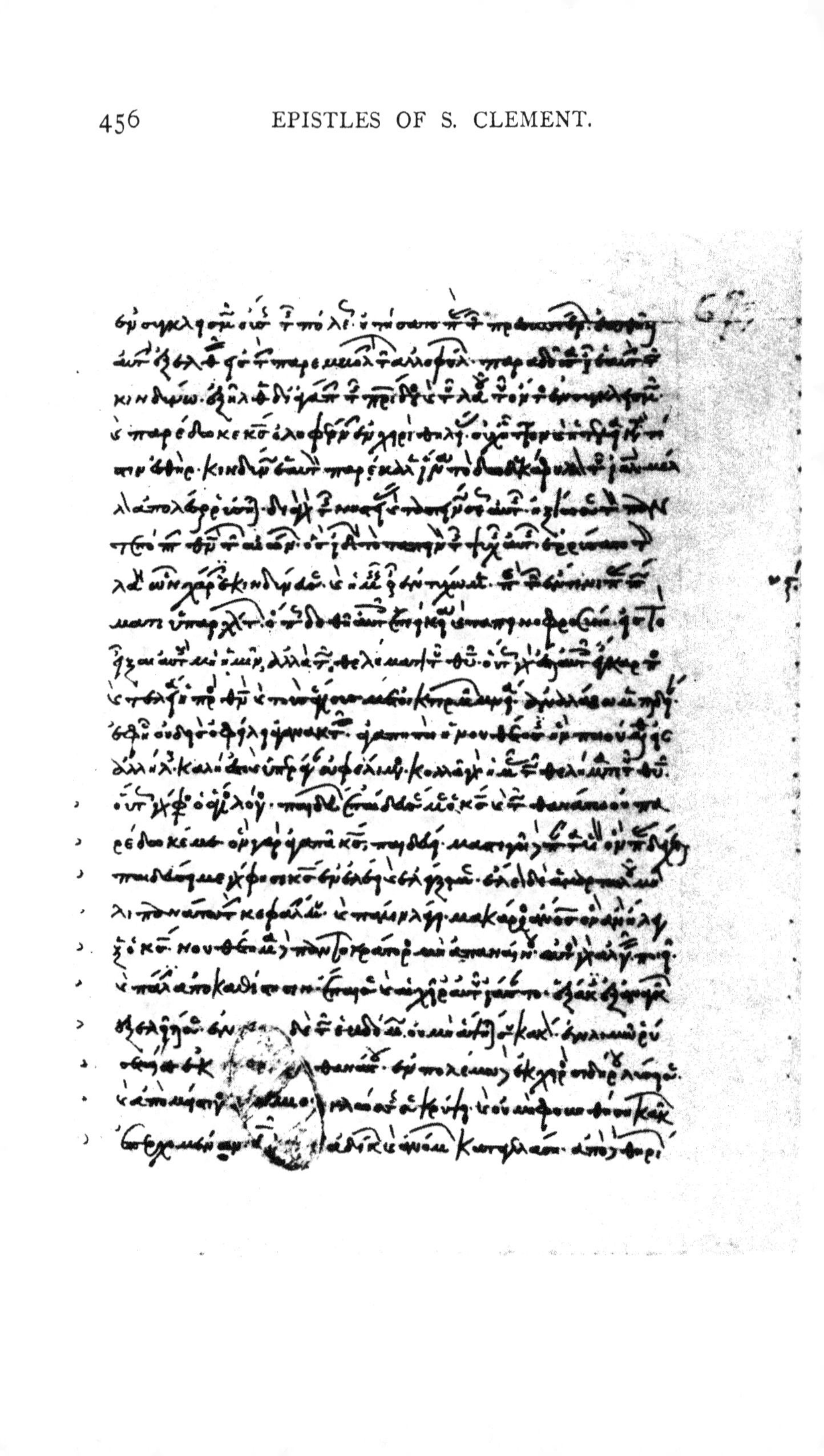

68

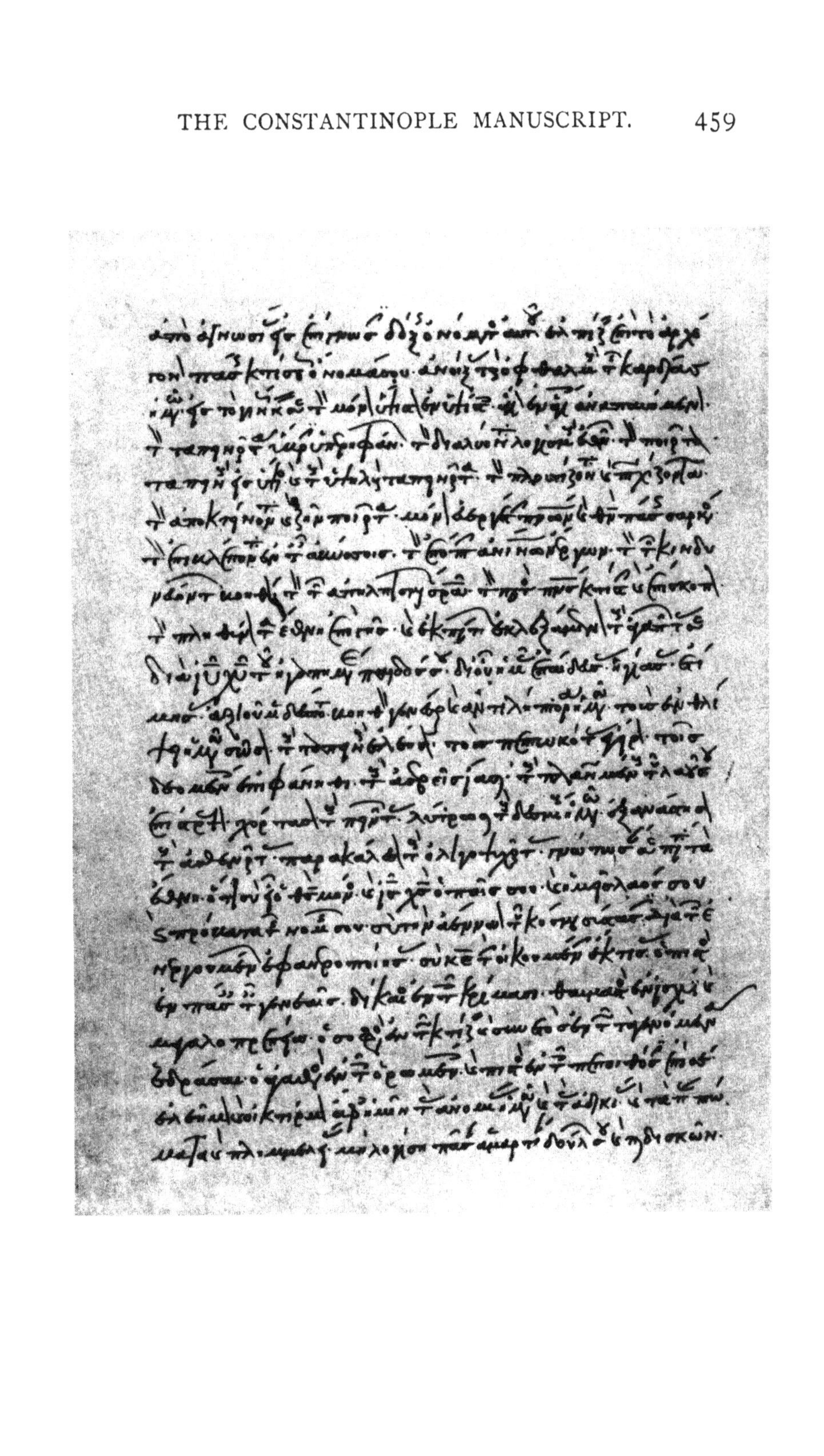

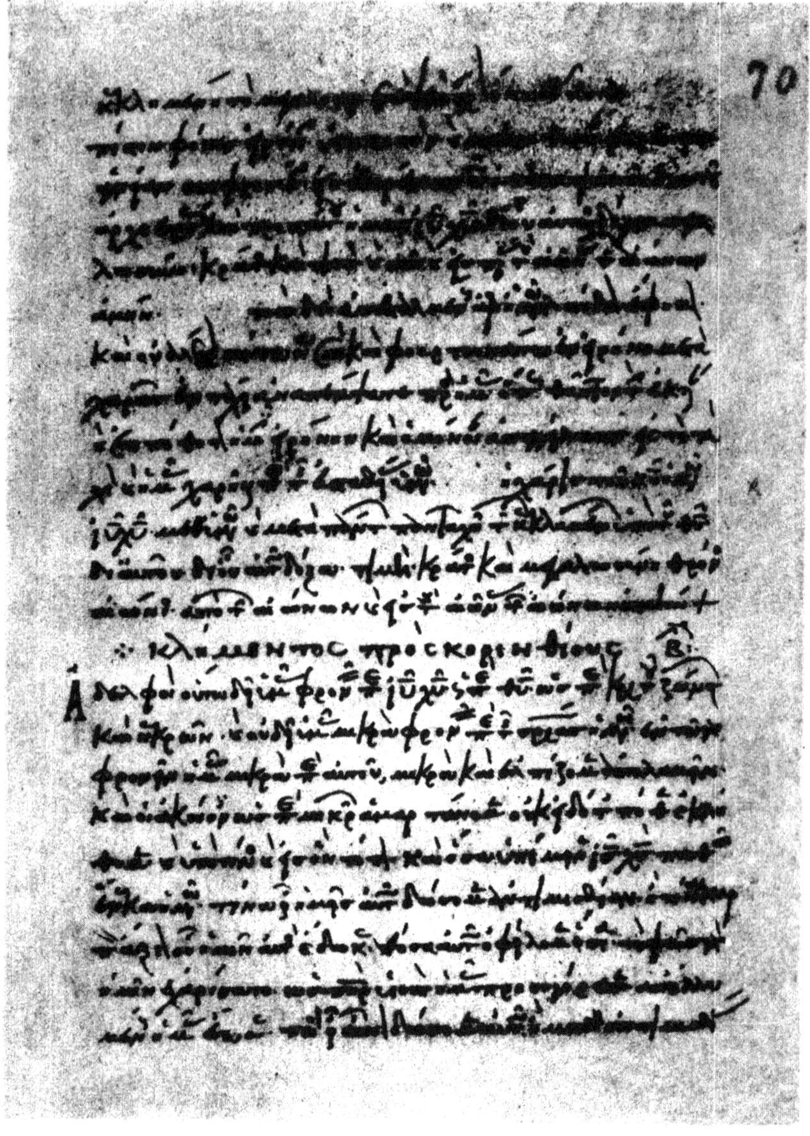

… πονηροὶ ὄντες τῇ διανοίᾳ προσκυνοῦντες λίθους καὶ
ξύλα καὶ χρυσὸν καὶ ἄργυρον καὶ χαλκὸν ἔργα ἀνθρώπων· καὶ ὁ βίος ἡμῶν ὅλος οὐδὲν
ἄλλο ἦν εἰ μὴ θάνατος. ἀμαύρωσιν οὖν περικείμενοι καὶ τοιαύτης ἀχλύ-
ος γέμοντες ἐν τῇ ὁράσει, ἀνεβλέψαμεν ἀποθέμενοι ἐκεῖνο ὃ περικείμε-
θα νέφος τῇ αὐτοῦ θελήσει. ἠλέησεν γὰρ ἡμᾶς καὶ σπλαγχνισθεὶς ἔσωσεν θεασάμενος ἐν ἡμῖν πολλὴν πλάνην καὶ ἀπώλειαν, καὶ μηδεμί-
αν ἐλπίδα ἔχοντας σωτηρίας, εἰ μὴ τὴν παρ' αὐτοῦ. ἐκάλεσεν γὰρ ἡμᾶς
οὐκ ὄντας καὶ ἠθέλησεν ἐκ μὴ ὄντος εἶναι ἡμᾶς. εὐφράνθητι στεῖρα
ἡ οὐ τίκτουσα· ῥῆξον καὶ βόησον ἡ οὐκ ὠδίνουσα· ὅτι πολλὰ τὰ τέκνα τῆς ἐρήμου μᾶλλον ἢ τῆς ἐχούσης τὸν ἄνδρα. ὃ εἶπεν εὐφράνθητι στεῖρα
ἡ οὐ τίκτουσα, ἡμᾶς εἶπεν· στεῖρα γὰρ ἦν ἡ ἐκκλησία ἡμῶν πρὸ τοῦ
δοθῆναι αὐτῇ τέκνα. ὃ δὲ εἶπεν βόησον ἡ οὐκ ὠδίνουσα, τοῦτο λέγει·
τὰς προσευχὰς ἡμῶν ἁπλῶς ἀναφέρειν πρὸς τὸν θεόν, μὴ ὡς αἱ ὠδίνουσαι
ἐγκακῶμεν. ὃ δὲ εἶπεν ὅτι πολλὰ τὰ τέκνα τῆς ἐρήμου μᾶλλον ἢ τῆς ἐ-
χούσης τὸν ἄνδρα· ἐπεὶ ἔρημος ἐδόκει εἶναι ἀπὸ τοῦ θεοῦ ὁ λαὸς ἡμῶν, νυνὶ δὲ
πιστεύσαντες πλείονες ἐγενόμεθα τῶν δοκούντων ἔχειν θεόν. καὶ ἑτέρα δὲ γραφὴ λέγει
ὅτι οὐκ ἦλθον καλέσαι δικαίους, ἀλλὰ ἁμαρτωλούς. τοῦτο λέγει ὅτι
δεῖ τοὺς ἀπολλυμένους σῴζειν. ἐκεῖνο γάρ ἐστιν μέγα καὶ θαυμαστόν, οὐ τὰ
ἑστῶτα στηρίζειν, ἀλλὰ τὰ πίπτοντα. οὕτως καὶ ὁ Χριστὸς ἠθέλησεν σῶσαι τὰ
ἀπολλύμενα, καὶ ἔσωσεν πολλούς, ἐλθὼν καὶ καλέσας ἡμᾶς ἤδη ἀπολλυμένους.
τοσοῦτον οὖν ἔλεος ποιήσαντος αὐτοῦ εἰς ἡμᾶς· πρῶτον μέν, ὅτι ἡμεῖς οἱ ζῶντες
τοῖς νεκροῖς θεοῖς οὐ θύομεν, ἀλλὰ ἔγνωμεν δι' αὐτοῦ τὸν πατέρα τῆς
ἀληθείας· τίς ἡ γνῶσις ἡ πρὸς αὐτόν, ἢ τὸ μὴ ἀρνεῖσθαι δι' οὗ ἔγνωμεν αὐτόν.

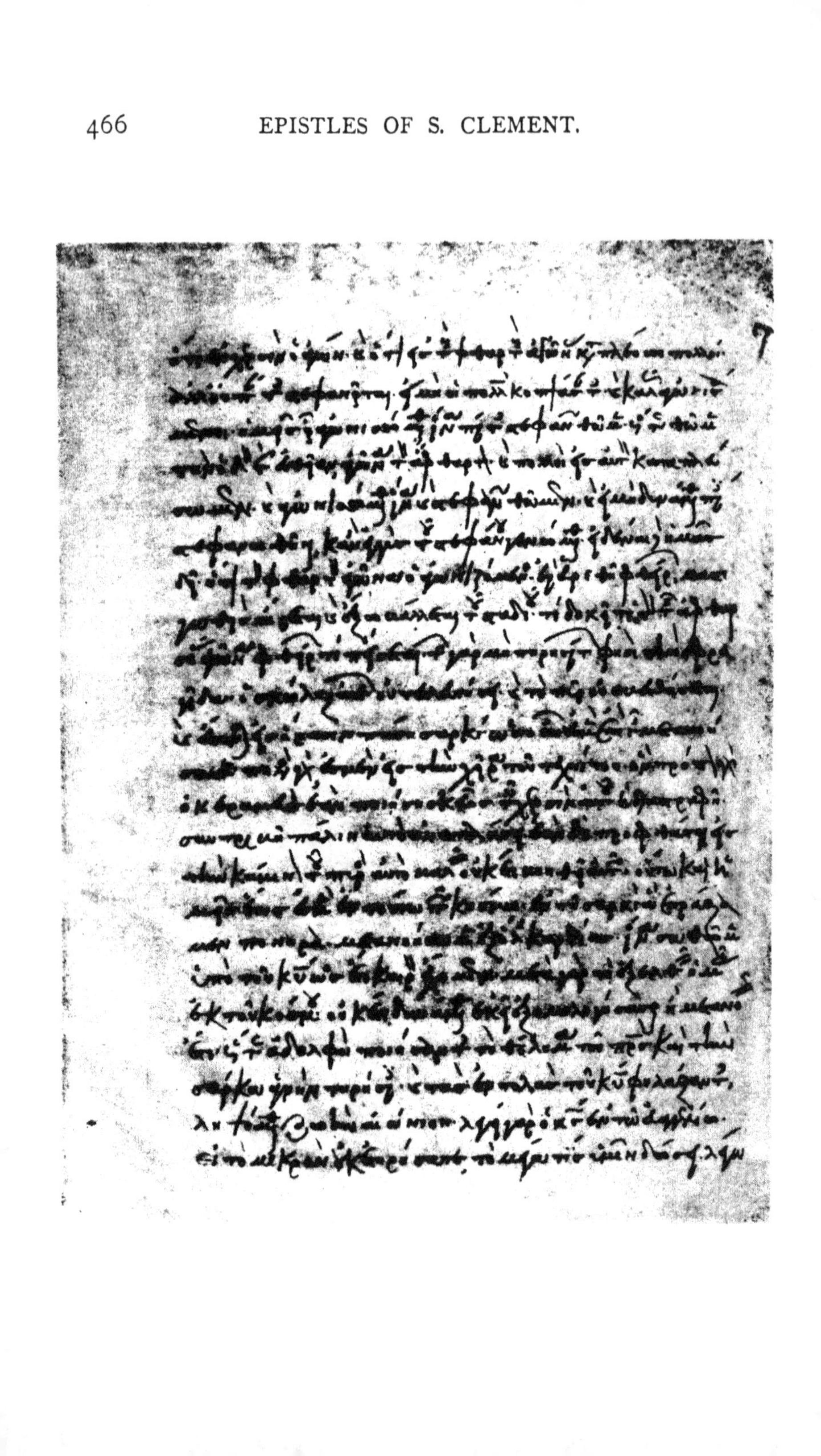

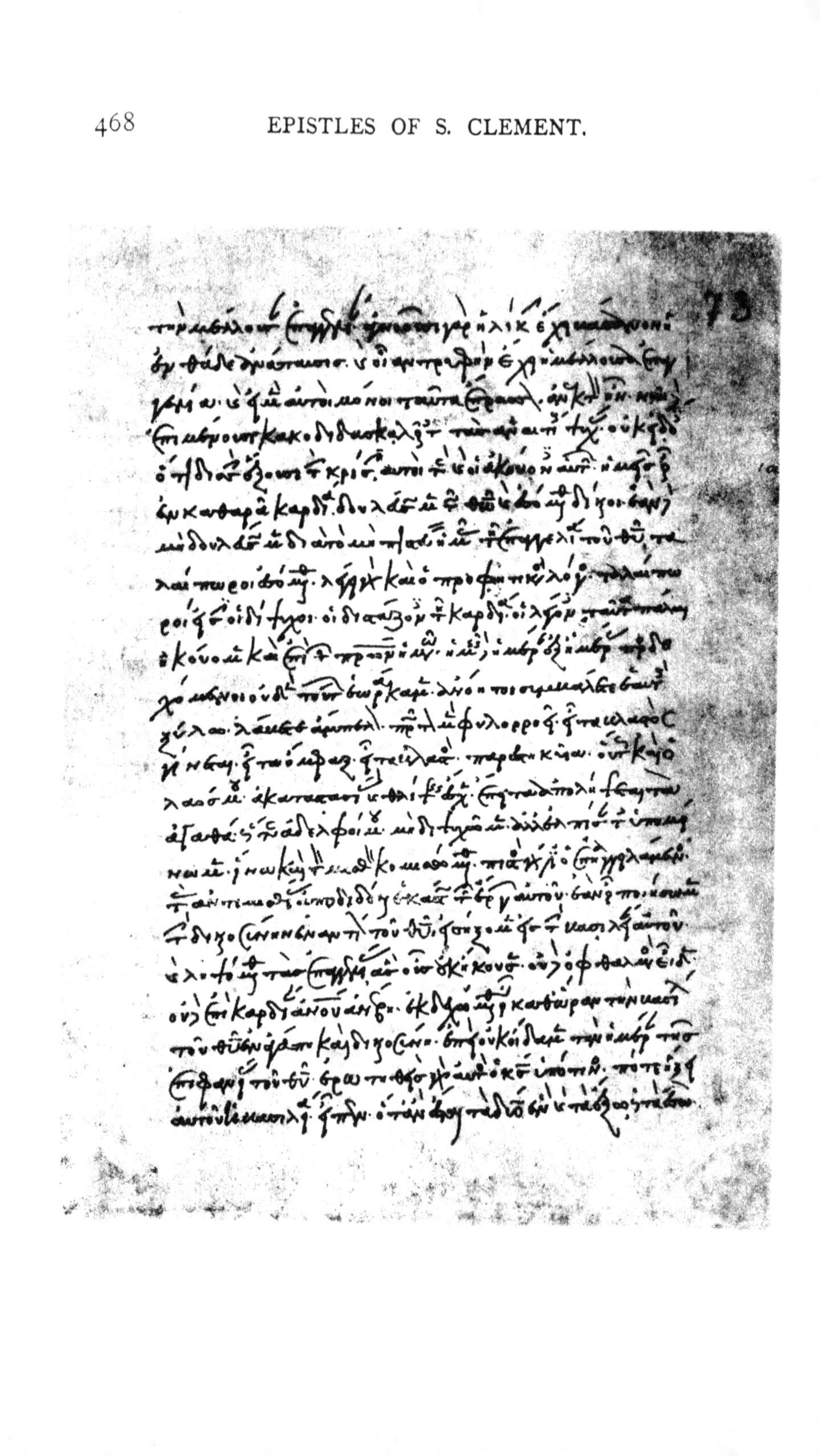

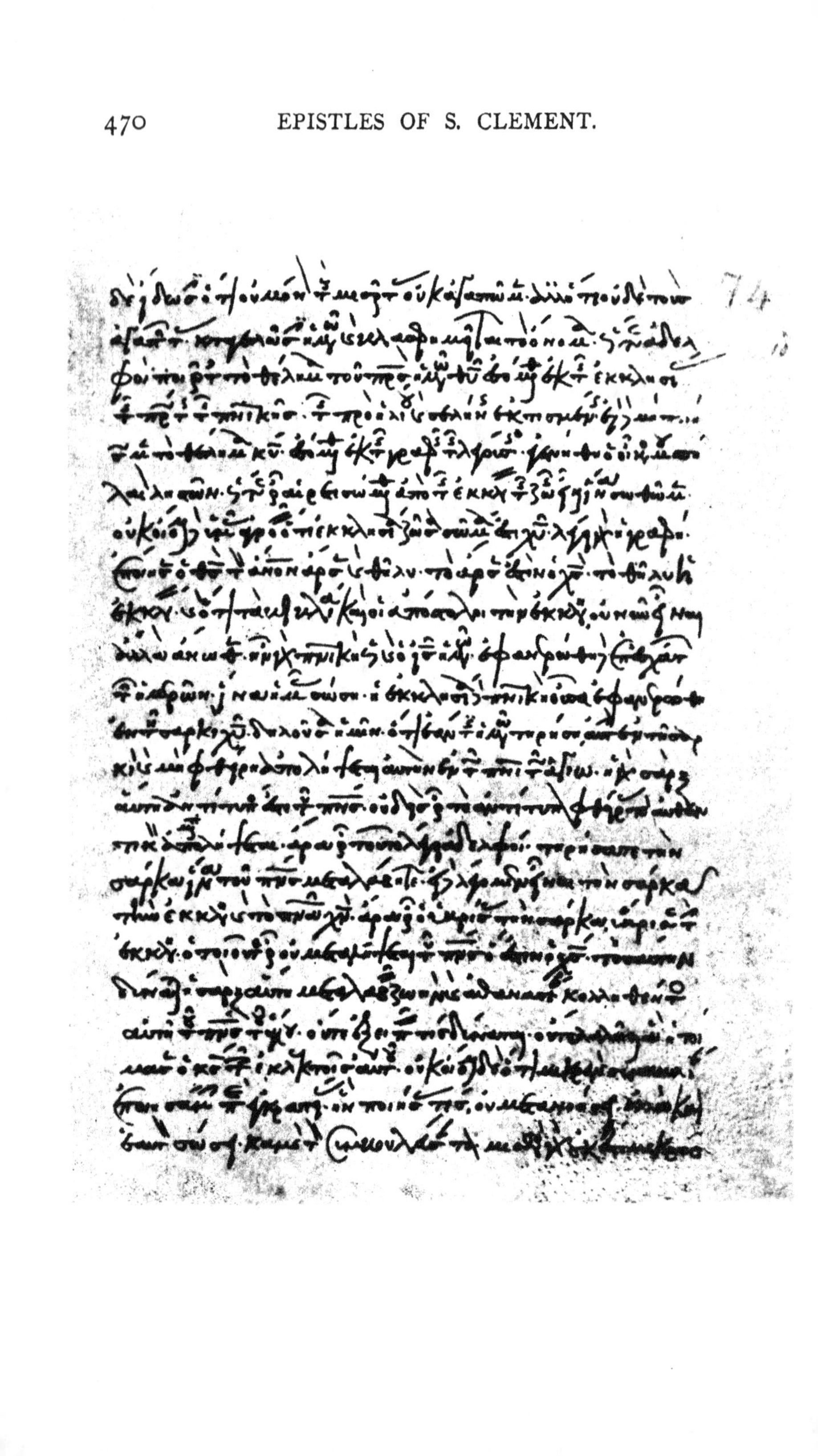

οὐ τὸ εὐσεβὲς ἀλλὰ τὸ κερδαλέον διώκοντες. διὰ τοῦτο θεία
κρίσις ἔβλαψε πνεῦμα μὴ ὂν δίκαιον καὶ ἐβάρυνε δεσμοῖς. τῷ μόνῳ
θεῷ ἀοράτῳ πατρὶ τῆς ἀληθείας, τῷ ἐξαποστείλαντι ἡμῖν τὸν σωτῆρα
καὶ ἀρχηγὸν τῆς ἀφθαρσίας, δι' οὗ καὶ ἐφανέρωσεν ἡμῖν τὴν ἀλήθειαν
καὶ τὴν ἐπουράνιον ζωήν, αὐτῷ ἡ δόξα εἰς τοὺς αἰῶνας τῶν αἰώνων.

στιχ. χ'. ρη'. ΤΑΚΒ:

∴ ὀνόματα τῶν βιβλίων παρ' ἑβραίοις·
γένεσις· βρησίθ· ἔξοδος· ἐλσιμώθ· λευϊτικόν· ὀδοικρα·
ἰησοῦ· ἰησοῦ ὁ τοῦ ναυῆ· δευτερονόμιον· ἐλεαδεββαρεί·
ἀριθμοί· οὐϊδαβήρ· ῥούθ· δαρούθ·
ἰώβ· δαϊώβ· κριταί· δασοφτιμ· ψαλτήριον· σφερτελίμ·
βασιλειῶν α'· διεμμιμοῦν· βασιλειῶν β'· δαδουδέ·
βασιλειῶν γ'· δαμαλαχήμ· βασιλειῶν δ'· ἀμαλαχήμ·
παραλειπομένων α'· δεβριϊαμίν· παραλειπομένων β'· δεριαμίν·
παροιμίαι· δαμαλεώθ· ἐκκλησιαστής· δακοέλεθ·
ᾆσμα ᾀσμάτων· σιρασιρίμ· ἱερεμίας· διερεμίου·
δωδεκαπρόφητον· δαθαριασαρ· ἡσαΐου· δησαΐου· ἰεζεκιήλ· διεεζεκιήλ·
δανιήλ· δαδανιήλ· ἔσδρας α'· δεσδρα α'· ἔσδρας β'·
δεσδρα β'· ἐσθήρ· δεσθήρ.

∴ διδαχὴ τῶν δώδεκα ἀποστόλων.

Διδαχὴ κυρίου διὰ τῶν δώδεκα ἀποστόλων τοῖς ἔθνεσιν. ὁδοὶ δύο
εἰσί, μία τῆς ζωῆς καὶ μία τοῦ θανάτου, διαφορὰ δὲ πολλὴ μεταξὺ
τῶν δύο ὁδῶν. ἡ μὲν οὖν ὁδὸς τῆς ζωῆς ἐστιν αὕτη· πρῶτον

INDEX.

INDEX.